FUNDAMENTALS OF SCM-EWM

A STEP-BY-STEP GUIDE

RAJESH GODWIN MENDONCA

JANET VEERA MASCARENHAS

ACKNOWLEDGMENTS

We want to thank our parents for their blessings, which are of paramount importance for any venture.

Special thanks to our two children, Gia and Nia, who had to endure many hours of our absence during the construction of this book.

We would also like to thank our family, friends, and colleagues, especially the many people who encouraged us to go forward with this project. In particular, we would like to thank Norbert Mendonca, Joe Vinod Mascarenhas, Suren Laad, Jerome Vikas Mascarenhas, and Prerna Laad for providing firsthand knowledge and valuable feedback on this book.

We would like to extend our heartfelt thanks to Suren Laad for singlehandedly conceiving and perfecting the logo and the book cover.

Printed in the United States of America

1st edition 2011

ISBN-13: 978-0983921103
ISBN-10: 0983921105

To our darling daughters

Gia and Nia

Whose share of our time and attention

We have most selfishly devoted to the construction of this book.

About the Authors

Rajesh Mendonca is a leading techno-functional consultant with more than a decade's worth of experience in SAP. His work includes extensive knowledge on extended warehouse management, warehouse management, and inventory and materials management. His clients have included several Fortune 500 companies from industries including manufacturing, chemicals, utility, mill products, and retail industries. He has worked with "The Big Four" consulting firms and currently works for Hitachi Consulting Corporation (USA).

Janet Mascarenhas is a graduate in electrical and electronics engineering. She worked briefly in the electrical industry before making a highly successful transition to SAP and has since worked on various aspects of SAP's warehouse management and logistics modules. Passionate about teaching SAP, Mascarenhas is dedicated to sharing her experience with those that are just beginning their careers in SAP.

With several years of teaching and implementation experience behind them and with a good understanding of what students and consultants want, they have put enormous effort in making this book simple and useful not only for experienced consultants, but also for beginners and clients.

SAP Training

Through this book, we have proved that the popular myth that SAP is a difficult application to learn is not the truth. For those who are interested in pursuing more in-depth training on SAP, we conduct instructor-led training, corporate training, and online e-training for various modules of SAP. Our wide range of services includes supervised training by qualified and experienced instructors. The course material is uniquely prepared to teach SAP, step by step, to any newcomer in the simplest way possible. During the training, we also prepare you to face daily challenges in your module as well as for the interview questions you may face. You can read more about the training we offer, on our website-www.ewmguru.com.

Contents

Preface

This book is intended to help beginners, experienced WM consultants, and SAP customers who are looking to implement SCM Extended Warehouse Management (SCM-EWM) solution.

With enormous experience in implementation and training in SAP Warehouse Management (WM) and EWM, we know the kinds of problems and questions consultants will have when learning and implementing the EWM solution. By incorporating all the insights that we have gained into this book, we hope to impart that same learning experience to our readers as well.

SCM-EWM is more complicated than SAP's WM module. Because of that, both beginners and experienced WM consultants often find it difficult to learn this module. Furthermore, SAP customers are often confused about which solution to select to manage their inventory and warehouse needs due to the variety of solutions available to them.

After reading this book, SAP customers will be able to get a good look at the different solutions SAP offers for managing inventory and be able to make an informed selection of the right solution for their warehouse needs. Similarly, this book will help beginners as well as experienced consultants master this module and configure the EWM system on their own. By understanding the hows and the whys, consultants will gain an understanding few have in this exciting field.

The following are the salient features of this book that will help you to read and understand the content easily.

Tables: By glancing at the table, you will able to absorb a sea of information that otherwise would require pages and pages of text. One look at the table informs you as to exactly where to configure what, which transaction code (TCode) to use for the configuration, what part of the configuration can be transported, and which settings have to be manually performed in each client. This is especially handy for consultants during integration testing and go-live cutover tasks.

Diagrams: One of the limitations of SAP's help-documentation is the lack of good diagrams explaining and connecting configuration objects. The addition of this feature in this book helps you to easily understand and remember the configuration in pictorial format, thus digesting the information faster, with fewer questions.

Step-by-Step Procedures: The sequence of steps involved in the configuration process is laid out in a very lucid, logical manner. This achieves two main objectives: it makes it easier to focus, and also makes it more interesting and understandable.

Screenshots: These help you to visualize the system without actually logging into it and connect the information to the practical environment. A glance at a screenshot gives you a good idea of what the system looks like, what parameter(s) to configure, and what value to select for the given option, besides indicating the actual physical location of various screen elements.

Live Examples: Any SAP book without real-life examples is only half complete. Through the examples provided in this book, you will observe warehouse challenges and how to provide solutions for them. Real-life examples and business scenarios walk consultants through the business requirements, giving them the confidence of an experienced consultant.

100% Guaranteed to Work: When we started authoring this book, we began with a system that had no data and no prior configuration loaded (not even BC sets). We activated everything from scratch and created our own data. During this process, we captured screenshots in every step and incorporated them into our book. Starting from the ground up also ensured a logical flow of information. This guarantees that those who reference our book will be able to confidently and successfully configure the system on their own.

Our aim is to provide a detailed guide on understanding various SAP solutions to manage the inventory and how to configure EWM system independently. Due to the vast amounts of information, we have divided the content of configuration of EWM into two parts: *Fundamentals of SCM-EWM* and *Advanced Concepts in SCM-EWM.*

"*Fundamentals of SCM-EWM*" covers the details of the various SAP solutions available to manage inventory and how to select the solution that best fits each client's requirements. In order to lay a strong foundation to EWM, this book covers in detail the basics of EWM, EWM architecture, how to set up data transfers between ERP and EWM systems, and master data configuration. In the later chapters, consultants will be guided through the configuration of goods receipts, goods issue, handling units (HUs), warehouse documents, internal warehouse movements, physical inventory (PI), Post-Processing Frameworks (PPFs), and exception handling, along with examples. This will build consultants' confidence on how to make the EWM system work. The "Lessons learned" section focuses on overcoming the challenges encountered in EWM implementation.

In "*Advanced Concepts in SCM-EWM*", we will cover additional functionalities like labor management, slotting, rearrangements, warehouse cockpit, and mobile or radio frequency (RF) functionalities, to name a few.

How to Read This Book

EWM is very technical and a highly complicated module to configure and understand. Some readers may find it difficult to understand and master the fundamentals of EWM in the first attempt; but perseverance and practicing it in the system will surely bear results.

Every chapter will have tables, diagrams, and configuration steps along with theory, examples, screenshots, and notes. Tables will help the reader to understand what configuration steps need to be performed, the sequence and importantly whether they can be transported to other systems or not. Diagrams will explain how the different objects are linked in pictorial format.

Configuration steps will cover the theory, information for the important fields, notes, configuration menu path, and screenshots. Theory and field level information will help the reader to understand the purpose of the configuration and the screenshots will help to visualize the system without actually accessing the system.

Readers who are comfortable reading the configuration section only after learning about master data and executing the transactions, can start reading chapters 14 though 20 after reading chapter 1, 2, and 3. Please note, reading chapters 14 through 20 without reading earlier chapters (4 through 13), may not give a clear understanding of the configuration, and abbreviations. On the other hand, if the reader is more comfortable reading and understanding the configuration first, then read this book as it is structured. Those who have already worked in SAP WM and EWM may skip chapters 1 and 2.

We hope you enjoy using this book as much as we have enjoyed writing it.

Software Used

When we wrote this book, the latest software version of EWM was SCM 7.0, and the ERP system connected to it was SAP ERP Central Component 6.0 with enhancement pack 4. Depending on your software version, some of the configuration paths mentioned in this book might vary. In such cases, you can use the transaction code to locate the required transaction.

Chapter 1: Introduction to Warehouse Management

This chapter provides a brief history of the warehouse, the definition of warehouse management, and key warehouse terminologies. For beginners we have also covered a short introduction to SAP, SAP jargon, abbreviations used in SAP, and an introduction to SAP menu.

1.1 Background and History

A warehouse is a building where goods may be received, labeled, catalogued, picked, packed, and shipped. The roots of the warehouse go back to the creation of storehouses to store food, which was historically available for purchase during times of famine. Slowly, as Europeans began to create shipping trade routes with neighboring nations, warehouses grew in importance for the storage of goods from afar.

Before the railroads, warehouses were often located near the major seaports or at the manufacturing facility. Warehouses were mainly operated by a team of workers. As railroads and, later, airports began to expand travel and transportation, the creation of warehouses near the rail depots or airports for the storage of materials became necessary. Since then the warehouse has gained importance in the supply chain, resulting in several different types of warehouses like public warehouses, private warehouses, commercial warehouses, contract warehouses, leased warehouses, and so on.

Warehousing companies are now striving to become more than simply storage facilities. Many companies or department stores like Sam's Club and Costco have turned their warehouses into true commercial buildings. They may be called warehouse stores, but the concept is that instead of spending a lot of money on merchandising and attractive displays, these companies concentrate on maximizing utilization of rack space, minimizing material handling, better control of inventory, and easy replenishment. This allows them to offer much lower prices to the consumers by minimizing the supply chain cost.

1.2 Warehouse Management Definition

Warehouse management is the process of coordinating the incoming goods, the subsequent storage and tracking of the goods, and, finally, the distribution of the goods to their proper destinations. In the past, warehouse management was very paper intensive in its coordination of a multitude of activities. Since early 1990, this has changed with the introduction of warehouse management system software.

Since 1990, warehouse management has drawn the attention of enough software companies to provide good solutions to manage the inventory, resources, and planning in the warehouse. SAP is one such company that has worked hard to provide better solutions to manage and trace inventory, helping companies and warehouse managers to overcome their daily challenges.

1.3 Warehouse Terminologies

Lack of understanding about warehouse terminologies will often make communication more complicated. Hence, it is important for the consultant to learn the warehouse terms. This helps the consultant in everyday consulting jobs. Below are some of the terms, acronyms, and abbreviations that are often used in the warehouse.

Putaway: Putaway is the process in which materials are put away after being received.

Material Handling: Material handling is the movement of the material to and from an original location. This includes the travel of both material and the warehouse workers.

Picking: Picking is the process in which materials are picked from the source and taken to a given destination, usually for shipping or production.

Loading and Unloading: Loading is the action in which the materials are loaded on trucks, trailers, or rail cars, usually for shipping. During unloading, materials are removed from trucks, trailers, or rail cars for storage in the warehouse or for consumption.

Cross-Docking: Cross-docking is the action of unloading materials from incoming trailers and immediately loading those materials on outgoing or outbound trailers, thus eliminating the need for warehousing.

Forklift Trucks: Vehicles used to lift, move, stack, and pick the materials in the warehouse.

Warehouse Operator: Person in the warehouse who unloads, does putaway, picks, or loads the materials in the warehouse.

Aisles, Racks, Bins: Aisles are spaces for walking or drive forklift trucks between racks. Racks are normally found either side of the aisles and contain several storage spaces or slots, usually labeled for easy identification. Bins are spaces dedicated to storing materials.

Fixed Bin: This is a fixed space dedicated to one or more materials from where the materials are issued to the production or shipping before picking from other bins.

Homogeneous Storage: All materials stored are the same kind.

Mixed Storage: Different materials are stored in the same bin.

Addition to Stock: This is usually performed to maximize the utilization of bin space by adding more stock to the bin.

Multipallet Bins: These are bins where more than one pallet can be stored, whether of the same or a different kind.

Pallet: This is a flat transport structure used to store materials in a stable fashion while being lifted by the forklift trucks.

ABC Indicators: These are used to identify the fast- and slow-moving materials.

Cycle Counting: Cycle counting is an inventory counting method that allows businesses to count materials in a number of areas within the warehouse without having to count the entire inventory.

Physical Inventory (PI): This refers to the process of counting all inventory in the warehouse.

Blind Count: This is a method of inventory where you provide the material numbers and location but no quantities.

Advanced Shipment Notification (ASN): ASN is used to notify a customer by a vendor of a shipment.

Direct or Drop Ship: Direct shipping and drop shipping are two terms generally used interchangeably. In this process, three parties interact with a sales transaction. The buyer orders a purchase from a seller, who then arranges with the supplier to ship the material directly to the buyers.

1.4 Introduction to SAP

SAP was founded in 1972 in Germany. It stands for Systems, Applications, and Products in Data Processing. Over the years, it has grown and evolved into the world premier provider of client/server business solutions for which it is so well known today.

The original SAP idea was to provide customers with the ability to interact with a common corporate database for a comprehensive range of applications. Gradually, the applications have been assembled, and today many corporations, including IBM and Microsoft, are using SAP products to run their own businesses.

The latest SAP R/3 enterprise application suite for open client/server systems has established new standards for providing business information management solutions. SAP applications, built around the R/3 system, provide the capability to manage financial, asset, and cost accounting; production operations; materials; inventory; warehousing; personnel; plants; and many other business needs.

Today, it is the world's largest interenterprise software company and the world's fourth-largest independent software supplier.

1.5 SAP Jargon and Abbreviations

It is important for both SAP consultants and their clients to know and understand the most commonly used SAP jargon and abbreviations and their meaning. In this section we have listed a little jargon and a few abbreviations used in SAP. Warehouse module–specific jargon is explained in the respective chapters in this book.

SAP Abbreviations: It is common to use abbreviations in SAP. In this book we have used several of them. They are ERP for ECC/ERP systems, EWM for SCM Extended Warehouse Management, WM for ERP Warehouse Management, Org Structure for Organizational Structure, IM for Inventory Management, MM for Materials Management, PI for Physical Inventory, FICO for Finance and Costing, QM for Quality Management, SD for Sales and Distribution, and PP for Production Planning.

CIF: In SAP, the term CIF refers to Core Interface. It is the interface that enables master data to be exchanged between an ERP system and a EWM system.

QRFC: In SAP, the term qRFC refers to queued Remote Function Call. It is the interface that enables transactional data to be exchanged between an ERP system and EWM system.

Handling Unit (HU): A HU is a term used in the SAP's packing module to identify a physical unit consisting of packaging materials and the goods contained in it. For example, a TV packed in a cardboard box.

Material Number: This is a unique identifier for each distinct product and services that can be procured internally or externally. It is also called a stock-keeping unit (SKU). In SAP retail, it is called an article number. In EWM, it is called a product number.

Batch: The quantity of a certain material or product that has been produced according to the same recipe, representing one homogenous, non-reproducible unit with unique specifications.

PGR and PGI: In SAP, the term PGR refers to Post Goods Receipts and PGI refers to Post Goods Issue. These are events in SAP that create the material document (i.e., the proof for goods receipts/issues and the accounting documents, if applicable).

1.6 Introduction to SAP Menu

SAP menu is broadly divided into user menu and configuration menu.

User menu is used in day-to-day operations for reporting purposes and to create, change, and display the master and transactional data. The configuration menu is mainly used for configuring the system, both during implementation and in the maintenance phase.

In SAP, any transaction can be accessed in two ways: by navigating through the menu path or by entering TCode in the command field. A TCode can be defined with up to 20 characters and is tied to the program. It is used more like a shortcut key to access the transaction. Instead of navigating through the menu path, one can simply enter the TCode in the command field, which will call the corresponding program and will display the transaction on the screen.

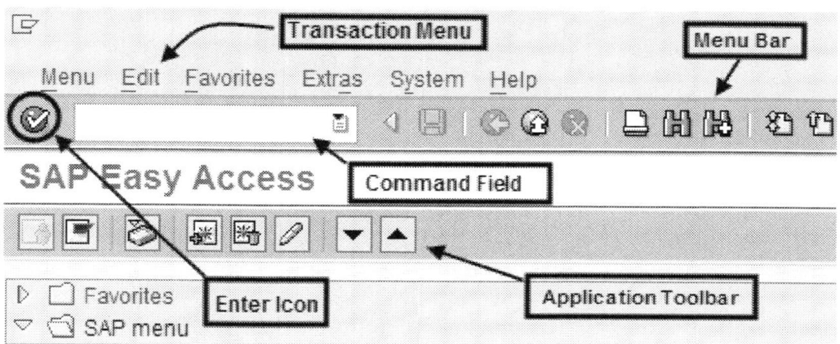

A configuration menu can be accessed by navigating through the menu path, for example: **SAP easy access menu | SAP menu | Tools | Customizing | IMG | Execute Project,** or by directly entering the TCode "**SPRO**" in the command field. In SAP the configuration menu is also referred as Implementation Guide Menu, or IMG menu.

Summary

In this chapter, you have learned the history of warehouse management; some of the most commonly used warehouse terminologies, SAP jargon, and how to navigate through the SAP menu. In the next chapter, we will look at the different solutions available in SAP to manage the inventory along with the advantages and limitations of each solution.

Chapter 2: Solutions to Manage Inventory in SAP

This chapter describes the different solutions available in SAP to manage inventory. It also describes how to choose the solution that would best fit each client's requirements by explaining the advantages and limitations of each solution. The authors hope this will help consultants in their day-to-day consulting jobs and guide clients in selecting the right solution for their warehousing needs.

2.1 Solutions to Manage Inventory in SAP

Since R/2, SAP has provided eight different solutions to manage and trace the inventory. These include simple solutions like managing the entire inventory in one storage location without bin visibility (IM managed stock); or complex solutions like EWM, where every movement of the stock—for example, unloading, staging, deconsolidating, packing, picking, and so on—is documented and recorded in the system.

Table 2.1A describes the different solutions available in SAP to manage the inventory.

Sol. #	SAP Solutions to Manage Ineventory	SAP Modules
1A	IM Managed Stock- No WM	IM Managed Solutions
1B	IM Managed Fixed Bin Warehouse (1 Material, 1 Bin) - No WM	
2A	Lean Warehouse Management	ERP WM Solutions
3A	ERP Standard WM Solution	
3B	ERP Standard WM Solution - with TRM Functionality	
3C	ERP EWM Solution (Yard Management, Cross Docking, VAS)	
3D	ERP EWM Solution & TRM Functionalities	
4A	Supply Chain Management - EWM Solution	SCM EWM Solutions

Table 2.1A

Solution 1A (IM Managed Stock—No WM): In this scenario, the stock is managed only at storage location level. Because the stock is not warehouse managed, in SAP it is called IM managed stock. This solution is more suitable for plants where only a small number of materials is stored in the plant, inventory can be managed without bin visibility, and (during the PI count) the entire stock of a storage location is counted for the selected material. This is the simplest way and a minimum requirement in SAP to manage inventory. However, this solution has certain limitations, namely:

i. There is no bin-level visibility for the stock

ii. No separate task can be created to pick or putaway the stock

iii. During PI, the entire stock of a particular material or material and batch (in case of batch management) needs to be counted

The benefit of this solution is that transactional overhead is at a bare minimum.

Solution 1B (IM Managed Fixed-Bin Warehouse (1 Material, 1 Bin)—No WM): This is almost the same as solution 1A, but with additional bin-level visibility. Here the stock is managed at storage location level, and the bin number is entered as text in the material master, which serves as the bin location for the stock in the system. The limitations of this solution are as follows:

i. Each material can have only one bin
ii. No separate tasks for picking and putaway can be created in the system
iii. As the bin number is just a text entered in the material master, without any bin validation, users can change the bin text in the material master, which can lead to problems during picking, putaway, and PI
iv. During PI, the entire stock of a particular material or material and batch (in case of batch management) needs to be counted

The benefits are as follows:

i. The bin number entered in the material master can be displayed in various inventory reports including the in PI document

ii. It gives the bin visibility without implementing the warehouse management module, hence avoiding all the warehouse management complexity

iii. Transactional overhead is at a bare minimum

This solution is particularly suitable for plants where the number of materials stored in the plant is few.

Solution 2A (Lean Warehouse Management): Solution 1B is further enhanced to provide some of benefits of warehouse management; this solution is called Lean Warehouse Management. This solution doesn't need the entire warehouse org structure, and no additional master data is maintained for materials. Like solution 1B, bin numbers are maintained in the material master as a text. An additional advantage of this solution over solution 1B is that the system can create a picking task (transfer order), and the warehouse personal can confirm the picking task in the system. The confirmation of the picking task automatically updates the picked quantity in the outbound delivery.

The limitations of this solution are as follows:

i. One material can have only one bin
ii. Because the bin number is just a text entered in the material master, without any bin validation, users can change the bin text in the material master, which can lead to problems during picking, putaway, and PI
iii. During PI, the entire stock of a particular material or material and batch (in case of batch management) needs to be counted

This solution gives all the benefits of solution 1B with the additional benefit of confirming the picking task for the warehouse personal. However, this solution is not recommended if any particular material is stored in more than one bin.

Solution 3A (ERP Standard WM Solution): To implement the standard ERP WM solution, one must implement the SAP WM module. This might be the right solution for a company if its warehouse has a medium to high volume of materials, stock of one material is managed in more than one bin, and most or all movements of the stock are recorded in the system.

It could also be the optimal solution for a company's warehouse if internal replenishment processes such as bin to bin transfer, addition to stock, fixed bin replenishment are followed in the warehouse to maximize bin utilization. Unlike solutions 1A and 1B, during PI, it is not required to count the entire stock of the material in the warehouse. Here, warehouse personnel can count the stock by bins to keep the bin inventory accurate. SAP has provided standard RF or mobile transactions to reduce human error. As of now, there are more than five thousand customers who are using this solution for their warehousing requirements.

Even though this solution has numerous advantages and flexibility in managing the inventory, it is not free from transactional overhead. If the warehouse is managed by only a few people, this solution may be more complicated to operate and can increase operational costs, unless some of the areas are customized and automated in the system.

It can also increase the complexity of warehouse operations if the warehouse stock is linked to HU, QM, PP, batch management modules and or hard allocated/unallocated to the customer sales orders. Changes to stock triggered by these modules could create posting change notices (PCNs) in the WM. Even though most of the transactions in WM can be automated, transactions like PCN cannot be completely automated, if the batch stock is stored in several bins, partially allocated or unallocated, the status of partial batch quantity is changed from one status to another, and so on. Before implementing this solution, the impact of other SAP modules on WM stock needs to be carefully considered.

The major limitation of this solution is that standard WM solutions don't consider labor management, kits, exception handling, warehouse resource capabilities, and internal warehouse routes when creating transfer orders. Hence, creating optimal tasks, optimizing the allocation of these tasks to warehouse resources, controlling task execution to prevent resource bottlenecks, and calculating resource performance in the warehouse is not possible.

Solution 3B (ERP Standard WM Solution—with TRM Functionality): Because of the limitations of solution 3A, in 2002, as part of ERP 4.7 extension set 1.1, SAP introduced a new functionality called Task and Resource Management (TRM).

TRM strengthens the SAP–ERP-WM solution by optimizing material flows via task execution and resource deployment. TRM breaks material movements down to the task and resource levels and optimizes the sequence in which they are executed, ensuring that the right task is completed by the best resource at the most optimal time.

This solution helps companies manage their warehouse processes more efficiently, because it achieves an unparalleled degree of process visibility within the system by tracking any activity performed on the warehouse floor. TRM uses the warehouse's physical layout to deploy resources according to the actual workload, the resource's qualifications, and the current geographic positions of the resources. The efficient deployment of resources can contribute to a considerable reduction of costs in material flow processing.

SAP-ERP-WM and TRM are closely integrated and work hand-in-hand to manage and maintain the workload in warehouses. SAP–ERP-WM provides the movement, operation demands, high-level scheduling, and planning, while TRM distributes the work among the various resources.

The major benefits of TRM are as follows:

i. Creating optimal tasks

ii. Optimizing the allocation of these tasks to warehouse resources

iii. Controlling task execution to prevent resource bottlenecks in the warehouse

iv. Providing visibility of all warehouse processes

In order get the benefits of task execution and resource management, TRM functionality needs to be implemented along with standard WM module.

Companies may need to opt for TRM solutions if the material movement is to be broken down to the task resource level to optimize the sequence in which the tasks are executed to ensure that the right task is executed by the right resource at the most optimal time.

Solution 3C (ERP EWM Solution): In 2002, when SAP released extension set 2.0 for ERP 4.7C, it introduced yard management, cross-docking, and value added services (VAS) functionalities in the warehouse management area and informally named the ERP warehouse management module "ERP Extended Warehouse Management." Since then, this solution has been available for all clients who have activated extension set 2 or implemented ECC systems. The name ERP EWM is applicable only if the client implements these three functionalities along with other WM functionalities.

This solution enables the following additional functionalities in the warehouse:

i. Cross-docking of materials from inbound to outbound doors without putting away the material in the bin, minimizing the material handling cost

ii. Additional value added services to the picked quantity, such as custom packaging

iii. Yard management to manage the incoming and outgoing trucks in the warehouse yard via check-in, check-out, sealing, loading, and so on

Since 2003, SAP has frozen all its new developments in the WM area and focused on developing EWM solutions.

Solution 3D (ERP EWM Solution with TRM Functionalities): The ERP EWM solution is just an extension of the standard WM solution with three additional functionalities. In order get the benefits of task execution and resource management and ERP EWM functionality, both TRM and ERP EWM must be implemented.

Between 2004 and 2009, many clients upgraded or implemented solution 3D for their warehouses to have system visibility in the areas of yard management, cross- docking, VAS, and warehouse resource optimization. But after the release of EWM 7.0, many new clients have opted for the EWM solution to get the maximum benefits of EWM functionalities and take advantage of SAP's continuous improvements in that domain.

Solution 4A (Supply Chain Management—EWM Solution): This is called the Supply Chain Management—Extended Warehouse Management (SCM-EWM) solution. It is the latest warehouse management solution from SAP, designed from the ground up, keeping in mind the needs of large, complex warehouses and distribution centers with high volume and velocity. Initially this was part of service parts management (SPM) solution. In version EWM 5.1, this function was made available to all customers outside SPM. We will cover this solution in greater detail in the following chapters.

Notes:

Apart from these solutions, some clients also use batch management and HU management to manage their inventory and to have bins visibility. These solutions have several limitations and are not dealt with here.

2.2 Guidelines for Selecting the Right Solution

The purpose of this section is to provide guidance in selecting an approach to managing inventory. Although some technical details are presented in support of the conclusions, intricate details of each solution are not the focus of this book. It is not the objective of this book to position any one approach as being the single best solution; rather, the reader is provided with information to help him or her understand why one approach might be a better fit for a given situation. All of the solutions discussed in this section are standard SAP solutions without any customization.

Guidelines:

Even though SAP has released advanced solutions in the warehouse area, like EWM, ERP EWM, TRM, etc., it is not necessary that companies select one of these advanced solutions for their warehouses. Selecting the right solution to manage inventory is a key thing in SAP. Choosing the wrong solution can have a negative impact on warehouse operations. In SAP, it is possible to implement simple solutions like inventory managed stock for some plants, standard warehouse solutions for small warehouses, and EWM or ERP EWM for large distribution centers.

While selecting a solution, companies should consider what their current and near-future warehouse requirements are and which solution best fit their list of requirements. Consultants also have to consider the transactional overhead and the impact of other SAP modules on the selected solution. It is very important to evaluate the overall impact of all modules on the warehouse management solution as a whole and not just the warehouse management module. Failure to do so can have a negative impact on everyday warehouse operations and might increase operational cost by reducing operational efficiency.

Tables 2.2A and 2.2B will help you understand each solution's supported functionalities, transactional overhead, and overall system complexity.

Notes: In table 2.2A:

i. The impact of serial number management, HU management, production planning, batch management, and quality management are not taken into account, as they do not have a straightforward effect on the transactional overhead and will give misleading results. Their effect on system complexity is dealt with in table 2.2B.

ii. Each solution described above has some transactional overhead. In table 2.2A, the numbers in the transactional overhead column indicates the transactional complexity of each solution. A higher number indicates more complexity.

iii. The numbers in the transactional overhead column are derived based on our consulting experience and might change, depending on the project scope and custom development. They should be used only as a guideline. Final decisions should be made after consulting with the implementation partners.

iv. Both WM and EWM are fantastic SAP products for managing bin managed inventory. The final decision, specific to each customer, depends on solution needs, along with licensing, implementation, and maintenance costs.

v. Two stars (**) in the warehouse requirements column indicate that implementation of HUM, QM, and PP modules required to support the respective functionalities. However, QM and HUM functionalities are built into solution 4A (SCM-EWM); hence, implementing these modules are not mandatory for solution 4A.

vi. Two checks against functionality indicate that the particular functionality is better supported by that solution in comparison with the others.

	Warehouse Requirements / Supported Functionalities	Solutions to Manage Inventory							
		1A	1B	2A	3A	3B	3C	3D	4A
	Transactional Overhead	1	1	2	5	6	7	8	7
1	Low Volume - Stock can be managed without bin visibilty	☑							
2	Low Volume - Single bin per material		☑						
3	Low Volume - Single bin per material and system driven picking			☑					
4	Pallet Tracebility or Handling Unit Management (HUM) **	☑	☑	☑	☑	☑	☑	☑	☑☑
5	Quality Inspection (QM) **	☑	☑	☑	☑	☑	☑	☑	☑☑
6	Production Support (PP) **	☑	☑	☑	☑	☑	☑	☑	☑
7	Bin to Bin Movements				☑	☑	☑	☑	☑
8	RF Support for Putaway, Picking, Loading, Unloading				☑	☑	☑	☑	☑
9	Replenishment				☑	☑	☑	☑	☑
10	Wave Picking / Wave Management				☑	☑	☑	☑	☑☑
11	Delivery Split for Outbound Orders				☑	☑	☑	☑	☑☑
12	Physical Inventory at Bin Level				☑	☑	☑	☑	☑☑
13	Multiple Bins per Material				☑	☑	☑	☑	☑☑
14	System Generated Placement and Picking				☑	☑	☑	☑	☑☑
15	Pallet Tracebility or Storage Unit Management				☑	☑	☑	☑	
16	Task Interleaving					☑		☑	☑☑
17	Task & Resource Management					☑		☑	☑
18	Yard Management						☑	☑	☑☑
19	Value Added Services						☑	☑	☑☑
20	Cross Docking						☑	☑	☑☑
21	Multiple Fixed Bins for the Materials								☑
22	Labor Management								☑
23	Deconsolidation, Kitting, Slotting and Rearrangement								☑
24	Stock IDs								☑
25	RF Screen Enhancement								☑
26	Serial Numbers, Contract Packaging								☑
27	Discrepancy Processing for Stock Transport Orders								☑
28	EH&S Integration								☑
29	Warehouse Cockpit - Standard Delivered BI content								☑
30	Service Parts Industry								☑
31	Material Flow System Support								☑

Table 2.2A

Table 2.2B will help you understand how other SAP modules like QM, PP, Batch Management, Serial Number Management, and HU Management affect the selected solution and what the overall system complexity will be. The numbers here represent the complexity of the everyday operations. For example, under solution 3A, QM module has its complexity listed as 2, which means solution 3A will be twice as complicated if the QM module is active for the stock.

Impact of Other SAP Modules on the Solutions	Solutions to Manage Inventory							
	1A	1B	2A	3A	3B	3C	3D	4A
Quality Management (QM) - A	1	1	1	2	2	2	2	1
Production Planning (PP) - B	1	1	1	2	2	2	2	2
Batch Management (BM) - C	1	1	1	2	2	2	2	2
Handling Unit Management (HUM) - D	1	1	1	2	2	2	2	1
Serial Number Management (SM) - E	1	1	1	2	2	2	2	1
Total Impact of Other SAP Modules (F) (F=A+B+C+D+E)	5	5	5	10	10	10	10	7
Transactional Overhead of WM Solution (G)	1	1	2	5	6	7	8	7
Overall System Complexity (F + G)	6	6	7	15	16	17	18	14

Table 2.2B

Conclusion

In some cases, transactional overhead may be higher, but it may still be the better solution if it reduces overall system complexity. For example, solution 3D along with batch management, QM, HU management, serial number management, and PP can make overall system complexity very high due to the number of transactions, posting change notices, transfer requirements, etc. Therefore, in such a case, 4A may be a better solution; even though it has more transactional overhead, it can be customized and simplified with some development objects. Finally, licensing fee, server fee and Return On Investment (ROI) may also need to be considered in case of solution 4A.

Summary

In the first part of this chapter, different solutions available to manage the inventory in SAP were discussed. In the second part, guidelines for understanding the transactional overhead and overall system complexity of each of these solutions was introduced. With this information, consultants should be able to guide their clients in choosing better solutions for their warehousing needs.

Chapter 3: Introduction to EWM and Org Structure

This chapter is an introduction to SCM EWM. It explains how EWM has evolved, how it is different from ERP WM, types of data transfer between ERP and EWM, various deployment options, and potential challenges during EWM implementation. It also covers in detail the org structure of warehouse and inventory management, which is the foundation for a good warehouse management solution design.

3.1 EWM Overview

EWM is the latest warehouse management solution from SAP. It was designed from the ground up, keeping in mind the needs of large, complex warehouses and distribution centers with high volume and velocity.

Because of the growing demands in warehouse, planning, and procurement areas, around 2002, SAP stopped all further development in ERP WM and started afresh, with a focus on designing a warehouse solution that could both meet customer demands and compete with the best of breed solutions in the warehouse area.

The development project lasted more than three years, and the first version of EWM (i.e., EWM 5.0) was made available to customers in 2005. Because the primary focus was on high-volume planning, service order fulfillment, and distribution of service parts, EWM became a part of the SCM solution—hence the name SCM-EWM.

Even though the initial focus was on service parts fulfillment, SAP's intent was to design a solution that could be used across multiple industries. Accordingly, it added new functionalities to support the requirements of complex, high-volume warehouses and distribution centers.

Many clients think that implementing EWM is just a technical upgrade from ERP WM. However, this is not true. Both ERP WM and SCM-EWM may share many common themes in terms of functionalities, but they are two different products of SAP and architecturally completely different from one another.

3.1.1 Key Differentiators between EWM and ERP WM

The following are some of the major differences between ERP EWM and EWM systems. They are broadly categorized into infrastructural and functionality differences.

3.1.1.1 Infrastructural and Master Data Differences

1. In ERP WM, organization structure elements like warehouse (WH) number, storage type, and storage sections are three characters long, whereas in EWM they are four characters long.
2. In ERP WM, the maximum length of bin number is ten characters, whereas in EWM it is eighteen.
3. In ERP WM, the bin number need not be unique across the warehouse, whereas it is a requirement of EWM that the bin number be unique across the warehouse.
4. In ERP WM, warehouse-related data is maintained in the material master in "warehouse view 1" and "warehouse view 2." In EWM, warehouse-related data is maintained in the product master of the EWM system.
5. Enhanced master data like supply chain unit, business partners, activity areas, and process types are not required for ERP WM but are mandatory for EWM.
6. In ERP WM, storage section is mandatory to create the bins, whereas in EWM it is not.

3.1.1.2 Functionality Differences

1. In ERP, storage type can be storage unit (SU) managed or non-SU managed. In EWM, the concept of storage unit is replaced with Handling Units (HU), and both HU and non-HU managed stock can exist in the same storage type.
2. In EWM, a graphical warehouse layout feature helps to manage the org elements and monitor material flow systems easily. This feature, however, does not exist in ERP WM.
3. Labor management is only available in EWM.
4. Kitting, slotting, rearrangement, and exception handling functionalities are not available in ERP WM.
5. EWM and ERP WM use different concepts, configuration objects, tables, structures, programs, and transaction codes.
6. Serial number visibility at bin level is possible in EWM. This feature, however, does not exist in ERP WM.
7. The warehouse cockpit is a new and useful feature of EWM that doesn't exist in ERP WM.

3.1.2 Evolution of SAP's EWM Solution

SAP released the first version (5.0) of EWM in 2005, and it was coupled with SCM. It was implemented as part of the SCM solution. In 2007, SAP launched the second version of EWM, version 5.1, with additional functionalities and able to be installed as an add-on to ECC 6.0. This was made available to customers in May 2008. In 2009, SAP released EWM 7.0 with additional functionalities like production staging support, resource management, task interleaving, and graphical warehouse layout. Currently, SAP has released EhP 1 for EWM 7.0. This is also called EWM 7.01. With this release, it is now possible to integrate EWM with ERP transportation management (TMS). You may have to implement EhP 5 in your ERP system in order to use all the functionalities available in EWM 7.01.

Table 3.1.2A will give an overview of the functionalities available in the different versions.

EWM Functionalities	EWM 5.0	EWM 5.1	EWM 7.0	EWM 7.1
Internal routing for Inbound and Outbound process	☑	☑	☑	☑
Warehouse Order creation (work bundle creation for picking)	☑	☑	☑	☑
De-consolidation / Packing	☑	☑	☑	☑
Exception Handling	☑	☑	☑	☑
Warehouse Monitor	☑	☑	☑	☑
Transportation Cross Docking	☑	☑	☑	☑
Value Added Services	☑	☑	☑	☑
Capacity checks using Weight, Volume and Dimension	☑	☑	☑	☑
Packaging Specification	☑	☑	☑	☑
Slotting and Re-arrangement	☑	☑	☑	☑
Yard Management	☑	☑	☑	☑
Kit to Order	☑	☑	☑	☑
Warehouse Cockpit		☑	☑	☑
Serial number Support		☑	☑	☑
Catch Weight Support		☑	☑	☑
Material Flow System		☑	☑	☑
Kit to Stock		☑	☑	☑
Centralized on ERP		☑	☑	☑
Labor Management		☑	☑	☑
RFID Enablement		☑	☑	☑
Batch Mgmt Enhancements		☑	☑	☑
Production Receiving		☑	☑	☑
Production Supply			☑	☑
Opportunistic Cross Docking			☑	☑
Graphical Warehouse Layout			☑	☑
Resource Management			☑	☑
Task Interleaving			☑	☑
Transportation Mgmt Integration				☑

Table 3.1.2A

3.1.3 Types of Data Transfer between ERP and EWM

Because ERP and EWM are two different systems, it is important to know how the data is transferred between the systems. For data transfer between ERP and EWM systems, SAP uses CIF and qRFC communication methods.

There are three main types of data transferred between ERP and EWM, namely, organizational data, master data, and transactional data.

3.1.3.1 Organizational Data

Organizational data includes plants, shipping points, and MRP areas. SAP uses CIF technology to transfer the organizational data from ERP to EWM system. If any changes need to be made to organizational data, they have to be made in the ERP system. Initially, all the data is transferred from ERP to the EWM system. After the initial transfer, only the changes or new entries can be sent to the EWM system. Once the data is transferred to the EWM system, the ERP organizational data will become part of the supply chain unit in EWM. Diagram 3.1.3.1A describes how the data is transferred between systems using CIF technology.

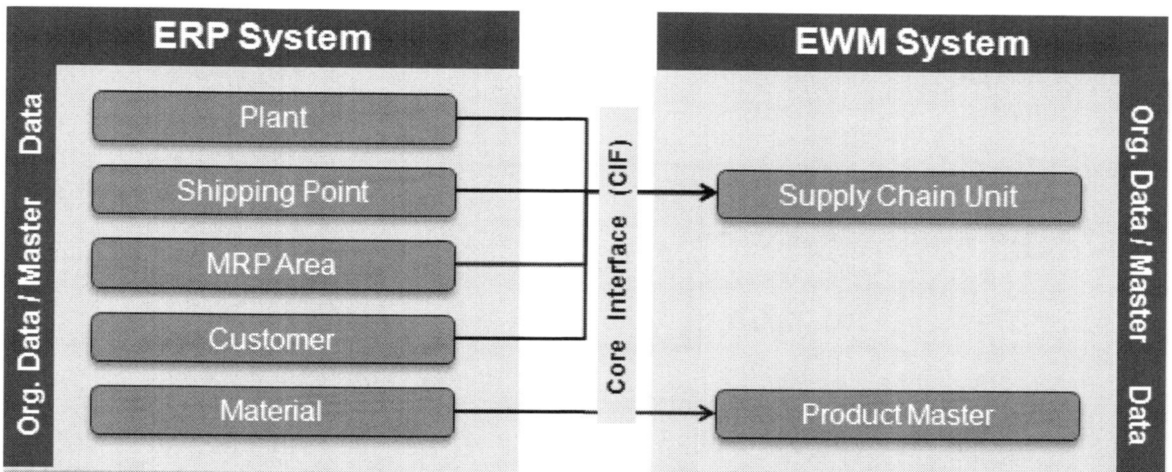

Diagram 3.1.3.1A

3.1.3.2 Master Data

In this context, master data includes material master data, supplier master data, and customer master data. SAP uses CIF technology to transfer the master data from ERP to the EWM system. If any changes must be made to the master data, they have to be made in the ERP system. Initially, all the data is transferred from the ERP to the EWM system. After the initial transfer, only changes or new entries will be transferred to the EWM system.

The supplier and customer master data will also become part of the supply chain unit in EWM, and material master data will become part of the product master data.

3.1.3.3 Transactional Data

Transactional data includes purchase orders, inbound deliveries, outbound deliveries, posting change requests, production order confirmations, and stock movements. SAP uses qRFC technology to move transactional data between ERP and EWM. Only the EWM-related information will be transferred to the EWM system. For example, when a purchase order is created in the ERP system, the plant and storage location have to be entered for the line items. Based on the plant and storage location of the line item, the warehouse number is determined and assigned to the line item. If the determined warehouse is a EWM warehouse, qRFCs will transfer the information to the EWM system. When goods movements like goods issue or goods receipt is posted in the EWM system, qRFC will send that information back to the ERP system. In this way, data in both the systems are synchronized automatically. Diagram 3.1.3.3A shows the type of transactional data transferred between the ERP and EWM systems.

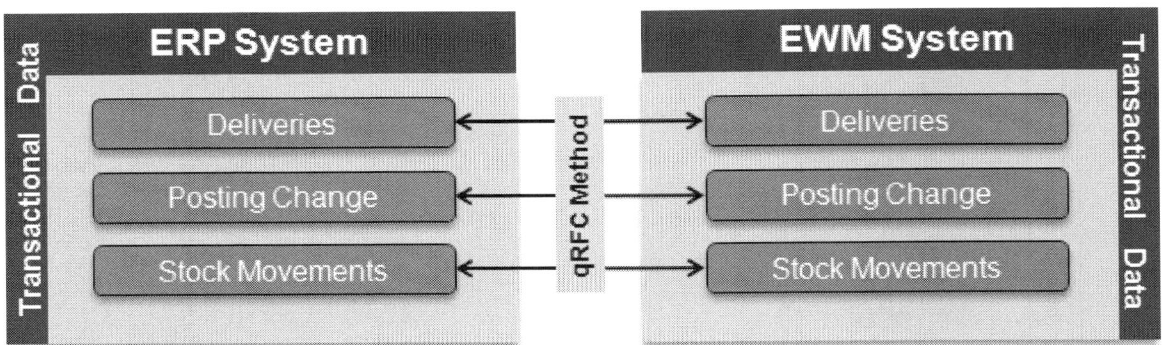

Diagram 3.1.3.3A

3.1.4 EWM Deployment Options

Once the decision is made to implement EWM, the next important task will be making a decision on how to deploy it. As of now, architecturally, EWM can be deployed in two ways: on an "SCM server," which is called a "decentralized warehouse"; or on an "ERP server," in which case it is called "add-on to ERP."

SAP recommends deploying EWM on a SCM server under a separate instance, which can yield better performance and availability and be less impacted with upgrades made to other modules. If the client decides to install EWM on a SCM server, along with other SCM components like APO (event management), then the future upgrades to the other components will have to be well thought out to avoid EWM downtime. SAP has given the option to deploy EWM as an add-on to provide the benefits of SCM to clients who are not using the SCM instance.

In either case, the method for integration between ERP and EWM systems will remain the same. The standard method for connecting EWM to ERP is via the Core Interface (CIF) for master data and via queued Remote Function Call (qRFC) for transactional data.

Table 3.1.4A will demonstrate the methods used to transfer data to the EWM system in each ERP release.

ERP Release	Communication Method Master Data	Transactional data
Below 4.6C	Custom IDOCs	Custom IDOCs
4.6C	CIF	IDOC
4.7 (EE Set 2.0)	CIF	IDOC
ECC 5.0	CIF	IDOC
ECC 6.0	CIF	qRFC
Ecc 6.0 (EhP 3.0 and above)	CIF	qRFC

Table 3.1.4A

3.1.5 EWM—Lessons Learned

When a company selects the EWM solution for its warehouse, the following points need to be considered.

Dedicated server: For better performance, it is recommended to have a separate dedicated server for EWM.

Plan enough support resources: EWM implementation is more complex than ERP WM implementation. It may require multiple consultants, depending on the type of implementation and the duration of the project.

Technical upgrade: Transitioning from ERP WM to EWM is not a technical upgrade but a reimplementation project. Proper training has to be given to the end users on the new system and new terminology.

Unique bin requirement: In EWM, the same bin numbers cannot exist more than once. This may require reorganization of the physical warehouse or relabeling of the bins in the warehouse.

Communication structure: Debugging and problem analysis take longer with EWM, and technical knowledge is desirable.

Additional master data: EWM requires more master data than ERP WM.

IT support: Implementation of both ERP WM and EWM solutions can complicate IT support. It may require more than one resource to support these solutions.

Different terminologies: Different terminologies used in ERP WM and EWM can confuse the end users/IT support, if the same resource supports both ERP WM and EWM solutions.

User training: Due to system complexity, a proper user training plan has to be developed, and training has to be initiated well in advance.

Knowledge transfer: EWM is extremely configurable and complex. It may be difficult for a part-time consultant to understand completely and manage the project after go-live. Hence, it is recommended to have full-time resources dedicated for EWM from the early stage of project.

Activate BC sets: SAP has delivered more than four hundred Business Configuration (BC) sets to jump-start your implementation project. Activating them can speed up your implementation process and avoid unnecessary errors during testing.

Future developments: All SAP's future developments in the WM area will remain only on EWM. Even though ERP WM will remain available on all ERP versions, SAP does not intend to extend its capabilities beyond those it has today.

3.2 Introduction to Org Structure

In SAP, every module has its own org structure. In most cases it looks somewhat like a pyramid with the company at the top level and the company code at the next level. Both these elements are part of Finance and Costing (FICO) org structure, usually defined by FICO consultants. Each company code can have several plants assigned to it.

As shown in figure 2.1A, in the IM org structure, plant is the topmost element, is mostly defined by the MM or PP consultant, and is assigned to a company code. Plant is an operating area or branch of the company. Each plant can have one or more physical or virtual storage locations to store the inventory. Storage locations usually represent a physical segregation of inventory within the plant.

An EWM or WM org structure starts with the warehouse number and is defined by the WM consultant. The warehouse number represents a physical warehouse complex and is assigned to one or more storage locations, if the stock is warehouse managed.

The shipping point, in SAP, is used to address the loading / unloading points or the group of people that is responsible for the shipping process. A plant can have more than one shipping point. Shipping points can also be shared by different plants.

In SAP, the company code, plant number, storage location code, and shipping points can be defined with a code having a maximum of four digits.

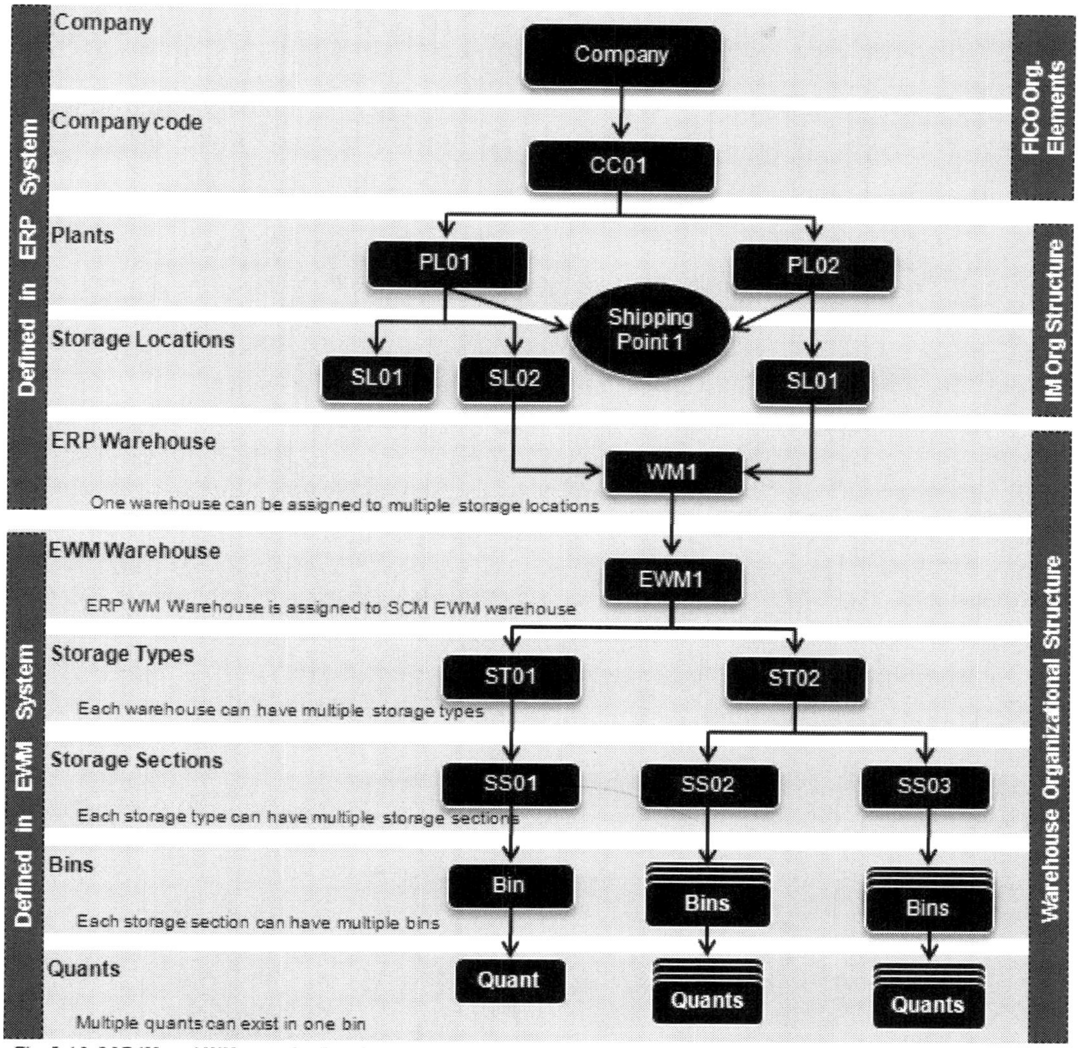

Fig. 2.1A SAP IM and WM organizational structure

3.2.1 IM Org Structure—Plant and Storage Locations

The IM org structure consists of plant and storage locations, the top element being plant. Plant is a subdivision of a company, where either materials are produced, or goods and services are provided.

In SAP, every plant must be assigned to one company code and may contain one or more storage locations. Each company code can have one or more plants, but a plant can be assigned to only one company code. At least one storage location must exist in the plant to manage the inventory. In the plant, if bin visibility is not required, the inventory can be managed at the storage location itself, in which case it will be called *inventory managed stock*. If bin visibility is required, the storage location must be assigned a warehouse org structure, in which case the stock is called *warehouse managed stock*.

3.2.2 WM Org Structure

The WM org structure consists of warehouse number, storage types, storage sections, bins, activity areas, and quants. The following sections will give an overview on each of these org elements.

3.2.2.1 Warehouse Number

The top element in the WM org structure is the warehouse number, which is assigned to the storage locations. In SAP, the warehouse number usually represents a physical warehouse and can be assigned to multiple storage locations of either the same or different plants.

3.2.2.2 Storage Types

The warehouse number is further divided into storage types. In SAP, storage types are segregated as interim and noninterim storage types.

Interim storage types are locations where the inventory is temporarily held until it is put away into the bin or issued from the warehouse. Goods receipt (GR) and goods issue (GI) areas are examples of interim storage types. In general these storage types form a link between WM and Inventory Management (IM).

Noninterim storage types are locations in the warehouse usually used to store the products, for example, finished goods, raw materials, fast-moving materials, etc.

In SAP, the warehouse must have both interim and noninterim storage types.

3.2.2.3 Storage Sections

Storage types are further divided into storage sections. In the physical warehouse, storage sections could represent the type of product (heavy products, small products), or a group of bins (upper level bins, lower level bins), or could represent the velocity of products (fast-moving, slow-moving, etc.). Physically, not all warehouses will have storage sections for each storage type. Even though storage section is required for every storage type in ERP WM, it is not a requirement in EWM to create the bins.

3.2.2.4 Bins

Storage sections are further divided into bins. Bins are locations in the warehouse where inventory is stored. In EWM, bin number should be unique across the warehouse.

3.2.2.5 Activity Area

An activity area is an organizational element and a new feature introduced in EWM. It is a logical group of bins that can have different sorting sequences and can be used in different warehouse activities like PI, picking, putaway, replenishment, and so on. In EWM, activity areas are required and are used by the warehouse-order-creation rules to create the warehouse orders.

Bins from different storage types can be assigned to a given activity area.

Within an activity area, you can also define an activity-dependent bin sorting sequence. The system uses these bin sorting sequences to optimize the execution of warehouse tasks and influence determination of warehouse queues. Diagram 3.2.2.5A is an example for how the activity areas can be created in the warehouse.

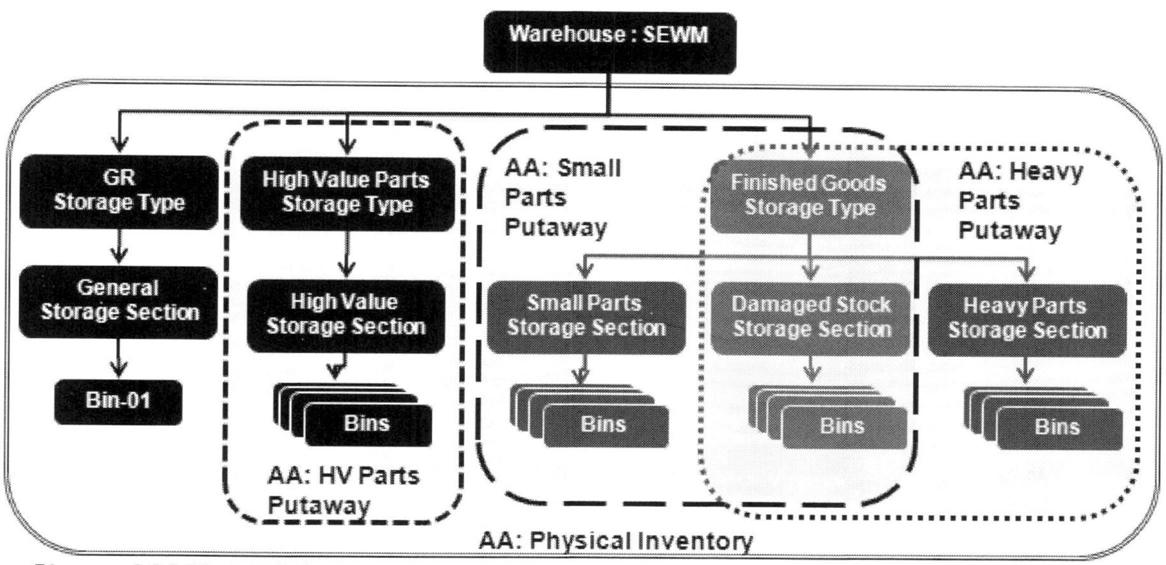

Diagram 3.2.2.5A - Activity Areas

3.2.2.6 Quant

Quant is the lowest level of org element in the warehouse and is within the bin. It represents the stock of material with the same features in one storage bin. It contains information that is used by the system for putaway and for picking from the bin. SAP generates a unique quant based on material number, batch number, stock type, special stock category, and party entitled to dispose.

Notes:

i. In case of warehouse-managed storage location, inventory is displayed both at the warehouse and the storage location levels.

ii. In the warehouse, the stock is managed by quantity at the bin level.

iii. The bin information is mainly used by warehouse personnel to move or manage the inventory inside the warehouse.

iv. All other modules like MM, IM, QM, PP, and SD only deal with the stock at the storage location level, and the corresponding request or notification is sent to the warehouse to pick, putaway, or change the status of the stock accordingly.

Summary

This chapter has examined how EWM has evolved, how it is different from ERP WM, different types of data transfer between ERP and EWM, various deployment options, and potential challenges during EWM implementation. Org structures covered here will help consultants to understand the configuration activities covered in the next chapter.

Chapter 4: Configuration Requirements in ERP

In chapter 3, we briefly covered the IM and WM org structure. This Chapter will cover how those organizational elements are configured in the ERP system. As EWM is not part of the ERP system, it is necessary to configure qRFC and CIF settings for data transfer between systems along with some basic configuration in the Logistic Execution (LE) section of the ERP system. The "Material Master Enhancements" section covers what EWM specific material master data can be stored centrally in the ERP material master and how to store it.

Diagram 4A gives an overview of how different configuration elements are linked to each other and what information flows to customer and material master.

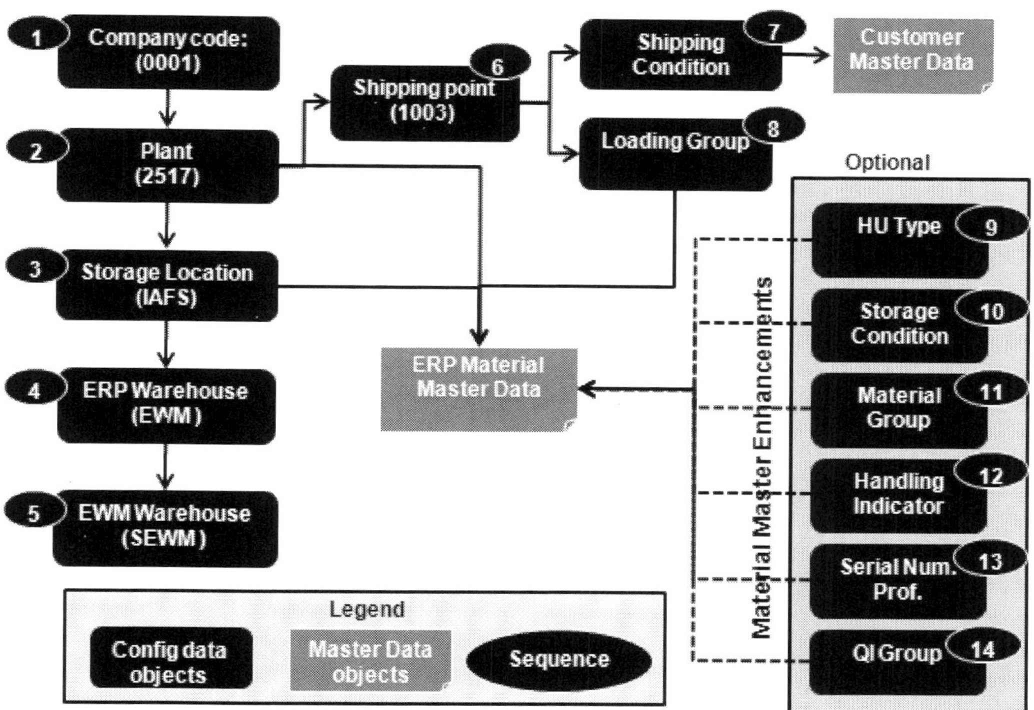

Diagram 4A

Notes:

i. Each section in this chapter has a table, which gives an overview of the configuration required in the ERP system.

ii. Items in the table are arranged in logical order to help readers understand better.

iii. Some configuration settings are highly technical and might require additional authorization or help from the basis team.

iv. Not all configurations done here are transportable. They are required to be maintained by each client manually.

v. Most of the configuration screens are accessed through the Implementation Guide (IMG) menu. Henceforth it will be referred as IMG.

4.1 Org Elements

Table 4.1A is the summary of the configuration covered in this section. The column "Transportable" refers to whether or not the configuration for the item can be transported to another system.

S. No	Configuration Check List	TCode	Transportable
1	Define Plants	SPRO	Yes
2	Define Storage Locations	SPRO	Yes
3	Define Warehouse Number	SPRO	Yes
4	Define Shipping Points	SPRO	Yes
5	Define Shipping Conditions	SPRO	Yes
6	Define Loading Groups	SPRO	Yes
7	Assign Plant to Company Code	SPRO	Yes
8	Assign Warehouse Number to Plant and Storage Location	SPRO	Yes
9	Assign ERP Warehouse to EWM Warehouse	SPRO	Yes
10	Assign Shipping Points to Plants	SPRO	Yes
11	Maintain Shipping Points for Outbound Deliveries	SPRO	Yes
12	Maintain Goods Receiving Points for Inbound Deliveries	SPRO	Yes

Table 4.1A

4.1.1 Define Plant

As explained in the chapter 3, the plant is the topmost org level entity in the IM org structure and is defined in the IMG.

Menu Path: SPRO | IMG | Enterprise Structure | Definition | Logistics—General | Define, Copy, Delete, Check Plant

In this menu, option "**Define plant**" can be used to create a plant without reference. Here consultants must define the entire required configuration manually. The other option is create a plant with reference to the existing plant. In such a case, the entire configuration defined for the existing plant is copied to the new plant. SAP recommends creating a new plant with reference. Option "**Copy, delete, check plant**" is used to create a plant with reference.

To create a plant with reference to existing plant, click on option "Copy, delete, check plant" and click on the "Copy org. object" icon located in the application toolbar. Here in the "From Plant," field enter the existing plant number from which you want to copy the configuration to the new plant; and in the "To Plant," field enter the new plant number. Click on green check. This will create a new plant and will copy the reference plant's configuration.

To change the name and address of the plant, click on define plant, select the plant name, click on the details icon on the application bar, and then change the name 1 and name 2 fields. The address can be changed by clicking on the address icon on the application toolbar.

In this example a plant with code 2517 has been defined, and it will be referenced throughout this book.

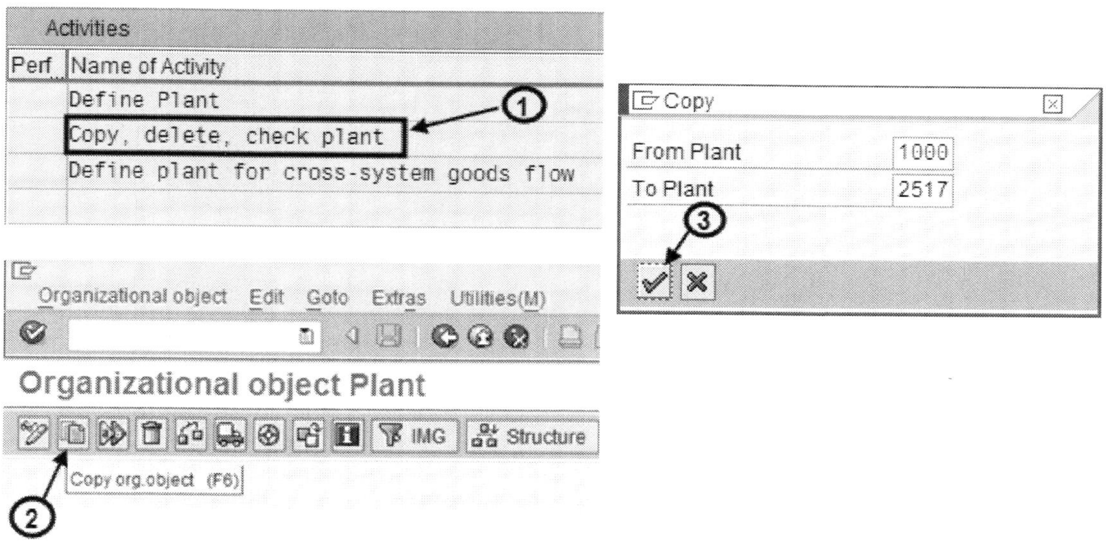

Notes:

i. The copy function will not copy all the number ranges for the plant automatically. They have to be maintained separately.

ii. To make a new plant operational, there may be some additional configuration required in other modules like FICO, MM, PP, SD and QM.

iii. During practice, we recommend that consultants use existing SAP delivered demo plants to avoid configuration dependency of other modules.

4.1.2 Define Storage Locations

Storage location is the place where stock is physically kept. Both for nonwarehouse managed stock and warehouse managed stock, storage location is required.

Menu Path: **SPRO | IMG | Enterprise Structure | Definition | Materials Management | Maintain Storage Location**

In this transaction, the system requires that the plant number be entered in the pop-up screen. When the pop-up screen appears, enter the plant number and click on the green check mark. This will display all the existing storage locations defined for the plant. To add a new storage location, click on the "New Entries" button on the application toolbar, enter the storage location code and description, and save the entries.

To delete storage locations, select the nonrelevant entries and click on the delete entries button on the application toolbar.

In this example, we have created three storage locations for plant 2517. Storage locations IAFS and NAFS are defined to manage the inventory at the warehouse bin. Storage location NEWM is defined to manage nonwarehouse managed stock.

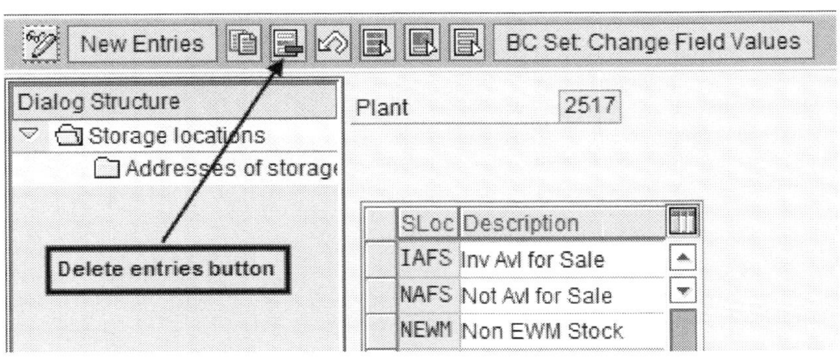

4.1.3 Define ERP Warehouse Number

Because EWM warehouses are configured in the SCM environment and cannot be directly linked to ERP storage locations, we have to first define the ERP warehouse and assign it to the ERP storage location. Later, the ERP warehouse has to be assigned to the EWM warehouse. This will form the link between ERP storage locations and the EWM warehouse. Here, the ERP warehouse will work only as a reference element between the storage locations and the EWM warehouse. No additional structure is required under the ERP warehouse.

Menu Path: **SPRO | IMG | Enterprise Structure | Definition | Logistics Execution | Define, Copy, Delete, Check Warehouse Number | Define Warehouse Number**

Click on the "New Entries" button on the application toolbar; enter the warehouse number and description, as shown below.

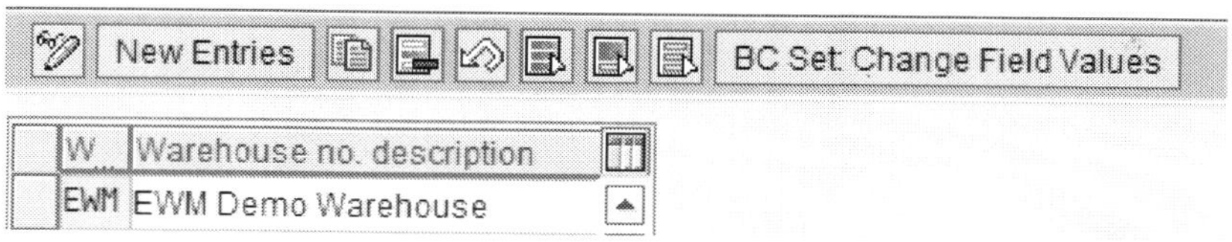

The ERP warehouse defined here will be assigned to storage locations in a later section of this chapter.

4.1.4 Define Shipping Point

In the ERP system, the shipping point is the organizational unit responsible for shipping process which is generally defined by the SD consultant and assigned to the plant. In this example we have defined one shipping point for plant 2517; however, more than one shipping point can exist for a plant.

Menu Path: SPRO | IMG | Enterprise Structure | Definition | Logistics Execution | Define, copy, delete, check shipping point

Here, select the "Define shipping point" option, click on the "New Entries" button on the application toolbar; enter shipping point code, name, and address.

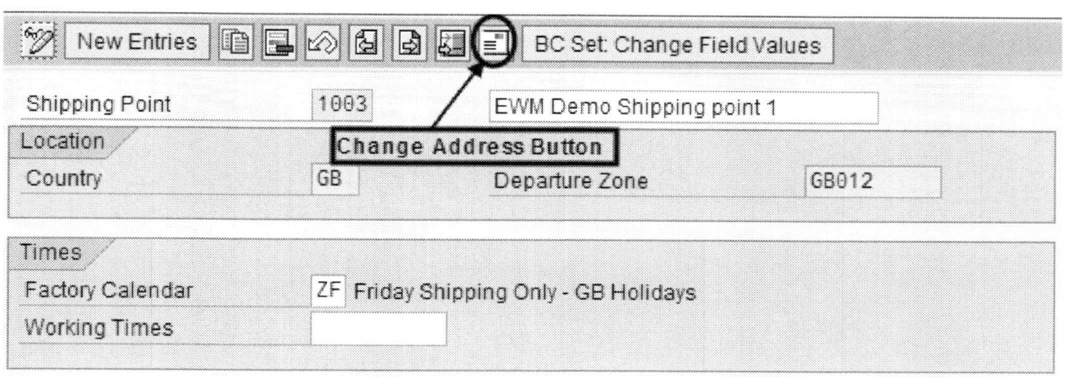

Notes:

i. It is recommended to create the shipping point using the "Copy, delete, check shipping point" option. This will copy the required configuration from the "FROM" shipping point to the "NEW" shipping point.

ii. Even though ERP systems allow it, do not create a shipping point with the same ID as the plant code. Shipping points and plants will become locations in the EWM system. Hence, having the same code will cause an error during the data transfer.

4.1.5 Define Shipping Condition

Shipping conditions are used to define how the materials are shipped to the customers. They can be by road, air, customer pickup, and so on. Shipping conditions defined here are assigned to the customer master. When the sales order is created for the customer, the shipping condition will be copied to the sales order from the customer master. The system uses this information along with loading group to determine the shipping points in the sales order.

Menu Path: SPRO | IMG | Logistics Execution | Shipping | Basic Shipping Functions | Shipping Point and Goods Receiving Point Determination | Define Shipping Conditions

Click on the "New Entries" button on the application toolbar; enter the shipping condition and the description of the shipping condition.

Shipping Conditions

SC	Description
01	Standard
02	Pick-up
03	Expedited
04	Truckload/Containers
05	Air
EW	EWM WH Pick-Up

4.1.6 Define Loading Group

"Loading group" refers to how the material is loaded to the delivery vehicle—for example, manually, by forklift, etc. Based on the combination of loading group and shipping condition, a shipping point is determined to load the materials. The loading group defined here is assigned to the material master. In order to determine the shipping point in the sales order, the appropriate loading group must be assigned to the material master.

Menu Path: SPRO | IMG | Logistics Execution | Shipping | Basic Shipping Functions | Shipping Point and Goods Receiving Point Determination | Define Loading Groups

Click on the "New Entries" button on the application toolbar; enter the loading group and the description.

Routes: Loading Groups

LGrp	Description
EWCR	Crane - EWM

4.1.7 Assign Plant to Company Code

A plant can belong to only one company code. To assign the plant to a company code follow the menu path **SPRO | IMG | Enterprise Structure | Assignment | Logistics—General | Assign Plant to Company Code**

Click on the "New Entries" button on the application toolbar; enter the company code and plant number and save your entries.

Assignment Plant - Company Code

Co...	Plnt	Name of Plant	Company Name	Status
0001	2517	EWM Demo	SAP A.G.	

4.1.8 Assign Warehouse Number to Plant and Storage Location

Any storage location that is warehouse managed needs to be assigned a warehouse number. Whenever an IM transaction is performed, the system will check whether the entered plant and storage location is warehouse managed. If so, the system will copy the warehouse information to the transaction. Therefore, to avoid any errors, it is recommended that this assignment be completed before creating any transactional data.

Menu Path: SPRO | IMG | Enterprise Structure | Assignment | Logistics Execution | Assign Warehouse Number to Plant/Storage Location

Click on the "New Entries" button on the application toolbar; enter the plant, the storage location, the warehouse number and click on the "Save" button.

Plnt	SLoc	W...	Warehouse no. description
2517	IAFS	EWM	EWM Demo Warehouse
2517	NAFS	EWM	EWM Demo Warehouse

4.1.9 Assign ERP Warehouse to EWM Warehouse

In this menu we have to specify which of the ERP warehouses is linked to the EWM warehouse. This link is used to transfer materials and transactional data from the ERP warehouse to the EWM warehouse for further processing.

Menu Path: SPRO | IMG | Integration with Other mySAP.com Components | Extended Warehouse Management | Additional Material Attributes | Assign Warehouse Number to Warehouse Number of Decentralized SCM System

The EWM warehouse number that needs to be linked to the ERP warehouse is entered here.

Assign Warehouse No. to Warehouse No. of Decentr. S		
W...	Whse no. description	WHN.DecS...
EWM	EWM Demo Warehouse	SEWM

Notes:

i. Here, column WHN.DecS is just a text field. The entries entered in this column are not validated against the EWM system. Hence, wrong entries can cause problems during the data transfer.

4.1.10 Assign Shipping Points to Plants

Menu Path: SPRO | IMG | Enterprise Structure | Assignment | Logistics Execution | Assign Shipping Point to Plant

Here, select the plant, click on the "Assign" button on the application toolbar, select the shipping point that should be assigned to the plant, click on the green check, and save the entries. This will assign the selected shipping points to the plant.

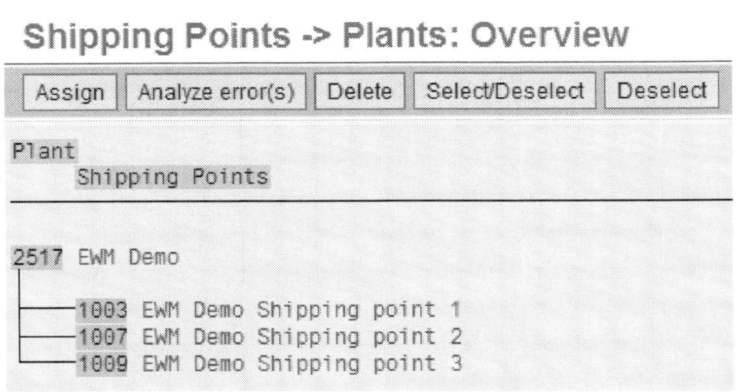

4.1.11 Maintain Shipping Points for Outbound Deliveries

In order to determine shipping points for the outbound deliveries, the entries for combinations of shipping condition, loading group, and plant must be maintained. This assignment is used only for outbound deliveries.

Shipping Point Determination					
SC	LGrp	Plnt	PrShP	MShPt	MShPt
EW	EWCR	2517	1009	1007	1003

Menu Path: **SPRO | IMG | Logistics Execution | Shipping | Basic Shipping Functions | Shipping Point and Goods Receiving Point Determination | Assign Shipping Points**

Here, click on the "New Entries" button on the application toolbar; enter the shipping condition, the loading group, the plant, and the shipping points. The shipping point entered in the "PrShp" column will be the default in the sales order. However, shipping points entered in the "MShPt" column can be selected manually in the sales order.

4.1.12 Maintain Goods Receiving Points for Inbound Deliveries

Here, the shipping points that are used for goods receipt are assigned. Only one shipping point per storage location can be assigned. In general, the goods receipt and goods issue points are represented by the same shipping point. In such cases, no separate shipping points are defined for goods receipts.

Menu Path: **SPRO | IMG | Logistics Execution | Shipping | Basic Shipping Functions | Shipping Point and Goods Receiving Point Determination | Assign Goods Receiving Points for Inbound Deliveries**

Click on the "New Entries" button on the application toolbar; enter the plant, the storage location, the shipping point, and click on the "Save" button to save the changes.

Assign Shipping Point as Goods Receiving Point to Plant/SLo

Plant	Stor. Loc.	Shipping P...	Sequence Number
2517	IAFS	1009	
2517	NAFS	1009	
2517	NEWM	1003	

4.2 Logistics Execution (LE) Requirements

In addition to org elements configuration, it is also necessary to define some additional configuration for EWM in the ERP logistics execution section. Table 4.2A covers an overview of the configuration required in the LE section.

S. No	Configuration Check List	TCode	Transportable
1	Define number range interval for unchecked deliveries	VN01	No
2	Assign unchecked delivery number range for outbound delivery type	SPRO	Yes
3	Assign unchecked delivery number range for inbound delivery type	SPRO	Yes
4	Define Delivery Split by Warehouse Number	SPRO	Yes
5	Activate Enhancements for Service Parts Management	SPRO	Yes
6	Maintain Extended Warehouse Management-Specific Parameters	SPRO	Yes

Table 4.2A

4.2.1 Define Number Range Interval for Unchecked Deliveries

In EWM, unchecked deliveries are used for planning purpose. They cannot be used for shipping or billing. In a direct delivery scenario, an unchecked delivery is created when the sales order is saved in CRM. Transferring these deliveries to the EWM system will lend visibility to the future workload and help in the planning of resources in the warehouse.

Creating a separate number range for unchecked deliveries is optional. To keep the actual deliveries separate from unchecked deliveries, it is recommended that a separate number range interval for unchecked deliveries be defined. This will help to easily identify unchecked deliveries by looking at the delivery number.

Menu Path: SPRO | IMG | Logistics Execution | Shipping | Deliveries | Define Number Ranges for Deliveries or TCode VN01

Click on the "Change Intervals" button to add a new number range. To define a new number range, click on the "insert interval" button on the application toolbar. The new number range should not overlap with a previously defined number range.

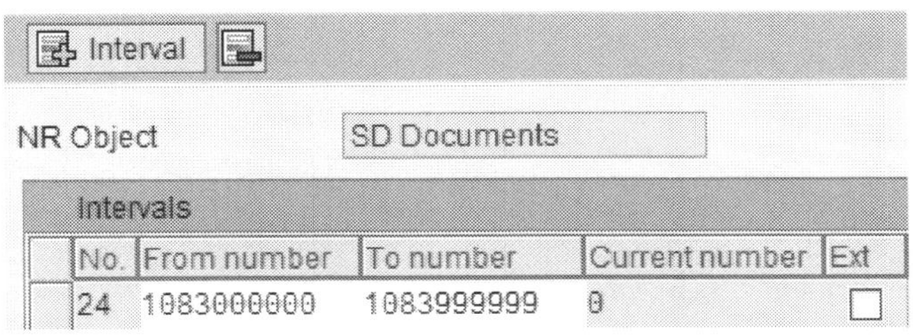

The number range defined here is assigned to an inbound and outbound delivery type in the later section.

4.2.2 Assign Unchecked Delivery Number Range for Outbound Delivery Type

Here, assign the unchecked delivery number range to the outbound delivery type. Whenever an unchecked or temporary outbound delivery is created, the system will assign the delivery number from the number range assigned here.

Menu Path: SPRO | IMG | Logistics Execution | Service Parts Management (SPM) | Outbound Process (SPM) | Unchecked Deliveries | Maintain Deviating Number Range for Unchecked Deliveries

Number Ranges for unchecked Deliveries

DlvTy	Description	Tmp...	Reuse
LF	Outbound Delivery	24	☑

4.2.3 Assign Unchecked Delivery Number Range for Inbound Delivery Type

Temporary inbound deliveries are similar to unchecked outbound deliveries. Whenever a temporary inbound delivery is created, the system will assign a number to the inbound delivery from this number range.

Menu Path: SPRO | IMG | Logistics Execution | Service Parts Management (SPM) | Extended Inbound Delivery Processing (SPM) | Settings for SPM Inbound Delivery Processing

Here, select the appropriate inbound delivery type, click on the "Details" button on the application tool bar, and enter the number range.

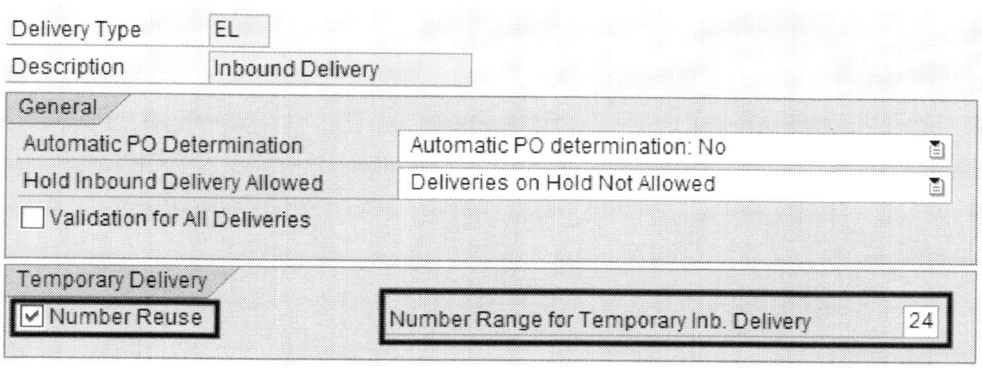

4.2.4 Define Delivery Split by Warehouse Number

Sales document may contain materials that need to be delivered from EWM warehouse, ERP warehouse- and non–warehouse–managed storage locations. Because EWM-specific delivery items are picked and post goods issued in the EWM system, a unique delivery must be created for materials belong to the EWM warehouse. Using the delivery split options, it can be ensured that, during the delivery creation process, a unique delivery is created for each warehouse, and only EWM-specific deliveries are sent to the EWM system. If the split indicator is only maintained for the delivery type, no individual delivery will be created for the warehouse number. Therefore delivery split has to be defined both per delivery type and per warehouse number.

Menu Path: SPRO | IMG | Logistics Execution | Shipping | Deliveries | Define Split Criteria for Deliveries | Delivery Split by Warehouse Number

Activities	
Perf	Name of Activity
	Define delivery split per delivery type
	Determine delivery split per warehouse number

Define delivery split for the delivery type: To define delivery split for the delivery type, click on "Define delivery split per delivery type," select the required delivery types (mainly EL and LF) and check the delivery split—WhNo check box and save the entries.

Delivery Split for Warehouse Number per Delivery Type		
Del. ty.	Description	Delivry Split - WhNo
EL	Inbound Delivery	☑
LF	Outbound Delivery	☑

Define delivery split by warehouse number: To define delivery split by warehouse number, click on option "determine delivery split per warehouse number," select the ERP warehouse defined for EWM warehouse, check the delivery split by warehouse number checkbox, and save the entries.

Delivery split by warehouse number		
Wareho	Warehouse no. description	Deliv.split by whse number
EWM	EWM Demo Warehouse	☑

4.2.5 Activate Enhancements for Service Parts Management (SPM)

One of the technical requirements of the EWM system is that SPM has to be active in the ERP system. Before activating SPM in the ERP system, all open business documents such as sales orders, deliveries, and invoices must be processed. Once SPM is activated, it may not be possible to process any open business documents created prior to activation.

Menu Path: SPRO | IMG | Logistics Execution | Service Parts Management (SPM) | Activate Enhancements for Service Parts Management (SPM) | Activate Enhancements for Service Parts Management

Click on "New Entries" button on the application toolbar; select the customer type as service parts management active. It will display a warning message. If all business documents are closed and SPM activation is ready, click on "Yes".

Enable SAP Solution	
Customer type	1 Service Parts Management active (SPM)

4.2.6 Maintain Extended WM-Specific Parameters

This configuration is required only for EWM-specific warehouses. It should not be activated for ERP warehouses. The WM system in ERP is activated by assigning the plant/storage location to the warehouse number. In this configuration, by setting the warehouse number to "ERP with EWM," as shown in the screenshot below, it is ensured that the warehouse stock is managed in the EWM system and not in the ERP WM system.

Menu Path: SPRO | IMG | Logistics Execution | Service Parts Management (SPM) | Integrate SPM with Other Components | Maintain Extended WM-Specific Parameters

In this configuration, enter the EWM warehouse number and maintain the values as follows: "ERP with EWM" for Ext. WM; "Queued and Serialized Asynchronous" for Comm. WM; check the UD check box; and for Dist. Mode, select "Distribution Immediately at Document Creation."

Extended Warehouse Management system

W...	Ext. WM	Comm. WM	UD	Dist. Mode	SN Dec. WM
EWM	E ERP with EWM	Q Queued and Seriali	☑	Distribution Immediatel	☑

Thus, in column Ext. WM, it is specified that the ERP warehouse is linked to the EWM warehouse. In case the warehouse is only an ERP warehouse, the entry selected should be "ERP with local WM."

The "Comm. WM" column specifies how the communication takes place between ERP and EWM warehouses.

Column "UD" controls whether unchecked deliveries are distributed to the warehouse.

The "Dist. Mode" setting is used to specify when an inbound/outbound delivery is distributed to the decentralized WMS. This setting is valid for all inbound/outbound deliveries that are processed in the relevant warehouse number.

"SN DEC. WM" indicator controls whether serial numbers can be maintained in the EWM system. Set this indicator if you want to maintain serial numbers in EWM. In this case, you should ensure that at the organization level, the serial numbers are unique across the system boundaries. In the SAP system, there is no cross-system check of serial numbers entered.

4.3 Material Master Enhancements

In ERP, material master data is one of the most important data elements for every module. Along with configuration, it drives the processes in the system. Since EWM is a different system, all master data settings for EWM are maintained in the EWM system under product master. Hence, maintaining EWM-specific data in the ERP material master is not required. But if, for various reasons a client wants to maintain some data elements (like handling unit type, serial number profile, or handling unit group) centrally in the ERP system and wants to transfer such information to the EWM system, they can do so by activating the material master enhancements.

When the material master enhancements are activated, the system will enable two additional views in the material master, called *WM Packaging* and *WM Execution,* along with a few additional fields in the Unit of Measure view. This can be used to maintain certain data centrally in the ERP system and transfer it to the EWM system.

During the material master data transfer from ERP to EWM, the system will transfer only data that is maintained in basic data view 1, basic data view 2, UOM view, WM packaging, and WM execution views. No data from other views will be considered during the data transfer. The data transfer will be done only through CIF technology.

Table 4.3A gives an overview of the configuration required to activate the material master enhancement and the configuration required to populate the values in the additional views.

S. No	Configuration Check List	TCode	Transportable
1	Material Master Enhancements or Activation of BC Sets	SCPR20	Yes
2	Maintain Additional Screen sequences	OMT3R	Yes
3	Attribute Values for Additional Material Master Fields like HU Type, material group etc.	SPRO	Yes

Table 4.3A

4.3.1 Material Master Enhancements or Activation of BC Sets

By default, WM Packaging and WM Execution views are not activated in the ERP system. SAP has developed a new Business Configuration (BC) set named "/SPE/MATERIAL_SCREENS," which has the entire configuration required for WM Packaging and WM Execution views. Activating this BC set will make these views visible in the material master to maintain the data in ERP. SAP stores these data in the MARA and MARM tables. Tables 4.3.1A, 4.3.1B, and 4.3.1C give an overview of all EWM-specific fields available in the material master after activating the BC set.

Table 4.3.1A - WM Packaging View

Field Description	Table Name	Field Name
Handling Unit Type	MARA	HUTYP
Standard HU Type	MARA	HUTYP_DFLT
Max. Allowed Capacity of Packaging Material	MARA	MAXC
Overcapacity Tolerance of the Handling Unit	MARA	MAXC_TOL
Form Name	MARA	PS_SMARTFORM
Variable Tare Weight	MARA	TARE_VAR
Max. Packing Length of Packaging Material	MARA	MAXL
Unit of Measure for Max. Packing Len/Wid/Hght	MARA	MAXDIM_UOM
Max. Packing Width of Packaging Material	MARA	MAXB
Max. Packing Height of Packaging Material	MARA	MAXH

Table 4.3.1B - WM Execution View

Field Description	Table Name	Field Name
Handling Indicator	MARA	HNDLCODE
Warehouse Material Group	MARA	WHMATGR
Warehouse Storage Condition	MARA	WHSTC
Standard HU Type	MARA	HUTYP_DFLT
Serial Number Profile	MARA	SERIAL
Pilferable	MARA	PILFERABLE
Relevant for Hazardous Substances	MARA	HAZMAT
Quarantine Period	MARA	QQTIME
Time Unit for Quarantine Period	MARA	QQTIMEUOM
Quality Inspection Group	MARA	QGRP

Table 4.3.1C - Additional Fields in Unit Of Measure View

Field Description	Table Name	Field Name
Remaining Volume after Nesting (in Percentage)	MARM	NEST_FTR
Max. Stacking Factor	MARM	MAX_STACK
Capacity Usage	MARM	CAPAUSE
EWM-CW: Category of Unit of Measure	MARM	TY2TQ

Notes:

i. After activating the BC sets and maintaining the screen sequence as described in section 4.3.1.1 and 4.3.1.2, if the above fields are not visible in the material master, it may be necessary to apply SAP note 958143.

ii. Activating the BC set might change the existing screen sequence. Hence, you may need to rearrange the appropriate screen sequence, as shown below in 4.3.1.2 (TCode OMT3R).

4.3.1.1 Activate Standard BC Set

To activate the BC set, enter TCode SCPR20, enter /SPE/MATERIAL_SCREENS in the BC set field, and click on the "Activate" button on the application toolbar. This will activate the entered BC set and add the additional views and fields in the material master.

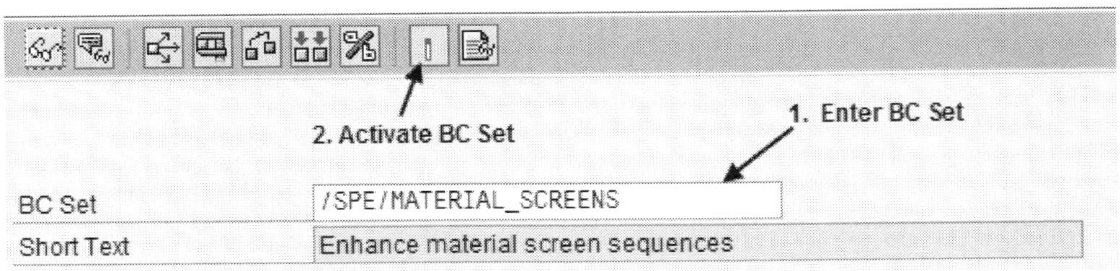

4.3.1.2 Maintain Additional Screen Sequence

After activating the BC set, it is important to adjust the screen display sequence. Prior to adjusting the screen sequence, the appropriate screen sequence for the material master should be identified. To do this, go to transaction OMT3E or follow the menu path **SPRO | IMG | Logistics—General | Material Master | Configuring the Material Master | Assign Screen Sequences to User/Material Type/Transaction/Industry Sector**. Here, double-click on option "Transaction screen reference" and locate the screen reference for the material master creation transaction.

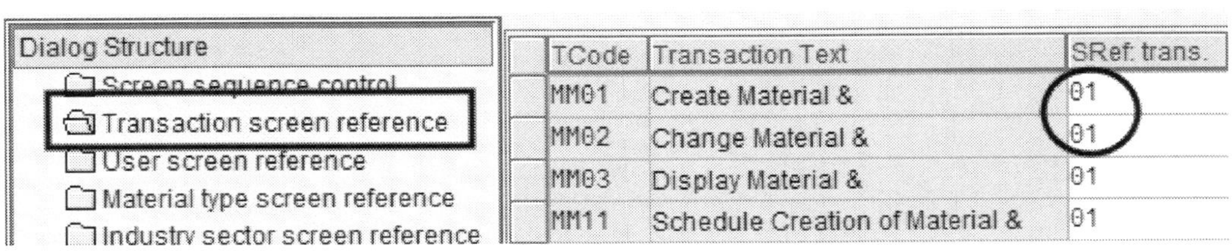

Once the screen reference is identified, double click on "Screen sequence control" and locate the appropriate screen sequence number. In most cases, it will be 21.

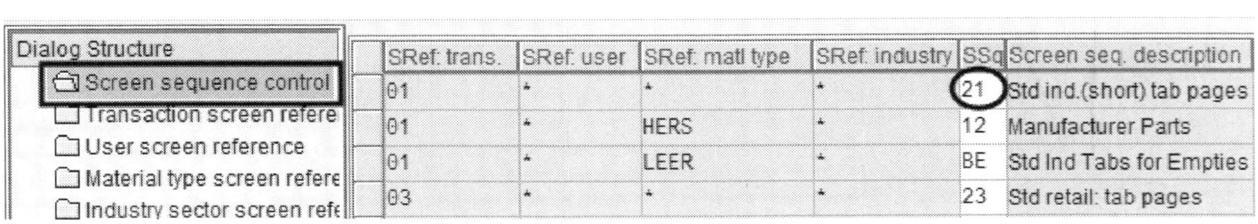

Once the screen sequence number is identified, the screen number in TCode OMT3R can be adjusted. This transaction can also be accessed from menu path **SPRO | IMG | Logistics - General | Material Master | Configuring the Material Master | Maintain Order of Main and Additional Screens**

Here, select the appropriate screen sequence, click on the "Details" button on the application toolbar, and hit the enter key. This will display the screen number, screen description, and each screen's assigned number. The screen numbers represent the views in the material master. The number represents in what sequence the views are arranged in the material master. The numbers for WM packaging and WM execution view can be changed or assigned as needed.

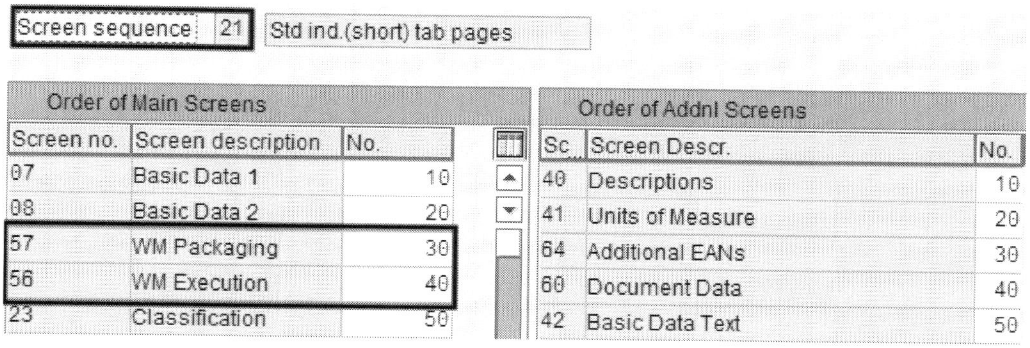

These changes can be verified in the material master. If the changes are not reflected in the material master, verify the configuration. If necessary, reactivate the BC set and follow the above instructions. If this does not solve the problem, it may be necessary to apply the SAP OSS notes.

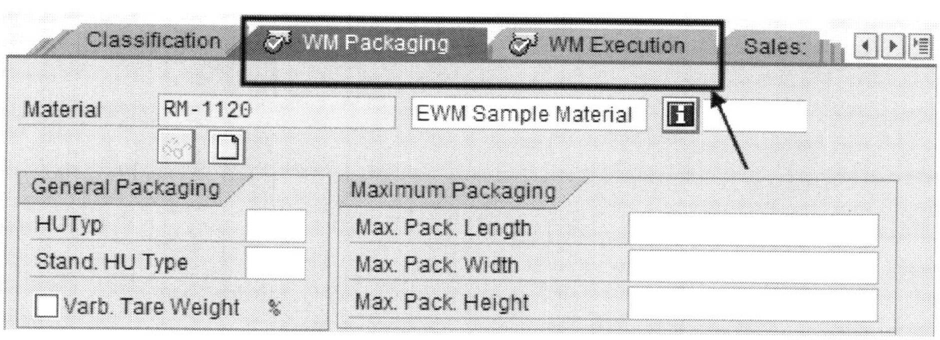

4.3.2 Attribute Values for Additional Material Master Fields

Once the WM Packaging and WM Execution views are activated, several fields will be enabled in these views to maintain data centrally in the ERP system. This information will be transferred to EWM system as part of the master data transfer in the CIF process. In order to populate the values in these two views, the following configuration is required in the ERP system.

4.3.2.1 Define Handling Unit (HU) Type

HU type is used to classify packaging materials and handling units with the same physical properties. Examples of HU types include steel pallet, cardboard box, wooden pallets, etc.

The HU type maintained in the ERP material master under WM packaging view can be transferred to the EWM as part of CIF. If maintaining HU types in the ERP material master is not a requirement, they can be maintained directly the EWM system in the product master.

Menu Path: SPRO | IMG | Integration with Other mySAP.com Components | Extended Warehouse Management | Additional Material Attributes | Attribute Values for Additional Material Master Fields | Define Handling Unit Type

Click on the "New Entries" button on the application toolbar; enter the HU type and the description.

Handling Unit Types

HUTyp	Description
STPL	Steel Pallet
WDPL	Wooden Pallet
CBOX	Cardboard Box

4.3.2.2 Define Warehouse Storage Condition

Storage conditions are specified when the materials need to be stored in specific conditions in the warehouse, for example, at a specific temperature. This information is useful for the warehouse operator when the goods are stored in the warehouse.

Menu Path: SPRO | IMG | Integration with Other mySAP.com Components | Extended Warehouse Management | Additional Material Attributes | Attribute Values for Additional Material Master Fields | Define Warehouse Storage Condition

Click on the "New Entries" button on the application toolbar; enter the WH storage condition and the appropriate description.

Warehouse Storage Condition

WHS...	Description
01	Cool
02	Dry

4.3.2.3 Define Warehouse Material Group

Warehouse material groups defined in this configuration are assigned to the ERP material master and used in EWM to specify that certain materials should always be stored in the same way.

Menu Path: **SPRO | IMG | Integration with Other mySAP.com Components | Extended Warehouse Management | Additional Material Attributes | Attribute Values for Additional Material Master Fields | Define Warehouse Material Group**

Click on the "New Entries" button on the application toolbar, enter the material group and description, and click on the "Save" button.

Warehouse Material Group

WHMatG	Description
HUMS	HU Managed Stock
NHUM	Non HU Managed stock

4.3.2.4 Define Handling Indicator

The handling Indicator is used to specify how the material should be handled in the warehouse. Examples include fragile materials, hazardous materials, etc.

Menu Path: **SPRO | IMG | Integration with Other mySAP.com Components | Extended Warehouse Management | Additional Material Attributes | Attribute Values for Additional Material Master Fields | Define Handling Indicator**

Click on the "New Entries" button on the application toolbar; enter the handling indicator and the description.

Handling Indicator

Hand.Ind.	Description
0001	Fragile handle with Care
0002	Transport in Upright Position
0003	hazardous substance

4.3.2.5 Define Quality Inspection Group

Quality inspection groups are used to group materials together that have to be inspected in a similar fashion. These groups are later used to simplify the maintenance of inspection rules in EWM. When the material is transferred to the EWM system, the quality inspection group is automatically transferred as well.

Menu Path: **SPRO | IMG | Integration with Other mySAP.com Components | Extended Warehouse Management | Additional Material Attributes | Attribute Values for Additional Material Master Fields | Define Quality Inspection Group**

Click on the "New Entries" button on the application toolbar; enter the quality inspection group (4 char code) and the description.

Quality Inspection Group	
QualInsGrp	Description
EXSP	Goods Receipts from External Supplier
PROD	Goods Receipt from Production

4.4 qRFC and CIF Configuration

Today, most applications are designed to communicate with other applications through an interface called Remote Function Call (RFC). RFC can be used to start an application remotely or to execute particular functions remotely. The main limitation of the RFC was that both the sending and receiving applications needed to be active to communicate and transfer data. Thus evolved the next generation of RFC, called *queued Remote Function Call* (qRFC). The main advantage of qRFC is that the receiving system doesn't need to be online at the time of data transfer. If the receiving system is not available, the data will be queued and later processed once the receiving system becomes available. SAP uses qRFC with inbound and outbound queues to transfer data between ERP and EWM systems.

Notes:

i. Some configurations may require additional authorization or Basis team support.

ii. Most of the configuration done in this section is not automatically transportable. Even though some of it can be transported manually, it is recommended to maintain them manually in each system.

iii. Some configurations might already exist, if the SCM system is already linked to the ERP system as a part of APO requirements.

4.4.1 Settings Required for Both CIF and qRFC

CIF and qRFC settings are required to transfer the master and transactional data between ERP and EWM systems. Table 4.4.1A gives an overview of the settings required to activate both CIF and qRFC in ERP systems.

Table 4.4.1A - Settings Required for Both CIF and qRFC

S. No	Configuration Check List	TCode	Transportable
1	Name Logical Systems for ERP and EWM Systems	SPRO	Yes
2	Assign ERP Logical System to a Client	SPRO	No
3	Assign EWM Release Version to EWM Logical System	SPRO	Yes
4	Create RFC User for RFC Connection	SU01	No
5	Define RFC Destination for EWM Logical System	SM59	No
6	Assign RFC Destinations to Different Application Cases	SPRO	No
7	Assign RFC Destinations to Method and BAPI Calls	BD97	No

4.4.1.1 Name Logical Systems for ERP and EWM Systems

During the data transfer, a system uses the “logical systems” to identify the sending and receiving systems. Therefore, we have to define two logical systems: one for the ERP system (sending) and the other for the EWM (receiving) system.

Menu Path: SPRO | IMG | Integration with Other mySAP.com Components | Extended Warehouse Management | Basic Settings for Setting Up the System Landscape | Name Logical System

Click on the "New Entries" button on the application toolbar; enter the logical system and the name. Click on "Save" to save the entries.

Here, we have defined two logical systems. In the name, the first three letters represent the system ID, and the last three digits represent the client number.

i. SE1CLNT410—ERP system

ii. SA1CLNT001—EWM system

Logical Systems

Log.System	Name
SA1CLNT001	SCM EWM Sandbox Client 001
SE1CLNT410	ERP Sandbox Client 410

4.4.1.2 Assign ERP Logical System to a Client

Once the logical systems are defined, the next step is to assign the ERP logical system to the client number. Here, the client number refers to the ERP client number, which will be connected to the EWM system. In SAP, this can be found at the right-hand corner of the status bar, as shown below.

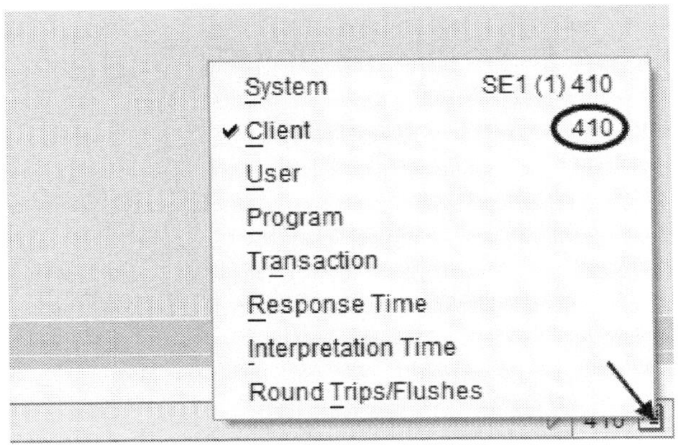

Menu Path: SPRO | IMG | Integration with Other mySAP.com Components | Extended Warehouse Management | Basic Settings for Setting Up the System Landscape | Assign Logical System to a Client

Click on the "New Entries" button on the application toolbar; enter the client number, description, and logical system, and set the client role as Customizing.

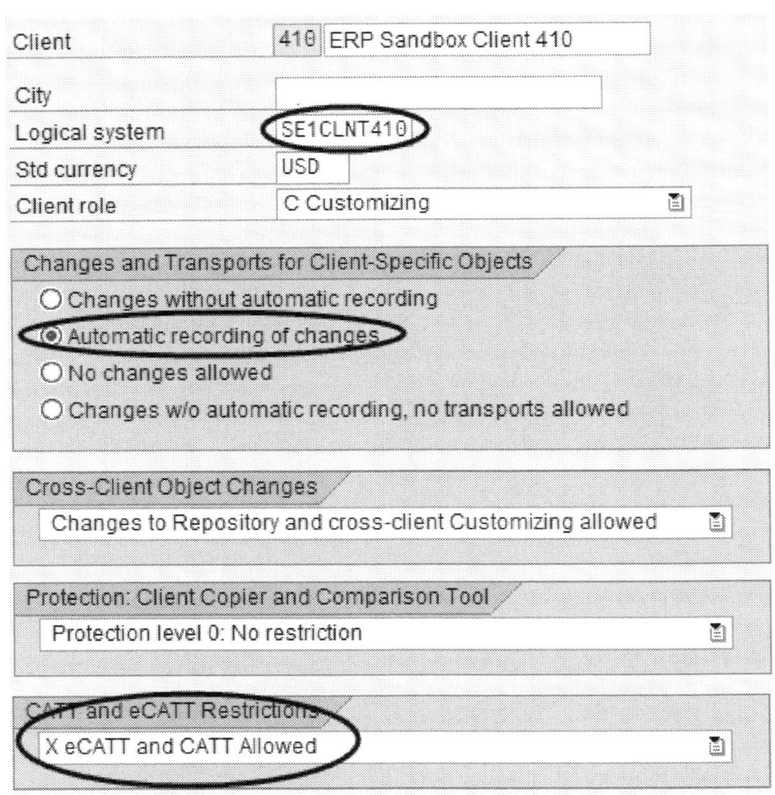

Notes:

i. Changes to this setting have to be discussed with the SAP Basis team.

ii. Assignment of a client number to the logical system is required only for the sending system. In the ERP system, ERP system is considered as a sending system.

iii. In this configuration, you may have to define settings are required for changes for client-specific objects, cross-client objects, and CATT and eCATT restrictions. It is important to discuss this with the Basis team before activating these settings.

4.4.1.3 Assign EWM Release version to EWM Logical System

SAP has released multiple versions of EWM software. In this menu, the appropriate release version must be assigned to the EWM logical system. This is a technical requirement for the data transfer.

Menu Path: SPRO | IMG | Integration with Other mySAP.com Components | Extended Warehouse Management | Basic Settings for Setting Up the System Landscape | Specify SAP APO Release

Click on the "New Entries" button on the application toolbar; select the EWM logical system defined, always enter Syst.type as "SAP_APO," and select the appropriate release version of the SCM system.

Log.System	Syst.type	Release
SA1CLNT001	SAP_APO	51

Notes:

i. This is a cross-client setting. Changes made in one client will apply to all clients in that system.

4.4.1.4 Create RFC User for RFC Connection

During the data transfer, the system uses an internally defined user ID and not the user ID of the user who created the data in the ERP system. Hence, a RFC user ID must be created for data transfer.

An RFC user ID is usually created by the basis team, with the user type "S Service." The RFC user must be assigned to S_BI-WX_RFC, S_ENTW_SHOW or SAP_ALL profiles.

To create a new user ID, enter the TCode SU01, enter user name and password, select the user type as "S Service," add all the above mentioned profiles under the "Profile" tab, and maintain all other required fields values (like name, address, etc.).

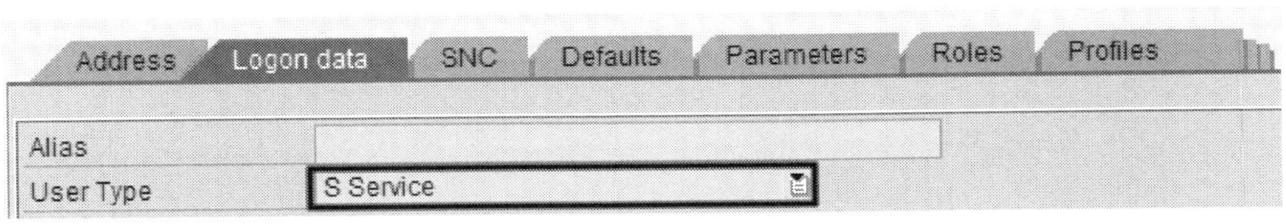

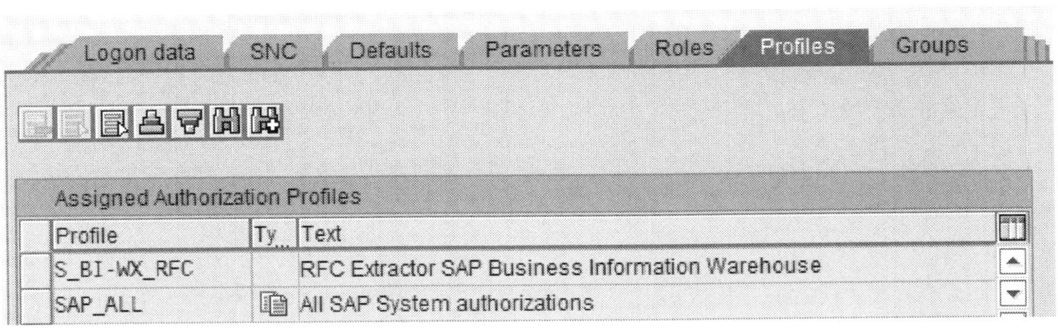

Notes:

i. In order to successfully process the data, the same user ID has to be created in the EWM system with the same password.

ii. Consult the Basis team before creating a RFC user for security reasons.

4.4.1.5 Define RFC Destination for EWM Logical System

To transfer the data from an ERP to EWM system, it is necessary to define a RFC destination for the EWM system and define technical parameters like the IP address of the destination, logon details, load balancing, and so on. Naming the RFC destination with the same name as the EWM logical system is recommended.

Menu Path: SPRO | IMG | Integration with Other mySAP.com Components | Extended Warehouse Management | Basic Settings for Setting Up the System Landscape | Set Up RFC Destination or TCode SM59

Here, click on ABAP Connections, choose "Create," and enter the connection type as 3.

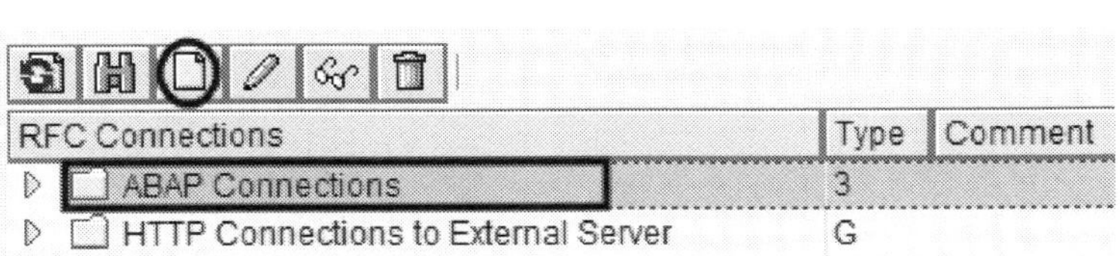

In the technical tab, specify the target host, system number, host name, or IP address.

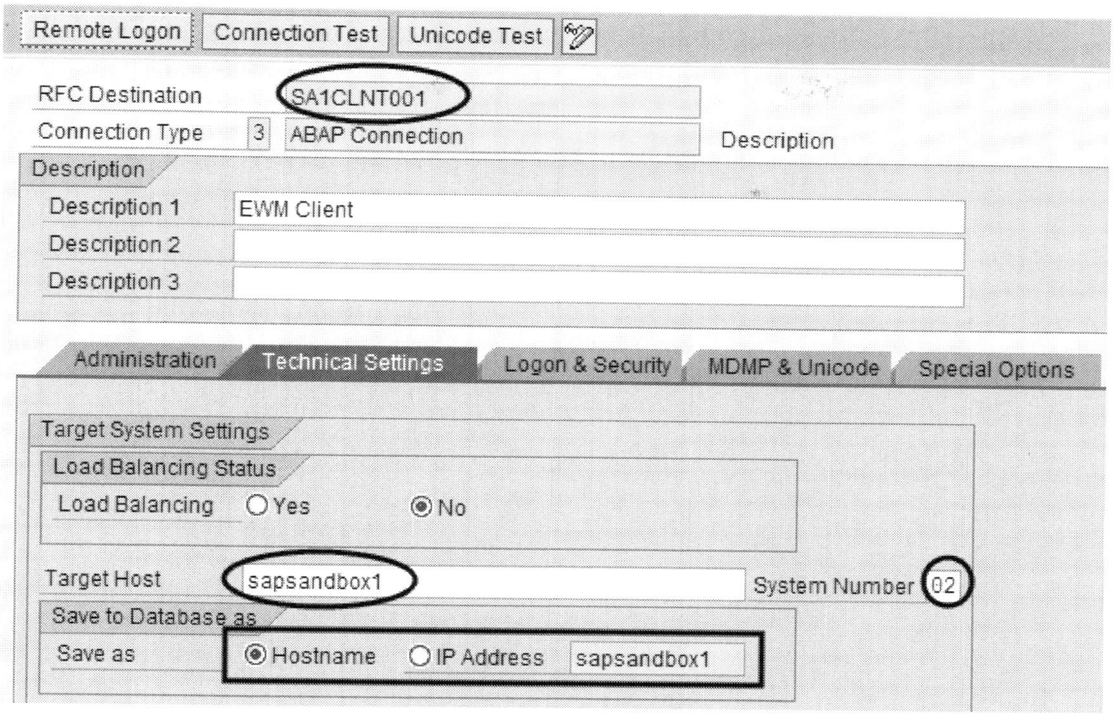

In the "Logon & Security" tab, enter the language as EN for English, the client number (EWM client), the user (RFC user ID) and the password (RFC user password).

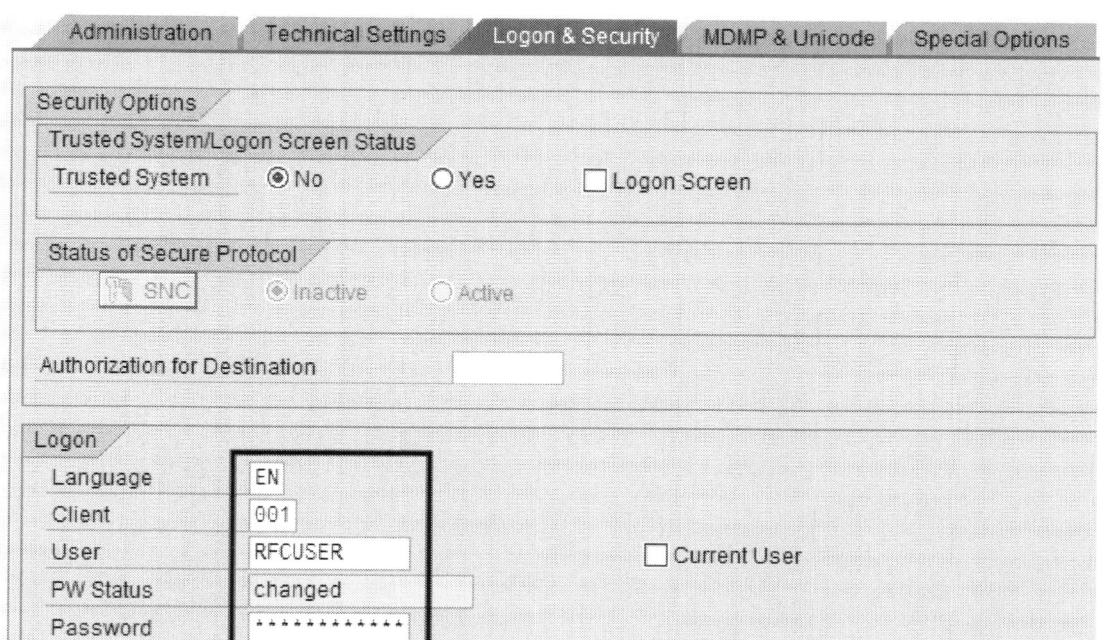

In the "Special Options" tab, for qRFC version, select "Classic qRFC." The remaining values can be set to default values. Logon details defined here will be used during the transfer of data.

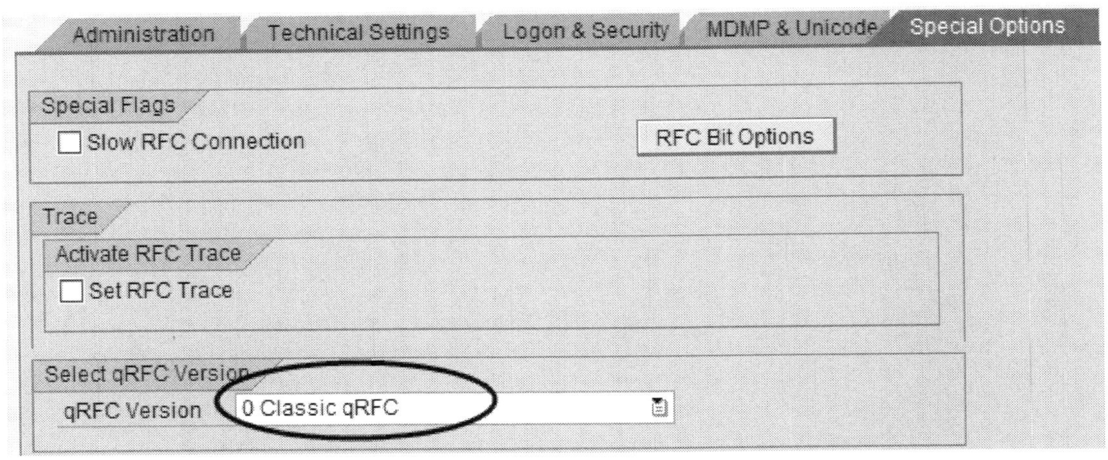

After creating RFC destination, click on "Connection Test Button" on the application toolbar to test the connection. In order to connect the EWM system successfully, the RFC user ID defined here must exist in the EWM system with the same user ID and password.

Connection Test SA1CLNT001

Connection Type SAP Connection

Action	Result
Logon	22 msec
Transfer of 0 KB	1 msec
Transfer of 10 KB	1 msec
Transfer of 20 KB	1 msec

Notes:

i. The Basis team must be consulted before making any changes to these settings.

4.4.1.6 Assign RFC Destinations to Different Application Cases

Integration via CIF is mostly based upon data transfers between the systems that run in the background without user interaction. However, in some cases (like Availability Check), it may be necessary for the user to access data in the target system, using a synchronous remote function call.

There are different cases available for RFC destinations. They are Availability Check (AC), Display Application Log of Another System (RL), Display qRFC Monitor of Another System (RQ), and Debugging (DG). More suitable cases for EWM are RL, RQ, and DG.

Menu Path: **SPRO | IMG | Integration with Other mySAP.com Components | Extended Warehouse Management | Basic Settings for Setting Up the System Landscape | Assign RFC Destinations to Different Application Cases**

Click on the "New Entries" button on the application toolbar; select the EWM logical system, enter the application case and RFC destination, and save the entries.

Log.System	Appl.	RFC Destination
SA1CLNT001	AC	SA1CLNT001
SA1CLNT001	RL	SA1CLNT001
SA1CLNT001	RQ	SA1CLNT001
SA1CLNT001	DG	SA1CLNT001

4.4.1.7 Assign RFC Destinations to Method and BAPI Calls

This section deals with assigning the RFC destinations for "synchronous BAPI calls" and "dialog methods."

To assign the BAPI destination to the logical system in the ERP system, enter TCode BD97, click on the logical EWM system, click on the standard BAPI destination button on the application toolbar, enter the RFC destination for BAPI calls, and click on the green check. This will assign the RFC destination for the BAPI calls, as shown below in the figure.

To assign the dialog destination, click on the logical system of the EWM system, click on the standard dialog destination button on the application toolbar, enter the RFC destination for dialog calls, and click on the green check. This will assign the RFC destination for the dialog calls.

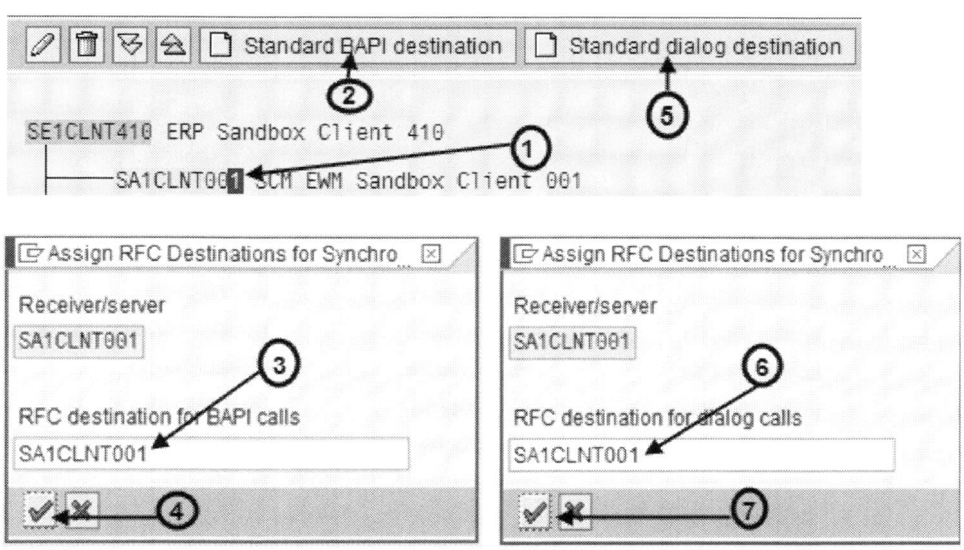

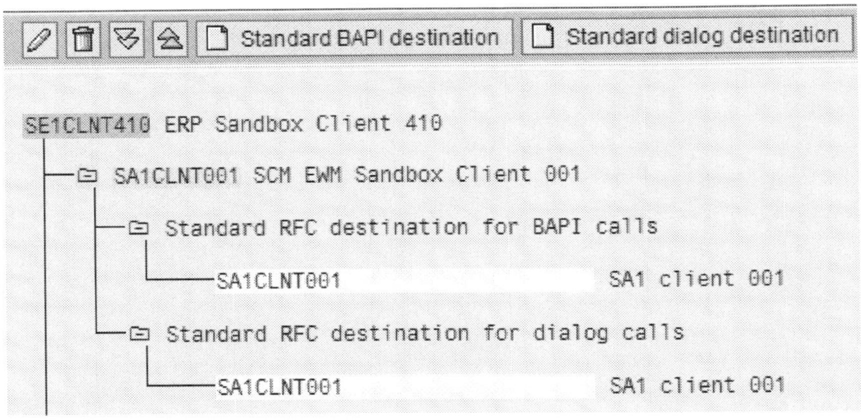

4.4.2 qRFC Specific Settings

Table 4.4.2A shows an overview of settings required to activate qRFC in the ERP system.

Table 4.4.2A - qRFC Specific Settings

S. No	Configuration Check List	TCode	Transportable
1	Maintain qRFC Monitor Settings for QIN Scheduler	SMQR	No
2	Maintain qRFC Monitor Settings for Qout Scheduler	SMQS	No
3	Maintain qRFC administration Settings	SMQE	No
4	Define Controller for RFC Queue Processing	SPRO	No
5	Create Distribution Model View to Transfer Delivery Information from ERP to EWM	BD64	No
6	Assign BAPIs and Message Types to Distribution Model View	/n/SPE/OL19	No
7	Define Log Recording for In and Out Messages	SPRO	No
8	Activate Detailed Navigation for Logs in qRFC Monitor	SPRO	No

4.4.2.1 Maintain qRFC Monitor Settings for QIN Scheduler

Normally, when the data records (LUW/inbound qRFC messages) are received from the EWM system they are automatically written to the inbound queues of the ERP system. However, they are not executed automatically in the ERP system. Each application in the ERP system can activate these queues using APIs. To avoid each application having to write a specific scheduler, qRFC supports a general scheduler, the QIN scheduler. The QIN scheduler looks for registered queues in the database tables and processes them. If a queue is not registered, it is not processed.

To register the QIN scheduler, enter the TCode SMQR, click on the "Registration" button on the application toolbar, enter Queue name = *, Mode = D, Max. Runtime = 30, USERDEST = <blank>, Attempts = 30, Pause = 300, and Scheduler Monitoring = 0.

Queue Name: Here, enter particular queue name, or enter * for all queue name. * will allow the system to process all the queues.

Mode: Mode refers to execution mode (i.e., D for Dialog work process and B for Batch work process).

MAX Runtime: This refers to maximum runtime that the QIN scheduler uses for activating a destination; default value is 30 seconds.

USERDEST: This field refers to the RFC destination with LOGON data. This field value can be left blank.

Attempts: Number of repetitions for failed calls; default value: 30.

Pause: Wait time between individual calls; default value: 300.

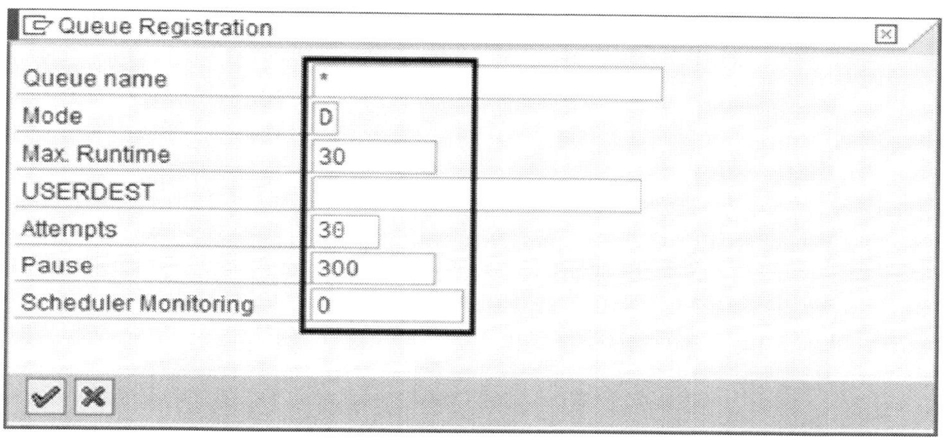

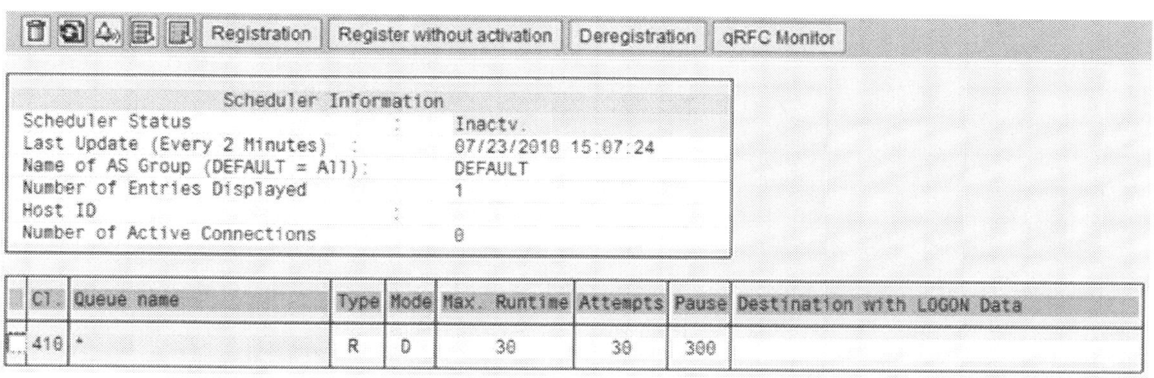

4.4.2.2 Maintain qRFC Monitor Settings for QOUT Scheduler

Like the QIN scheduler, ERP system has a QOUT scheduler to manage the outgoing qRFC messages. The QOUT scheduler was introduced to improve the performance when sending the qRFC messages.

Here, available options at the time of registration are as follows:

Type: Following types are available. The appropriate type for the QOUT scheduler is R.

i. R: The destination is registered; that is, it is started using the QOUT scheduler.

ii. U: The destination is not registered; that is, it is not processed.

iii. N: The destination is not registered using the QOUT scheduler; it is sent at the time of the COMMIT WORK by the program.

Max. Connections: Number of connections used to send the qRFC.

Max. Runtime: Time allotted to process the destination for the QOUT scheduler. The default value is 60 seconds.

To maintain the QOUT scheduler enter the TCode SMQS, click on the "Registration" button on the application toolbar, enter RFC destination = <EWM system RFC destination>, MaxConn = Allowable number of processes depending on app servers, Maxtime = 3600, scheduler_Watch = 0, and save the entries.

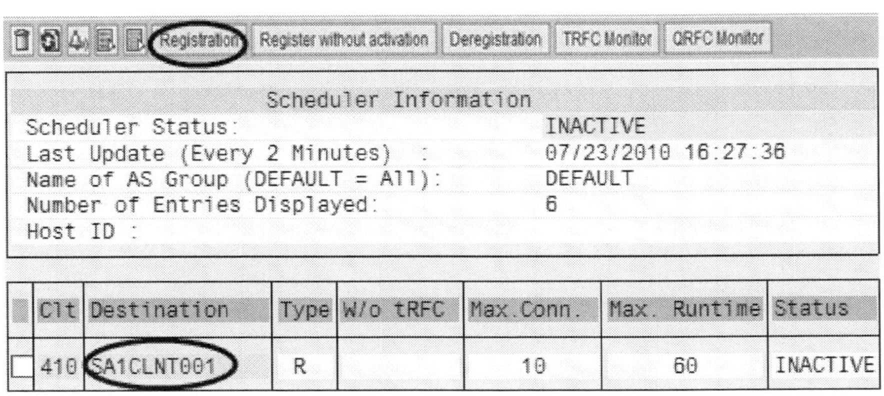

4.4.2.3 Maintain qRFC Administration Settings

The qRFC monitor makes it possible to monitor the faulty queue entries, which might occur during delivery data transfer; view the contents of the queues; and carry out follow-up processing for the objects affected. To do this, one must register the program /SPE/QUEUE_DISPLAY_TOOLS as the display program for DLV*, EWM* and QM* queues.

In case of CIF data transfer, if faulty queue entries occur, the CIF queue display can be used to view the contents of the queues and carry out follow-up processing for the objects affected. It is also possible to setup qRFC administration to make it possible to call the CIF queue display from the qRFC monitor.

To do this, the program CIFQEV02 must be registered as the display program for CF* queues, as shown below.

To register the programs, enter the TCode SMQE, click on EDIT menu, register display programs, and enter the queue name and program names mentioned above.

qRFC Administration

CF*	P			CIFQEV02
DLV*	P			/SPE/QUEUE_DISPLAY_TOOLS
EWM*	P			/SPE/QUEUE_DISPLAY_TOOLS
QM*	P			/SPE/QUEUE_DISPLAY_TOOLS

4.4.2.4 Define Controller for RFC Queue Processing

In qRFC, delivery data is stored temporarily in RFC queues, and the queue type (inbound or outbound) determines whether queue processing is controlled by the sending (ERP) or receiving (EWM) system.

In this configuration, the ERP system defaults the queue type as "Inbound Queue." This setting means that queue processing is controlled by the EWM system. This setting is recommended if a large amount of data is expected or if the EWM system does not have sufficient work processes available to process the queue. If there are not enough work processes available in the EWM system, the data is saved upon entering the EWM system and then processed at a later time.

Queue type "outbound" means that queue processing is controlled by the ERP (sending) system. This may lead to problems if the EWM (receiving) system does not currently have enough free work processes to process the queue. Therefore, it is recommended to set the queue type as inbound.

Menu Path: SPRO | IMG | Logistics Execution | Service Parts Management (SPM) | Integrate SPM with Other Components | Define Queue for Transfer to Extended WM

Configuration of EWM communication via Queues

Receiver	Queue Type	Agg SQueue	MQueue Act	MQueue Par
SA1CLNT001	Inbound Queue	No Agregatic	Mass queue disable	1

4.4.2.5 Create Distribution Model View to Transfer Delivery Information from ERP to EWM

A distribution model is a group of BAPIs and message types used to move outbound and inbound deliveries from ERP to EWM systems. The first step in defining the distribution model is creating or naming the distribution model view.

In BD64 transaction, click on the "Create model view" button on the application toolbar, enter the name for the distribution model in the short text field, enter the technical name, enter a valid start date and end date, and click on the green check mark. This will create a distribution model view.

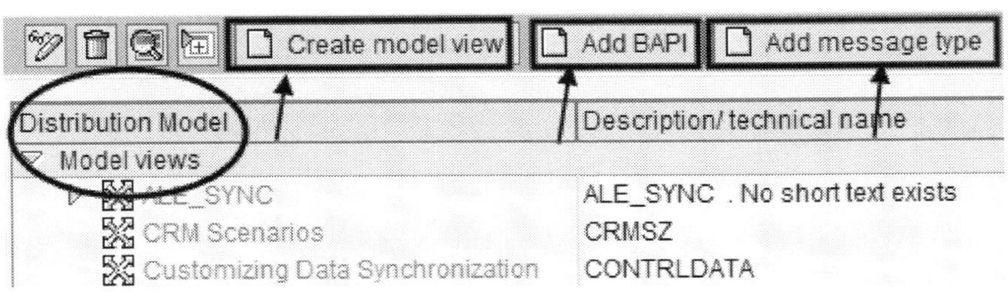

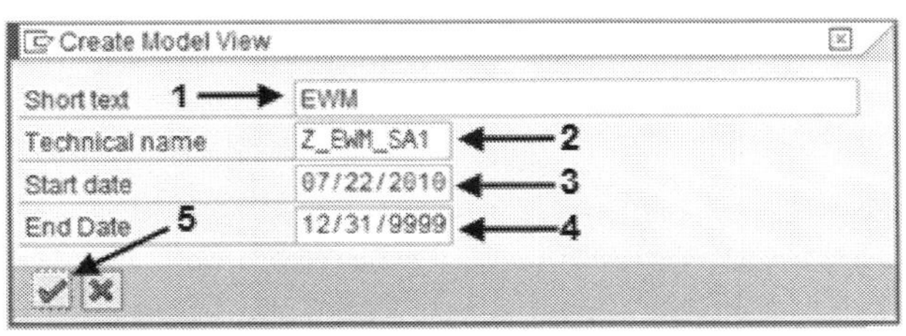

4.4.2.6 Assign BAPIs and Message Types to Distribution Model View

Once the distribution model view is created, the transaction /n/SPE/OL19 can be used to automatically generate the required object types (BAPIs) and methods (Message Types) for the delivery-related data transfer.

To automatically generate the BAPIs and methods automatically in the distribution model view, go to transaction /n/SPE/OL19, enter the ERP warehouse number, select the EWM's logical system, select the distribution model view, select the radio button "Both" for objects section, select the radio button "Create Entries," for the action section and click on the "Execute" button.

This will assign the BAPIs and methods required to transfer both inbound and outbound deliveries.

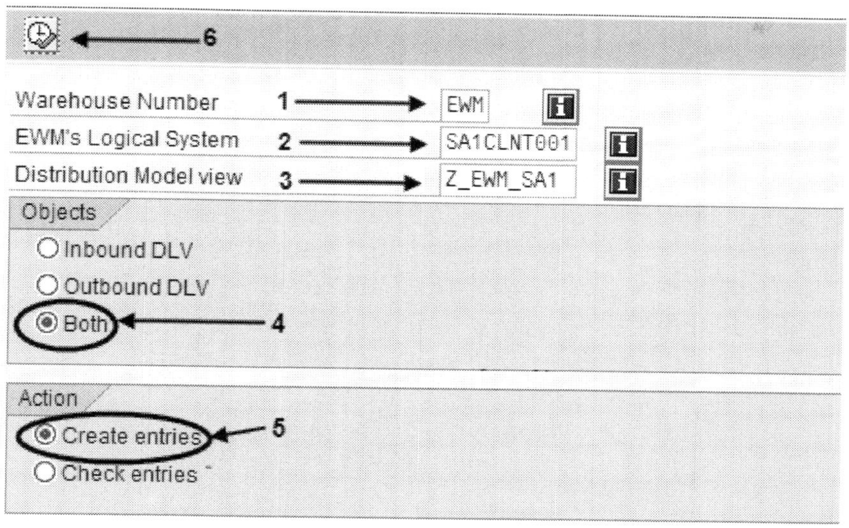

Go to transaction BD64 to verify the results.

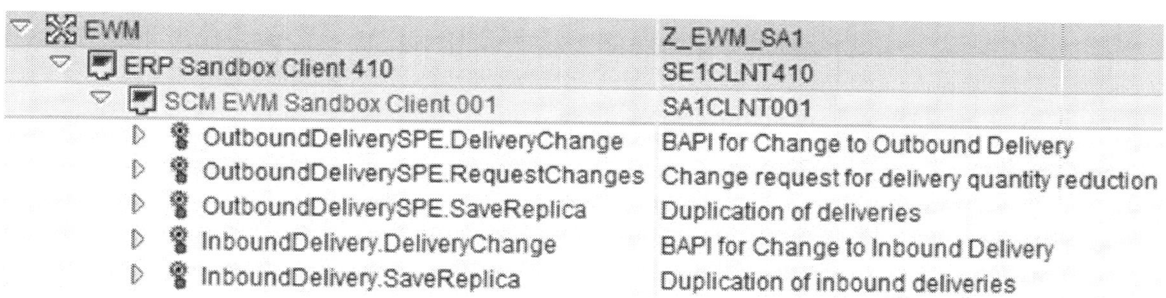

Notes:

i. In BD64, it is possible to manually add BAPI and message type. In case of manual generation, filter values have to be entered manually.

4.4.2.7 Define Log Recording for IN and OUT Messages

Here, you can define the settings for logging messages that are sent to or received from EWM systems. Due to the high volume of messages, SAP recommends logging only error messages in a production environment. System default settings are set to record only error messages.

Menu Path: SPRO | IMG | Logistics Execution | Service Parts Management (SPM) | Integrate SPM with Other Components | Log Sent and Received Messages

Click on the "New Entries" button on the application toolbar and select the appropriate entries for the log received and for the log send options.

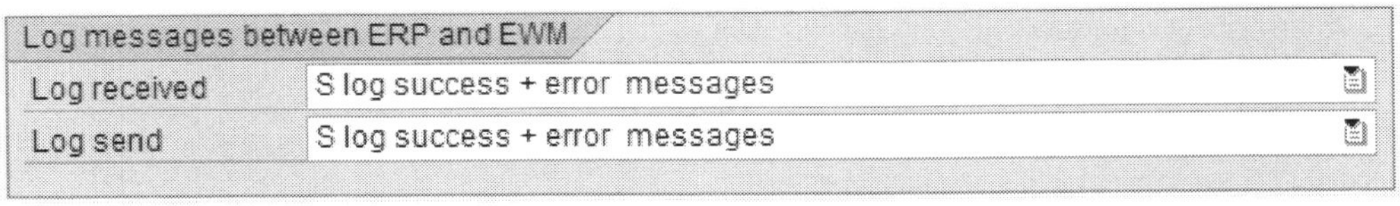

4.4.2.8 Activate Detailed Navigation for Logs in qRFC Monitor

In case of an error during data transfer, qRFC monitor displays the status as SYSFAIL in the status column. More details about the error can be found by double-clicking on the status, if the navigation is activated.

Menu Path: SPRO | IMG | Logistics Execution | Service Parts Management (SPM) | Integrate SPM with Other Components | Register Navigation from Queue

Here, select the "Register" radio button and click on the "Execute" button. This will activate the navigation.

4.4.3 CIF Specific Settings

Table 4.4.3A provides an overview of settings required to activate CIF in the ERP system.

Table 4.4.3A - qRFC Specific Settings

S. No	Configuration Check List	TCode	Transportable
1	Configure Data transfer Log for CIF	SPRO	No
2	Set User Parameters for RFC Mode - CIF	CFC2	No
3	Activate Business Transaction Events (BTEs) for Master Data Changes - CIF	FIBF	Yes
4	Define Master Data Change Transfer Settings - CIF	SPRO	No
5	Activate ALE Change Pointers for Master Data Transfer - CIF	BD61	No
6	Activate ALE Change Pointers by Message Type for Automatic Data Transfer in Background - CIF	SPRO	No
7	Define Controller for Master Data Processing - CIF	CFC1	No
8	Define Number Ranges for Parallelized Data Transfer - CIF	CFC8	No
9	Set Maximum Runtime for CIF Integration Model - CIF	SE38	No

4.4.3.1 Configure Data Transfer Log

Every CIF data transfer is recorded in the transfer log. By default, the system records the log with minimum information. This log can be viewed in transaction CFG1. If you want to record more detailed log or deactivate some of the unimportant data, you can do so in this configuration menu.

SAP recommends restricting the number of object types to be logged, in section "Set User Parameters for RFC Mode". The interface parameters required for most analyses in the CIF application log are already set by default.

Menu Path: SPRO | IMG | Integration with Other mySAP.com Components | Extended Warehouse Management | Basic Settings for Data Transfer | Configure Application Log

Under "Select Object Type" (for example, Material Master Data), double click on "Select Parameters," select "Interface Parameters," double-click on "Select Fields," and then check the required fields.

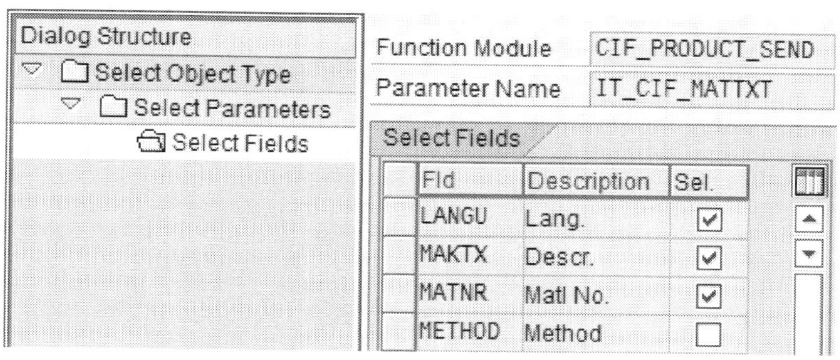

4.4.3.2 Define User Parameters for Data Transfer

Here, user-specific settings can be established for the master data transfer. For example, RFC mode's "no calls" can be useful if a certain user makes changes that are not to be transferred to EWM. In the RFC mode, "no calls" or "Queued RFC" can be selected. Queued RFC means data transfer is allowed. Under logging, one can specify how to record the logs, like no logging or normal (X) or detailed (D) logging. Under the "Debug" column, debugging can be activated or deactivated for a specific user. The user name "*" means changes apply to all the users.

Menu Path: SPRO | IMG | Integration with Other mySAP.com Components | Extended Warehouse Management | Basic Settings for Data Transfer | Set User Parameters or TCode CFC2

Click on the "New Entries" button on the application toolbar; enter user name and select the appropriate values in the RFC mode, Logging, and Debug columns.

User Name	RFC Mode	Logging	Debug
*	Q	D	X

Notes:

i. * means the system will maintain the log for all users.

ii. Since the log can cause performance issues, it is recommended to set user parameters for the required users.

4.4.3.3 Activate Business Transaction Events (BTEs)

By activating BTEs, the system keeps track of master data changes in the ERP system and replicates them in the EWM system.

To activate BTEs, enter TCode FIBF, click on menu "Settings," "Identification," and "SAP Application," then check the check box for ND-APO and NDI, as shown below.

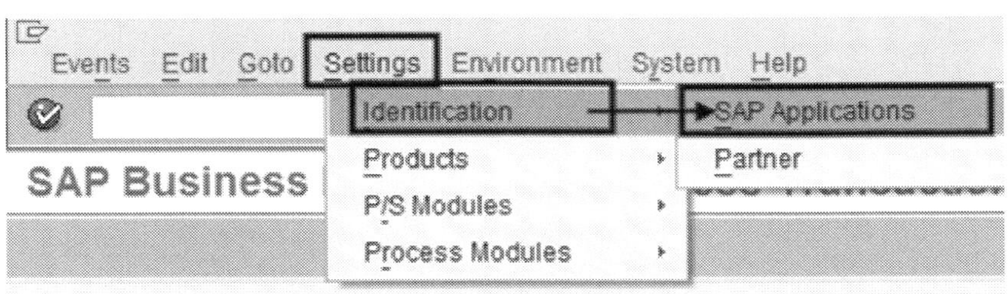

Appl.	A	Text
ND-APO	☑	New Dimension PlugIn APO
NDI	☑	New Dimension Integration

4.4.3.4 Define Master Data Change Transfer Settings

Here, how master data changes are transferred from the ERP system to the EWM system is specified. If the changes are moved manually, select "No Change Transfer." In case of periodic transfer, select "ALE Change Transfer Periodic." To transfer changes immediately, select the option "BTE transfer, immediately."

Menu Path: SPRO | IMG | Integration with Other mySAP.com Components | Extended Warehouse Management | Basic Settings for Data Transfer | Change Transfer for Master Data | Configure Change Transfer for Master Data or TCode CFC9

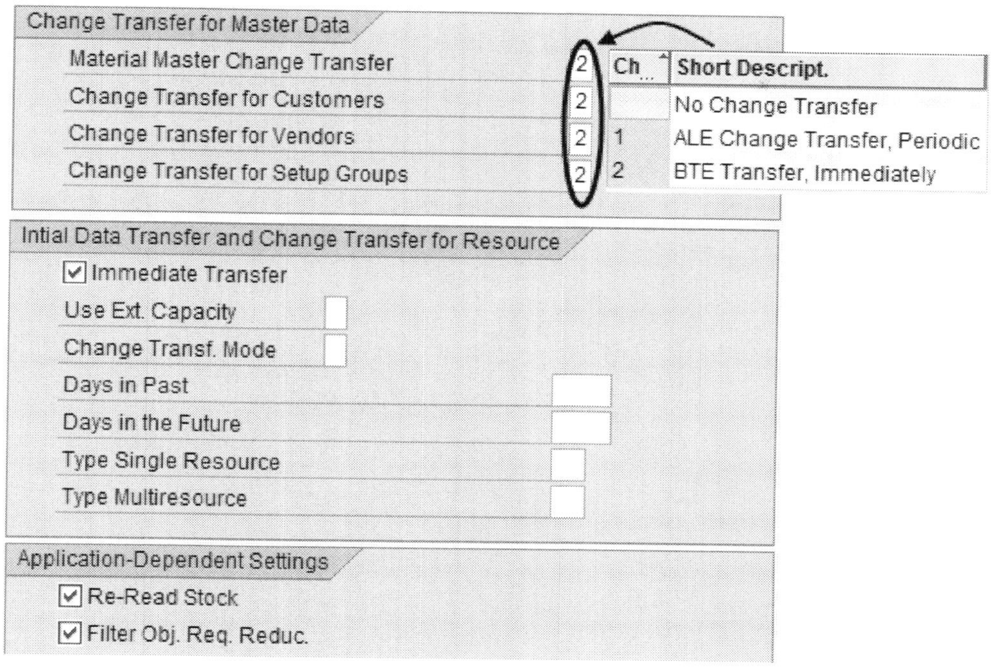

4.4.3.5 Activate ALE Change Pointers for Master Data Transfer

One of the requirements to move master data changes from ERP to EWM system is the activation of ALE change pointers. This can be done in menu path **SPRO | IMG | Integration with Other mySAP.com Components | Extended Warehouse Management | Basic Settings for Data Transfer | Change Transfer for Master Data | Activate ALE Change Pointers Generally or TCode BD61**

4.4.3.6 Activate ALE Change Pointers By Message Type for Automatic Data Transfer in Background

After activating the ALE change pointers, it is also necessary to activate the ALE change pointers by message type for message types CIFCUS, CIFMAT, CIFVEN, and CIFMTMRPA, and the background jobs should be scheduled for the data transfer. With this configuration, whenever the master data is changed for the selected objects in the ERP system, those changes will be pushed to the EWM system automatically by the background jobs.

Menu Path: **SPRO | IMG | Integration with Other mySAP.com Components | Extended Warehouse Management | Basic Settings for Data Transfer | Change Transfer for Master Data | Activate ALE Change Pointers for Message Types**

Activate Change pointers for Message Type

Messg.Type	active
CIFCUS	☑
CIFMAT	☑
CIFMTMRPA	☑
CIFVEN	☑

4.4.3.7 Define Controller for Master Data Processing

Just like "delivery data processing," it is necessary to specify who controls the processing of master data transfer queues. Just like controller for RFC queue processing, the controller for the master data queue must be specified. The queue type (inbound or outbound) determines whether the queue processing is controlled by the sending (ERP) or receiving (EWM) system. In this config, the target system and the queue type for the master data transfer are specified.

As explained earlier, when expecting large amounts of integration data and insufficient work process resources, it is recommended to change this setting to Inbound Queues. This means that the queue processing is controlled by the receiving system (EWM). If there are not enough work processes available here, the data is saved upon entering EWM and then processed at a later point in time.

Menu Path: **SPRO | IMG | Integration with Other mySAP.com Components | Extended Warehouse Management | Basic Settings for Setting Up the System Landscape | Set Target System and Queue Type or TCode CFC1**

Click on the "New Entries" button on the application toolbar; select the EWM system, and the Q-Type. System will determine the appropriate OPMode automatically.

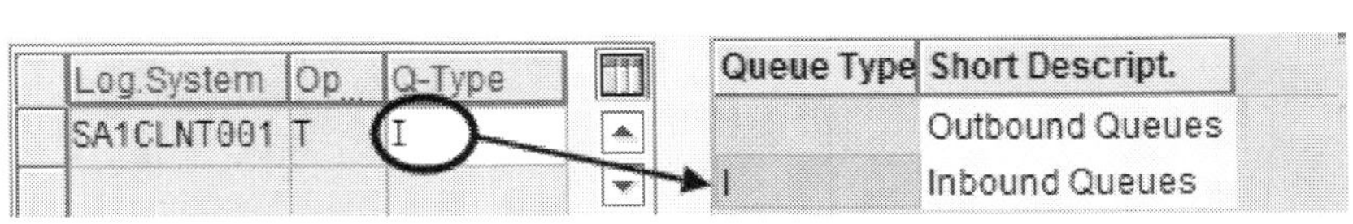

4.4.3.8 Define Number Ranges for Parallelized Data Transfer

While transferring the master data, one can use the parallelized transfer to influence the performance of the data transfer (covered in chapter 6). If the option "Parallelize Selection in ERP System" is selected, the system will use the number range defined here to identify each data transfer process uniquely. Therefore, the number range defined here should be an internal range.

Menu Path: SPRO | IMG | Integration with Other mySAP.com Components | Extended Warehouse Management | Basic Settings for Data Transfer | Initial Data Transfer | Determine Number Ranges for Parallelization or TCode CFC8

Click on the "Change interval" button, click on the "Insert interval" button, and add the number range.

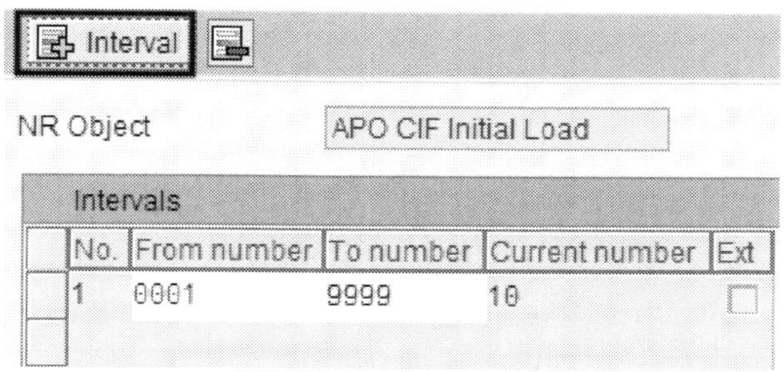

4.4.3.9 Set Maximum Runtime for CIF Integration Model

Finally, before initiating the master data transfer in the CIF integration model, execute the program RCIFIMAX to set the maximum runtime of the active integration model. This is the technical requirement for CIF to avoid program dump during the data transfer.

To execute the program, enter TCode SE38, enter the program name as RCIFIMAX, and click on the "Execute" button on the application toolbar.

Select action to execute = generation, enter the object types = *, logical target system = <EWM logical system name>, and click on the "Execute" button.

Once the program is executed successfully, the following message will appear on the status bar:

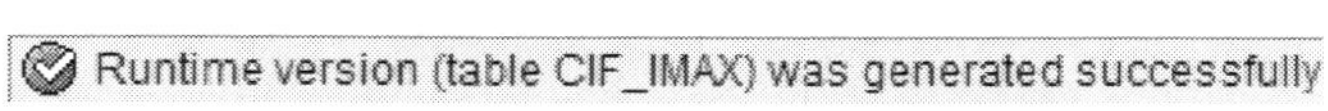

Summary

In order to implement the EWM solution, consultants must know the configuration that needs to be performed in the ERP system as well as in the EWM system. This chapter explained the configuration required in the ERP system. The CIF and qRFC topics of this chapter gave a detailed explanation of how data transfer can be configured between the two systems.

Chapter 5: Basic Configuration in EWM

Before delving deeper into EWM configuration, consultants must know the basic configuration that needs to be completed in the EWM system for successful communication with the ERP system during the data transfer. Such basic configuration is discussed here under the qRFC section. In the warehouse organizational elements section, the definition and mapping of various warehouse organizational elements is discussed.

5.1 qRFC Settings

In chapter 4, we have discussed in detail the qRFC configuration in the ERP system. Most of the qRFC configurations done in this section are similar to the ERP system.

Usually, qRFC configuration is considered a technical task and is done by the Basis team. But it is very important for every EWM consultant to understand what this configuration is and how it is used for data transfer between ERP and EWM systems. This understanding will help the consultant identify and fix any communication-related issues quickly.

Diagram 5.1A describes how the qRFC settings are defined and mapped in the EWM system.

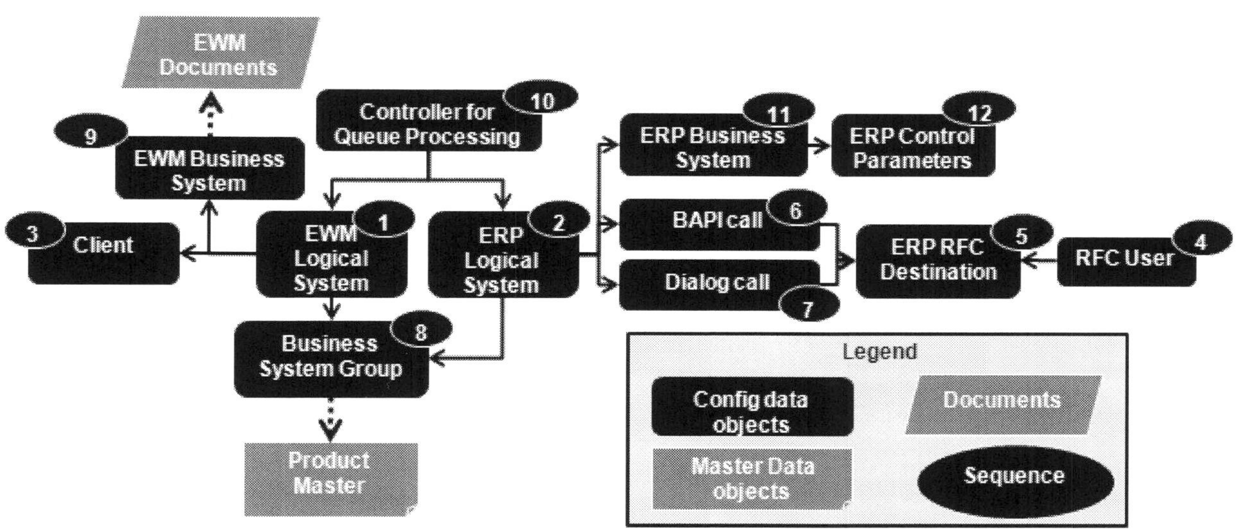

Diagram 5.1A: qRFC Configuration Mapping in EWM System

The following table provides an overview of the configuration required to integrate the EWM and ERP systems. The column transportable shows which of these configurations can be transportable automatically.

Table 5.1B qRFC Settings

S. No	Configuration Check List	TCode	Transportable
1	Name Logical Systems for ERP and EWM Systems	SPRO	Yes
2	Assign EWM Logical System to a Client	SPRO	No
3	Verify APO Model and Planning Version	SE38	No
4	Create RFC User for RFC Connection	SU01	No
5	Define RFC Destination for ERP Logical System	SM59	No
6	Assign RFC Destinations to Method and BAPI Calls	BD97	No
7	Create Business System Groups (BSG)	/n/SAPAPO/C1	No
8	Assign Logical System and Queue Types to BSG	/n/SAPAPO/C2	No
9	Maintain qRFC Monitor Settings for QIN Scheduler	SMQR	No
10	Maintain qRFC Monitor Settings for QOUT Scheduler	SMQS	No
11	Maintain qRFC administration Settings	SMQE	No
12	Define Business System for EWM	SPRO	No
13	Define Business System for ERP	SPRO	No
14	Define Controller for RFC Queue Processing	SPRO	Yes
15	Set Control Parameters for ERP Version Control	SPRO	Yes
16	Activate BC Sets	SCPR20	Yes

Notes:

i. In EWM systems, we do not need CIF configuration, because CIF is used to transfer master data from the ERP system to the EWM system.

ii. Since most of the qRFC configuration is covered in detail in chapter 4, we have given only a brief description and the configuration path for it.

iii. Most of the configurations described in this section are not automatically transportable. Even though some of them can be transported manually, it is recommended to maintain them manually in each system.

iv. If the SCM system is already linked to the ERP system as part of APO implementation, some of the configurations might already exist.

v. The configurations described here may require additional authorization and Basis team help.

5.1.1 Name Logical Systems for ERP and EWM Systems

Like ERP systems, EWM systems also require "logical systems" to identify the sending and receiving systems during data transfer. Here we will define two logical systems i.e. one for EWM (sending) and the other for ERP (receiving) system.

Menu Path: **SPRO | IMG | SCM Basis | Integration | Basic Settings for Creating the System Landscape | Name Logical Systems**

Logical Systems

Log.System	Name
SA1CLNT001	EWM System SA1 Client 001
SE1CLNT410	ERP System SE1 Client 410

5.1.2 Assign EWM Logical System to a Client

In this step, assign the EWM logical system to the client number. Here, the client number refers to the EWM client number, which will be connected to the ERP system.

Menu Path: **SPRO | IMG | SCM Basis | Integration | Basic Settings for Creating the System Landscape | Assign Logical Systems to a Client**

Client	001 APO / EWM Client
City	Walldorf
Logical system	SA1CLNT001
Std currency	USD
Client role	C Customizing

5.1.3 Verify APO Model and Planning Version

Because the EWM system was designed as part of an APO system, for technical reasons, an active APO model and planning version 000 should be active in the EWM system. Before activating an APO planning version and model, verify in **TCode /SAPAPO/MVM** if version 000 exists for APO Planning and Model in the EWM system.

Model/Planning version	D	Description
000		000 - Active model
000		000 - ACTIVE VERSION

To create the planning version, enter TCode SE38 in the command bar, enter the program name /SAPAPO/VERSION_CREATE_NO_APO, and click on the "Execute" button on the application toolbar.

If the following dialog box appears, choose "Cancel" and check if the planning version 000 and model 000 exist in TCode /SAPAPO/MVM.

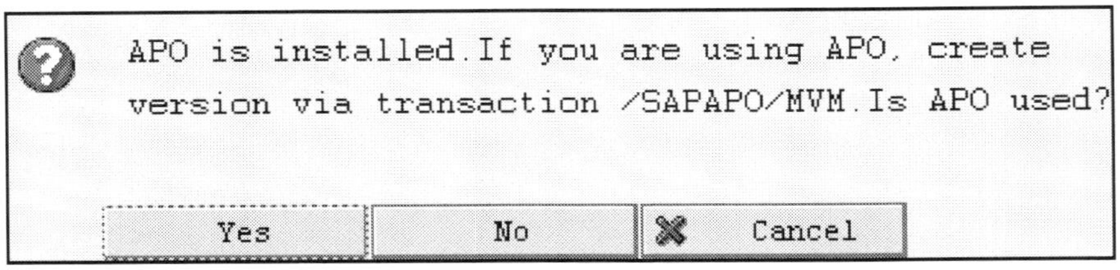

5.1.4 Create RFC User for RFC Connection

Creating a RFC user ID (TCode SU01) in the EWM system is the same as was explained in the previous chapter. In the EWM system, create an RFC user ID, which will be assigned to the RFC connection and will be used to transfer the data from the EWM to ERP system.

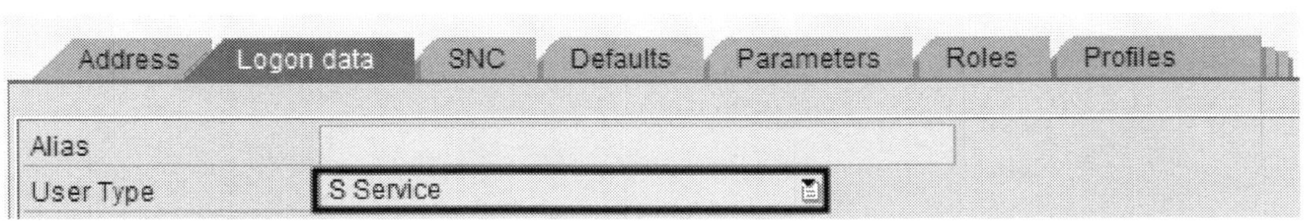

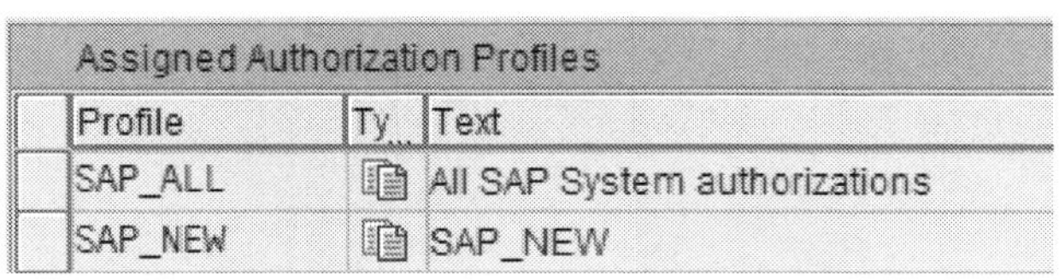

Assigned Authorization Profiles

Profile	Ty..	Text
SAP_ALL		All SAP System authorizations
SAP_NEW		SAP_NEW

5.1.5 Define RFC Destination for ERP Logical System

To transfer the data from the EWM to ERP system, a RFC destination for the ERP system must be defined and technical parameters like the IP address of the destination, logon details, load balancing, and so on must also be defined. It is recommended that the RFC destination be named the same as the ERP logical system.

Menu Path: SPRO | IMG | SCM Basis | Integration | Basic Settings for Creating the System Landscape | Set Up RFC Destination or TCode SM59

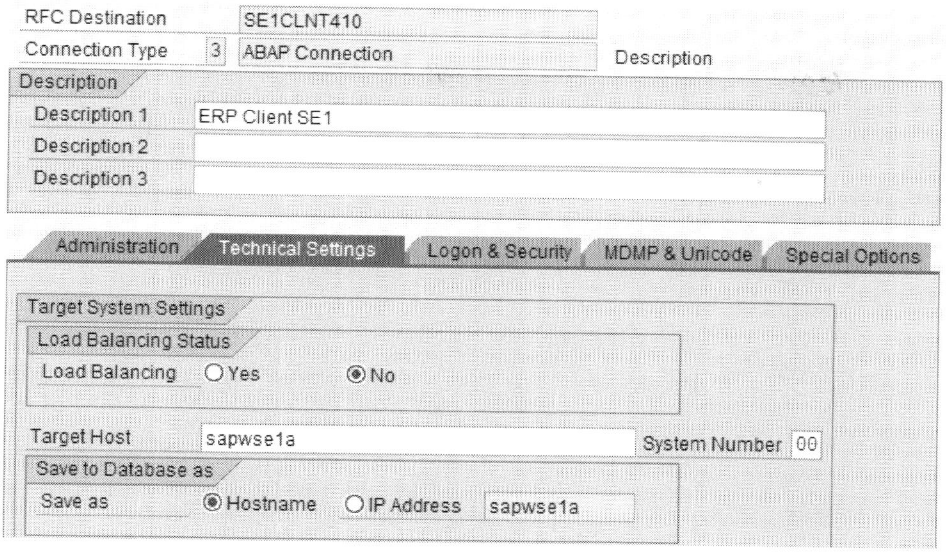

5.1.6 Assign RFC Destinations to Method and BAPI Calls

Assigning the RFC destinations for "synchronous BAPI calls" and "dialog methods" is done as described in the previous chapter. In TCode BD97, select the ERP logical system name and maintain the RFC destination for both BAPI and dialog calls.

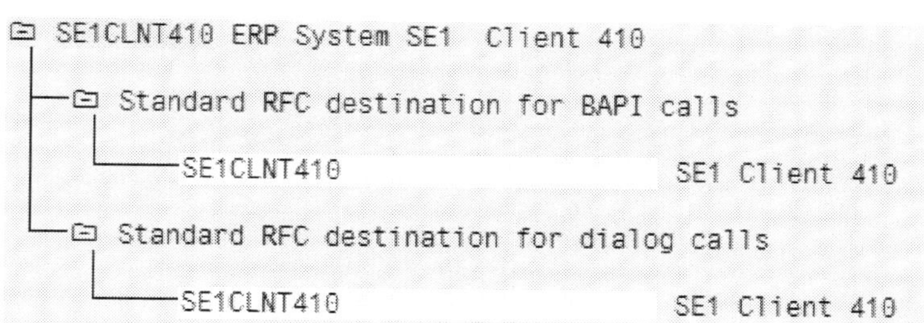

5.1.7 Create Business System Groups (BSG)

The BSG integrates ERP and EWM systems into one higher-level logical unit. By doing this, you create areas with the same naming convention that guarantee the unique naming of master data and its synchronization in distributed system landscapes. It is mainly used during master data transfer. The following two scenarios will explain how it can be useful in EWM systems.

Scenario 1

An EWM System is to be linked with two ERP Systems (A and B), in which two different materials (for example, a hammer and a screw) have the same material number (100). Both materials are to be represented as two different products in the EWM System.

Assign both ERP systems to different BSGs and assign the EWM system to one of the BSGs whose data does not have to be renamed. For example:

SAP ERP System A -> BSG A

SAP ERP System B -> BSG B

EWM System -> BSG A

In order to avoid having two identical names in the EWM system, you need to use SAP enhancement APOCF005 (inbound processing product).

In this example, material number 100 from BSG A receives product number 100 in the EWM system, and material number 100 from BSG B gets product number 100_BSGB. This allows you to uniquely identify both materials in the EWM system.

Scenario 2

An APO System is to be linked with two SAP ERP Systems (A and B). In system A, a screw has material number 110, and in system B, it has material number 120. Both material numbers are represented in the EWM system by one product, with product number 110.

Assign both ERP systems to different BSGs and assign the EWM system to one of the BSGs whose data does not have to be renamed. For example:

SAP ERP System A -> BSG A

SAP ERP System B -> BSG B

EWM System -> BSG A

In order to rename the material, use SAP enhancement APOCF005 to convert material number 120 to the EWM product number 110.

Notes:

i. For the time being, this second scenario is only supported for material masters and product masters. If, for example, the same customer is used with different BSGs in ERP Systems A and B, you must create two separate customer locations in the EWM System. This applies for the vendor, plant, and other master data.

ii. ABAP developer will know how to activate the BADIs.

iii. For inbound processing in the EWM System, the following SAP enhancements are available for master data:

a. APOCF001: Inbound processing location

b. APOCF005: Inbound processing product

c. APOCF008: Inbound processing resource

d. APOCF0012: Inbound processing production process model

In the next section, we will see how to assign the ERP and EWM logical systems to the BSG.

Menu Path: SPRO | IMG | Integration with SAP Components | Integration via APO Core Interface (CIF) | Basic Settings for Creating the System Landscape | Maintain Business System Group

BusSys	Description
ZBUSGRP	BSG for ERP (SE1) and EWM (SA1) System

5.1.8 Assign Logical System and Queue Types to BSG

In this IMG activity, logical systems are assigned to appropriate business system groups (BSG). Additionally, a queue type (inbound queue or outbound queue) is assigned to the BSG. In "SAP Sys." field (for ERP logical system), set an indicator "X," which indicates that the logical system belongs to SAP R/3 system.

Menu Path: SPRO | IMG | Integration with SAP Components | Integration via APO Core Interface (CIF) | Basic Settings for Creating the System Landscape | Assign Logical System and Queue Type

Assignment of Logical System to Business System Group

BusSys	Logical sys	SAP I	Rel	Queue Type	Err. Hndlg	Role
ZBUSGRP	SA1CLNT001		70	I Inbound	Strict (Ter	Not Specifie
ZBUSGRP	SE1CLNT410	X	600	I Inbound	Strict (Ter	Not Specifie

5.1.9 Maintain qRFC Monitor Settings for QIN Scheduler

Just as we defined QIN scheduler settings for ERP systems, we must also maintain similar qRFC monitor settings in the EWM system (TCode SMQR). Here, enter Register Queue Names = *, Mode = D, Max. Runtime = 60, USERDEST = <blank>, Attempts = 30, Pause = 300, and Scheduler Monitoring = 0.

	Cl.	Queue name	Type	Mode	Max. Runtime	Attempts	Pause	Destination with LOGON Data
☐	001	*	R	D	60	30	300	

5.1.10 Maintain qRFC Monitor Settings for QOUT Scheduler

The QOUT scheduler in the EWM system is configured much like the QOUT scheduler settings of the ERP system. In TCode SMQS, enter destination as ERP RFC destination name, Max Conn = 10, Max.Runtime = 60, w/o tRFC = <blank>, click on enter, and save the entries.

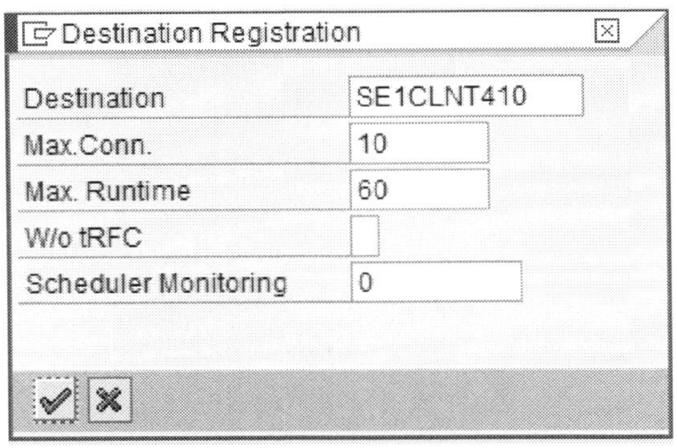

5.1.11 Maintain qRFC Administration Settings

In TCode SMQE, register the queues for the following programs to monitor the faulty queue entries occur during delivery data transfer.

Queue Name	Type	Action	Event Function	Display Program
CF*	P			/SAPAPO/CIF_QUEUE_EVENT2
DLV*	P			/SCWM/QRFC_APPL_LOG_DISPLAY
QI*	P			QIE_RFC_DISPLAY_QUEUE_LOG
QM*	P			QIE_RFC_DISPLAY_QUEUE_LOG
X*	P			RSXMB_SHOW_ENTRY

5.1.12 Define Business System for EWM

In the EWM system, instead of the EWM logical system name, a business system name is stored in the EWM documents, and this business system name is linked to the logical system. This allows flexibility to change the logical system if required at a later time. During the data transfer, the system uses the business system name to identify the logical system. Therefore, while defining the business system, it is recommended to enter the same name as the EWM logical system name.

Menu Path: SPRO | IMG | Extended Warehouse Management | Interfaces | ERP Integration | General Settings | Define Own Business System

Name of Own Business System
Business System
SA1CLNT001

5.1.13 Define Business System for ERP

In this step, the business system for ERP logical system is defined, and the EWM logical system is assigned to the EWM business system. This creates the mapping between the logical and business systems. The following are reasons this mapping should exist in the system:

i. The deliveries sent from the ERP system to EWM contain only the information for the logical system. As EWM stores only the business system name in the warehouse request, when the document is posted, the system performs a mapping of the logical systems to the business systems.

ii. When sending confirmations from EWM to the ERP system, EWM uses the logical system that originally contained the delivery. EWM therefore maps the business system onto the logical system to send the confirmations.

It is important to assign only one logical system to a business system. Only then can EWM send messages or transfer data to the ERP system.

Menu Path: SPRO | IMG | Extended Warehouse Management | Interfaces | ERP Integration | General Settings | Define Business System

Buffer for SLD Data of Business Systems

Business System	Logical sys...	Manual Maint.
SA1CLNT001	SA1CLNT001	X Flag set. Event has occurred.
SE1CLNT410	SE1CLNT410	X Flag set. Event has occurred.

5.1.14 Define Controller for RFC Queue Processing

This is an optional setting. As discussed earlier, the EWM system uses the RFC-enabled function modules to transfer data to the ERP system. When the data is transferred, the following types of messages are sent from EWM to the ERP system:

- **Messages with reference to a delivery in the ERP system**: Reporting delivery changes (for example, quantity changes), reporting goods movements for the delivery (goods receipt or goods issue)
- **Messages without reference to a delivery in the ERP system**: Reporting stock postings without reference to a delivery, posting changes without reference to a delivery, reporting inventory differences, scrapping without a delivery in the ERP system

Here, consultants can specify whether the RFC queue processing is controlled by the sending system or the receiving system. If the processing is to be controlled by the sending system, select the queue type as "Outbound Queues." If it is to be controlled by the receiving system, select the queue type as "Inbound Queue." If these settings are not defined, EWM systems use the inbound queue type for the target system.

Menu Path: SPRO | IMG | Extended Warehouse Management | Interfaces | ERP Integration | General Settings | Control for RFC Queue

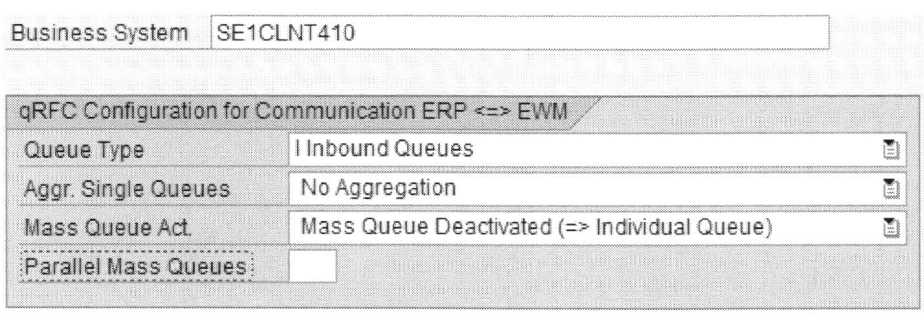

5.1.15 Set Control Parameters for ERP Version Control

Here define what and how to communicate the changes made to EWM documents like inbound deliveries, goods movements, quality inspection, batch management, or outbound deliveries to the ERP system.

Menu Path: SPRO | IMG | Extended Warehouse Management | Interfaces | ERP Integration | General Settings | Set Control Parameters for ERP Version Control or TCode SCPR20

Business System	SE1CLNT410
SAP Release	603
Package Name	SAPKA70102

General Settings

Duplicate Check	Do Not Suppress Check
Perform Inb. Deliv. Split	Carry Out Inbound Delivery Split and R
Report In Yard to ERP	Report In Yard to ERP
Confirmation Type of SNs	1 Communicate All SNs Correspondin

Batch Control

Batch Update	Joint Update of Batch and Classificati(
Changeability of Externally Specified Batch in EWM	Batch Change Can Be Changed Usin(
Communication of Batch Split of Inbound Delivery Item	Immediate Communication of Batch S
Report Batch Changes Immediately to ERP	Send Batch Chnage Immediately to EF

Create / Delete Inbound Deliveries

Local Creation of Inbound Delivery in EWM	Local Creation of Inbound Delivery in E
Local Creation of an Inbound Delivery Item	Inbound Delivery Item Can Be Created
Delete Inbound Delivery	Inbound Delivery Can Be Deleted
Delete Inbound Delivery Item	Inbound Delivery Item Can Be Deleted

Goods movement

Goods Receipt Mode	Immediately Send GR Postings and P
Posting Change wrt Inbound Delivery	Post. Change in Relation to Inb. Deliv.

Quality Inspection

Possible Usage Decisions	All Inspection Decsions Can Be Made
Quality Confirmation for Returns	Maximum Returns Functionality

Outbound Delivery

Check for Kit Header Item in HU at Goods Issue	1 Carry Out Kit Check
Handling Cross-Delivery HUs	Normal Creation and Communication
Perform GI Cancelation	Perform GI Cancelation
Invoice Creation Before Goods Issue	2 Invoice Creation Before Goods Issue
Delete Outbound Delivery	Outbound Delivery Can Be Deleted
Send Pick Denial Message to ERP	Send Pick Denial Message to ERP
Batch Split Communication of an Outbound Delivery Item	Immediate Communication of Batch S
Split Reversal	Split Reversal Allowed
Distributability of Locally Created Outbound Delivery Orders	1 Outbound Deliveries Cannot Be Crea

5.1.15 Activate Business Configuration (BC) Sets

BC sets contain important data required for EWM deliveries, non-warehouse–dependent configuration, and the configuration required for the reference warehouse number 0001. During system install, not all required data will be activated in the EWM configuration tables. Hence, BC sets need to be activated in order to populate the required data in the configuration tables. As of SCM 7.0, there are more than four hundred BC sets available. Even though it is not necessary to activate all the BC sets, it is recommended to activate them, as this can minimize configuration efforts and avoid system errors during testing. SAP recommends that minimum the following BC sets must be activated in the following order:

- /scwm/basic_whs_indep_basis
- /scwm/basic_whs_indep
- /scwm/basics
- /scwm/basic_number_ranges
- /scwm/process
- /scwm/inventory
- /scwm/we_process
- /scwm/wa_process
- /scwm/internal_wh_process
- /scwm/dlv_standard_cw (if you use at least one material for catch weight management)
- /scwm/dlv_standard (if you do not use any materials for catch weight management)

To activate BC sets in EWM, enter **TCode SCPR20** in the command field, search for *SCWM* relevant BC sets, select the BC set, and click on the "Activate" button. This will copy all the data from the BC set into the relevant config tables. In case of errors, it may be necessary to activate some BC sets more than once or to activate some dependent BC sets first to avoid errors during activation.

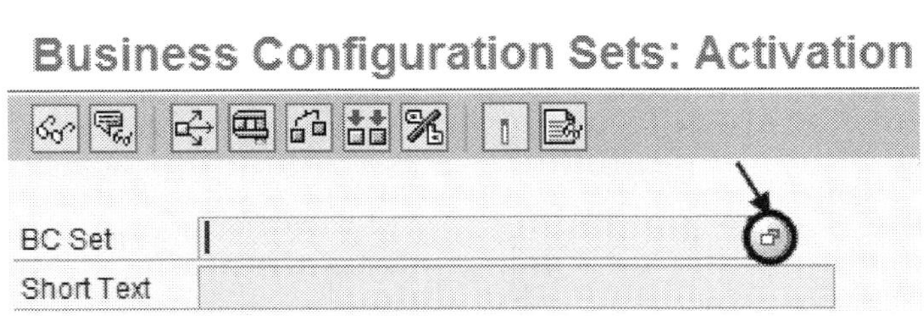

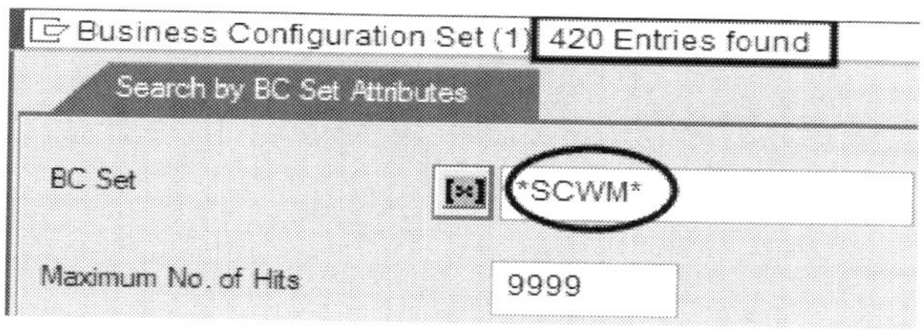

Notes:

In the EWM system, the reference warehouse is not activated at the time of basis system installation. Activation of reference warehouse is part of activating BC sets. A reference warehouse is a standard SAP delivered warehouse (0001), which can be used as a reference during the configuration.

5.2 Warehouse Org Elements and Master Data

In chapter 3, the "warehouse org structure" section briefly covered the key elements of warehouse structure and how they are linked to each other. This section will cover how to configure those org elements in detail.

Before starting the warehouse configuration, consultants should have a clear idea of what their client's WM org structure will look like; what it will be named; how many storage types, storage sections, and bin types are needed for the warehouse; and so on. Once those requirements are ready, they can be configured in the EWM system. Table 5.2A is a summary of the configuration and the master data settings that will be completed in this section. Some settings are done outside SPRO. Some of them are transportable, and some are not. Nontransportable settings have to be performed in every client manually.

Table 5.2A Warehouse Org Elements and Master Data			
S. No	**Configuration Check List**	**TCode**	**Transportable**
1	Define Warehouse Number	SPRO	Yes
2	Define Supply Chain Unit (SCU) for Warehouse	/SCMB/S	No
3	Assign an SCU and Default Business Partners to the Warehouse	/SCWM/L GNBP	No
4	Assign the EWM Warehouse to the ERP Warehouse	SPRO	Yes
5	Define Availability Group	SPRO	Yes
6	Define ECC Stock Type	SPRO	Yes
7	Define Stock Types for Warehouse	SPRO	Yes
8	Define Stock Removal Rule	SPRO	Yes
9	Define Storage Types	SPRO	Yes
10	Define Storage Sections	SPRO	Yes
11	Define Storage Bins	SPRO	Yes
12	Define Number Ranges for Warehouse Documents	SPRO	No
13	Define Activity Areas	SPRO	Yes
14	Define Staging Areas and Warehouse Doors	SPRO	Yes
15	Define Work Centers	SPRO	Yes
16	Map Storage Locations from ERP System to EWM	SPRO	Yes
17	Assign Control Parameters to Warehouse	SPRO	Yes

5.2.1 Define Warehouse Number

When creating a new warehouse, it is highly recommended to create one with reference to the SAP-delivered template warehouse "0001," using "copy warehouse function." This will copy all the configuration settings from the template warehouse to the new warehouse. This way, it is not necessary to build the entire required configuration from the ground up. Once the configuration is copied, the required settings for the new warehouse can be changed. However, in this section, the warehouse has been created from scratch (without using the copy function) so consultants are cognizant of both methods.

In chapter 4, the ERP warehouse called "EWM" was defined and assigned to the SCM-EWM warehouse called "SEWM." Here, the "SEWM" warehouse in the EWM system will be defined.

Menu Path: SPRO | IMG | Extended Warehouse Management | Master Data | Define Warehouse Numbers

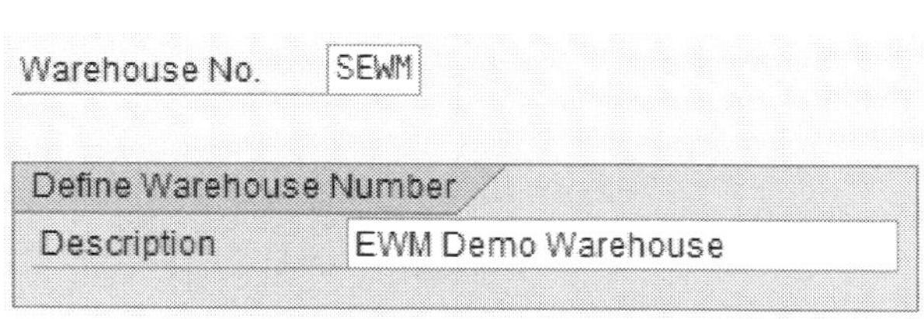

Click on the "New Entries" button on the application toolbar; enter the warehouse number and the description and click on the "Save" button.

Note:

i. SAP recommends defining separate warehouse numbers for each warehouse complex.

ii. The copy warehouse function is available in **SPRO | IMG | Extended Warehouse Management | Cross-Process Settings | Copy Warehouse Number Customizing**. Here, the existing setup of the warehouse can be copied to the new warehouse. This will copy all data in the dependent tables automatically, except the number range intervals. It is also necessary to define the assignment of the warehouse to the supply chain unit separately.

5.2.2 Define Supply Chain Unit (SCU) for Warehouse

SCU is a master data that contains information like country, region code, time zone, address, and essential business attributes of the warehouse. Business attributes describe how the SCU is used in the EWM system, like whether it is a warehouse; goods receipt office, ship-to party, and so on.

For every EWM warehouse, there should be one SCU assigned to it. The SCU assigned to the warehouse should be defined with the category code 1008—warehouse. The system uses the time zone information of the SCU when displaying all date and time fields for the warehouse.

Since SCU is part of master data and is not transportable, it has to be manually maintained in every client. Assigning the SCU to a warehouse can be done either as part of configuration or in the user menu (SAP easy access menu), which is covered in the next section.

Menu Path: SAP Easy Access | SAP menu | Extended Warehouse Management | Master Data | Maintain Supply Chain Unit or TCode /SCMB/SCUMAIN.

Here, enter the name of Supply Chain Unit, select the category as 1008 (warehouse), and click on the "Create" button.

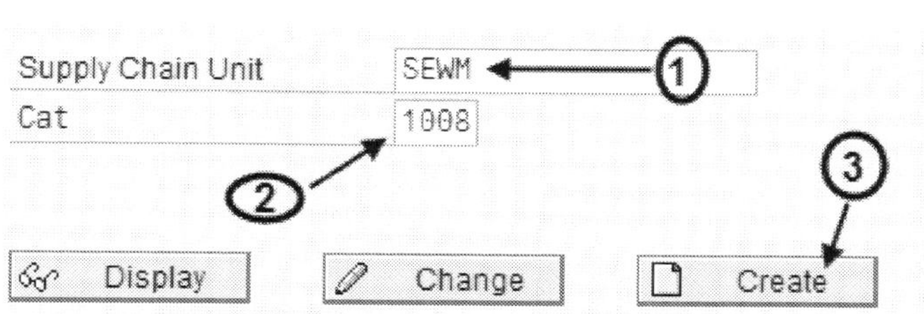

In the "General" tab, maintain the time zone. Other details like geographical data and partner data are optional. Under the "Address" tab, specify the country and the region. In the "Alternative" tab, click on the "Add Role" button to select the essential business attributes for the warehouse. Multiple business attributes can be assigned to one warehouse, as shown below.

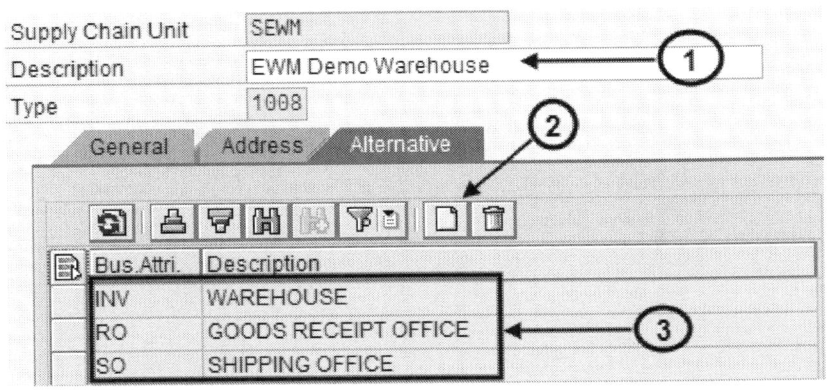

5.2.3 Assign an SCU and Default Business Partners to the Warehouse

In this step, an SCU and default business partners are assigned to the warehouse. The assignment can be done in the configuration menu or from the SAP easy access menu. Even though the assignment can be done in configuration menu path, this setting is not transportable. Hence, it must be manually maintained in every client.

A default party entitled to dispose and a default ship-to party should be assigned only if the warehouse is linked to only one ERP plant. The default data maintained here will be used as default data when maintaining the product master and in some of the transactional data.

Menu Path: SPRO | Extended Warehouse Management | Master Data | Assign Warehouse Numbers or TCode /SCWM/LGNBP.

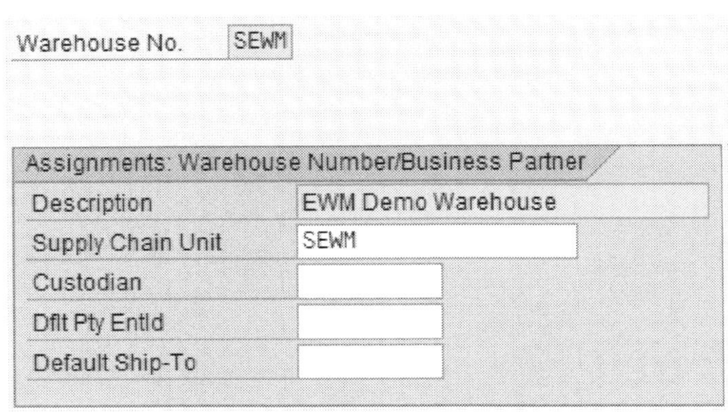

✎ **Note:**

i. SAP recommends that the assignment of SCU to a warehouse should not be changed after defining the product master data or transactional data. Doing so can cause errors.

5.2.4 Assign the EWM Warehouse to the ERP Warehouse

Now that the warehouse has been defined in the SCM system, it is important to link it to the ERP warehouse. In this menu link the EWM warehouse to the ERP warehouse and ERP business system. This link is used to transfer the transactional or goods movement data from EWM to the ERP warehouse.

Menu Path: SPRO | IMG | Extended Warehouse Management | Interfaces | ERP Integration | General Settings | Map Warehouse Numbers from ERP System to EWM

Here, select the ERP business system in "Business System" field; enter the ERP warehouse number in the WHoERP field and the EWM warehouse number in the warehouse number field.

Mapping for Warehouse Number

Business System	WNoERP	Warehouse Number
SE1CLNT410	EWM	SEWM

5.2.5 Define Availability Group

The availability group is used to group different stock types (Unrestricted-use stock, Stock in quality inspection, Blocked stock, Restricted-use Stock) in the EWM system. Once it is defined, this group can be assigned to a storage type to allow certain stock types in the storage type. Other than this, the availability group is also used for communication with the ERP system.

In the configuration, storage type, stock type, and WPTs are assigned to the availability group, and the availability group is assigned to the ERP storage location. In this way, the system can find an ERP stock type and a specific storage location for every EWM stock type during the data transfer.

Menu Path: SPRO | IMG | Extended Warehouse Management | Goods Receipt Process | Configure Availability Group for Putaway | Define Availability Group

Customizing Table - Availability Groups

War	AGr	Description	DType ERP
SEWM	001	Goods in Putaway	IDRECDOCK
SEWM	002	Goods Available to Sell	IDAVAILFS
SEWM	003	Stock in Production	

Diagram 5.2.5A shows how different org elements are linked to the availability group.

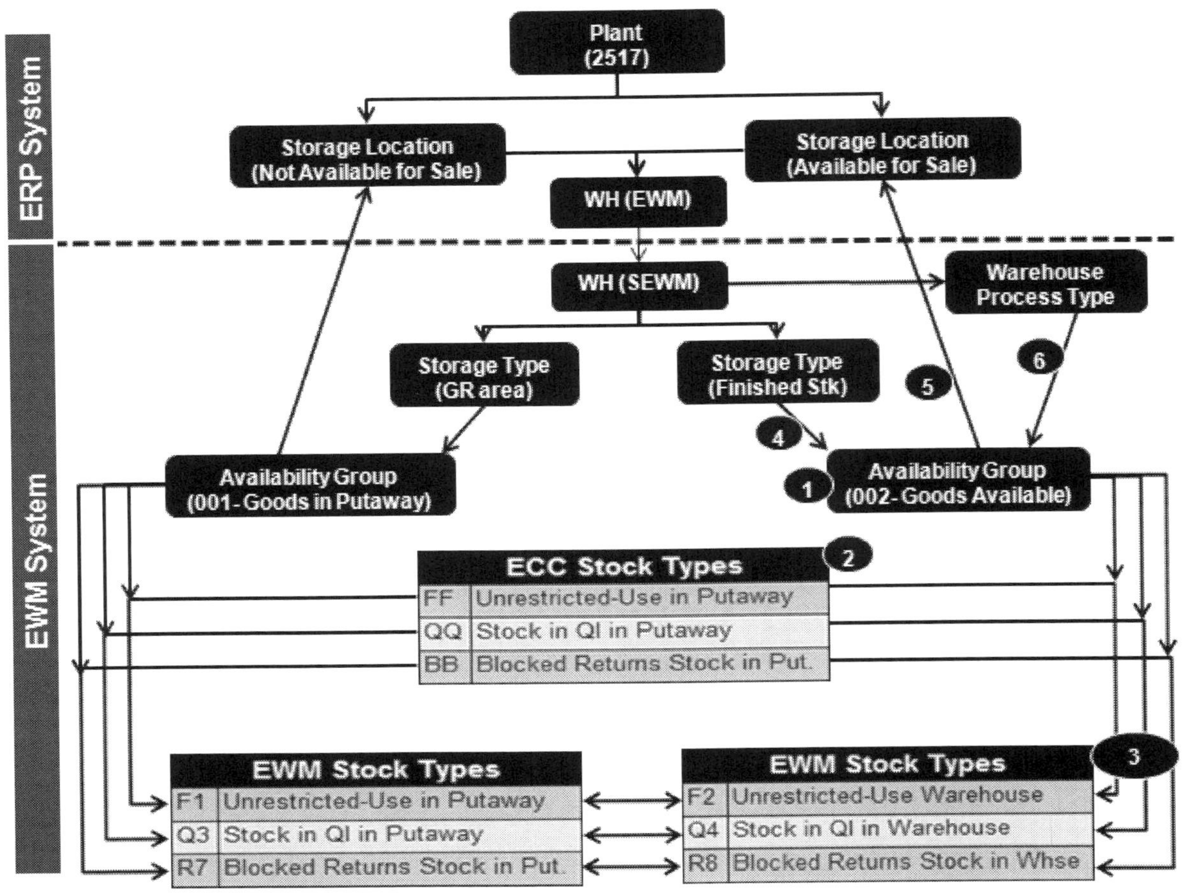

Diagram 5.2.5A Availability Group

The numbers specified in the diagram are the steps involved in defining and setting up the availability group, stock types, and their assignments.

The availability group must also be assigned to a WPT, because when the system defines the stock type of a delivery, it uses the availability group of the WPT and not the availability group of the storage type.

5.2.6 Define ECC Stock Types

In the ERP system, stock type is referred to as unrestricted-use, quality inspection, or blocked. In EWM, they are referred as non-location–dependent stock types.

In EWM, these stock types can be further divided into multiple different stock types like unrestricted under putaway, unrestricted available to sell, and so on. But they all have to be assigned to non-location–dependent stock types, because during the data transfer, the ERP system recognizes only the non-location–dependent stock types.

In this section, we will define the following nondependent stock types for the warehouse.

- FF: Unrestricted-use stock
- QQ: Quality inspection stock
- BB: Blocked stock
- RR: Returns blocked stock (non-valuated and not visible in SAP APO)

The main usage of non-location–dependent stock types in the EWM system is determining the subsequent stock type for a transfer between two storage types that belong to different availability groups or mapping between EWM stock type and ERP stock type.

Menu Path: SPRO | IMG | Extended Warehouse Management | Goods Receipt Process | Configure Availability Group for Putaway | Define Non-Location–Dependent Stock Type

Customizing Table: Non-Location-Specific Stock Type

War...	N	Description
SEWM	BB	Blocked Stock
SEWM	FF	Unrestricted-Use Stock
SEWM	QQ	Stock in Quality Inspection
SEWM	RR	Blocked Stock Returns

Note:

i. The SAP ERP system only recognizes the above stock types.

5.2.7 Define Stock Types for Warehouse

In this configuration, the non-location–dependent stock types are further divided into multiple warehouse specific stock types and assigned to different availability groups. This helps maintain more meaningful stock status in the warehouse under different storage types—for example, stock under putaway and not available for picking, stock available for picking, and so on.

Menu Path: SPRO | IMG | Extended Warehouse Management | Goods Receipt Process | Configure Availability Group for Putaway | Configure Stock Type

Customizing View - EWM Stock Types									
War...	ST	Description Stoc...	S	SG	AGr	Description	N...	Description	R.
SEWM	B5	Blocked in Puta			001	Goods in Putaway	BB	Blocked Stock	N Normal Stock
SEWM	B6	Blocked Wareho			002	Goods Available to	BB	Blocked Stock	N Normal Stock
SEWM	D1	Free for Cross-			004	Cross Docking	FF	Unrestricted-Use	N Normal Stock
SEWM	F1	Unrestricted-Us			001	Goods in Putaway	FF	Unrestricted-Use	N Normal Stock
SEWM	F2	Unrestricted-Us			002	Goods Available to	FF	Unrestricted-Use	N Normal Stock
SEWM	P2	P2			003	Stock in Productior	FF	Unrestricted-Use	N Normal Stock
SEWM	P4	P4			003	Stock in Productior	QQ	Stock in Quality In	N Normal Stock

5.2.8 Define Stock Removal Rule

The stock removal rule defines the sequence in which the quants found by the program should be sorted before proposing the bins and quantity for picking. For example, First in First Out (FIFO), Last in First Out (LIFO), and so on. In ERP WM, stock removal rules are preconfigured, and very few changes can be made to the existing defined rules without a user exit. In EWM, SAP has provided more flexibility to define one's own rules.

Menu Path: SPRO | IMG | Extended Warehouse Management | Goods Issue Process | Strategies | Specify Stock Removal Rule

Here, enter the warehouse number, stock removal rule code and the description for each warehouse. Hit "Enter" and save the entries. Select the stock removal rule and double-click on "Stock Removal Rule" in the dialog structure to assign the sort fields, sort type and the sequence.

Dialog Structure
▽ Definition of Stock Remov
Stock Removal Rule

Definition of Stock Removal Rules		
War...	Re...	Description
SEWM	FIFO	First In First Out
SEWM	LIFO	Last in First Out
SEWM	BIND	By Bin (Desending order)

Consultants can add thirty sort fields for the stock removal rules and then specify how the results should be sorted (i.e., ascending or descending order).

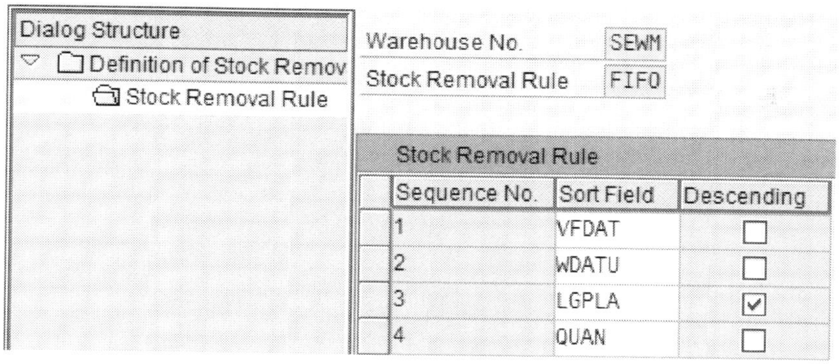

5.2.9 Define Storage Types

The above sections covered the data elements required to configure storage types.

In EWM, storage types are a further division of warehouse number and play an important role during product movement and storage in the warehouse. There are several control indicators available for storage types, which can influence the behavior of putaway, stock removal, replenishment, and goods movement. This is further explained below.

Menu Path: SPRO | IMG | Extended Warehouse Management | Master Data | Define Storage Type

Storage type configuration is broadly divided into five sections. They are general control, putaway control, stock removal control, replenishment settings, and goods movement control. Each section will have many control keys, representing the configuration for that section of the storage type.

Notes:

i. Settings made under storage type are storage-type specific. Therefore, these settings have to be defined for every storage type. The settings can be copied from one storage type to another with the copy function.

ii. In EWM, interim storage types are normally defined with starting number 9. This helps the consultant and warehouse team to easily distinguish between the interim and noninterim storage types.

5.2.9.1 General Controls

This section controls some of the important settings of the storage type, like storage type role, fixed bin settings of the storage type, storage behavior, and HU requirements. Some of the important settings in this section are covered in detail below.

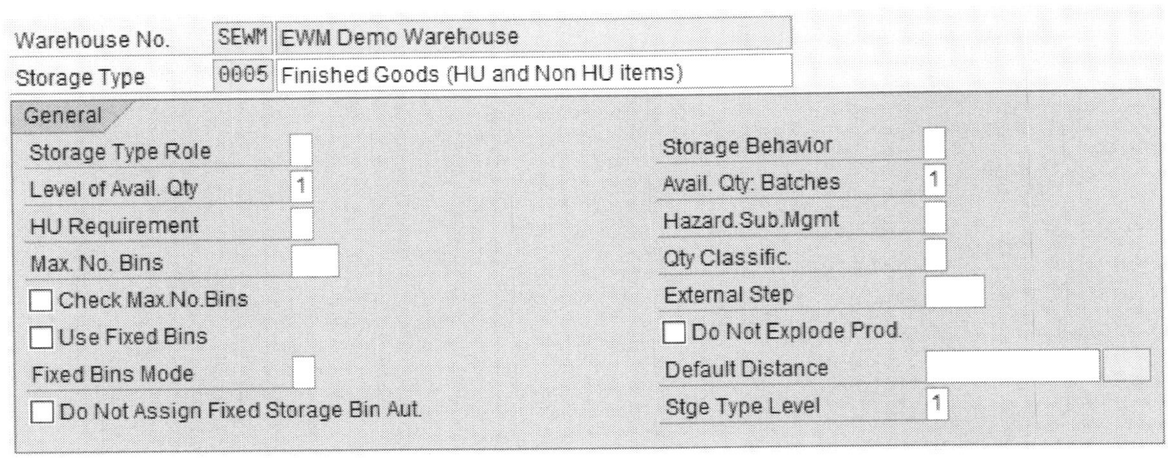

Storage Type Role

Storage type role is used to define how the storage type is used in the warehouse. Each storage type will be defined for a specific purpose or to play a specific role and will influence the goods movements. Following is the list of storage type roles provided by SAP:

Role	Description
	Standard Storage Type
A	Identification Point
B	Pick Point
C	Identification and Pick Point
D	Staging Area Group
E	Work Center
F	Doors
G	Yard
H	Automatic Storage Retrieval (Material Flow Control)
I	Work Center in Staging Areas Group
J	Automatic Warehouse (Controlled by MFS)
K	Production Supply

- **Standard Storage Type**: This represents a physical area in the warehouse where the products are finally stored as the last step in the putaway process. Control parameters configured for putaway and picking will influence product putaway and picking from this storage type. In the warehouse, the majority of storage types usually have "standard storage" roles assigned to them, which are used for final storage of products.
- **Identification point (ID point)**: ID point represents an area in the warehouse where the products are taken for verification, labeling, and so on during goods receipt and before final putaway. It is mainly used in the Automated Storage and Retrieval System (ASRS).
- **Pick Point**: Just like ID point, pick points are used at the time of goods issue for labeling, inspection, or packing. They are mainly used for ASRS.
- **Identification and Pick point**: If the ID and pick points comprise one common area in the warehouse, this role can be assigned to the storage type.

- **Work Center**: This is the area within the warehouse where inspection, packing, labeling, and value added services are performed for both incoming and outgoing products.
- **Yard**: For yard management, define a yard as a storage type and each space or dedicated area for truck in the yard is defined as a bin.
- **Material Flow Control**: This role is used for storage types that represent ASRS or conveyor systems.

Level of Available Quantity

If the stock is HU managed, sometimes it is more practical if warehouse personnel makes the decision on which HU to pick from the bin for delivery, rather than having the system suggest which HU to pick. This gives more flexibility to the warehouse personnel. On the other hand, if the products have batch constraints or shelf life expiry, it is appropriate if the system suggests what to pick. This can reduce human error at the time of picking. In this configuration, consultants specify which of these options they want for the storage type.

The two available options are "Highest-Level HU," in which case the system is suggesting the HU in the warehouse task, and the user has to pick the system-suggested HU. If it is preferable for the user to make the decision at the time of picking, the value in this field should be "storage bin."

HU Requirement:

In EWM, SAP has withdrawn the functionality of storage units and provided HU functionality to track pallets and products. Now it is possible to store both HU and non-HU–managed stock in the same bin. In this setting, consultants specify whether HU functionality is required for the storage type or not. The default value for this setting is that HU is allowed but not a requirement. Available options are as follows:

- HU Allowed but not a Requirement
- HU Requirement
- HU not Allowed

Max No. Bins

One of the common problems in the warehouse is that a few materials occupy most of the storage space, leaving very little or no space for other materials in the primary storage type. This often triggers rearrangement of the stock or delay in picking for outbound deliveries. To avoid such problems, SAP has a "Max No. Bins" provision, allowing consultants to specify the number of bins for each material in the primary storage type. This ensures that all materials will get space in the primary storage type, and overflow of product stock will be stored in the secondary storage types.

The setting at storage type is applicable for all the products stored in that storage type. The same option is available at the product level. If it is specified in the product master as well as at the storage type, the product master settings will take precedence.

Check Max. No. Bins

The value entered in the "Max No. Bins" field will be active only if the "Check Max No. Bins" indicator is active. If it is not checked, the value entered in the "Max. No. Bins" field (both in product master and storage type) has no impact.

Use Fixed Bins

If the storage type defined is fixed-bin storage, the check box "Use Fixed Bins" should be checked. If this indicator is checked, the system will consider the value in the “Fixed Bins Mode” field to determine the proper fixed bin.

Fixed Bins Mode

The fixed bins mode defines how the fixed bins will be selected for stock putaway. The system uses the following two options to select the bins:

- **Put Away to Optimum Fixed Storage Bins Only**: Here, only those bins that the system has determined, with a combination of putaway and slotting algorithm, will be selected for putaway. The slotting algorithm plays an important role here in determining bins.
- **Put Away to Optimum Fixed Storage Bins Preferred**: In this case, the system will first try to suggest optimal bins. If none are found, it will suggest other available bins in the storage type.

Do Not Assign Fixed Storage Bin Automatically

The EWM system allows multiple fixed bins for the products. If the fixed bins are not assigned to the product, or the assigned fixed bins are full, new fixed bins will be determined for the products at the time of putaway. The system will automatically add those bins to the fixed bin table for the products, if this checkbox is not checked. Fixed bins can be assigned in TCode /SCWM/FBINASN **(menu path: SAP Easy access | Extended Warehouse Management | Master Data | Storage Bin | Assign Fixed Storage Bins to Products)**.

Storage Behavior

Storage behavior describes how the products, or pallet of products, are managed in the storage type. Options available include the following:

- **Standard Warehouse**: Here Standard warehouse is referred to normal storage space where products are stored with or without pallets in the bin.

- **Pallet Storage**: For pallet storage, identical subdivision will be done, depending on the pallet type at the time of initial putaway. These divisions are used to know the exact position of the pallets in the bin, and they become part of the bin name.
- **Bulk Storage**: If the bins are large, or the products are stored in the open where pallets are stacked on top of another, a bulk storage option is recommended.

Available Quantity (Batches)

If the products are batch managed, in some industries it is more practical if the warehouse personnel decides which batch to pick from the bin for the delivery. This can reduce the picking effort. On the other hand, if the products have shelf life expiry or batch dependency (all pick quantity of the product should belong to same batch), it is more practical to pick a system-suggested batch.

If the warehouse personnel specifies which batch is picked for the warehouse task at the time of picking, then the selected option in this field for the storage type should be "Available Quantity: Batch-Neutral."

If the system suggests the batch based on sales order or delivery, select the option "Available Quantity: Batch-Specific."

Hazardous Substance Management (HSM)

HSM is used to check whether products can be mixed in the storage type, according to hazardous substance rules. If the value in this field is blank, it means no check will be performed. The other two available options are "Hazardous substance check only at storage type level" and "Haz.sub.check at stor.type and stor.section levels."

Quantity Classification

Quantity Classification describes the packaging in which the products are stored in the storage type. For example, pallets, loose products, bags, boxes, and so on. This information is used, along with the packaging specification, to determine the right storage type for picking based on the pick quantity. This can help in reducing partial pallets in the storage type. The allowed values for quantity classification can be configured in the menu path **SPRO | IMG | Extended Warehouse Management | Cross-Process Settings | Warehouse Task | Define Quantity Classifications**

External Step

External steps represent the actions or activities performed in the warehouse—for example, Unload, Count, Deconsolidate, Putaway, Remove from Stock, Pack, Stage, Load, and so on.

External steps assigned to the storage type are used only for HU-managed stock, if the crucial step is not performed before the process is completed. If the material has not yet achieved the assigned external step, the last completed step will be replaced with the assigned external step.

In EWM, SAP has predefined internal process steps, which have to be assigned to the external steps. This is covered in more detail in chapter 15. To define external steps, follow the menu path **SPRO | IMG | Extended Warehouse Management | Cross-Process Settings | Warehouse Task | Define Process-Oriented Storage Control**

Do Not Explode Product

In the warehouse, products can be moved with a product warehouse task (WT) or as a HU WT (if the product is HU managed). For HU WT, it is also possible to track the warehouse movements of the products individually by product. If tracking the movements individually by product is not desired, check this box.

The effect of checking this indicator is that in the warehouse monitor, it will not be possible to query the warehouse tasks by product. If the indicator is not checked, the system will populate the additional values for the products in the tracking table. This gives more visibility in the warehouse monitor and can be queried by product. The other impact of selecting this indicator is confirming the HU WT can take more system resource and can cause performance issue.

Default Distance

The default distance defined in the storage type is used to record the distance traveled in labor management, if the warehouse task is confirmed using desktop transactions. In case of RF devices, the system uses the last WT confirmation bin and the current WT bin to calculate the actual distance traveled, using the bin coordinates and travel path defined in labor management.

Storage Type Level

This field value is used to show the different levels in the graphical view of the warehouse. It defines what level the storage type is located, for example, ground floor, first floor, or second floor. If the value in this field is not maintained, the system will consider that all storage types are located in the same levels.

5.2.9.2 Putaway Control

The parameters defined here are used to control the putaway into the storage type. Putaway here refers to all inward movements of products into the storage type. It could be goods receipts putaway, transfer of products between two storage types, replenishment, bin to bin movements, and so on.

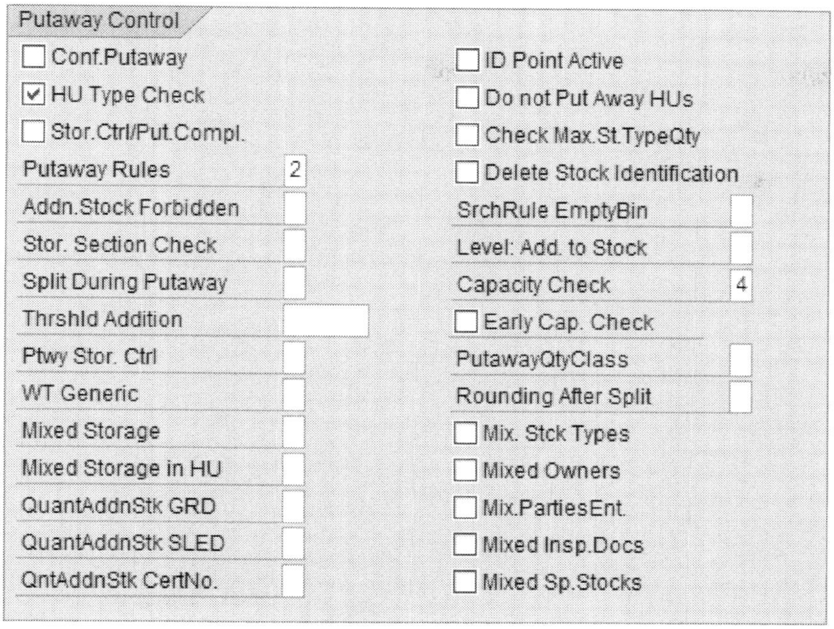

Confirm Putaway:

In the warehouse, WTs are used to confirm goods movements and update the bin stock. They can be confirmed manually by an operator or can be confirmed automatically by the system in the background. If you preferred the operator to confirm the WT manually, check this indicator. To confirm the WT automatically in the background, the "Confirm putaway" indicator should not be checked for the destination storage type, and the "Confirm removal" checkbox should not be checked for the source storage type.

HU Type Check

The warehouse may use more than one type of HU to store the materials. For example, small boxes, large boxes, industrial size pallet, and so on. If not all types of HUs are allowed in a storage type, this box must be checked. If this indicator is active, the system will check whether the HU type associated with the HU in the warehouse task is allowed in the storage type.

Storage Control/Putaway Completed

This indicator determines that the storage type is a final destination for the putaway activity. This indicator is useful only for process-oriented storage control (POSC), which is covered in chapter 15.

Putaway Rules

The putaway rule specifies the logic that the EWM system will use to find destination bins during putaway of products. The following four rules are available for the storage type. (If these rules do not meet some companies' warehouse requirements, consultants can activate available Business add-ins

(BADIs) and write their own custom logic in addition to standard code to find the appropriate destination bins.)

- **Empty Bin:** During putaway, the system only searches for empty bins in the storage type.
- **Addition to Existing Stock/Empty Bin:** The system searches for partially occupied bins first. If it does not find partially occupied bins, the system then searches for empty bins. While searching the partial bins, the system also will consider other rules specified for the storage type, such as mixed stock types, mixed storage, split during putaway rules, and so on.
- **Consolidation Group:** Storage bins from the storage type assigned to the consolidation group. If this option is selected, during putaway the system searches for the bin that matches the stock consolidation group. This is very useful in the packing area, where products being stored in a bin by consolidation group help to speed up the packing process. Consolidation groups help clarify what products can be packed and stored together.
- **General Storage Area:** This is more applicable for interim storage types, staging areas where there is only one bin and there are no restrictions on the stock that can be stored in the bin. These storage types allow mixed stock, addition to existing stock, and mixing of all types of products.

Addition to Stock Forbidden

In some storage areas, it is practical to add stock to the existing stock in the bin to make use of maximum bin capacity. To manage this feature in EWM, there are three options: addition to stock allowed, addition to stock not allowed, or product putaway profile decides. The selected option in this configuration will affect what can be defined in other fields of storage type configuration. For example, if "addition to stock not allowed" is selected for the storage type, the putaway rule "addition to existing stock" cannot be selected. If such conflicts occur, the system will give an error message.

Storage Section Check

It is possible that some storage types might have many storage sections, and some restrictions might apply while putting away products in the storage sections. For example, heavy products may not be suitable for putaway in the top-level bins. In case of such restrictions, the storage section check should be activated. During putaway the product master drives the products to the appropriate storage section. If the warehouse operator tries to locate the product in the wrong storage section, the system will indicate an error at the time of WT creation or confirmation.

Split During Putaway

This configuration controls how the quantity should split in the warehouse task, in case the full quantity does not fit into one bin. This is applicable only for non-HU stock.

Split during putaway is performed only for product WTs as per maximum storage type quantity, weight, volume, and capacity key figures. Options available are "Do Not Split," "Split During Putaway," and "Product Master Decides".

Threshold Addition

If either the "Split During Putaway" or "Product Master Decides" option is selected in split during putaway configuration, the system will refer the value of "threshold addition" before the warehouse task created for the split quantity. If the quantity expected in the bin is less than the threshold value, the system will not split the putaway quantity. This field will avoid unnecessary small quantity split, which could reduce operational efficiency. The threshold value is defined in percentage of the storage bin capacity.

Rounding after Split

This configuration controls how the split quantity should be rounded. If the "no rounding" option is selected, the total quantity will be put away into one bin. In case selected option is round down WT qty to a multiple of a unit, the system will round down the WT quantity to multiples of the pallet quantity, and the remaining quantity will be put away in a different bin. For example, if the putaway quantity is two and a half pallets, and the rule is round down the WT quantity to the multiple of pallet quantity, there will be two WTs: one WT for two pallets and one for the partial pallet.

Putaway Storage Control

This configuration defines how to create a warehouse task for a handling unit. You can specify whether the putaway is to be performed with a HU WT, performed with a product WT, evaluated dynamically based on the settings of the field "Create Putaway WTs," or HU Pick-WTs.

This is only valid in the case of process-oriented storage control. If process-oriented storage control is not used, the setting is made at WPT level based on the field value of "Select HU w/o Storage Process."

WT Generic

This configuration lets you define how generic the WT destination data should be. WTs can have all three destination data, that is, destination storage type, storage section and the bin, or only storage type or only storage section and storage type.

For example, if the storage type is a packing station, it is not necessary for the WT created to move the stock to the packing station to contain the destination storage bin. Instead, the WT can contain only destination storage type, and when the WT is confirmed, the warehouse personnel can specify the destination storage bin for putaway based on physical availability.

Mixed Storage

This parameter indicates how the mixed stock is managed in the bin. In case of non-HU stock, the entire bin behaves like a HU, and the option specified for HU will apply to the bin. Here, the following options are available:

- **Mixed Storage without Limitations:** More than one HU can be stored in the storage bin. There are no dependencies between the individual HUs. However mixing of products and batches within an HU is controlled by the "Mixed Storage in HU" indicator.
- **Several Non-Mixed HUs with the Same Product/Batch:** Several HUs can be stored in a storage bin simultaneously. However, the individual HUs must contain the same product and the same batch number.
- **Several HUs with Different Batches of the Same Product:** Several HUs can be stored in a storage bin simultaneously. However, the HUs must contain the same product. If the product is batch managed, several batches of the product can be stored in the bin.
- **One HU Allowed per Bin:** Here, only one HU can be stored in a bin. Because the system treats the bin also as one HU, storing of both non-HU and HU materials in the same bin is not allowed.

Mixed Storage in HU

This configuration describes how products and batches can be mixed in one HU. Options available include the following:

- **Mixed Storage Not Allowed:** This means only the same product and batch can be stored in one HU.
- **Several Batches of the Same Product per HU:** Different batches can be packed together, but the product should be same.
- **Mixed Storage Without Limitation in HU:** This means any products of any batches can be packed into one HU.

Quant

Quant is the unique number in the bin that represents the quantity of a specific product with the same characteristics. It contains product number, batch number, stock type, stock category, and stock usage. You can alter the quant by adding more stock to existing stock. In such cases, the system will first determine if there is an existing quant for the stock; if so, certain values like GR date, SLED, and certificate number will be updated based on the configuration specified in the storage type. The following few sections will describe how this can be configured in the storage type.

Quant Addition Stock GR Date

If addition to stock is allowed in the storage bin, it is possible that the GR date of the new stock could be different than the date already existing in the quant. The quant can contain only one GR date. In this scenario, define how the system should behave when updating GR date for the quant. Here, the options available include the following:

- **Allowed—Most Recent Date Dominant:** In case of addition to stock, if the quant already exists for the product or batch, the GR date of the quant will be replaced with the latest GR date of the stock.
- **Allowed—Earliest Date Dominant:** In case of addition to stock, if the quant already exists for the product or batch, the GR date of the quant will be replaced with the oldest GR date of the stock.
- **Not Allowed**: If the new stock has a different GR date than the GR date of the existing quant, the system will not allow addition to stock.
- **Product Putaway Profile Decides**: In this case, the product profile will decide at the time of putaway.

Quant Addition Stock Shelf Life Expiry Date (SLED)

If addition to stock is allowed in the storage bin, it is possible that the SLED date of the new stock could be different than the one existing in the quant. The quant can contain only one SLED date. In this scenario, it is necessary to define how the system should behave while updating SLED date for the quant. The options available are very similar to the GR date explained above.

Quant Addition Stock Certificate No.

If the addition to stock allowed in the storage bin, it is possible that the certificate number of the new stock could be different than the one existing in the quant. The quant can contain only one certificate number. In this scenario, define how the system should behave while updating the certificate number for the quant. The options available are very similar to the GR date explained above.

ID Point Active

ID points are areas in the warehouse where the products are moved to soon after unloading for further processing, like palletizing or labeling, before putting them away in the bin. This indicator should be checked if the storage type is one of those interim points.

Do Not Putaway HUs

This indicator is used when Process Oriented Storage Control (POSC) is being used in the goods putaway process, and the retaining of the HU number is not required in the in final storage type. If the HU is not removed when the stock is confirmed in its final putaway bin location, at the time of picking, it is necessary to specify the HU. If this parameter is checked, the system will use a product WT for the final putaway step instead of HU WT.

Check Maximum Storage Type Quantity

This indicator specifies whether or not the product should be put away into the storage type, if the maximum storage type quantity is exceeded for the product. If this indicator is not set, the product is put away, even though the maximum storage type quantity is exceeded. The maximum storage type quantity can be defined in the product master in storage type view.

Delete Stock Identification

Stock ID is a unique number that can be used to identify the stock with all of its attributes like product number, batch, stock type, stock category, quantity, and so on. This can be printed on labels and can be used to track the products throughout the picking and putaway process. If POSC is used, and the storage type is checked as final destination (i.e., the "Stor. Ctrl/Put. Compl" indicator is checked), the "Delete Stock Identification" check box must be checked for the storage type.

Search Rule Empty Bin:

In addition to the putaway rule, the system will consider the configuration defined here to search the empty bin. Here, specify how the system should select the empty bins for putaway strategy (e.g., "Next Empty Bin"). The options available are as follows:

- **Sorting According to Definition**: If this option is selected, the system will use the sort field defined in the storage bin master to sort and select the empty bins.
- **Near To Fixed Bin:** The empty bins are prioritized according to their closeness to a fixed bin.
- **Product Decides**: The setting for the search rule in the product decides the course of action.

Level: Addition to Stock

If addition to existing stock is allowed in the storage type, the system uses this configuration to control at which level the stock should be added at the time of WT creation, for example, whether the warehouse personnel or the system will decide which HU to add the stock to. The following two options are available:

- **Addition to Stock at Bin Level**: If this option is selected, the system will not suggest any HUs in the WT. Warehouse personnel will manually decide which HU to add the stock to. This will give more flexibility to the operator to make the decision at the warehouse.
- **Addition to Stock at Highest HU level**: In this case, the system determines the HU during the WT creation, and the operator can't change the HU.

Capacity Check Method

In many warehouses, bin capacity is strictly followed during putaway to avoid bin damage, due to overloading the bins, or damage to the product due to the product dimensions.

To calculate total capacity of the bin, required parameters should be maintained in the product master under the “unit of measure” view, and also for HU type (in case of HU management).

In this configuration, specify whether the capacity check is active for the storage type, and if so, how the capacity is calculated. Options available include the following:

- **No Check According to Key Figure:** According to this option, the system will not perform any capacity check against the total capacity assigned to the bin. But the system will always perform a capacity check against the weight and volume if they are maintained in the storage bin.
- **Check Acc. to Key Figure Product:** Only product master capacity consumption information (defined under the "Unit of Measure" tab) is used to check the total capacity assigned to the bin.
- **Check Acc. to Key Figure HU Type:** Only the packaging material capacity consumption information (defined in the "Unit of Measure" tab) is used to check the total capacity assigned to the bin.
- **Check Acc. to Key Figures Product and HU Type:** Here, both products and packaging material capacity consumption information (defined in the "Unit of Measure" tab) is used to check the total capacity assigned to the bin.
- **No Check Against Key Figure, Weight, and Volume:** No capacity check is carried out, either against capacity consumption or against the maximum weight and volume. This option should be selected for all storage types where the capacity check should not be carried out.

Note:

i. If no capacity check should be performed for the storage types, the "No Check Against Key Figure, Weight, and Volume" option should be selected. If this is not selected, the system will always perform a capacity check against weight and volume, if they are maintained in the storage bin.

Early Capacity Check

If this indicator is checked, the EWM system does the early check on the bin type capacity before it checks the individual bins, eliminating all bins and bin types that are not suitable for the putaway. This helps increase the performance of the system.

Mix. Stock Types

In this configuration, specify whether or not multiple stock types are allowed in the bin (for example, unrestricted stock, inspection stock, or blocked stock). If multiple stock types are allowed in a bin, a unique quant will be created for all owners, parties entitled, material, batch, stock type, and stock category combination. Check this indicator if mixed stock types should not be allowed in the bin.

Mixed Owners

Every stock in EWM is assigned to an owner. Hence, bins may contain stock belonging to different owners. Check this indicator if multiple owners' stock should not be allowed within a bin.

Mixed Parties Entitled

Every stock in EWM is assigned to a party entitled to dispose. In this configuration, specify whether or not stock belonging to multiple parties should be allowed in a bin; check this indicator if not.

Mixed Insp. Docs

Usually, stock belonging to multiple inspection documents is allowed in one bin. Check this indicator if multiple inspection documents should not be allowed in a bin.

Mixed Sp. Stock

If this indicator is checked, the system will not allow mixed special stock in one bin. Special stock is customer stock, project stock, consignment stock, and so on.

5.2.9.3 Stock Removal Control

The parameters defined here are used to control the picking behavior from the storage type. "Picking" here refers to all outward movements of products from the storage type. Examples include outbound delivery, bin to bin movement, replenishment, and so on.

Confirm Removal

In the warehouse, WTs are used to confirm goods movements and update the bin stock. These can be confirmed manually by an operator or can be confirmed automatically by the system in the background. If it is preferred that the operator confirm the WT manually, check this indicator. To confirm the WT automatically in the background, the "Confirm Removal" indicator should not be checked for the source storage type, and the "Conf. Putaway" indicator should not be checked for the destination storage type.

Stock on Resource

If this indicator is selected, while searching the storage types for stock removal, the system will consider both stocks in the bin as well as stock that is on resources like forklifts, conveyer belts, and so on.

Negative Stock

This configuration controls whether negative stock is allowed in the storage type. The available options include the following:

- **Negative Stocks Not Allowed**: In this case, the system will not allow picking quantity more than the available quantity in the bin.
- **Negative Available Quantity Allowed:** In this case, at the time of WT creation, warehouse personnel can specify the removal quantity more than bin available quantity. In this case, the total available quantity is "available quantity plus total quantity scheduled for putaway."
- **Negative Stocks Allowed:** In this case, stock removal quantity can be more than the available plus scheduled for putaway quantity.

HU Picking Ctrl

Here, what should be the pick HU is defined. The available options are as follows:

- **Adopt Source HU with Lower-Level HUs into Pick HU:** In this case, the system will create a new pick HU and adopt the source and lower-level HUs into the pick HU.
- **Propose Source HU as Destination HU:** Here, the system will use the picked source HU as the destination HU.
- **WPT Controls Proposal for Destination HU:** In this case, the WPT determines the destination HU.
- **Only Adopt Contents (Prod. and Lower-Level HUs) into Pick HU:** Only the contents of the source HU are copied to the destination pick HU.

Pick Point Active

The pick point is the actual place in the warehouse to where the entire pallet is taken and only the required quantity is picked, in case of partial picking.

In case of partial picking, if all Hus should be directed to the pick point, this checkbox should be checked.

Use for Rough Bin Determination

If this indicator is checked, the storage type will be assigned to the delivery line item during the rough bin determination, even though the storage types do not have sufficient stock to fulfill the picking requirement. This information is used to drive the order-related replenishment in the warehouse.

Stock Removal Rule

Here, select the stock removal rule for the storage type. These rules can be defined in **SPRO | IMG | Extended Warehouse Management | Goods Issue Process | Strategies | Specify Stock Removal Rule**.

Round Whole Units

Here, configure how the picking WT quantity should be rounded. This can be defined at the storage type level as well as in the WPT. For example, if the pick quantity is 2.5 pallets, the system will behave following way:

- **No Rounding**: One WT will be created for quantity 2.5 pallets
- **Round Down WT Quantity to Single Unit:** Three WTs will be created: two WTs for full pallets and one WT for partial pallet
- **Round Down WT Quantity to a Multiple of a Unit:** There will be two WTs: one for two pallets and one for partial pallet
- **Round Up WT Quantity to a Multiple of a Unit:** In this case, there will be one WT for three pallets.

5.2.9.4 Goods movement control

In this section, the goods movement control parameters, which influence the goods movements in the ERP system, will be defined.

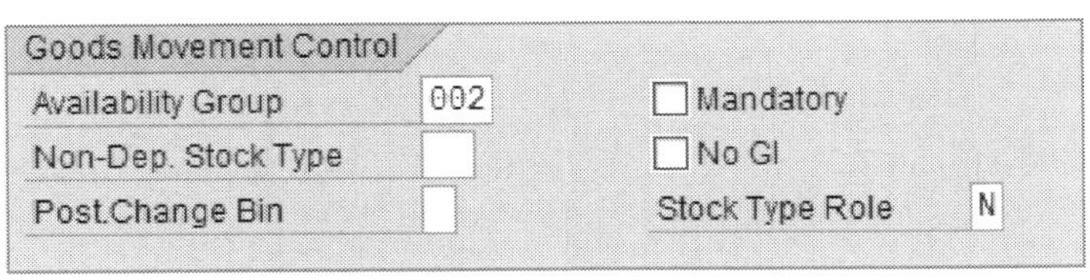

Availability Group

Availability groups were explained in detail earlier in the "Define Availability Group" section. Here, the appropriate availability group is assigned to the storage type. When putaway is confirmed, the stock type will be automatically changed to the stock type of the availability group. If required, posting change will be performed to move the stock from one storage location to another.

Nondependent Stock Type

This is explained earlier in the "Define Nondependent Stock Type" section. This configuration is required only if the stock in storage type belongs to one particular nondependent stock type. In such cases, assign the relevant value.

Posting Change Bin

Posting change in SAP refers to change of stock status with or without physical movement of the stock. For example, posting change will be created when the stock type is changed from blocked stock to unrestricted stock, or the stock category is changed from customer stock to own stock, and so on. This configuration specifies how to process the posting changes created in the system. The available options are:

- **Posting Change Always in Storage Bin:** For example, if the stock category is changed for the stock, it is not necessary that for the stock to be physically picked from the bin. In such cases, posting change can be performed in the same bin. Hence, no WT will be created.
- **Posting Change According to Mixed Storage Setting:** In this case, if mixed stock is allowed in the storage type, posting change will be performed in the same bin. If mixed stock is not allowed in the storage type, the system will create a WT to move the stock to a different storage bin.
- **Posting Change Never in Storage Bin:** In this case stock will always be moved to a different bin whenever posting change occurs.

Mandatory

This indicator specifies that stock can be posted only to the assigned availability group for the storage type. If a stock quantity is put away with a stock type from a different availability group into the storage type, the system automatically performs a posting change for the quantity into the relevant stock type of the mandatory availability group, during warehouse task confirmation.

No GI

This indicator restricts the storage type from posting goods issue from the storage type. In the warehouse, this indicator should be set to all storage types, which should not allow goods issue directly from the storage type without moving material to the interim storage type.

Stock Type Role

In the warehouse, if the storage type is always used to store a particular stock type (scraped stock, customs blocked stock, or blocked stock), select the appropriate stock type role for the storage type. Based on this indicator, whenever the stock is put away into the storage bin, the stock type will be changed automatically for the material.

5.2.9.5 Replenishment

In this section, the controls required for replenishment will be defined.

Replenishment Level

Replenishment level specifies whether the replenishment in this storage type is requested at storage bin level (fixed-bin storage only) or at storage type level. Options available include the following:

- **Storage Bin Level for Fixed Bins:** In this option, the replenishment quantities will be calculated for individual fixed bins as per the stock levels defined for the bins.
- **Storage Type Level:** In this option, the stock levels will be read for the entire storage type, and the replenishment quantities will be calculated based on the available stock in the storage type, compared with the stock level at the storage type.

Tolerance

Tolerance is defined in percentages, and it is used to check whether the replenishment quantity is sufficient to create a WT for replenishment.

5.2.10 Define Storage Sections

Storage types are further divided into storage sections. In the physical warehouse, storage sections could represent the type of product stored in the area (for example, heavy materials, small products, etc.), or a combination of bins (high racks, upper-level bins, lower-level bins, etc.) or could represent the velocity of products (fast-moving, slow-moving, etc.).

Not all warehouses will have storage sections for every storage type. This was mandatory until EWM 5.0 version. From EWM 5.1 onward, it is no longer the requirement to create bins and for bin determination for putaway. Stock can be put away into bins without a storage section. For example, interim storage types usually do not need a storage section.

Even though multiple storage sections can be created for a type, it should be thought out carefully. Increased storage sections can affect maintenance.

Menu Path: SPRO | IMG | Extended Warehouse Management | Master Data | Define Storage Section

Storage Sections

WhN	Typ	Sec	Description
SEWM	0005	0001	Heavy Parts
SEWM	0005	0002	Small Parts
SEWM	0005	0003	Damaged Stock
SEWM	0006	0001	High Value
SEWM	9002	0001	High Value Parts Staging Area
SEWM	9002	0002	Regular Parts Staging Area
SEWM	9020	0001	GI Staging Area

5.2.11 Define Storage Bins

Storage bins represent the physical location in the warehouse where the products are physically stored. This contains the details of the bin attributes, stock information, bin sectioning, production supply areas (PSA), activity areas, and PI data.

Even though creating bins is not part of configuration, the required information to create bin like different bin types, bin access types are defined in the configuration. This information is stored in the bin master and used during the products storage. This section will cover the required bin-related configurations and how to create and change them in EWM.

In EWM, a minimum of one storage bin should exist in every storage type. Bins can be created individually from SAP easy access menu (**Menu Path: SAP Easy Access | Extended Warehouse Management | Master Data | Storage Bin | Create Storage Bin or TCode /SCWM/LS01**) or automatically through a bin structure (**Menu Path: SAP Easy Access | Extended Warehouse Management | Master Data | Storage Bin | Generate Storage Bins or TCode /SCWM/LS10**).

TCode /SCWM/LS01 is mostly used to create individual bins as a daily maintenance activity, and bin structures are mostly used to create a large group of bins automatically, especially at the time of go-live.

While defining the bins following configuration data may be used depending on the warehouse requirements and the type of products storage.

5.2.11.1 Define Storage Bin Types

If a warehouse uses different bin types to store products, the bin types have to be defined in the configuration. Bin types are used to guide the right products into the right bins to avoid damage to the bins or products. For example, in an electronics warehouse, small bins may be used to store small products like cell phones, USB drives, and so forth; large bins may be used to store products like large refrigerators, TVs, and so on, and standard-sizes bins may be used to store products like microwaves, air conditioning units, and so on.

In EWM, different types of bins can be configured. Usage of bin types in the bin master is an optional feature. However, if storage types are HU managed, knowing the bin type is mandatory for creating the bins. Here, bin types are used to specify what HU types are allowed for each bins, for example standard-sized pallets, large-sized pallets, medium-sized boxes, etc. Based on this information, HU putaway will be restricted to those bins that are not suitable for the storage of HU.

Storage Bin Types

War...	Stor...	Description
SEWM	BIGB	Big Bins
SEWM	REGB	Regular Bins
SEWM	SMAB	Small Bins

Menu Path: SPRO | IMG | Extended Warehouse Management | Master Data | Storage Bins | Define Storage Bin Types

For capacity management, maximum weight, volume, capacity, length, width, and height must be defined for the bin types. The system will automatically copy this information to the bins at the time of bin creation.

5.2.11.2 Define Bin Access Types

Bin access types are used to better manage resources in EWM. They can represent a qualification of a resource type. For example, if a warehouse has bins at different heights or levels (say, five levels), some resources like forklifts may be capable of reaching only to certain levels (i.e., one or two), and some may be capable of reaching all the levels in the warehouse. In such scenarios, for the system to use proper resources for the WTs, it is very important to assign bin access types to the bins and resources. This information is used by resource management in determining the right resources for the execution of tasks.

Menu Path: SPRO | IMG | Extended Warehouse Management | Master Data | Storage Bins | Define Bin Access Types

Bin Access Types

War	Acc. Type	Description
SEWM	LVL1	Level 1
SEWM	LVL2	Level 2
SEWM	LVL3	Level 3
SEWM	LVL4	Level 4
SEWM	LVL5	Level 5

5.2.11.3 Define Storage Bin Identifiers for Storage Bin Structures

In the warehouse, the storage bin name usually consists of aisle identification, level identification, and the position of the bin. In some cases, the bin name might have additional information like stack, subdivision, and so on. For example, if the warehouse has triple-deep bins, with aisles and multiple levels, the bin name might look like A01-001-01-01, where A01 could be an aisle, 001 could be a level, 01 might represents the bin position, and the last two digits might represent the depth of the bins.

Subdivisions of the bins are mostly used in most cases where the warehouse has multiple depth bins like double-deep or triple-deep bins. Double-deep and triple-deep bin concepts are used for maximum utilization of the warehouse space by reducing aisle space used.

In EWM, storage bin identifiers represent Aisle, Stack, Level, Subdivision, and Bin depth. You can define a letter as the storage bin identifier for these identifiers. These are later used to define the storage bin structures and the activity areas independently of the storage type.

Menu Path: SPRO | IMG | Extended Warehouse Management | Master Data | Storage Bins | Define Storage Bin Identifiers for Storage Bin Structures

Warehouse No. SEWM

Storage Bin Identifier

Aisle ID	A
Stack Descriptn	S
Level Descriptn	L
ID for Bin Subdivsn	B
Bin Depth Indicato	D

5.2.11.4 Define Storage Bin Structure

Bin structure is a template where all the required values for the bins like storage type, section, bin types, bin access types, weight, volume, capacity, fire containment sections, XYZ coordinates, bin start value, bin end value, and increment number are defined. The bin attributes defined in bin structure will be copied to the bins when the bins are generated from the bin structures. In order to create bin structures, bin identifiers are essential.

The bin structure template can be defined using the characters N, A, and C, where N is used for numerical values, A is used for alphabetic characters, and C is used for a constant value. For example, template **A**CCCCC**N**C**NN**CCCCCCCC can be used to define the bin structure that starts with A01-001-01 and ends at D01-001-09. In the template, "A" represents an alphabetic character, "N" represents numeric values, and C represents the constant value (i.e., dashes and numbers that don't change). In the above example, the last five Cs represent the blank spaces. Because the bin number is eighteen digits, the template also should have eighteen digits.

Menu Path: SPRO | IMG | Extended Warehouse Management | Master Data | Storage Bins | Define Storage Bin Structure

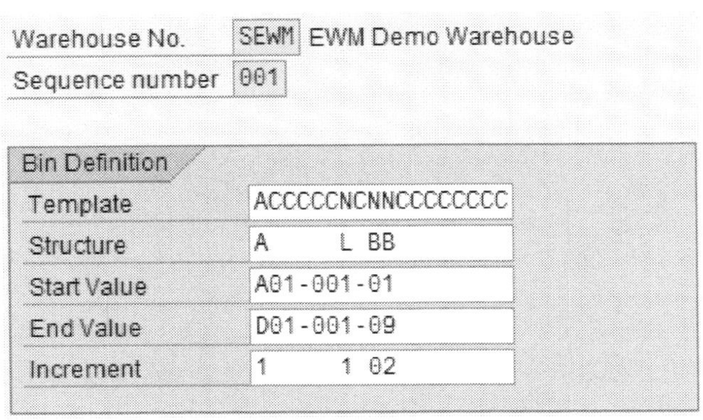

Warehouse No.	SEWM EWM Demo Warehouse
Sequence number	001

Bin Definition	
Template	ACCCCCNCNNCCCCCCCC
Structure	A L BB
Start Value	A01-001-01
End Value	D01-001-09
Increment	1 1 02

The X, Y, and Z coordinates specify the location of the bin and the distance between bins. In this template, aisle is defined in the X-axis; level is defined in the Y-axis, and bin ID is defined in the Z-axis.

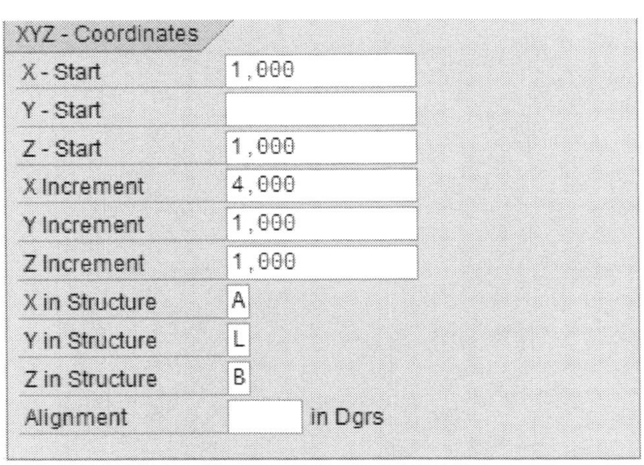

XYZ - Coordinates	
X - Start	1,000
Y - Start	
Z - Start	1,000
X Increment	4,000
Y Increment	1,000
Z Increment	1,000
X in Structure	A
Y in Structure	L
Z in Structure	B
Alignment	in Dgrs

Additional Data		
Storage Type	0005	Finished Goods (HU and Non HU
Storage Section	0001	Heavy Parts
Stor. Bin Type	BIGB	Big Bins
Bin Access Type	LVL1	
Maximum Weight	20.000,000	LB
Max. Volume		M3
Total Capacity		
Fire-Cont.Sect.		
Storage Group		

This structure can create twenty bins for storage type 0005, storage section 0001, and bin type Big Bins, with a maximum bin capacity of 20,000 pounds. There is no unit of measure for bin coordinates. Hence, they can be defined as per the warehouse diagram or by manually measuring in meters, feet, or yards.

Based on the fire containment section indicator, the storage bin is assigned to a particular fire-containment section in the warehouse. This field appears in reports (for example, the inventory list for the fire department) that list the different hazardous substances per fire-containment section.

Storage Bin Generation

War...	Sq...	Stor...	Stor...	Template	Start Value	End Value	Acc. ...	Storage Section
SEWM	001	0005	BIGB	ACCCCCNCNNCCCCCCCC	A01-001-01	D01-001-09	LVL1	0001
SEWM	002	0005	BIGB	ACCCCCNCNNCCCCCCCC	A01-001-02	D01-001-10	LVL1	0001
SEWM	003	0005	BIGB	ACCCCCNCNNCCCCCCCC	A01-002-01	D01-002-09	LVL2	0001
SEWM	004	0006	SMAB	ACCCCCNCNNCCCCCCCC	F01-001-01	I01-001-09	LVL1	0001

5.2.11.5 Generating Storage Bins from Bin Structures

After defining the bin structures, TCode /SCWM/LS10 can be executed to generate storage bins automatically. In the transaction, enter the warehouse number, select the structure, click on the "Choose" button on the application toolbar, and click on the "Create Bins" button located on the application toolbar. This will display a preview of the number of bins the system will generate, along with the bin details. Verify the bin details and click on the "Create" button to create the bins.

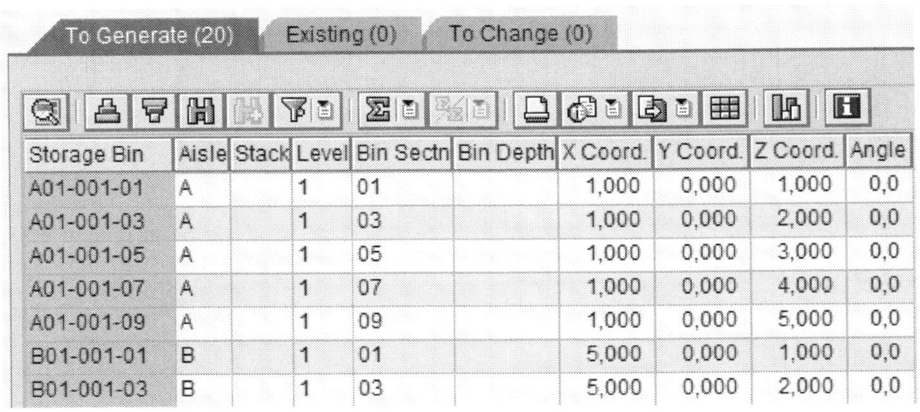

Storage Bin	Aisle	Stack	Level	Bin Sectn	Bin Depth	X Coord.	Y Coord.	Z Coord.	Angle
A01-001-01	A		1	01		1,000	0,000	1,000	0,0
A01-001-03	A		1	03		1,000	0,000	2,000	0,0
A01-001-05	A		1	05		1,000	0,000	3,000	0,0
A01-001-07	A		1	07		1,000	0,000	4,000	0,0
A01-001-09	A		1	09		1,000	0,000	5,000	0,0
B01-001-01	B		1	01		5,000	0,000	1,000	0,0
B01-001-03	B		1	03		5,000	0,000	2,000	0,0

Notes:

i. The "storage group" field, under additional data for Resource Execution Constraint (REC), can be used to control the number of working resources in different storage groups of the warehouse. Each bin of the warehouse can be grouped into different REC storage groups. With this assignment, the number of working resources in each REC managed warehouse area can be restricted to optimize warehouse resource efficiency. In the bin structure, the REC cannot be specified. However, it is possible to enter REC when creating a bin individually in TCode /SCWM/LS01 or the bins can be mass updated in TCode /SCWM/LS11. The values for the REC field come from the configuration table (**SPRO | IMG | Extended Warehouse Management | Cross-Process Settings | Resource Management | Control Data | Assign Resource Execution Constraints to REC Storage Group**).

ii. In case the bins are created using bin structure, the bin values can be mass updated using TCode /SCWM/LS11—Mass Change to Storage Bins.

5.2.11.6 Maintain Verification Field

A verification field value is used on RF or mobile devices to ensure that warehouse personnel confirm the task in the right bin. The values in this field can be defined the same as bin name or different, depending on the warehouse requirements.

To maintain verification field data for a bin, go to TCode /SCWM/LX45; enter the warehouse number, storage type, and the bin details. For updating all the bins in the warehouse, leave the storage type and bin numbers blank. Check the radio button "Adopt bin completely" to copy the bin name into the verification fields. Under the "Adopt bin partially" option, it is possible to specify what position value of the bin name should be copied to the verification field. If these two options do not solve the problem, BADI can be used to write a custom code.

After entering the required values, click on the "Execute" button on the application toolbar. This will provide a preview. After verifying the data, click on the "Update" button. This will update the values for the selected bins.

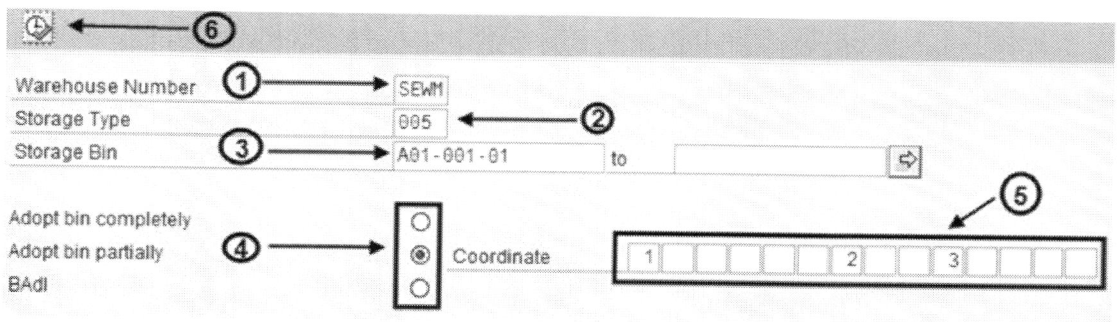

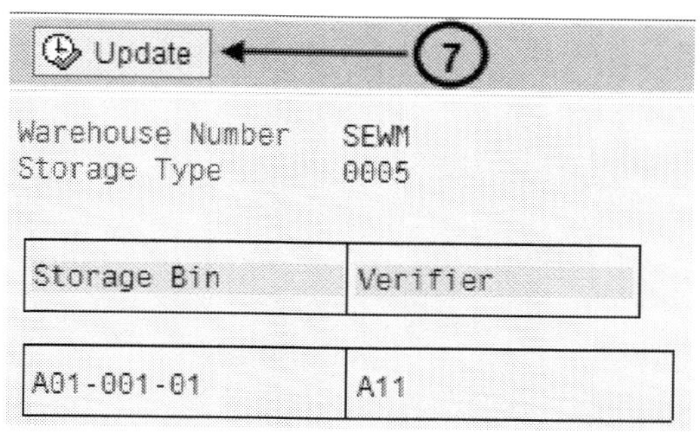

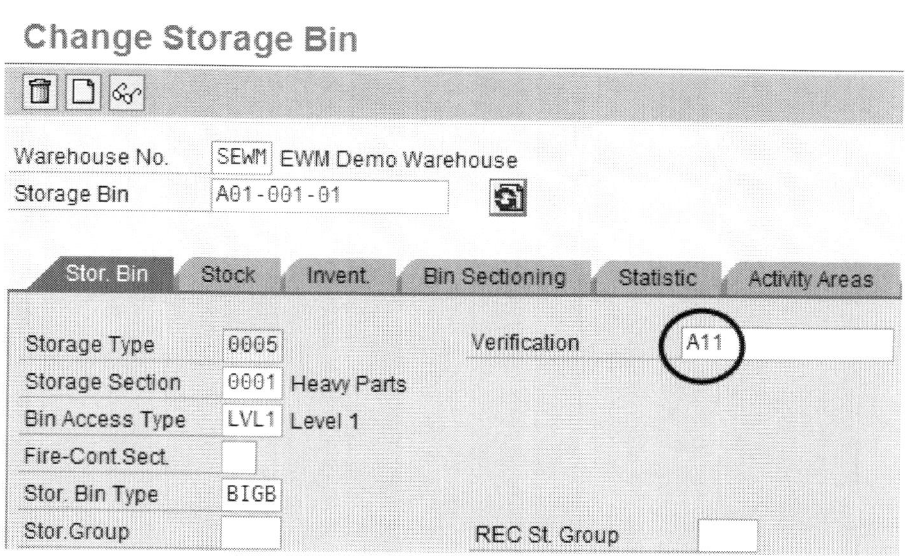

5.2.11.7 Other Important TCodes

The following TCodes are available for different bin-related activities. TCodes /SCWM/SEBA and /SCWM/SBST are used for the activity area, which will be covered in the Activity Area section. TCodes /SCWM/BINMAT, /SCWM/FBINDEL, /SCWM/FBINASN, and /SCWM/PRFIXBIN are related to fixed bins, which are covered in the replenishment section of chapter 19. TCode /SCWM/PRBIN can be used to print the storage bin labels.

System	Transaction code	Description
EWM	/SCWM/LS02	Change Single Storage Bin
EWM	/SCWM/LS03	Display Storage Bin
EWM	/SCWM/SBST	Sort Storage Bins
EWM	/SCWM/SEBA	Assign Start/End Storage Bin for Activity Area
EWM	/SCWM/BINSTAT	Add User Status for Storage Bins
EWM	/SCWM/BINMAT	Maintain Fixed Storage Bin
EWM	/SCWM/FBINDEL	Delete Fixed Storage Bin Assignment
EWM	/SCWM/FBINASN	Assign Fixed Storage Bins to Products
EWM	/SCWM/PRFIXBIN	Print Fixed Bin Label
EWM	/SCWM/PRBIN	Print Storage Bin Label

5.2.12 Define Number Ranges for Warehouse Documents

In EWM, number ranges should be defined to the following warehouse documents and have to be assigned to the warehouse. These number ranges are used to identify the warehouse documents uniquely.

- Warehouse Tasks/Warehouse Documents
- Wave
- Warehouse Order
- Consolidation Group
- VAS Order
- Indirect Labor Tasks
- PI Documents

These warehouse documents are covered in detail in chapter 10.

Menu Path: SPRO | IMG | Extended Warehouse Management | Master Data | Define Number Ranges

1	Define Number Ranges for Warehouse Tasks/Warehouse Documents
2	Define Number Range Intervals for Wave
3	Define Number Range Intervals for Warehouse Order
4	Define Number Range Intervals for Consolidation Group
5	Number Ranges for VAS Order
6	Define Number Ranges for Indirect Labor Tasks
7	Number Ranges for Physical Inventory Documents
	Assign Number Range Intervals to Warehouse Number (8)

Here, the number ranges for each warehouse document types must first be defined, and then assigned to the warehouse as a last step. To define number ranges for each document type, double-click on the documents, enter the warehouse number, click on the "Change Interval" button, click on the "Insert Interval" button (in the following screen), in the popup window enter the sequence number, the number range (“From number” and “To number”), click on the "Insert" button, and save the entries.

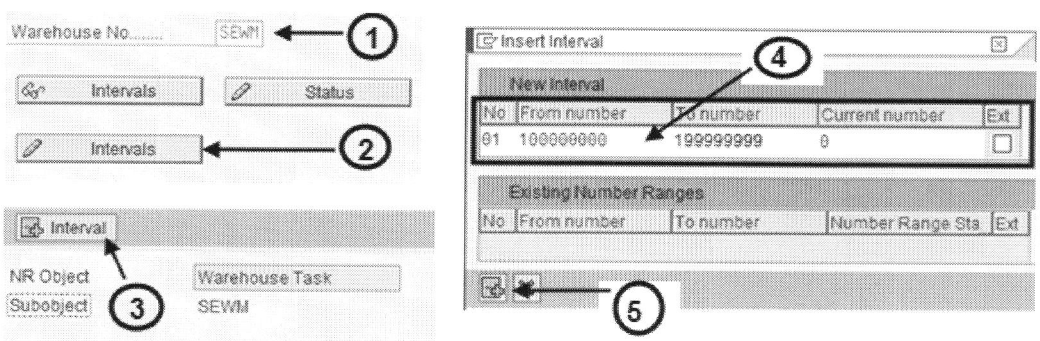

Repeat the steps for all document types. After defining the number ranges, click on the "Assign Number Range Intervals to Warehouse Number" menu to assign the defined number ranges to the warehouse.

Number Ranges for Whse Management

Wareh...	No.Rng	No. Range	WaveNoRg	NRInt. WO	VAS No.Rge	NRI Ind...	NRI PI Docum...
SEWM	01	01	01	01	01	01	01

Number ranges defined for the consolidation group are assigned to the warehouse in **SPRO | IMG | Extended Warehouse Management | Goods Receipt Process | Deconsolidation | Assign Number Range Intervals to Consolidation Groups**

Here, click on the "New Entries" button on the application toolbar, enter warehouse number, select the type of consolidation group, enter the number range, and click on the "Save" button.

Number Ranges for Using Consolidation Groups

War	Tpe	Int
SEWM	A Internal Consolidation Group for	01
SEWM	B Unique Consolidation Group for St	01
SEWM	C Consolidation Group for Putaway	01
SEWM	D Manual Consolidation Group	01
SEWM	E External Consolidation Group for	01

Notes:

i. Even though number ranges can be transportable, it is recommended to maintain them manually in every client.

ii. Assignment of number ranges is transportable.

5.2.13 Define Activity Areas

An activity area is an organizational element and a new feature introduced in EWM. These areas are logical groups of bins that can have different sorting sequence and can be used in different warehouse activities like PI, picking, putaway, replenishment, and so on. In EWM, activity areas are required and are used by warehouse-order-creation-rules to create warehouse orders.

Bins from different storage types can be assigned to activity areas.

Within an activity area, an activity-dependent bin sorting sequence can also be defined. The system uses these bin-sorting sequences to optimize the execution of warehouse tasks and influence determination of warehouse queues. Diagram 3.2.2.5A is an example of how activity areas can be created in the warehouse.

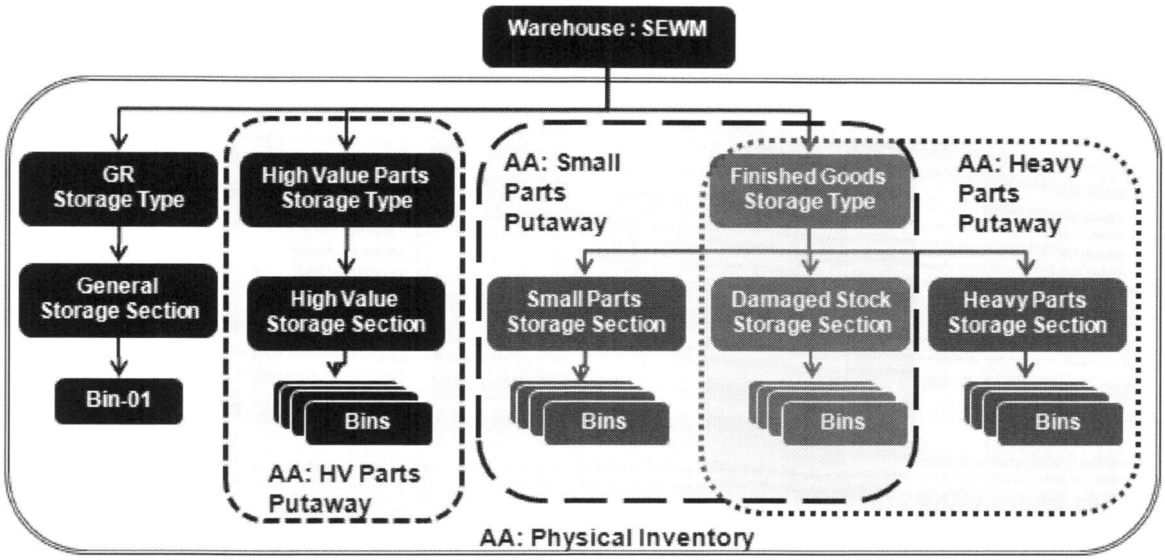

Diagram 3.2.2.5A - Activity Areas

The next few sections will cover the required configuration for activity areas.

5.2.13.1 Define Activities

In EWM, an activity triggers the goods movements. In this section, different activities can be defined. All defined activities must be assigned to a warehouse process category. Warehouse process categories are predefined in the system and used to classify the type of goods movements of the activities. More than one activity can be assigned for the same warehouse process category; for example, one activity can be defined for bin-to-bin movement and another for replenishment with the same warehouse process category, "Internal Stock Transfer."

The following warehouse process categories are predefined in the system. Only goods receipt and goods issue warehouse process categories are not available for the activities. They are used by the system internally during goods receipt and issue.

- Putaway
- Stock removal
- Internal stock transfer
- PI
- Posting change
- Cross-line stock putaway
- Goods Receipt
- Goods Issue

Menu Path: SPRO | IMG | Extended Warehouse Management | Master Data | Activity Areas | Activities | Define Activities

Click on the "New Entries" button; enter warehouse number, activity code, description, process category, and process step. Process step is required only for labor management.

Define Activity

War...	Activity	Description	C	Pro...
SEWM	CLSP	Cross Line Stock Putaway	8	
SEWM	INTM	Internal Warehouse Movements	3	
SEWM	PCNS	Posting Change Notices	7	
SEWM	PHYS	Physical Inventory Movement	4	
SEWM	PICK	Picking	2	
SEWM	PUTW	Putaway	1	
SEWM	REPL	Replenishments	3	

5.2.13.2 Define Activity Areas

As mentioned earlier, activity areas play an important role in the warehouse and are used by warehouse-order-creation rules to create warehouse orders. The system uses these bin-sorting sequences to optimize the execution of warehouse tasks. It is also an influencing parameter in determining warehouse queues.

Notes:

i. Bin sorting must be performed whenever activity areas or the bin master data are changed (i.e., addition, change, or deletion).

ii. To work with activity areas, bin sorting is essential.

Menu Path: SPRO | IMG | Extended Warehouse Management | Master Data | Activity Areas | Define Activity Area

Here, click on the "New Entries" button on the application toolbar; enter warehouse number, activity area, and the description.

Define Activity Area			
War...	AA	Description	Joined
SEWM	HPIK	Heavy Parts Picking	☐
SEWM	HPUT	Heavy Parts Putaway	☐
SEWM	PHYS	Physical Inventory	☐
SEWM	PICK	Picking	☑
SEWM	PUTW	High Value Parts Putaway	☐
SEWM	SPIK	Small Parts Picking	☐
SEWM	SPUT	Small Parts Putaway	☐

It is also possible to define an activity area that groups more than one activity area by checking the "Joined" checkbox.

To assign an activity area to a group activity area, follow the menu path **SPRO | IMG | Extended Warehouse Management | Cross-Process Settings | Warehouse Order | Join Activity Areas Together**

Assign Activity Areas to Joined Activity Areas			
War...	H.Act.Ar...	AA	Sort Sequence
SEWM	PICK	HPIK	1
SEWM	PICK	SPIK	2

5.2.13.3 Assign Storage Bins to Activity Areas

An activity area consists of one or more storage bins. Bins can be assigned explicitly to more than one activity areas if the entire storage type bins do not belong to one activity area. Bins can be assigned using aisle, stack, level, and bin section. For every activity area, you can define a unique consolidation group ID by clicking on the "Pull Consolidation Group" button, or manually enter a consolidation group if more than one activity area shares a consolidation group. Consolidation groups are used to determine which products are packed together or can be stored together. This helps to initiate deconsolidation activity, if required.

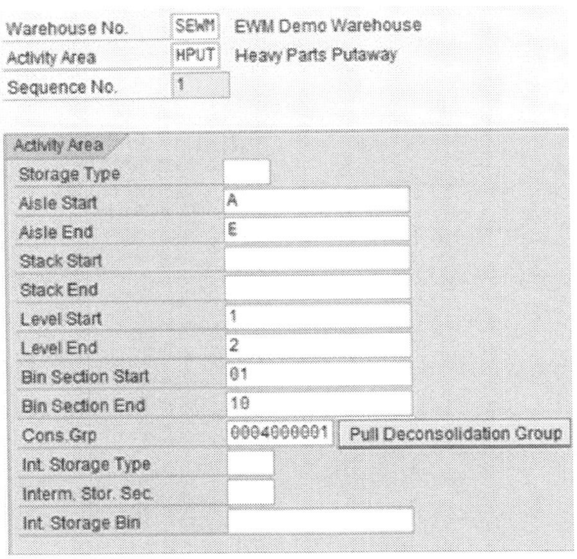

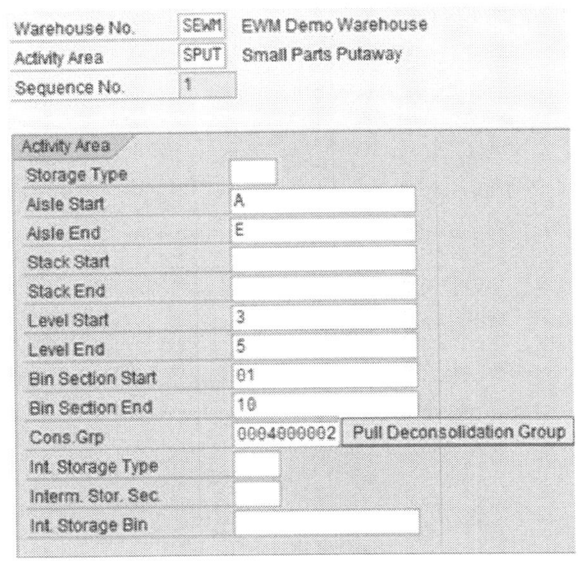

Menu Path: SPRO | IMG | Extended Warehouse Management | Master Data | Activity Areas | Assign Storage Bins to Activity Areas

Here, click on the "New Entries" button on the application toolbar; enter warehouse number, select the activity areas previously defined, specify the bin parameters, and assign a consolidation group manually or by clicking on the "Pull Consolidation Group" button.

5.2.13.4 Define Sort Sequence for Activity Area

In this section, the sort sequences for the activity area and for the activity are defined. Bins can be sorted differently for different activities to optimize WTs. Many activities can be assigned to one activity area.

Menu Path: SPRO | IMG | Extended Warehouse Management | Master Data | Activity Areas | Define Sort Sequence for Activity Area

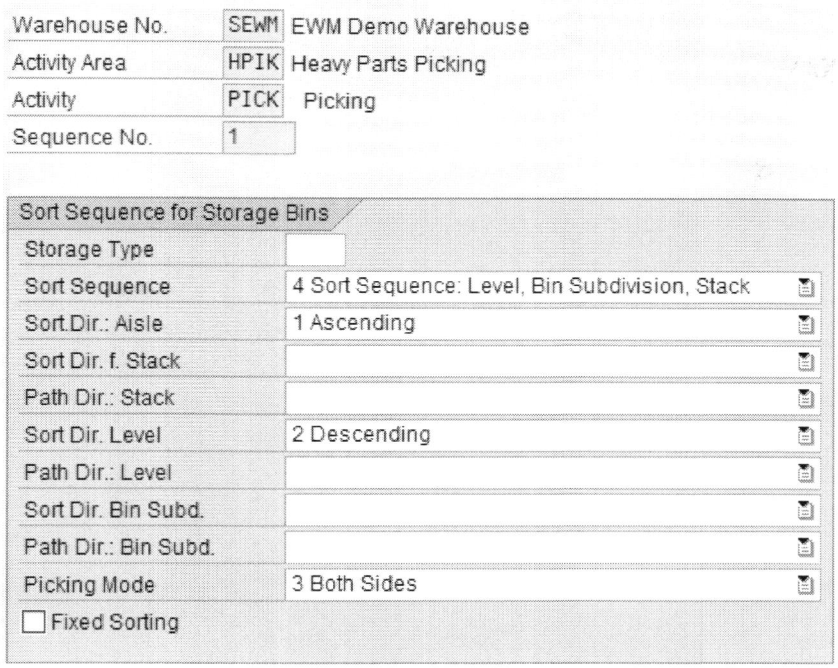

5.2.13.5 Generate Activity Area from Storage Type

If you do not want to define activity areas manually, storage type–dependent activity areas can be generated in menu path **SPRO | IMG | Extended Warehouse Management | Master Data | Activity Areas | Generate Activity Area from Storage Type**

Here, enter the warehouse number, storage type, and activity. To assign all activities automatically to the activity areas, leave the activity blank. However, the bin sort sequence for the activity area must be specified manually.

5.2.13.6 Generate Bin Sorting

In this final step, perform the bin sorting that creates the internal sequences the system uses in warehouse order (WO) creation and sequencing warehouse tasks within the warehouse order. This is not part of configuration and cannot be transportable. It has to manually maintained in every system in menu path **SAP Easy Access | Extended Warehouse Management | Master Data | Storage Bin | /SCWM/SBST—Sort Storage Bins or TCode /SCWM/SBST**

Here, enter warehouse number, activity area, and activity, and click on the "Execute" button. This will display the results in a simulation screen. Click on the "Execute" button in the simulation screen to create the sequence.

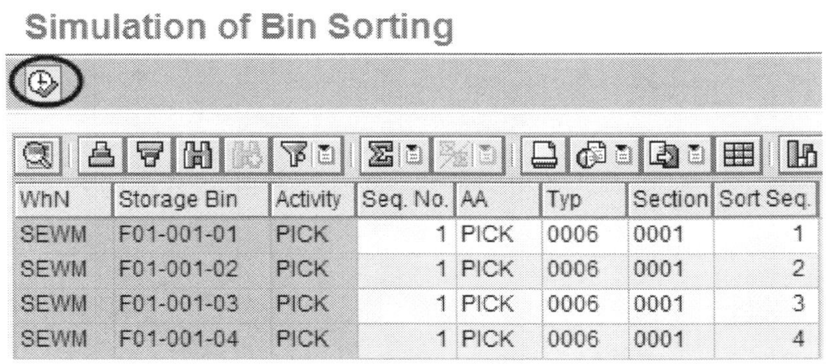

Simulation of Bin Sorting

WhN	Storage Bin	Activity	Seq. No.	AA	Typ	Section	Sort Seq.
SEWM	F01-001-01	PICK	1	PICK	0006	0001	1
SEWM	F01-001-02	PICK	1	PICK	0006	0001	2
SEWM	F01-001-03	PICK	1	PICK	0006	0001	3
SEWM	F01-001-04	PICK	1	PICK	0006	0001	4

5.2.14 Define Staging Areas and Warehouse Doors

Staging areas are used for the interim storage of goods in the warehouse and are usually located near the doors assigned. They are used mainly for unloading and loading activities.

This section will cover the details and required configuration for staging areas and warehouse doors. Diagram 5.2.14A gives an overview of the configuration of staging areas and warehouse doors and its mapping.

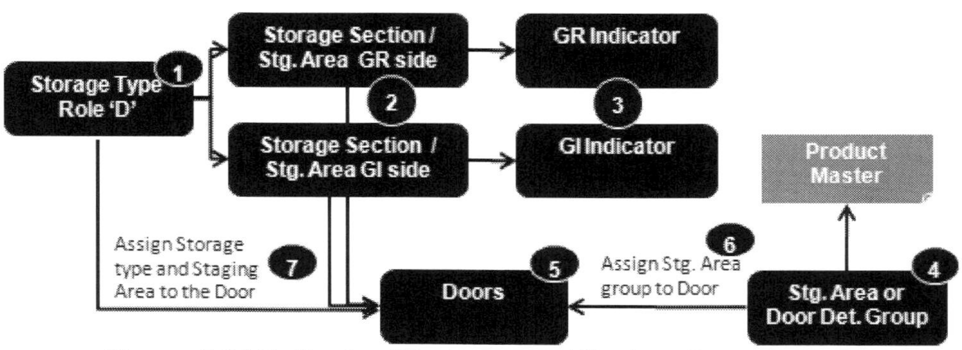

Diagram 5.2.14A - Mapping of Staging Areas and Warehouse Doors

5.2.14.1 Define Staging Areas

In EWM, staging areas can be defined to specific or multiple purposes, for example, only for goods receipt, only for goods issue, or for both. They are defined as storage sections to the storage type with role "D."

A loading rule can also be selected for the staging areas. Possible options include the following:

- HUs should be sent to the warehouse door immediately after arrival
- All HUs must arrive before loading can begin
- There needs to be a wait of twenty-four hours before loading can begin

Multiple bins can be created in each staging area (storage sections), which can represent the loading sequence of the products.

Menu Path: **SPRO | IMG | Extended Warehouse Management | Master Data | Staging Areas | Define Staging Areas**

Click on the "New Entries" button on the application toolbar; enter warehouse number, select storage type, select storage section, and specify the type of staging area.

Define Staging Areas

War	Stor	Stor	GR	GI	Load.Rule
SEWM	9002	0001	☑	☐	
SEWM	9002	0002	☑	☑	
SEWM	9020	0001	☐	☑	

5.2.14.2 Define Staging Area and Door Determination Groups

Staging area groups and door determination groups are used for door determination for the loading and unloading of products. For example, in large distribution centers, products like frozen products are loaded and unloaded at different doors than are regular products. This configuration is used for such warehouse requirements.

These staging area and door determination groups are assigned to the product master, which then influences the staging area and door determination for loading and unloading activities.

Menu Path: **SPRO | IMG | Extended Warehouse Management | Master Data | Staging Areas | Define Staging Area and Door Determination Groups**

Staging Area/Door Determination Group

War	SA/DDetGrp	Description
SEWM	HEVY	Heavy Products (Stg. Group)
SEWM	HVAL	High Value Products (Stg. Group)
SEWM	REGL	Regular and Small Products(Stg. Group)

5.2.14.3 Define Warehouse Door

In EWM, a door is a location assigned to the warehouse where vehicles drive up to load or unload products.

Menu Path: **SPRO | IMG | Extended Warehouse Management | Master Data | Warehouse Door | Define Warehouse Door**

Here, specify loading direction, action profile, default staging area group, default staging area, and means of transport.

The system will use the default values defined here in the warehouse documents if it cannot find staging area group, staging area, or means of transport.

Door Definitions

War	Whse Door	Load.Dir.	Action	NR	DfStgArGrp	DfStgAre	Def. MTr
SEWM	IS01	O Outbound		01	9020	0001	0001
SEWM	IS02	O Outbound		01	9020	0001	0001
SEWM	IS03	O Outbound		01	9020	0001	0001
SEWM	RE01	I Inbound		01	9002	0002	0001
SEWM	RE02	I Inbound		01	9002	0002	0001
SEWM	RE03	I Inbound		01	9002	0001	0001

5.2.14.4 Assign Staging Area/Door Determination Group to Door

Here, a staging area group can be assigned to permitted warehouse doors.

Menu Path: SPRO | IMG | Extended Warehouse Management | Master Data | Warehouse Door | Assign Staging Area/Door Determination Group to Door

Staging Area/Door Determination Gro

War	Whse Door	SA/DDetGrp
SEWM	RE01	REGL
SEWM	RE02	REGL
SEWM	RE03	HEVY
SEWM	RE03	HVAL

5.2.14.5 Assign Staging Area to Warehouse Door

Here, staging areas are assigned to warehouse doors. During this assignment, the system takes into account the possible loading and unloading activities for the staging areas and doors. These assignments form the basis for the determination rules (staging area, group, and door) in the delivery.

Menu Path: SPRO | IMG | Extended Warehouse Management | Master Data | Warehouse Door | Assign Staging Area to Warehouse Door

Assignment of Staging Area to Warehouse Door

War..	Whse Door	StgAreaGrp	StgArea
SEWM	IS01	9020	0001
SEWM	IS02	9020	0001
SEWM	IS03	9020	0001
SEWM	RE01	9002	0001
SEWM	RE02	9002	0001
SEWM	RE03	9002	0002

5.2.15 Work Center

The work center is the physical location in the warehouse where warehouse activities such as deconsolidation, counting, quality inspection, value added service, or packing are performed. In EWM, the following transactions or activities can be performed in the work center:

- **Packing General—TCode /SCWM/PACK**: Work center can be used for all general packing. The transaction code for general packing is /SCWM/PACK. Menu path is **SAP Easy Access | Extended Warehouse Management | Execution | Packing—General**
- **Deconsolidation in Goods Receipt—TCode /SCWM/DCONS**: This transaction is used to segregate the mixed HUs into non-mixed HUs using deconsolidation groups. Menu path is **SAP Easy Access | Extended Warehouse Management | Execution | Deconsolidation in Goods Receipt**
- **Quality Inspection and Count—TCode /SCWM/QINSP**: This transaction is used for counting, recording, and confirming inspection results. Menu path is **SAP Easy Access | Extended Warehouse Management | Execution | Quality Inspection and Count**
- **Create Confirmation for VAS—TCode /SCWM/VASEXEC**: This transaction is used to perform value added services like packing, printing, and relabeling products with customer-specific labels and so on. Menu path is **SAP Easy Access | Extended Warehouse Management | Execution | Create Confirmation for VAS**

The following configuration and master data must be set up for the work center:

- Define storage type with an appropriate role
- Minimum of one storage section should exist for the storage type
- At least one bin must be created
- Specify work center layout
- Define a work center

- Define master data attributes (/SCWM/TWORKST)
- Define scales (/SCWM/SCALE)
- Determine work center in goods issue (/SCWM/PACKSTDT)
- Printer control (/SCWM/TWCPRINT)
- Optimize work center determination in goods issue

Diagram 5.2.15A provides an overview of how the work center is linked to different configuration objects in EWM.

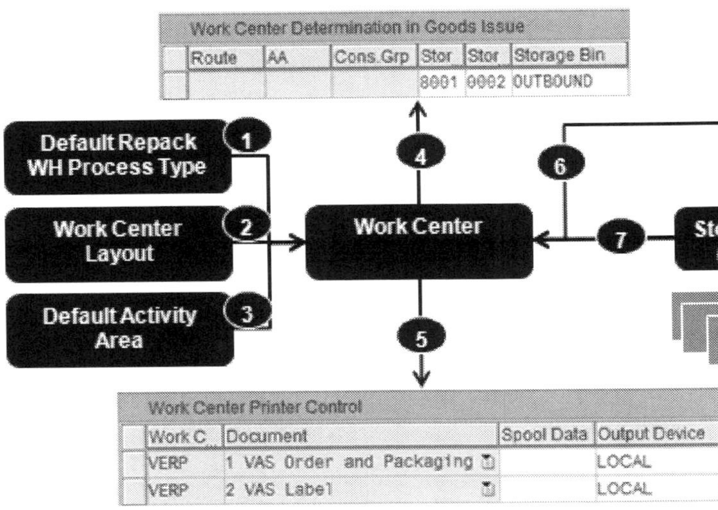

Diagram 5.2.15A – Mapping of Work Center

In EWM, to define work centers, storage types should be created with the role "Work Center (E)," "Pick Point (B)," or "Identification and Pick Point (C)." Defining the storage type, section, and bin has already been covered above. Here, the remaining configuration and master data setup for the work center will be covered.

5.2.15.1 Specify Work Center Layout

The work center layout is used to specify which options to make available, which functions to allow, and which tab pages to show in the work center–related transactions. In this IMG activity, define which of the available tab pages the user should be offered for the transaction.

Menu Path: SPRO | IMG | Extended Warehouse Management | Master Data | Work Center | Specify Work Center Layout

Here, enter the warehouse number and layout code; select the transaction type; and specify the values for the "tab pages in scanner area," "tab pages in detail area," and "different functions" that the work center can perform.

- **Tab pages in the scanner area**: These tab pages appear in the upper right screen. These tab pages are necessary when working in a work center with a keyboard scanner or without a mouse.
- **Tab pages in the detail area**: These tab pages appear in the lower right screen. This is used to see detailed information about the storage bin and HU. The detail area can only be used in connection with tree control. Double-click on the object in the tree control (HU, storage bin, and so on), and the system adds the detailed information to the tab page.
- **Tree control**: The tree control appears in the left screen of the work center. This can used to perform repacking transactions using Drag & Drop.
- **Different Functions**: Here, different functions for the work center like packing in bin, delete HU, empty HU etc. can be enabled.

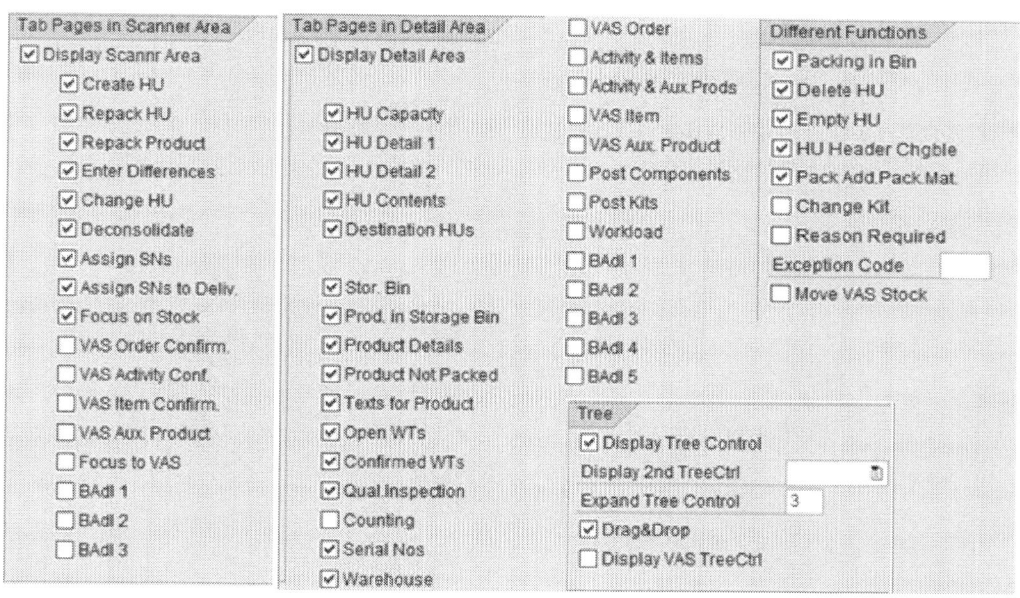

5.2.15.2 Define Work Center

In this configuration, one can create a work center for a warehouse and assign attributes like storage type, inbound and outbound section, repack process type, and storage bin. The following are the details of the attributes that are assigned to the work center:

- **External Step**: The external step represents the action or activity performed in the work center. It is applicable only to HU-managed stock.

- **Storage Type**: This specifies the storage type of the work center.
- **Inbound Section**: This is defined as storage section under storage type and is used in the work center to store products that need to be processed.
- **Outbound Section**: This is also defined as storage section under storage type and is used in the work center to store products that have been already processed.
- **Repack Warehouse Process Type**: This is the WPT that needs to be used for repacking. You can specify default WPT for repacking for warehouse number. If the WPT is not assigned here, and no process type is determined, the system will use the WPT defined for the warehouse number. WPT is covered in chapter 11.
- **Layout**: Specify which layout to use for the work center.
- **Return Storage Type and Return Storage Section**: These are used if the work center is to be used as a pick point.

Menu Path: SPRO | IMG | Extended Warehouse Management | Master Data | Work Center | Define Work Center

Define Work Center

War...	Work...	Description	Step	Stor...	ISec	OSec	R...	Layout	RF: HU	Print...	Process	Ret...
SEWM	VERP	Packaging Work		8001	0001	0002		VPMX	☑			

5.2.15.3 Define Master Data Attributes

The storage bin and scales assignment is not a configuration activity. You can specify the bin and name of the scale in case the weight is automatically captured using program SCALE_FOR_SCM.exe or some other custom program. This assignment can be done in SAP's easy-access menu: **Extended Warehouse Management | Master Data | Work Center | Define Master Data Attributes or TCode /SCWM/TWORKST**

Warehouse No.	SEWM
Work Center	VERP

Work Center: Define Master Data Attributes

Description	Packaging Work Center
Storage Bin	OUTBOUND
Terminal	
Pack. Material	
Scales	
Weight Tolerance	
Storage Type	8001

5.2.15.4 Define Scales

Defining scales is required only if it is necessary to capture the weights directly from the scales and update the weights in EWM. For this, the RFC destination has to be defined for the PC connected to the scales. Once the RFC destination is defined, it has to be assigned to the scales in EWM. These are the settings required in the EWM system. Additionally, to pull the data from the PC, the SCALE_FOR_SCM.exe program must be registered on the PC connected to the scales. In addition to this, there may be some additional programs/services that need to be registered on the PC to transfer the data from the scales to the PC, depending on the hardware.

More help on SCALE_FOR_SCM.exe along with software to download is available at service.sap.com/scm.

The menu path to define scale and assign the RFC destination is **SAP Easy Access Menu | Extended Warehouse Management | Master Data | Work Center | Define Scales or TCode /SCWM/SCALE**

Scales

Scales	Description	RFC Dest. for Scale
METTLER	VERTEX Floor Scales	CALL_MLR

5.2.15.5 Determine Work Center in Goods Issue

Here, specify which work center should be used for outbound-related activities like packing, VAS, and so on. The work center is assigned to the combination of route, activity area, and consolidation group.

Menu Path: **SAP easy access menu | Extended Warehouse Management | Master Data | Work Center | Determine Work Center in Goods Issue or TCode /SCWM/PACKSTDT**

Work Center Determination in Goods Issue					
Route	AA	Cons.Grp	Stor..	Stor..	Storage Bin
			8001	0002	OUTBOUND

5.2.15.6 Printer Control

Here, consultants can specify which printer to be used to print the labels, delivery note, or packaging specifications in the work center. This transaction can be accessed from **SAP easy access menu | Extended Warehouse Management | Master Data | Work Center | Printer Control or TCode /SCWM/TWCPRINT**

Warehouse No. SEWM

Work Center Printer Control			
Work C..	Document	Spool Data	Output Device
VERP	1 VAS Order and Packaging		LOCAL
VERP	2 VAS Label		LOCAL
VERP	3 Delivery Note		LOCAL

5.2.15.7 Optimize Work Center Determination in Goods Issue

In the "Optimize Work Center Determination" table, the sequence to use to determine the work center during work center determination can be specified for better performance. The system will first determine the work center defined in "Determine Work Center in Goods Issue." If it doesn't find one, it will use the access optimization table to find work center.

Menu Path: **SPRO | Extended Warehouse Management | Master Data | Work Center | Optimize Work Center Determination in Goods Issue**

Optimize Work Center Determination in Goods Issue				
Wareh..	Sequence No.	Route	Activ.Area	CnsGrp
SEWM	1	☑	☑	☐
SEWM	2	☑	☐	☑
SEWM	3	☐	☑	☑

5.2.16 Map Storage Locations from ERP System to EWM

Earlier in this chapter, the topics of availability group, warehouse stock types, ERP stock types, were covered in detail. This section will explore how to map ERP storage locations to the availability group. The major advantage of this setting is that when the putaway is confirmed, stock can be transferred from one storage location to another automatically (for example, from "not available to sell" storage location to "available to sell" storage location), based on the availability group assigned to the source and destination storage types.

Menu Path: SPRO | Extended Warehouse Management | Interfaces | ERP Integration | Goods Movements | Map Storage Locations from ERP System to EWM

Here, click on the "New Entries" button on the application toolbar; enter plant, storage location, and logical system as the ERP logical system; warehouse number as the EWM warehouse number; and the appropriate availability group for the storage location.

Customizing Mapping Table for ERP Plant Storage Location

Plnt	SLoc	Logical sys...	War...	AGr	Ent. to Dispose	Desc.Person Ent. to Dis...
2517	IAFS	SE1CLNT410	SEWM	002	2517	EWM Demo Plant
2517	NAFS	SE1CLNT410	SEWM	001	2517	EWM Demo Plant

Notes:

i. Entries made in plant, storage locations, and logical systems are not verified by the system. Therefore, wrong entries can cause incorrect results.

ii. Value for "Ent. To dispose" will be copied automatically from the supply chain unit master data of the plant (i.e., value from business partner field). This is covered in chapter 6.

5.2.17 Assign Control Parameters to Warehouse

Here, the basic data and default values for each warehouse number are defined. Default values will be used if the system does not find the required configuration to process the transaction.

Menu Path: SPRO | Extended Warehouse Management | Master Data | Define Warehouse Number Control

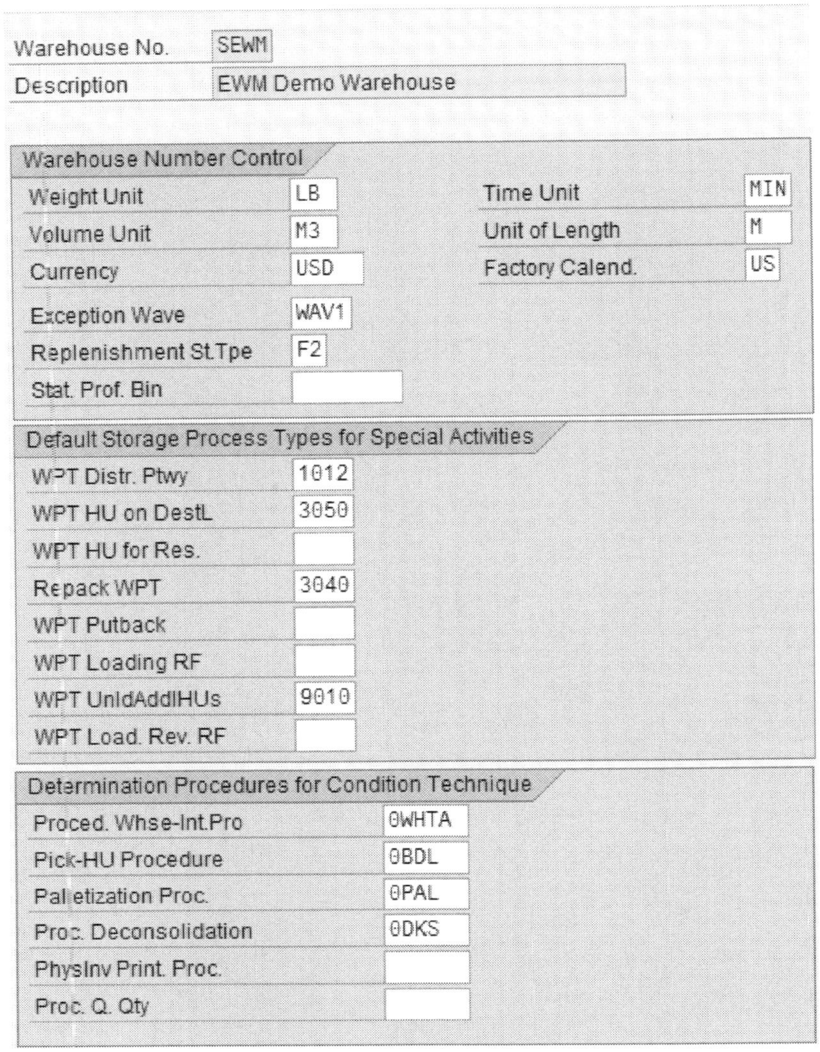

5.3 Number Ranges for Other Documents

In addition to the number ranges defined in 5.2.12, it is necessary to define number range intervals for inbound deliveries, outbound deliveries, expected goods receipt documents, and handling units, which are created in the EWM system; and for ERP inbound deliveries and outbound deliveries, which are transferred from the ERP system. The following sections will cover more details on this.

5.3A Number Ranges for Other Documents			
S. No	**Configuration Check List**	**TCode**	**Transportable**
1	Number Range Intervals for Other EWM Documents	SPRO	No
2	Define Number Ranges for ERP Delivery Documents	SPRO	No
3	Define Number Range for HU Identification	SPRO	No

5.3.1 Number Range Intervals for Other EWM Documents

In this section, define the number range intervals for various other EWM documents like outbound deliveries, inbound deliveries, outbound delivery orders, posting changes, and for expected goods receipts (EGR). These documents are originated in the EWM system and not transferred from ERP. Details of these documents are covered in chapter 10.

Menu Path: SPRO | Extended Warehouse Management | Cross-Process Settings | Delivery Processing | Number Ranges

Number Ranges

- Define Number Range Intervals for Technical Keys
- Define Number Range Intervals for Outbound Deliveries
- Define No. Range Intervals for Inbound Deliveries and Outbound Del. Orders
- Define Number Range for Posting Changes and Stock Transfers
- Define Number Range Intervals for Expected Goods Receipt

NR Object: Technical key

Intervals

No.	From number	To number	Current number	Ext
01	00000000000000000001	99999999999999999999	0	☐

NR Object: Outbound Delivery **Object Name: /SCDL/FD**

Intervals

No.	From number	To number	Current number	Ext
01	00000000000000000001	00000000009999999999	0	☐
02	00000000010000000000	00000000019999999999		☑

NR Object: Processing Document **Object Name: /SCDL/PRD**

Intervals

No.	From number	To number	Current number	Ext
01	00000000000000000001	00000000009999999999	0	☐
02	00000000010000000000	00000000019999999999		☑

NR Object: Expected GR **Object Name: /SCDL/EGR**

Intervals

No.	From number	To number	Current number	Ext
01	0009000000	0009999999	0	☐

5.3.2 Define Number Ranges for ERP Delivery Documents

Here, number ranges must be defined for inbound delivery notification (IDN) and outbound delivery requests (ODR) created in the EWM system due to delivery split.

When the ERP inbound and outbound deliveries are transferred to the EWM system, they become IDN and ODR in the EWM system. During this transfer, the system copies the same number to the IDN and ODR, which in turn helps users search the corresponding EWM documents or refer to document flow created in the EWM system for ERP documents.

In certain cases, it is possible that the delivery quantities may need to be adjusted in the EWM system due to reasons like short supply and short pick, in which case the EWM system adjusts the original document quantity and creates the new document, using delivery split functionality. In such scenarios, the new IDN/ODR documents are being created in the EWM system, using the internal number range of the EWM system, and will be transferred to the ERP system. In order to avoid any data transfer issues, the internal number range defined for IDN/ODR should be the same as the one defined for the deliveries (external number range) in the ERP system. If the number ranges are not defined properly in both systems, it can cause errors while transferring the data.

The number ranges for deliveries in the ERP system can be found under **SPRO | Logistics Execution | Shipping | Deliveries | Define Number Ranges for Deliveries.**

Intervals **Number ranges in ERP system**

No.	From number	To number	Current number	Ext
17	8880000000	8883999999	8880032282	☐
18	8885000000	8888999999		☑
41	1180000000	1182999999	1180000288	☐
42	1185000000	1186999999		☑

In this screenshot, number ranges 18 and 42 are defined as external number ranges and assigned to inbound delivery type EL and outbound delivery type LF.

In the following menu, these number ranges are defined as an internal number range in the EWM system.

Intervals **Number ranges in EWM system**

No.	From number	To number	Current number	Ext
01	1185000000	1186999999	1185000000	☐
02	8885000000	8888999999	8885000000	☐

Menu Path: **SPRO | Extended Warehouse Management | Interfaces | ERP Integration | Delivery Processing | Define Number Ranges for ERP Documents**

5.3.3 Define Number Range for HU Identification

To use handling unit functionality in EWM, it is necessary to define the internal or external number ranges and should be assigned to packaging material types. The internal number range of the EWM system should be defined as an external number range and should be assigned to the appropriate packaging material types in the ERP system. Otherwise, it can cause errors during data transfer.

Menu Path: **SPRO | Extended Warehouse Management | Cross-Process Settings | Handling Units| External Identification | Define Number Range for HU Identification**

Summary

This chapter has explained qRFC configuration, warehouse org structure, and basic configurations required for various master and transactional data in the EWM system. By now, readers have a good understanding of basic configuration requirements in both ERP and EWM systems. The following chapters will build on the information defined in these two chapters, rather than explaining it again.

Chapter 6: Data Transfer and Business Partners

Before data transfer to the EWM system is initiated, certain data-dependent settings must be enabled in the EWM system. This includes product master–dependent settings; delivery-related settings, and business partner–dependent settings. This chapter covers configurations required for such data transfer settings as well as actual transferring of master data from the ERP system to the EWM system via CIF. The business partner sections explain how to create business partner data for the transferred master data (customers, vendors, employees, and plants) in the EWM system.

6.1 Master Data–Dependent Settings

In order to initiate the data transfer from ERP system to EWM system, we must define product master–dependent settings; delivery-related settings, and business partner–dependent settings. Once these settings are completed it is recommended to do the table comparison between ERP and EWM system to verify if any data inconsistencies exist in the database tables. Following sections will cover more details on each of these settings.

6.1.1 Product Master–Dependent Settings

In chapter 4, section 4.3.2 covered how to define "Attribute Values for Additional Material Master" in the ERP system. This section will cover how to define those values in the EWM system. Table 6.1.1A gives an overview of required product master dependent settings in the EWM system.

6.1.1A Product Master Dependent Settings

S. No	Configuration Check List	TCode	System	Transportable
1	Define HU Types	SPRO	EWM	Yes
2	Define Warehouse Storage Condition	SPRO	EWM	Yes
3	Define Warehouse Product Group	SPRO	EWM	Yes
4	Define Handling Indicator	SPRO	EWM	Yes
5	Define Quality Inspection Group	SPRO	EWM	Yes
6	Maintain Transportation Group	SPRO	EWM	Yes

6.1.1.1 Define HU types

In EWM, storage unit management is replaced with HU management. In order to activate HU management, an HU type is essential. HU type is used to classify packaging materials and HUs with the same physical properties—for example, steel pallet, cardboard box, or wooden pallet.

HU type can be centrally maintained in the ERP material master under WM packaging view and can be transferred to EWM as part of CIF. In such cases, HU types defined in the ERP system should match the HU types defined in the EWM system.

If maintaining HU type in the ERP material master is not a requirement, it can be directly maintained in the EWM product master.

Menu Path: SPRO | IMG | Extended Warehouse Management | Cross-Process Settings | Handling Units | Basics | Define HU Types

Handling Unit Types

Han...	HU Type Description
BOX	Box
CBOX	Cardboard Box
E1	Europallet - 1m Height
E2	Europallet - 2m Height
STPL	Steel Pallet
WDPL	Wooden Pallet

6.1.1.2 Define Warehouse Storage Condition

Storage conditions are defined when the materials need to be stored in specific conditions in the warehouse, for example, at a specific temperature. This information is useful for the warehouse operator when the goods are placed in the warehouse.

Like HU type, warehouse storage condition can also be maintained centrally in the ERP material master under the WM Execution view and can transferred to EWM as part of CIF. If it is maintained in ERP, the storage condition defined in EWM should match with the warehouse storage condition of ERP.

If maintaining storage condition in the ERP material master is not a requirement, it can be maintained in the product master of EWM.

Menu Path: SPRO | IMG | Extended Warehouse Management | Master Data | Product | Define Warehouse Storage Condition

Warehouse Storage Condition

Wareh...	Description
01	Cool
02	Dry

6.1.1.3 Define Warehouse Product Group

In ERP system, the warehouse product group is called *warehouse material group*. It is used to specify that certain materials should always be stored in the same way.

This can be centrally maintained in the ERP material master under the WM execution view and transferred to EWM as part of CIF. If maintaining warehouse product group in the ERP material master is not a requirement, it can be maintained in the EWM product master. If it is maintained in ERP, warehouse product group defined in EWM should match with the warehouse product group of ERP.

Menu Path: SPRO | IMG | Extended Warehouse Management | Master Data | Product | Define Warehouse Product Group

Warehouse Product Group

Warehou..	Description
0001	Small Parts
0002	Large Parts
HUMS	HU Managed Stock
NHUM	Non HU Managed stock

6.1.1.4 Define Handling Indicator

The handling indicator is used to specify how the material should be handled in the warehouse. Examples include fragile materials, hazardous materials, and so on.

The handling indicator can be centrally maintained in the ERP material master under the WM execution view and transferred to EWM as part of CIF. If maintaining the handling indicator in the ERP material master is not a requirement, it can be maintained in the EWM product master. If it is maintained in ERP, the handling indicator defined in EWM should match the ERP handling indicator.

Menu Path: SPRO | IMG | Extended Warehouse Management | Master Data | Product | Define Handling Indicator

Handling Indicator

Hand.Ind.	Description
0001	Fragile handle with Care
0002	Transport in Upright Position
0003	hazardous substance

6.1.1.5 Define Quality Inspection (QI) Group

Quality inspection groups are used to group materials together that have to be inspected in a similar fashion. These groups are used to simplify the maintenance of inspection rules in EWM. If the QI group is maintained in the ERP material master under the WM execution view, when the material is transferred to the EWM system, the quality inspection group is automatically transferred as well.

If maintaining a QI group in the ERP material master is not a requirement, it can be maintained in the EWM product master. If it is maintained in ERP, the QI group defined in EWM should match the HU QI group of the ERP system.

Menu Path: SPRO | IMG | Extended Warehouse Management | Cross-Process Settings | Quality Management | Settings for Inspection Rules | Define Quality Inspection Group

Quality Inspection Group

QualInsGrp	Description
EXSP	Goods Receipts from External Supplier
PROD	Goods Receipt from Production

6.1.1.6 Maintain Transportation Group

When the material master data is transferred to EWM, the transportation group assigned to the material master gets copied to the product master. It is used by EWM to determine the route assignment for deliveries.

Menu Path: SPRO | IMG | SCM Basis | Master Data | Product | Maintain Transportation Group

Transportation groups defined in EWM should match the transportation groups defined in ERP under the menu path **SPRO | IMG | Logistics Execution | Shipping | Basic Shipping Functions | Routes | Route Determination | Define Transportation Groups**

6.1.2 Delivery-Related Settings

When deliveries are transferred to the EWM system, along with product and quantity details, some of the delivery header information like delivery priority, shipping conditions, and incoterms are transferred also. In the warehouse, this information is used to determine the appropriate WPT to process the deliveries. Table 6.1.2A provides an overview of what delivery related settings need to be configured in the EWM system.

6.1.2A Delivery Dependent Settings				
S. No	**Configuration Check List**	**TCode**	**System**	**Transportable**
1	Define the Delivery Priority	SPRO	EWM	Yes
2	Define Shipping Condition	SPRO	EWM	Yes
3	Define Incoterms	SPRO	EWM	Yes

6.1.2.1 Define Delivery Priority

In ERP, delivery priority is used to control delivery processing and give priority to individual customers. When the deliveries are created, this information is automatically copied into the delivery header from the sales order, and when the ERP delivery is sent to EWM for picking, the same information will be copied into the item details of the warehouse delivery request document.

In EWM, this information is used to determine the appropriate WPT through which the warehouse can initiate expedited picking for high-priority deliveries and normal picking for regular orders.

To avoid errors during data transfer, the delivery priorities defined in the EWM system should match the delivery priorities defined in the ERP system. In ERP, these can be found in **SPRO | IMG | Sales and Distribution | Master Data | Business Partners | Customers | Shipping | Define Delivery Priorities**

To define delivery priority in the EWM system, follow the menu path **SPRO | IMG | Extended Warehouse Management | Cross-Process Settings | Delivery Processing | General Settings | Define Delivery Priority**

Delivery Priority	
Del.Prio.	**Description**
1	High
2	Normal
3	Low
4	Next day
5	2 day

6.1.2.2 Define Shipping Conditions

Shipping conditions are used to define how the materials are shipped to the customers. This can be by road, air, customer pick-up, and so on.

This is assigned to the customer master, and the same will be copied to the sales order from the customer master record. The shipping condition and loading group are used to determine the shipping points in the sales order. Shipping points and shipping conditions get copied to the header of the ERP delivery number. When the delivery is transferred to EWM for picking, the shipping condition will be copied to the item details of the warehouse delivery request document.

Menu Path: SPRO | IMG | Extended Warehouse Management | Cross-Process Settings | Delivery Processing | General Settings | Define Shipping Conditions

Click on the "New Entries" button on the application toolbar; enter the shipping condition and the description of the shipping condition.

Shipping Conditions

SC	Description
01	Standard
02	Pick-up
03	Expedited
04	Truckload/Containers
05	Air
EW	EWM WH Pick-Up

6.1.2.3 Define Incoterms

Incoterms specify certain internationally recognized procedures that both the shipper and the receiving party must follow for the shipping transaction to be successfully completed.

This is assigned to the customer master and will be copied to the sales order from the customer master record. When delivery is created for the sales order, this information is copied to the header of the ERP delivery number. When the delivery is transferred to EWM for picking, this information will be copied into the header details of the warehouse delivery request document.

Incoterms defined here should match those defined in ERP system. In ERP, these can be found in **SPRO | IMG | Sales and Distribution | Master Data | Business Partners | Customers | Billing Document | Define Incoterms**

To define incoterms in the EWM system, follow the menu path **SPRO | IMG | Extended Warehouse Management | Cross-Process Settings | Delivery Processing | General Settings | Define Incoterms**

Incoterms	
Incoterms	Description
EXW	Ex Works
FCA	Free Carriage and Freight
FOB	Free On Board ship

6.1.3 Business Partner (BP) Dependent Settings

In order to transfer master data like vendor, sold-to-party, ship-to-party, customer, plant, and so on to the EWM system, BP–dependent settings need to be configured in the EWM system. Table 6.1.3A gives an overview of the configuration required to transfer this data into the EWM system. Later, in section 6.3, more details will be provided on who BPs are, why they are needed, and how they are mapped in the EWM system.

6.1.3A Business Partner Dependent Settings				
S. No	Configuration Check List	TCode	System	Transportable
1	Verify BP Identification Categories	SPRO	EWM	Yes
2	Verify Business Partner (BP) Role	SPRO	EWM	Yes
3	Verify Number Ranges and Groupings for BP	SPRO	EWM	Yes

6.1.3.1 Verify BP Identification Categories

In order to transfer the data, the identification types CRM002 and CRM004 should not be defined as "Display Only" in the EWM system. This indicator influences the creation of business partners for vendors and customers. Creation of business partners can be automated as part of CIF data transfer, or it can be done manually in the EWM system.

Menu Path: SPRO | Cross-Application Components | SAP Business Partner | Business Partner | Basic Settings | Identification Numbers | Define Identification Categories

Identification Categories			
Identifi...	Description	ID Unique	Display Only
CRM002	R/3 Customer Number	☐	☐
CRM003	External System Identifier for ICM	☐	☐
CRM004	R/3 Vendor Number	☐	☐

6.1.3.2 Verify BP Role

Before initiating the data transfer, it is important to verify that the following business partner roles exist in EWM. If they do not exist, they must be defined—one for each BP role category, as show below.

Menu Path: **SPRO | Cross-Application Components | SAP Business Partner | Business Partner | Basic Settings | Business Partner Roles | Define BP Roles**

BP Roles

BP Role	Title	Description
000000	Business Partner (Gen.)	Business Partner (General)
BBP000	Vendor	Vendor
BBP003	Plant	Plant
BUP004	Organizational Unit	Organizational Unit
CRM000	Sold-To Party	Sold-To Party
CRM002	Ship-To Party	Ship-To Party
CRM003	Payer	Payer
CRM004	Bill-To Party	Bill-To Party
CRM008	Customer	Customer

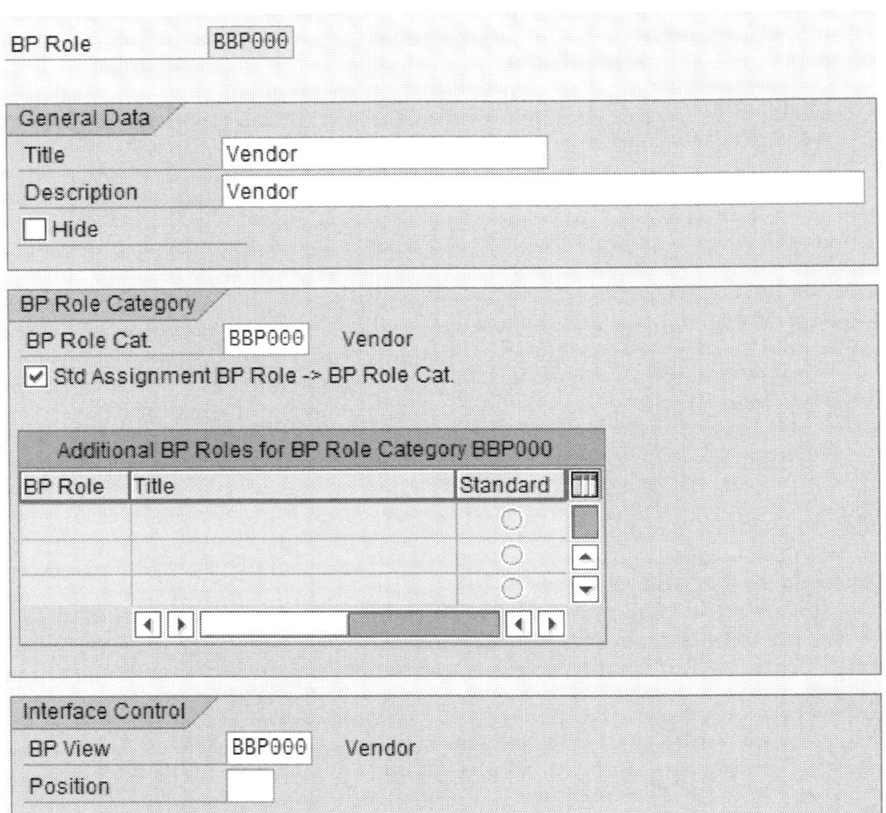

6.1.3.3 Verify Number Ranges and Groupings for BP

In EWM, BP data is master data created for customers, vendors, carriers, plants, and employees. This can be created either as part of CIF data transfer or manually in the EWM. In order to create a BP, number ranges should be defined and assigned to the BP groups. To create BPs with the same number as the ERP number, appropriate external number range must be defined.

Menu Path: SPRO | Cross-Application Components | SAP Business Partner | Business Partner | Number Ranges and Groupings | Define Number Ranges

NR Object: Business partner

Intervals

No.	From number	To number	Current number	Ext
1	0000000001	0000400000	0	☐
AA	AAAAAAA	ZZZZZZZ		☑

After defining the number range, define the groups and assign the number range to the groups in **SPRO | Cross-Application Components | SAP Business Partner | Business Partner | Number Ranges and Groupings | Define Groupings and Assign Number Ranges**

Group...	Short name	Description	Nu...	External	Int.Std....	Ext.St...	Hide
0001	Int.no.assgnmnt	Internal number assignment	1	☐	◉		☐
0002	Ext.no.assgnmnt	External number assignment	AA	☑		◉	☐

6.1.4 Verify Table Entries between ERP and EWM Systems

Finally, before initiating the data transfer, it is recommended to compare the data in following tables to check for any inconsistencies between the ERP and EWM systems. Most errors during data transfer are caused by such inconsistencies. Tables can be compared manually, using TCode SE16 in both systems.

SNo	Table Description	EWM Table	ERP Table
1	Handling ID	/SCMB/THNDLCD	THNDLCD
2	Handling Unit Type	/SCWM/THUTYP	THUTYP
3	Packing Material Type	/SCWM/TPMTYP	V_TVTY
4	Packing Group	/SCWM/TPACKGR	V_TVEGR
5	Warehouse Product Group	/SCMB/TWHMATGR	TWHMATGR
6	Warehouse Storage Condition	/SCMB/TWHSTC	TWHSTC
7	Delivery Priority	/SCDL/TDLVPRIO_V	V_TPRIO
8	Shipping Condition	/SCDL/TSRVLVL	V_TVSB
9	Incoterms	/SCMB/TSINC	V_TINC
10	Address Types	TB009	TB009
11	Unit of measure	T006	T006
12	Dangerous Goods Ind. Profile	/SEHS/DGC_041	TDG41

6.2 Master Data Transfer—CIF

This section will cover how to transfer plants, shipping points, customers, vendors, and materials master data from ERP to EWM systems. If the materials are batch managed, it is necessary to complete batch management–related configuration settings to transfer additional data like batches, classes, and characteristics. This is discussed in chapter 8. Table 6.2A provides an overview of the topics covered in this section.

Table 6.2A Master Data Transfer - CIF

S. No	Configuration Check List	TCode	System	Transportable
1	Create Customers	XD01	ERP	Not Applicable
2	Create Vendors	MK01	ERP	Not Applicable
3	Create Materials	MM01	ERP	Not Applicable
4	Creating an Integration Model in the ERP System	CFM1	ERP	Not Applicable
5	Activate the Integration Model in the ERP System	CFM2	ERP	Not Applicable
6	Display CIF Log	CFG1	ERP	Not Applicable
7	Send Changes Manually	CFP1	ERP	Not Applicable
8	Create Variants for Background Jobs	SE38	ERP	Not Applicable
9	Define Background Jobs	SM36	ERP	Not Applicable
10	Monitor the Queues	CFQ1	ERP	Not Applicable
11	Verify Data Transfer in EWM System		EWM	Not Applicable

6.2.1 Create Customers

Customer master data is created in the ERP system (TCode XD01) and transferred to the EWM system via CIF data transfer. In EWM, customers are called BPs. Once customer data is transferred to the EWM system, appropriate ID types and roles should be assigned. This is covered in more detail in section 6.3. During the data transfer, all or selected customers to can be transferred to the EWM system. Creating customers is part of the sales process; hence, it will not be covered in detail in this book.

6.2.2 Create Vendors

Vendor master data is also created in the ERP system and transferred to EWM as part of a CIF data transfer. In EWM, vendors are also called BPs. After transferring vendors to the EWM system, appropriate ID types and roles should be assigned. This is covered in more detail in section 6.3. Vendors are usually created as part of the purchasing process in transaction MK01.

All or selected vendors can be transferred to the EWM system.

6.2.3 Create Materials

Material master data is created in the ERP system and transferred to the EWM system via CIF data transfer. In EWM, material master data is called product master data. After transferring material master data to the EWM system, warehouse-specific data must be maintained for the products; this is covered in detail in chapter 7.

In ERP, creation of material master is managed by the master data team. The TCode to create material master is MM01.

As discussed in chapter 4, it is not necessary to maintain EWM-specific data in the ERP material master. However, if a client wants to maintain certain data centrally in the ERP system, this can be done by activating BC sets. This will enable the WM execution view, WM packaging view, and some additional fields for unit of measure in the material master, which can be used to maintain EWM-specific data. This data will be transferred to the EWM system when the CIF interface is activated.

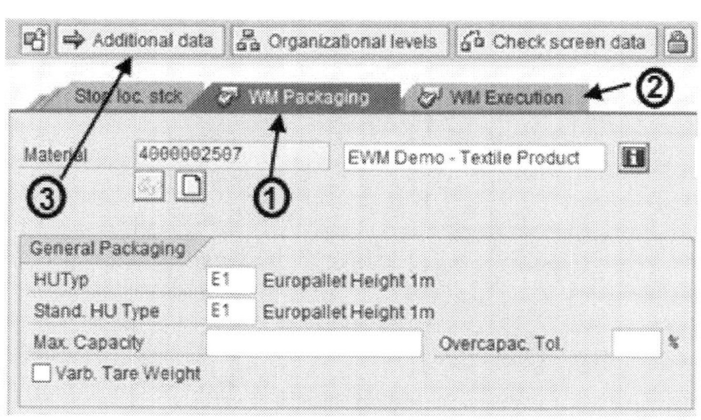

6.2.4 Creating an Integration Model in the ERP System

Once the master data (materials, vendors, customers) and org elements (plants, shipping points, classes/characteristics, batches) are created in the ERP system, they need to be transferred to the EWM system. This can be done using CIF—or IDOCs, (for older ERP versions).

To transfer data, first create a CIF integration model specifying what data should be transferred. Either all data or selected data can be transferred by adding filters in the selection screen. If the SCM system has other components like APO, additional precautions should be taken when defining the integration model. Wrong selections or data without appropriate filters can cause problems like unwanted data getting transferred to the SCM system or overwriting existing data. This can have a negative impact on other components of the SCM system, such as APO. Hence, it is recommended to have fewer integration models and not to include the same data in multiple models.

Menu Path: SAP Easy Access | SAP menu | Logistics | Central Functions | Supply Chain Planning Interface | Core Interface Advanced Planner and Optimizer | Integration Model | Create or TCode CFM1

Here we have used the following data to demonstrate the creation of an integration model and transferring of the data from the ERP system.

Table 6.2.4A Master Data

Materials	Vendors	Customers
4000014262	1003387	1002845
4000014264	P2517	C2517

Table 6.2.4B Org Elements

Plants	Shipping Points
2517	1003
	1007
	1009

Table 6.2.4C Batch Characteristics Data		
Batch	**Class**	**Characteristics**
FINISHED_TILE	023	Quality
		Off Quality Reason
		Roll Width
		Roll Width
		Batch Number
		Country of Origin
		Expiration date, shelf life
		Status of Batch
		Date when Batch Was Produced
		Deletion Ind. for Batches
		Availability Date
		Next Insp. Date for Batch

In order to create an integration model for CIF data transfer, go to transaction CFM1, enter model name <free text>, select the logical system as EWM logical system, and enter "free text" in the APO application field, as shown in the screenshot below. Under "Material Dependent Objects," select materials and plants, and maintain the filter values under "General Selection Options for Materials." Under "Material Independent Objects," select batch, customers, vendors, shipping points, and Classes/Charact. You can also maintain filter values for each of these objects.

For both vendors and customers, select value "2" in “create Loc/BP” field. This is required to create both location and business partners in the EWM system for vendors and customers.

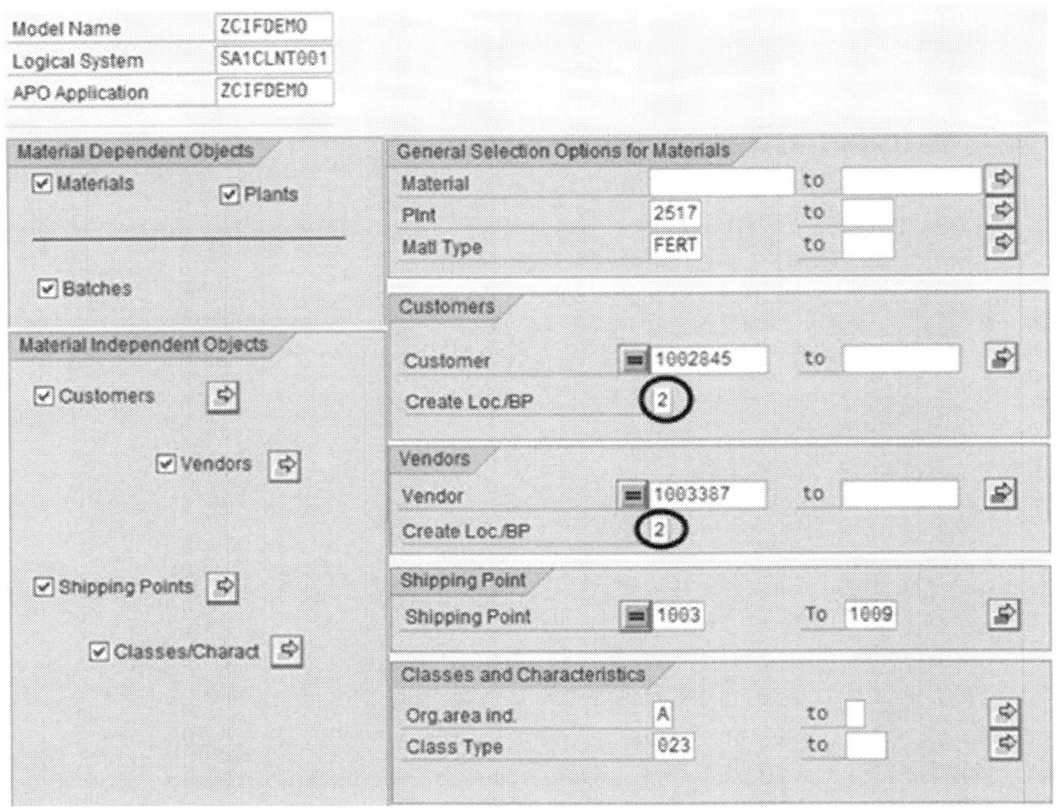

Click on the "Execute" button (F8) on the application toolbar. This will display a summary of the data transfer. After verifying the data, click on the "Generate IM" button. This will generate a CIF integration model.

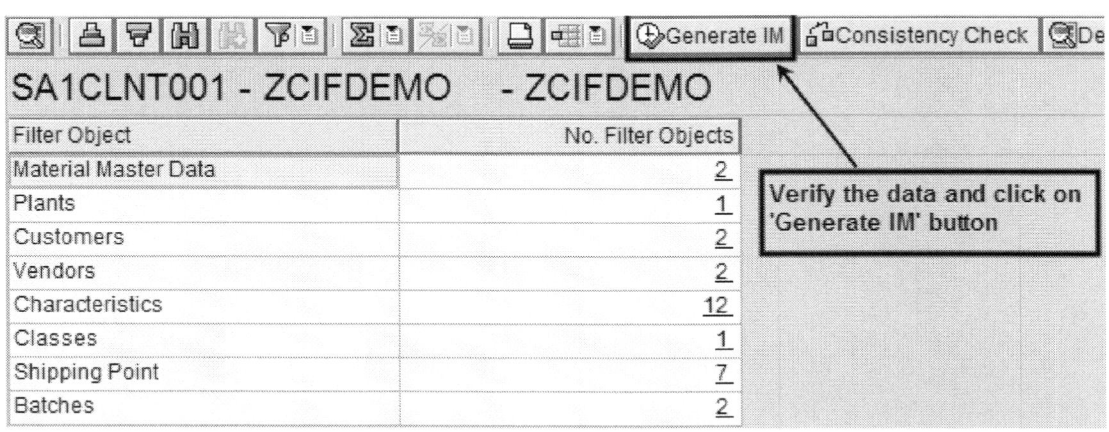

6.2.5 Activate the Integration Model in the ERP System

After creating an integration model, the model should be activated in order to initiate the data transfer from the ERP to EWM system. Once the CIF integration model is activated, the data will be transferred to the EWM system, and any changes to the data elements specified in the integration model will be redistributed automatically. If new data is added, the integration model has to be recreated and reactivated. This can be automated with a background job.

Menu Path: SAP Easy Access | SAP menu | Logistics | Central Functions | Supply Chain Planning Interface | Core Interface Advanced Planner and Optimizer | Integration Model | Activate or TCode CFM2

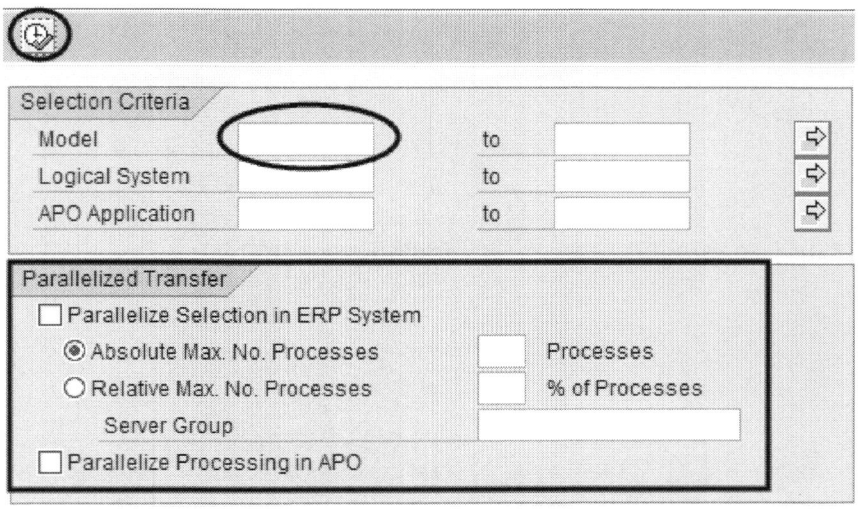

Here, enter the model name or EWM logical system and click on the "Execute" button. This will display the integration model on the left side of the screen. Click on the integration model to display the status of the integration model on right side of the screen.

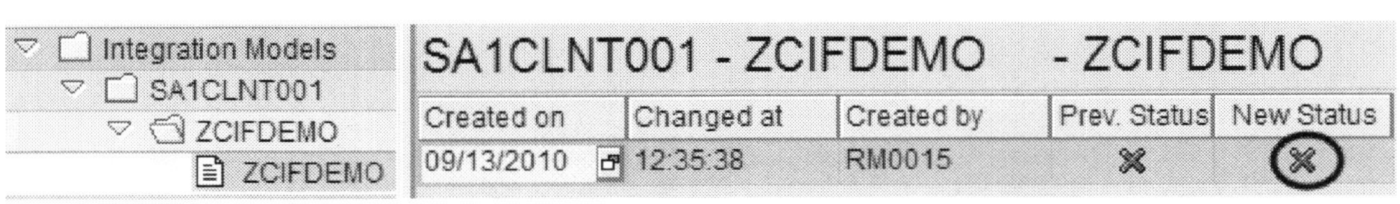

Click on "New Status" to change the status from inactive to active.

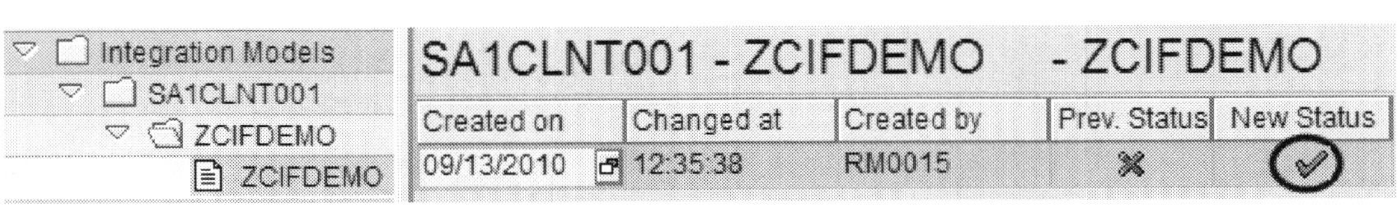

Click on the "Start" button to activate the integration model. If all values are transferred to the target system, it will display the following popup. Click "yes" to show the status of the data transfer. If the data is transferred properly, the green message will be displayed.

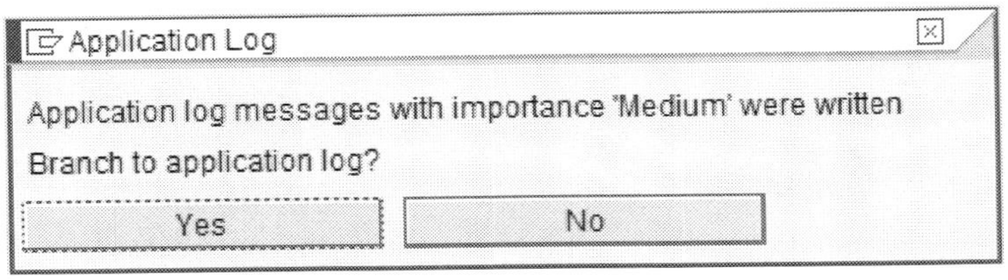

Date/Time/User	Numb	External...	Object txt	Sub-object text	Tran	Program	Mode
09/13/2010 12:55:31 RM0015	16	CIFLOA...	Core Interface A...	Initial Data Tran...	CFM2	SAPLCIFG	Dialog pro...
09/13/2010 12:55:31 RM0015	73	CIFLOA...	Core Interface A...	Initial Data Tran...	CFM2	SAPLCIFG	Dialog pro...
09/13/2010 12:55:31 RM0015	80	CIFLOA...	Core Interface A...	Initial Data Tran...	CFM2	SAPLCIFG	Dialog pro...
09/13/2010 12:55:32 RM0015	42	CIFLOA...	Core Interface A...	Initial Data Tran...	CFM2	SAPLCIFG	Dialog pro...
09/13/2010 12:55:32 RM0015	28	CIFLOA...	Core Interface A...	Initial Data Tran...	CFM2	SAPLCIFG	Dialog pro...

6.2.6 Display CIF Log

The TCode to display the CIF log is CFG1. Here, enter CIF in the object field; enter date and other required filter values like user, transaction code, program name, and so on. Click on F8 to display the log.

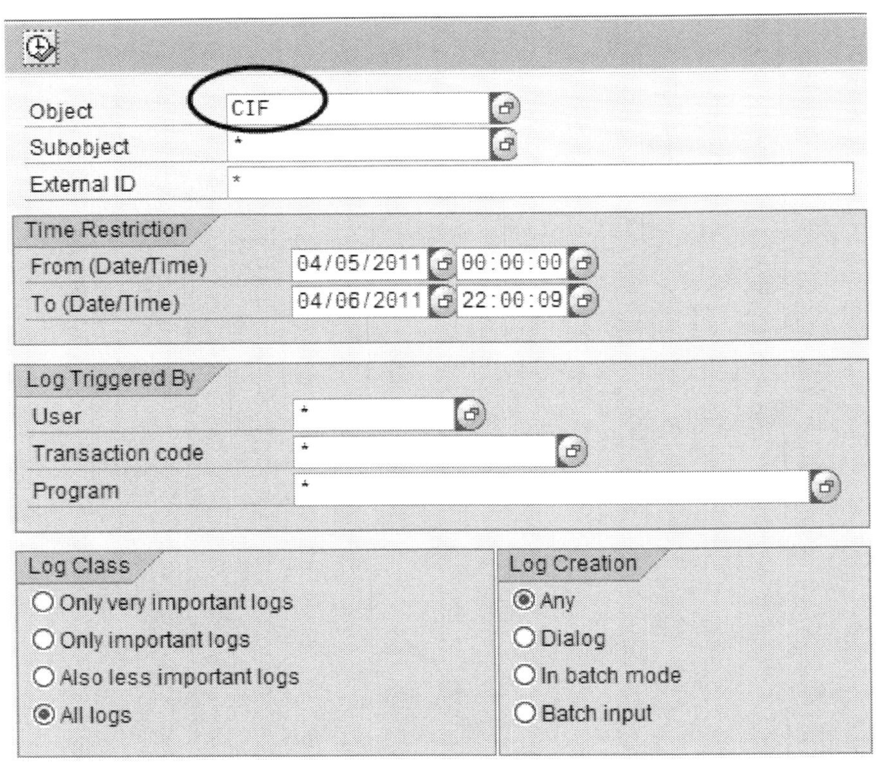

6.2.7 Send Master Data Changes Manually

After the initial data transfer, it is possible to transfer the changes manually or automatically with background jobs. To transfer the data manually, the transaction code is CFP1. This transaction can be accessed from **SAP Easy Access | SAP menu | Logistics | Central Functions | Supply Chain Planning Interface | Core Interface Advanced Planner and Optimizer | Integration Model | Change Transfer | Master Data**

Here, enter the logical system, select the object types, and click on the "Execute" button on the application toolbar to initiate the data transfer.

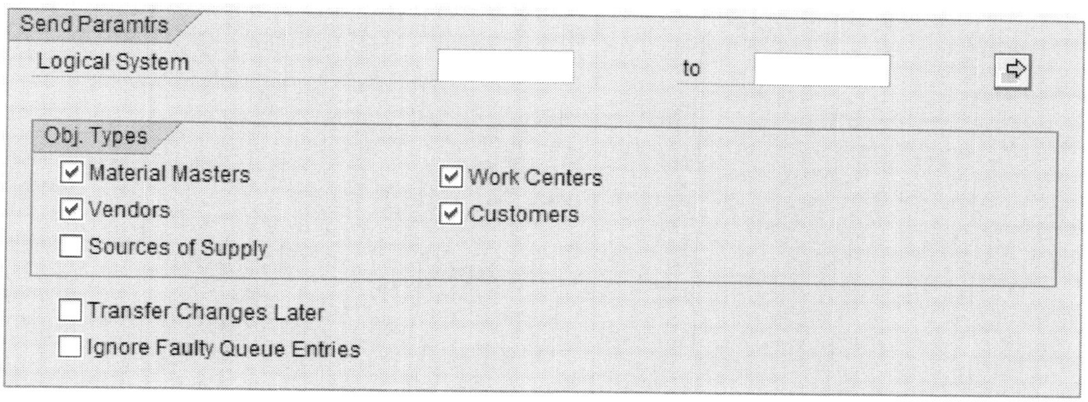

6.2.8 Create Variants for Background Jobs

If the master data is constantly changed in the ERP system, it is recommended to schedule a background job to regularly update the integration model to the newest status and transfer the changes to SAP APO. It is also necessary to delete the old versions of the integration model on a regular basis to avoid any performance issues. To do this, SAP recommends creating the following programs as periodic jobs:

i. Generate new versions of the integration model (RIMODGEN)
ii. Activate the newest versions (RIMODAC2)
iii. Optional: Delete the old versions (RIMODEL)

► Generate new versions of the integration model (RIMODGEN)

In this step, create a variant for the integration model, which will be used in the background job later. To create a variant, go to transaction SE38, enter program name RIMODGEN, select the "Variants" radio button, and click the "Display" button.

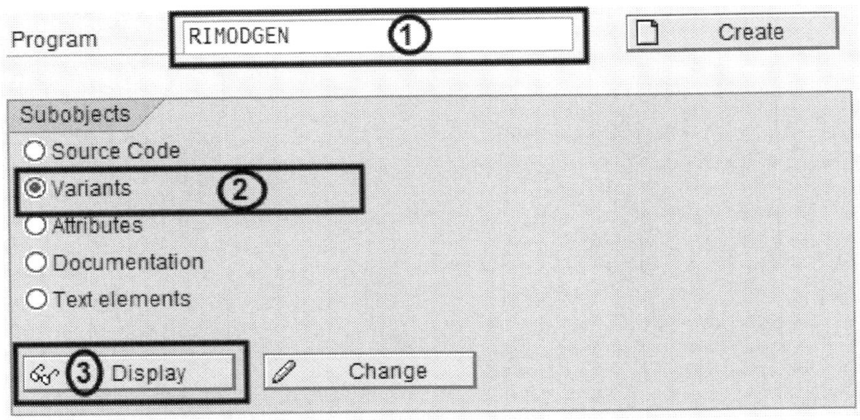

In the next screen, enter a variant name, select the "Values" radio button, and click the "Create" button.

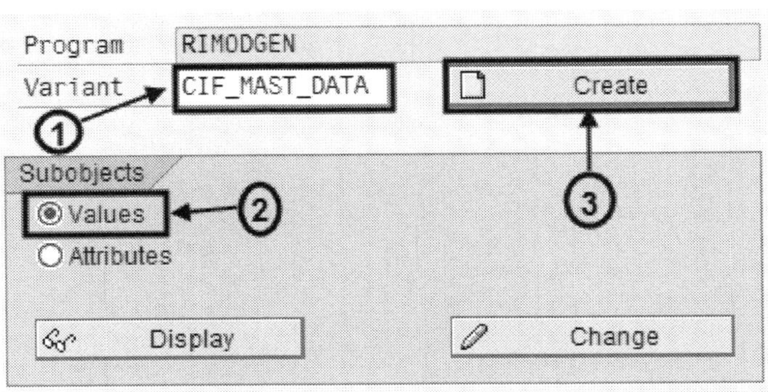

In the following screen, enter model name, logical system name, and APO application name; select the objects; enter the filter values; and click the "Save" button.

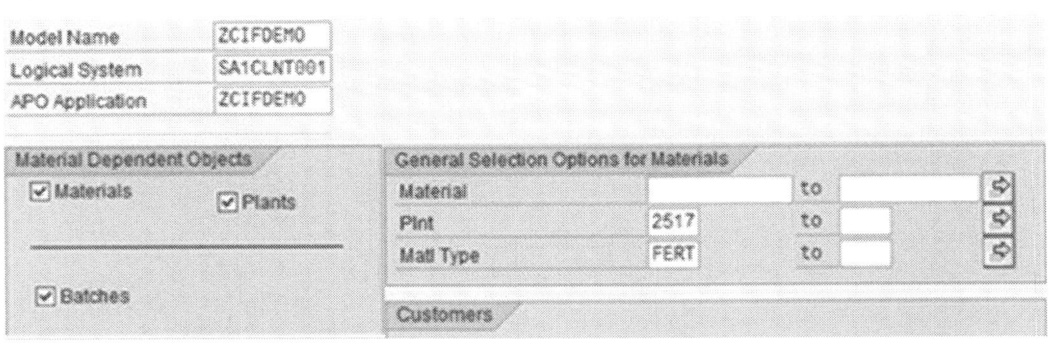

In the following screen, enter the description in the meaning field and click on save button.

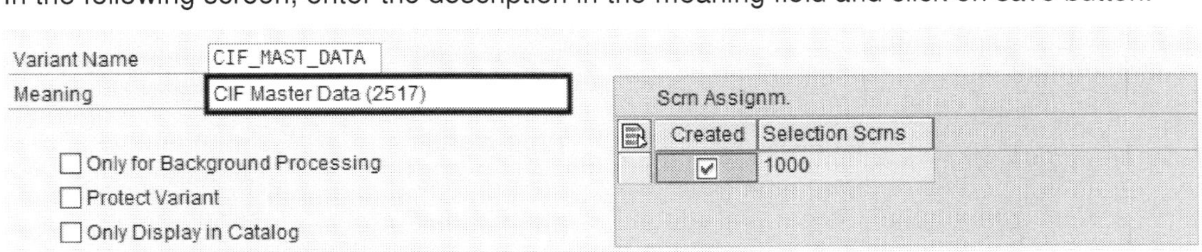

This will create a variant, which will be used later while defining the background job.

- **Activate the newest versions (RIMODAC2)**

As explained in the above step, create two variants for program RIMODAC2: one variant to activate the newest integration model version and one to deactivate the all older active integration model versions, as explained below.

In the active version, enter the model, logical system, and APO application that were created in the earlier step. In the "Action to Execute" section, select "Activate Newest Version." In the special CIF settings, check "Ignore Faulty Queues" and other appropriate options. Click on the "Attributes" button on the application toolbar to create a variant.

In the deactivate version, enter the model, logical system, and APO application that were created in the earlier step. In the "Action to Execute" section, select "Deactivate all versions." Deactivation is required, because in the system, only deactivated versions can be deleted.

- **Optional: Delete the old versions (RIMODDEL)**

Even though this is optional, it is still recommended to delete the older versions, because these can hinder performance. Create a variant for program RIMODDEL.

6.2.9 Define Background Jobs

After defining the variants, background jobs can be created and scheduled to run as per client requirement. To create a background job,

i. Enter TCode SM36 in the command bar, specify a job name, and click the "Step" button.

ii. In the screen, change the user name to the one created to run the background job. In the production system, usually a separate user ID is created to run background jobs.

iii. To delete the older versions, it is necessary to first deactivate all active versions of the integration model. Therefore enter the program name RIMODAC2 and select the variant created to deactivate the integration model. Click the "Save" button.

iv. Click the "Create" button, repeat step 2, enter the program name RIMODDEL, and select the variant created above. Click the "Save" button. This will delete all inactive versions of the integration model.

v. Click "Create," repeat step 2 for program RIMODGEN, and select the variant created above. Click "Save." This will create a new integration model for CIF.

vi. Click "Create," repeat step 2 for program RIMODAC2, and select the variant created to activate the integration model. Click "Save." This will activate the integration model, and the data transfer will begin.

vii. Click on back button (arrow key) or F3 to define start condition.

viii. Click the "Start condition" button, click the "Immediate" button, check the "Periodic Job" checkbox to define a periodic job, click on the "Periodic Values" button, select appropriate values (like hourly, daily), and click "Save." Click "Save" again. Click "Save" once more to save and release the job.

The following screenshot shows the job log of a background job that was executed successfully.

Time	Message text
07:53:04	Job started
07:53:04	Step 001 started (program RIMODAC2, variant CIF_2517_VER_D, user ID RM0015)
07:53:07	Step 002 started (program RIMODDEL, variant CIF_2517_DEL, user ID RM0015)
07:53:07	You have deleted 14 models
07:53:07	Step 003 started (program RIMODGEN, variant CIF_MAST_DATA, user ID RM0015)
07:53:07	Integration model ZCIFDEMO generated for target system SA1CLNT001 and application ZCIFDEMO
07:53:07	Step 004 started (program RIMODAC2, variant CIF_2517_VER, user ID RM0015)
07:53:11	Application log messages with importance 'Medium' were written
07:53:11	Job finished

Notes:

Usually, scheduling jobs is managed by the Basis team. Consultants may need to consult with their Basis team before scheduling jobs.

6.2.10 Monitor Error Queues

To monitor errors, go to TCode CFQ1. Here, double-click on the status column to analyze the cause for the error. To reactivate the failed records, click the activate button.

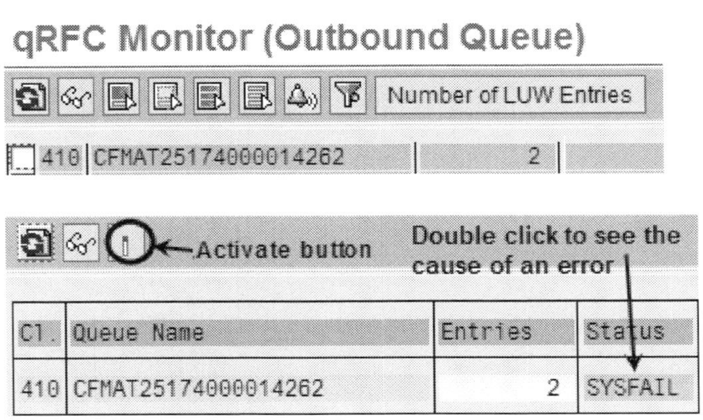

✎ **Notes:**

i. Some screenshots might show a destination as APO_00_001, and in a few cases the destination might appear as SA1CLNT00. However, they both refer to the EWM system.

6.2.11 Verify Data Transfer in the EWM System

Finally, verify the data transfer in the EWM system. In our example, we have transferred two types of data: material master data, which becomes the product master in the EWM system; and other master data like plant, shipping point, customer, and vendor become part of the locations and Supply Chain Unit (SCU) in EWM.

Product master data can be verified in TCode /SAPAPO/MAT1. To verify SCU-specific data, go to TCode /SCMB/SCUMAIN.

Supply Chain Unit	Type	Description
0001002845	1010	EWM Demo Customer
2517	1001	EWM Demo Plant
1003	1003	EWM Demo Shipping point 1
1007	1003	EWM Demo Shipping point 2
1009	1003	EWM Demo Shipping point 3
0001003387	1011	EWM Demo Vendor
P2517	1011	EWM Demo Vendor (Plant)

All location data can be viewed in TCode /SAPAPO/LOC3.

Location	LT	Location Description
2517	1001	EWM Demo
0001002845	1010	EWM Demo Customer
1003	1003	EWM Demo Shipping point 1
1007	1003	EWM Demo Shipping point 2
1009	1003	EWM Demo Shipping point 3
0001003387	1011	EWM Demo Vendor
P2517	1011	EWM Demo Vendor (Plant 2517)

Customers and vendors will also become BPs automatically. This data can be accessed in TCode BP.

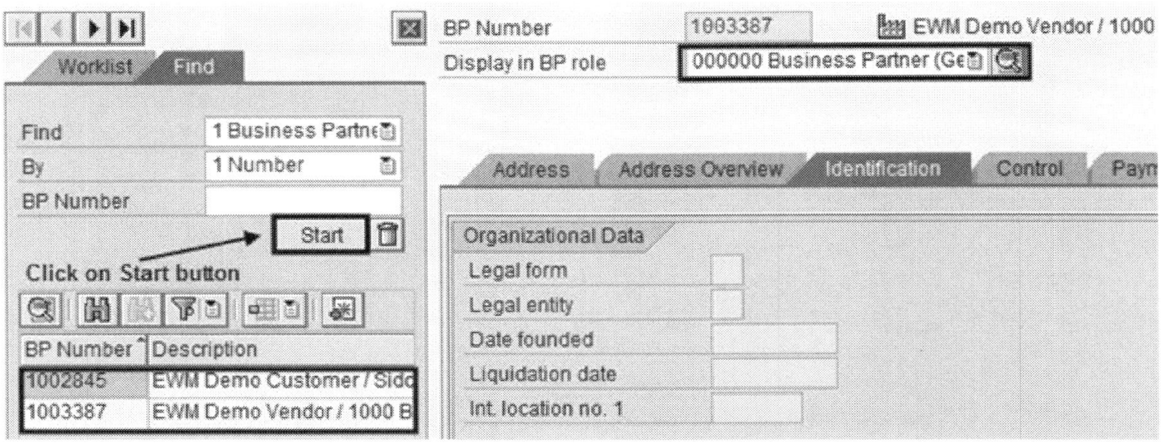

6.3 Business Partner (BP) Data

Business partners are parties with whom business transactions are conducted. Examples include customers, vendors, plants, and so on. The key business partners are the sold-to, ship-to, bill-to, and payer. In EWM business partners must also be created for vendors, plants, employees, carriers, and freight forwarders. Each of these business partners can be classified as a person, organization, or group. They can be manually created in TCode BP, or created automatically for parties like vendor and customer, if the data is transferred via CIF. The menu path to access transaction code is **SAP Easy Access | SAP menu | Extended Warehouse Management | Master Data | Maintain Business Partner**

The same transaction can be used to create, locate, change, or delete existing BPs.

Each BP can be assigned to multiple roles. For example, customers may be defined strictly as sold-to or ship-to, or both. To assign multiple BP roles to an existing BP, first locate the BP with the "Start" button, double-click on the BP, and click on the "Change" button, as shown below.

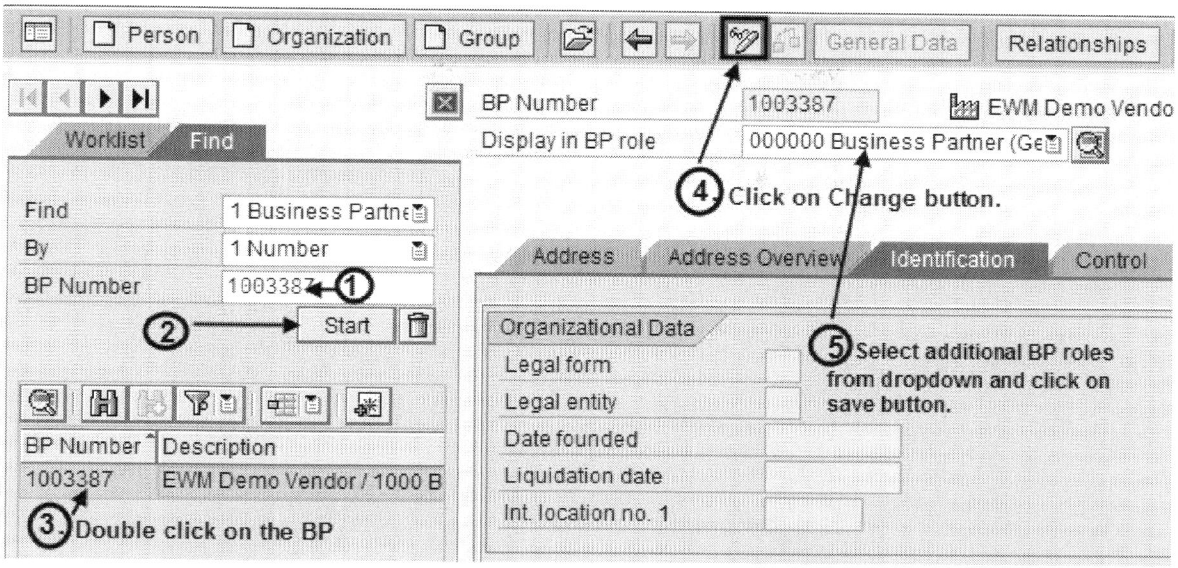

To assign a new BP role, select a BP role from the dropdown list and click on "Save" button. This will add the new role to the existing BPs. All assigned BP roles can be viewed by clicking the "Role Detail" button as shown below.

From the BPs, information like address, identification numbers, responsible institution, and business hours are used in the warehouse documents. Addresses can be updated in the "Address" tab; business hours like calling hours, GR hours, and visiting hours can be maintained in the "Control" tab. The identification numbers and responsible institution can be maintained in identification tab.

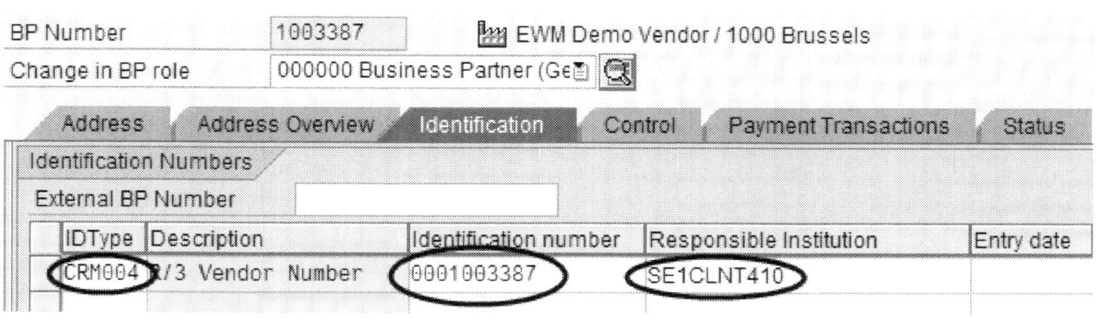

One BP can have more than one ID type. Maintaining ID type, number, and responsible institution is important in the EWM system, because they are used to determine the relevant BP data to be used for warehouse documents based on the BP number in the source document. For example, the identification type CRM004 is used to determine the vendor number for the IDN, with inbound delivery based on the vendor number assigned to the inbound delivery in ERP.

It is not necessary that the ID number be the same as the BP number; however, in most cases it will be defined the same for easy identification.

An example of IDN in the EWM system follows.

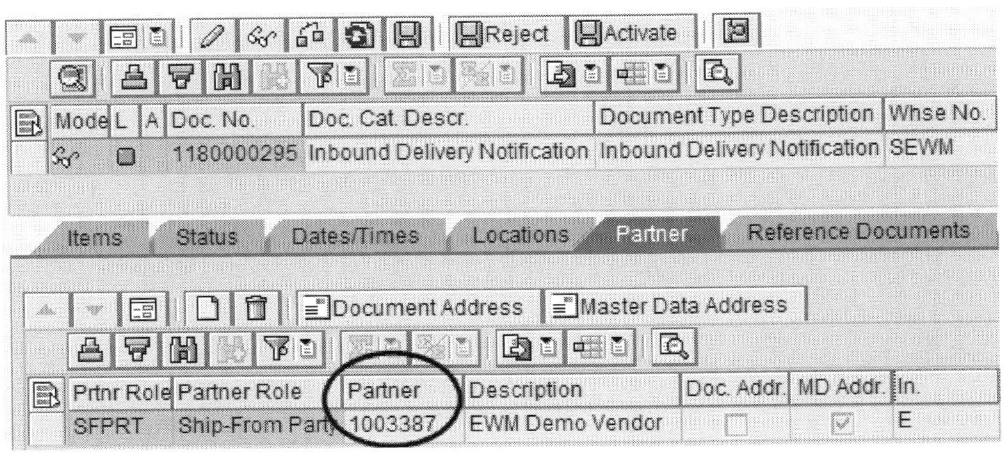

Even though there are several types of business partners, only vendor, customer, employee and plant BPs are generally used in EWM documents. They are usually created in the ERP system and transferred to the EWM system as part of a CIF data transfer. Business partners for plants have to be created manually. The following section will give an overview of each of these master data and what ID types are defined for them.

6.3.1 Customer BP Data (TCode BP)

Customers are created in the ERP system and transferred to EWM system as part of the CIF data transfer process. As explained earlier, BP records for customers can be created automatically by selecting value 2 in field "Create Loc/BP" in the CIF integration model. Once the business partner record is created, ensure that the identification type CRM002—customer; identification number (can be the same as the BP number); responsible institution; and appropriate BP roles like business partner general, sold-to, ship-to, and financial services BP are assigned to the customer BP record. TCode BP is used to create, edit or view customer BP data in EWM.

Diagram 6.3.1A provides an overview of how the customer BP data is linked to different BP objects and how they are linked to different warehouse documents.

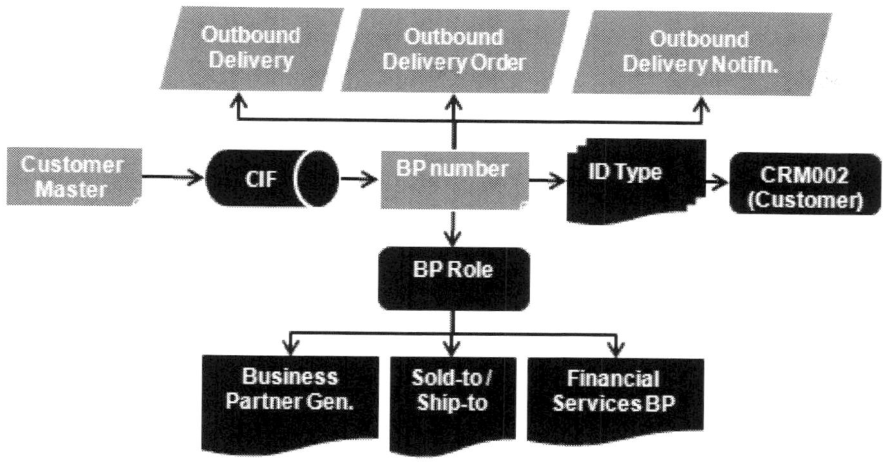

Diagram 6.3.1A – Mapping of Customer BP Data

6.3.2 Vendor BP Data

Vendors are created in the ERP system and transferred to the EWM system as part of the CIF data transfer process. For vendors, BP records can be created automatically by selecting value 2 in field "Create Loc/BP" in the CIF integration model. Once the business partner record is created, ensure that the identification type CRM004—vendor; identification number (can be the same as the BP number); responsible institution; and appropriate BP roles like business partner general, vendor, and financial services are maintained to the vendor BP. TCode BP is be used to create, edit or view vendor BP data in EWM.

Diagram 6.3.2A is an overview of how vendor BP data is linked to different BP objects and how they are linked to different warehouse documents.

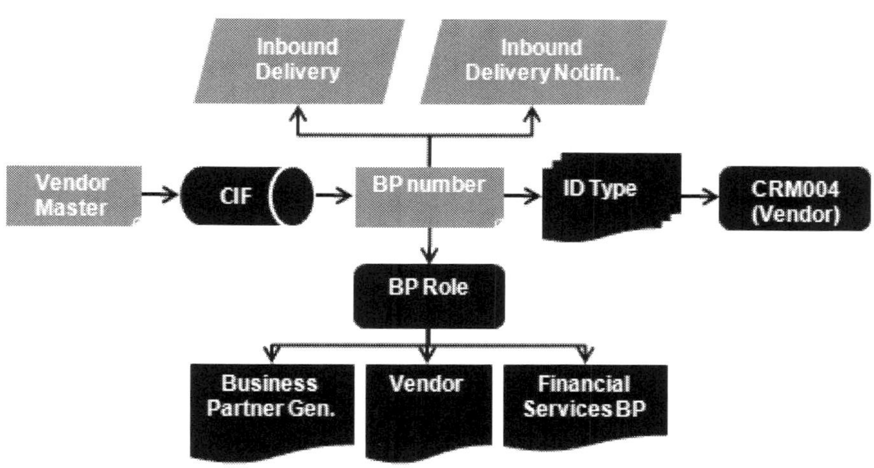

Diagram 6.3.2A – Mapping of Vendor BP Data

6.3.3 Employee BP Data

Employee data created in the Human Capital Management (HCM) module of the ERP system can be transferred to the EWM system as part of a CIF data transfer process. For employee data, BP records can be created automatically by selecting value 2 in field Create Loc/BP in the CIF integration model. Once the business partner record is created, only the appropriate BP roles need to be assigned. ID types are not applicable for employee BP data. The typical BP roles used for employees are business partner general, financial services BP, and employee. In EWM, employee data is required only if labor management performance data is interfaced with HCM or Human Resource (HR) applications. In BP roles, a personal number and user name can be assigned to the employee BP record. TCode BP is used to create, edit or view employee BP data in EWM.

Diagram 6.3.3A shows how employee BP data is linked to different BP objects and how they are linked to warehouse documents.

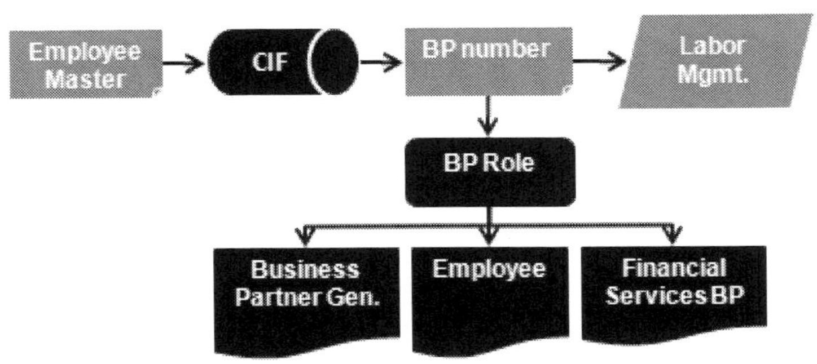

Diagram 6.3.3A – Mapping of Employee BP Data

6.3.4 Plants BP Data

Plants are created in the ERP system and transferred to EWM as part of the CIF data transfer process. Like customers, BP records for plants cannot be created automatically as part of a CIF data transfer. They have to be manually created in TCode BP.

Plants require business partner records mainly for stock transfers. They are created with the BP roles of business partner general, financial service BP, vendor, and sold-to/ship-to party, and assigned to ID types CRM002—Customer, CRM004—Vendor, and CRM011—Plant. Like other BP records, ID type, ID number, and responsible institution are essential for plant BP records.

Diagram 6.3.4A demonstrates how plant BP data is linked to different BP objects and how they are linked to different warehouse documents.

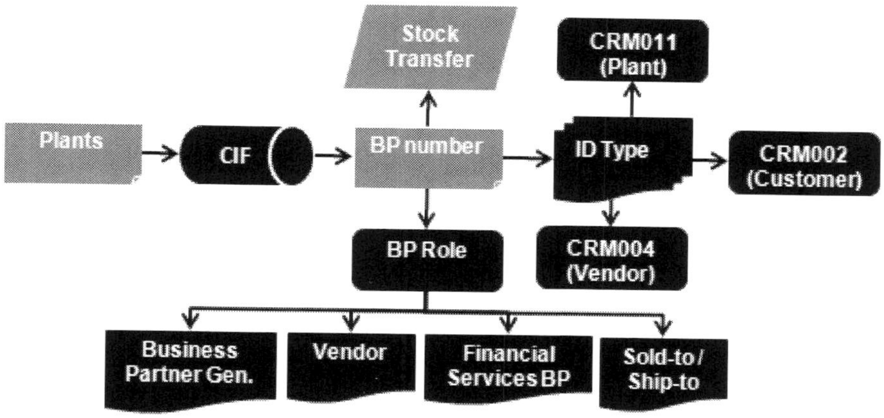

Diagram 6.3.4A – Mapping of Plant BP Data

6.4 Supply Chain Unit (SCU) Data

SCU is master data containing information like BP number, country, region code, time zone, addresses, and essential business attributes. Business attributes describe how the SCU is used in the EWM system, like whether SCU is a warehouse, goods receipt office, ship-to party, and so on.

SAP will create a SCU record for every ERP plant, customer, vendor, shipping point, and MRP area when the data is transferred from ERP to EWM. SCU records have to be created manually for the data defined locally in the EWM system, such as warehouse doors, shipping zones, and so on.

Supply Chain Unit	Description	Type
0001002845	EWM Demo Customer	1010
2517	EWM Demo Plant	1001
1003	EWM Demo Shipping point 1	1003
0001003387	EWM Demo Vendor	1011

SCU data can be created, changed, or displayed in transaction **/SCMB/SCUMAIN (SAP Easy Access | SAP menu | Extended Warehouse Management | Master Data | Maintain Supply Chain Unit).** Here, select SCU and click the "Change" button.

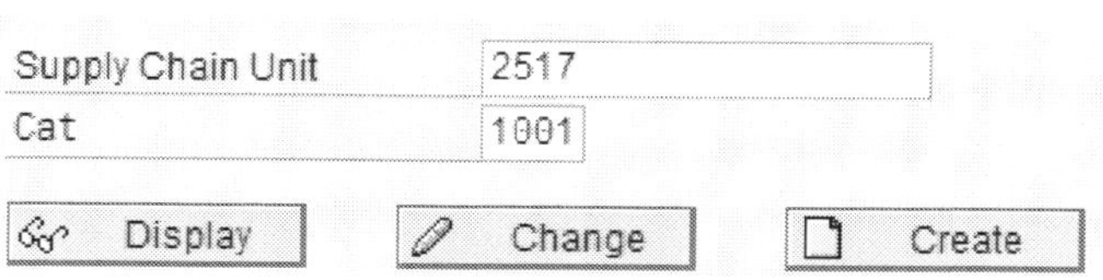

In the general tab, maintain the business partner data and the time zone.

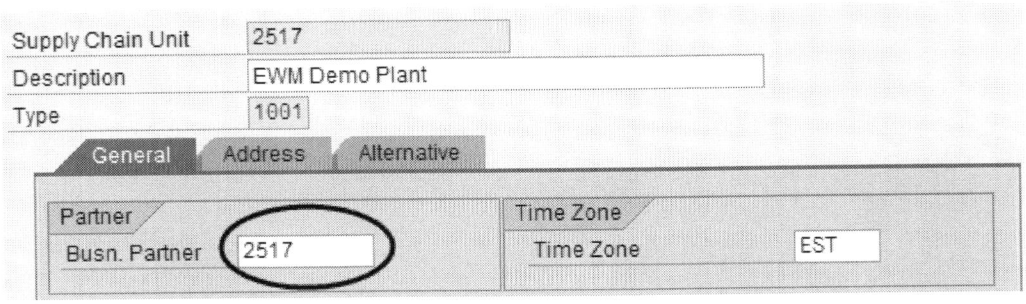

In the "Alternative" tab, click on the "Add Role" button to specify the essential business attributes. Business attributes can be selected from the dropdown list.

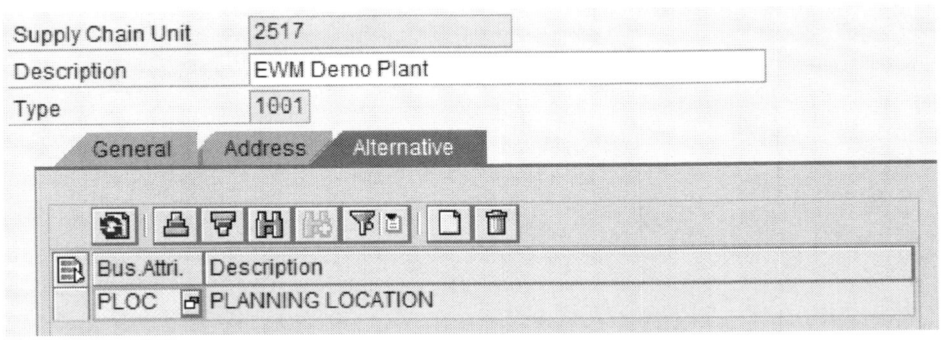

Notes:

Even though the SCU entry is created automatically for plants, business partner information has to be updated manually in the SCU record. This information will be automatically copied to the "Map Storage Locations from ERP System to EWM" configuration.

Summary

This chapter has explained how to define integration models for CIF data transfer, transferring master data from ERP to EWM systems, and configuring business partners in the EWM system. In the next chapters, the information defined here will be used in various examples, rather than be explained again.

Chapter 7: Product Master in EWM

In every system, master data play an important role. In EWM, both product master data and the configuration are used to guide the products into appropriate warehouse processes during different warehouse activities like putaway, picking, and internal warehouse movements. It is important for consultants and users to understand product master data and maintain appropriate values to achieve the desired results. This chapter will cover the various product master views in EWM in detail.

7.1 Product Master Data Views

In EWM systems, the product master data are broadly divided into two parts:

i. Basic product master data

ii. Warehouse-specific product master data

Basic Product Master Data (TCode /SAPAPO/MAT1)

Basic product master data are also known as global data. This information is used by all warehouses and other SCM components like APO, SNP, and Event Management. Hence, any changes to this data should be done with caution.

Basic product master data can be accessed from **SAP Easy Access | SAP menu | Extended Warehouse Management | Master Data | Product | Maintain Product or TCode /SAPAPO/MAT1**

Here, enter the product number, select the "Global Data" radio button, and click the "Display" button. This will display the global data of the product master data.

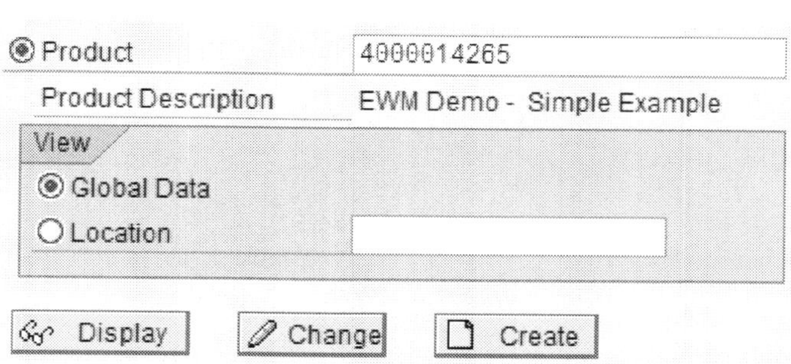

The global data of product master have eight views, but only the "Properties," "Classification," "Unit of Meas.," "Pkg Data," and "Storage" views are applicable for warehouses. Any changes in global data of product can affect all the warehouses as well as APO, SNP, and Event Management. Therefore, caution should be used when changing any existing data there.

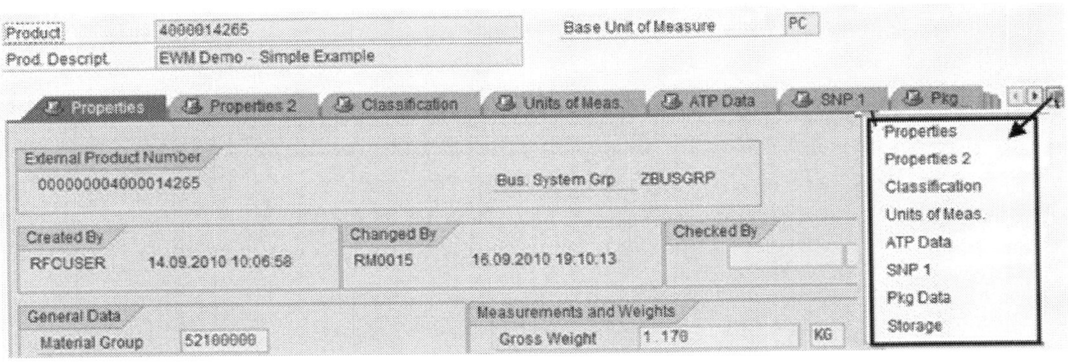

Warehouse-Specific Product Master Data (TCode /SCWM/MAT1)

Warehouse-specific product master data is accessed using TCode /SCWM/MAT1. In order to display the warehouse product data, it has to be first created. The CIF data transfer creates only the global data for the product and not the warehouse-specific data. To create warehouse-specific data, go to TCode /SCWM/MAT1 and enter product number, warehouse number, and party entitled to dispose, and click "Create."

Here, the warehouse number and party entitled to dispose fields are mandatory because the warehouse dependent data is created only to the specified warehouse and to the party entitled to dispose. It is one of the limitations of ERP warehouse where the data for plant and warehouse combination can't be defined. For example, two different putaway or picking indicators for different plants cannot be defined for the same warehouse, whereas this is possible in EWM systems. This allows more flexibility for storing products from different plants separately in large distribution centers (DCs).

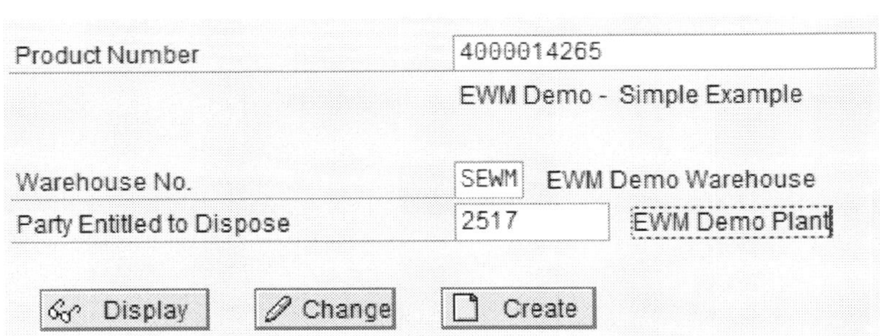

The warehouse-specific product master data also shows eight views. The first five views (properties, unit of measure, classification, package data, and storage) are part of the basic product master data or global product master data. The last three views (Whse Data, Slotting, and St. Type Data) belong to the warehouse, and the data maintained in these views is specific to the warehouse and party entitled to dispose.

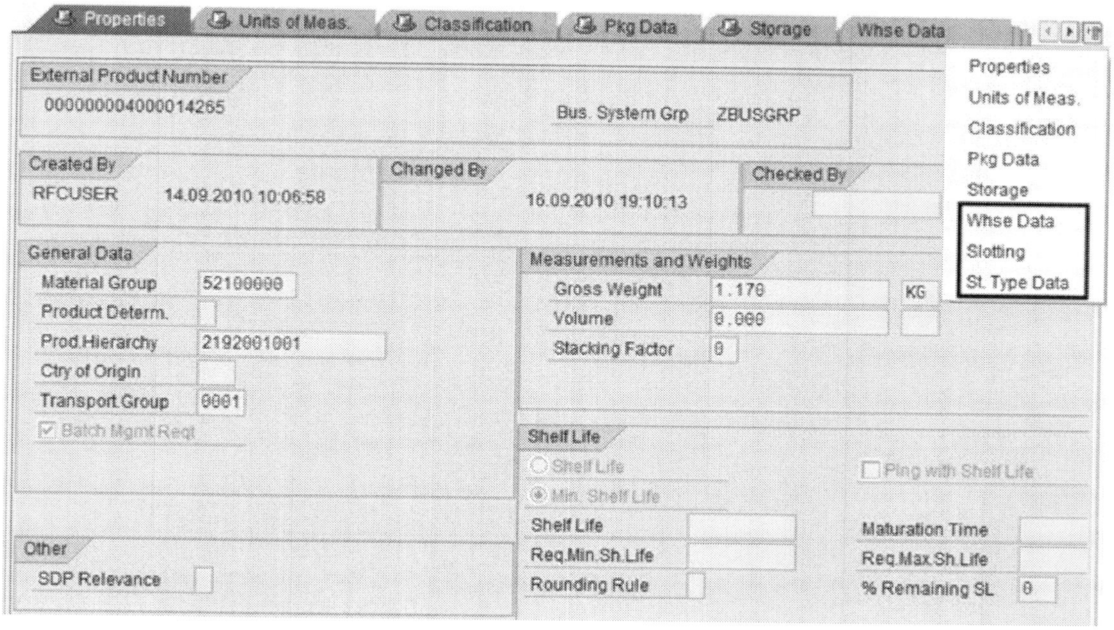

7.1.1 Unit of Measure View

This view contains the unit of measure (UOM) conversion data from alternative UOM to base UOM. Here, alternative UOMs, dimensions, capacity consumption, and so on can be defined. For the most part, this information is used during packing, capacity check at the time of putaway, and slotting.

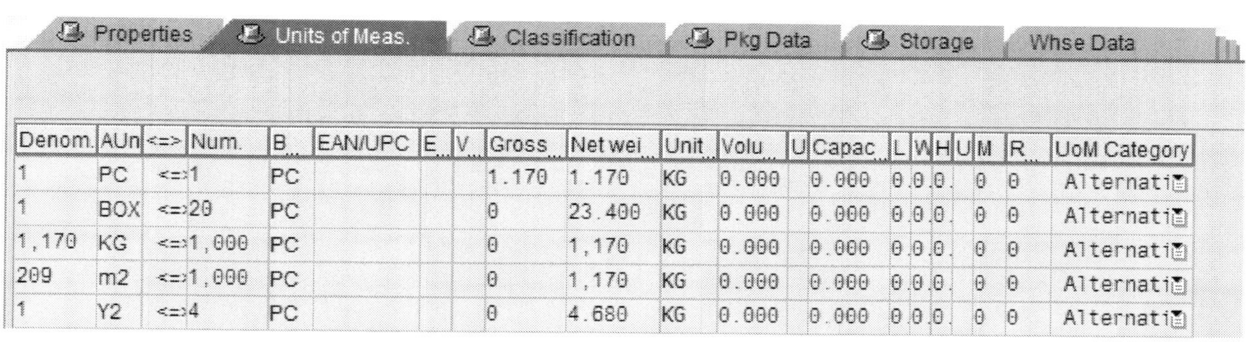

7.1.2 Properties View

This view contains general information related to the product such as description, weight, volume, grouping codes, and shelf life related information. Even though most of this information is transferred from the ERP system, not all field values are used in the day-to-day warehouse operation. Some field values defined here are used only for information purpose. Fields that are currently used in EWM include transportation group, to determine the route assignment for deliveries; batch management requirement, filed to specify whether or not products are batch managed; gross weight and volume, which are used at the time of packing and capacity check; and shelf life, minimum shelf life, required minimum shelf life, and percent remaining shelf life, to calculate the shelf life expiry of the products. As of now, all other fields are used for information purposes only.

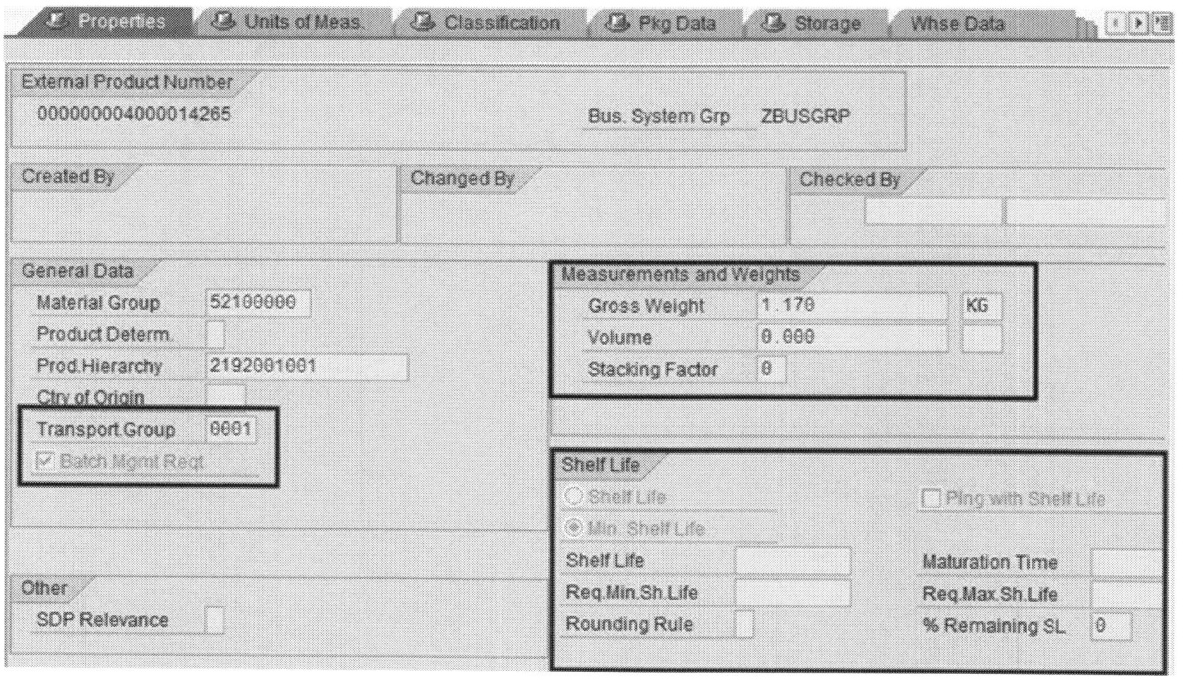

7.1.3 Classification View

This view provides information for batch-managed products like reference products, class name, and characteristics of the class. This is required when products are batch managed.

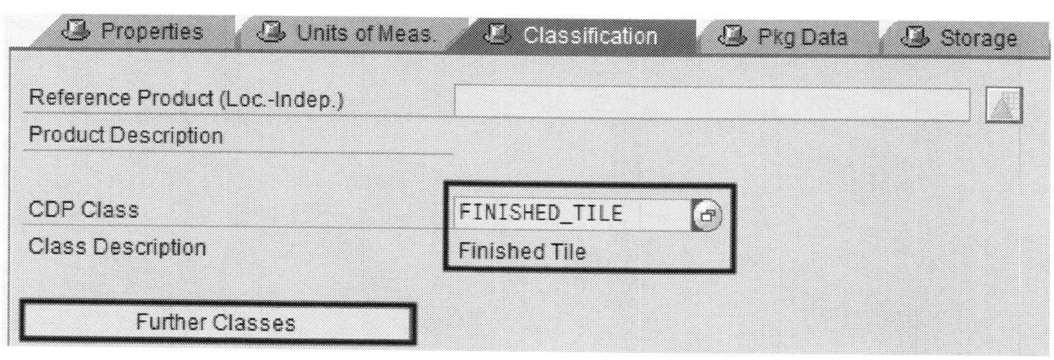

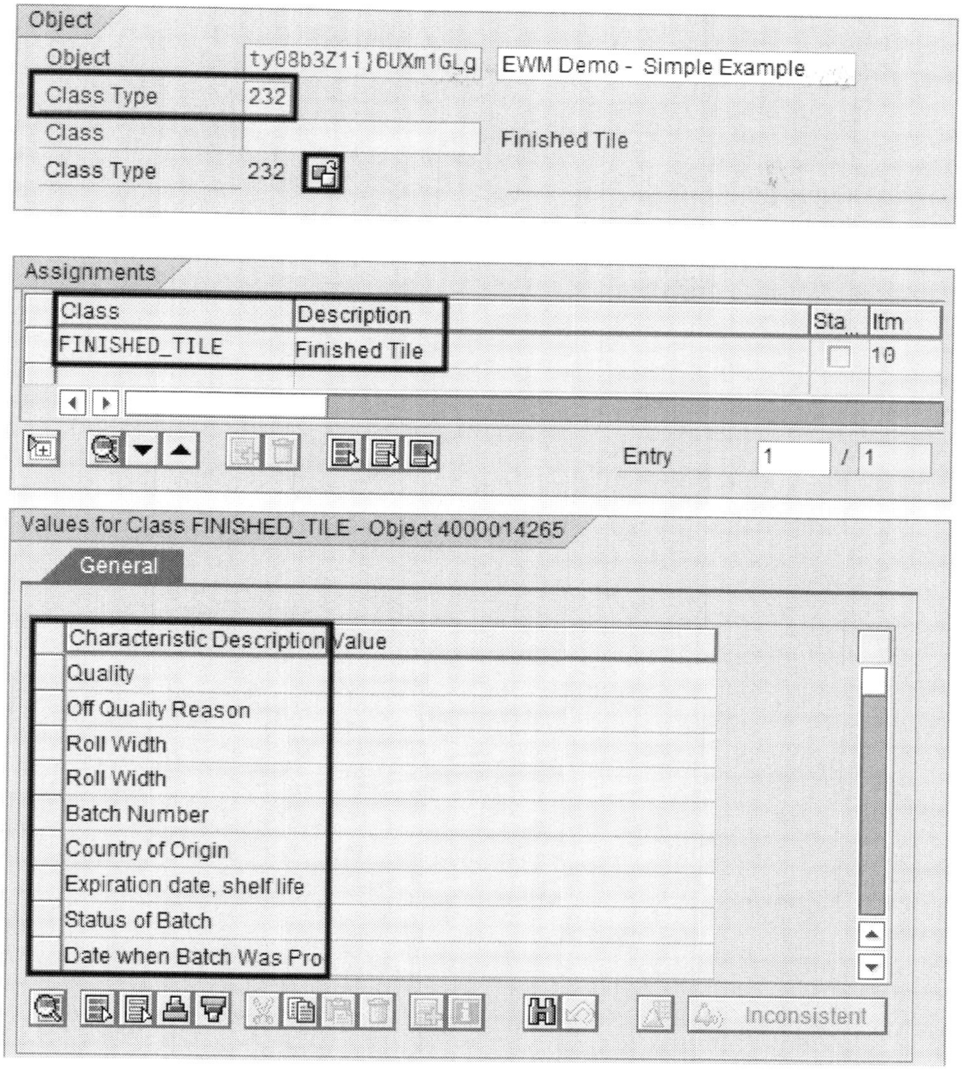

7.1.4 Packaging Data (Pkg Data) View

The fields defined here are mainly used for product master data that represent packaging materials. The data is broadly divided into three sections.

Pack section: This is used to define packing group, reference products for packing and standard HU type for the products that go inside packaging materials at the time of packing.

Packaging Material Section: This is mainly used for packing products to define the packaging material type, HU type, and label forms. Either smart or PDF forms can be used to define the labels' format; and are assigned to the packing material here.

Capacities: The information in the capacities sections is also mainly used for packing materials to define the capacities of the packing materials. Values that can be maintain here include maximum weight, excess weight tolerance in percentage, maximum volume, excess volume tolerance in percentage, tare weight variable, maximum capacity, and excess capacity tolerance, along with maximum length, width, and height.

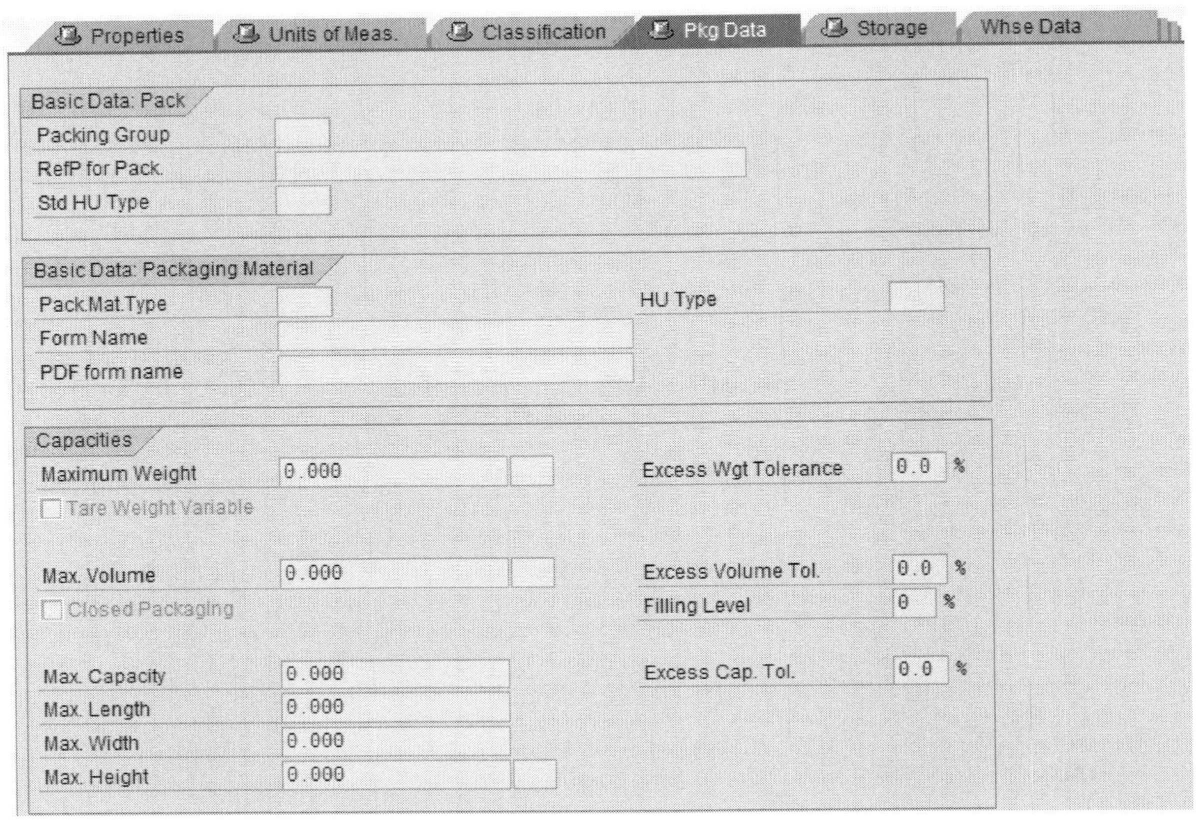

7.1.5 Storage Data View

The storage data view contains data pertaining to the storage of the product. Since it belongs to global data and any changes to values of these fields will be applicable to all warehouses which use this information. The values for the following fields of storage data view can be transferred from the ERP system.

Warehouse product group: This groups products by warehousing points of view.

Warehouse storage condition: This describes how the product should be stored in the warehouse.

Warehouse handling indicator: This is used to determine how the product should be handled when moving from one location to another.

Item category group: As of now, this is used for information purposes only.

Serial number profile: This controls the serialization level and number assignment of serial numbers.

Quality inspection group: This is the group that identifies products that behave or are handled in the same way in a quality inspection. It is used for various purposes, like to group materials together for determination of quality inspection relevance, determination of value intervals for counting, to specify the forbidden goods movements from inspection, and so on.

Pilferable: The product is pilferable, and possibly requires special storage in a secure storage type/section within the warehouse. As of now, it is not used in EWM. This indicator can be used in BADI.

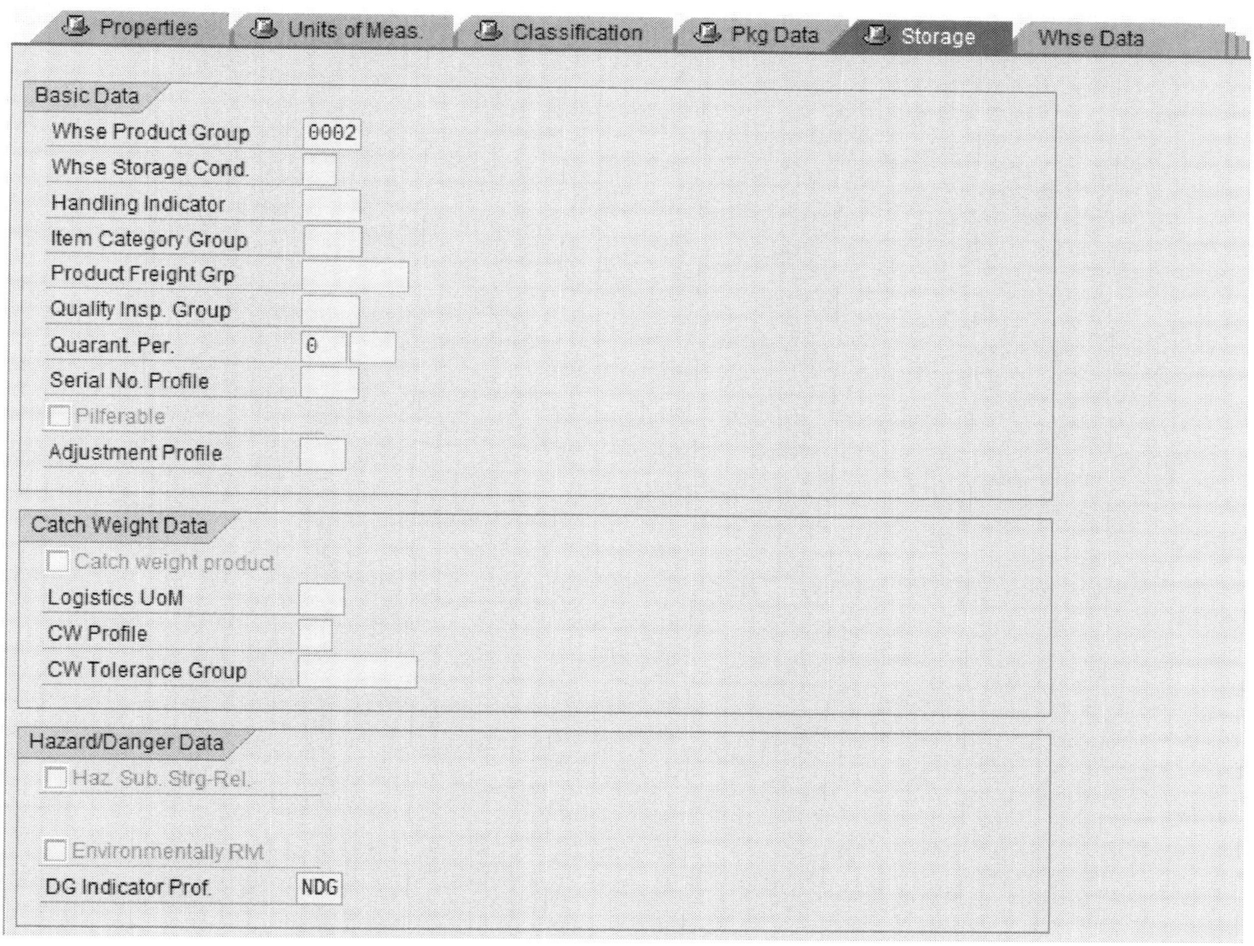

7.1.6 Warehouse Data (Whse Data) View

The fields in this view influence the product movement, putaway, and picking in the warehouse.

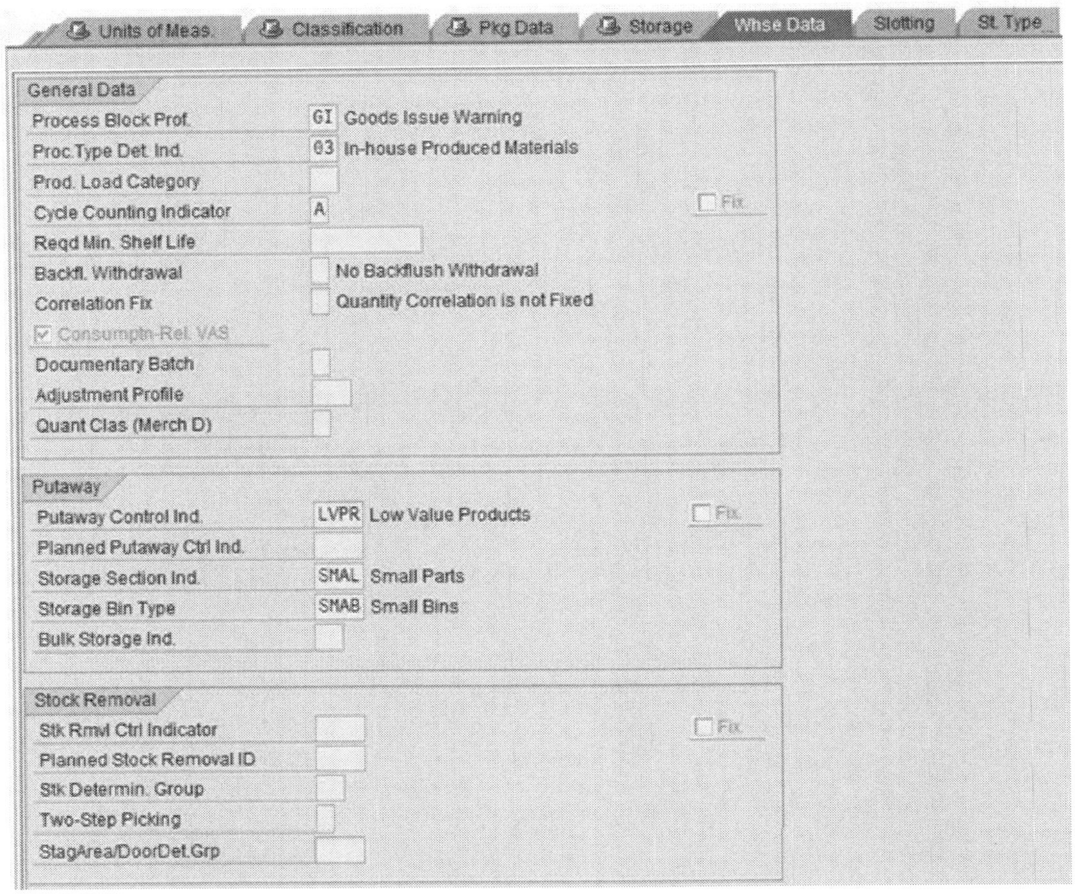

Process block profile: A process block profile can be used to trigger an error or warning message when certain processes are performed in the warehouse for a product. For example, it can display a warning message when the product is goods issued. To enable this feature, the process block profile must be defined and assigned to the product master. The supported warehouse processes are as follows: create warehouse task, confirm warehouse task, post goods receipt, post goods issue, create inventory document, and count inventory document.

To define process block profile go to **SPRO | IMG | Extended Warehouse Management | Master Data | Product | Define Process Block Profile**

Here, click on the "New Entries" button on the application toolbar, enter warehouse number, process block profile code, and description. Hit the "Enter" key and click "Save."

Dialog Structure
- Create Process Block Profile
  - Define Process Block Profile

Create Process Block Profile

War	PrBlckProf	Description
SEWM	GI	Goods Issue Warning

Select the entry previously defined and double-click on "Define Process Block Profile" under "Dialog structure." Click on "New Entries," enter warehouse number, process block profile, select the process, and process block type, and click "Save." After it is created, assign it to the product master.

The process block profile will be ignored if, in the WPT, the "Skip Process Block Profile" indicator is checked.

Dialog Structure
- Create Process Block Profile
  - Define Process Block Profile

Define Process Block Profile

War	PrBlckProf	Process	PrBlk Type
SEWM	GI	B Post Goods Issue	W Warning

Process type determination indicator: The WPTs are similar to movement types in ERP WM, which is covered in detail in chapter 11. It provides the information required for putaway, stock removals, internal stock transfers, and stock postings. The process type determination indicator assigned to the product master is used to determine the relevant process type for warehouse activities.

Process type determination indicators can be defined in **SPRO | IMG | Extended Warehouse Management | Cross-Process Settings | Warehouse Task | Define Control Indicators for Determining Warehouse Process Types**

Here, click the "New Entries" button on the application toolbar; enter warehouse number, process type indicator, and description. Click "Save" to save the entries.

Control Indicator for Warehouse Process Type Determination

War	ProTyp	Description
SEWM	03	In-house Produced Materials

Cycle Counting (CC) Indicator: This is also called the ABC indicator. They are used to define the frequency of counting for the products. Category A products are counted more often than those in category C.

Cycle count indicators can be defined in **SPRO | IMG | Extended Warehouse Management | Internal Warehouse Processes | Physical Inventory | Warehouse-Number-Specific Settings | Configure Cycle Counting**

Here, enter the warehouse number, CC indicators, interval for physical inventories in workdays, and the allowed buffer time.

Cycle Counting Counting Cycle

War...	CC Ind.	InPl	BT
SEWM	A	30	5
SEWM	B	60	5
SEWM	C	90	5

The "Fix" check box in the general data section indicates that the CC indicator is fixed and should not be changed by slotting function.

Backflush Withdrawal: This is used to specify that the product is consumed automatically at the time of production order confirmation and not explicitly issued to the production order.

Correlation Fix: This information is used when creating kits with value added services (VAS) orders. If the quantities have a fixed correlation, the quantity of the kit components is automatically adjusted if the kit header quantity is changed. If the quantity correlation is not fixed, the quantities are not adjusted automatically.

Consumption-Relevant for VAS: It defines the consumption relevance for VAS auxiliary products. If the product is an auxiliary product and consumption is to be posted at the time of VAS order confirmation, this indicator needs to be checked.

To consume the stock of the auxiliary products during the VAS order confirmation, you also have to assign a storage bin to the VAS work center.

Documentary Batch: This indicator specifies whether the product is documentary batch relevant or not. It is covered in more detail in chapter 8.

Putaway Control Indicator: This indicator defines the number of storage types that are relevant for the putaway of the product. It can be used to specify that during putaway, certain products are put away only in certain storage types. The indicator assigned in the product master helps to search the appropriate storage types during product putaway.

Putaway Control Indicators can be defined in **SPRO | IMG | Extended Warehouse Management | Goods Receipt Process | Strategies | Storage Type Search | Define Putaway Control Indicator**

Putaway Control Indicator			
War...	PACI	Description	Storage T...
SEWM	HEVY	Heavy Products	
SEWM	HVPR	High Value Products	
SEWM	LVPR	Low Value Products	
SEWM	SMAL	Small Products	

Later, in chapter 14, the storage type search sequence will be covered in more detail.

Storage Section Indicator: Like the putaway control indicator, the storage section indicator is used to determine appropriate storage sections during putaway.

Menu Path: SPRO | IMG | Extended Warehouse Management | Goods Receipt Process | Strategies | Storage Section Search | Create Storage Section Indicators

Storage Section Indicators		
War...	SecIn	Description
SEWM	SMAL	Small Parts
SEWM	HEVY	Heavy Parts
SEWM	HVAL	High Value Parts

Planned Putaway Control Indicator: This indicator is set when the slotting results are saved. Once the slotting run is activated, planned putaway control indicator is copied to the putaway control indicator. If the Fix check box is checked, system will ignore the planned putaway control indicator and will not update the putaway control indicator when the slotting run is activated.

Storage Bin Type: Storage bin type indicator is used to determine appropriate storage bin type during putaway.

Bulk Storage Indicator: This classifies products according to the way they are stored in a bulk storage area. It is used to define how the products can be stacked in the bulk storage bin. This indicator is a decisive factor in the definition of the structure of a block within a bulk storage area. It is applicable only for bulk storage type putaway.

Menu Path: SPRO | IMG | Extended Warehouse Management | Goods Receipt Process | Strategies | Putaway Rules | Storage Behavior: Bulk Storage | Define Bulk Storage Indicators

Bulk Storage Indicator		
War...	BSI	Description
SEWM	05	5 Stacks
SEWM	04	4 Stacks

Stock Removal Indicator: The stock removal indicator is used to determine the appropriate storage types during picking.

Menu Path: SPRO | IMG | Extended Warehouse Management | Goods Issue Process | Strategies | Define Stock Removal Control Indicator

Stock Removal Control Indicator

War	SRCI	Description
SEWM	PICK	Stock Removal Strategy

Two-Step Picking: This indicator is used to specify the relevance of two-step picking. In EWM, you can pick products directly with one step or with two-step picking. If two-step picking is active in EWM for the warehouse number, and product-dependence is defined (the appropriate field in the Extended Warehouse Management view of the product master record indicates two-step picking), this key controls whether or not the two-step method will be used to pick the product.

Staging Area/Door Determination Group: This indicator is used to determine the staging area or doors during loading and unloading activities.

It is defined in **SPRO | IMG | Extended Warehouse Management | Master Data | Staging Areas | Define Staging Area and Door Determination Groups**

Staging Area/Door Determination Group

War	SA/DDetGrp	Description
SEWM	HVAL	High Value Parts (Stg. Group)
SEWM	REGL	Regular Parts (Stg. Group)

To assign staging area groups to the warehouse doors, go to **SPRO | IMG | Extended Warehouse Management | Master Data | Warehouse Door | Assign Staging Area/Door Determination Group to Door**

Staging Area/Door Determination Gro

War	Whse Door	SA/DDetGrp
SEWM	RE01	REGL
SEWM	RE02	REGL
SEWM	RE03	HVAL

In addition to the above config, the following settings have to be defined in the SAP easy access menu.

i. **Define settings for inbound and outbound to determine the staging area and doors**: Transactions are /SCWM/STADET_IN for inbound and /SCWM/STADET_OUT for outbound.

ii. **Access Sequence to Staging Areas and Door Determination**: Access sequence can be defined in transaction /SCWM/STADET_ASS.

All these transactions are available under **SAP Easy Access | SAP menu | Extended Warehouse Management | Settings | Shipping and Receiving**

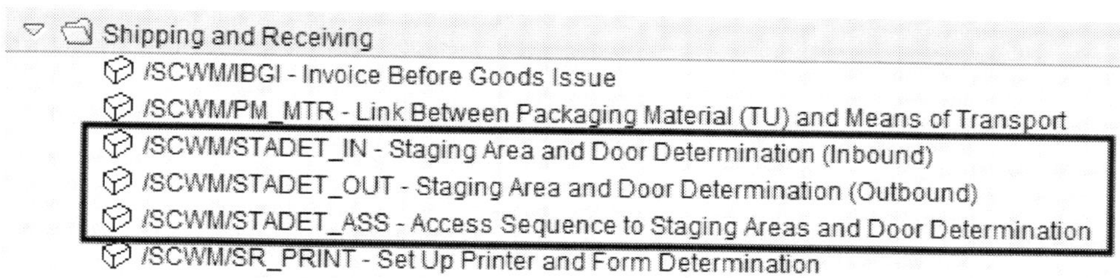

7.1.7 Slotting View

In this view, maintain the parameters that are required for the slotting and rearrangement process.

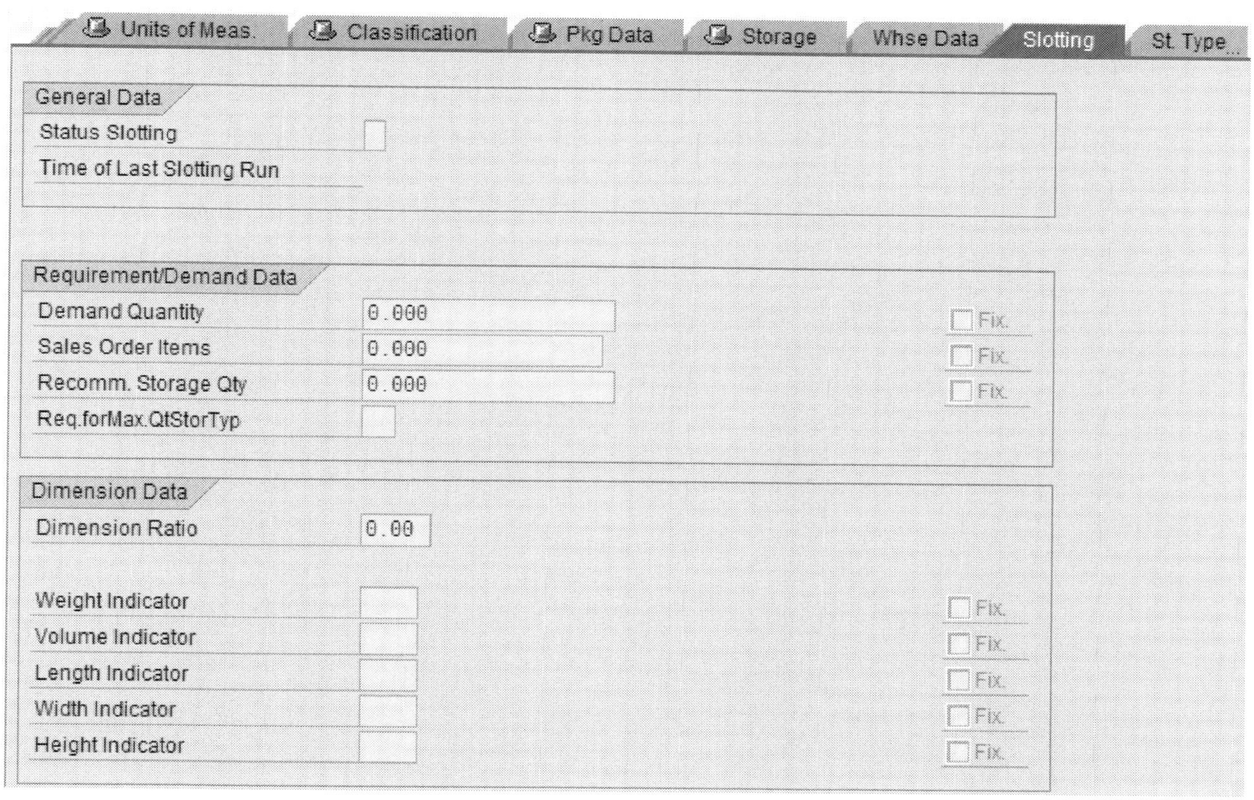

Status Slotting: This indicator specifies whether slotting is allowed or not. The available options are:

i. Product not yet slotted/slotting allowed

ii. Product not yet slotted/slotting not allowed

iii. Product already slotted/reslotting allowed

iv. Product already slotted/reslotting not allowed

Time of Last Slotting Run: This displays the date and time of the last slotting run.

Demand Quantity: This field is used during the slotting run to determine the total quantity that must be shipped from the warehouse during a given time frame. The data in this field can come from APO or through manual input or custom program.

Sales Order Items: Like demand quantity, the sales order item field value is used during the slotting run to determine the total number of sales order items to be shipped from the warehouse during a given time frame. The data in this field can come from APO or through manual input or custom program.

Recommended Storage Quantity: During the slotting run, this information is used to determine the recommended storage quantity in the warehouse for the product.

Request for Calculation of Maximum Quantity in Storage type: Based on the value in this field, the slotting program decides which value to use to calculate the maximum quantity in the storage type. Options available include demand quantity, sales order items, and recommended storage quantity.

7.1.8 Storage Type Data View

In this view, data can be maintained specific to a particular storage type in which a product will be stored. This data generally consists of indicators used for replenishment, stock placement, and removal.

Some indicators are found in both storage type data view and warehouse data view. In such cases, the values defined in the storage type data view are used for bin determination. If the values are not defined in the storage type data view, the values defined in the warehouse data view is used for bin determination. The same logic will apply even with slotting.

If some of the values defined here should not be affected with the slotting results, then the "Fix" indicator should be checked on.

It is possible for products to be stored in more than one storage type. In the storage type data view, more than one storage type data can be defined. To define the storage type data, click on the "Create" button, enter the values in the desired fields, and click on the "Adopt" button. This will display the storage type on the left side of the storage type panel. Data that can be maintained will be displayed on the right hand side of the storage type panel.

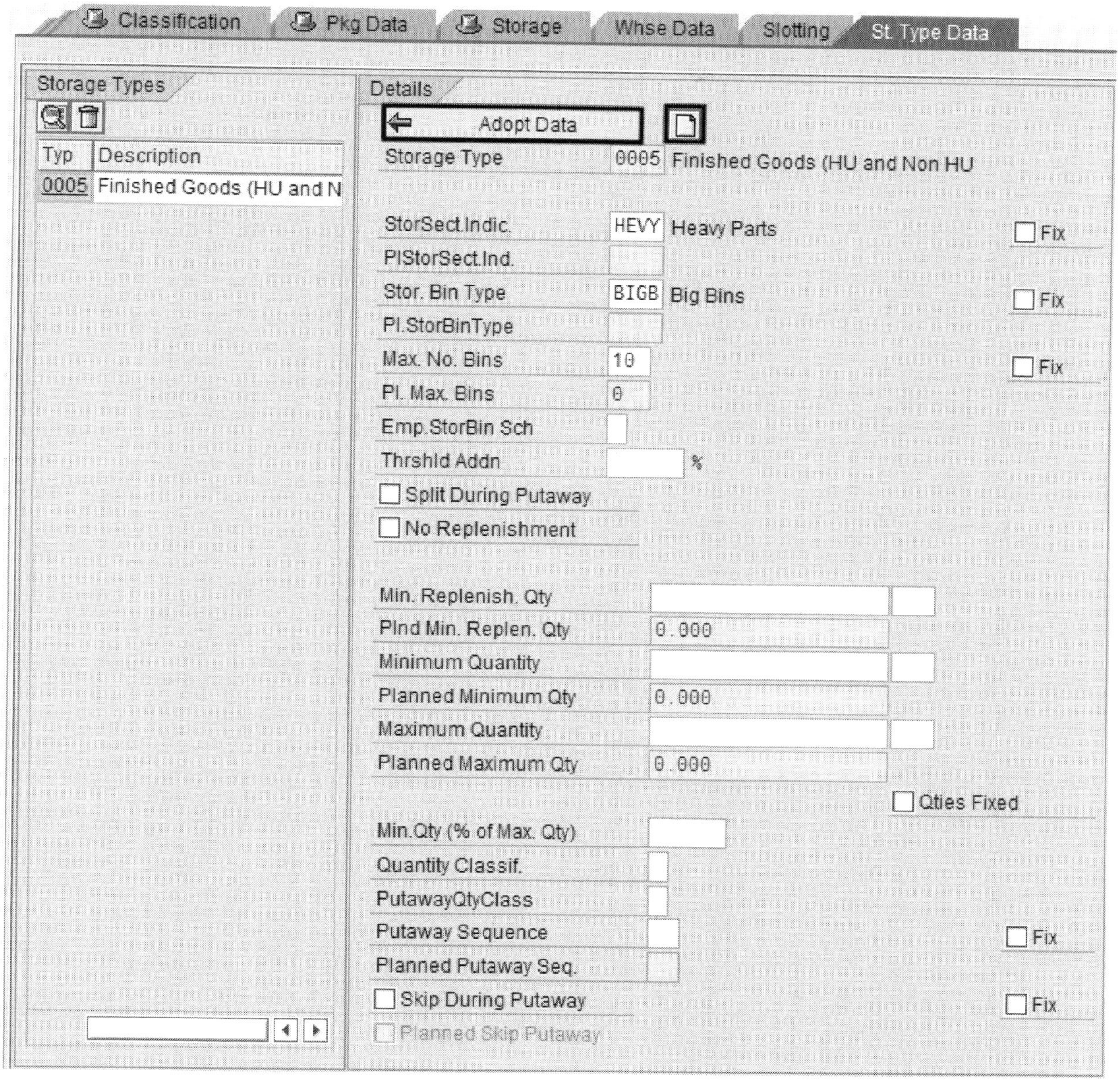

Maximum Number of Bins: This is used to specify the maximum number of bins that products can occupy in a specified storage type. This way you can avoid having one product occupy all or most of the storage type bins, leaving little or no space for other products.

Planned Maximum Number of Bins: The slotting program determines the maximum number of bins, as per the slotting logic.

Empty storage bin search: In addition to the putaway rule, the system will consider the settings defined here to search the empty bin. Here, it is possible to specify how the system should select the empty bins for putaway. The options available include the following:

i. **Sorting According to Definition**: If this option is selected, the system will use the sort field defined in the storage bin master to sort and select the empty bins.

ii. **Near To Fixed Bin:** Empty bins are prioritized according to their closeness to a fixed bin.

iii. **Product Decides**: The setting for the search rule in the product decides the course of action.

Threshold Addition: If a "Split During Putaway" option is active at the storage type, the system will refer to the value of "threshold addition" before the WT created for the split quantity (qty). If the qty expected in the bin is less than the threshold value, the system will not split the putaway qty. This field will avoid unnecessary small qty split, which can reduce the operational efficiency. The threshold value is defined in the percentage of the storage bin capacity.

Split During Putaway: This indicator is effective for the storage type configuration if the value is defined as "product master decides" for the "split during putaway" field.

No Replenishment: It is possible that in the storage type, some products require replenishment and some do not. If the products are not related to replenishment, the check box should be checked.

Minimum Replenishment Qty: This field is used to specify the minimum qty that should be considered for replenishment. Examples include full pallet, full box, and so on.

Planned Minimum Replenishment Qty: The value in this field is populated when the slotting results are saved. Once the results are activated, the value in this field gets copied to the minimum replenishment quantity field.

Minimum Qty: This field is used to specify the minimum quantity of stock that should be stored for this product in the storage type.

Maximum Qty: This field is used to specify the maximum quantity of stock that should be stored for this product in the storage type.

Quantities Fixed: If the slotting program should not change the minimum and maximum quantities, check this check box.

Minimum Quantities (% of Max. Qty): This field maintains the minimum qty in the percentage of maximum qty. In this case, minimum qty is calculated as per the percentage defined.

Putaway Sequence: The value in this field is used to sort the storage types within a storage type group during putaway for bin determination.

Skip during Putaway: If this indicator is checked, this storage type will be skipped during the determination of the destination bin.

Summary

This chapter has explained all about product master data (i.e., different views of product master data and the fields that are applicable to WM). The next chapter will explore how to activate batch management in the EWM system.

Chapter 8: Batch Management

Batch management is used by many industry sectors to differentiate products by characteristic. In ERP, it is a module by itself, tightly integrated with MM, PP, WM, EWM, QM, and SD. Because batches do not have master data attributes, all batch-related information is stored as characteristics. This chapter will discuss the configuration of batch management in the EWM system. It covers configuration for both Documentary and Non-Documentary batches.

8.1 Batch Management in EWM

Batch management in EWM was introduced as part of the EWM 2007 release, which requires ECC 6.0 enhancement pack 3. One of the requirements to activate batch management in EWM is that in the ERP system, batch number needs to be set unique for each material. The characteristics and batches of the batch-managed materials must be transferred from ERP to EWM systems as part of a CIF data transfer process.

Table 8.1A gives an overview of the configuration required in the ERP and EWM systems to effectively communicate batches between these two systems.

Table 8.1A Batch Management Configuration

S. No	Configuration Check List	System	Transportable
1	Define Organizational Area for Class Type BATCH	Both	Yes
2	Assign Organizational Area to Class (TCode CL02)	ERP	No
3	Define Number Range for Batch	Both	No
4	Activate LOG_LE_INTEGRATION business function	ERP	No
5	Maintain EWM Specific Parameters	ERP	Yes
6	Setting for New Batches	EWM	Yes
7	Settings for Warehouse Task Creation	EWM	Yes
8	Activate Documentary Batch in EWM	EWM	Yes
9	Activate Documentary Batch in Product Master	EWM	Not Applicable
10	Distribute Documentary Batch Settings from ERP	EWM	No
11	Define Update Control for Batches	EWM	Yes
12	Create Batches for Products	EWM	Not Applicable
13	Batches in Goods Receipt Process	EWM	Not Applicable
14	Batches in Goods Issue Process	EWM	Not Applicable
15	CIF Batch specific data from ERP to EWM (Tcode CFM1, CFM2)	EWM	Not Applicable
16	Verify Classes and Classification Data	EWM	Not Applicable

8.1.1 Define Organizational Area for Class Type BATCH—Both Systems

In general, the "Organizational Areas" indicator is used to group the batch characteristics by business like Purchasing, Engineering and so on. Here, this functionality is used to identify the EWM-related batch characteristics. This will be useful to filter the EWM-specific batch characteristics in the CIF integration model.

The "Organizational Areas" indicator defined for EWM must be assigned to the appropriate material classes as well as to the characteristics.

Menu Path (in ERP System): SPRO | IMG | Cross-Application Components | Classification System | Classes | Maintain Object Types and Class Types

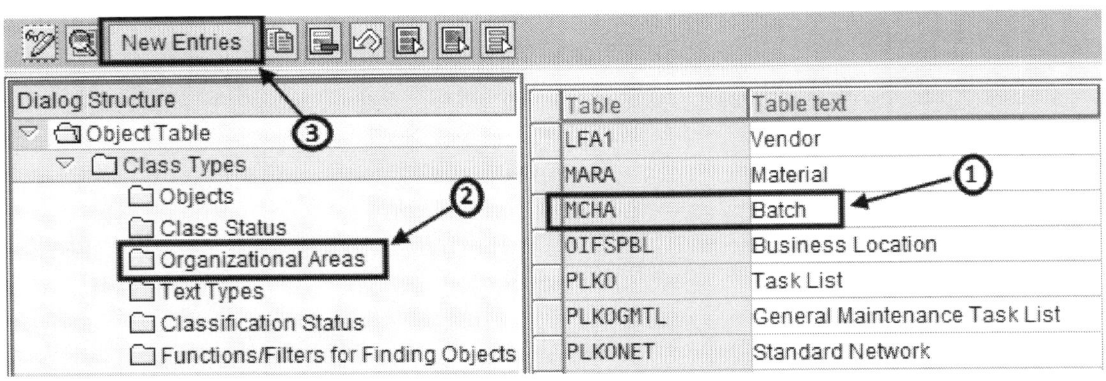

Here, select the table entry MCHA—Batch, and double-click on "Organizational Areas," click the "New Entries" button on the application toolbar, and define the organizational area for EWM in class type 023.

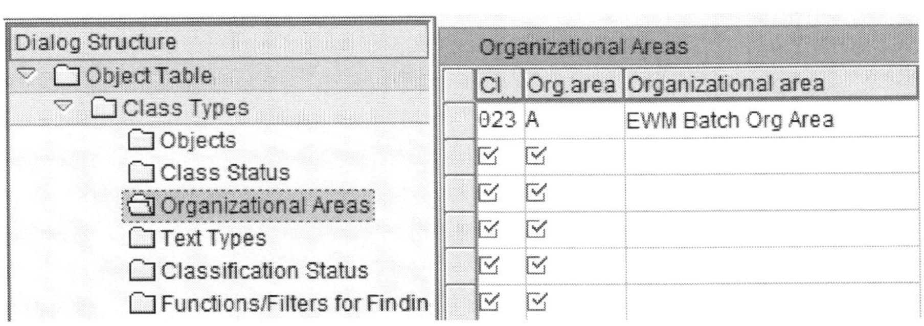

To define the organizational area in the EWM system, follow the menu path **SPRO | IMG | Cross-Application Components | Classification System | Classes | Maintain Object Types and Class Types**

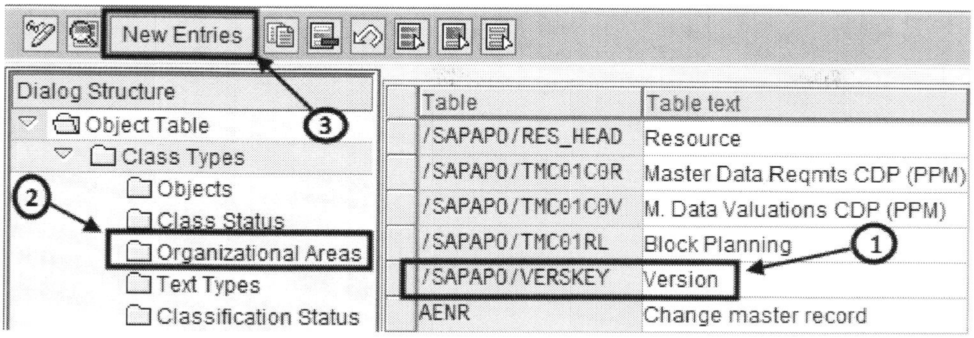

Here, select the table entry "version /SAPAPO/VERSKEY" double-click on "Organizational Areas," click on the "New Entries" button on the application toolbar, and define the organizational area for class type 230.

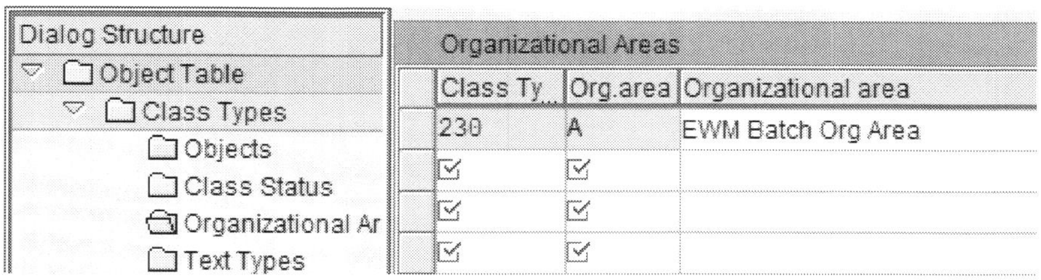

8.1.2 Assign Organizational Area to Class

In the ERP system, after the organizational area is defined, it has to be assigned to the appropriate classes (class type 023) and to the characteristics of the class as shown below. The TCode is CL02.

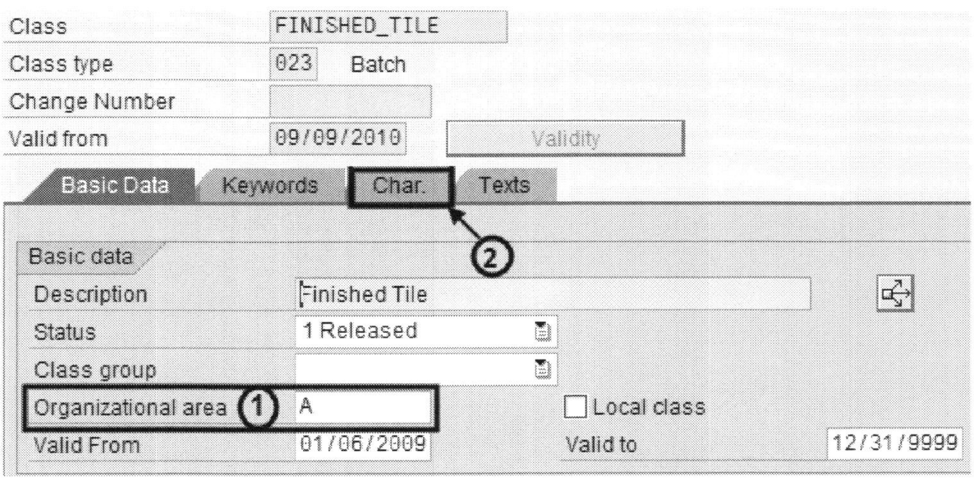

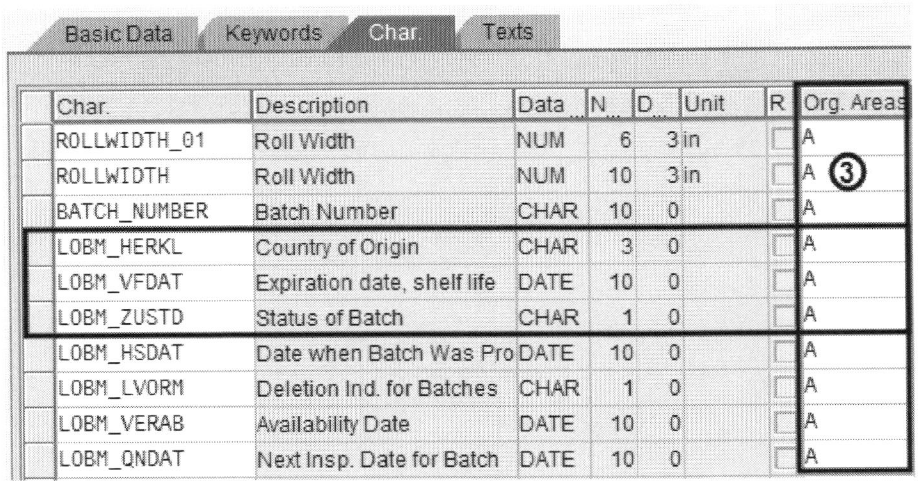

Additionally, if the batches are to be managed with restricted or unrestricted status, it is necessary to add LOBM_ZUSTD batch characteristics to the class. This is required because in EWM, batch status is stored as part of batch characteristics. Characteristics LOBM_HERKL, LOBM_VFDAT, and LOBM_ZUSTD represent the stock attributes in the EWM system. Other available characteristics include the following:

Batch Characteristics
LOBM_HERKL - Country Of Origin
LOBM_VFDAT - Shelf Life Expiration Date
LOBM_ZUSTD - Status of Batch
LOBM_HSDAT – Production Date
LOBM_LVORM - Deletion Ind. for Batches
LOBM_VERAB - Availability Date
LOBM_QNDAT - Next Insp. Date for Batch

8.1.3 Define Number Range for Batch

Number range defined here is used to assign the batch number at the time of batch creation. IT should match ERP batch numbers. The EWM internal number range should be defined as an external ERP number range, and the EWM external number range should be defined as an internal ERP number range in the ERP system.

Menu Path: SPRO | IMG | Extended Warehouse Management | Cross-Process Settings | Batch Management | Define Number Range for Batch

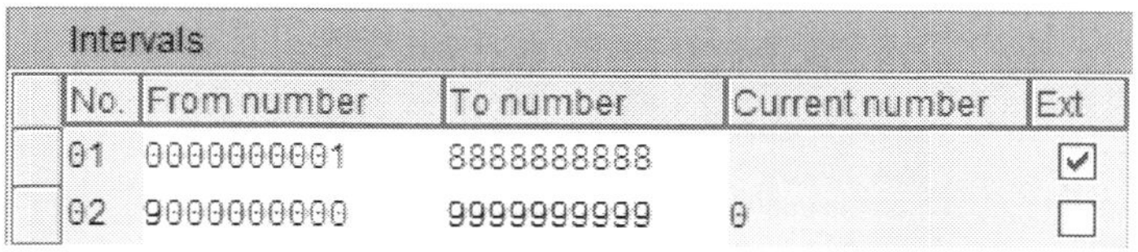

To define number ranges in the ERP system, follow the menu path **SPRO | IMG | Logistics – General | Batch Management | Batch Number Assignment | Maintain Internal Batch Number Assignment Range**

Here, enter the object type "BATCH_CLT," click on the "Number ranges" button on the application toolbar. In the number range intervals screen, click on the "Change Intervals" button to enter or change the existing number range.

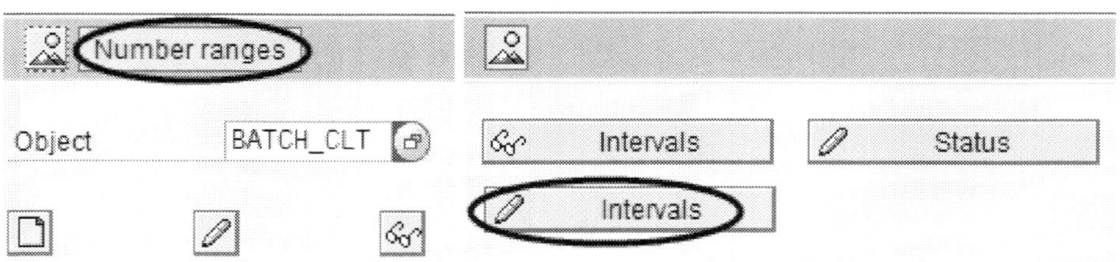

In the "maintain number range interval" screen, define the internal and external number, range as explained above.

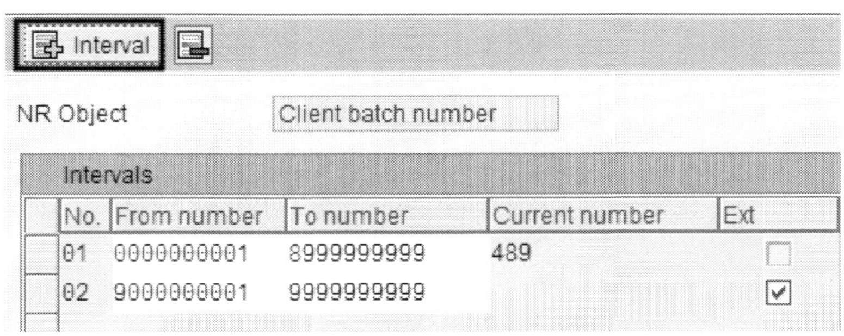

8.1.4 Activate the LOG_LE_INTEGRATION Business Function in ERP

In order to work batch management properly in EWM, it is necessary to check the "BatchDetEW" checkbox in the "Maintain Extended WM-Specific Parameters" in the ERP system for your warehouse. As of ECC 6.0 EHP 3.0, this configuration is not available unless the LOG_LE_INTEGRATION business function is activated in Switch Framework (TCode SFW5).

To activate this business function, login to the ERP system, enter TCode SFW5, click on ENTERPRISE_BUSINESS_FUNCTIONS, locate object LOG_LE_INTEGRATION, check the checkbox in the "Planned Status" column, and click on the "Activate" button. This will create a background job and might take several hours to complete. Once this job is executed successfully, a new column "BatchDetEW" will be displayed in the **Maintain Extended WM-Specific Parameters** configuration menu. If this object is already active in the ERP system, there will be no checkbox displayed in the "Planned Status" column for object LOG_LE_INTEGRATION. In this case, no further activation is required.

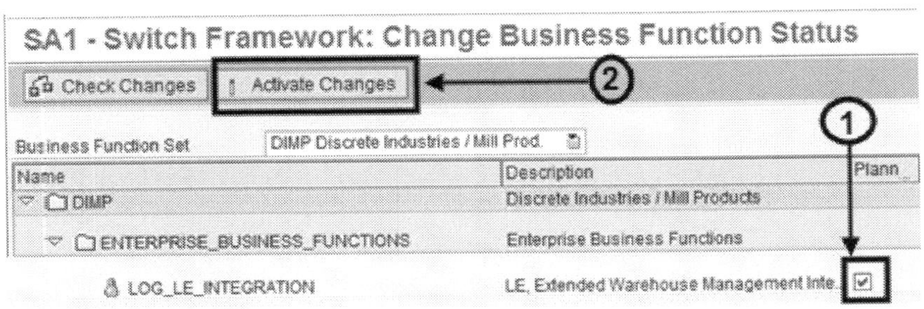

This will activate the following functionalities in ERP system:

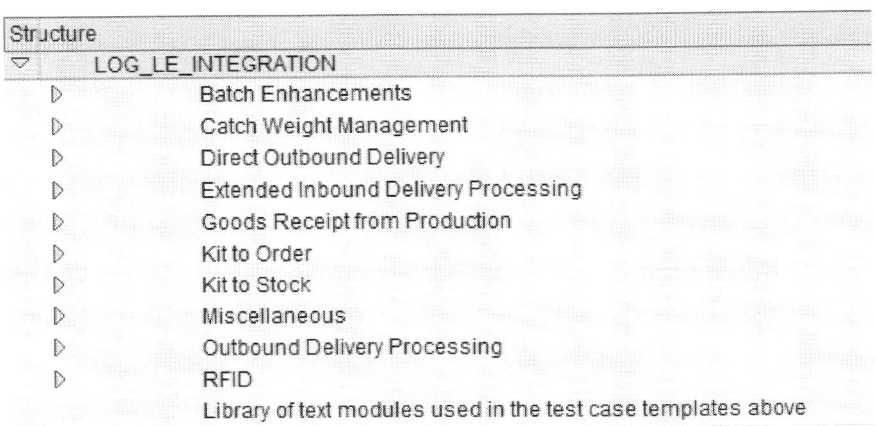

8.1.5 Maintain EWM-Specific Parameters

After activating the LOG_LE_INTEGRATION object, the "BatchDetEW" checkbox must be checked in the "Maintain Extended WM-Specific Parameters" menu.

Menu Path: SPRO | IMG | Logistics Execution | Service Parts Management (SPM) | Integrate SPM with Other Components | Maintain Extended WM-Specific Parameters

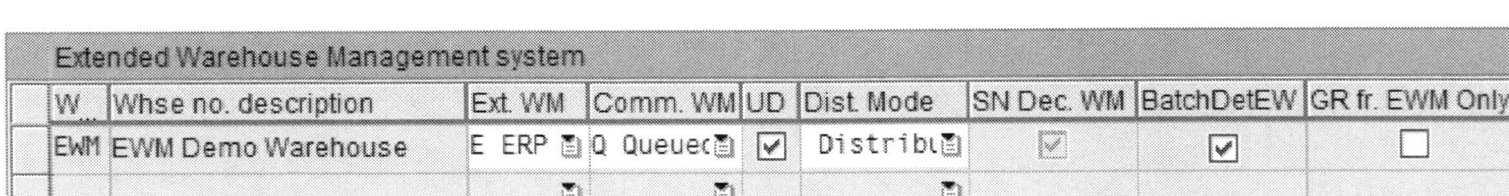

Extended Warehouse Management system

W...	Whse no. description	Ext. WM	Comm. WM	UD	Dist. Mode	SN Dec. WM	BatchDetEW	GR fr. EWM Only
EWM	EWM Demo Warehouse	E ERP	Q Queuec	☑	Distribu	☑	☑	☐

8.1.6 Setting for New Batches

This configuration specifies how the batch will be created and the criteria to display on the classification screen at the time of new batch creation.

Menu Path: SPRO | IMG | Extended Warehouse Management | Cross-Process Settings | Batch Management | Make Setting for Delivery

Doc. Categ.	PDI
Warehouse No.	SEWM
Item Type	IDLV
Document Type	INB

Batch Management and SLED Check in the Delivery

Sel. Criteria	
☐ GdsMvt 'Restricted'	
Create Batch	C Create Batch in the Background, Ext. and Int. Number Assgmt
Classif. Create	Classification Using SAP Default Characteristics Only
Check BBD/SLED	Do Not Lock Item, Minimal Check

8.1.7 Settings for WT Creation

This specifies what the batch status should be for the WPT. The status defined in the WPT will be copied to the WTs at the time of WT creation. If the "Sts Restr." check box is checked, the system will always post the batch into restricted status.

Menu Path: SPRO | IMG | Extended Warehouse Management | Cross-Process Settings | Batch Management | Batch Status Management | Settings for Warehouse Task Creation

Controlling WT Creation for Batch Status

Ware...	Whse P...	Sts Restr.
0001	1010	☑
0001	1011	☑
0001	1012	☐
0001	1013	☐

8.1.8 Activate Documentary Batch in EWM

Documentary batches are more useful for tracking purposes. Batches that are classified as a documentary batch are not inventory managed by the system. Hence, not all of the functionalities of batch management can be used. The system creates a documentary batch as additional information prior to goods receipt. This additional information is then located in the batch field of inbound or outbound delivery.

In this configuration, for the combination of item type and document category, activate the documentary batch management. This enables the tracing of a product without having to manage the stock of the product in batches.

Menu Path: SPRO | IMG | Extended Warehouse Management | Cross-Process Settings | Batch Management | Set Documentary Batch

Item Types: Delivery: Add-On Data

Item Ty...	Doc. ...	Description	Doc. Batch
ITCD	PDI	Inbound Delivery Stock Transfer TCD	☐
IVAS	PDI	Standard Item with VAS	☐
OKC	PDO	Assembly Component Item	☑

8.1.9 Activate Documentary Batch in Product Master

After activating documentary batch management in the EWM system, it must also be activated for the products by setting the value "1" in the "Documentary Batch" field in the "Whse Data" view of the product master data (TCode /SCWM/MAT1). Only then can documentary batch numbers be maintained for products in the inbound and outbound delivery.

It is also possible to specify documentary batch numbers at the time of WT task creation. If it is specified in the WT, the operator has to confirm or enter the documentary batch at the time of WT confirmation or putaway confirmation.

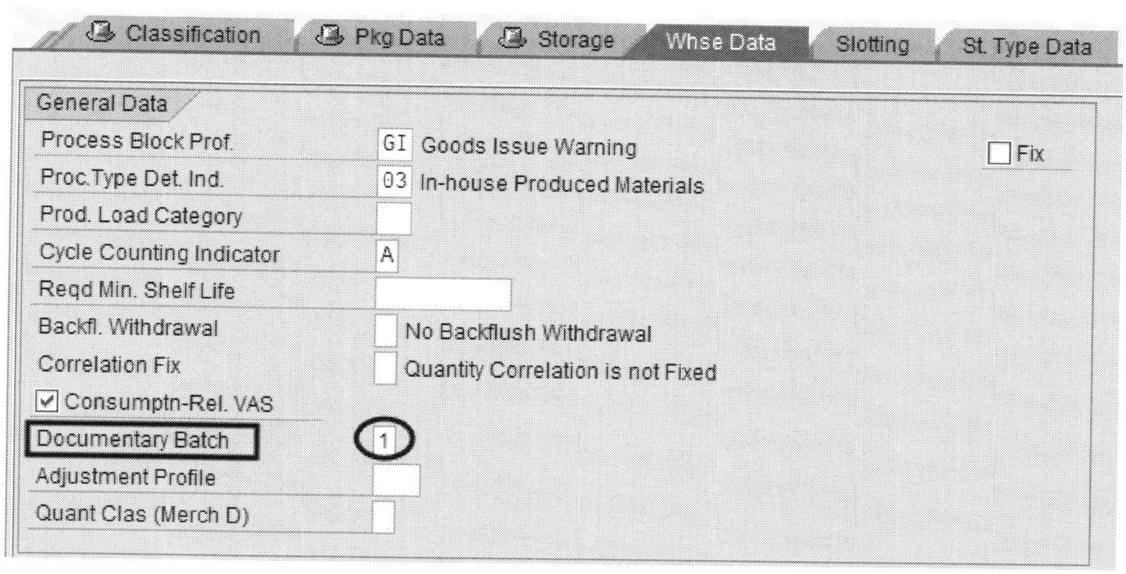

8.1.10 Distribute Documentary Batch Settings from ERP

In ERP, documentary batch can be activated in the configuration (**SPRO | IMG| Logistics – General | Batch Management | Documentary Batches**) and can be distributed to EWM system. Since documentary batch management is not activated at material level this information cannot be transferred as part of CIF. In EWM, TCode **/SCWM/DBATCHSYNC (SAP easy access menu | Extended Warehouse Management | Master Data | Product | Synchronize ERP/EWM Settings for Documentation Batches**) can be used to pull the required information from ERP and update the product master automatically. This transaction can be executed online or in background.

8.1.11 Define Update Control for Batches

Whenever there is a change to the existing batch, or a new batch is created in EWM, the system will automatically make a call to the ERP system to transfer the data in real time. In case of any error (like unavailability of the ERP system, the batch is locked by another application, and so on), the system will display an error to the user. To avoid such interruptions, the update control value can be set to 1 or 2.

Menu Path: SPRO | IMG | Extended Warehouse Management | Cross-Process Settings | Batch Management | Set Update Control (Centralized, Decentralized)

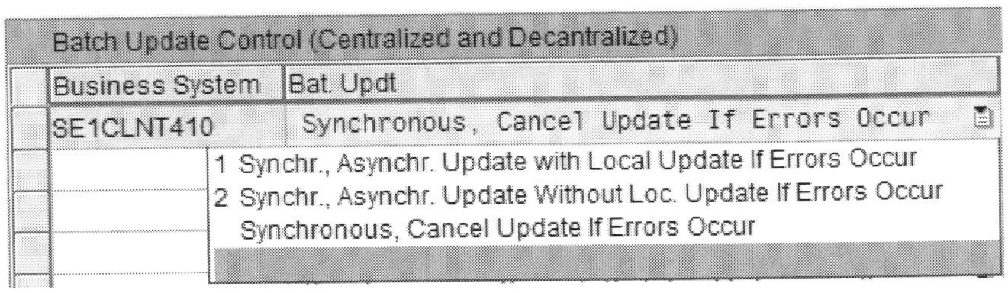

8.1.12 Create Batches for Products

In EWM system, TCode /SCWM/WM_BATCH_MAINT can be used to update or create a new batch for products.

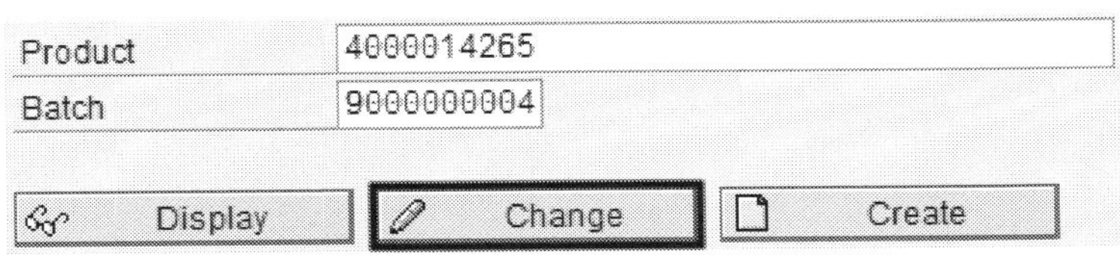

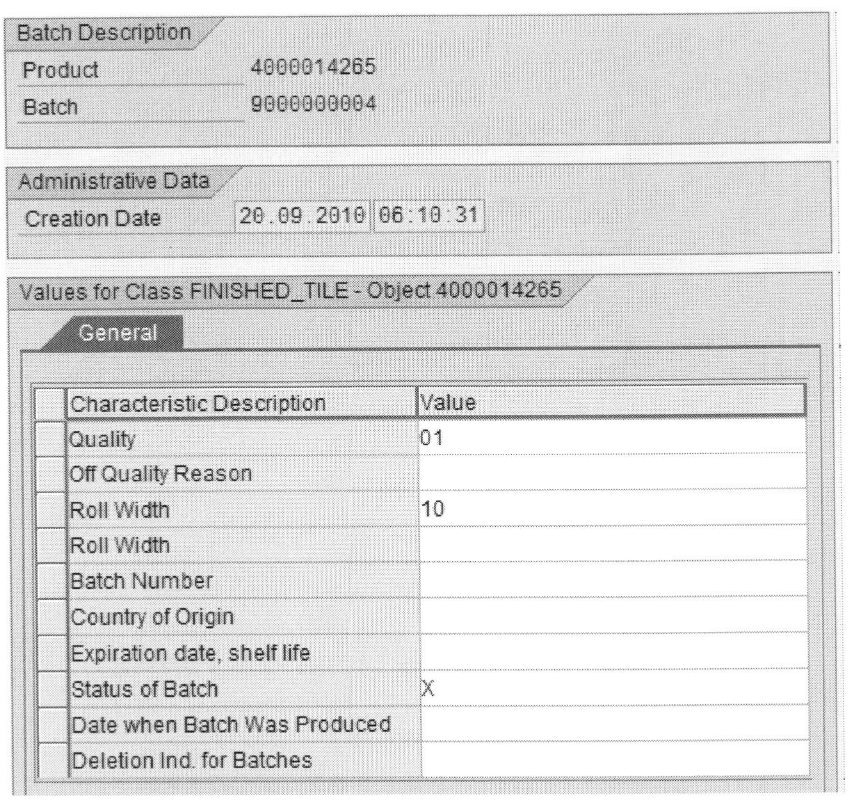

8.1.13 Batches in Goods Receipt Process

In ERP, if a batch number is specified in an inbound delivery, the same will be transferred to the EWM system as part of the delivery item. If batch data is not transferred to the EWM system, it can be created manually in the foreground or automatically in the background (internal number range used) at the time of inbound delivery creation. Once the batch master is created, the products can be put away in the warehouse.

8.1.14 Batches in Goods Issue Process

Picking of batches in EWM can be initiated in the following two ways:

- Specify a batch in the ERP outbound delivery and pick the specified batch in the EWM system. In case of a batch split in EWM, it will be communicated back to the ERP system, and the outbound delivery will be updated.
- Specify batch selection criteria in the ERP outbound delivery (for example, specify the value for one of the batch characteristics). This information will be transferred to the EWM system along with outbound delivery, which will be used to determine the appropriate batch for the picking WT. A batch can be manually specified in the WT, instead of the system deciding on the batch. In such a scenario, the system will ensure that the selection criteria mentioned in the outbound delivery are met. If multiple batches are picked to satisfy the delivery quantity, a batch split will be initiated and updated in the ERP outbound delivery.

8.1.15 CIF Batch-Specific Data from ERP to EWM

The batch classes and characteristics defined in the ERP system should be transferred to the EWM system as part of CIF transfer. In the CIF integration model (TCodes CFM1, CFM2), select "Batches" and "Classes/Characteristics" as shown in the following screenshot. Organization area indicator and class 023 can be used in the filter data option to filter the EWM specific data. CIF integration models are covered in detail in the next section.

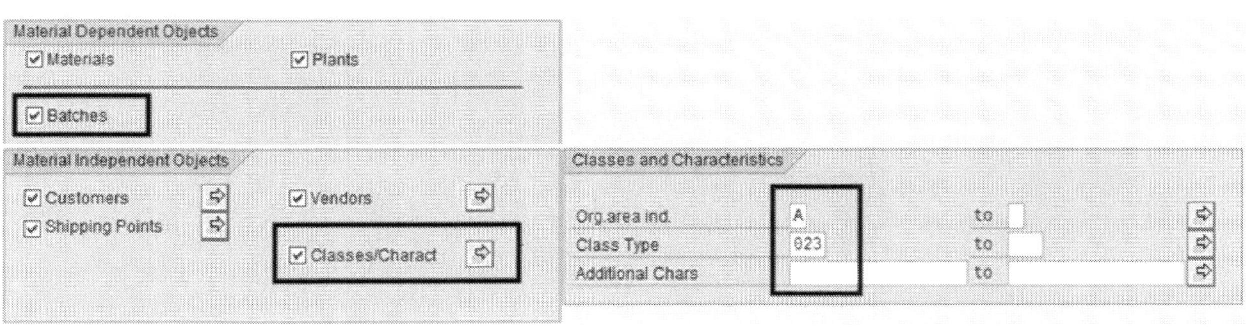

8.1.16 Verify Classes and Classification Data

In the EWM system, after the data transfer, verify the transferred characteristics in TCode CT04 and classes in TCode CL02.

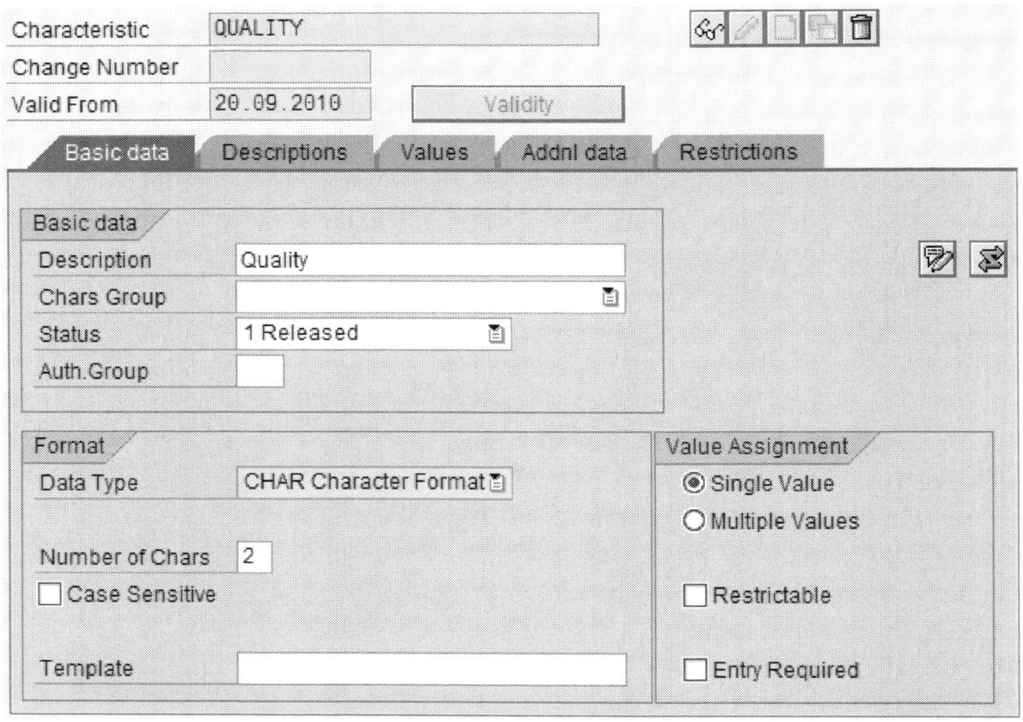

Summary

This chapter has explained batch management functionality in EWM. It has also covered the configuration required in both ERP and EWM systems to create and transfer batch-related information from one system to another. The next chapter will discuss handling units and packaging specifications.

Chapter 9: HUs and Packaging Specifications

In EWM, HUs and packaging specifications are essential for certain types of picking and putaway processes in the warehouse. The topics covered in this chapter include the configuration of HUs, packaging specifications, and how to set up the master data for the packaging specifications in the EWM system.

9.1 Handling Units

An HU is a physical unit consisting of packaging materials (load carriers/packing material) and the goods contained on/in it. It is usually created with a combination of products and packaging materials. It has a unique, scannable identification number that can be generated by the system, or it can be specified externally. The HU ID can be constructed according to industry standards such as EAN 128 or SSCC.

In the warehouse, it is a required feature for some of the process like process-oriented putaways, layout-oriented putaways, value added services, and so on. It contains attributes like identification number, dimension, weight, volume, status, products, quantity, packaging material, and packaging specifications. HU contents can be broadly categorized as header data and item data. Header data contains information like HU ID, packaging materials, packaging material type, and so on. Item data contains the details of the products, qty packed, and so on.

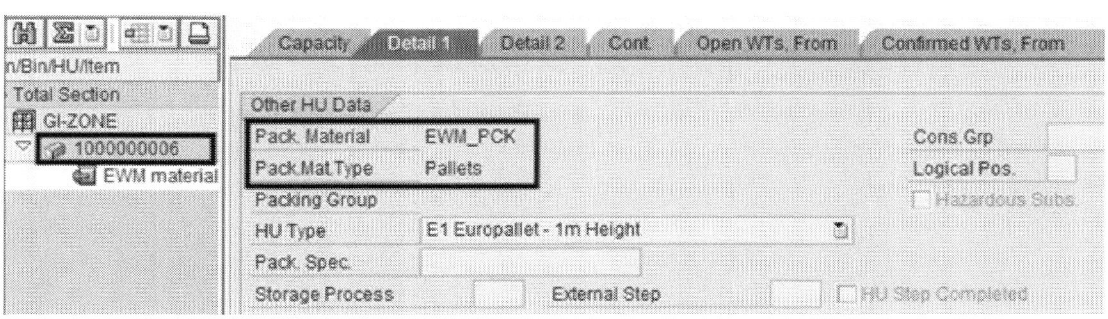

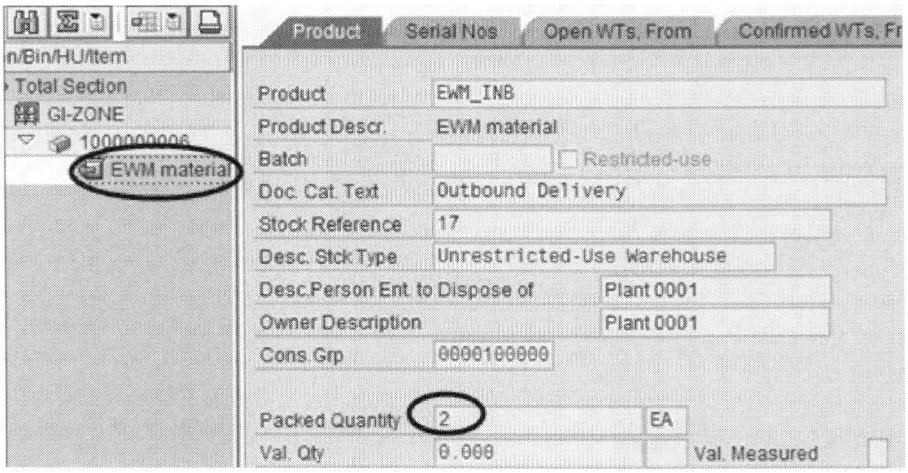

In the system, the action of creating a HU is called "packing." The process to remove the products from HU is called "unpacking." At the time of packing, a unique ID can be explicitly assigned, or the system can internally assign one for the HU, called an HU number.

To create HUs in the warehouse, warehouse product master data must exist for packaging materials, and the "Pkg Data" view must be maintained. The HUs created in the warehouse can be used temporarily only for internal processes and can be deleted when the products are finally put away in the bin or can be retained in the bin and used at the time picking, depending on the storage type settings. They can also be communicated to the ERP outbound delivery at the time of post goods issue (PGI). In order to retain HU numbers in the warehouse bin, storage type should be configured to allow HUs. In case of yard and transportation management, HU IDs are created internally by the system, which represents the vehicle and the content.

Table 9.1A provides an overview of the HU configuration. The number range configuration is not transportable automatically and may be required to maintain every client.

9.1A HU Configuration

S. No	Configuration Check List	TCode	Transportable
1	Define Number Range for HU Identification	SPRO	No
2	Define Packaging Material Types	SPRO	Yes
3	Assign Number Range Intervals to Packaging Material Types	SPRO	Yes
4	Define Packing Groups for Products	SPRO	Yes
5	Maintain Allowed Packaging Material Types for Packing Group	SPRO	Yes
6	Define HU Types	SPRO	Yes
7	Define HU Type Groups	SPRO	Yes
8	Assign Default HU Type and HU Group for Warehouse	SPRO	Yes
9	Define HU Types for Each Storage Type	SPRO	Yes

9.1.1 Define Number Range for HU Identification

In order to create handling units in the warehouse, the number ranges for HUs must be defined and assigned to the packaging material types. To avoid errors during the data transfer, the internal number ranges of EWM should be defined as external number ranges in ERP, and internal number ranges of the ERP system should be defined as external number ranges in the EWM system.

Menu Path: SPRO | Extended Warehouse Management | Cross-Process Settings | Handling Units| External Identification | Define Number Range for HU Identification

9.1.2 Define Packaging Material Types

The packaging material type groups the packaging materials and contains the settings that are valid for the relevant packaging material. The system uses the number range assigned to the packaging material type to generate the HU number.

The controls available in packaging material types include the following:

- **Packaging material category**: The packaging material category specifies the type of packaging material that this packaging material type is. Examples include auxiliary types, vehicle, transportation unit, and so on. The auxiliary packaging material category cannot be used to generate HU number. It is used to categorize packaging material like plastic wrap, box lids which are not used as the main packaging materials. The most widely used category is "C Packaging Materials."
- **Variable tare weight**: This indicates that the tare weight of a packaging material is variable. This means that the tare weight is adjusted when the total weight of a handling unit changes.
- **Number assignment**: The type of number range assigned here controls the generation of the HU number when a handling unit is created with this packaging material type.
- **Closed**: Indicates whether the packaging material is a closed package.
- **Status profile**: Can be used to assign a custom user status profile for better control of handling unit usage.
- **Print Determ. Pro**: This is used for printing the HU.
- **Size**: Max. number of nesting allowed for HU.
- **Delete**: Indicates how the system is designed to manage empty HUs. This indicator controls whether
    i. The bin also becomes empty: This is recommended for pallets and boxes that, in principle, no longer occupy the bin when they are empty.
    ii. The bin is still occupied by the empty HU and must first be emptied by a WT.

Menu Path: **SPRO | Extended Warehouse Management | Cross-Process Settings | Handling Units| Basics | Define Packaging Material Types**

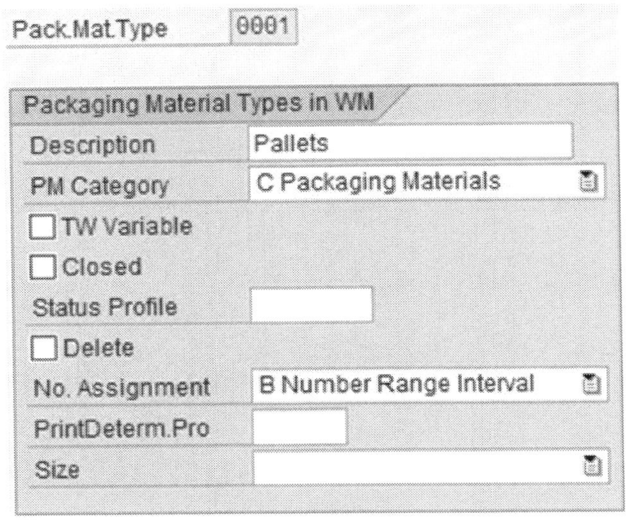

9.1.3 Assign Number Range Intervals to Packaging Material Types

In order to generate HU numbers in the packing process, internal or external number ranges must be assigned to the packaging material type. For an external number range, the user has to specify the HU number. With an internal number range, the system will automatically assign a HU number at the time of packing.

Menu Path: **SPRO | Extended Warehouse Management | Cross-Process Settings | Handling Units| External Identification | Assign Number Range Intervals to Packaging Material Types**

9.1.4 Define Packing Groups for Products

Packing group refers to the grouping of products that have similar packing requirements. The values defined here will be used in the product master data in the "Basic Data: Pack under Pkg Data view" section.

Menu Path: **SPRO | Extended Warehouse Management | Cross-Process Settings | Handling Units| Basics | Define Packing Groups for Products**

Packing Groups

PackGrp	Description
PG01	On Pallets
PG02	On Container

9.1.5 Maintain Allowed Packaging Material Types for Packing Group

This specifies what packaging material types are allowed for each packing group. At the time of packing, the system checks if the entered packaging material is allowed for the product based on the packing group specified in the product master.

Menu Path: SPRO | Extended Warehouse Management | Cross-Process Settings | Handling Units| Basics | Maintain Allowed Packaging Material Types for Packing Group

Allowed Pack. Mat. Types

PackGrp	Unit	PkMtT
PG01		0001
PG01		0004
PG01		Y007

9.1.6 Define HU Types

HU types are discussed in detail in chapters 4 and 6. In the EWM system, they can be defined in SPRO **| IMG | Extended Warehouse Management | Cross-Process Settings | Handling Units | Basics | Define HU Types**

9.1.7 Define HU Type Groups

HU type groups can be used to group together similar HU types. They are used as an optional parameter in slotting. During putaway, an HU type check can be activated at the storage-type level. To determine a deconsolidation station, all HU types used must be assigned to the HU type group. HU type groups are mandatory for resource management.

Menu Path: SPRO | Extended Warehouse Management | Cross-Process Settings | Handling Units| Basics | Define HU Type Groups

Warehouse No.	SEWM
HU Type Group	0001

Handling Unit Type Group Definition

Description	Pallets

9.1.8 Assign Default HU Type and HU Group for Warehouse

Here, the default HU type and HU group is assigned to a warehouse.

Menu Path: **SPRO | Extended Warehouse Management | Cross-Process Settings | Handling Units| Basics | Define HU Types for Each Warehouse Number and Assign HU Type Group**

Here, enter the warehouse number, HU type, and HU type group.

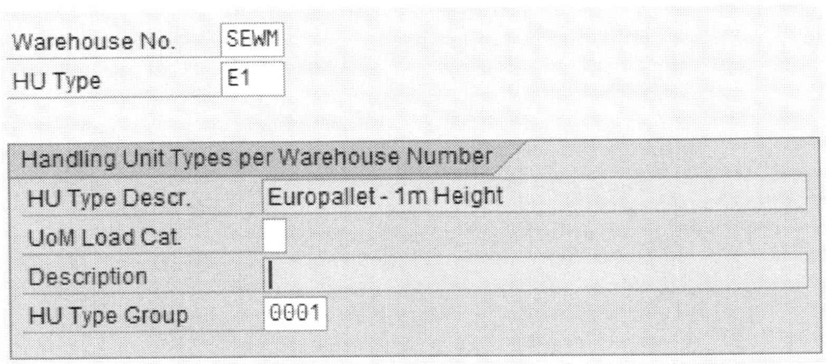

9.1.9 Define HU Types for Each Storage Type

This menu defines the allowed HU types for each storage type. In EWM, the total number of permitted HU types for a storage type is 30. This configuration is required only if the HU type check box is active in the storage type.

Menu Path: **SPRO | Extended Warehouse Management | Cross-Process Settings | Handling Units| Basics | Define HU Types for Each Storage Type**

HU Types per Storage Type

WhN	Typ	HU Ty...	HU Ty...	HU Ty...	HU Ty...	HU Ty...
SEWM	0005	E1	E2			
SEWM	0001	E1	E2	STPL	WDPL	

9.2 Packaging Specifications

Packaging specifications are another set of important master data in EWM. This is used to define the packing requirements for products to be put away and transported. Internally, the packing specifications use the Integrated Product and Process Engineering (iPPE) engine to store the packing specifications. Once they are configured, a condition technique is used to determine its application. Other than EWM, supplier network collaboration (SNC) and service parts planning applications also use the packaging specifications for automatic HU creation, for inbound delivery in SNC and in rounding rules in service parts planning.

Table 9.2A shows an overview of the usage, structure, and configuration of packaging specifications.

9.2A Packaging Specification Configuration			
S. No	Configuration Check List	TCode	Transportable
1	Usage of the Packaging Specifications	N/A	N/A
2	Packaging Specification Structure	N/A	N/A
3	Define Number Range for Packaging Specification	SPRO	No
4	Define General Packaging Specification Parameters	SPRO	Yes
5	Define Work Step Type	SPRO	Yes
6	Assign Work Step Type to Packaging Material Type	SPRO	Yes
7	Define Level Type	SPRO	Yes
8	Define Element Type	SPRO	Yes
9	Assign Packaging Material Type to Element Type	SPRO	Yes
10	Define Level Set	SPRO	Yes
11	Define Packaging Specification Group	SPRO	Yes
12	Define Access Sequences	SPRO	Yes
13	Define Condition Types	SPRO	Yes
14	Define Determination Procedure	SPRO	Yes
15	Create Condition Maintenance Group	SPRO	Yes
16	Create Packaging Specification	SPRO	Yes
17	Determination of Packaging Specification	SPRO	Yes

9.2.1 Usage of Packaging Specifications

In EWM, packaging specifications can be used not only to determine how the products should be palletized; but also they can also be used extensively in the packing process to provide information on how products should be packed into HUs, what packaging and auxiliary materials to use, how much qty, and so on. This information can also be printed as instructions to the operator.

In EWM, packaging specifications are used in the following processes:

i. Automatic packing for inbound delivery
ii. Packing in the work center
iii. Packing during putaway and picking WTs confirmation
iv. Slotting
v. Packaging material determination in the WO creation, or during deconsolidation.
vi. Palletization
vii. Packing using RF framework
viii. Deconsolidation using RF framework

One of the most common usages of packaging specifications is to specify how products are palletized in the warehouse. For example, in electronic goods storage warehouse, printing and labeling a pallet ID for, say, refrigerators may not add much value to the warehouse. But the palletization of refrigerators may be important and can influence how many refrigerators can be assigned to the storage bin and how many WTs should be created during the putaway process. For example, if one qty of refrigerator per pallet is specified, but fifty quantities is received, the system will determine fifty bins and split the quantity into fifty WTs.

Most importantly, the introduction of a good deal of flexibility into the packaging specification determination helps the warehouse in many ways. Using the condition techniques, a warehouse can decide how the same product should be packed or palletized differently for different customers, vendors, and so on. It also resolves one of the known limitations of the storage unit: a maximum of three different types of palletization data can be defined in WM view 2 in the material master.

The following section will cover the structure and configuration of packaging specification and HU in detail.

9.2.2 Packaging Specification Structure

It is important to understand the structure of packaging specifications before they are configured in the EWM system. The main components of packaging specification structure are header, contents, levels, element group, elements, packaging materials, and the steps. Diagram 9.1.2A makes the structure easy to understand.

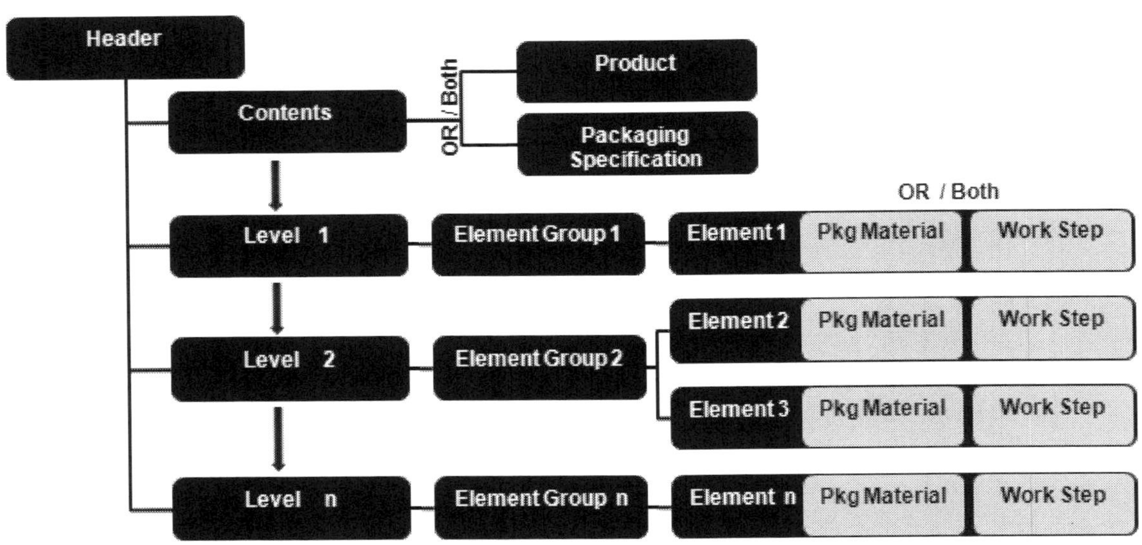

Diagram 9.1.2A – Packaging Specification

There can be many levels in the packaging specification.

Header: The header contains information like name, description, status, and other administrative information such as the user who created it, creation date and so on.

Content: The content can contain only the product (or products) to be packed or a reference to another packing specification or both.

Level: Packaging specifications can have one or more levels. Each level contains the overall instructions for packing a previous level. If the current level is the first level in a packaging specification, the level quantity describes the number of units that should be packed in this level.

Element Group: Each level consists of only one element group. The element group can have more than one element. Element groups can be created separately and assigned to the packaging specifications or can be defined at the time of creating packaging specifications. Elements groups, once created, can be reused in multiple packaging specifications.

Elements: An element can consist of packaging material, a work step, or both. Packaging materials have to be defined as products in EWM systems. Work steps can be simply texts or instructions for packing defined with a code, which can be reused in other packing specifications. In EWM, work steps can be defined separately and assigned in many packaging specifications.

9.2.3 Define Number Range for Packaging Specification

In EWM, every packaging specification is stored with a unique identification number. This identification number can be entered manually, or the system can generate it automatically when the packaging specifications are created from the internal number range. The same rule applies to element group and work steps. Hence, it is necessary to decide what will be the number ranges. If necessary, up to three different sets of number ranges can be defined (i.e., one for element group, one for work step, and one for packaging specification), or one number range can be used for all three.

Menu Path: SPRO | Extended Warehouse Management | Master Data | Packaging Specification | Define Number Range for Packaging Specification

NR Object: Packaging Spec.

Intervals

No.	From number	To number	Current numb...	Ext
01	00000000000000000001	00000000000000009999	0	☐
02	00000000000000010000	00000000000000040000	0	☐
03	00000000000000040001	00000000000000060000	0	☐
09	00000000000000090000	00000000000000099999		☑

9.2.4 Define General Packaging Specification Parameters

The previous menu showed how to define a number range. In this menu, that number range is assigned to the work step and element group. Here, the form name can also be assigned to print the packaging specifications.

Menu Path: SPRO | Extended Warehouse Management | Master Data | Packaging Specification | Define General Packaging Specification Parameters

Global attributes for packaging specifications	
NR Work Step	02
NR Elem. Group	03
Max.Rows	900
Alert Category	SCM_ANOT
Form Name	
PDF form name	
Document MS	
Document Object	
☑ Save Det. Analysis	
☑ Change Documents	

9.2.5 Define Work Step Type

As mentioned earlier, work steps can be either instructions or certain actions in the packing activity. The work step types ensure a logical grouping of work steps. Each work step can be assigned to exactly one work step type. This means that similar work steps can be assigned to the same work step type. The work step type can be used to restrict permissions of work steps for a packaging material. These permissions are ensured by assigning work steps to packaging material types.

Menu Path: SPRO | Extended Warehouse Management | Master Data | Packaging Specification | Maintain Structure of Packaging Specification | Define Work Step Type

Customizing: Work Step Type

Work Step Type	Description
0001	Plan Packing
0002	Packing

9.2.6 Assign Work Step Type to Packaging Material Type

Permitted work step types can be assigned to a packaging material type. The system takes this assignment into account during maintenance of packing instructions. Several work step types can be assigned to a packaging material type. If no work steps are assigned to a packaging material type, then all work step types are permitted during maintenance of a level element in a packing instruction, a packaging material from the given packaging material type is being used.

Menu Path: **SPRO | Extended Warehouse Management | Master Data | Packaging Specification | Maintain Structure of Packaging Specification | Assign Work Step Type to Packaging Material Type**

Assign Work Step Type to Packaging Material Type

PkMtT	Description	Wor...	Description
YQ01	Box	0001	Plan Packing
YQ01	Box	0002	Packing

9.2.7 Define Level Type

Level type is essential for creating a level set. It consists of settings for level qty, performing entity, HU type, and HU creation. If the current level is the first level in a packaging specification, the level quantity describes the number of units that should be packed in this level. Here, also it can be specified whether a level of this type can be deleted in a packaging specification. An icon can be used to display the symbol for a level of this level type on the packaging specification user interface.

Menu Path: **SPRO | Extended Warehouse Management | Master Data | Packaging Specification | Maintain Structure of Packaging Specification | Define Level Type**

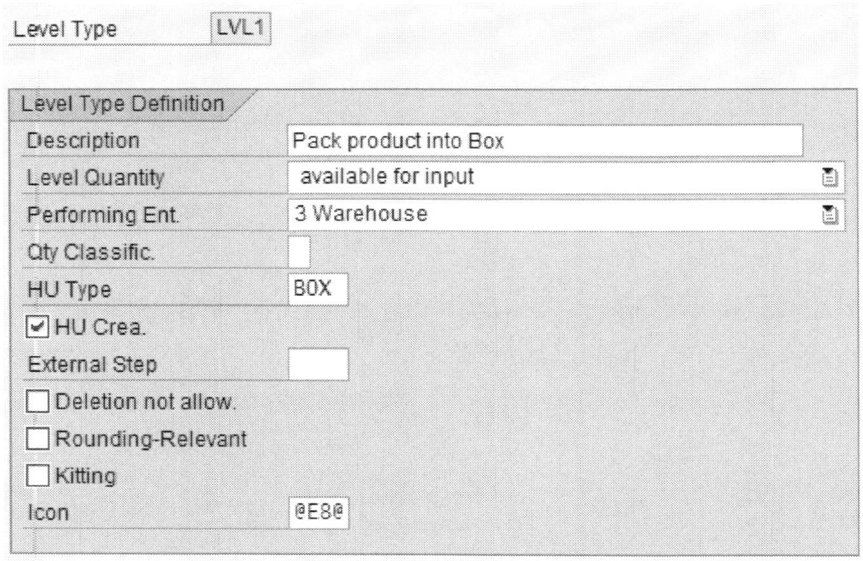

9.2.8 Define Element Type

Ar element type is also required to create a level set. Here, we can specify "HU relevancy", "Icon", and "Delete" indicator "i.e." whether this element can be deleted from the packaging specification. HU relevancy in the element type guides whether or not the system can create a HU number during packing.

Element Type Definition

ET	Description	HU-Rel.	D	Icon
AUX	Auxiliary Packaging Mtrl	2 Auxiliary Packaging Materia	☐	
NRHU	Non Relvent for HU	Not Relevant for HU	☐	
NRWT	Non Relvent but Consider Wei	3 not rel., but consider weig	☐	
PACK	Main Packaging Mtrl	1 Main Packaging Material	☐	@77@

Menu Path: SPRO | Extended Warehouse Management | Master Data | Packaging Specification | Maintain Structure of Packaging Specification | Define Element Type

9.2.9 Assign Packaging Material Type to Element Type

This makes it possible to assign more than one packaging material type to an element type. If packaging material types are assigned to an element type, then only packaging materials that belong to these packaging material types are valid for this level element in a packing instruction. If no packaging material types are assigned to an element type, then all packaging materials are valid in the level element.

Menu Path: SPRO | Extended Warehouse Management | Master Data | Packaging Specification | Maintain Structure of Packaging Specification | Assign Packaging Material Type to Element Type

Assign Packaging Material Type to Level Element Type

ET	Description	PkMtT	Description
PACK	Main Packaging Mtrl	0001	Pallets
PACK	Main Packaging Mtrl	YQ01	Box

9.2.10 Define Level Set

A level set defines the structure of a packaging specification. It consists of level types and element types. It enables us to predefine a uniform structure for packaging specifications in their system. If a user creates a packaging specification with reference to the level set, the system adopts all the default values of the level set to the newly created packaging specification.

Menu Path: SPRO | Extended Warehouse Management | Master Data | Packaging Specification | Maintain Structure of Packaging Specification | Define Level Set

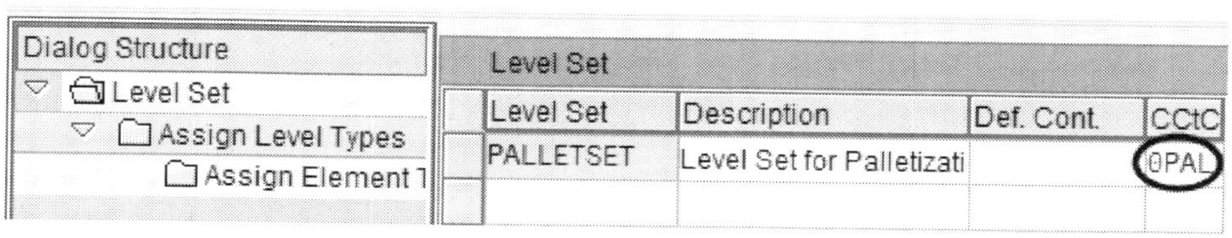

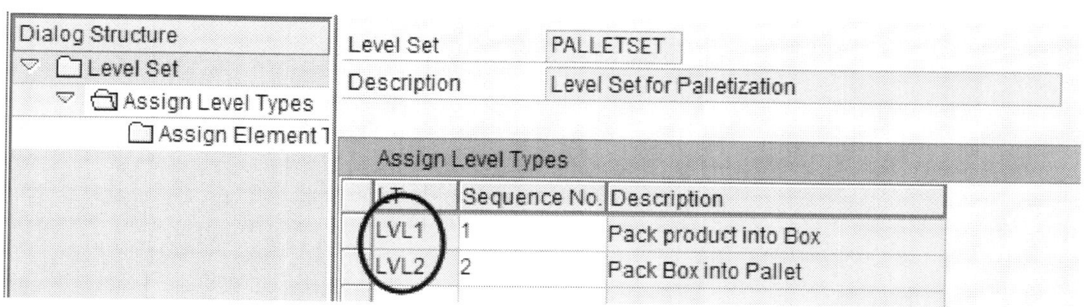

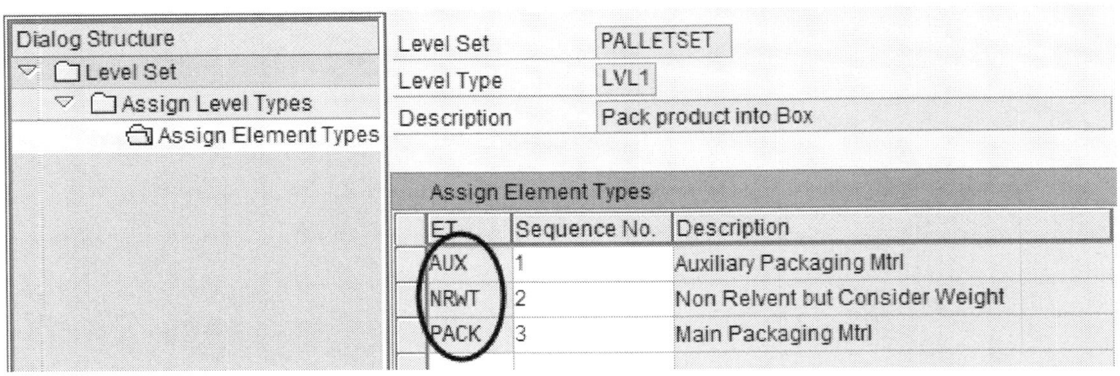

9.2.11 Define Packaging Specification Group

A group consists of a description, the assignment of a number range interval, and a level set. It is used in the authorization object for packaging specifications. The system will use the number range assigned here to uniquely identify each packaging specifications. In case the number range is internal, the system will automatically assign the number from the number range. If it is external, the user has to specify manually at the time of packing.

Menu Path: SPRO | Extended Warehouse Management | Master Data | Packaging Specification | Define Packaging Specification Group

Here, enter the group name; assign the number range and level set and check the "Act. With CT" check box "ON" to respect the condition types.

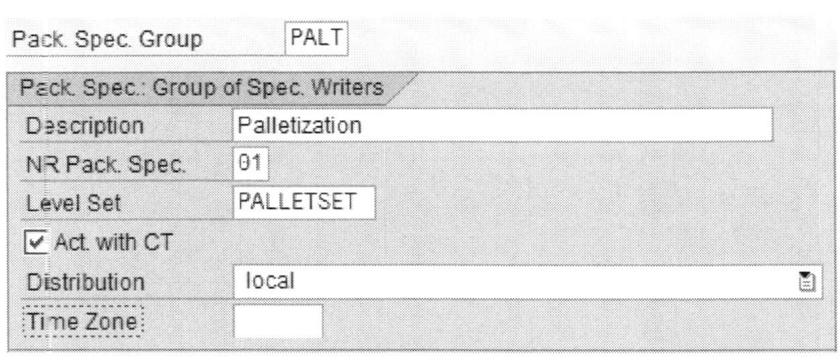

9.2.12 Define Access Sequences

The access sequence is a search strategy that the SAP system uses to search for valid determination records for a packing instruction condition type. Each condition table contains a particular combination of fields that the system uses to search for the condition records. The search sequence should go from specific to general condition records.

For example, in packaging specification determination, it can be set up so that the SAP system first searches for a packing instruction, using only the combination of product and supply chain unit. If no results found, then system can search packing instruction specific for the product.

Menu Path: SPRO | Extended Warehouse Management | Master Data | Packaging Specification | Maintain Structure of Packaging Specification | Define Access Sequences

SAP has delivered access sequences for each of the areas. Users can define these manually or use those delivered by SAP. For palletization, the SAP-delivered access sequence is 0PAL—Palletization Data.

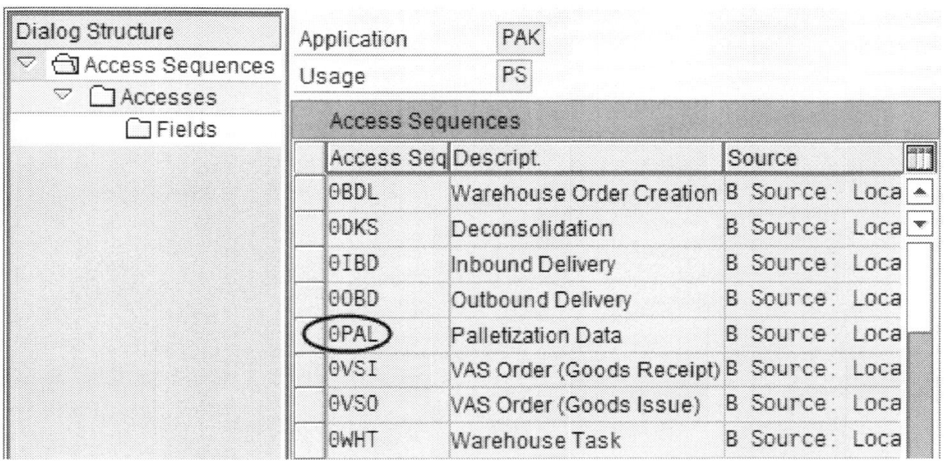

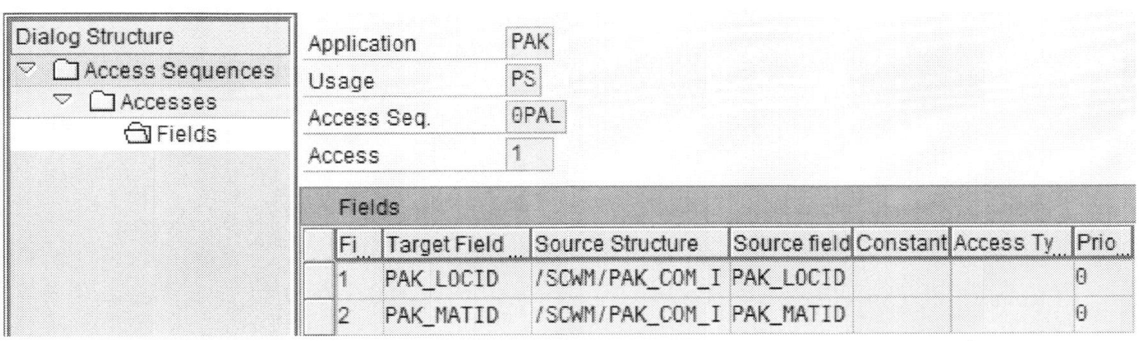

Notes:

The SAP-delivered application for packing is "PAK—Pack. Specification," and the usage is "PS—Packaging Specification." Access sequence, condition types, and determination procedure have to be maintained for both application (PAK) and usage (PS).

9.2.13 Define Condition Types

The condition type is used in SAP for different functions like pricing, output type determination, packaging specification determination, and so on. Under packaging specification, it is used to determine the level set for the product that needs to be packed based on access sequence and condition records maintained in the system. The access sequence contains a list of accesses to condition tables. The condition tables are searched to find the right key combination.

Menu Path: SPRO | Extended Warehouse Management | Master Data | Packaging Specification | Maintain Structure of Packaging Specification | Define Condition Types

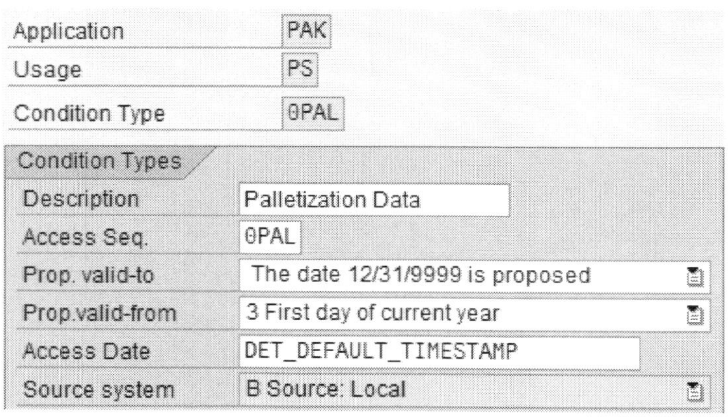

9.2.14 Define Determination Procedure

Packaging specification determination procedure defines which condition types are taken into account and in which order. When determining the packaging specification, the system automatically determines which procedure is valid for a business transaction and takes into account the condition types contained within, one after the other.

Menu Path: SPRO | Extended Warehouse Management | Master Data | Packaging Specification | Determination of Packaging Specifications | Define Determination Procedure

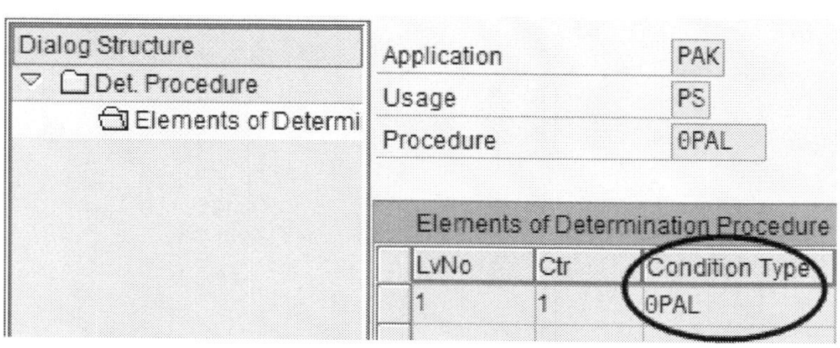

9.2.15 Create Condition Maintenance Group (CMG)

The CMG groups together the condition tables and condition types for condition maintenance. SAP delivered CMG is PAK—Packing Instruction. Here, the application, usage, condition table, and condition types are registered.

Menu Path: SPRO | Extended Warehouse Management | Master Data | Packaging Specification | Determination of Packaging Specifications | Create Condition Maintenance Group

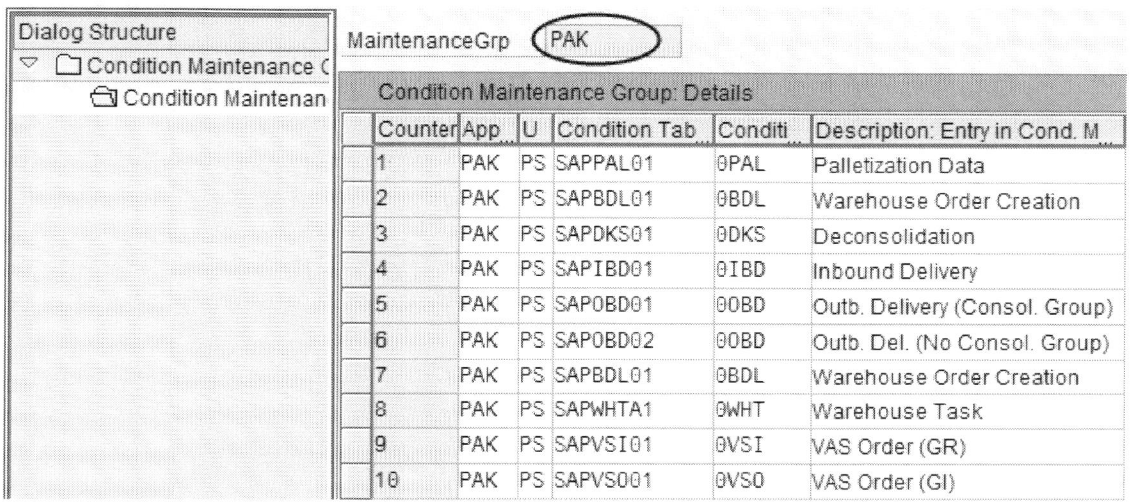

Counter	App...	U	Condition Tab...	Conditi...	Description: Entry in Cond. M...
1	PAK	PS	SAPPAL01	0PAL	Palletization Data
2	PAK	PS	SAPBDL01	0BDL	Warehouse Order Creation
3	PAK	PS	SAPDKS01	0DKS	Deconsolidation
4	PAK	PS	SAPIBD01	0IBD	Inbound Delivery
5	PAK	PS	SAPOBD01	0OBD	Outb. Delivery (Consol. Group)
6	PAK	PS	SAPOBD02	0OBD	Outb. Del. (No Consol. Group)
7	PAK	PS	SAPBDL01	0BDL	Warehouse Order Creation
8	PAK	PS	SAPWHTA1	0WHT	Warehouse Task
9	PAK	PS	SAPVSI01	0VSI	VAS Order (GR)
10	PAK	PS	SAPVSO01	0VSO	VAS Order (GI)

9.2.16 Create Packaging Specifications

The above described configuration maintains the required master data for the packaging specification. This section will cover the master data requirement for packaging specifications. Most of the transactions explained below are not available under SPRO menu. They are part of master data and have to be maintained in the SAP easy access menu.

9.2.16.1 Maintain Packaging Data in Product Master

In order to create packaging specifications, users have to maintain packing groups for products that get packed. In the packaging material, users have to maintain packaging material type and HU type. Following screenshots displays the products master data for packaging and finished products (TCode /SCWM/MAT1).

Master data for product (that needs to be packed):

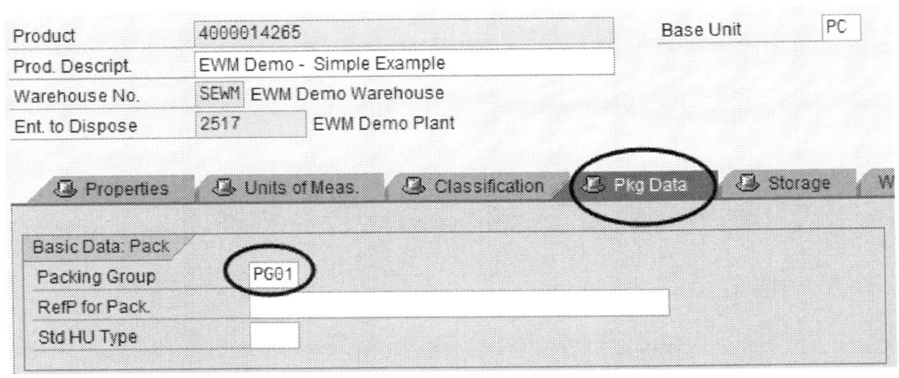

Product master data for packaging material:

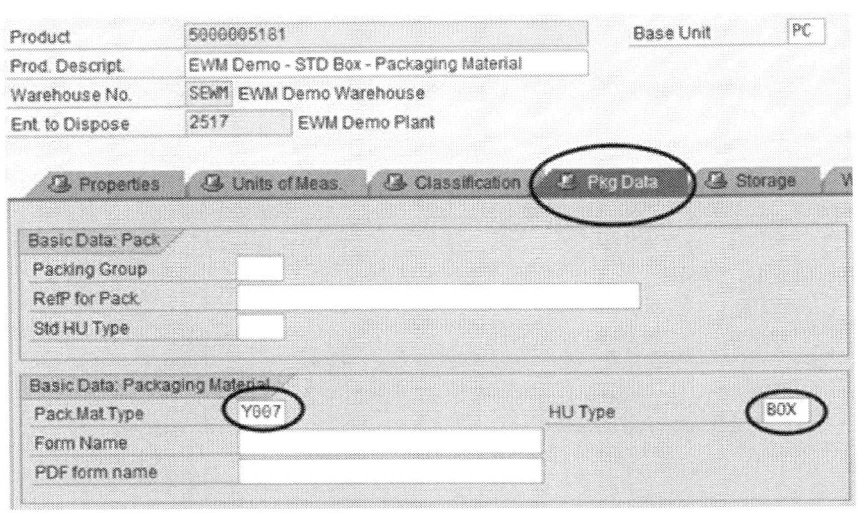

9.2.16.2 Maintain Packaging Work Step

Work steps are another type of master data used in packaging specification. They can be created in menu path **SAP Easy Access | Extended Warehouse Management | Master Data | Packaging Specification | Maintain Packaging Work Step or using TCode /SCWM/PSWORKSTEP**

If the number range assigned to the work step is an external number range, both the work step ID and the work step description must be entered.

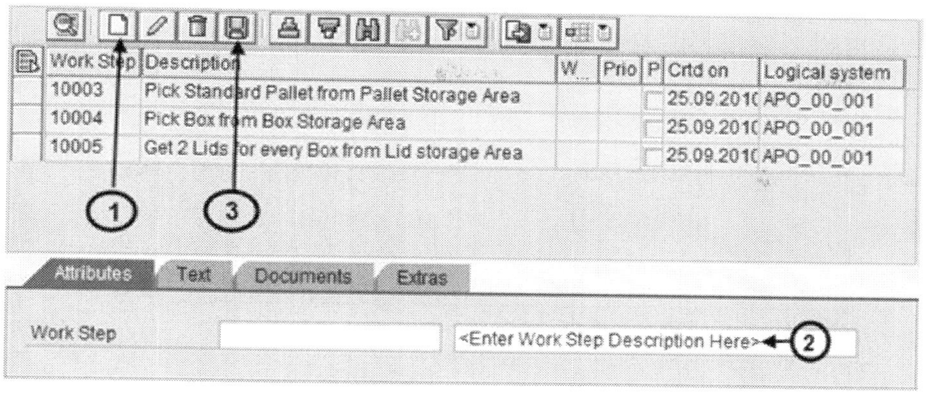

9.2.16.3 Maintain Level Element Group

Once element groups have been created, they can be reused in multiple packaging specifications. In EWM, element groups can be created in menu path **SAP Easy Access | Extended Warehouse Management | Master Data | Packaging Specification | Maintain Level Element Group or using TCode /SCWM/PSEG**.

If the number range assigned to an element group is external, both the element group ID and element group description must be entered.

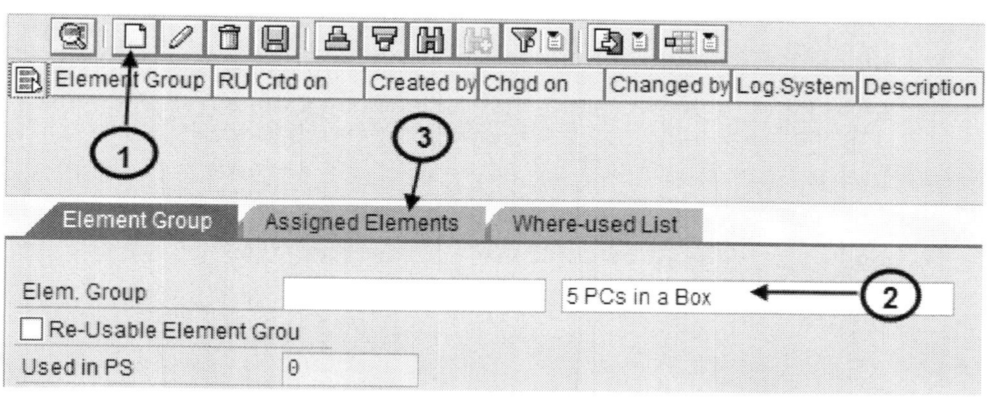

Under "Assigned Elements" tab, enter the element type, packaging material, and work step.

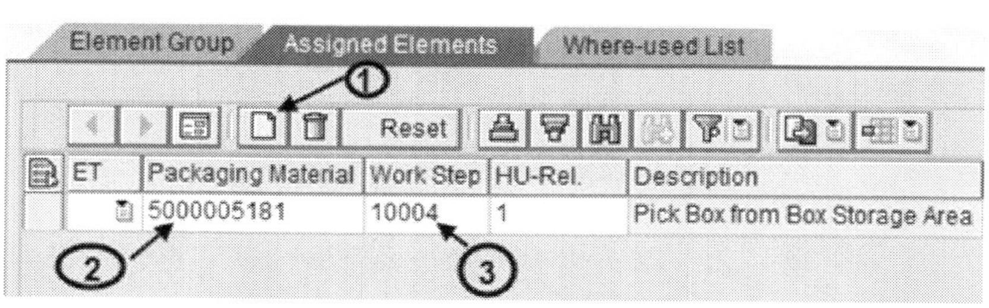

9.2.16.4 Maintain Packaging Specification

Packaging specifications can be created in maintain packaging specification transaction.

Menu path: SAP Easy Access | Extended Warehouse Management | Master Data | Packaging Specification | Maintain Packaging Specification (TCode /SCWM/PACKSPEC)

Here, click on "add new line," select the appropriate PS Group, enter description, and click "Save." This will create a packaging specification with a unique ID.

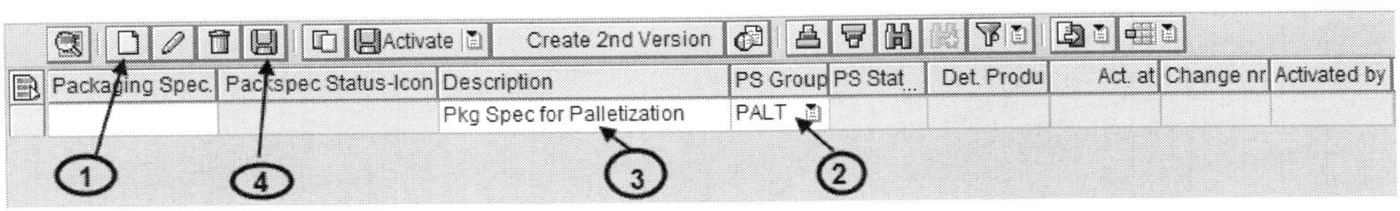

Now, select the packaging specification line and click on the "Details" or "Change" button to maintain the content.

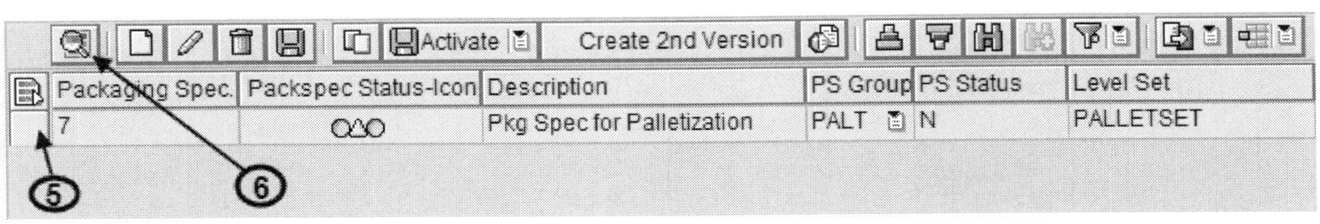

In the determination tab, select the appropriate condition type and enter the appropriate details, like SCU, product, condition sequence, and validity. Hit the "Enter" key to add more records.

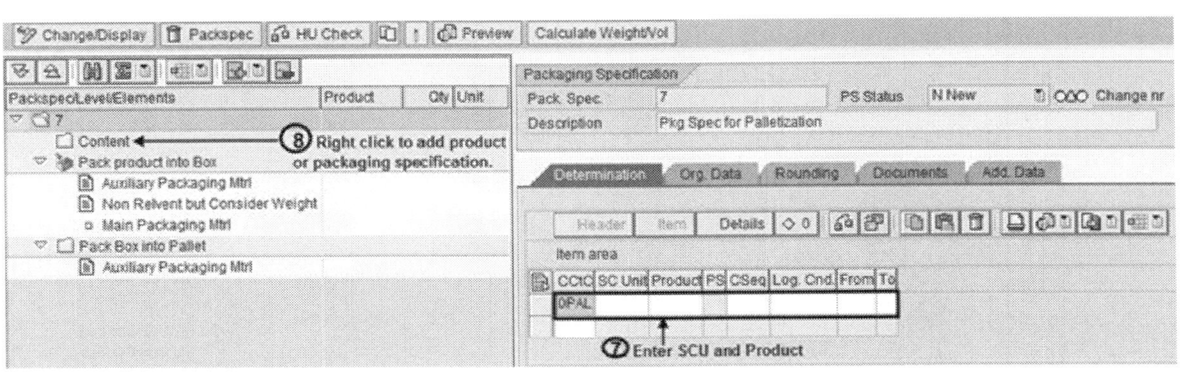

Right-click on the "Content" folder icon and select the product content or packaging specification option. This will add a new option called "Product" or "Packaging specification" under the content folder.

Expand the content to see the added content. Click on the product line under the content folder; enter the product number and the qty that needs to be packed, and click "Save."

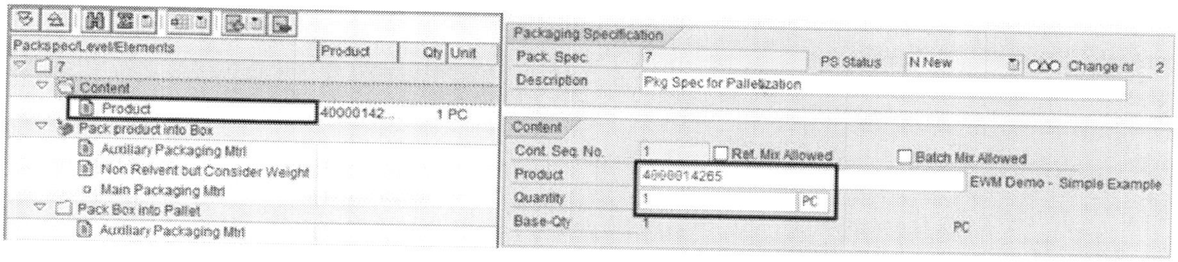

To add level content, double click on the level type. Add the target qty i.e. the pack qty, enter packaging material and or work step. Click "Save." If there are multiple level types in the packaging specification, repeat the instructions in this step for other level types.

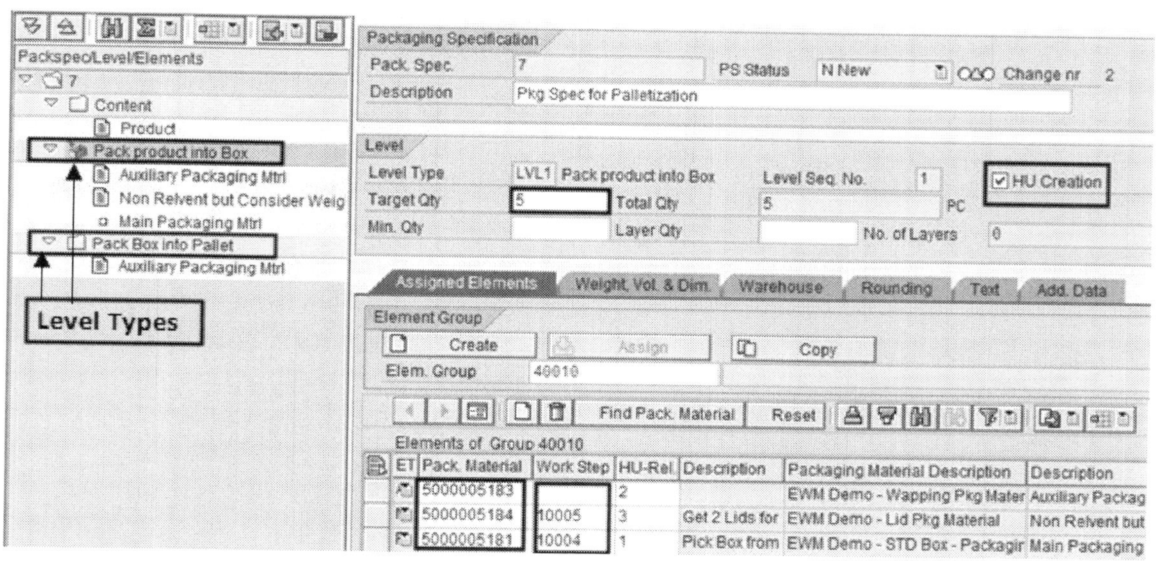

9.2.16.5 Activate Packaging Specification

Once all the data is maintained in the packaging specification (TCode /SCWM/PACKSPEC), click on Activate/Deactivate button on the application toolbar.

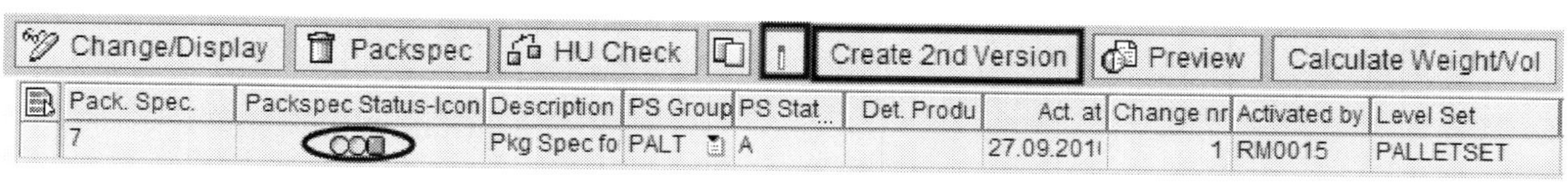

After activating the packaging specification, to change the content, the packaging specification must be deactivated (click on the "Activate/Deactivate" icon on the application toolbar), and a new version of the packaging specification must be created (click on the "Create 2nd Version" button on the application toolbar). After completing the changes, click "Activate" to activate the packaging specification.

9.2.16.6 Condition Maintenance

To use the packaging specifications, maintain the condition records in TCode /SCWM/PSCT6. Here, select the condition type, enter SCU and product number, select the packaging specification, and enter the validity period.

9.2.17 Packaging Specifications Determination Diagram

To determine when the packaging specification is to be applied, the condition technique is used. As seen in the condition maintenance group, it is necessary to assign a conditional table and condition type to the application code "PAK" and usage code "PS," which helps the EWM system to know that the objects assigned are used in packaging specification determination.

Diagram 9.2.17A demonstrates how different configuration objects are linked and how they are determined at the time of creation of the packaging specification.

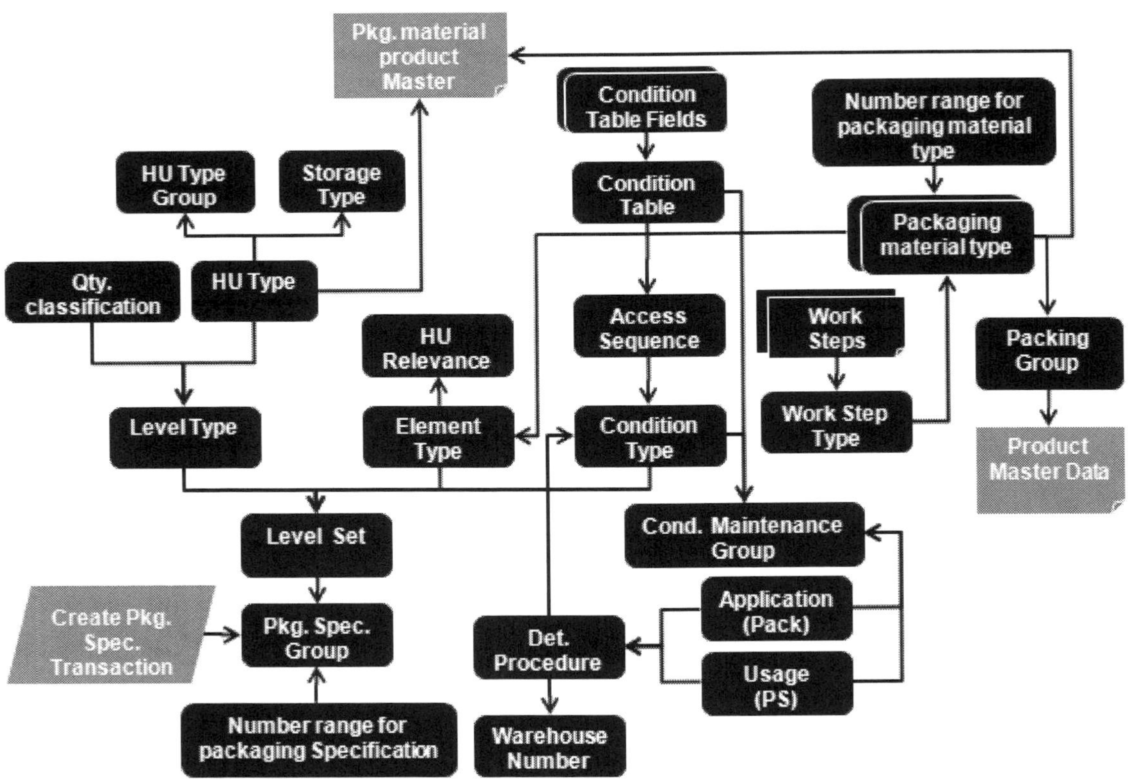

Diagram 9.2.17A – Packaging Specification Determination

Summary

This chapter has demonstrated how to configure HUs and packaging specifications and how to maintain required master data for packaging specifications. The data maintained here will be used later in the goods receipts (GR) and putaway chapter to palletize the GR products and create the HUs.

Chapter 10: EWM Documents

In this chapter the various documents used in the EWM system will be discussed. These documents are usually triggered during inbound, outbound, and internal warehouse processes. It is important for consultants to understand what these documents are, where they are used, and what information they contain. Table 10A is an overview of different documents used in EWM system during different processes.

S. No	Warehouse Documents	System	Process
1	Inbound Delivery Notification	EWM	Inbound
2	Inbound Delivery	EWM	Inbound
3	Outbound Delivery Request	EWM	Outbound
4	Outbound Delivery Order	EWM	Outbound
5	Outbound Delivery	EWM	Outbound
6	Posting Change Request	EWM	Posting Change
7	Posting Change	EWM	Posting Change
8	Warehouse Request Documents	EWM	All
9	Warehouse Task Documents	EWM	All
10	Warehouse Order	EWM	All
11	Wave	EWM	Outbound
12	Transportation unit	EWM	Yard Management
13	Vehicle	EWM	Transportation Management

Table 10.A EWM Documents

10.1 Inbound Process

Generally inbound process starts with purchase order and ends with goods receipt. Diagram 10.1A shows different documents used in both ERP and EWM systems in connection with the inbound process.

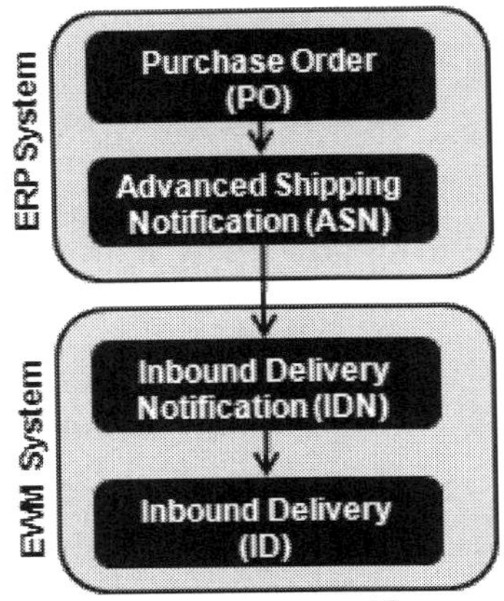

Diagram 10.1A – Inbound Documents

10.1.1 Inbound Delivery Notification (IDN)

In an EWM system, the IDN is a document created automatically with reference to the inbound delivery of the ERP system. The information from the advanced shipping notification from the supplier is stored in an inbound delivery document in ERP, which gets automatically transferred to the EWM system in the form of incoming messages and gets converted into an IDN document. The IDN number will remain same as the inbound delivery number of the ERP system. The IDN can be converted manually or automatically using PPF into inbound delivery. Using IDN, incoming changes to an existing inbound delivery can also be processed or rejected.

The standard document category used in IDN is IDR, and the document type is INB.

Menu Path: SAP Easy Access | Extended Warehouse Management | Delivery Processing | Inbound Delivery | Maintain Inbound Delivery Notification or TCode /SCWM/IDN

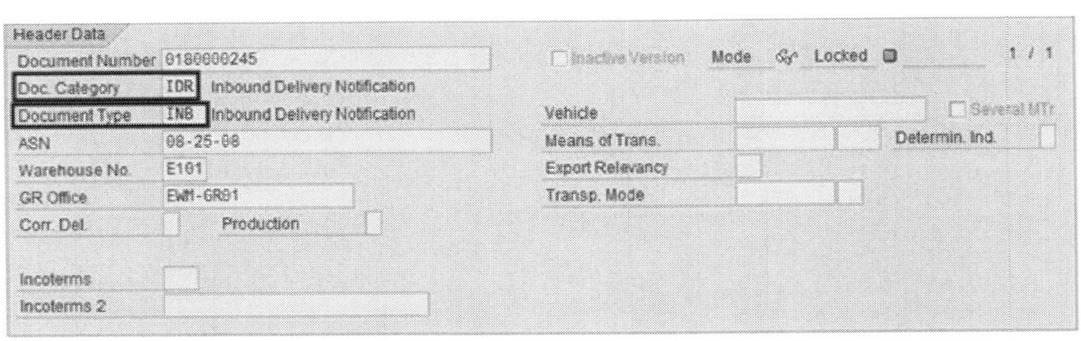

10.1.2 Inbound Delivery (ID)

In EWM, Inbound Delivery is a document, containing all the data required for triggering and monitoring the complete inbound delivery process. This is also called a warehouse request document. This process starts with receipt of the goods in the delivery process or in the yard and ends with transfer of the goods at the final putaway. From the Inbound delivery, the WTs are created to control the putaway and other associated process such as unloading, packing, and staging.

An inbound delivery can be created automatically after activating the IDN, and it adopts all the relevant data from the IDN. In EWM, inbound delivery is referenced when executing the following actions:

- Registering the delivery in the yard
- Unloading the delivery
- Canceling the unloading of the delivery
- Placing the delivery into stock (putaway)
- Canceling the delivery putaway
- Adjusting the delivery quantity (in case of over delivery or under delivery).
- Posting a goods movement
- Canceling a goods movement

The standard document category used in inbound delivery is PDI, and the document type is INB.

Menu Path: SAP Easy Access | Extended Warehouse Management | Delivery Processing | Inbound Delivery | Maintain Inbound Delivery or TCode /SCWM/PRDI

10.2 Outbound Process

Diagram 10.2A provides an overview of different documents used in both ERP and EWM systems in connection with the outbound process. The process begins in the ERP system when the created outbound delivery document contains one or more items which are EWM relevant. In such cases the delivery document is replicated to the EWM system automatically via qRFC. In the EWM system, the document created for ERP outbound delivery is an outbound delivery request (ODR). It is a copy of the ERP outbound delivery document and identified with the same number as the ERP outbound delivery.

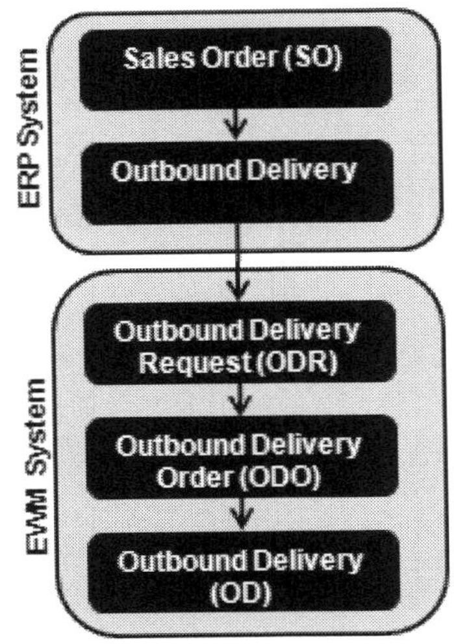

Diagram 10.2A – Outbound Documents

10.2.1 Outbound Delivery Request (ODR)

The ODR contains all the relevant logistics data in the outbound delivery process, taken directly from the ERP outbound delivery and sales order.

The ODR is created automatically by incoming messages and is converted manually or automatically into an ODO. This document can used to plan warehouse resources or calculate the estimated workload for the outbound process. In ODR, the standard document category used is ODR, and the document type is OUTB.

Menu Path: SAP Easy Access | Extended Warehouse Management | Delivery Processing | Outbound Delivery | Maintain Outbound Delivery Request or TCode /SCWM/ODR

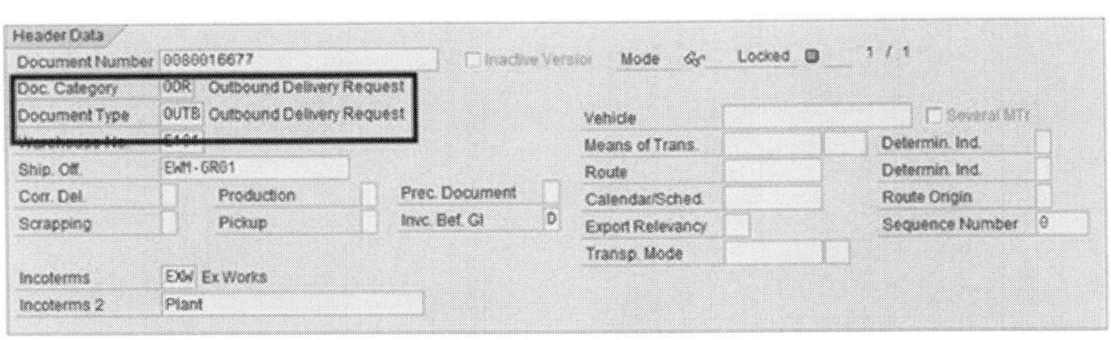

10.2.2 Outbound Delivery Order (ODO)

Based on PPF configuration settings, when the ODR is activated, the system creates the outbound delivery order (ODO) automatically. This is also called Warehouse Request document. The ODO contains all the data required for triggering and monitoring the complete outbound delivery process. The process starts with the first planning activities for the outbound delivery and continues until the finished goods have been loaded and sent.

The ODO is created automatically after activating the ODR. You can use ODO to preview the planning of pending warehouse activities or to execute the following actions:

- Picking the delivery
- Canceling the delivery picking
- Loading the delivery
- Canceling the delivery loading
- Setting the status "Leave Yard"
- Adjusting the delivery quantity to the picked quantity
- Posting a goods movement
- Canceling a goods movement

The standard document category used in ODO is PDO, and the document type is OUTB.

Menu Path: SAP Easy Access | Extended Warehouse Management | Delivery Processing | Outbound Delivery | Maintain Outbound Delivery Order or TCode /SCWM/PRDO

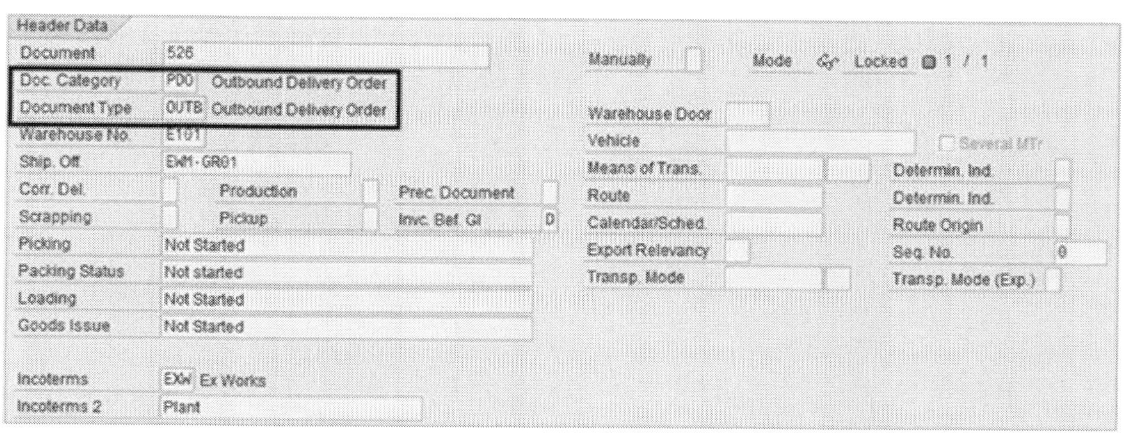

From the ODO, the WTs are created to control the picking and other associated processes such as packing, staging, and loading. Finally, when all the tasks are confirmed, the goods issue will be performed; this will create an outbound delivery in the EWM system, which is a proof of goods issue.

10.2.3 Outbound Delivery (OD)

Outbound delivery can be created manually by selecting action "Create Outbound Delivery" or automatically while posting goods issue, canceling goods issue, or setting the status "Leave Yard." The standard document category used in OD is FDO, and the document type is OUTB.

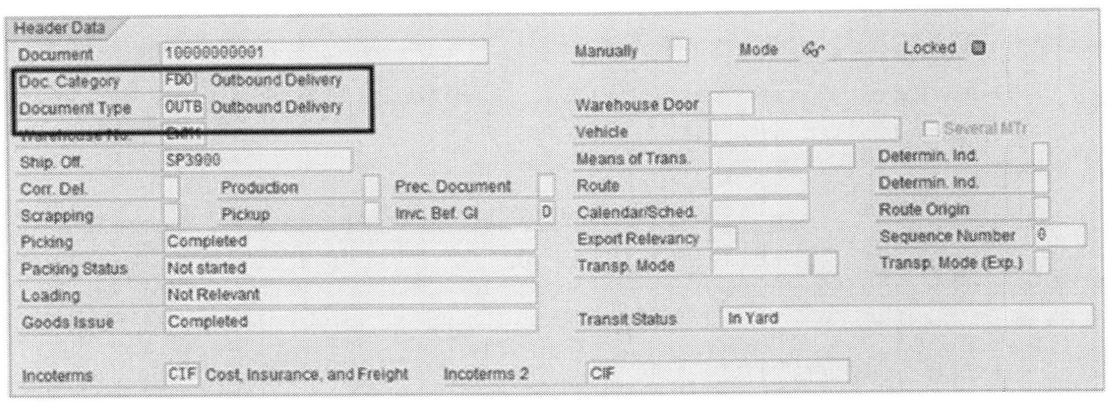

Menu Path: SAP Easy Access | Extended Warehouse Management | Delivery Processing | Outbound Delivery | Maintain Outbound Delivery or TCode /SCWM/FD

10.3 Posting Change Process

Diagram 10.3A provides an overview of posting change documents and process flow in both ERP and EWM. Posting changes can be initiated in the EWM system and communicated to the ERP, or they can be initiated in the ERP system and processed in the EWM system. In EWM, the term "posting change" is used to refer to a change in product, batch, stock type, or stock usage. This may or may not trigger the physical product movement in the warehouse. For example, if the stock type is changed from quality stock to unrestricted, it is not necessary that the stock also be physically moved out and placed back in the bin.

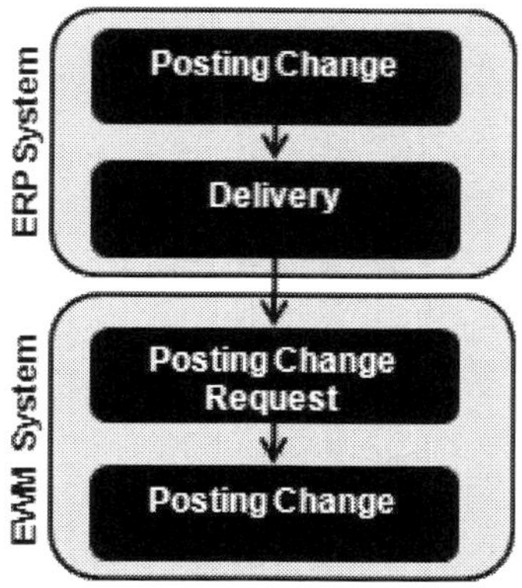

Diagram 10.3A – Posting Change Process

10.3.1 Posting Change Request

This is a document into which the system copies all relevant logistics data from the initiator of this process. For example, if it is initiated in ERP, it will copy all the data from posting change–related delivery. It is used to transfer the data to the posting change to create WTs.

Menu Path: SAP Easy Access | Extended Warehouse Management | Monitoring | Warehouse Management Monitor | Documents | Posting Changes or TCode /SCWM/MON

10.3.2 Posting Change

This is generated after activating a posting change request. From this document, WTs are created to initiate the posting change–related movements.

Menu Path: SAP Easy Access | Extended Warehouse Management | Work Scheduling | Make Posting Change for Product or TCode /SCWM/POST

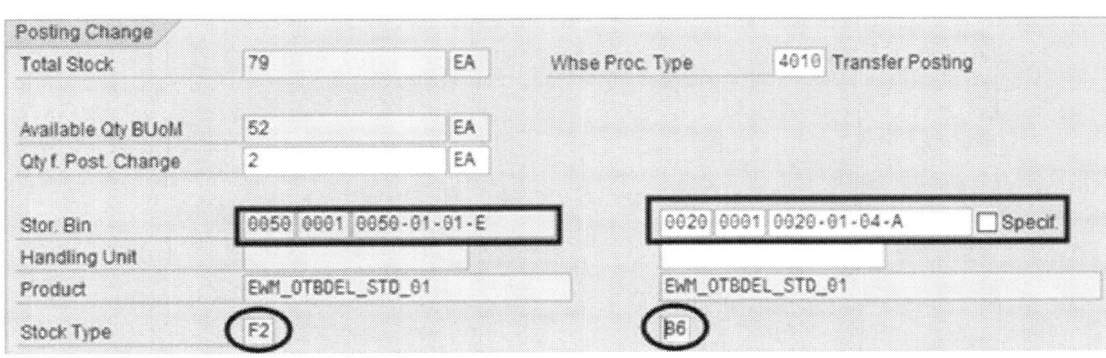

10.4 Warehouse Request Document

This is a document used for planning and processing various warehouse activities for a specific product. "Warehouse request" is a generic term used in the warehouse to refer to outbound delivery orders in case of picking; inbound delivery in case of putaway; and posting change in case of stock transfer, scrapping, and product-to-product movement; and so on. One of the key pieces of information in the warehouse request documents is the WPT, which contains the configuration settings required to complete the process. The following types of warehouse requests can be created in the EWM system.

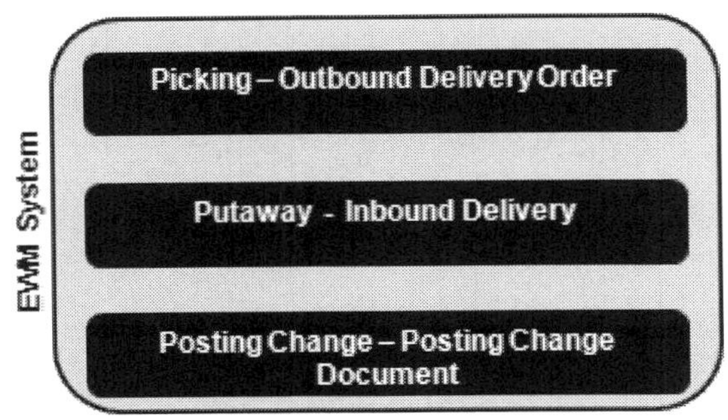

Table 10.4A – Warehouse Request Documents

When the system creates the warehouse request, the following activities are generally carried out in the background and updated in the warehouse request:

- Determination of WPT
- Determination of staging area
- Determination of door assignment
- Rough bin determination
- Wave assignment
- Creation of VAS order

In case of inbound delivery, the following additional activities are carried out, along with the above-mentioned activities:

- Automatic packing
- Determination of a counting for each delivery item
- Check of the handling unit type for notified handling units
- Creation of batches
- Creation of Inspection Document

In case of outbound deliveries, the following additional activities are carried out, along with the above-mentioned activities:

- Determination of which products can be packed together for a shipment

- Route determination

10.5 Warehouse Tasks

WTs are documents used in the EWM system for executing goods movements that are logical or physical, including pick, putaway, posting change, packing, internal warehouse movements, goods receipt postings, and goods issue postings. They are created either with reference to warehouse request document or created manually without reference. They contain all the necessary information on a planned goods movement, such as:

- What should be moved?
- Which quantity should be moved?
- From where products should be moved (source storage bin)
- To where products should be moved (destination storage bin)

The data in WTs are controlled by the WPTs. There are two types of warehouse tasks:

- **Product WT:** Product WTs contain all the required information to move products in and out of the warehouse, such as the product to be moved, the qty to be moved, source location, and the destination location.

- **HU WT:** A HU WT represents a goods movement of a HU. It contains all the required information to move the HU stock in and out of the warehouse like HU to be moved, source and destination location, and so on. HU tasks can also be used in loading and unloading warehouse activities.

Menu Path: SAP Easy Access | Extended Warehouse Management | Execution | Warehouse Management Monitor | Documents | Warehouse Task or TCode /SCWM/MON

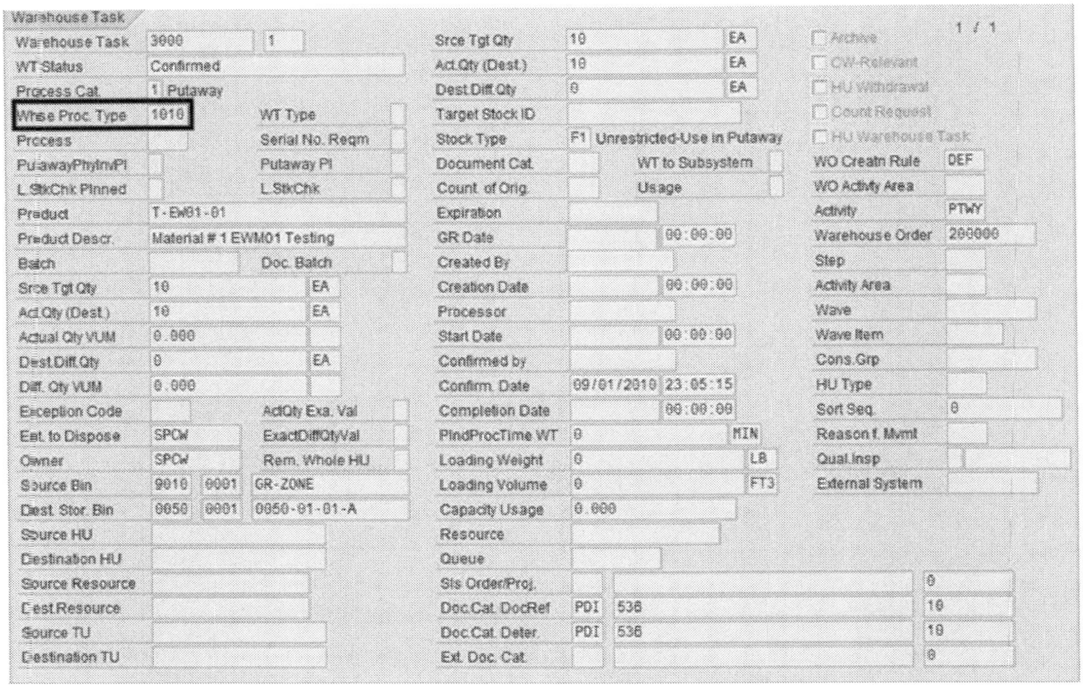

10.6 Warehouse Orders (WO)

This is a warehouse document that represents an executable work package that a warehouse employee should perform at a specific time. It consists of WTs or PI items. WTs are assigned to a WO, based on a WOCR. WOCRs are defined as part of configuration and assigned to activity areas. The source or destination information from the WTs are used to determine the activity areas to be used to obtain WOCR to be applied to the WT.

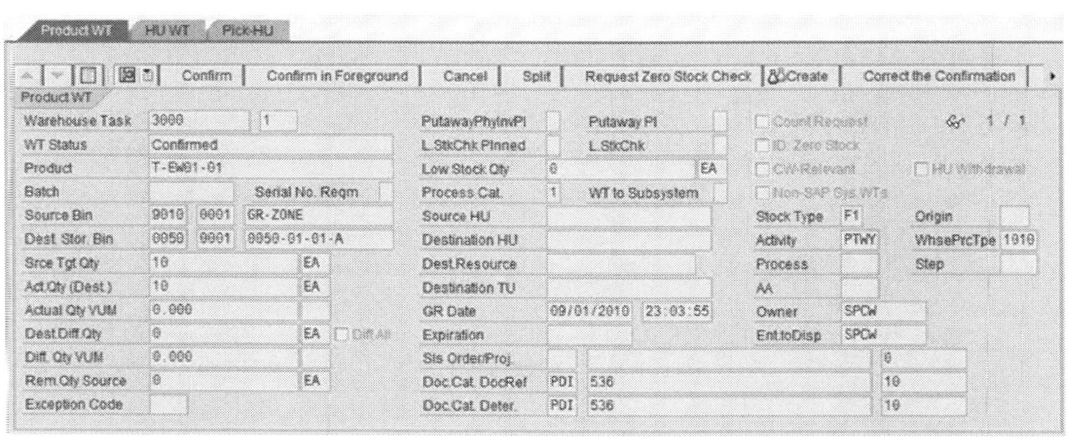

10.7 Wave

In EWM, wave documents can be used to group delivery items and to process them together at the same time to optimize the picking process and facilitate monitoring. They can be created automatically or manually via a batch program. For the automatic wave creation process, wave templates will be used. The parameters like capacity, lock time, planned pick and release time from the template will influence the creation of waves.

Wave templates can be created in transaction code /SCWM/WAVETMP. To determine the appropriate wave template condition, records have to be maintained in TCode /SCWM/WDGCM. To create waves manually, the TCode is /SCWM/WAVE. All these transaction codes are available under the SAP easy access menu.

Menu Path: SAP Easy Access | Extended Warehouse Management | Work Scheduling | Wave Management

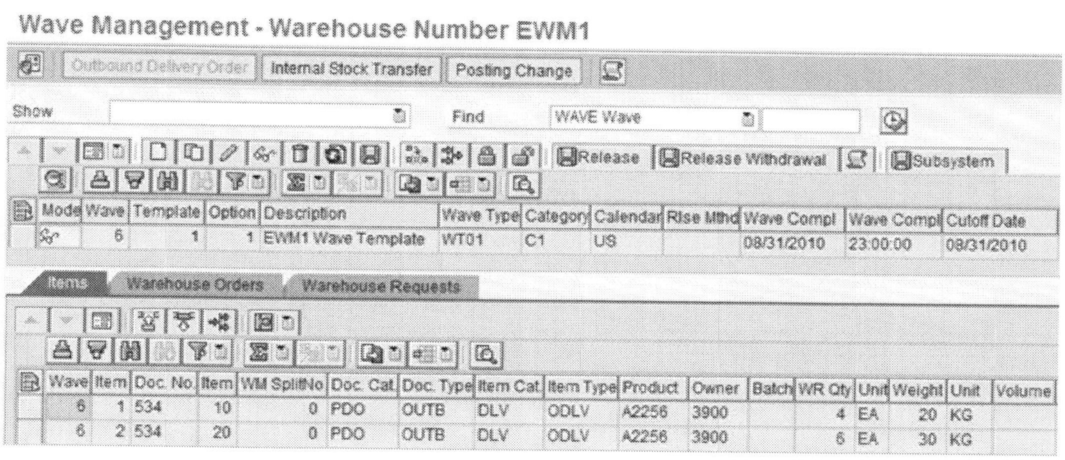

10.8 Transportation Unit (TU)

This is the smallest loadable unit of a vehicle used to transport goods. Examples for TU include a semitrailer truck with one compartment, a truck with a cargo area and trailer (two TUs), or a train with multiple wagons (multiple TUs). TUs and vehicles are used in yard management. The details will be covered in the "Advanced Concepts in SCM-EWM (A Step by Step Guide)" book.

TUs can be created in three different ways.

i. Create them from the TU user interface (UI)

ii. Create them from the check-in/check-out transaction

iii. Create them automatically during the interface with advance shipping notification from ERP

TUs are important master data about the conveyances used to transport the products to and from the warehouse. In EWM, TUs represent HUs. In the TU master data user can enter TU ID number, carrier, SCAC, means of transport, packaging material, route, direction (i.e., shipping or receiving), and the start and end date time.

If daily creation of a new TU is not mandatory, (if the same carrier ships the data) the existing TUs can be reused. This helps eliminate unnecessary data entry and data maintenance in day-to-day warehouse operations.

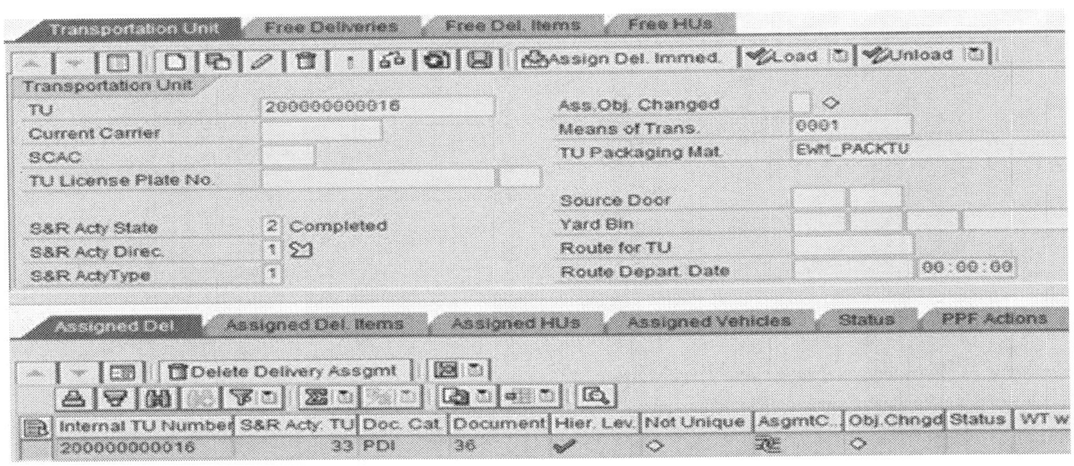

10.9 Vehicle

A vehicle is the equipment used to transport TUs. This can comprise one or more TUs. Examples of vehicles include trucks, locomotive engines, ships, and so on.

In EWM, vehicles can be created either in vehicle UI or check-in/out transactions.

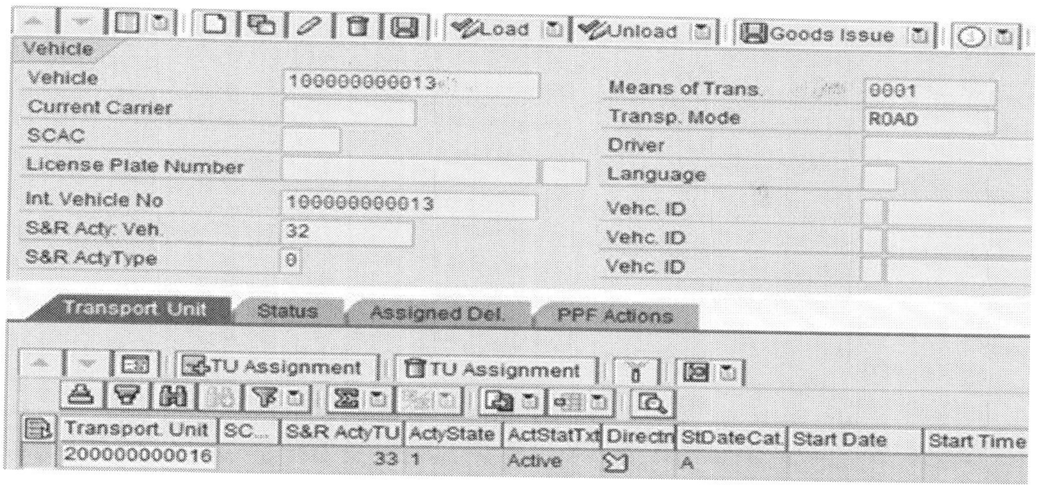

10.10 Handling Units (HUs)

A HU is a physical unit consisting of packaging materials and the goods contained on/in it. It is always a combination of products and packaging materials. All the information contained in the product items (for example, information about batches, quantity, stock type, etc.) is retained in the handling units. Therefore, when the HU is moved from one location to another, the entire content of the HU moves along with it.

For unique identification, every HU has a unique, scannable identification number that can either be generated by the system or be specified externally. In EWM, HUs are mandatory for some of warehouse processes, such as process-oriented putaways, layout-oriented putaways, value added services, and so on.

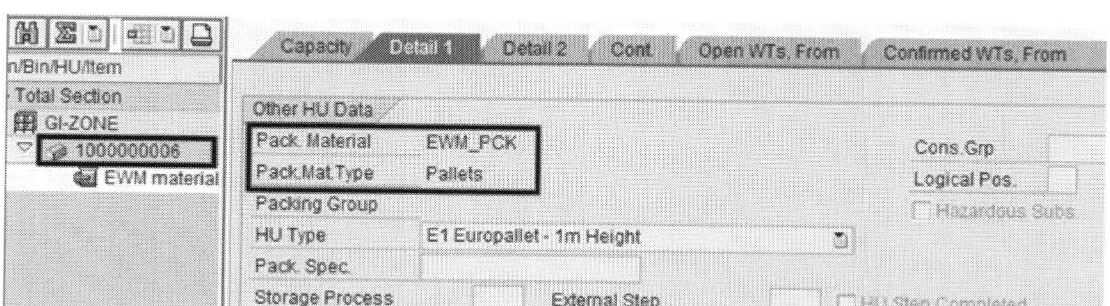

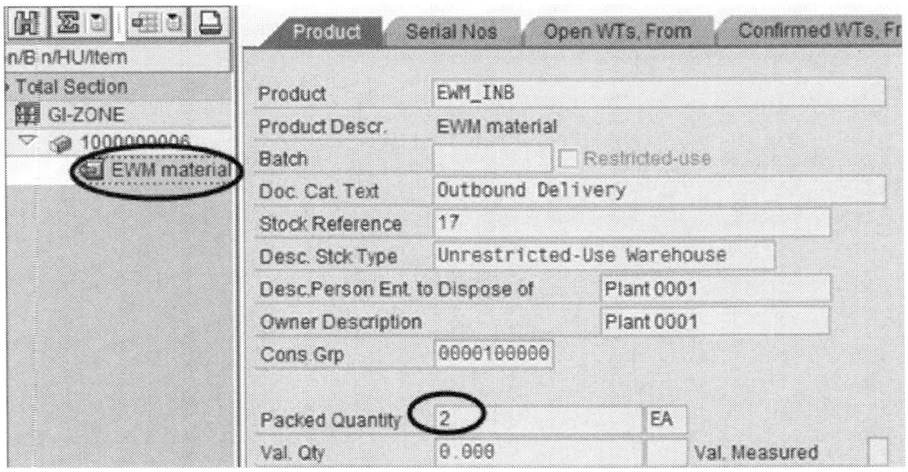

Summary

This chapter described different warehouse documents used in EWM. This should provide a basic understanding of what these documents are. The coming chapters will further explain these documents, along with examples.

Chapter 11: Warehouse Process Type (WPT)

WPT plays an important role in warehouse movements. Similar to warehouse movement types in ERP WM, WPT controls the movement of products in the EWM system. In EWM, WPT is required to control every warehouse process, such as goods receipt, goods issue, repacking, and so on. Thus, it becomes crucial to understand how to configure WPT and how it is determined in the warehouse request documents. This chapter will explain how to define WPT, the meaning of different indicators in WPT and how it is determined in the warehouse request document.

11.1 Define Warehouse Process Type (WPT)

In EWM, WPT is assigned to a warehouse process category and warehouse activity together, which shows the direction of the goods movement in the warehouse. As with ERP WM movement type, source and/or destination storage type and bin information can be included in the WPT definition. One important difference between ERP WM movement type and EWM WPT is that in EWM, dynamic storage bins cannot be used for the interim storage types.

WPT settings are broadly divided into six sections. They include the following:

i. General settings

ii. Control for putaway and stock removal

iii. Control indicators for HUs

iv. Settings for storage process

v. Posting change settings

vi. Settings for warehouse requests

Menu Path: SPRO | IMG | Extended Warehouse Management | Cross-Process Settings | Warehouse Task | Define Warehouse Process Type

11.1.1 General WPT Settings

General WPT settings consist of several indicators that facilitate the movement of products in the warehouse.

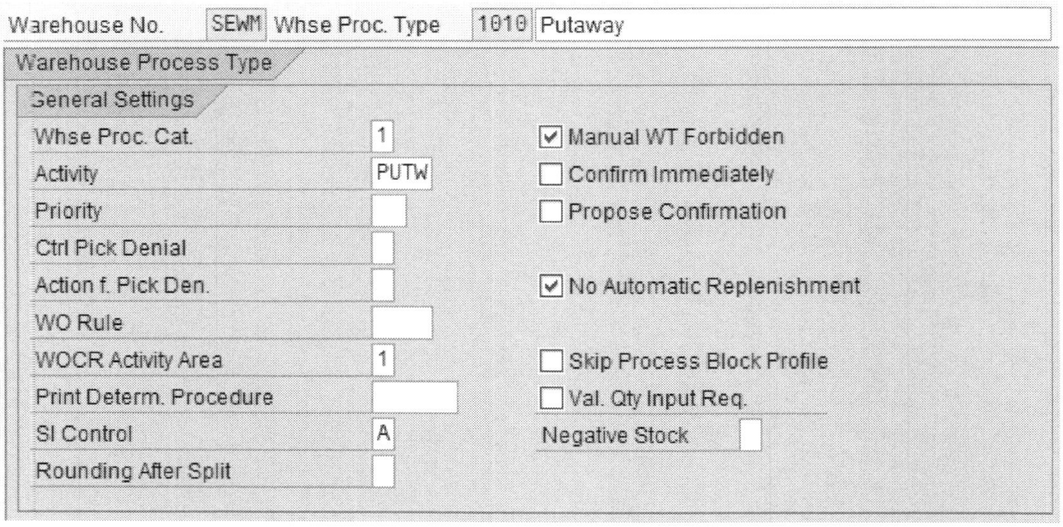

- **Whse Proc. Cat**: The warehouse process category is used to classify the type of goods movements such as putaway, stock removal, internal warehouse movement, PI, goods receipt posting, goods issue posting, posting change, and cross-line stock putaways. All these process categories are predefined by SAP, and most of them are available for selection during the WPT definition, except for goods receipts and issue. For technical reasons, goods receipts and issue categories are not available for selection and are used by SAP internally to identify the relevant process.

- **Activity**: In EWM, activities trigger goods movements. Warehouse activity together with warehouse process category show the direction of the movement in the warehouse. This is used to select the appropriate activity for the WPT.

- **Ctrl Pick Denial**: This is used to specify how pick denial should be processed on both dialog and background modes. It can be "Warning for dialog, automatic follow-up action in background" or "Automatic follow-up action in dialog and in background."

- **Action for Pick Denial**: This defines the action to be performed in case of pick denial. Options include "No action," "qty to be adjusted in warehouse request," or "adjust the qty to pick qty and send a message."

- **Stock Identification Control (SI Control)**: This is a unique number that you use to identify non-HU stock with all its stock attributes, such as quantity, batch, or stock type. When the goods movements are performed in the warehouse, for every goods movement, the system creates a new WT with a unique WT number. If the values chosen in the WPT "B—Create Stock Identification if none exists," the system automatically creates the stock identification in every product WT, which can be bar-coded and used to confirm the warehouse task. For technical reasons, it is necessary to delete the SI in the final destination putaway storage type. If the SI is not deleted, the putaway status will not be updated as completed.

- **Skip Process Block Profile**: A process block profile can be used to trigger an error or warning message when certain processes are performed in the warehouse for a product. For example, a warning message may be displayed when the product is goods issued. A process block profile is assigned to the product master. If this indicator is set in the WPT, the system does not take into account the process block profile assigned in the product master.
- **Negative Stock**: This is used to specify whether or not negative stock should be allowed. If the indicator is set to "A," the system will allow the posting of negative quants for movements with this WPT.

11.1.2 Control for Putaway and Stock Removal

This defines process type groups for putaway and picking along with source and destination bin information.

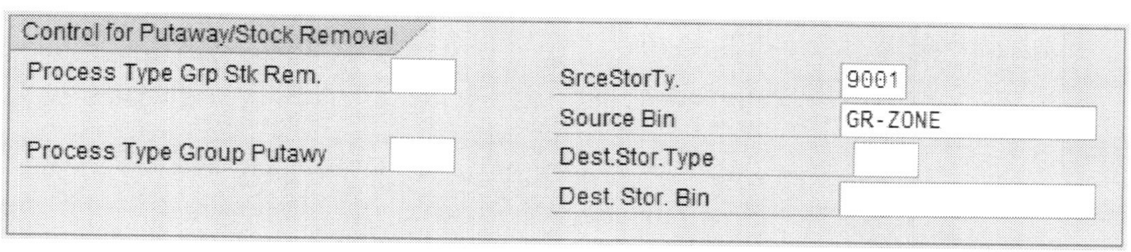

- **Process Type Group for Stock Removal and Putaway**: You can assign a WPT group for stock removal and putaway to summarize the WPTs for putaway and removal strategies.
- **Source & Destination Stor. Type/Bin:** Storage Type and Storage Bin defined here are used as a default source or destination bin during putaway/picking with this WPT.

11.1.3 HU Control

These control indicators are used only for HU-managed stock.

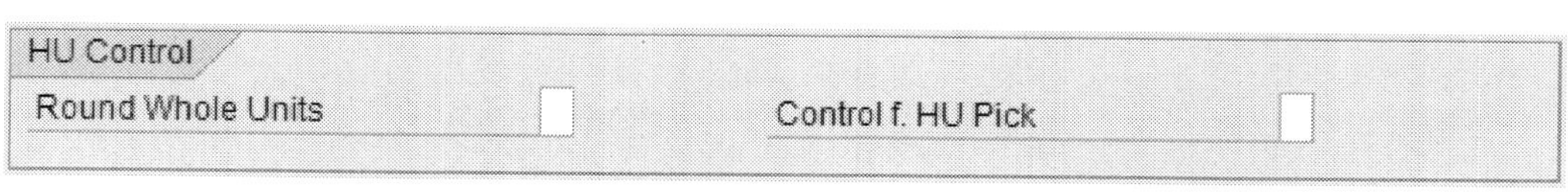

- **Round Whole Units**: This is used for rounding the WT quantity to whole units. The available options are as follows:

    i. Round down to a single unit

ii. Round down to a multiple of a unit

iii. Round up to a multiple of a unit

- **Control for HU Pick**: This indicator guides the system in determining what should be the pick HU; that is, while picking, whether the source HU should be used as pick HU or product and source HU should be adopted into pick HU.

11.1.4 Settings for Storage Process

Incicators defined here are used during the process oriented putaway.

- **Storage Process**: Activities and storage process steps can be summarized into a storage process. The storage process describes the activities that must be performed and their sequence. For example, in the goods receipt process, the internal storage process steps allowed could be in the sequence of unload, count, deconsolidate, and putaway. The storage process steps can be defined in the menu "Define Process-Oriented Storage Control."

- **Deactivation Allowed**: If this check box is activated, manual changes to storage control are allowed. This means that if a user wants to create a WT directly for a destination storage bin, without the product or HU passing through interim steps, then the parameter "Storage Control Is Not Relevant" can be set in the transaction at the time of creating the WTs. Changing this indicator is possible only if this check is on.

11.1.4 Settings for Posting Changes

Indicators defined here are used during the posting change.

- **Posting Change in Bin:** This decides whether the posting change should transfer the stock to different bin with creation of WT or it should direct transfer in the same Bin.

- **Exception Code for Posting Change**: An exception code can be entered here to trigger the subsequent action after posting change.

- **Goods Movement before Warehouse Task**: In EWM, goods movement for posting change can happen in three ways: goods movement before creating and confirming WTs, after the creating and confirming the WT, or without creating of a WT. If this check box is checked, the goods movement will occur before creation and confirmation of WTs.

11.1.5 Settings for Warehouse Request

Indicators defined here are used in the warehouse request.

- **Doc. and Item Type Whse Intrnl**: If a warehouse request is created as a follow-up action to an internal warehouse process, it is necessary to specify a document and item type for this warehouse request. One default document type can be defined for each process type.
- **Pick Completely**: Activate this indicator if the entire requested quantity in the warehouse request should be picked and a minimum coverage of the quantity to pick is not allowed.
- **Rough Bin Determination**: Performs a rough bin determination for warehouse request item. Rough bin determination is used for wave picks and planning the replenishment of orders.
- **Automatic Wave Creation:** if this is set, warehouse request items with this WPT are transferred for auto wave pick assignment.
- **Availability Group**: When the system defines the stock type of a delivery, it uses the availability group of the WPT and not the availability group of the storage type. If this WPT is delivery relevant, an appropriate availability group must be assigned to this WPT.
- **Select HU without Storage Process**: Set this indicator if a HU is to be put away (placed in storage) without a storage process. A HU WT is created for this purpose. If this indicator has not been set, the product items of a HU are put away without a storage process via product WTs.

11.2 Define Control Indicators for Determining WPT

This IMG activity defines the product-specific control indicator for determining the WPT. This indicator can be used to group products for which the same WPT will always be used. The control indicator can be assigned to the relevant products in the warehouse data view of the product master.

If this indicator is maintained in the product master, whenever the warehouse request is created, EWM takes the product master attribute to determine the WPT.

Menu path: SPRO | IMG | Extended Warehouse Management | Cross-Process Settings | Warehouse Task | Define Control Indicators for Determining Warehouse Process Types

Control Indicator for Warehouse Process Type Determination

War...	ProTyp...	Description
SEWM	01	Storage Process Active
SEWM	02	VAS Storage Process Active
SEWM	03	In-house Produced Materials
SEWM	04	Direct Putaway without Storage Process

11.3 Determine Warehouse Process Type

While creating a warehouse request, the system uses warehouse number, document type, item type, delivery priority, control indicator, and process type determination indicators to determine the WPT. Diagram 11.3A shows how the information flows to determine the WPT.

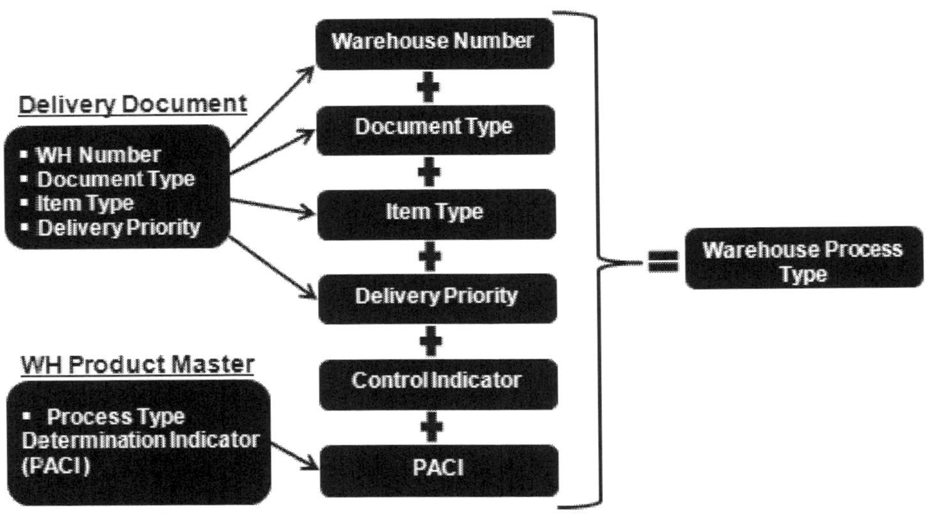

Diagram 11.3A – Determination of WPT

If the warehouse request is with reference to the delivery documents (inbound or outbound deliveries), the warehouse number, document type, item type, and delivery priority information flows from delivery documents, and the process type determination indicator is derived from the warehouse product master.

The system determines the WPT according to the following logic, which means that it is not always necessary to make entries in all the fields. The table values are read in the following sequence:

- All key fields are specified
- Document type, item type, and processing priority are specified
- Document type, item type, and control indicator are specified
- Document type and item type are specified
- Item type, processing priority, and control indicator are specified
- Item type and processing priority are specified
- Item type and control indicator are specified
- Item type is specified
- Document type, processing priority, and control indicator are specified
- Document type and processing priority are specified
- Document type and control indicator are specified
- Only the document type is specified

Menu path: SPRO | IMG | Extended Warehouse Management | Cross-Process Settings | Warehouse Task | Determine Warehouse Process Type

Determination of Warehouse Process Type

War.	Doc. Type	Item Type	Del.Prio.	ProTypeDet	Process Ind.	WhsePrcT
SEWM	INB			04	No Specia	1010

11.4 Assign Control Indicator to the Products Master

One of the keys used in determining the WPT is the control indicator from the product master. You can assign the control indicator to the relevant products in the warehouse data view of the product master in TCode /SCWM/MAT1.

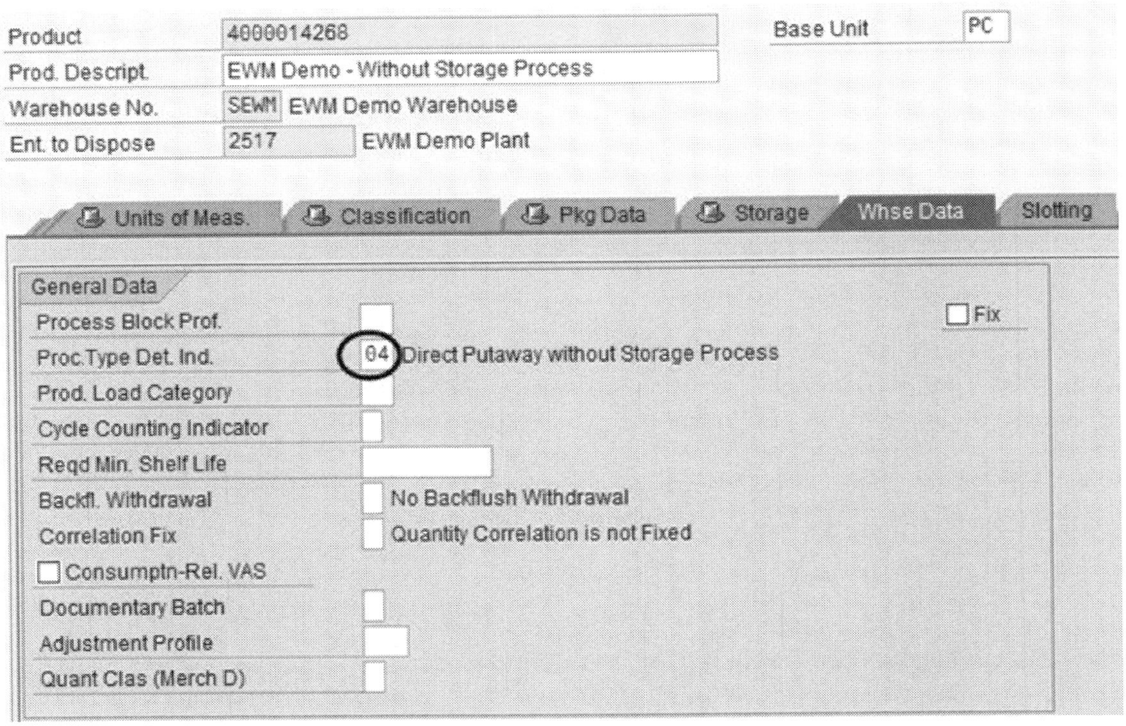

Summary

This chapter has explained what a WPT is and its importance in the warehouse. Chapters 14, 15, 16, 19, and 20 will show how the WPT is determined in the warehouse request document, along with examples.

Chapter 12: Warehouse Order

A Warehouse Order (WO) is a document that represents an executable work package for a warehouse employee to perform at a specific time. This chapter will discuss how WTs are processed and grouped into warehouse orders, the role of the warehouse order creation rules (WOCR), and how they can be configured to meet the client's requirements.

12.1 Overview of WO Creation Process

WOs consist of WTs or PI items. At the time of the WO creation process, all WTs pass through a function called WOCR, which determines the number of WTs for a given WO. During this process, as shown in diagram 12.1A, WOCR might bundle more than one WT into one WO or can create multiple WOs for one WT, depending on rules defined in the WOCR.

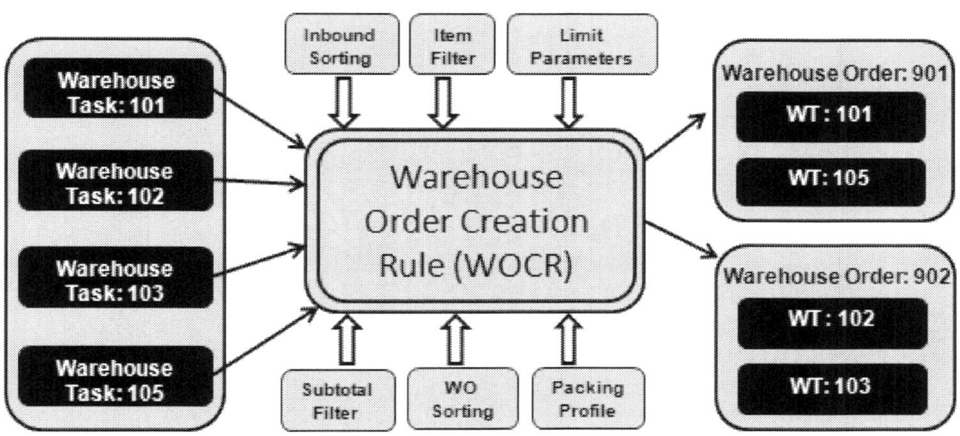

Diagram 12.1A – WO Creation Process

WOCR is a set of rules defined as part of a configuration and assigned to the activity areas. Multiple WOCRs can be assigned to each activity area. Based on the activity area and activity code from the WPT, the system determines the appropriate WOCR. Once the WOCR is determined, the system uses WOCR to decide how and which WTs should be grouped together and how many WOs should be created for the WTs. Once the WOs are created, they are available for processing in the warehouse. In a RF environment, the WO acts like a RF queue. Resources can be assigned manually or automatically to the WO, using resource management to execute the WO.

Diagram 12.1B provides an overview of how the WOCRs get determined and how the WOs are created. In this diagram, outbound delivery has been used as an example.

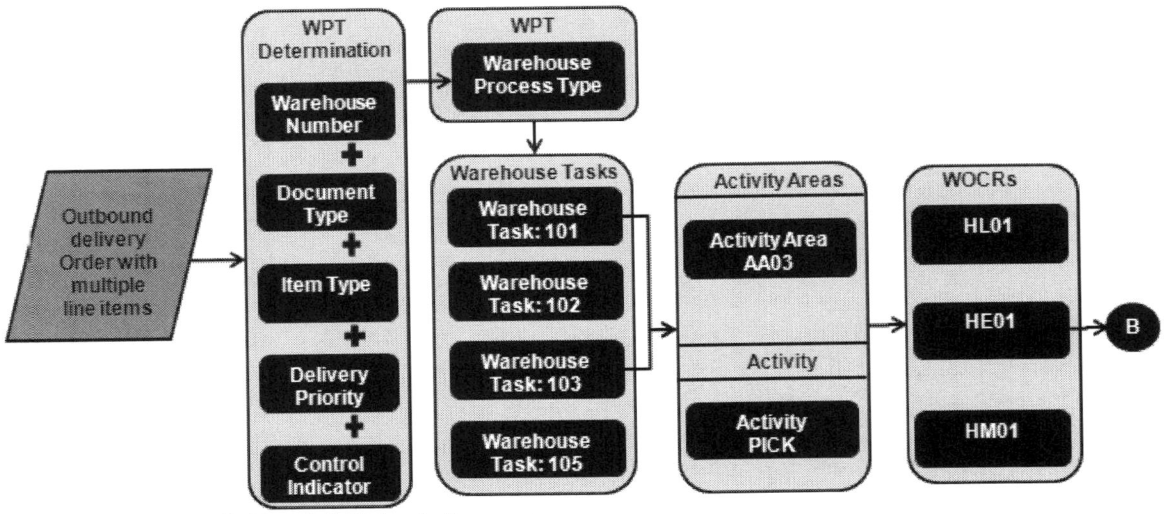

Diagram 12.1B – WOCR Determination

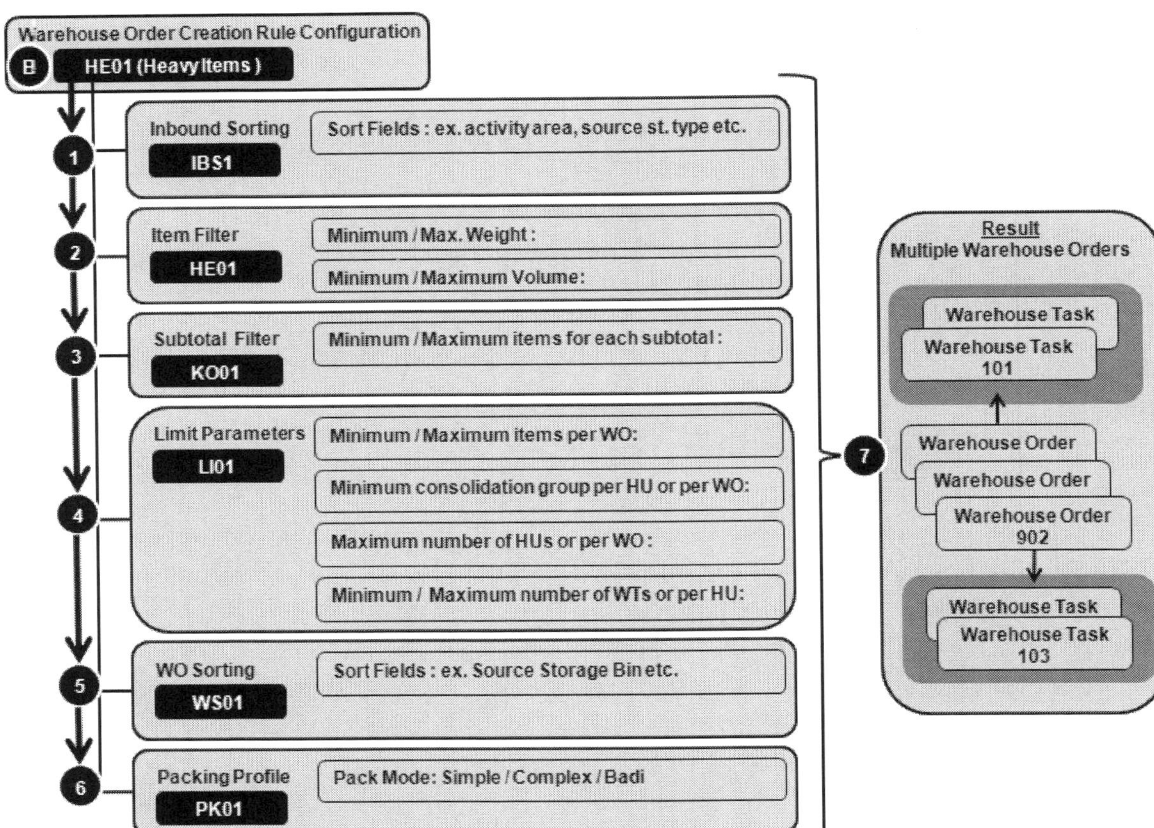

Diagram 12.1C – WOCR Determination

As explained in the above diagram, when the warehouse request (WR) is created, the WPT gets determined. WPT helps to create the WTs. When creating the WTs, EWM first searches for the stock and creates one or more WTs. These WTs will then go through the WO creation process.

In the WO creation process, all WTs will be grouped by activity area. Activity areas are determined as per the WPT configuration setting (i.e., WOCR Activity Area, source or destination bin, along with the activity code). Based on the activity areas, the system determines the WOCRs for the activity areas. Each activity area can have more than one WOCR. EWM system will first pass all the WTs to the first WOCR. If any tasks fail, the system stops processing the WT and continues with the next task in sequence.

12.1.1 Inbound Sorting

As soon as system applies a WOCR, WTs will be sorted as per the sort rules defined for the WOCR. These items will then move through the item filter rules defined for the WOCR.

The sort rules and fields can be defined by following **menu path**: **SPRO | IMG | Extended Warehouse Management | Cross-Process Settings | Warehouse Order | Define Sort Rules for Warehouse Tasks**

12.1.2 Item Filter

An item filter checks an individual WT for the defined filter criteria. This is used to filter out all tasks that do not meet the filter criteria mentioned for the WOCR. For example, it may be set to filter out all heavy items whose weight is more than 20,000 kg. If the filter fits the WT, the system continues processing the WT. If it does not fit, the system stops processing the WT and continues with the next task in sequence.

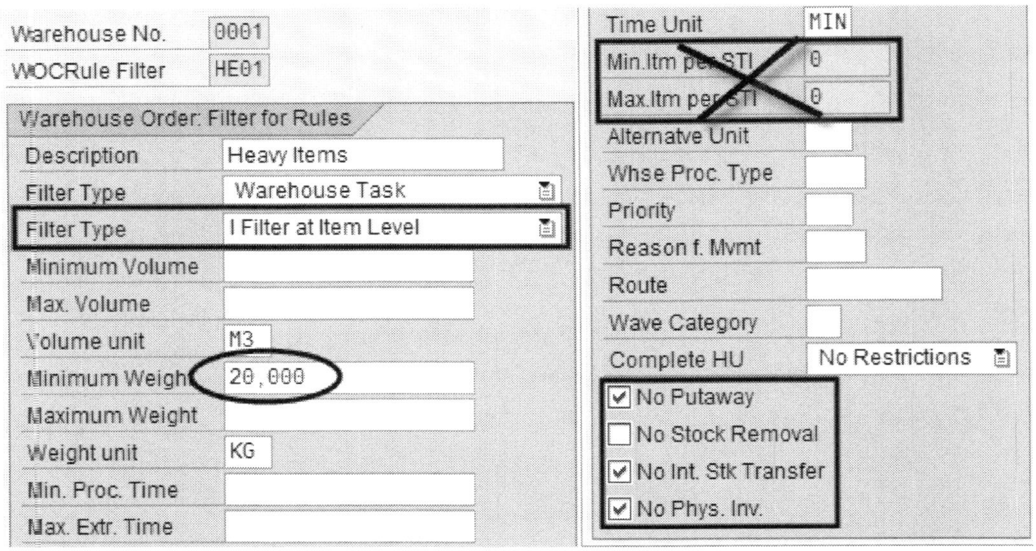

In the item filter we can specify minimum/maximum values for volume, weight, and processing, and extract time for each item filter, priority, route, wave category, and HU withdrawals restrictions. If this filter should not be applied for putaway, picking, internal stock transfer, or PI, check the respective check boxes in the item filter configuration screen.

Menu Path: **SPRO | IMG | Extended Warehouse Management | Cross-Process Settings | Warehouse Order | Define Filters for Warehouse Order Creation Rules**

12.1.3 Subtotal Filter

This can be used to specify minimum/maximum values for volume, weight, and number of item per subtotal, along with minimum processing time and maximum extract time. An example might be a minimum of five items per subtotal. In addition, we can also specify minimum processing time and maximum extract time for each subtotal filter.

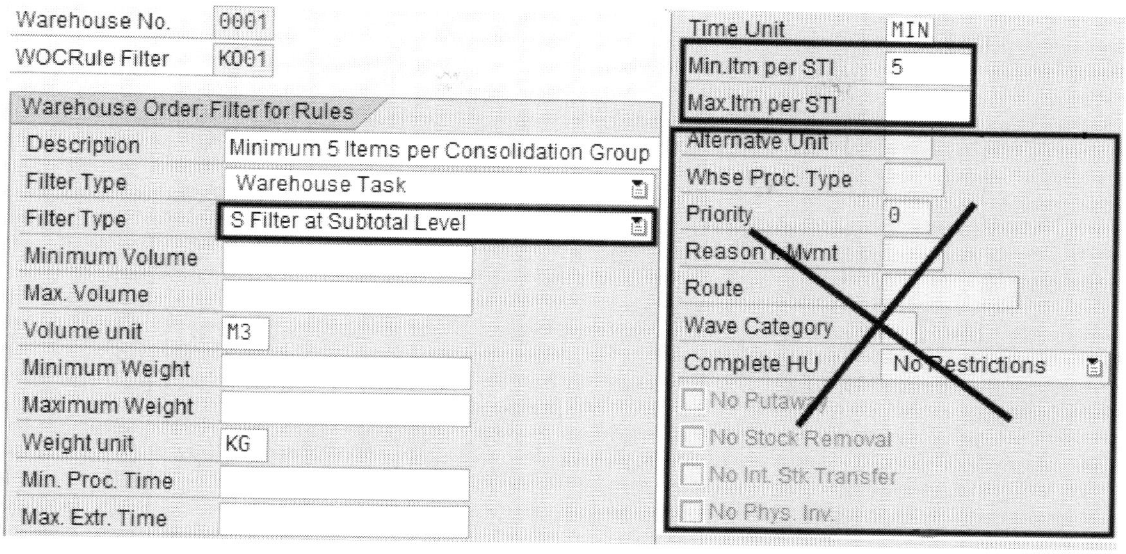

The subtotal filter is based on the consolidation group (CG). It will be determined based on the customizing settings of the activity area. CG helps to determine which items can be packed and shipped together. The subtotal filter can be used to specify minimum and/or maximum number of items per subtotal.

If the filter fits the WT, the system continues processing it. If it does not fit, the system stops processing the WT and continues with the next task in sequence.

Menu Path: SPRO | IMG | Extended Warehouse Management | Cross-Process Settings | Warehouse Order | Define Filters for Warehouse Order Creation Rules

12.1.4 Limit Parameters

This defines the size and/or scope of the warehouse order. This means that, using this profile, the number of WTs assigned to a WO can be restricted. The parameters defined here are maximum/minimum values for number of items per WO, weight, volume, minimum processing time, maximum extract time, maximum number of consolidation groups per WO/per HU, and minimum/maximum WTs per HU. As soon as the value exceeds the defined maximum limit, the system will create a WO for all the WTs processed to that point. This process will continue for the remaining WTs.

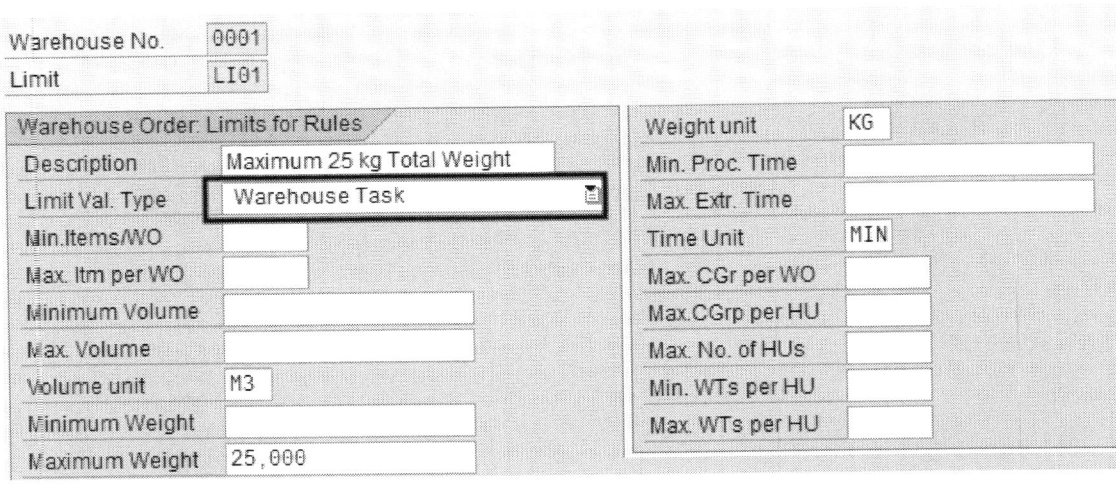

After the WO creation has checked the values for the maximum limits, it checks the values for the minimum limits. If the filter fits the WT, the system continues processing it. If it does not fit, it stops processing the WT and continues with the next task in sequence.

Menu Path: **SPRO | IMG | Extended Warehouse Management | Cross-Process Settings | Warehouse Order | Define Limit Values for the Size of a Warehouse Order**

12.1.5 WO Sorting

In this step, the system will sort the WTs, as per the WO sorted rule before creating the WO. Sorting rules for WO sorting are defined under the same menu as inbound sorting.

12.1.6 Packing Profile

This defines packing profiles for WO creation. This helps to control how WO creation determines pick-handling units for a WO. The system uses the data from the WTs of a WO (such as weight, volume, or dimensions) to perform this determination. It compares this data with possible packaging materials and determines the number and category of the required pick-handling units. In addition to these values, when determining the pick-handling units, the system also considers limit values for the size of a WO. Limit values considered are maximum number of different deconsolidation groups in a pick-handling unit, maximum number of pick-handling units, maximum number of items for each handling unit, or minimum number of items for each handling unit.

When defining packing profile, select appropriate modes for determining the pick-handling units. Available modes are simple algorithm, complex algorithm, or BADI. A simple algorithm can have one packaging material.

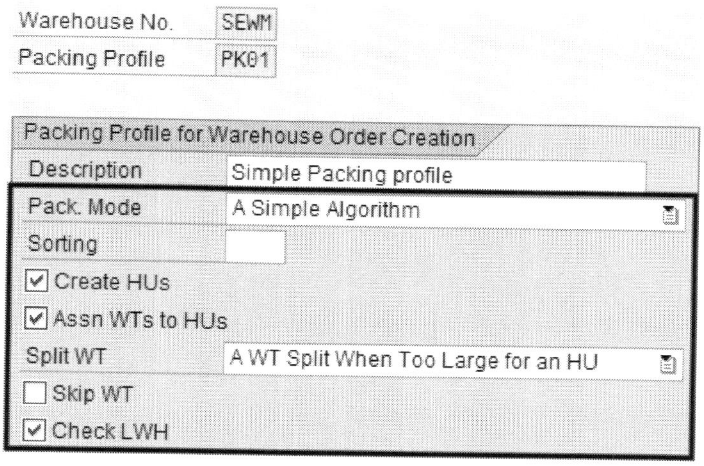

12.1.7 Result

At the end of step 6, the system will create the required amount of WOs for the completely processed WTs. There can be one or several WOs. Each WO might contain one or more WTs.

All skipped WTs will then get processed with the next available WOCR and will follow all seven steps explained above.

12.1.8 Exceptions

If the system has applied all the WOCR defined for the activity area, and there are still unprocessed WTs, the system uses a SAP-defined WOCR called the *remainder rule* (UNDE). This rule creates WOs for the remaining WTs. Under this rule, the system summarizes the WTs, according to the following criteria:

- For each activity area
- For each queue
- For each consolidation group

If there are no defined WO creation rules for the current activity area, the system uses a standard WOCR called DEF (default rule). This rule attempts to group deliveries according to the following criteria:

- For each activity area
- For each queue
- For each delivery

12.2 Define Number Ranges for Warehouse Order

This configuration helps to generate the unique number for each WO. This menu defines an internal number range for WOs and assigns it to the warehouse number.

NR Object: Warehouse Order

Subobject: SEWM

Intervals

No.	From number	To number	Current number	Ext
01	0003000000	0003999999	0	☐

Assign WO Number Range Interval to Warehouse Number

War...	Description	NRInt. WO
SEWM	EWM Demo Warehouse	01

Menu Path: **SPRO | IMG | Extended Warehouse Management | Cross-Process Settings | Warehouse Order | Define Number Ranges for Warehouse Order**

12.3 Define Warehouse Order Creation Rule (WOCR)

In the overview of WO creation process section we have discussed how to configure the required filter profiles for the WOCR. After the WOCR profiles have been created, they need to be assigned to the WOCRs.

Menu Path: **SPRO | IMG | Extended Warehouse Management | Cross-Process Settings | Warehouse Order | Define Creation Rule for Warehouse Orders**

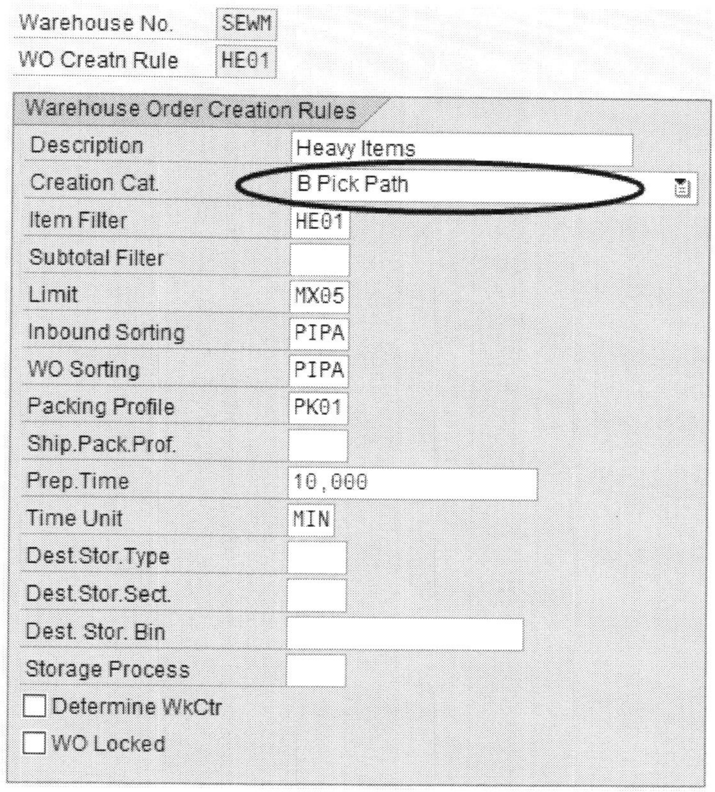

Creation Category: WOCR categories are different ways in which WO creation occurs. The available options are:

- Consolidation Group: System keeps together WTs that belong to the same consolidation group
- Pick Path: System optimizes the picking process along the pick path
- Pick, Pack, and Pass (system-driven): System predefines the sequence of WOs created for different activity areas, according to customizing settings
- Pick, Pack, and Pass (user-driven): User can select the sequence of WOs
- Load and Unload: Used to load and unload transportation units.
- Distributive Putaway: Used to put away a HU with several products, according to the pick path
- Physical Inventory: Used to create WOs for PI items

The destination storage type, section, bin, and determine work center fields are not available for Pick, Pack, and Pass (system-driven), Pick, Pack, and Pass (user-driven), Pick and Pack, Load and Unload, Distributive Putaway, or PI. Additional fields not applicable for the physical inventory option include subtotal filter, packing profile, and shipment packing profile.

12.4 Define WOCR Search Sequence for Activity Areas

This menu assigns one or more WOCRs to an activity area. These rules are processed during WO creation for each activity area, according to the sequence defined.

Warehouse Order: Search Sequence for Rules per Activity Area

War	AA	Activity	Sequ...	WOCR	Description
SEWM	PICK		1	HE01	Heavy Items
SEWM	PICK		2	KO01	Minimum 5 Items per Consolidation Group
SEWM	PICK		3	LI01	Light Items to Max. 25 kg Total Weight
SEWM	PICK		4	HU01	Complete Pallet Withdrawal
SEWM	PICK		5	PU01	Putaway

Menu Path: SPRO | IMG | Extended Warehouse Management | Cross-Process Settings | Warehouse Order | Define Search Sequence of Creation Rules for Activity Areas

WOCR can also be assigned to WPT when defining the WPT. The system uses this WOCR for creation of WO for all the tasks that have this WPT.

Summary

This chapter has explained what a WO creation rule is and its importance in processing WTs. It has also demonstrated how to define and assign multiple WOCRs to activity areas.

Chapter 13: Delivery Processing in EWM

The delivery document plays a key role in the EWM system. It is the trigger for the majority of warehouse movements and serves as the key document in the integration between ERP and EWM. This chapter will describe various delivery processing profiles, the basic configuration settings related to delivery document integration, data mapping between the ERP and EWM documents/item types, and EWM delivery document determination.

13.1 Overview of Delivery Document Integration

From an integration point, it is important to understand the basic EWM integration setting for delivery documents. Delivery documents are very important for data exchange between the ERP and EWM systems. Diagram 13.1A provides an overview of delivery document process flow and integration between ERP and EWM systems. Most of the communication between ERP and EWM systems is two-way, and the qRFC technology is used to communicate the data.

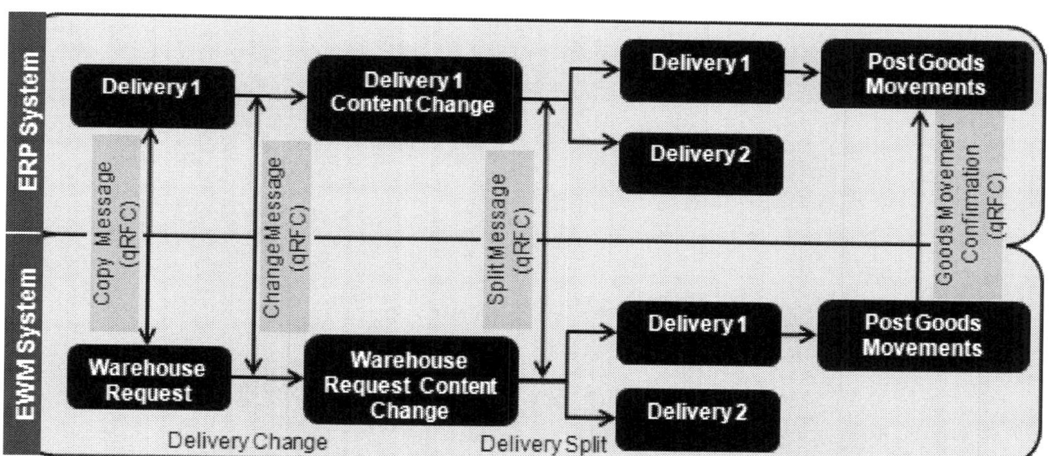

Diagram 13.1A–Delivery document Process Flow

Even though, in most cases, the creation of delivery documents is initiated in the ERP system, it is possible that in certain cases, the EWM system initiates the creation of delivery documents. For example, manual inbound delivery can be created in the EWM system. In such cases, the content of the delivery document must be transferred to the ERP system using qRFC. The other possible reasons for the data exchange between the two systems are changes in the delivery document, delivery split, PCN, or the goods movement confirmation in the EWM system. In order to transfer data between the ERP and EWM systems, both systems need to be configured, and the delivery document integration must exist in the EWM system.

Diagram 13.1B shows how the inbound delivery created in the ERP system gets processed in the EWM system, and the following documents are created and communicated between two systems.

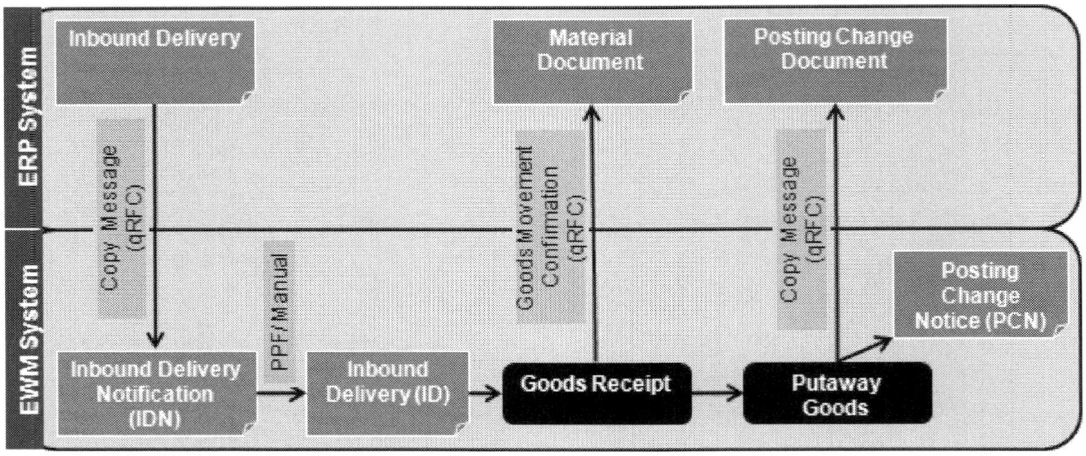

Diagram 13.1B – Inbound Delivery Document Overview

13.1.1 Delivery Document Structure

Every delivery document contains a document header and one or more document items. Document header data is valid for the entire document, and item-specific information is stored in the document items.

13.1.1.1 Delivery Document Header

The document header contains the general data information that is relevant for the entire document. Two key parameters in the header data include document category and document type.

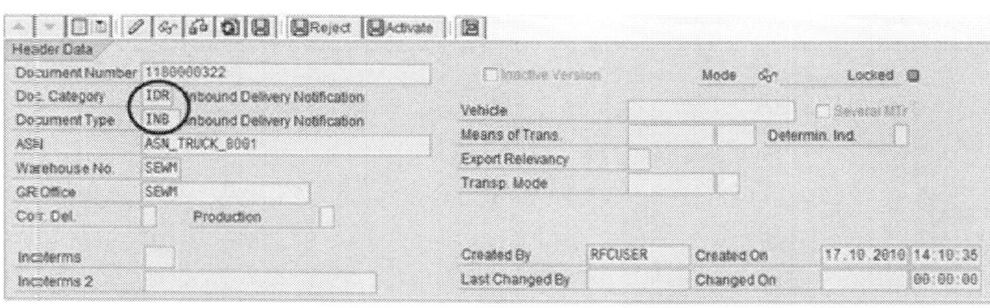

Document Category: The document category classifies the different type of documents that can be processed by the system in delivery processing. Examples include expected goods receipt, inbound or outbound delivery, posting change, stock transfers. These are predefined in the EWM system and cannot be changed.

Table 13.1.1.1A contains some of the most frequently used document categories in the EWM system.

Document Category	Description
EGR	Expected Goods Receipt
GRN	Goods Receipt Notification
IDR	Inbound Delivery Notification
PDI	Inbound Delivery
FDO	Outbound Delivery
ODR	Outbound Delivery Request
PDO	Outbound Delivery Order
POR	Posting Change Request
SPC	Posting Change
WMR	Stock Transfer

Table 13.1.1.1A - Document Categories

Document Type: The document type classifies the document with regard to the complete delivery process. It defines the primary business use of the document. Custom document types can be created in the EWM system. Table 13.1.1.1B contains some of the most frequently used document types in the EWM system.

Document Type	Description
INB	Inbound Delivery
INBI	Inbound Delivery Production
OUTB	Outbound Delivery
SREA	Warehouse Reorganization
SRPL	Replenishment
SWHI	Stock Transfer
TWPR	Posting Change

Table 13.1.1.1B - Document Types

Mapping of Document Category and Document Type: Every document (goods receipt, goods issue, stock transfers, posting change, etc.) in EWM has a document type and document category. It is possible for each document type may have one or more document category, or every document category might have more than one document type. Table 13.1.1.1C shows some of the important document types and their respective document category codes.

Document Type	Document Category	Description
OUTB	FDO	Outbound Delivery
OUTB	PDO	Outbound Delivery Order
OUTB	ODR	Outbound Delivery Request
INB	IDR	Inbound Delivery Notification
INB	PDI	Inbound Delivery
SPRL	WMR	Replenishment
SWHI	WMR	Stock Transfer
TWPR	POR	Posting Change Request
TWPR	SPC	Posting Change

Table 13.1.1.1C - Mapping of Document Type and Document Category

13.1.1.2 Delivery Document Item

Delivery document items contain information related to products, such as product number, delivery quantity, picking quantity, weight and volume details, and so on. Every item is uniquely identified by item number. Like the document header, the document item also contains document category, item category, and item type.

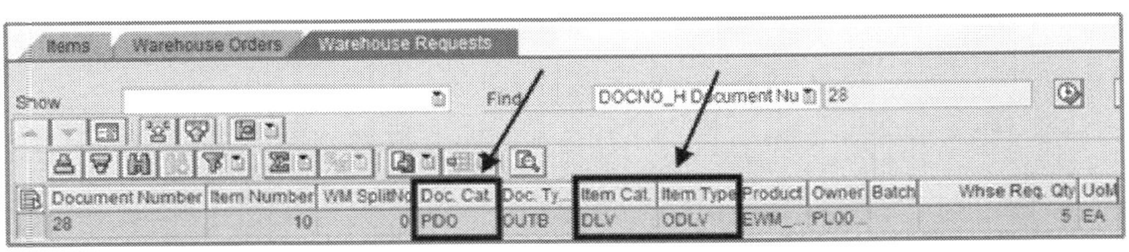

Delivery document items can be broadly classified as delivery item, packing item, return item, text item, or value item. System uses the item category for this classification. Item categories are defined by SAP and cannot be changed. Table 13.1.1.2A shows a list of item categories widely used in the EWM system.

Item Category	Description
DLV	Delivery Item
PAC	Packing Item
RET	Return Item
TXT	Text Item
VAL	Value Item

Table 13.1.1.2A - Item Categories

The delivery item type defines the business characteristics or type of delivery item like inbound delivery item, outbound delivery item, or posting change item, and so on. Table 13.1.1.2B shows a list of item types commonly used in the EWM system. You can configure your own item types to represent your business needs.

Item Type	Description
IDLV	Inbound Delivery Item
ODLV	Outbound Delivery Item
TWPR	Posting Change Item

Table 13.1.1.2B - Item Types

SAP has provided a set of standard settings for the common delivery documents. For custom delivery types, some of these settings may have to be defined manually.

13.2 Delivery Processing Profiles

One of the important configuration objects of the delivery processing are the various delivery processing profiles, which influence the processing of goods receipt, goods issue, and internal warehouse process. These profiles are used to define how the document types and item types are processed within EWM. These profiles are broadly categorized as follows:

System Profiles: System profiles are standard profiles delivered by SAP. They cannot be configured or changed. They are used internally by the system as default options during the delivery processing, if the customer specific profiles are missing. Internally, these profiles are linked to document categories and item categories.

Customer Profiles: SAP has provided this option for users to define their own profiles to meet their business needs. SAP has also delivered various customer profiles. This section will discuss customer profiles and how they are linked to the item types and document types.

Table 13.2A provides an overview of various delivery processing profiles used in EWM. The following section will cover how they are configured and their usage in the delivery documents.

S. No	Delivery Processing Profiles	TCode	System	Transportable
1	Delivery Qty Adjustment	SPRO	EWM	Yes
2	Text Management	SPRO	EWM	Yes
3	Quantity Offsetting	SPRO	EWM	Yes
4	Reference Documents	SPRO	EWM	Yes
5	Partner Processing	SPRO	EWM	Yes
6	Dates / Times Profile	SPRO	EWM	Yes
7	Status Management	SPRO	EWM	Yes
8	Field Control	SPRO	EWM	Yes
9	Incompleteness Check	SPRO	EWM	Yes
10	Process Management & Control	SPRO	EWM	Yes

Table 13.2A Delivery Processing Profiles

In the following screenshot, the various delivery processing profiles used in the inbound delivery document can be seen. Each profile is defined for a specific purpose. For example, a reference documents profile is defined to keep track of the reference documents created against the original document. These profiles are explained below.

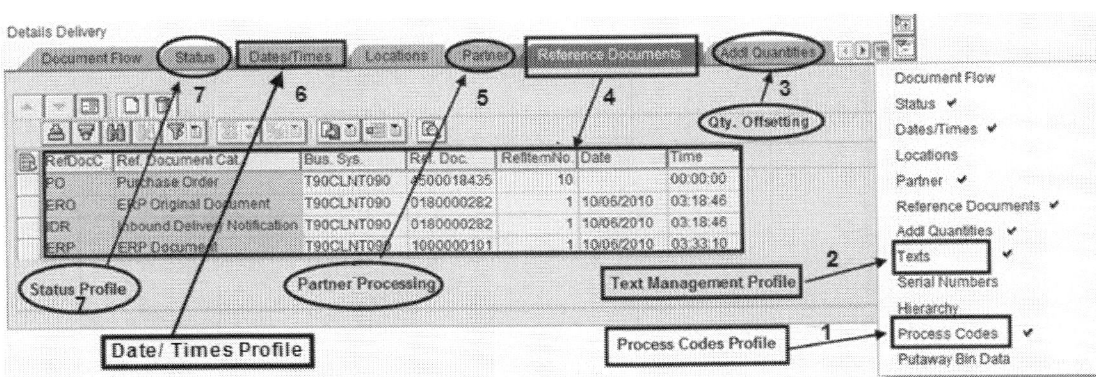

13.2.1 Process Codes (Delivery Quantity Adjustment) Profile

Process code profile is also called as delivery quantity adjustment profile. In the warehouse, for various reasons, it is required to alter the delivery quantity in the system—for example, if the delivery document quantity is different than the actual delivered quantity. In this case, it is required to update the delivery document quantity to the delivered quantity and create a new delivery document for the open quantity. In such scenarios, process codes are used to update the delivery quantity and trigger the required follow-up action.

13.2.1.1 Process Codes

Process code controls the way delivery quantity is adjusted. Here the available options include the following:

- **No Quantity Adjustment**: In this case, the system does not adjust the delivery document quantity, but the process code will be saved in the delivery for future reference.
- **Adjustment of delivery quantity**: In this case, the system does adjust the delivery quantity and saves the process code in the delivery.
- **Adjustment of delivery quantity and delivery quantity transferred**: Here, the system updates the delivery quantity and also initiates the split delivery process for the open quantity.

Menu Path: SPRO | IMG | Extended Warehouse Management | Cross-Process Settings | Delivery Processing | Process Codes | Define Process Codes

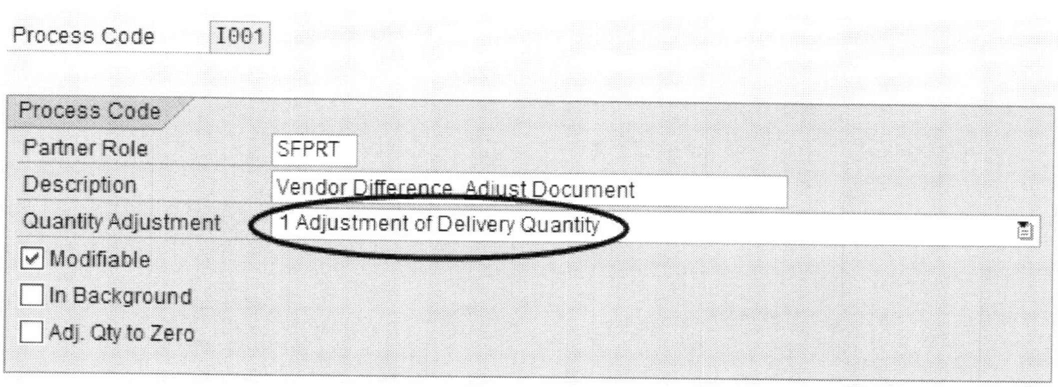

13.2.1.2 Process Code Profiles

Even though quantity adjustment settings are configured under process code, delivery quantity adjustment is governed by process code profiles, which consist of process codes.

In the configuration, each process code profile has to be assigned to the system profile. When creating a process code profile with a copy function, all the predefined process codes are automatically copied to the new process code profile. The process codes that are not required can manually be deactivated, or users can assign custom defined process codes to the process code profiles. The profiles defined here can be used for both inbound and outbound deliveries.

Menu Path: **SPRO | IMG | Extended Warehouse Management | Cross-Process Settings | Delivery Processing | Process Codes | Maintain Process Code Profiles**

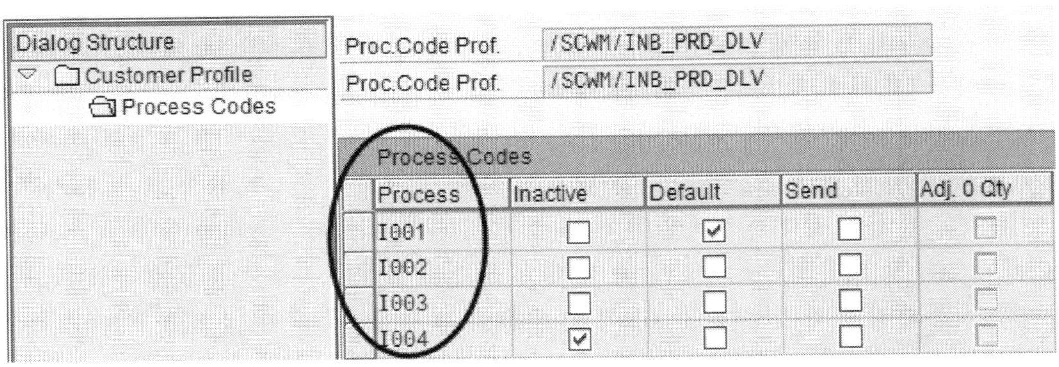

13.2.1.3 Assign Process Code Profiles to Item Types

In order to use the process code profile, it is necessary to assign it to the item types.

Menu Path: SPRO | IMG | Extended Warehouse Management | Goods Receipt Process | Inbound Delivery | Manual Settings | Define Item Types for Inbound Delivery Process

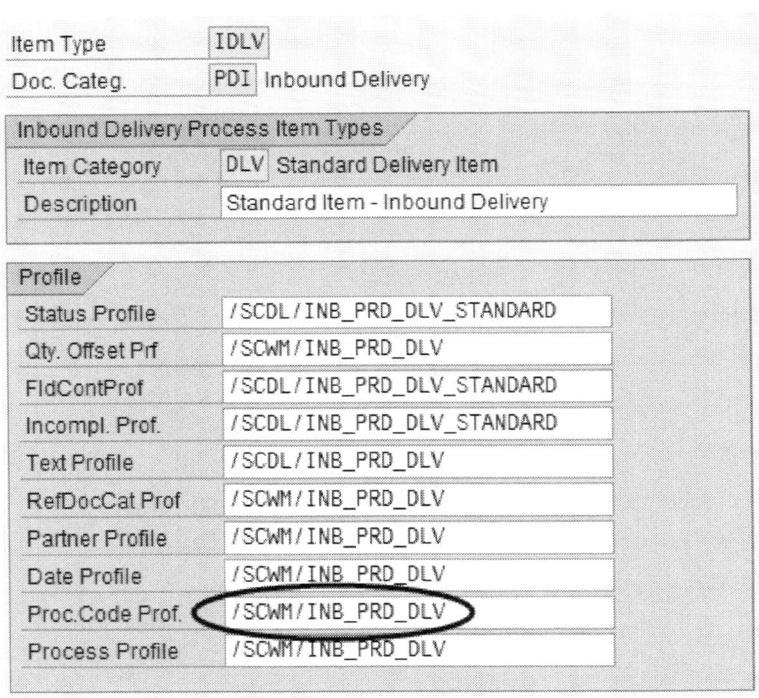

13.2.1.4 Test Configuration

To verify the configuration, go to transaction /SCWM/PRDI and locate your partially or not processed inbound delivery. Under delivery item details, click on "Process Codes" button. Three options discussed above for the process codes can be seen here.

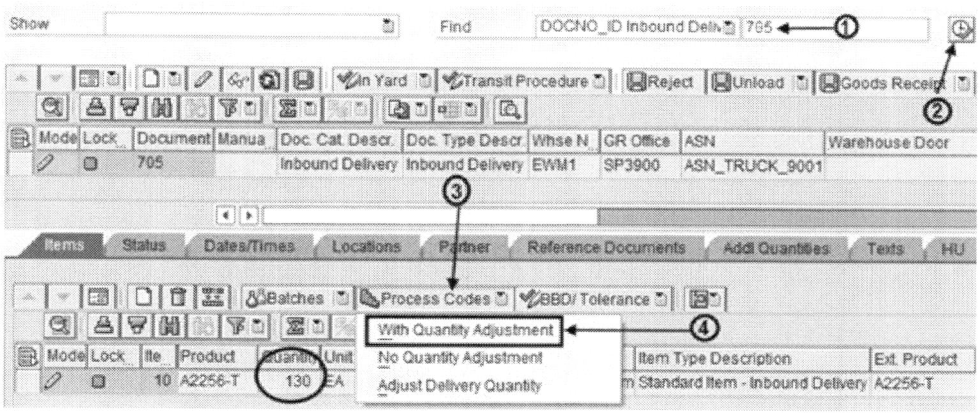

To change the delivery quantity, select "With Quantity Adjustment" option, enter the quantity and click "Enter," as shown below.

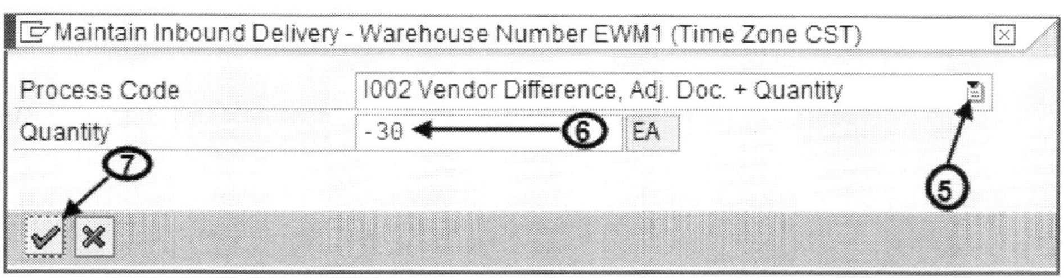

Click "Save." This will change the delivery quantity in the IDN and in the warehouse request (inbound delivery) document. In this example, it is reduced to quantity 100 EA. You can verify the changes in the "Process Codes" tab.

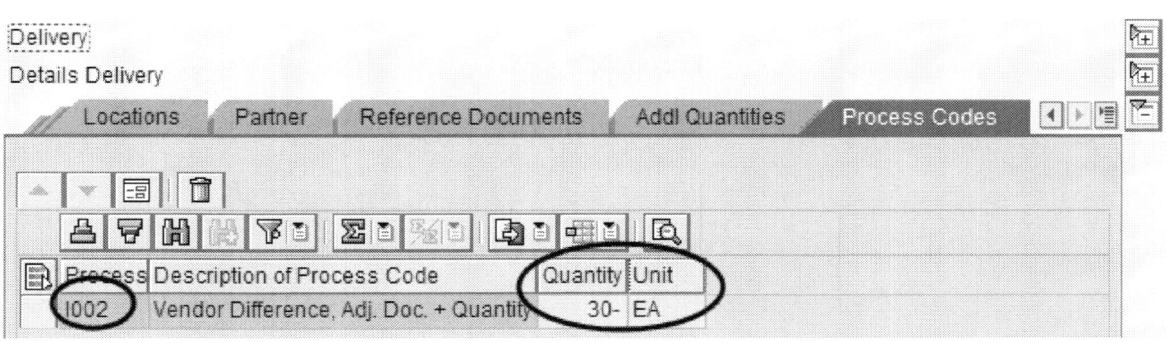

This will also create a new inbound delivery in the ERP system for the split quantity. This document can be verified in the "Reference Documents" tab.

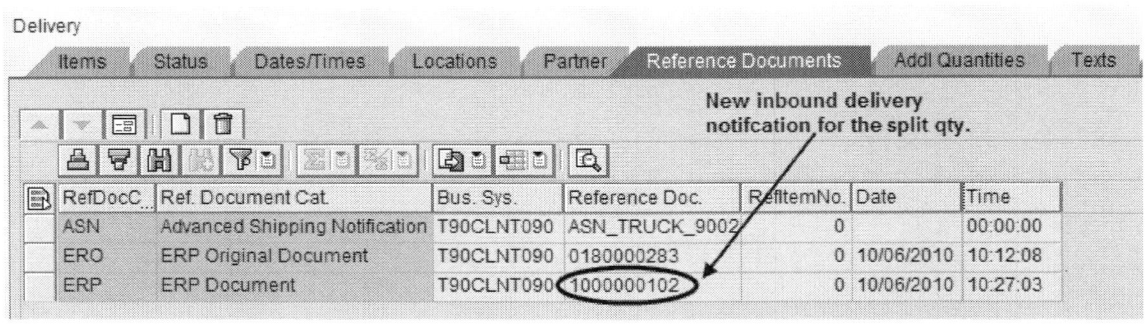

In the background, the EWM system will send a message to the ERP system to update the quantity in the original inbound delivery (i.e., 100 in this example), a message with the details of the new IDN for the split quantity (i.e., quantity 30) created in the EWM system, and the IDN number. The ERP system will process these messages and update the purchase order status accordingly.

Note:

Delivery splits for outbound delivery orders work the same way as for inbound delivery.

13.2.2 Text Management Profile

In EWM, Text Management profile is used to create, change, display, or delete additional texts. Texts can be received from the ERP system via delivery documents. New texts also can be created and saved within the EWM delivery document. This can be maintained in the delivery header as well as at the items level.

The following example demonstrates how to use text types to add the text in the delivery header.

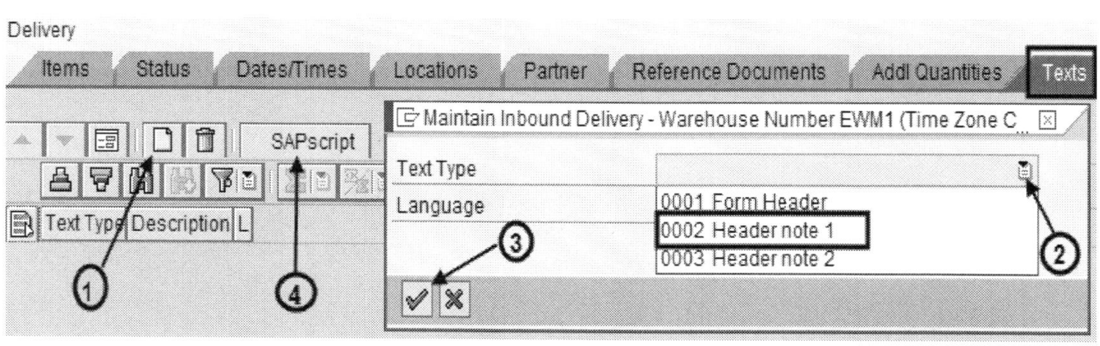

Once the third step is completed, a new line item will be added under the text type/description area. To enter the actual text, select the line item under text type and click the "SAPscript" button (step 4). This will open a word document. Here, add text and click "Save."

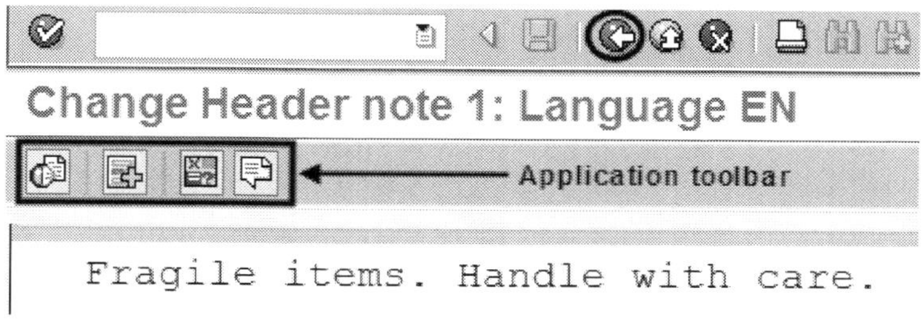

Once the document is saved, the text will be available for future reference. Click on the form view to display the long text.

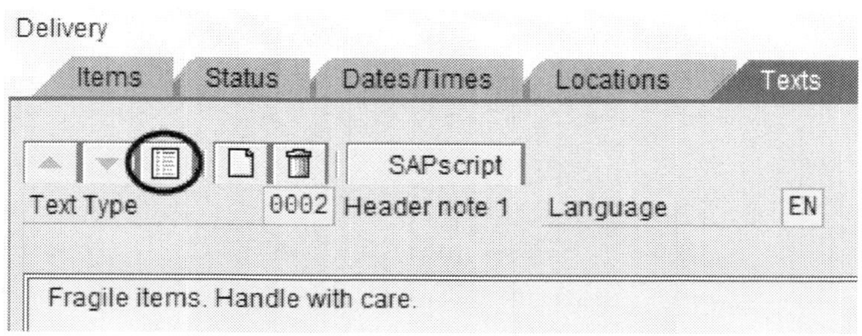

Text Management in delivery is governed by the text profile, which consists of text types and their access sequences. Each text profile is assigned to the system profile and to the delivery document and item types.

Defining and assigning text profile is similar to process codes profile. First, the text types for delivery header and delivery item must be defined. Second, a text profile with an access sequence must be defined.

Menu Path: SPRO | IMG | Extended Warehouse Management | Cross-Process Settings | Delivery Processing | Text Management

Once these things are defined, the text profile can be assigned to the delivery document types and/or item types.

13.2.3 Quantity Offsetting Profiles

Quantity offsetting is used to calculate the open quantities for a warehouse document for each item. This is also used to calculate the requested quantity and reduced quantity. It is always executed at the item level of a delivery document. It contains quantity calculation and quantity offsetting rules to be used by the quantity offsetting profile to calculate the desired quantity.

The following is an example shows the open quantity calculated for the inbound delivery.

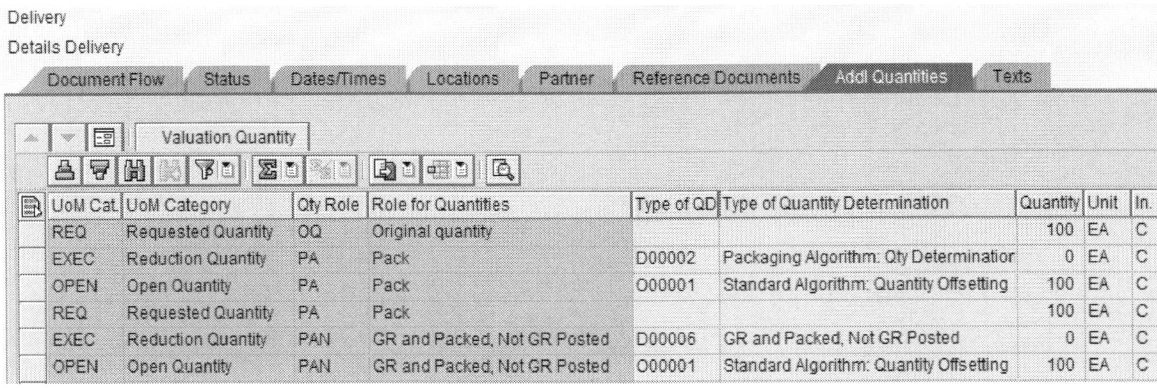

Delivery
Details Delivery

Document Flow | Status | Dates/Times | Locations | Partner | Reference Documents | Addl Quantities | Texts

Valuation Quantity

UoM Cat.	UoM Category	Qty Role	Role for Quantities	Type of QD	Type of Quantity Determination	Quantity	Unit	In.
REQ	Requested Quantity	OQ	Original quantity			100	EA	C
EXEC	Reduction Quantity	PA	Pack	D00002	Packaging Algorithm: Qty Determinatior	0	EA	C
OPEN	Open Quantity	PA	Pack	000001	Standard Algorithm: Quantity Offsetting	100	EA	C
REQ	Requested Quantity	PA	Pack			100	EA	C
EXEC	Reduction Quantity	PAN	GR and Packed, Not GR Posted	D00006	GR and Packed, Not GR Posted	0	EA	C
OPEN	Open Quantity	PAN	GR and Packed, Not GR Posted	000001	Standard Algorithm: Quantity Offsetting	100	EA	C

A quantity offsetting profile consists of the following components:

13.2.3.1 Quantity Categories

These classify the different quantities for each warehouse document item. Examples include requested quantity, reduced quantity (i.e., already processed quantity), open quantity (quantity remaining to process), and so on.

Menu Path: **SPRO | IMG | Extended Warehouse Management | Cross-Process Settings | Delivery Processing | Quantity Offsetting | Define Quantity Roles and Quantity Types**

You can view the existing quantity categories by double-clicking on "Quantity Category" under the dialogue structure. Here, enter the quantity category code and description.

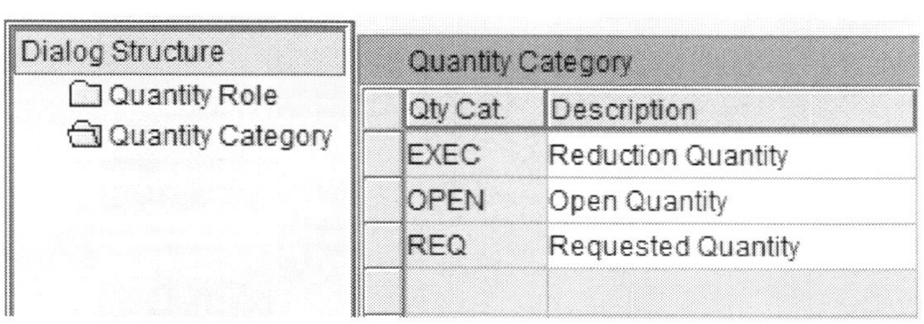

Dialog Structure
- Quantity Role
- Quantity Category

Quantity Category

Qty Cat.	Description
EXEC	Reduction Quantity
OPEN	Open Quantity
REQ	Requested Quantity

13.2.3.2 Quantity Role

Quantity Role is used to group quantity calculation or quantity offsetting rules for certain applications or processes. With this approach, quantity determination/offsetting rules can be defined to be either application dependent or process dependent—for example, packing, goods receipts, and goods issue. A quantity role can have several quantity types, like requested quantity, reduced quantity, and open quantity.

Menu Path: **SPRO | IMG | Extended Warehouse Management | Cross-Process Settings | Delivery Processing | Quantity Offsetting | Define Quantity Roles and Quantity Types**

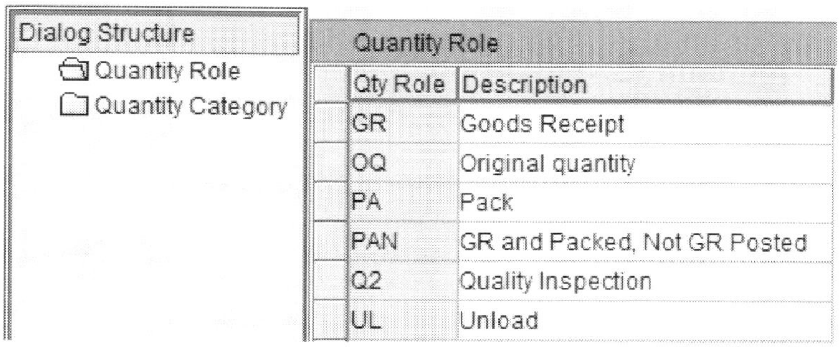

13.2.3.3 Quantity Determination Rules

Quantity determination rules define the quantity calculation rule for the relevant quantity for offsetting. It decides which algorithm is to be used to calculate the quantity for a particular combination of quantity role and quantity type. It also decides whether proceeding/follow-up documents (in document flow) should be referenced for quantity calculation.

Menu Path: **SPRO | IMG | Extended Warehouse Management | Cross-Process Settings | Delivery Processing | Quantity Offsetting | Define Quantity Determination Rules**

From the "Dialog Structure", both "Quantity Determination Algorithms" and "Quantity Determination Rules" can be accessed.

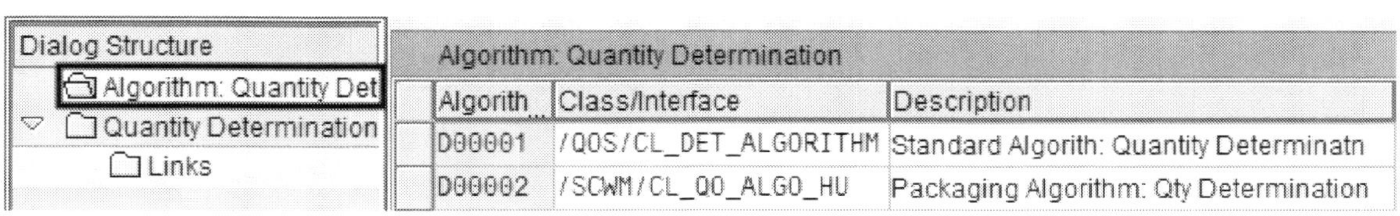

SAP has delivered several standard quantity determination algorithms. To define custom quantity determination algorithm, it is necessary to create custom class and that class has to implement interface /QOS/IF_DET_ALGORITHM.

To define the "Quantity Determination Rule", assign the quantity role, quantity category, and algorithm for quantity determination. Check the "Document Flow" check box and provide the relevant document category, if quantity is calculated from reference documents.

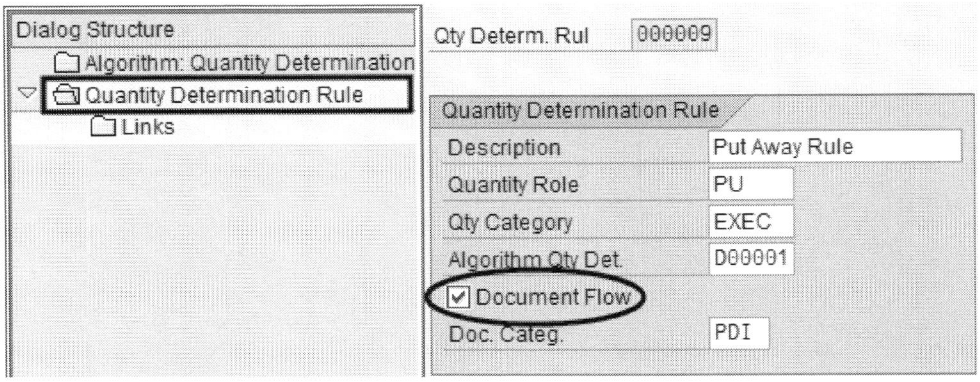

Under “Links” option, links to the reference documents (“i.e.” preceding and follow-up) can be provided from the document flow table.

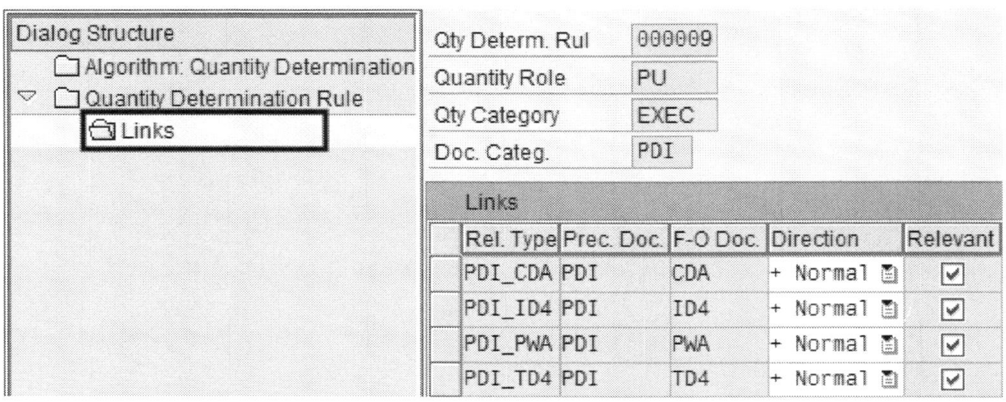

13.2.3.4 Quantity Offsetting Rules

The quantity offsetting rule is similar to the quantity determination rule. It defines the rule for calculating the open quantity. It decides offsetting algorithm and quantity determination rules used for a particular quantity role to calculate the open quantity. To define custom quantity determination algorithm, it is necessary to create custom class and that class has to implement interface /QOS/IF_OFF_ALGORITHM.

Menu Path: SPRO | IMG | Extended Warehouse Management | Cross-Process Settings | Delivery Processing | Quantity Offsetting | Define Quantity Offsetting Rules

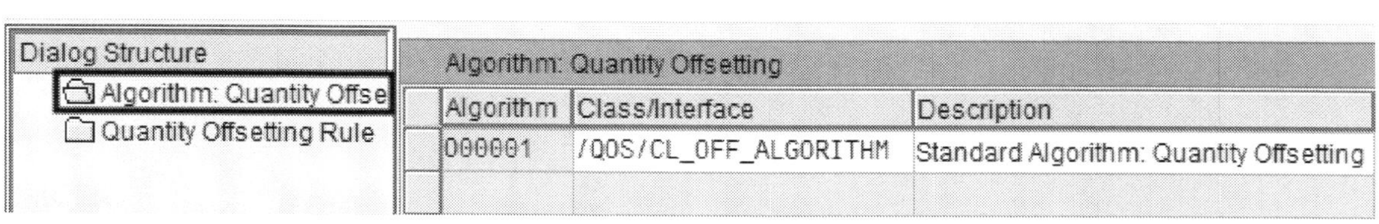

The appropriate quantity determination rule can be assigned under the quantity offsetting rule.

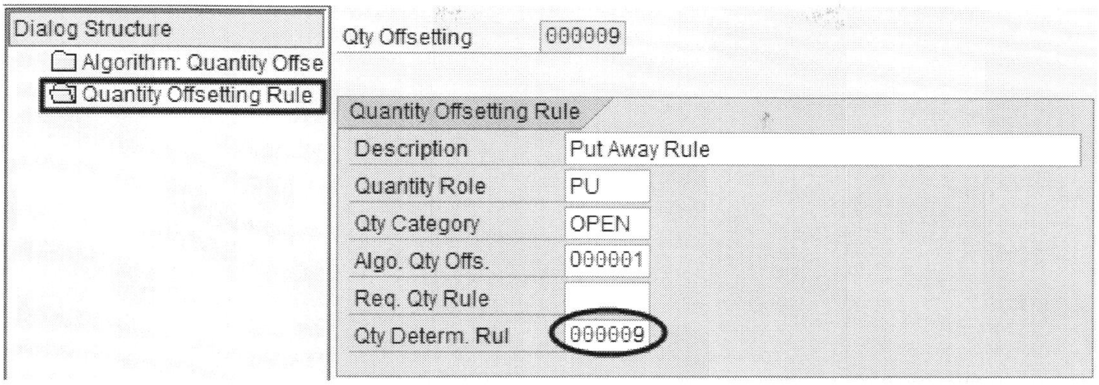

13.2.3.5 Quantity Offsetting Profile

The quantity offsetting profile is defined for a particular application to execute quantity offsetting automatically. Each quantity offsetting profile is assigned to the system profile. When the quantity offsetting profile is assigned to the system profile, all the predefined quantity roles are copied to quantity offsetting profile, where they can be used to activate or deactivate the quantity roles that are not marked as mandatory.

Menu Path: **SPRO | IMG | Extended Warehouse Management | Cross-Process Settings | Delivery Processing | Quantity Offsetting | Define Quantity Offsetting Profile**

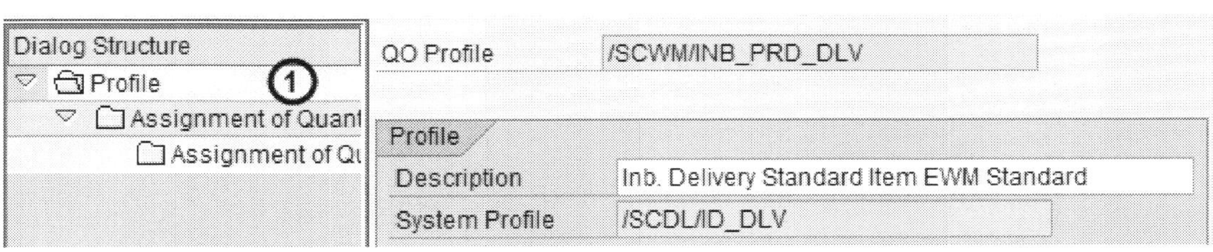

During assignment of quantity roles, any custom defined quantity roles can be assigned or can change the attribute of the existing roles to inactive as shown in the following screenshot.

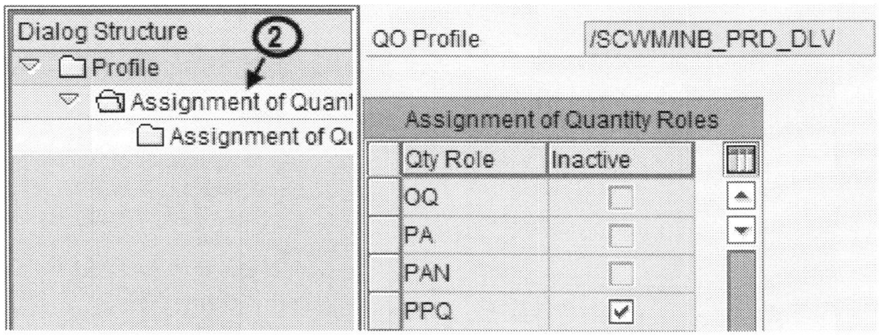

Under “Assignment of Quantity Categories”, the custom defined quantity categories are assigned. Check the checkbox “Dynamic” to determine the quantities dynamically.

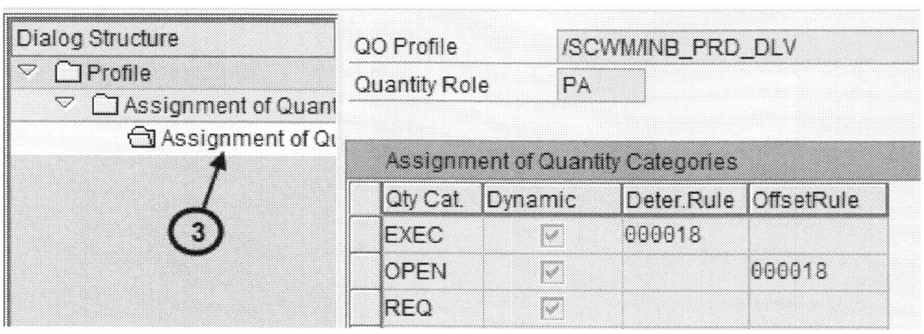

13.2.3.6 Assign Quantity Offsetting Profile to Item Type

In order to use the custom defined quantity offsetting profile, it is necessary to assign it to the document types or item types. The quantity offsetting profile defined here can be used for both inbound and outbound deliveries.

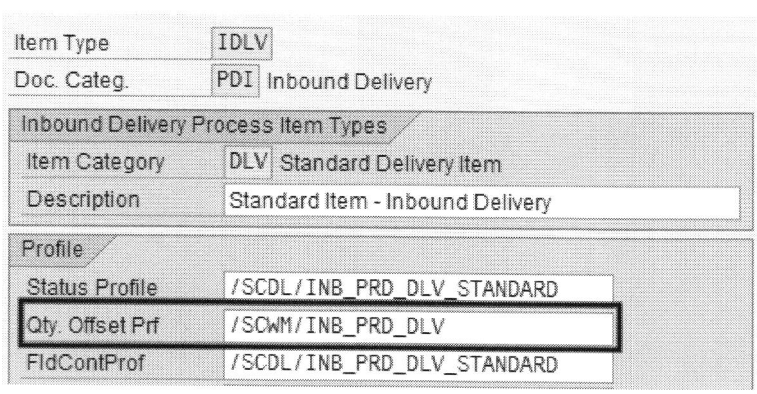

Menu Path: **SPRO | IMG | Extended Warehouse Management | Goods Receipt Process | Inbound Delivery | Manual Settings | Define Item Types for Inbound Delivery Process**

13.2.4 Reference Document Profiles

Reference document profiles determine which reference documents are allowed for a delivery document. The reference documents profile is assigned to the document categories. SAP provides a set of preconfigured profiles for the standard delivery document and item category.

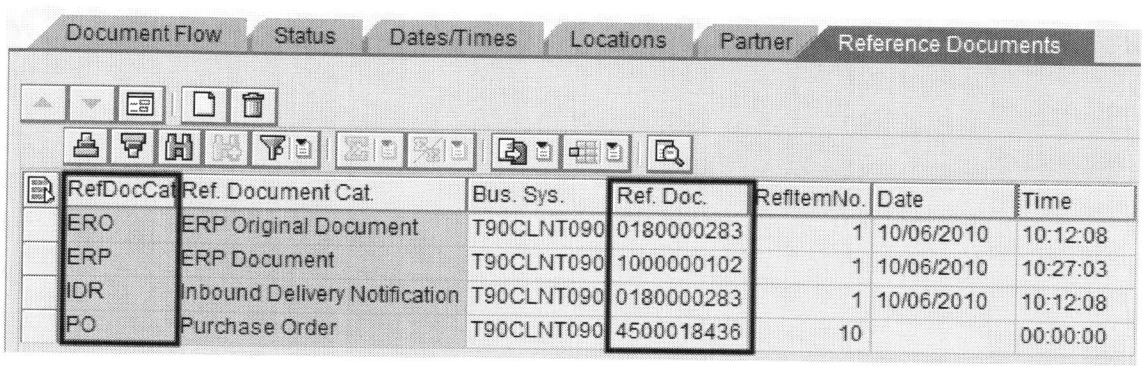

RefDocCat	Ref. Document Cat.	Bus. Sys.	Ref. Doc.	RefItemNo.	Date	Time
ERO	ERP Original Document	T90CLNT090	0180000283	1	10/06/2010	10:12:08
ERP	ERP Document	T90CLNT090	1000000102	1	10/06/2010	10:27:03
IDR	Inbound Delivery Notification	T90CLNT090	0180000283	1	10/06/2010	10:12:08
PO	Purchase Order	T90CLNT090	4500018436	10		00:00:00

13.2.4.1 Reference Document Categories

Reference document categories are used for linkage with the documents used in delivery processing. The data is copied from the reference document to the linked document.

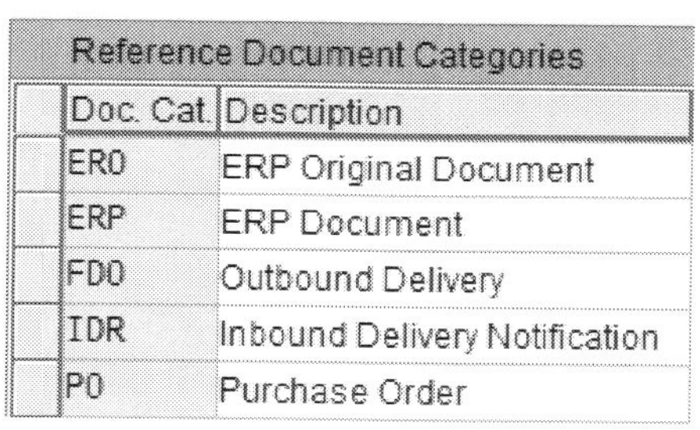

Reference Document Categories

Doc. Cat.	Description
ERO	ERP Original Document
ERP	ERP Document
FDO	Outbound Delivery
IDR	Inbound Delivery Notification
PO	Purchase Order

Menu Path: SPRO | IMG | Extended Warehouse Management | Delivery Processing | Reference Documents | Define Reference Document Categories

13.2.4.2 Reference Document Type Profiles

Reference document type determination is governed by the reference document type profile, which consists of reference document categories. The reference document type profile is also assigned to the system profile.

Menu Path: SPRO | IMG | Extended Warehouse Management | Delivery Processing | Reference Documents | Define Reference Document Type Profiles

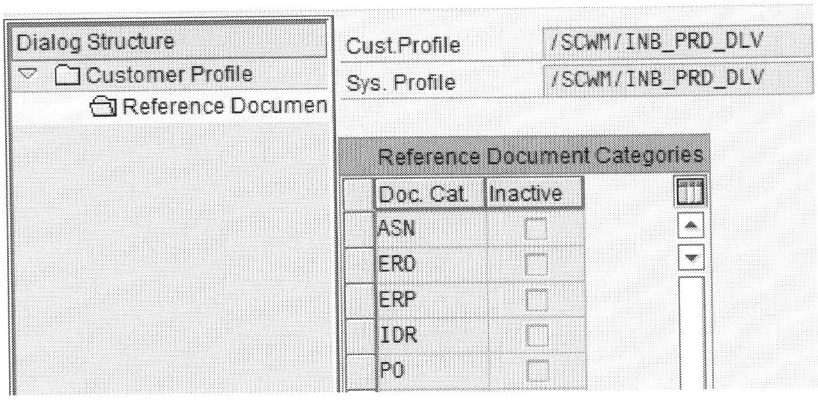

13.2.4.3 Assign Ref. Doc. Type Profiles to the Document or Item Type

If a custom profile is defined, it must be assigned to the appropriate document type or item type.

13.2.5 Partner Processing

Partner processing is the function that makes it possible to maintain partner information in the header and/or item level in the delivery documents. In this section we will explore the configuration of defining partner roles and partner profiles and assigning the partner profiles to the document or item types.

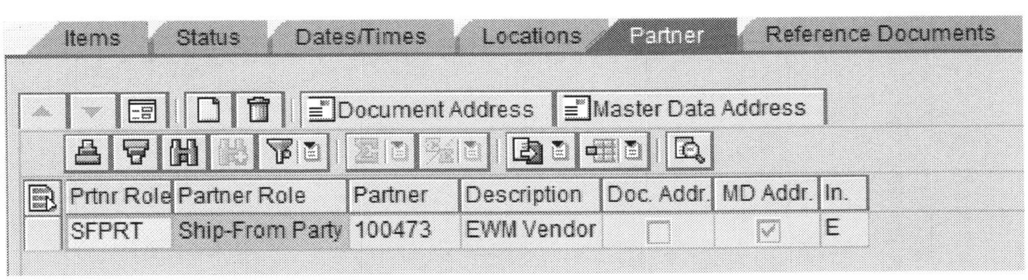

13.2.5.1 Partner Roles

Partner roles are used to represent a role or function in the business process such as suppliers, ship-to, buyer, and so on. They are defined with a unique key, description, and role category. The role categories are predefined by SAP. They include business partner, location, and organization. Once the partner roles defined, they need to be assigned to the appropriate partner profiles. If the master data is to be referenced for the partner data, the "MD" check box must be active.

Menu Path: SPRO | IMG | Extended Warehouse Management | Delivery Processing | Partner Processing | Define Partner Roles

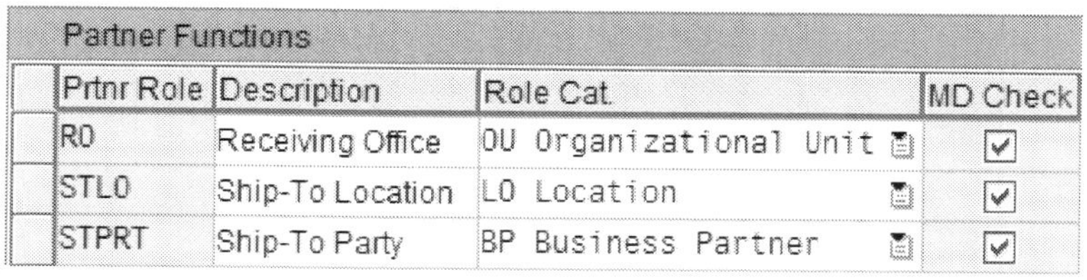

Prtnr Role	Description	Role Cat.	MD Check
RO	Receiving Office	OU Organizational Unit	☑
STLO	Ship-To Location	LO Location	☑
STPRT	Ship-To Party	BP Business Partner	☑

13.2.5.2 Partner Profiles

Partner profiles contain partner roles and are assigned to the delivery document types and item types. SAP has provided several predefined partner profiles. In the predefined profiles, SAP has assigned mandatory as well as optional partner roles. If these profiles are not sufficient, customers can define their own partner profiles in menu path **SPRO | IMG | Extended Warehouse Management | Delivery Processing | Partner Processing | Define Partner Profiles**

13.2.5.3 Assign Partner Profiles to the Document or Item Type

Once the partner profiles are defined, they must be assigned to the appropriate document or item type of inbound or outbound delivery.

13.2.6 Dates/Times Profile

The dates that are supported in EWM are defined as date types—for example, delivery date, GR date, GI date, and so on. Time is always recorded as part of a date type. In EWM, new date types can be configured using the date type functionality.

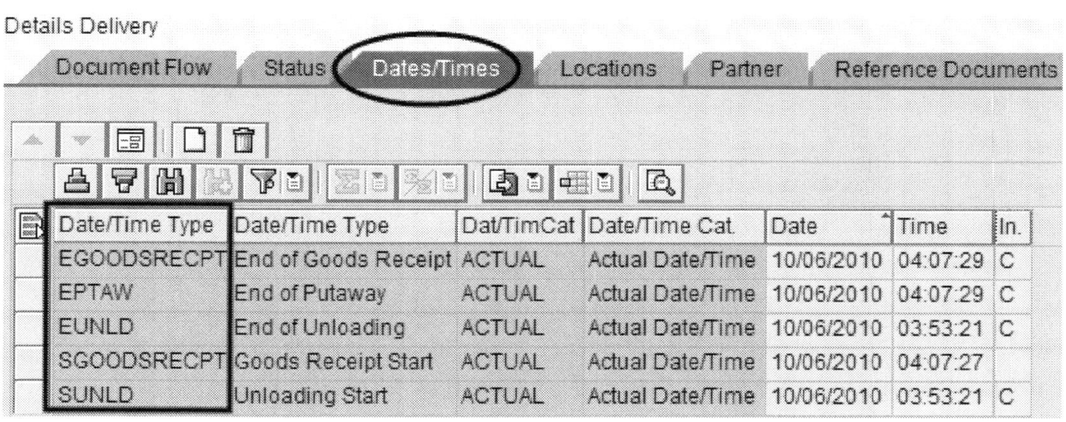

Date/Time Type	Date/Time Type	Dat/TimCat	Date/Time Cat.	Date	Time	In.
EGOODSRECPT	End of Goods Receipt	ACTUAL	Actual Date/Time	10/06/2010	04:07:29	C
EPTAW	End of Putaway	ACTUAL	Actual Date/Time	10/06/2010	04:07:29	C
EUNLD	End of Unloading	ACTUAL	Actual Date/Time	10/06/2010	03:53:21	C
SGOODSRECPT	Goods Receipt Start	ACTUAL	Actual Date/Time	10/06/2010	04:07:27	
SUNLD	Unloading Start	ACTUAL	Actual Date/Time	10/06/2010	03:53:21	C

Importantly, the EWM date types should match the date types defined in configurable process scheduling. **Menu Path: SPRO | SCM Basis | Configurable Process Scheduling | Scheduling Schema | Define Elements of Schema > Date/Time Types**

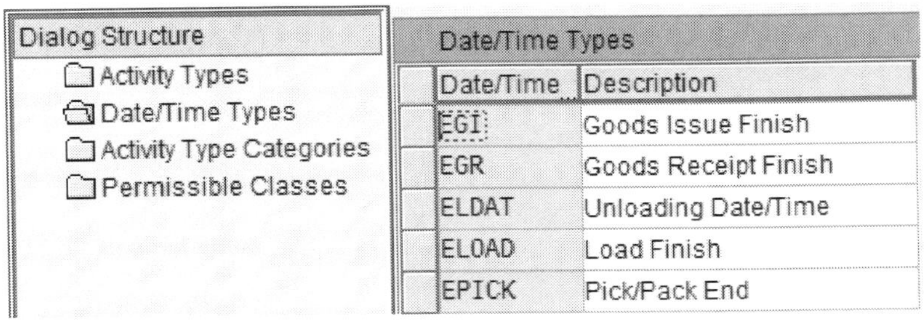

Dialog Structure
- Activity Types
- Date/Time Types
- Activity Type Categories
- Permissible Classes

Date/Time Types

Date/Time	Description
EGI	Goods Issue Finish
EGR	Goods Receipt Finish
ELDAT	Unloading Date/Time
ELOAD	Load Finish
EPICK	Pick/Pack End

13.2.6.1 Define Date Types

This defines the date type key (maximum of twelve characters long) and a description for the date type.

Menu Path: SPRO | Extended Warehouse Management | Cross-Process Settings | Delivery Processing | Dates/Times | Define Date Types

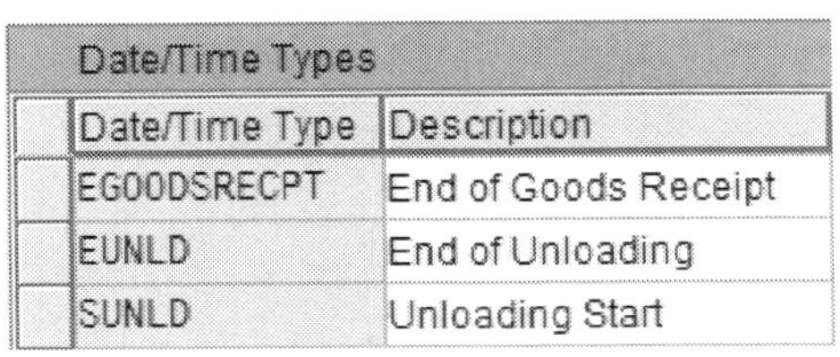

Date/Time Types

Date/Time Type	Description
EGOODSRECPT	End of Goods Receipt
EUNLD	End of Unloading
SUNLD	Unloading Start

13.2.6.2 Define Date Profiles

Date type determination in delivery is governed by the date type profile, which consists of date types. Each date type profile is assigned to the system profile. When the date type profile is assigned to the system profile, all the predefined date types are copied to the date type profile. As with any other profile, the existing values of the date types that are not mandatory can be changed, or customers can define their own date types.

Menu Path: SPRO | Extended Warehouse Management | Cross-Process Settings | Delivery Processing | Dates/Times | Define Date Profiles

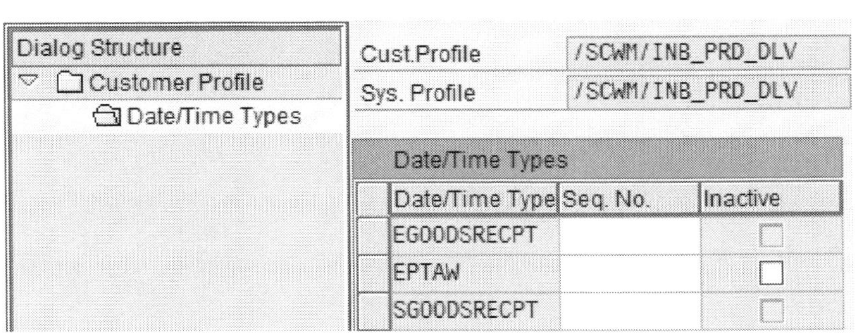

Dialog Structure
- Customer Profile
  - Date/Time Types

Cust.Profile /SCWM/INB_PRD_DLV
Sys. Profile /SCWM/INB_PRD_DLV

Date/Time Types

Date/Time Type	Seq. No.	Inactive
EGOODSRECPT		☐
EPTAW		☐
SGOODSRECPT		☐

13.2.6.3 Assign Date Profile to the Document or Item Type

Finally, like any other profile, the date profile must be assigned to the document or item type.

13.2.7 Status Management

In EWM, the status management configuration is used to allow and restrict certain functionalities in the warehouse document. It also shows the sub status of each status type (i.e., started, in process, or completed). Status management in delivery is governed by the status profile, which consists of status types and status values, as shown below.

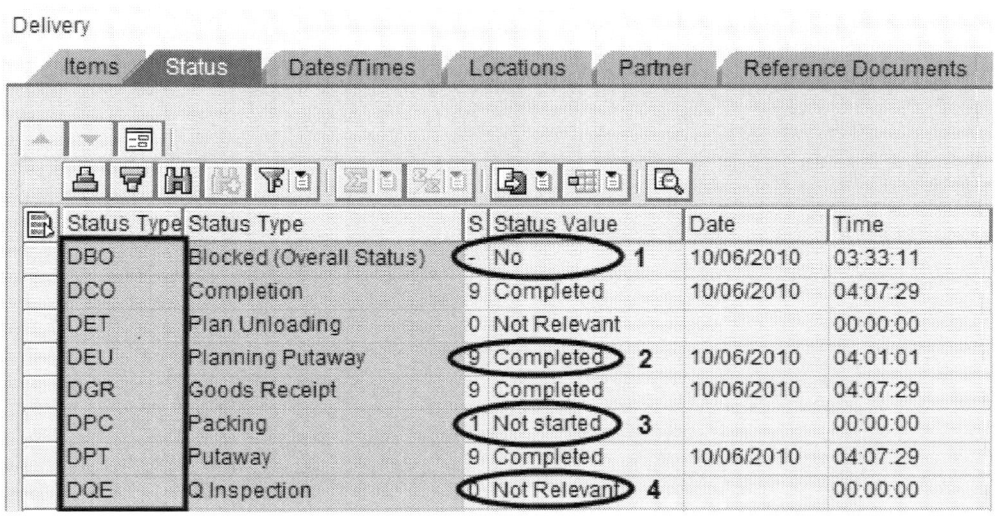

13.2.7.1 Status Profiles

A status profile consists of various status types and is assigned to the system profile. When it is assigned to the system profile, all the predefined status types are copied to the status profile. You can manually change the settings of attributes for status types that are not marked as mandatory. The system will not allow changes to the settings of attributes for mandatory status types in the status profile.

Menu Path: SPRO | IMG | Extended Warehouse Management | Cross-Process Settings | Delivery Processing | Status Management | Define Status Profiles

The following is an example of a standard status profile used in the EWM system for inbound delivery. Users can define their own status profile by clicking on "New entries."

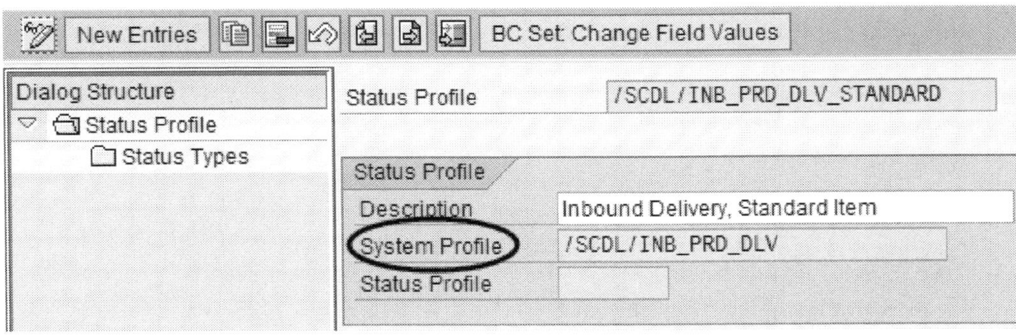

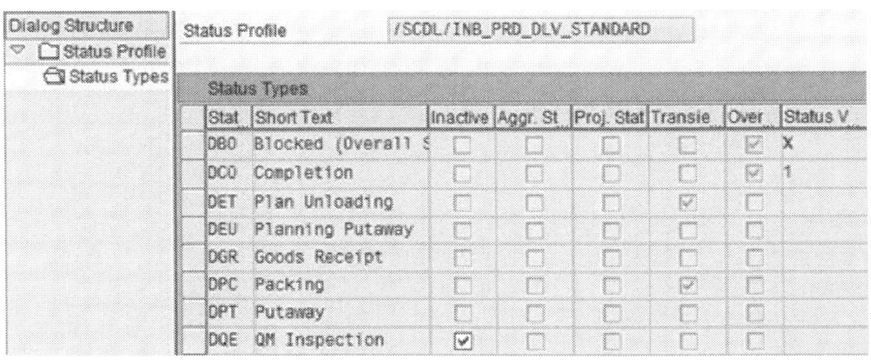

The following attributes are available for each status types.

- **Inactive:** Not all statuses can be changed to inactive. If changes are permitted, you can change the attributes of status types as per your requirement
- **Aggregated Status:** The system calculates the status value of such a status type from the status values of all the partial objects in a lower document level
- **Projected Status:** The system calculates the status value of such a status type from the status type with the same name from higher document levels
- **Overall Status:** The status value for this is calculated from current status values of a predefined quantity of status types from the same partial object
- **Transient Status:** The system only calculates this status type for the runtime. The status type is not saved permanently

13.2.7.2 Assign Status Profile to Item Type

In order to use the status profile, it must first be assigned to the document types or item types. The status profiles defined here can be used for inbound and outbound deliveries.

Menu Path: **SPRO | IMG | Extended Warehouse Management | Goods Receipt Process | Inbound Delivery | Manual Settings | Define Item Types for Inbound Delivery Process**

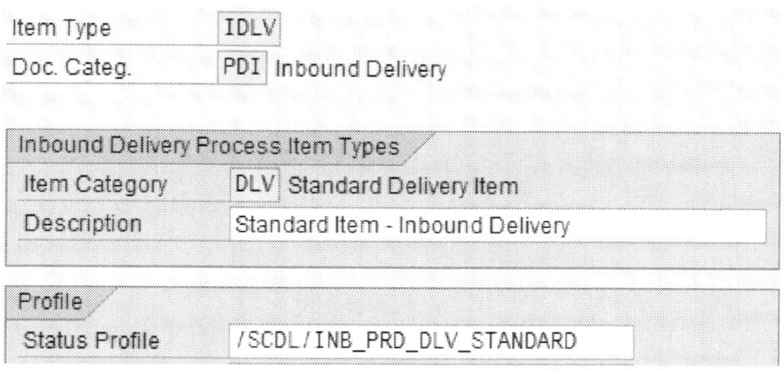

13.2.8 Field Control

Field Control decides which fields in a delivery document should be display only and which can be edited or hidden at various statuses of the document. Field control supports fields at the header and item level of a document. It is also dependent on status management.

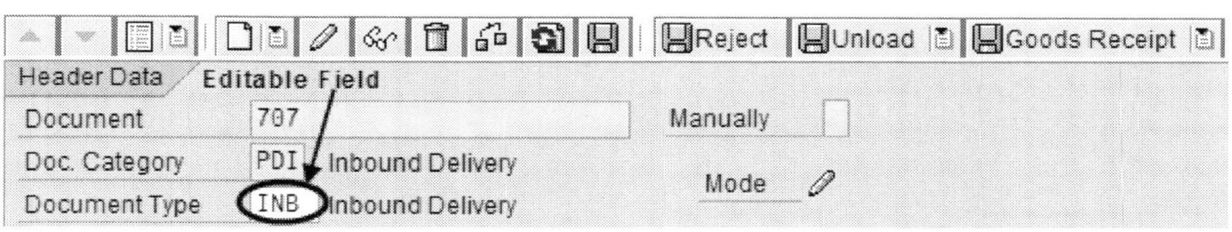

The field control can be accessed at the time of creation, change, or display of a document or a document item. It is governed by the field control profile, which consists of structures. All fields in a delivery document are defined in the system as components of structure. Every component in a structure is uniquely identified by the logical field name and can be addressed directly.

Each field control profile is assigned to the system profile. Like other profiles, when the field control profile is assigned to the system profile, all the predefined logical field names along with the attributes (display, hide) are copied to the field control profile. The attributes of the fields are controlled by the field group. By default, most of the fields belong to group number 0001 and are display only.

The following example demonstrates how to make the document type field "inbound delivery" editable.

- **Define a new field group:** Here, copy group 0001 to a new group a new group. We have created a new group called 9999.

Menu Path: SPRO | IMG | Extended Warehouse Management | Cross-Process Settings | Delivery Processing | Extend Delivery Processing | Extend System Profiles for Field Control

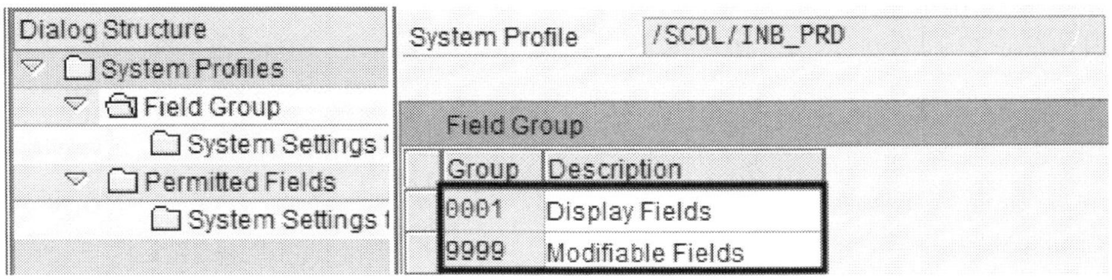

Verify the attribute values for field group 0001.

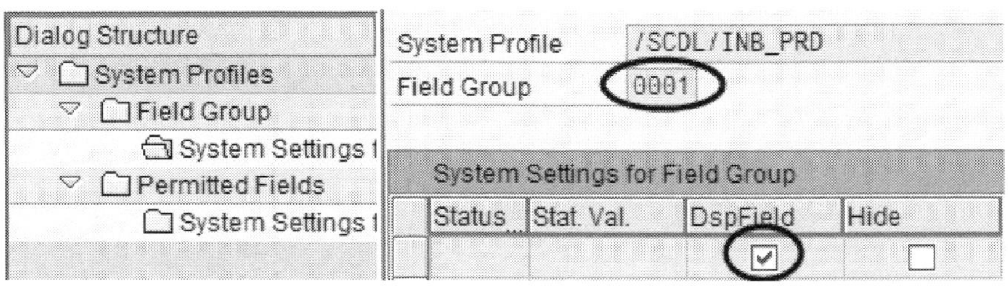

For group 9999, uncheck the "DSPFIELD" check box to allow changes.

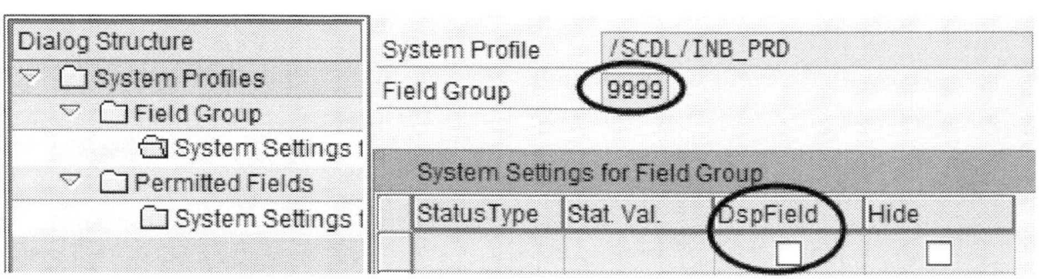

Next, assign the group to the logical fields under permitted fields.

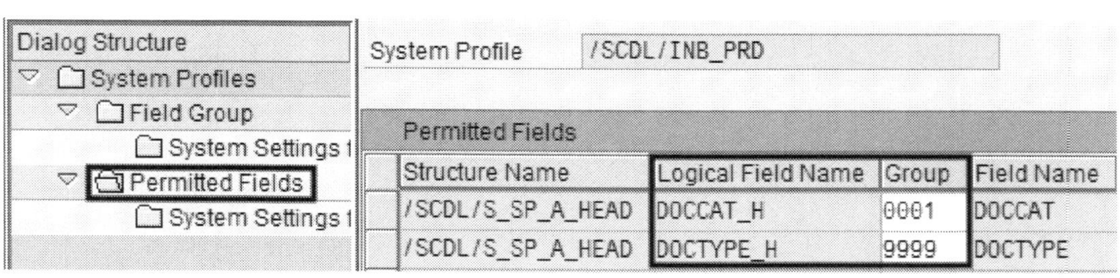

Once the required configuration is completed, the changes can be verified in the delivery document. The following is the example of inbound delivery (TCode /SCWM/PRDI), for which group 9999 is active and the document type field is now editable.

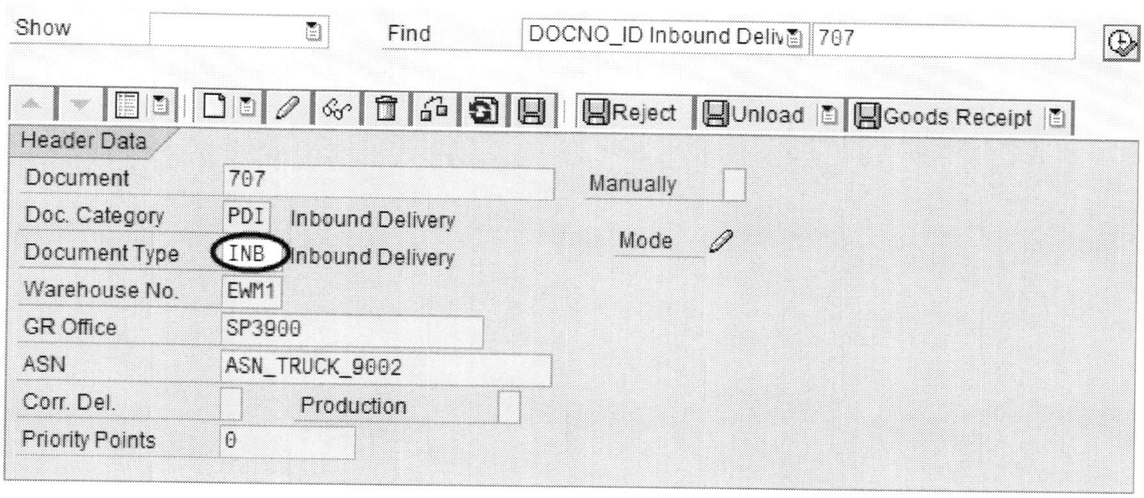

Filed control settings can be configured in the following configuration menu:

- **Define logical field names:** This option is available under **SPRO | IMG | Extended Warehouse Management | Cross-Process Settings | Delivery Processing | Extend Delivery Processing | Define Logical Field Names**
- **Extend system profiles for field control:** This can be accessed under **SPRO | IMG | Extended Warehouse Management | Cross-Process Settings | Delivery Processing | Extend Delivery Processing | Extend System Profiles for Field Control**

Finally, depending on the requirement, the field control profile has to be assigned to the document type and item type.

13.2.9 Incompleteness Check

This is used to ensure that all required fields in the delivery documents have been filled or completed before initiating the next process. If the required condition is not fulfilled, the system will set the status of the document as an error or inactive, and the document will be blocked for inconsistency.

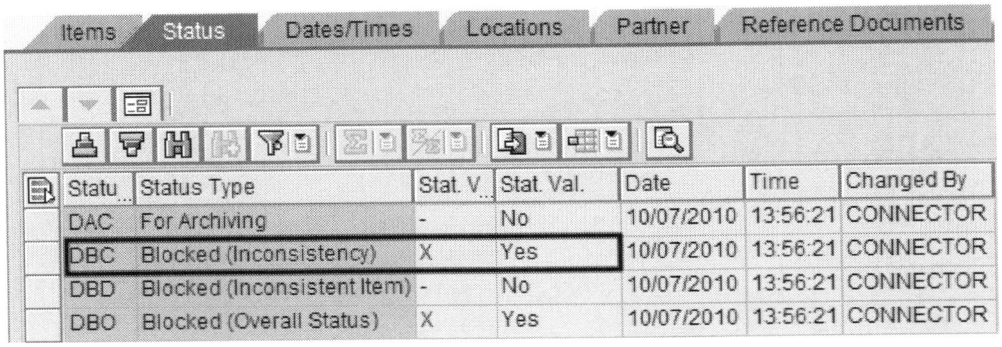

13.2.9.1 Incompleteness Profiles

The incompleteness check in the delivery is governed by the incompleteness profile. In configuring the incompleteness profile, the settings of the logical fields can be changed. Each field consists of a business action code such as "Save", "Goods issue", or "Check", which determines when the field is checked for completeness.

Menu Path: SPRO | IMG | Extended Warehouse Management | Cross-Process Settings | Delivery Processing | Incompleteness Check | Define Incompleteness Profiles

Here, select the required incompleteness profile and click on the "Required Fields" option under the dialog structure. To add new logical fields, click the "New" button. It is possible to inactivate the verification for various fields, by selecting the "Inactive" check box.

In the following example, inbound delivery is allowed to process in the warehouse without an ASN document number (REFDOCNO_ASN_H) in the inbound delivery.

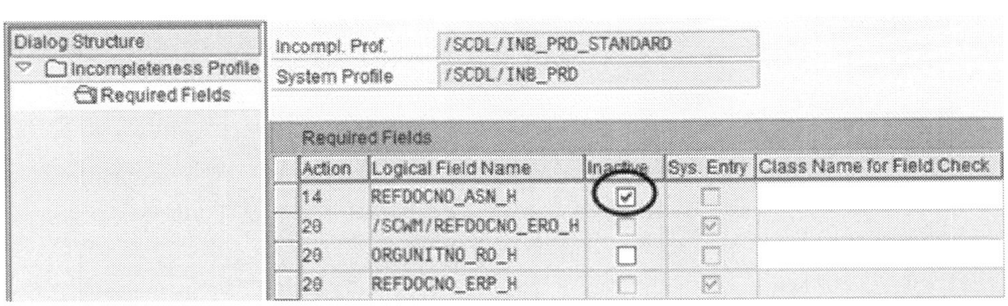

13.2.9.2 Assign Incompleteness Profile to the Doc. or Item Type

Depending on where the incompleteness check is to be used, the profile can be assigned to the document or item type.

13.2.10 Process Management (Mgmt.) and Control

Process management and control plays an important role in delivery processing. It controls whether certain process are allowed for a delivery type. Process control indicators can be set for header and item level. The following screenshot shows that invoice creation before goods issue is not allowed in outbound delivery 80016725.

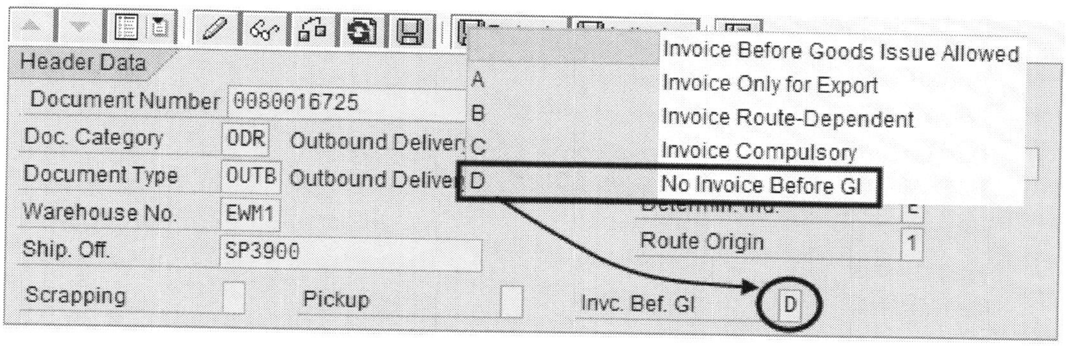

13.2.10.1 Process Profile for Delivery Document Header

The following indicators can be set for the delivery header profile:

- **Manual Creation:** Specify whether a document can be created manually or not.
- **Preceding Document:** Specify whether a reference to a preceding document is allowed or not.
- **Scrapping:** Specify whether scrapping is mandatory or disallowed for the document. If it is set to mandatory, it shows that the document type is relevant for the scrapping process.
- **Pickup:** Specify whether a pickup is mandatory or disallowed for the delivery document. For example, for a construction project, the tools can be issued to a worker directly from the warehouse without a sales order and with reference to a cost center. In this case, the workers will pick up the stock directly from the warehouse and no transportation is involved. In this scenario, stock is issued by creating an outbound delivery order locally in EWM system without reference to a sales order. For these deliveries, once the goods issue is complete, the process is complete.
- **Invoice before goods issue:** This does allow creating an invoice before the goods issue.
- **Correction Delivery:** Allows posting of a differences to the stock and the difference to be cleared using a correction delivery document.

Menu Path: **SPRO | IMG | Extended Warehouse Management | Cross-Process Settings | Delivery Processing | Process Management and Control | Define Process Profile for Delivery Document Header**

Process Profile	/SCWM/INB_PRD

Process Profile Delivery

Description	Inbound Delivery Standard
Process Prof. Syst.	/SCWM/INB_PRD
Create Manually	A Allowed
Preceding Document	Predecessor Document Allowed
Production	Disallow
Scrapping	Disallow
Pickup	Disallow
Inv Bef GI	D Disallow
Correction Delivery	Disallow

13.2.10.2 Process Profile for Delivery Document Item

The following indicators can be set for the delivery item:

- **Manual Creation:** This allows creating an item in the delivery manually without reference to a line item in the preceding document.
- **Invoice before Goods Issue:** This allows billing of a line item before its goods issue posting.

Menu Path: SPRO | IMG | Extended Warehouse Management | Cross-Process Settings | Delivery Processing | Process Management and Control | Define Process Profile for Delivery Document Item

Process Profile	/SCWM/INB_PRD_DLV

Process Profile Delivery Item

Description	Inbound Delivery Standard Item Standard
Proc. Prof Syst	/SCWM/INB_PRD_DLV
Create Manually	A Allowed
Invoice Bef. GI	Disallow

13.2.10.3 Assign Process Mgmt. and Control to the Doc. or Item Type

Depending on where the process management and control is to be used, the profile is assigned to the document or item type.

13.3 Delivery Processing—ERP Integration

From an integration perspective, it is important to understand the basic EWM integration setting for delivery documents. This section will review those settings. Table 13.3A provides an overview of configurations covered under this section.

S. No	Delivery Processing - ERP Integration	TCode	System	Transportable
1	Define ERP Document Types for Differentiation Attribute	SPRO	EWM	Yes
2	Map Document Types from ERP System to EWM	SPRO	EWM	Yes
3	Map Item Types from ERP System to EWM	SPRO	EWM	Yes
4	Map Date Types from ERP System to EWM	SPRO	EWM	Yes
5	Define Account Assignment Category	SPRO	EWM	Yes
6	Map Routes and Route Schedule from ERP System to EWM	SPRO	EWM	Yes

Table 13.3A Delivery Processing Integration Overview

13.3.1 ERP Document Types for Differentiation Attribute

The differentiation attribute makes it possible to map an ERP item type onto various item types in EWM. This means that the items can be controlled in different ways in EWM under different scenarios.

SAP has delivered four predefined profiles that can be assigned to ERP delivery type. They include the following:

- **RETCU:** Customer returns.
- **SCRAP:** Scrapping deliveries.
- **TRANS:** Stock transfers.
- **ITEM:** This can be used as a general differentiation attribute.

These profiles cannot be changed or enhanced. Each profile has exactly one field of the delivery interface for the ERP system. The field receives the values from the ERP system that were defined for a specific domain. The value of the field can be used as a differentiation attribute for mapping item types from ERP to EWM, which is covered below in section 13.3.3.

SAP has provided mapping for all the standard document types. Hence, no additional configuration is required for the standard ERP document types.

Menu Path: SPRO | IMG | Extended Warehouse Management | Interfaces | ERP Integration | Delivery Processing | Define ERP Document Types for Differentiation Attribute

Determine Differentiation Attribute for Item Type Mapping

DocTypeE...	Business System	Profile
DIG		TRANS
DOG		TRANS
DTR		SCRAP
EL		TRANS
NL		TRANS
SRCL		RETCU
SRNP		RETCU
SRUP		RETCU

13.3.2 Map Document Types from ERP to EWM

For data exchange between ERP and EWM systems, document types from the ERP system must be mapped to the document types of the EWM system.

SAP has provided mapping for all the standard delivery document types. Hence, no additional configuration is required for the standard document types. All these settings exist in a table used to cross-reference the ERP delivery document type to the EWM delivery document type. Diagram 13.3.2A shows how the EWM delivery document type gets determined for the ERP delivery document type. The system will always search for a more specific entry rather than a generic entry in the table.

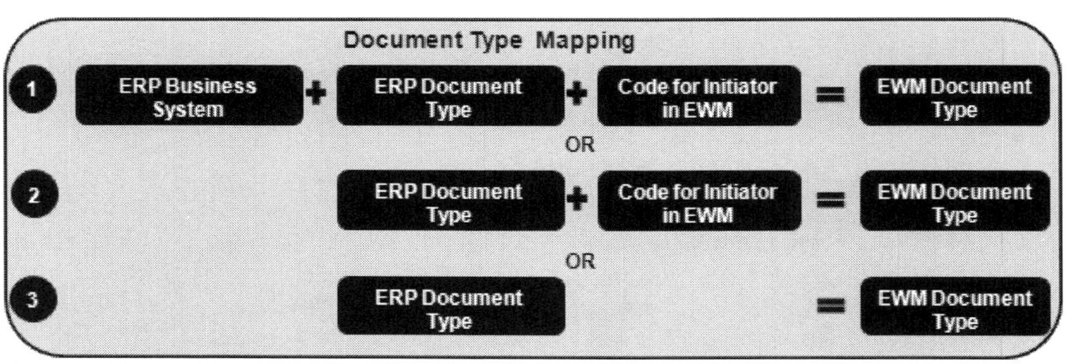

Diagram 13.3.2A - ERP and EWM Document Type Mapping

Menu Path: SPRO | IMG | Extended Warehouse Management | Interfaces | ERP Integration | Delivery Processing | Map Document Types from ERP System to EWM

Mapping Delivery Type - Document Type			
Business System	DocTypeERP	Cde Init. Com.	Doc. Type
	EL		INB
	EL	GRN	EGRE
	LF		OUTB

13.3.3 Map Item Types from ERP to EWM

In addition to mapping the delivery document types, the integration between the ERP and EWM system includes mapping item types from the ERP to EWM systems. SAP has delivered mapping for all the standard delivery item types. Hence, no additional configuration is required for the standard item types.

Diagram 13.3.3A shows how the EWM delivery item type gets determined for the ERP delivery item type. The system will search for a more specific, rather than generic, entry in the table. The ERP item type is referred as "item category" in the ERP system.

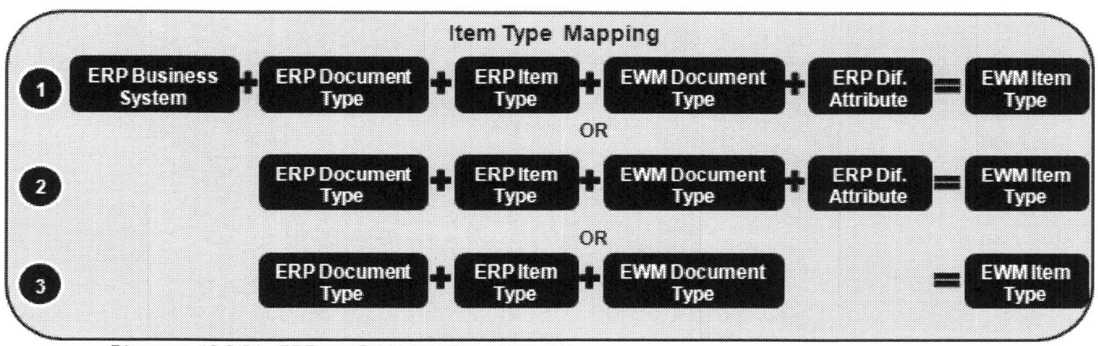

Diagram 13.3.3A - ERP and EWM Item Type Mapping

Menu Path: SPRO | IMG | Extended Warehouse Management | Interfaces | ERP Integration | Delivery Processing | Map Item Types from ERP System to EWM

Mapping of ERP Item Type						
Busin...	DocTypeERP	ItmTpERP	Doc. Type	Diff.Attr.	CW Product	Item Type
	EL	ELN			☐	IDLV
	EL	ELN			☑	IDCW
	EL	ELN		A	☐	IDTR
	EL	ELN		A	☑	ITCW
	EL	ELN		D	☐	IDTR

13.3.4 Map Date Types from ERP to EWM

Like delivery item types, the system uses business system, ERP date type, and EWM document and item type to determine date types in the EWM system. SAP has provided mapping for all the standard date types. Hence, no additional configuration is required for the standard date types.

Menu Path: SPRO | IMG | Extended Warehouse Management | Interfaces | ERP Integration | Delivery Processing | Map Date Types from ERP System to EWM

Mapping ERP Date/Time Types

Busin...	DType ERP	Doc. Type	Item Type	Start Date	End Date	Conf.D/T
	WSHDRLFDTI	INB	IDCW	SGOODSRECPT	EGOODSRECPT	E Confirm End Date
	WSHDRLFDTI	INB	IDLV	SGOODSRECPT	EGOODSRECPT	E Confirm End Date

13.3.5 Account Assignment Category in Warehouse Number

The system uses the settings of the allowed account assignment categories in a warehouse number to determine which account assignments can be created or displayed in outbound delivery orders in EWM. SAP has the following account assignment categories as standard:

- "10 - Cost center"
- "11 – Order"
- "12 – Project"

When working with the standard account assignment categories, consultants should assign the existing account assignment categories to their client's warehouse number.

Menu Path: SPRO | IMG | Extended Warehouse Management | Interfaces | ERP Integration | Delivery Processing | Define Account Assignment Category and Allow in Warehouse Number

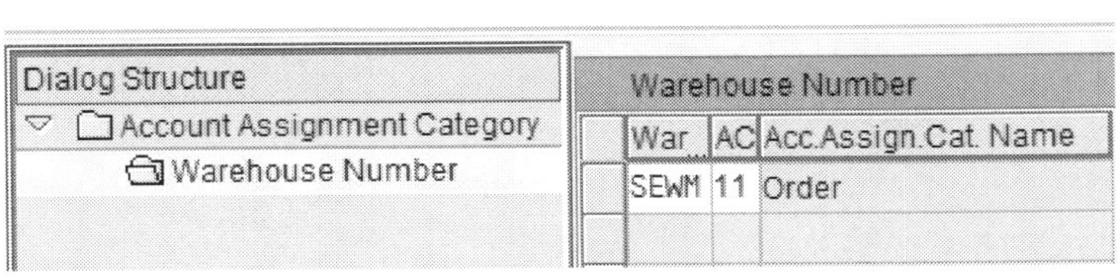

13.3.6 Map Routes and Route Schedule

This configuration sets which route data or route schedule data is to be copied from ERP to EWM. Here, the two important terms are Route (SD) and Route (SCM).

- **Route (SD):** A route that can be entered in the sales order in ERP or determined by ERP route determination. This route is called an ERP route.

- **Route (SCM):** A route used in SCM/EWM route determination. This can be also transferred from a CRM system. This route is called the Geo route.

Menu Path: SPRO | IMG | Extended Warehouse Management | Interfaces | ERP Integration | Delivery Processing | Map Routes and Route Schedule from ERP System to EWM

Here, enter ERP business system name in the business system field, ERP warehouse number in the Whs. No. ERP field, and select one of the following values in mapping route field:

- **Standard setting use route (SCM):** The route may come from a SCM system. This route is usually filled when working with CRM, in which routes from an SCM system are used (e.g., by availability check).

- **Use route (SD) if route (SCM) is initial or blank**: An SD route that may exist in documents is only used if the route (SCM-EWM) is not filled at the same time.

- **Use route (SD) if route (SD) and route schedule are filled:** An SD route that may exist in documents is only used if the SD route and route schedule are transferred from ERP.

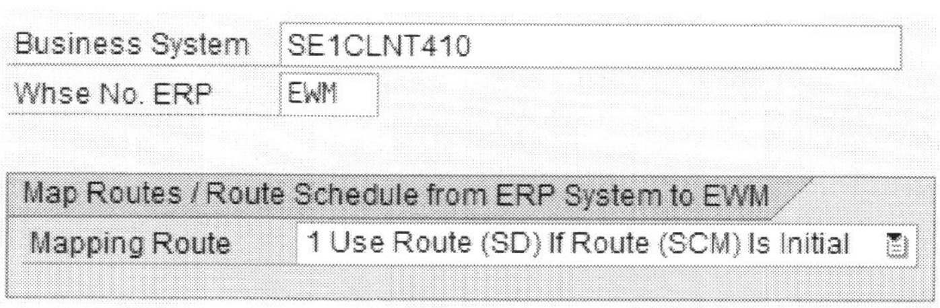

The following example demonstrates that the SD route is copied to EWM delivery because the SCM route is blank.

- **ERP Sales Order—Transaction VA01:**

In ERP system, create a sales order and verify that the route is filled in the sales line items. Make sure that the plant and storage location is EWM relevant.

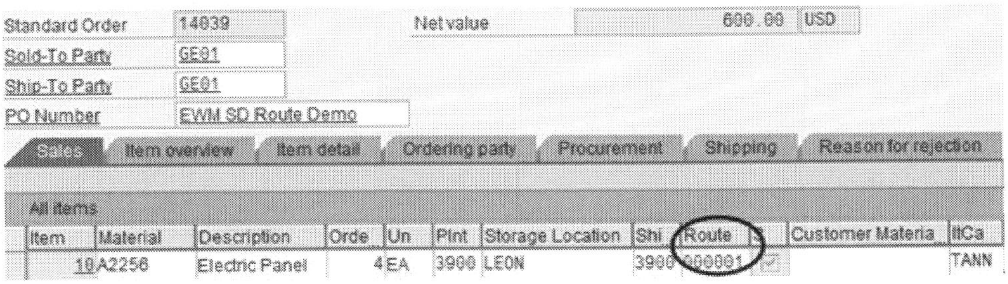

- **ERP Delivery (TCode VL01N)**

After creating the sales order got to transaction VL01N and create a delivery document. Verify that the route is copied to the outbound delivery from the sales order. This information is available in the shipment tab, as shown below.

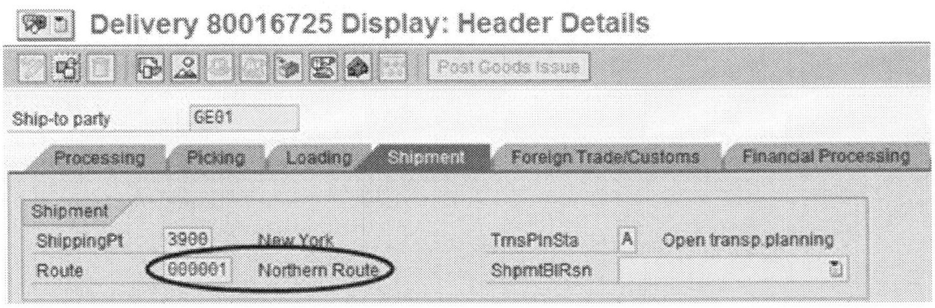

- **Outbound Delivery Request (ODR) in EWM system (TCode /SCWM/ODR)**

Because the plant and storage location is EWM managed, the system will automatically transfer the content of the ERP delivery document to the EWM system, and the corresponding ODR document will be created. The ODR number will be same as the ERP delivery document number. In ODR, route information should show in the header data of the ODR document, as shown below.

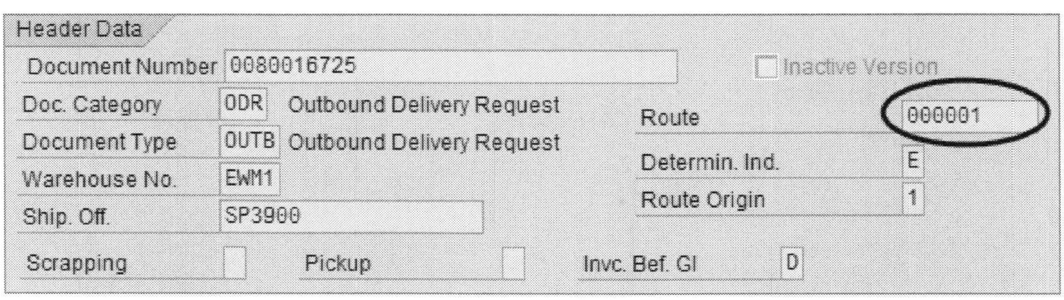

Summary

This chapter explained the delivery document structure, various delivery processing profiles used in the delivery document, integration with ERP document types, and delivery processing. It also demonstrated how delivery processing profiles influence the delivery document.

By now, all the required settings in the ERP and EWM system have been covered. The next chapter will discuss how to process documents in the EWM system and will also cover the goods receipt and putaway process in both the ERP and EWM systems.

Chapter 14: Goods Receipts and Putaway

This chapter covers, along with examples, the goods receipts (GR) process overview, configuration of the direct putaway process, unloading, GR, creating WTs, and processing of WOs. By the end of this chapter, it should be clear how to perform GR, create various putaway-related documents in the warehouse, and how to confirm WTs and WOs.

14.1 GR Process Overview

In general, there are four major ways that goods can be received in the EWM system. They include:

- Advanced Shipping Notification (ASN/inbound delivery document)
- Expected Goods Receipt (EGR)
- Returns
- Production Receipt

14.1.1 Advanced Shipping Notification (ASN)

ASN is a document or delivery confirmation received from the vendor, containing the details of the customer purchase order, products, and the quantities that are dispatched from the vendor location to the customer location. Based on the ASN information, inbound delivery will be created either manually or through Electronic Data Change (EDI) in the ERP system, which gets automatically transferred to the EWM system in the form of incoming messages. In the EWM system, these messages are converted into an IDN document. The IDN number will remain same as the inbound delivery number of the ERP system. IDN documents are mainly used for planning purposes.

In order to process IDN, it has to be converted into inbound delivery (ID) which is also called a warehouse request. This can be done manually or automatically, using PPF. In the standard system, by default it is automated, using PPF.

GRs can be posted manually with reference to inbound delivery, before the WTs are created, or they can be posted automatically when the WO is confirmed.

WTs cannot be created with reference to IDN. In order to create WTs for GRs, the IDN has to be converted into ID. WTs are used to create WOs, which are then used to putaway the products in the warehouse.

The following screenshot shows how to perform unloading and GR activities with reference to ID without creating the WTs.

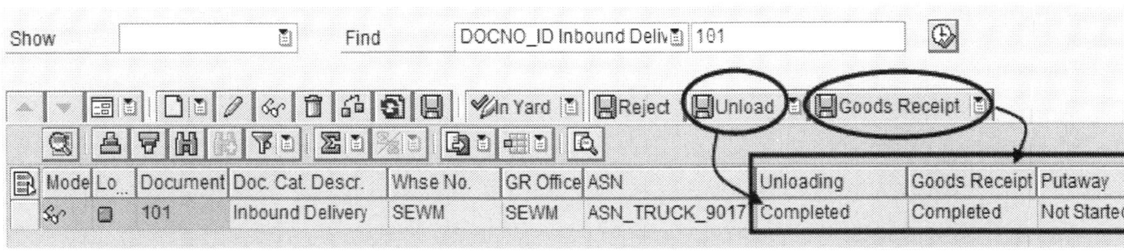

14.1.2 Expected Goods Receipt (EGR)

Usually, EGR is used in the absence of ASN. Diagram 14.1.2A shows the process flow followed in case of EGR. The GRN (Expected Goods Receipt Notification) document is created in the EWM system with reference to either a purchase order or a production order. It contains a copy of all the data from the source document. The EGR document is created from the GRN after it has been activated. Once the EGR is created, it is possible to create an inbound delivery from an EGR document.

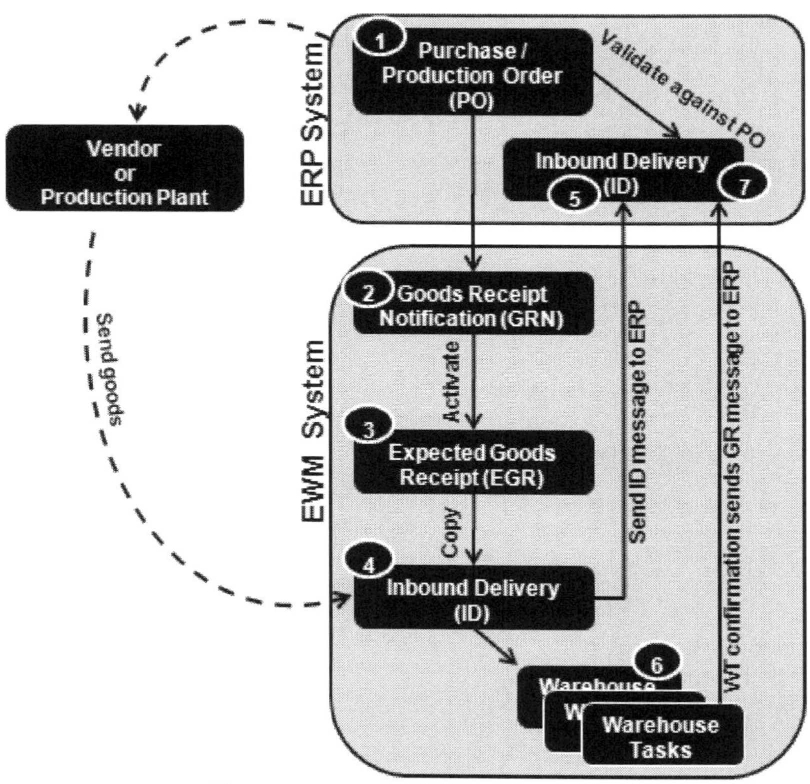

Diagram 14.1.2A – EGR Process Flow

EGR is a temporary document, and when EWM no longer requires it, the system deletes it. It only acts as a template for copying existing data from GRN, and none of this data can be changed. In the related inbound delivery, however, the data like quantity can be changed. When the inbound delivery is created in the EWM system, the system sends the message to the ERP system, which creates the inbound delivery with reference to the source document in the ERP system.

During this process, EWM neither updates the EGR nor offsets the quantity for EGR. It is also important to note that as of EWM 7.0, the system does not show EGR in the document flow of the inbound delivery.

The document type used for EGR is EGRE, and the document category is GRN and EGR.

Expected Goods Receipt Document Types

Doc. T	Doc. Cat.	I...	Description
EGRE	EGR	01	Expected Goods Receipt
EGRE	GRN	01	Expected Goods Receipt

In the EWM system, report /SCWM/ERP_DLV_DELETE can be used to delete the existing EGR and request new EGR from the ERP system for selected criteria.

The configuration for EGR can be found in the menu path **SPRO | IMG | Extended Warehouse Management | Goods Receipt Process | Expected Goods Receipt**

Just like ASN, in TCode /SCWM/PRDI, GRs can be posted manually with reference to inbound delivery before the WTs are created, or they can be posted automatically when the WO is confirmed.

14.1.3 Returns

In EWM, the term *returns* refers to returns from customers (i.e., from ship-from party or from ship-from location). Usually, once these goods arrive in the warehouse, they need to be putaway again may be after the quality inspection, if required, or they may be scrapped.

For returns, the item type used in EWM is ICR, the item category is RET, and the document categories are IDR and PDI.

Inbound Delivery Process Item Types

Item Type	Doc. Cat.	Item Cat.	Description
ICR	IDR	RET	Customer Returns
ICR	PDI	RET	Customer Returns

14.1.4 Production Receipt

As explained in the EGR section, in EWM, it is possible to post GRs for produced goods via EGR or using an inbound delivery. Inbound delivery can be initiated from the ERP side or from the EWM side.

In case of inbound delivery, when the last production step is confirmed for a EWM warehouse-managed product, ERP generates an inbound delivery instead of a material document. This delivery document provides information about material and quantity being produced. The document type used here is INBI (Inbound Delivery from Production) to differentiate from inbound delivery from Purchase Order (INB), and the document categories are IDR and PDI.

Inbound Delivery Process Document Types

Doc. Type	Doc. Cat.	Int. NRI	Description
INBI	IDR		Inbound Delivery Notif. GR Production
INBI	PDI	01	Inbound Delivery GR Production

14.2 Warehouse Putaway

In the warehouse, product putaway can be done in four different ways:

- Direct Putaway
- Process-Oriented Putaway
- Layout-Oriented Putaway
- Combination of Both Process- and Layout-Oriented Putaway

This chapter will cover direct putaway. In the next chapter, process-oriented putaway and layout-oriented putaway are covered in detail under storage control.

14.3 Direct Putaway

Direct putaway can be used for all the GR scenarios explained above. Here, an ASN example will be used to putaway the stock. This section will explain how to define the configuration, set up the required master data, and process the various documents, with an actual example all the way from purchase order to putaway in the warehouse, along with TCodes.

14.3.1 Product Master

In the warehouse, the putaway process is derived by the product master (TCode /SCWM/MAT1). In order to use a direct putaway process, the process type determination indicator for the product must be set in the product master, as shown below. SAP delivered process type determination indicator for direct putaway is "04—Direct Putaway". This is the key that drives this process.

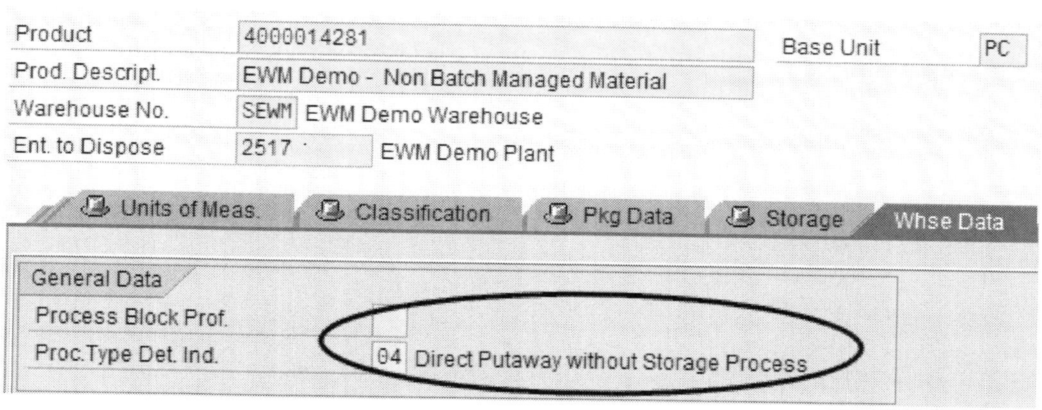

14.3.2 Purchase Order

To demonstrate the direct putaway process, we created a purchase order in the ERP system (TCode ME21n). In the purchase order we used a material that has setup for direct putaway in the EWM system, the plant, and vendor, were already transferred to the EWM system and the storage location entered for the material in the purchase order is configured as EWM relevant.

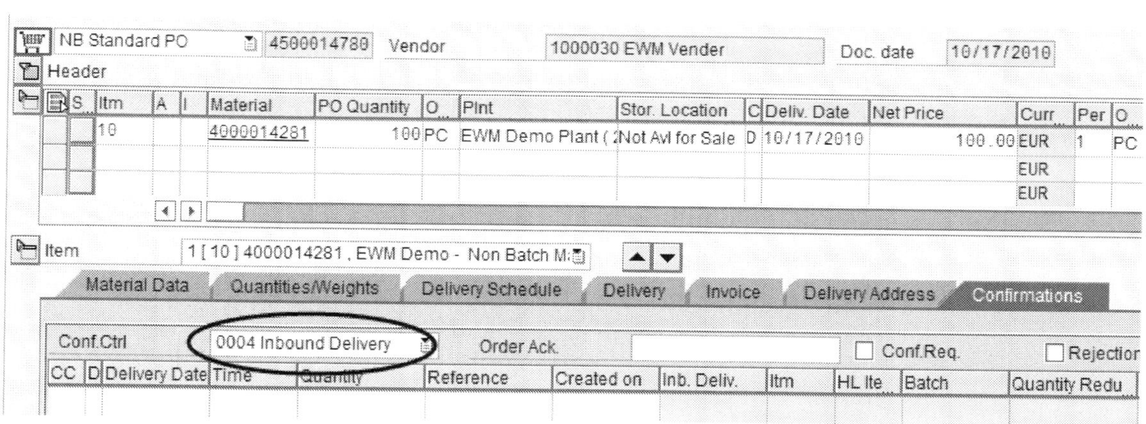

One of the requirements for the ASN process is that a purchase order line item must have confirmation control key, which allows the creation of inbound delivery. The SAP-delivered control key to create inbound delivery is "0004—Inbound Delivery".

14.3.3 Inbound Delivery (ASN)

When a vendor sends delivery confirmation (ASN), inbound delivery can be created in the ERP system manually, using transaction VL31N, or automatically through an EDI process. To create an inbound delivery in the ERP system, go to transaction VL31N, enter vendor, purchase order number, and the external ID, and hit "Enter." Change the proposed quantity to ASN quantity, if it is different.

Under the stock placement tab, verify the warehouse number, putaway status, and WM status. Because the warehouse number is linked to the EWM warehouse, neither putaway nor WM status are applicable in the ERP system.

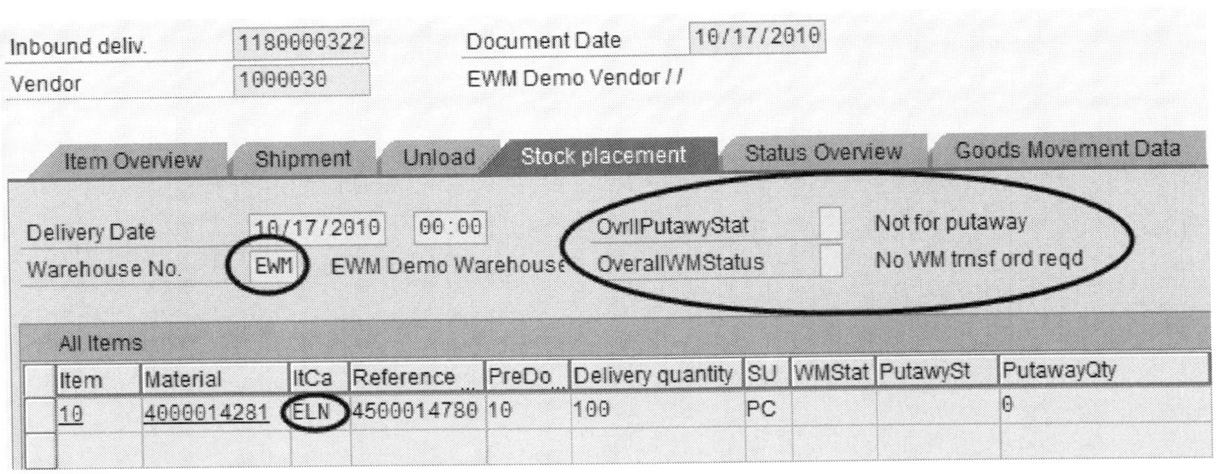

When the inbound delivery is saved, the system will automatically transfer the inbound delivery to the EWM system via qRFC. The message issued at the time of saving the inbound delivery confirms that inbound delivery is transferred to the EWM system. This status will be saved in the header data of inbound delivery under the stock placement tab in the decentralized warehouse field.

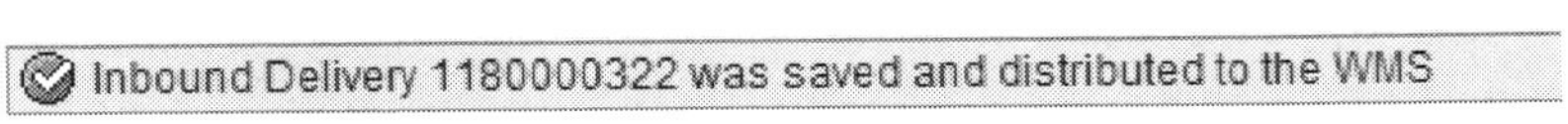

In the standard EWM system, usually the ASN number is set to "mandatory" in the incompleteness profile. In this case, the inbound delivery should contain the ASN number, which can be entered in the "External ID" field of the inbound delivery at the time of inbound delivery creation.

14.3.4 Document and Item Type Determination in the EWM System

As explained earlier, in order to create an IDN, the system should determine the document type and item type for the IDN.

Based on the settings in the EWM system, under menu path **SPRO | Extended Warehouse Management | Interfaces | ERP Integration | Delivery Processing | Map Document Types from ERP System to EWM**, the EWM system will determine the document type for the IDN. In this case, the document type of ERP inbound delivery is EL, and the corresponding EWM document type will be INB.

Mapping Delivery Type - Document Type

Business System	DocTypeERP	Cde Init.	Doc. Type
	EL		INB
	EL	GRN	EGRE

Next, based on the settings in **SPRO | Extended Warehouse Management | Interfaces | ERP Integration | Delivery Processing | Map Item Types from ERP System to EWM**, the EWM system will determine the item type for IDN based on the ERP document type and item type. In this example the item type IDLV is determined for ERP document type EL and item category ELN.

Mapping of ERP Item Type

Busine...	DocT	ItmTpERP	Doc.	Diff.A	CW Product	Item Type
	EL	ELN			☐	IDLV
	EL	ELN			☑	IDCW

14.3.4 Status Profiles Determination in the EWM system

Once the document and item type are determined, the EWM system will determine the various profiles for the document header and document items.

For the header, the system will use the document type and category to determine the appropriate profiles. The document category gets determined internally by the system.

For the header profiles, settings are made under menu path **SPRO | Extended Warehouse Management |Goods Receipt Process | Inbound Delivery | Manual Settings | Define Document Types for Inbound Delivery Process**

To keep the IDN number the same as the ERP IDN, no internal number range should be assigned for document type INB or document category IDR, as shown below.

Inbound Delivery Process Document Types

Doc. Type	Doc. Cat.	Int. NRI	Description	Ret.Period	C	Act. Prof.	Inc.Prof.
INB	IDR		Inbound Delivery Notification	365	☑	/SCDL/IDR	/SCDL/INB_REQ_STANDARD
INB	PDI	01	Inbound Delivery	365	☑	/SCDL/PRD_IN	/SCDL/INB_PRD_STANDARD

For item-related profiles, the system uses the item type, document category, and item category information. For IDN, the item type is IDLV, document category is IDR, and item category is DLV.

Inbound Delivery Process Item Types

Item Type	Doc. Cat.	Item Cat.	Description	StatuPrf.
IDLV	IDR	DLV	Standard Item - Inbound Delivery	/SCDL/INB_REQ_DLV_STANDARD
IDLV	PDI	DLV	Standard Item - Inbound Delivery	/SCDL/INB_PRD_DLV_STANDARD

14.3.5 Verify IDN

Once the required data is determined from the configuration tables, the system will create an IDN in the system. The IDN can be located in transaction /SCWM/IDN.

In EWM, the IDN screen is mainly divided into three parts, as shown below. They are as follows:

- IDN header data
- Details of IDN
- Details of IDN Item

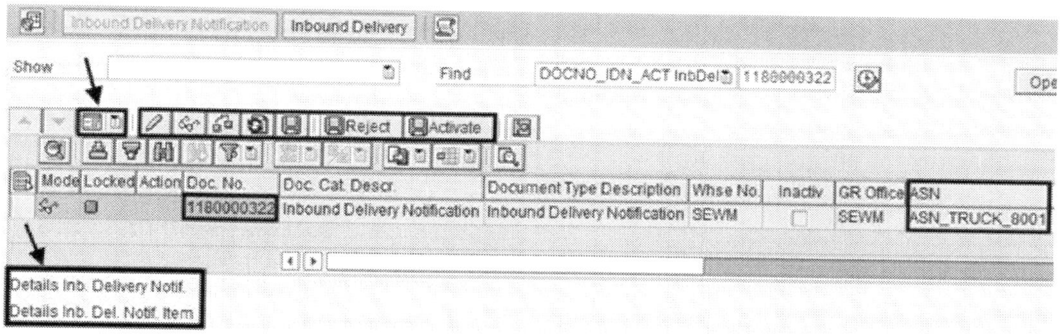

IDN header data can be viewed using a form view or list view. The above screenshot is an example of the list view. This can easily be switched to the form view by selecting the line and clicking on "switch to form view" icon.

In the form view, verify the document type and document category for the IDN.

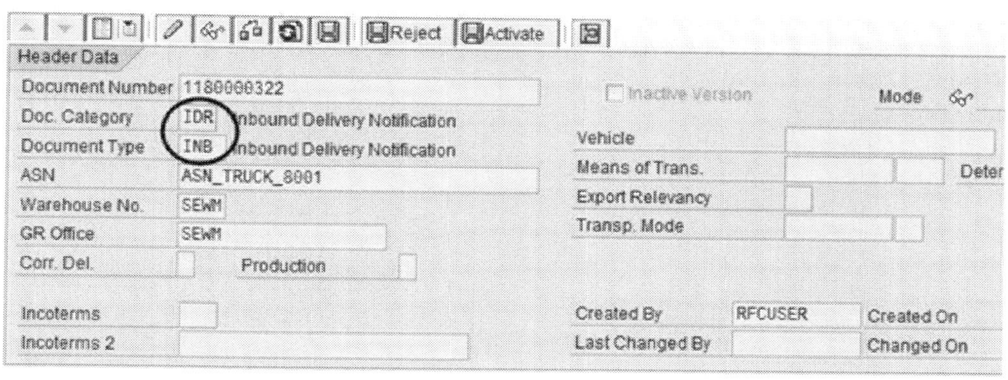

In the details section of IDN, verify the quantity, stock type, and item type.

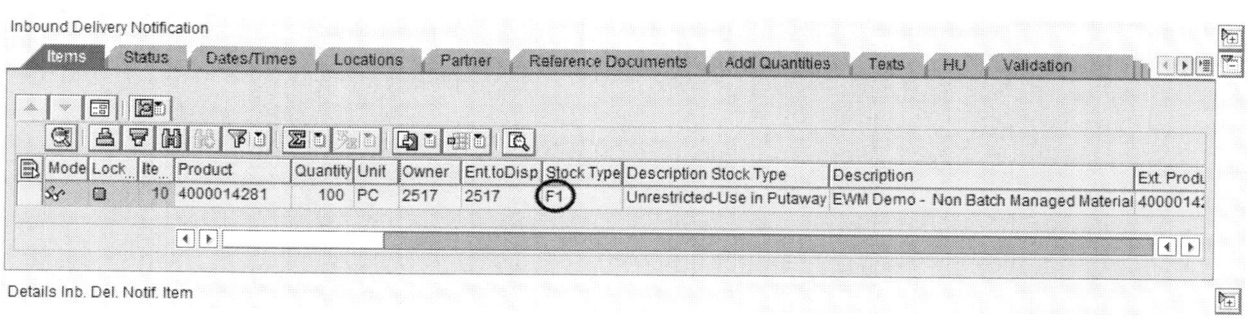

In the details section of IDN item, verify the various other statuses for the line item. It is also possible to navigate to ID by clicking on the inbound delivery button located on application toolbar or via transaction /SCWM/PRDI

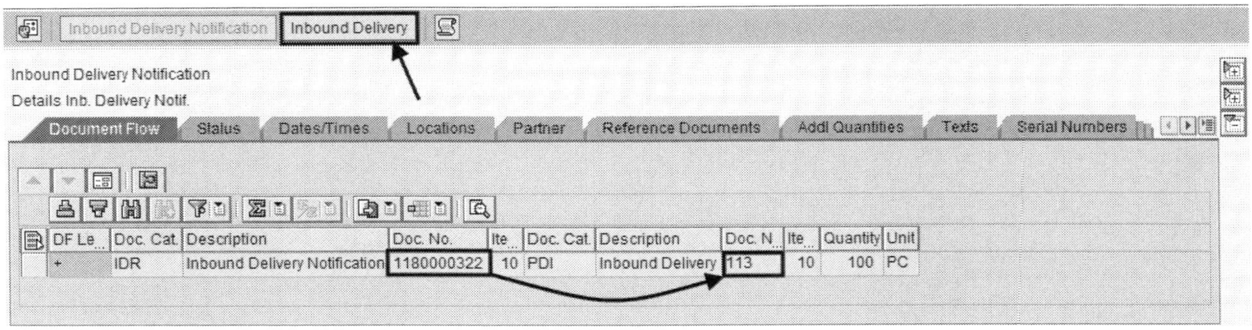

14.3.6 Inbound Delivery (ID) in EWM system

In EWM, PPF is used to create ID from IDN. The standard behavior of the system is that, if the IDN processed successfully and is active, the system will automatically convert the IDN into ID. ID is a very important document in the warehouse. It serves as a basis for product putaway WTs.

ID is broadly divided into three parts, which are as follows:

- delivery header information
- delivery details
- delivery item details

The delivery header contains various controls required to process the ID—for example, change icon, add new item, reject, unload, GRs, and so on. The form view can be used to verify the document type and category of the ID. The ID can be located in transaction /SCWM/PRDI.

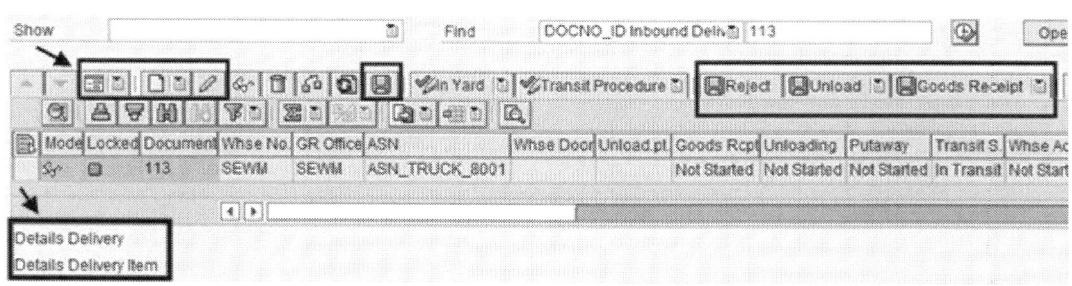

The standard document category and document type for ID are PDI and INB.

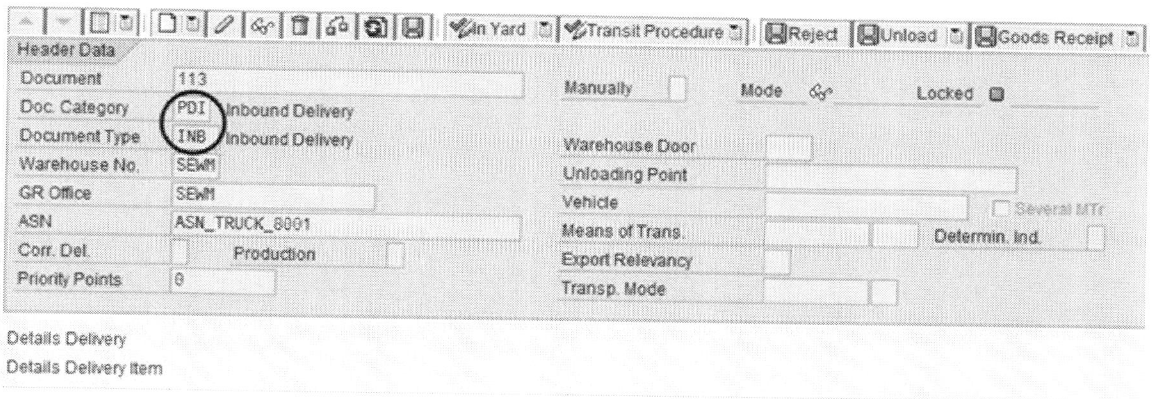

In the delivery details, the process codes are used mainly for delivery split. One of the important pieces of information in the delivery details is WPT, which plays important role in the putaway activity.

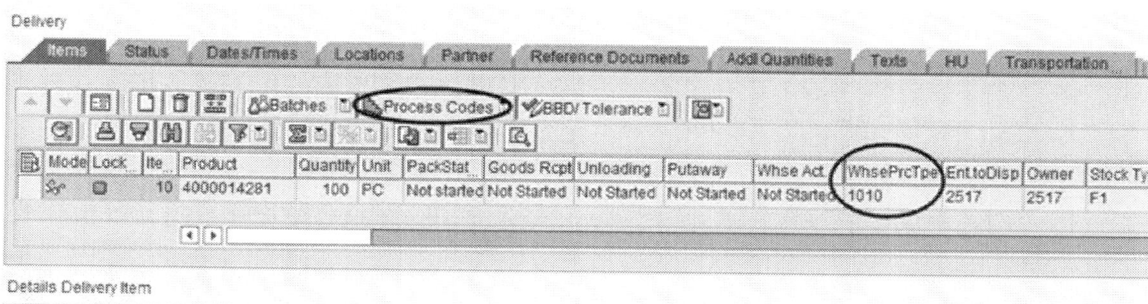

14.3.7 WPT Determination

WPT is needed to create WTs. It is determined based on the information stored in IDN and the warehouse product master. In the above example, WPT 1010 is determined based on warehouse number, document type, and the process type determination indicator. Warehouse number (SEWM) and document type (INB) is derived from IDN, and the process type determination indicator (04) is derived from the warehouse product master.

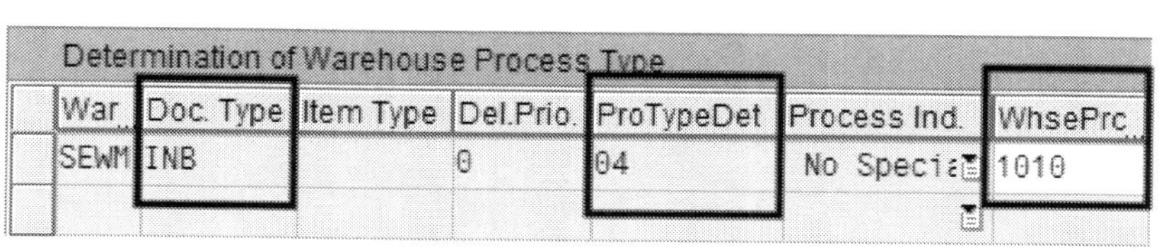

WPT contains various settings required for the next process in the warehouse. In this example, WPT 1010 contains the activity, availability group, source storage type, and source bin, which is passed to the warehouse task document.

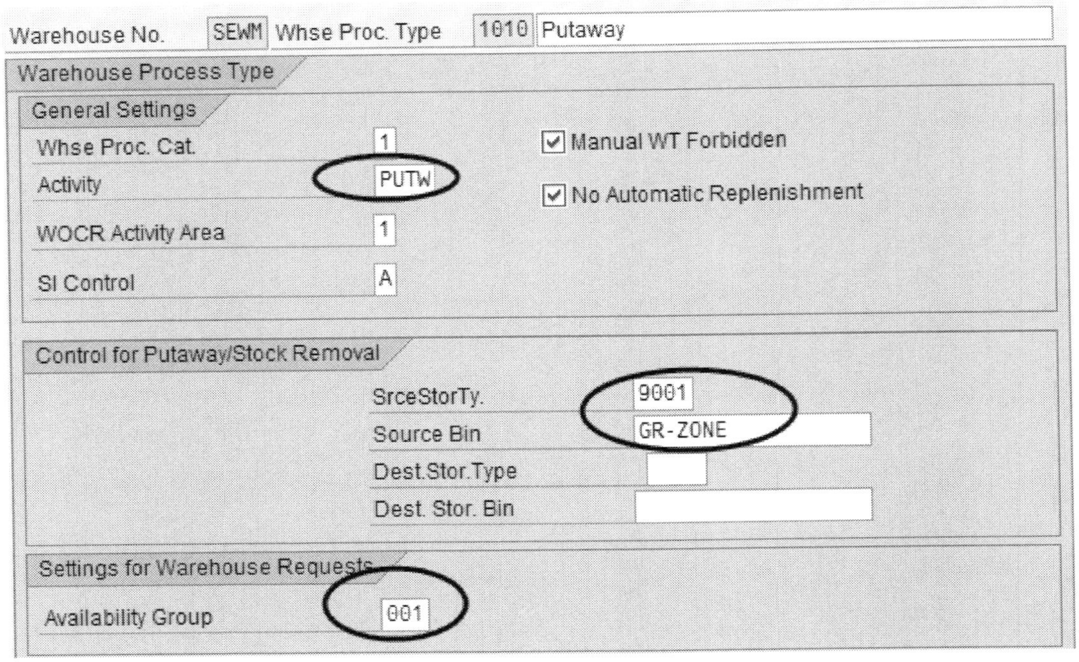

14.3.8 Availability Group

An earlier chapter already covered details of the availability group.

In this example, availability group 001 is mapped to the stock type F1, which means that in the warehouse, it is unrestricted stock in putaway; and in the ERP system, this stock belongs to storage location NAFS (not available for sale). Once the stock is put away in the destination storage type (005), the stock type will change to the availability group of destination storage type. Availability group 002 means in the EWM system, the stock type is mapped to "F2—unrestricted use in the warehouse"—and in the ERP system, the stock will be automatically moved to IAFS (available to sell) storage location. PCN documents will be created and posted for the stock change in both systems.

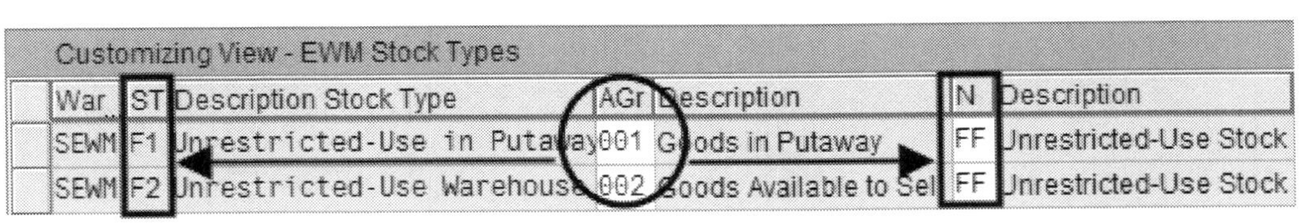

Customizing View - EWM Stock Types

War	ST	Description Stock Type	AGr	Description	N	Description
SEWM	F1	Unrestricted-Use in Putaway	001	Goods in Putaway	FF	Unrestricted-Use Stock
SEWM	F2	Unrestricted-Use Warehouse	002	Goods Available to Sell	FF	Unrestricted-Use Stock

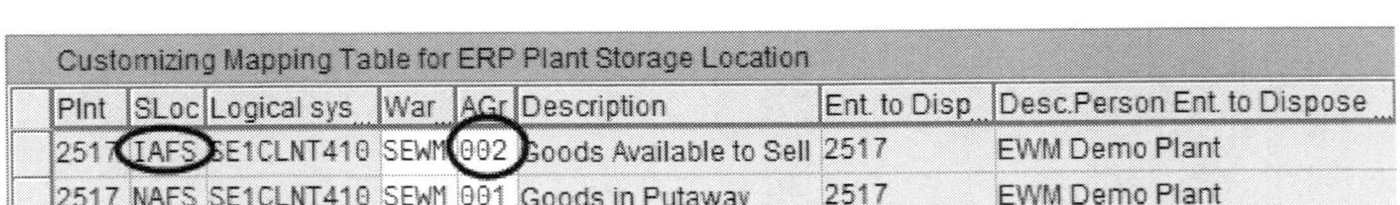

Customizing Mapping Table for ERP Plant Storage Location

Plnt	SLoc	Logical sys	War	AGr	Description	Ent. to Disp	Desc.Person Ent. to Dispose
2517	IAFS	SE1CLNT410	SEWM	002	Goods Available to Sell	2517	EWM Demo Plant
2517	NAFS	SE1CLNT410	SEWM	001	Goods in Putaway	2517	EWM Demo Plant

14.3.9 Storage Type and Storage Section Settings

Storage type and storage sections are covered in detail in chapter 5. This section explains the settings required for final and interim storage types and how they influence processing of putaway.

Menu Path: **SPRO | IMG | Extended Warehouse Management | Master Data | Define Storage Type**

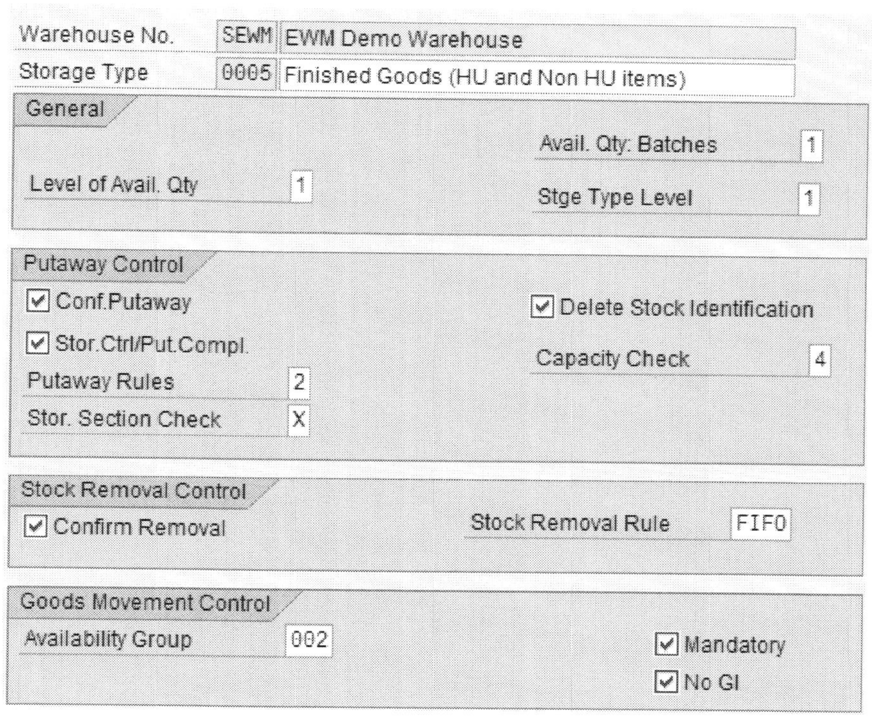

The availability group of the final storage type along with the check in the mandatory check box will control the stock type for the stock that has been put away. If the mandatory check is not active, the availability group will not be considered during putaway confirmation. Only if this checkbox is active will the system create a PCN to move the stock to the destination storage type availability group.

If the confirm putaway indicator is not active, the system will confirm the WT and WO immediately in the background, when the WT is created.

The "Storage.Ctrl/Put.Compl" indicator controls the putaway status in the warehouse request. If this indicator is not set for the final storage type putaway, the status will not be updated in the inbound delivery.

The following screenshot describes the settings required for the interim storage type. For GR, there must be an interim storage type and a bin.

To test our configuration, we have created storage type 9001, storage section 0001, and bin GR-ZONE. The storage type settings for 9001 are shown below.

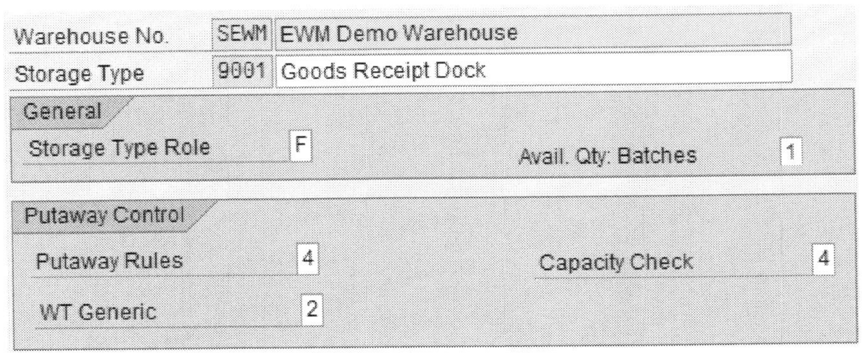

Storage sections defined for this example are as follows:

Storage Sections

WhN	Typ	Sec	Description
SEWM	0005	0001	Heavy Parts
SEWM	0005	0002	Small Parts
SEWM	0005	0003	Damaged Stock
SEWM	9001	0001	General Storage Section

14.3.10 Storage Type, Section, and Bin Determination:

Product master settings play an important role in the storage type, storage section, and storage bin determination process. The Putaway Control Indicator (PACI) from the product master guides the system to search for the appropriate storage types for the product putaway. In this example, PACI has been set to "SMAL – Small Products". The following sections will explain how PACI is configured and influences the storage type search sequence.

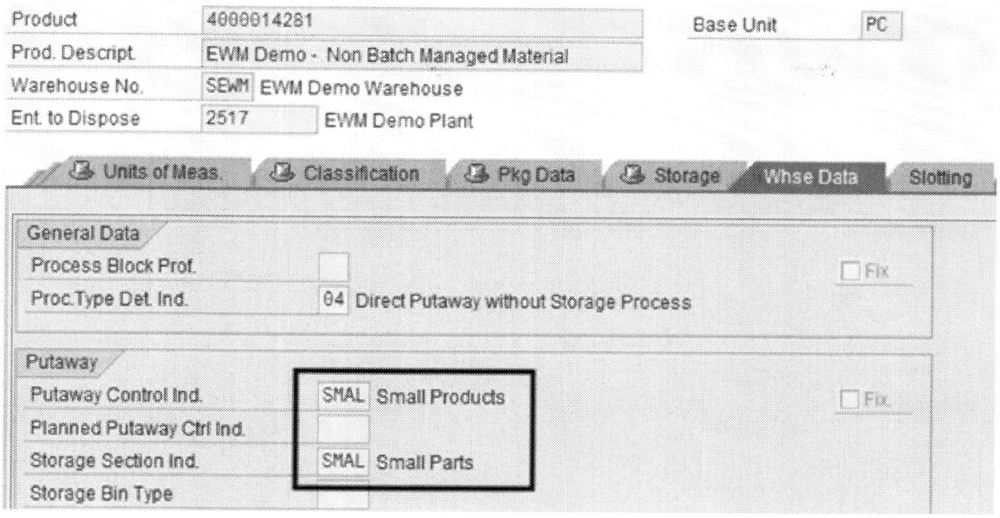

14.3.10.1 Define Putaway Control Indicator (PACI)

In EWM, the PACI is defined in menu **SPRO | IMG | Extended Warehouse Management | Goods Receipt Process | Strategies | Storage Type Search | Define Putaway Control Indicator**

Once this indicator is defined, it can be used to determine the appropriate storage type search sequence indicator required for product putaway.

Putaway Control Indicator

War..	PACI	Description	Stor..
SEWM	HEVY	Heavy Products	
SEWM	SMAL	Small Products	

14.3.10.2 Define and Assign S. Type Search Seq. Ind. for Putaway

The storage type search sequence indicator is used to assign appropriate storage types for the product putaway in a sequence. It is defined under **SPRO | IMG | Extended Warehouse Management | Goods Receipt Process | Strategies | Storage Type Search | Define Storage Type Search Sequence for Putaway**

Storage Type Search Sequence for Putaway - Definition

War..	Stor..	Description
SEWM	0005	Put Away in Storage Type 0005

Once the indicator is defined, you assign the appropriate storage types and the putaway sequence to it, as shown below.

Menu path: **SPRO | IMG | Extended Warehouse Management | Goods Receipt Process | Strategies | Storage Type Search | Assign Storage Types to Storage Type Search Sequence**

Storage Type Search Sequence for Putaway

WhN	Srch Seq.	Seq	Typ	STG	Evl	Description
SEWM	0005	1	0005			Put Away in Storage Type 0005

14.3.10.3 Specify Storage Type Search Sequence for Putaway

This menu is used to assign the storage type search sequence indicator to the combination of PACI and WPT, along with other available indicators.

Menu Path: **SPRO | IMG | Extended Warehouse Management | Goods Receipt Process | Strategies | Storage Type Search | Specify Storage Type Search Sequence for Putaway**

Search Sequence: Putaway

WhN	PACI	Proc.	Qty Class.	Sto	Type	Use	Ent.toDisp	H	H	Srch Se	Putaway Rules
SEWM	SMAL	1010								0005	No Putaway Rule

During the WT creation process, WPT gets determined from the warehouse request, and PACI is derived from the product master. These two values, along with other available options, help the system to determine the storage type search sequence indicator, which in turn helps the system determine the appropriate storage types for putaway.

14.3.10.4 Optimize Access Strategy for Storage Type Search

In EWM, various indicators influence the storage type search. To reduce the number of entries, consultants can define an access strategy for the storage type search table. This can improve system performance. Each sequence number is an access combination that the system uses while determining the storage type search. The system will use a more specific search first, broadening to a more generic search as needed.

It is defined in menu path **SPRO | IMG | Extended Warehouse Management | Goods Receipt Process | Strategies | Storage Type Search | Optimize Access Strategy for Storage Type Search: Putaway**

Optimization of Access for Stor.Type Determ. at Putaway

WhN	Seq	Put.Strat.	ProcTyp	Q	Stk	Sto	Use	Pa	Ris	Hzd
SEWM	1	☑	☑	☐	☐	☐	☐	☐	☐	☐

14.3.10.5 Storage Section Search Sequence

Like with storage type search, the system can be set up to determine the appropriate storage sections for putaway. The storage section search starts after determination of destination storage type. The system uses the storage section indicator assigned in the product master to determine the allowed storage sections for product putaway. They are defined in menu path **SPRO | IMG | Extended Warehouse Management | Goods Receipt Process | Strategies | Storage Section Search | Create Storage Section Indicators**

Storage Section Indicators

War	SecIn	Description
SEWM	HEVY	Heavy Parts
SEWM	SMAL	Small Parts

Once the storage section indicators are defined, they can be used in the storage section search sequence table to assign the appropriate storage sections and sequence.

Menu Path: SPRO | IMG | Extended Warehouse Management | Goods Receipt Process | Strategies | Storage Section Search | Maintain Storage Section Search Sequence

Storage Section Search

WhN	Typ	HazRat1	HazRat2	SecIn	Sequence No.	Sec	EvlWhsItem
SEWM	0005			SMAL	1	0002	

Finally, the storage section indicators are assigned to the product master. Once the system identifies the appropriate storage type, the storage section indicator of the product master will be used to determine the appropriate storage sections for product putaway.

14.3.10.6 Storage Section Check

In EWM, storage section search is not mandatory for putaway. This is defined in the storage type under option "storage section check." When the storage section search and storage section check are active, goods are put away only in storage sections that are found in the storage section search.

The storage section check can also be defined under **SPRO | IMG | Extended Warehouse Management | Goods Receipt Process | Strategies | Storage Section Search | Storage Section Check**

Storage Section Check and Haz. Subst. Mgmt per Storage Type

WhN	Typ	SC
SEWM	0005	X Storage section determination and check
SEWM	0006	X Storage section determination and check
SEWM	0007	Y Storage section determination, no check
SEWM	0009	No storage section determination or check

14.3.11 Warehouse Order Creation Rule (WOCR) Determination

WOCR plays an important role in creating WOs. It can be determined from two sources: if it is specified in the WPT, it will be used to create the WO. If it is not specified here, it will be determined from the activity area of the destination bin, as in this example.

The following screenshot shows the defined activity areas for the destination storage bins (TCode /SCWM/SBST)

WhN	Storage Bin	Activity	Seq. No.	AA	Typ	Section	Sort Seq.
SEWM	A01-003-01	PUTW	1	SPUT	0005	0002	120
SEWM	A01-003-02	PUTW	1	SPUT	0005	0002	119
SEWM	A01-003-03	PUTW	1	SPUT	0005	0002	118
SEWM	A01-003-04	PUTW	1	SPUT	0005	0002	117

In the configuration, the PU01 WOCR has been assigned to activity area SPUT.

Warehouse Order: Search Sequence for Rules per Activity Area

War...	AA	Activity	Sequence No	WOCR	Description
SEWM	SPUT		1	PU01	Putaway

14.3.12 Unloading

In EWM, unloading functionality can be used even without yard management. This action will not update stock in the warehouse or the ERP system. It is only used to update the unloading status in inbound delivery. Unloading can be performed directly in inbound delivery or separately in TCode /SCWM/UNLOAD—Unload.

14.3.13 Goods Receipt

As explained earlier, GR can be posted manually in the inbound delivery or automatically when the putaway is confirmed. If the GR is performed manually in the inbound delivery, stock will be updated in the interim storage type (GR area) of the warehouse as well as in the ERP system, and the status of ID will be set to Goods Receipt—Completed.

Stock overview in ERP system: Transaction MMBE

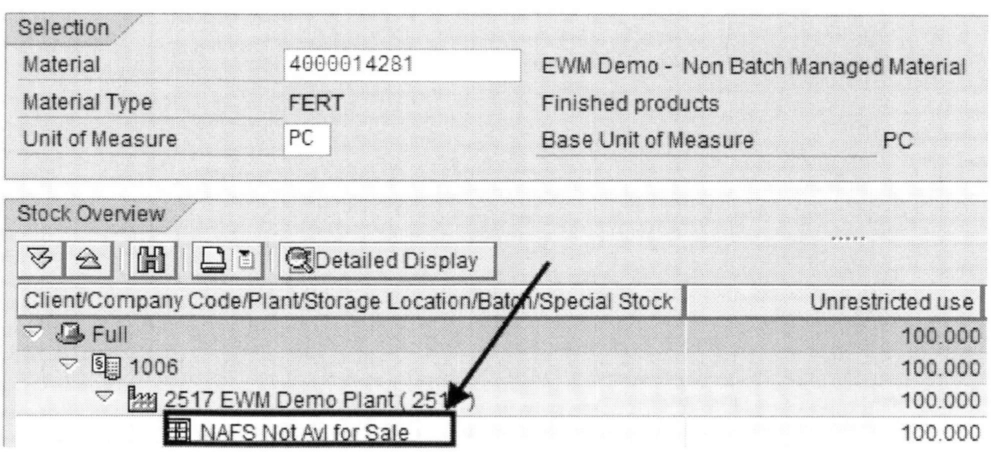

14.3.14 Create Warehouse Task

In EWM, WTs can be created several different ways. One way is by manually creating it from the inbound delivery, as shown below. Here, go to the inbound delivery menu, select "Follow-On Functions," and click on the "Warehouse Task" option. This will bring up the WT creation screen.

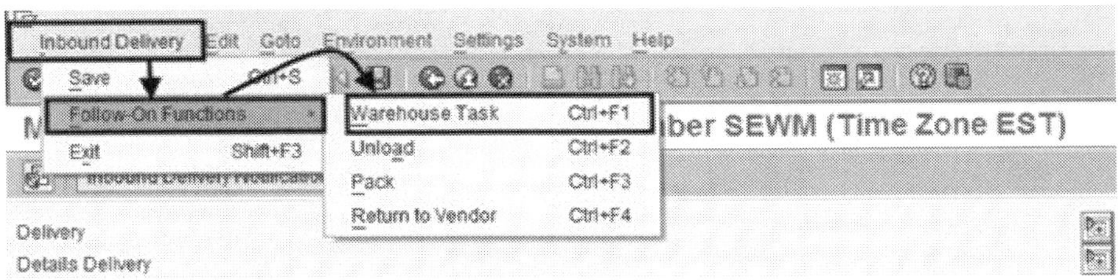

In the WT creation screen, select the line item, and click on the "Create" button. This will display the target quantity and destination location details. The system will determine the destination storage type, section, and bin based on settings in the product master. Verify the destination storage bin details and quantity and click "Save." This will create the WT.

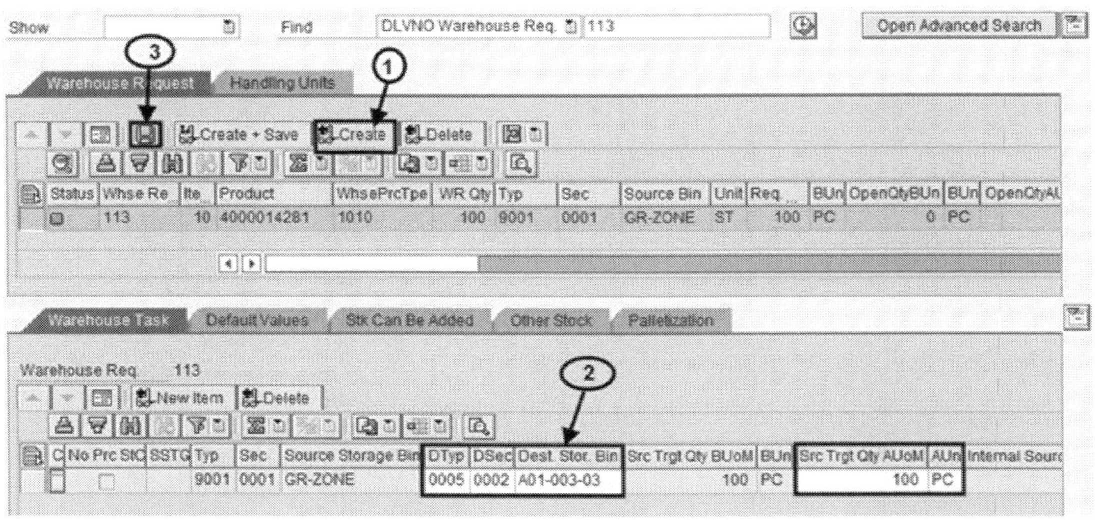

Depending on the WPT settings, the WOCR will be determined, and the WT will be processed in the WOCR to create a WO. At the end of the WT creation process, the system will automatically create a warehouse order.

Stock Overview in the EWM system: (TCode /SCWM/MON)

Because the putaway is not complete, and the WO is not confirmed, the system will show the outgoing quantity from GR area and the incoming quantity to the destination bin, as shown below.

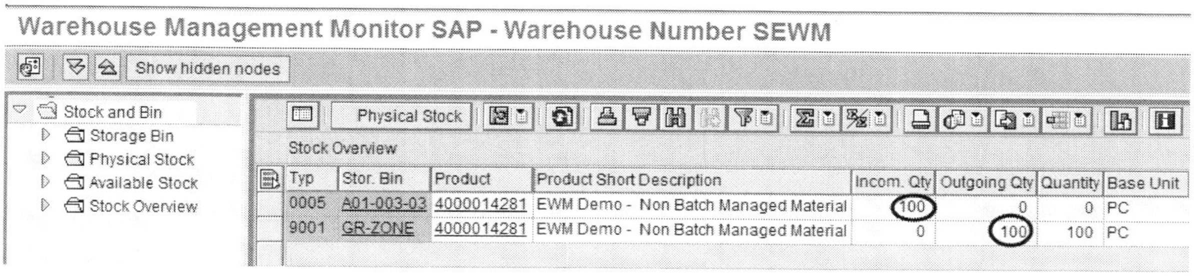

14.3.15 Warehouse Monitor

One of the important tools in the EWM system is the warehouse monitor. This is a central monitoring tool and can be used to display any type of data in the warehouse, for example, warehouse documents, stocks, PI documents, open tasks, open orders, and so on. In addition to displaying data, it can also be used to execute transactions, like confirming warehouse orders and so on.

Menu Path: **SAP Easy Access | Extended Warehouse Management | Monitoring | Warehouse Management Monitor (TCode /SCWM/MON)**

In this transaction, enter warehouse number, enter monitor ID, and click on "Execute." SAP has assigned its monitor ID as "SAP."

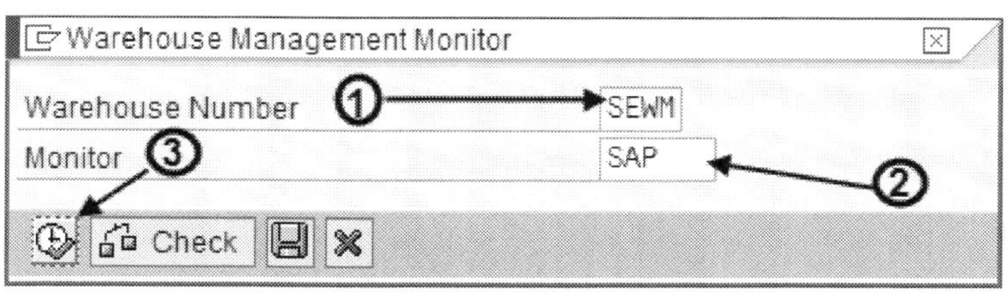

The warehouse monitor display screen is divided into three parts. They are as follows:

- **Navigation Tree Section**: This is located on the left side of the screen and contains all the predefined nodes and their objects—for example, inbound, outbound, stock and bin, document, and so on.
- **Parent Data Section**: The upper portion of the right side of the screen is used to display the header or parent data of the object.
- **Child or Item Details Section**: The child, or item details, section is displayed at the lower portion of the right side of the screen and can be used to display the item details of the parent data.

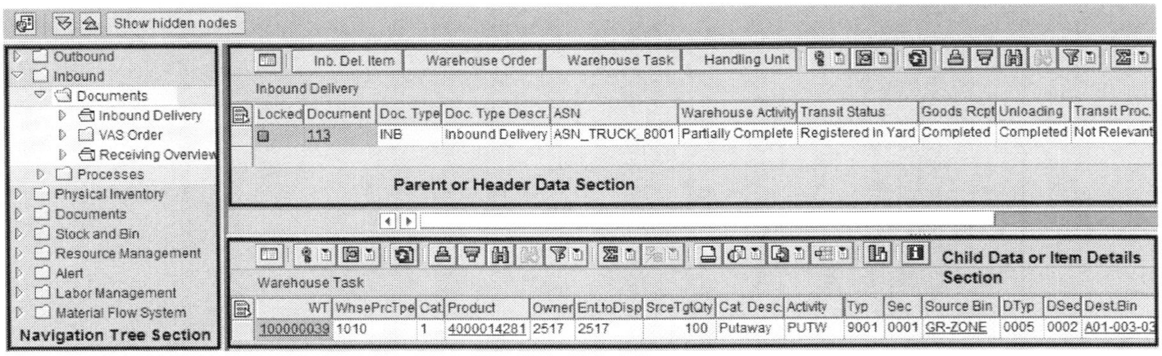

14.3.16 Confirm WT

In order to confirm the WT, the WTs must first be located. The open WT can be found in the warehouse monitor (TCode /SCWM/MON). In the monitor, select inbound, then documents, and double-click on inbound delivery. A window will pop up with the selection fields. Here, enter the inbound delivery number or products. This will display the inbound delivery in the parent data screen. Select the "Inbound Delivery" line item and click on the WO button. This will display the WO in the child data screen.

Click on the WO number. This will open the WO confirmation screen. Select the WO line item and click on the "Confirm + Save" button. This will confirm the WT and update the putaway status in the inbound delivery to be completed.

Alternatively, TCode /SCWM/TO_CONF can also be used to confirm the WT.

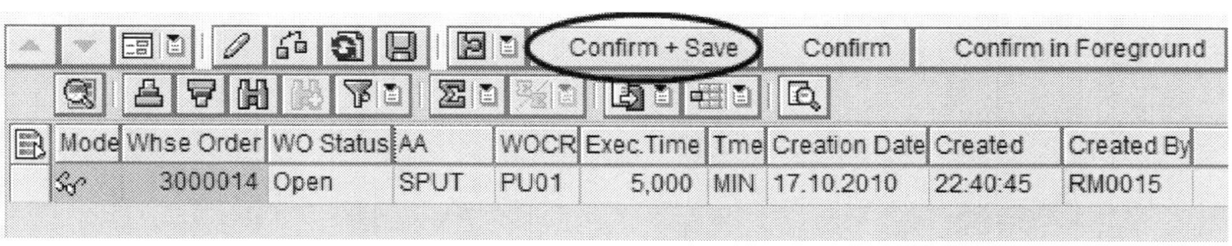

14.3.17 Verify EWM Stock

Notice that in the warehouse monitor (TCode /SCWM/MON), the stock is now displayed under the available quantity column, and the stock type is moved from F1 to F2. Change of stock type happened as per the availability group of the storage type. In the background, when the WO was confirmed, a posting change was initiated for the stock type from F1 to F2. In this example, in the ERP system, the stock will be posted to "available to sell" storage location.

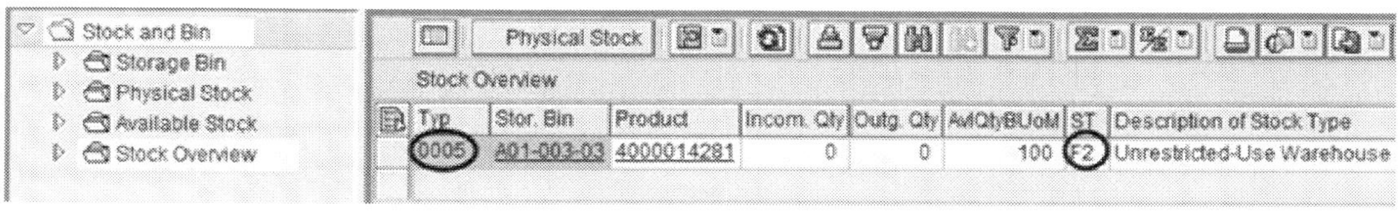

Typ	Stor. Bin	Product	Incom. Qty	Outg. Qty	AvlQtyBUoM	ST	Description of Stock Type
0005	A01-003-03	4000014281	0	0	100	F2	Unrestricted-Use Warehouse

14.3.17 Posting Change Document

A WT number created for the posting change is saved in the document flow of inbound delivery, which can be accessed in TCode /SCWM/PRDI under the document flow tab in the delivery item details screen.

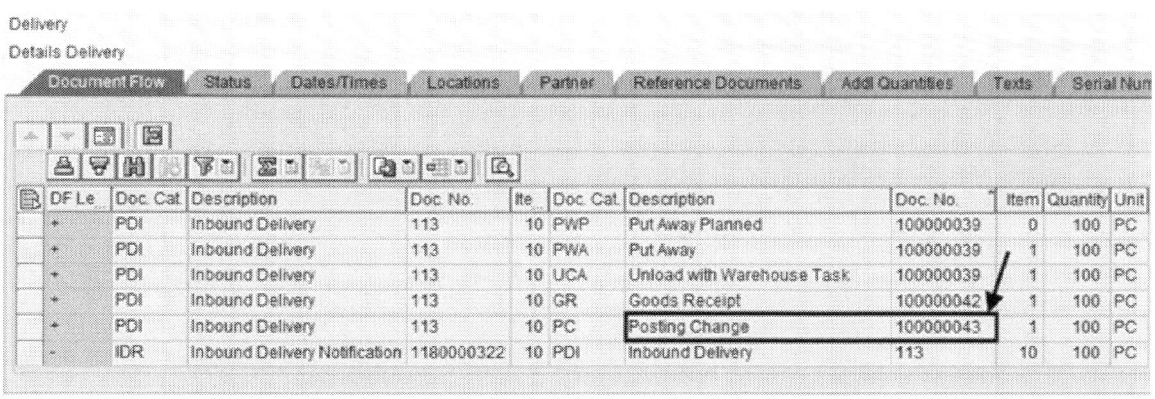

DF Le...	Doc. Cat.	Description	Doc. No.	Ite...	Doc. Cat.	Description	Doc. No.	Item	Quantity	Unit
+	PDI	Inbound Delivery	113	10	PWP	Put Away Planned	100000039	0	100	PC
+	PDI	Inbound Delivery	113	10	PWA	Put Away	100000039	1	100	PC
+	PDI	Inbound Delivery	113	10	UCA	Unload with Warehouse Task	100000039	1	100	PC
+	PDI	Inbound Delivery	113	10	GR	Goods Receipt	100000042	1	100	PC
+	PDI	Inbound Delivery	113	10	PC	Posting Change	100000043	1	100	PC
-	IDR	Inbound Delivery Notification	1180000322	10	PDI	Inbound Delivery	113	10	100	PC

The WT number can be displayed in the warehouse monitor.

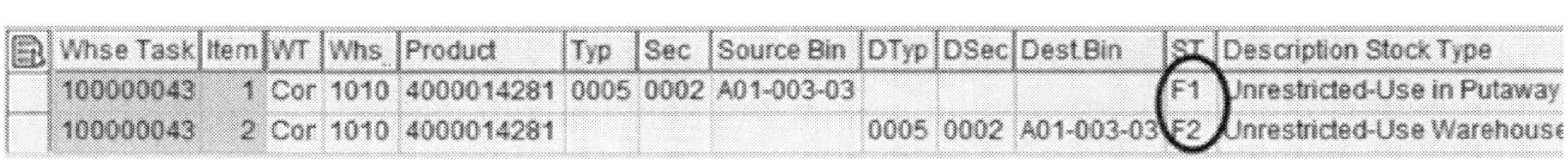

Whse Task	Item	WT	Whs.	Product	Typ	Sec	Source Bin	DTyp	DSec	Dest.Bin	ST	Description Stock Type
100000043	1	Cor	1010	4000014281	0005	0002	A01-003-03				F1	Unrestricted-Use in Putaway
100000043	2	Cor	1010	4000014281				0005	0002	A01-003-03	F2	Unrestricted-Use Warehouse

14.3.18 Verify IM Stock in ERP System

Before confirming the WT the stock was displayed in the "not available to sell" storage location. As shown below, after the confirmation of the WT the stock is automatically moved to "available sell" storage location. Verify the stock in the ERP system in TCode MMBE.

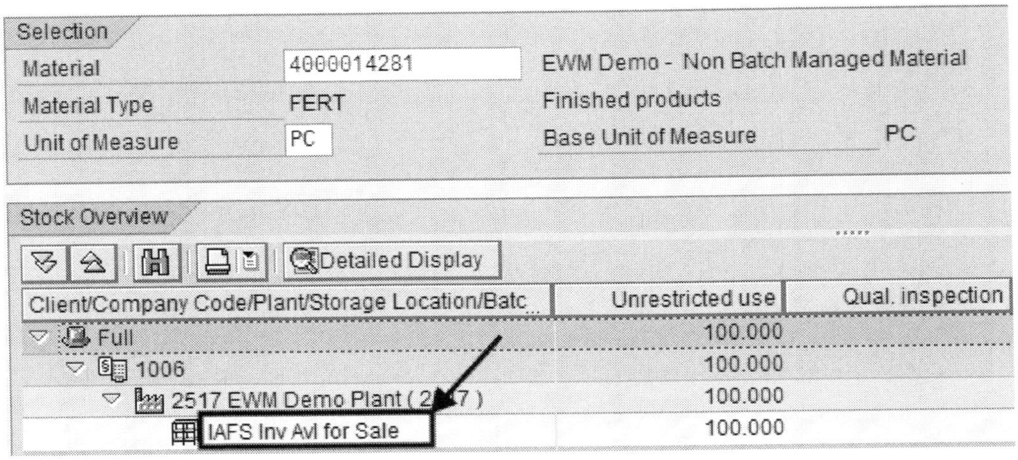

14.3.19 Verify Material Documents in ERP System

In the ERP system, two material documents are created. One is for GR and the other is for warehouse posting change (i.e., stock transfer between storage locations). TCode MB51 can be used to verify the material documents in the ERP system.

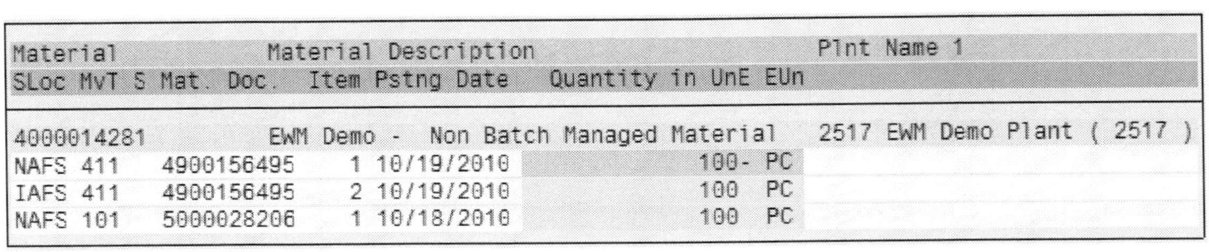

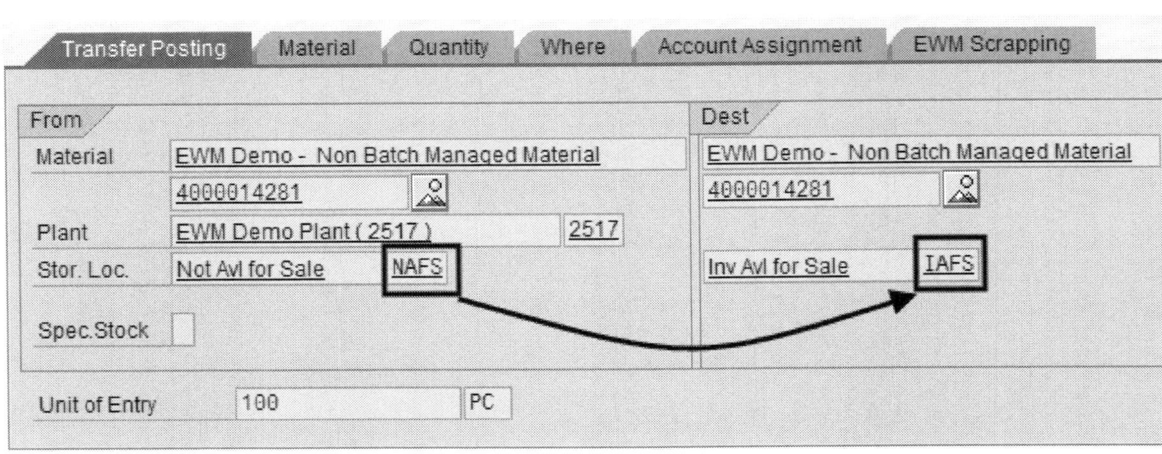

Summary

This chapter has explained how to configure direct putaway. This process is used for single-step putaway or simple putaway. To manage multistep putaway in the warehouse, SAP has defined a process called storage control, which is covered in the next chapter.

Chapter 15: Storage Control (SC)

This chapter covers the storage control technique used to determine the process steps required to perform product movements in the warehouse. The goal of storage control is to process complex putaway or stock removals, based on warehouse processes or the physical layout of the warehouse, and provide traceability and stock visibility for each of those process steps.

The storage control processes in EWM are broadly divided into two types. They are:

- Process-Oriented Storage Control (POSC)
- Layout-Oriented Storage Control (LOSC)

POSC can also be combined with LOSC. In this case, EWM always executes the POSC first. The LOSC then verifies whether the sequence of putaway process step is possible in the warehouse layout view. If required, it will adjust the flow of putaway or stock removal.

This section will discuss LOSC and combined LOSC and POSC for warehouse putaway and picking, along with an example of how to use POSC.

15.1 Process-Oriented Storage Control (POSC)

POSC is mainly used in complex warehouses where additional tasks are performed in addition to basic putaway and picking. Example for complex putaway could be unloading, quality inspection, deconsolidation, packing, and putting away the products in the warehouse. Depending on the product processing requirements, it may be required that some products have to go through several steps before the product is actually put away in the bin or shipped to customers. Under POSC, all of these individual storage process steps are combined into one storage process, and the system traces the status of each individual process step.

One of the requirements for the POSC process is that the product should be HU managed. During the GR or GI, as soon as a HU is created or changed, the system copies the predefined process steps from the storage process type to the HU. Also, POSC only supports GR, GI, and internal warehouse processes. It determines the internal routing based on the processes to be carried out within the warehouse before the final putaway or after the stock removal.

Diagram 15.1A is an example for an inbound POSC scenario.

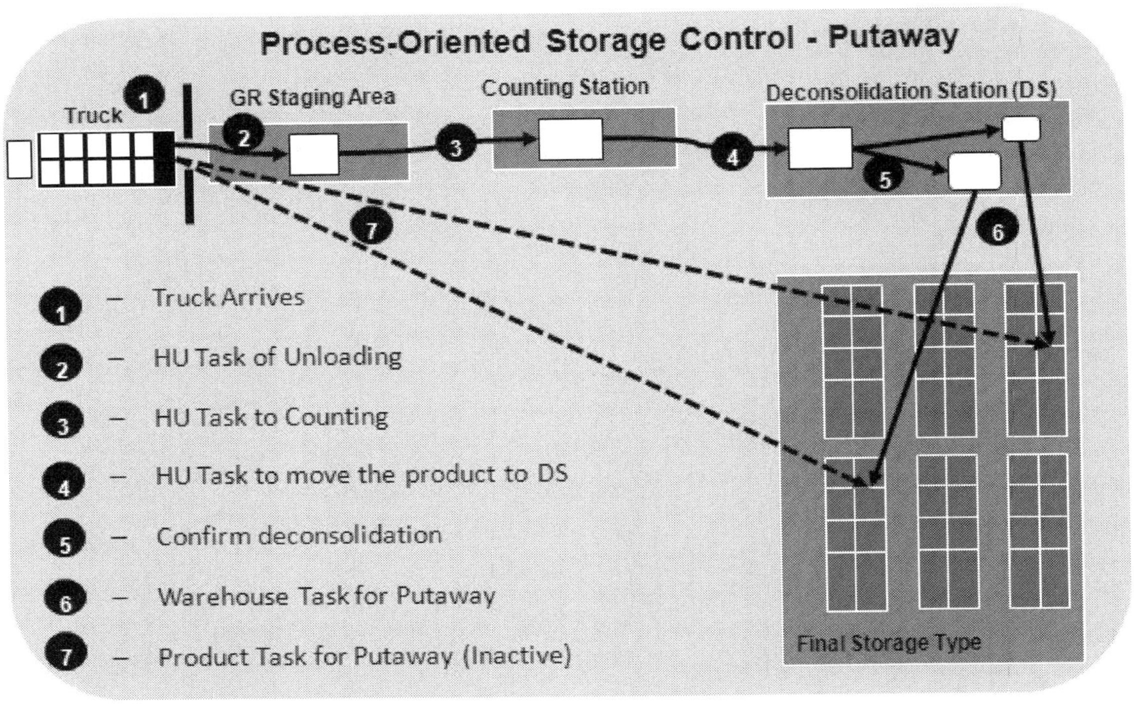

Diagram 15.1A – Process-Oriented Storage Control - Putaway

The following illustration will describe how the system creates multiple tasks and how they are processed in sequence.

1. Truck arrives at the warehouse door.
2. Unloading: When the products are unloaded, the system will create tasks for each process with the status "B—Waiting," other than the HU task for unloading. All waiting tasks will be inactive and can't be processed until the active unloading task is completed. Confirmation of the unloading task will update the HU stock in the GR staging area, and the next task to move the HU to the counting station will be set to active. The WO will be created automatically for the next active WT.
3. Counting: when the active WT is confirmed, the system will update the stock in the counting station and will activate the counting task. When the operator confirms the counting activity, the system will automatically activate the next task to move the HU to the deconsolidation station for product deconsolidation.
4. Confirmation of the WO will update the stock in the deconsolidation work center.
5. Once the HU is deconsolidated, new HUs will be created. The confirmation of a new HU will set the status of the putaway product WT to active.

6. Finally, WOs will be created to putaway the products into the final destination bin. Confirmation of the putaway will update the stock in the final bin.

Diagram 15.1B is an example for the simple POSC picking process.

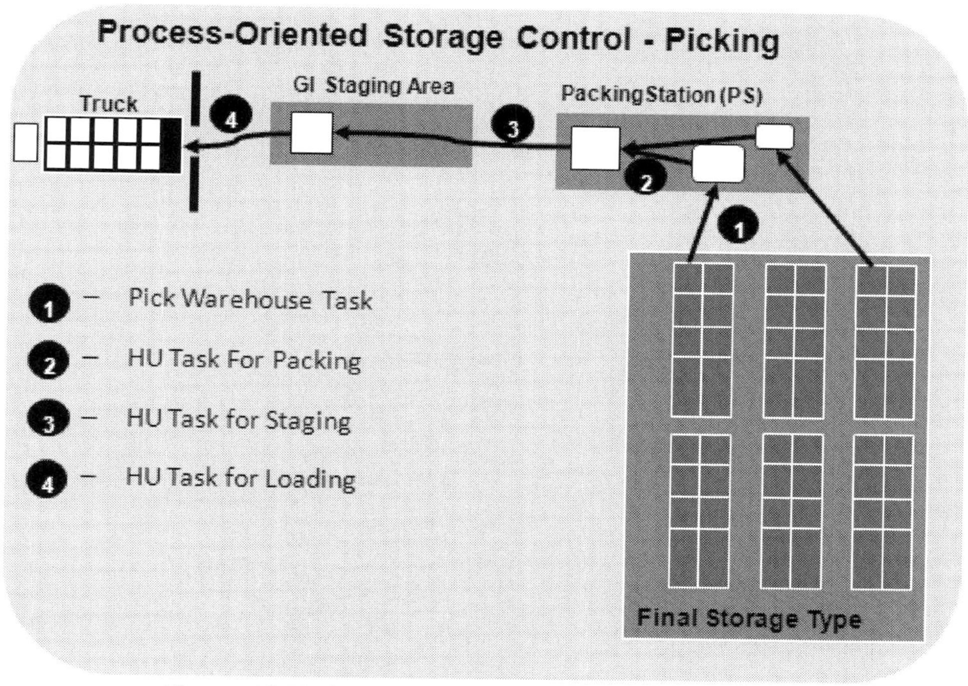

Diagram 15.1B – Process-Oriented Storage Control – Picking

POSC Business Scenario

In order to provide a better understanding of POSC configuration and process flow, we have used a business scenario in which a vendor ships product A and product B as one packed unit. In the truck, they both will arrive as one product. However, in the warehouse, they will be stored as two different products in two different bins. Hence, the product has to be taken to the deconsolidation work center. In the work center products will be segregated and packed into two different products and finally put away in their respective bins.

In order to demonstrate this scenario, three external steps are described below:

- Unloading (IB01): In this step, warehouse personnel will unload the truck.
- Deconsolidation (IB02): Here, warehouse personnel will deconsolidate and repack the products into two different HUs.
- Putaway (IB03): This is the last step. Here, warehouse personnel will putaway the products into the bins.

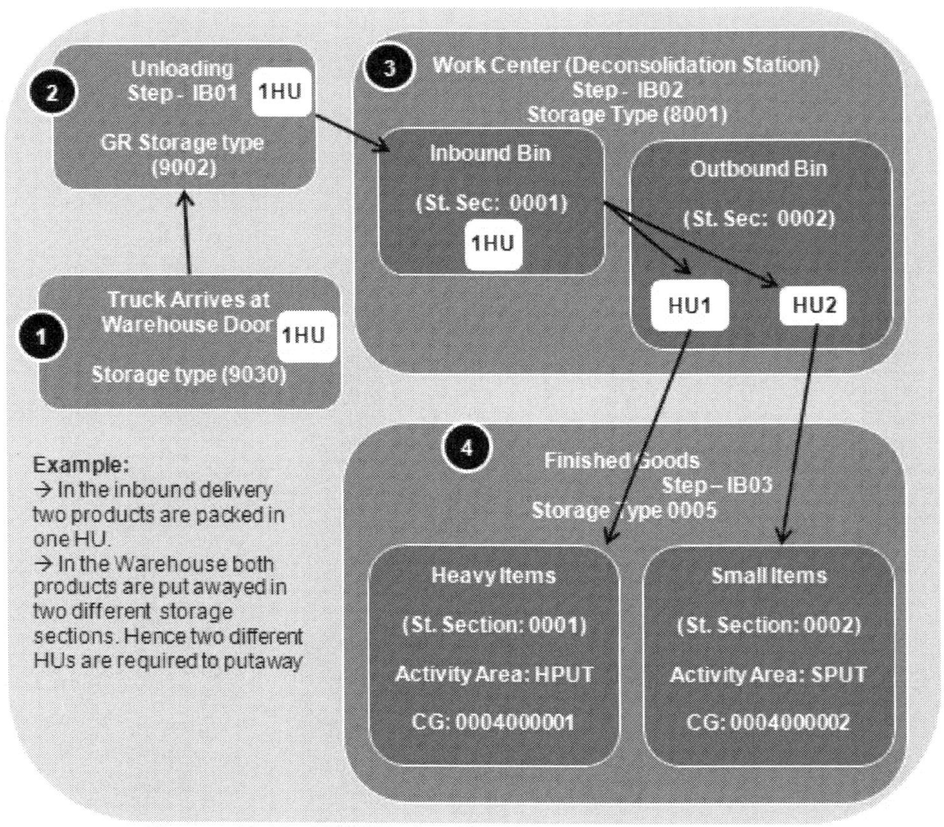

Diagram 15.1C – POSC Business Scenario

Following sections describe the POSC configuration in step by step.

15.1.1 Storage Process Step

The storage process step is nothing but a warehouse operation or task performed as part of the putaway or removal process. Examples include unloading, deconsolidation, packing, quality inspection, and so on. Under POSC they are defined as external storage process steps.

SAP has predefined several internal steps that describe the standard warehouse operations. These internal process steps are not modifiable. When the external process steps are defined, they must be assigned to the internal process steps.

To define the external storage process steps, follow menu path **SPRO | IMG | Extended Warehouse Management | Cross-Process Settings | Warehouse Task | Define Process-Oriented Storage Control**

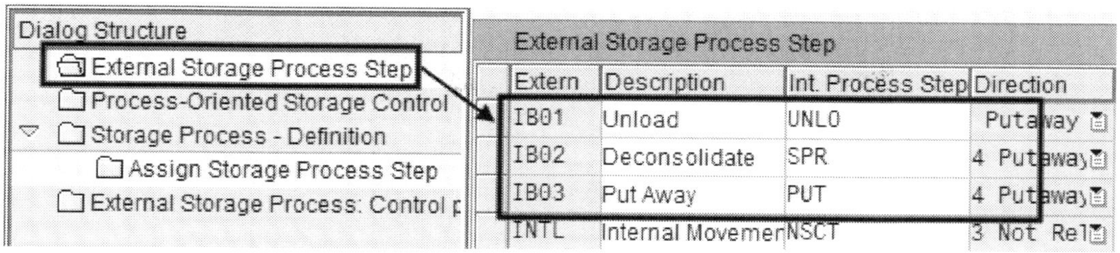

As per the business scenario, three external process steps (IB01, IB02, and IB03) have been defined and assigned to the appropriate internal process steps.

15.1.2 Process-Oriented Storage Control

Under the POSC option, maintain the required data like WPT, destination storage bin, source and destination storage types, for intermediate external process steps.

Menu Path: SPRO | IMG | Extended Warehouse Management | Cross-Process Settings | Warehouse Task | Define Process-Oriented Storage Control

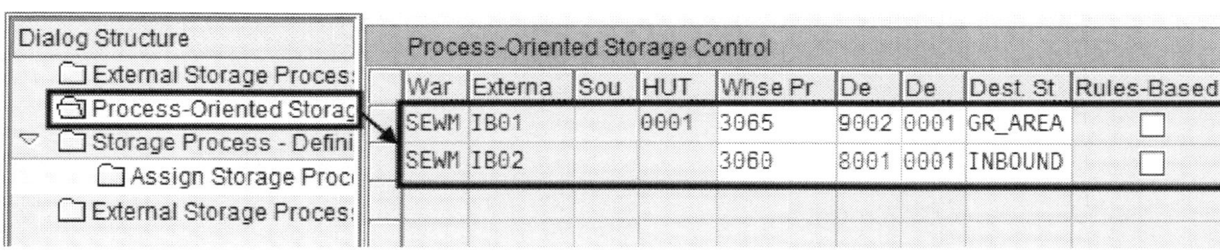

The destination bin for the last step (IB03) will be determined as per product master. Hence, it is not defined here.

- **Source storage type** enables users to control whether the HU should be moved via this intermediate storage type.
- **HU type group**: This is determined from the HU type of the material that is used for packaging. This assignment can be used to always specify that a particular HU type should be always moved via this intermediate storage type.
- **WPT:** This is required to create the WT for the external step.
- **Destination details**: This specifies a destination storage type, destination section, and destination bin for the intermediate external steps that will be used in the WT. Rule-based determination can also be used to determine the destination storage bin details. In this case, the system will use search sequences to determine the bins. If the system should search for the intermediate storage type, section, or bin using specific rules, set the "Rules-Based" indicator.

15.1.3 Storage Process—Definition

Third important step under POSC is defining storage process. Storage process contains the external process steps in a sequential order. For technical reasons, it is always necessary to maintain the process steps in the following sequential order. For putaway, it should always be

- Unload
- Count
- Deconsolidate
- Quality Inspection
- Perform Value Added Services
- Putaway

Some of the above steps may be optional, but putaway should always be the last step in the sequence.

For, the process steps must be defined in the following sequence:

- Remove from Stock (Pick)
- Perform Value Added Services
- Pack
- Stage
- Load

Some of the above steps may be optional, but picking should always be the first step in the storage process for removal.

For internal movements, the internal storage process steps are allowed in the following sequence:

- Remove from Stock
- Pack
- Deconsolidate
- Putaway

If there is stock to be removed, that should be the first step. If there is putaway, that should be the last step.

Menu Path: **SPRO | IMG | Extended Warehouse Management | Cross-Process Settings | Warehouse Task | Define Process-Oriented Storage Control**

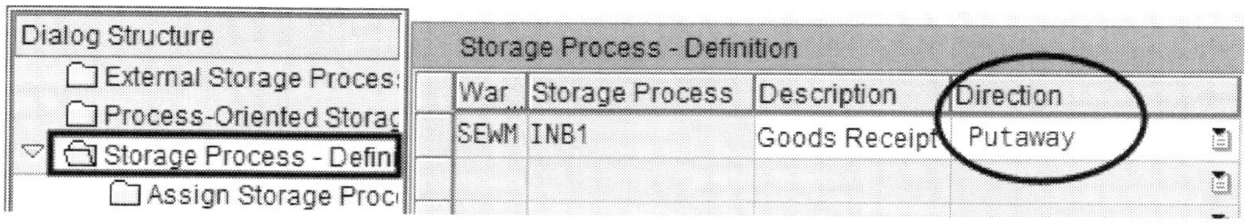

Here "Storage Process" INB1 is defined for Putaway. In the "Assign Storage Process Step" option, all the external storage process steps are assigned to the storage process (INB1) in appropriate sequence.

Duration can also be maintained for each of these steps in "Duration" field. The "Auto WT" check box will determine whether the WT will be created automatically. If the check box is not checked, the WT has to be created manually.

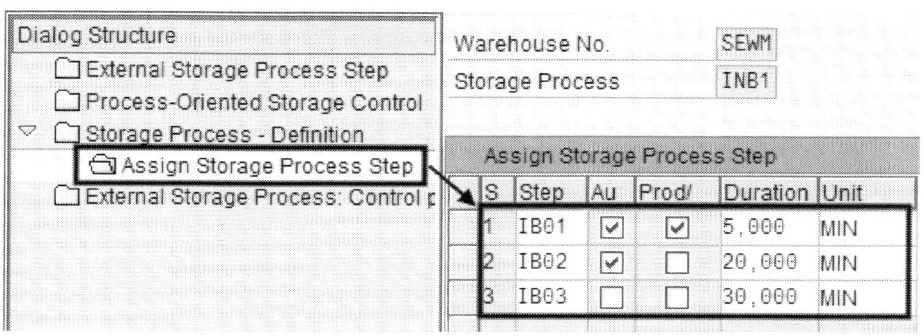

15.1.4 Assign Storage Process to WPT

Next step in case of "Inbound Process" is assigning the storage process to the WPT. For "Outbound Processing (Removal)," the storage process is assigned to the WOCR used to create WO for picking. Assignment of storage process to WPT can be done in the following menu path.

Menu Path: **SPRO | IMG | Extended Warehouse Management | Cross-Process Settings | Warehouse Task | Define Warehouse Process Type**

In the above example, because the IB01 is the first external step in INB1 and IB01 is assigned to WPT 3065, Storage Process Step INB1 must be assigned to WPT 3065. During WT creation, if WPT "3065" gets determined and the stock is HU managed, system will automatically trigger INB1 storage process. This will create one or more WTs for every step and the WT for first external step IB01 will be set to active.

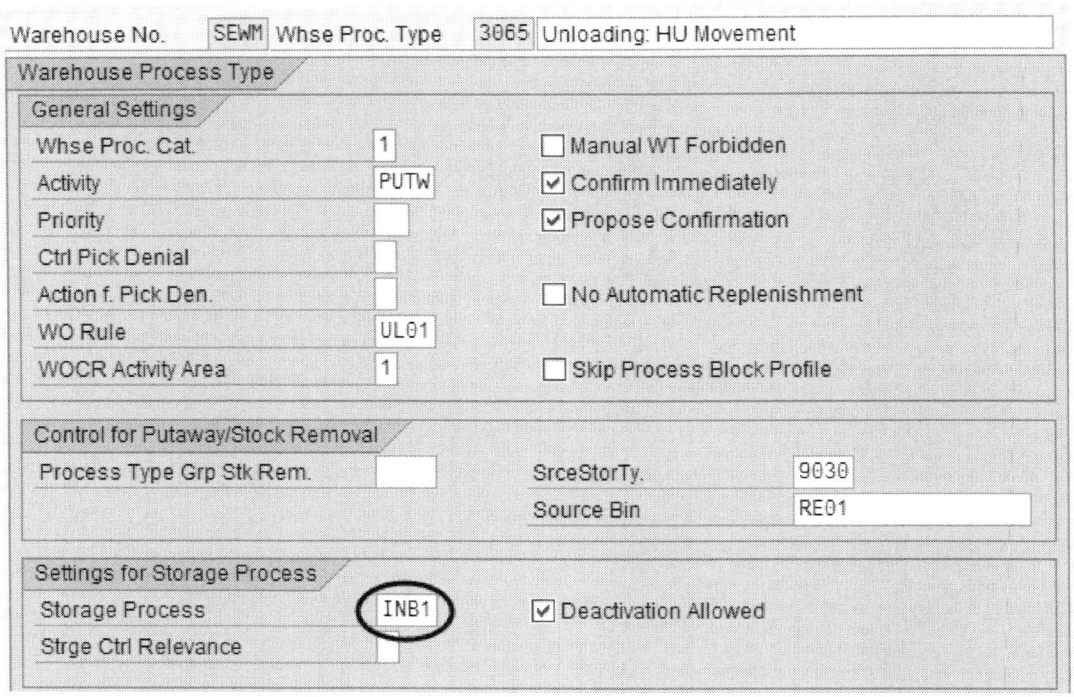

The following screenshot shows the settings for WPT 3060. Because WPT 3065 triggers before WPT 3060, INB1 must be assigned to the WPT 3065.

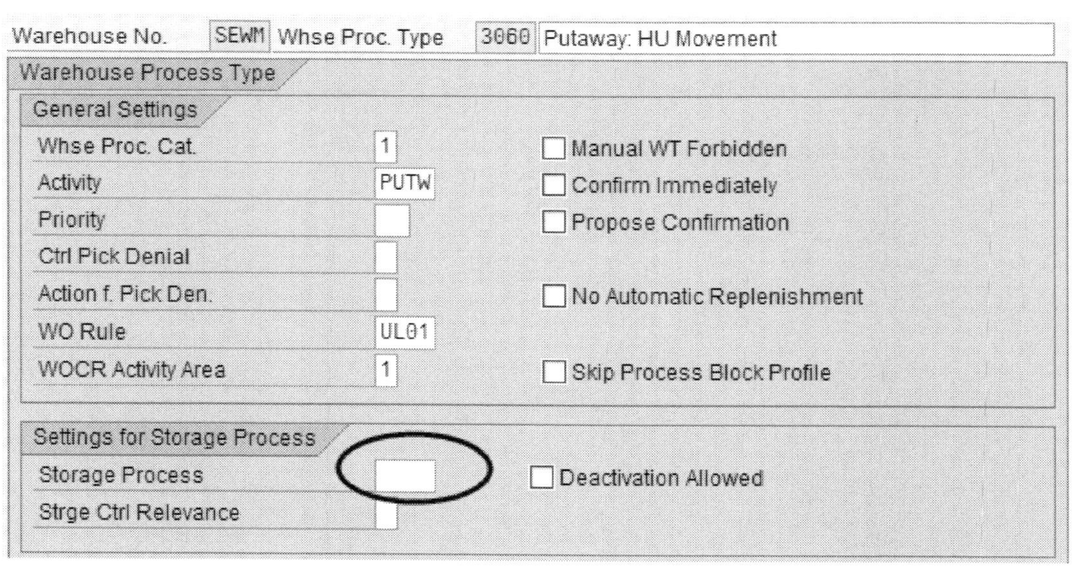

15.1.5 WPT Determination

WPT always gets determined based on delivery document type, delivery item type, delivery priority, and process type indicator. Values for delivery document type, delivery items type, and delivery priority come from the source document. The process type indicator is derived from the product master.

Menu Path: SPRO | IMG | Extended Warehouse Management | Cross-Process Settings | Warehouse Task | Define Warehouse Process Type

Determination of Warehouse Process Type

War...	Doc....	Item ...	Del.Prio.	ProTypeDet	Process Ind.	Whse...
SEWM	INB		0	01	No Special	3065
SEWM	INB		0	04	No Special	1010

15.1.6 Storage Type and Storage Section Settings

Storage type and storage sections are covered in detail in the chapter 5. The following screenshots will show you how the storage types and storage sections are defined in the system for the above mentioned POSC business scenario. These setting might change depending on your business requirements.

Menu Path: SPRO | IMG | Extended Warehouse Management | Master Data | Define Storage Type

The availability group of the final storage type along with the mandatory check will control the stock type for putaway. If the "Mandatory" check box is not active, the availability group will not be considered during putaway confirmation. Only if this check box is active will the system create a PCN to move the stock to the destination storage type availability group.

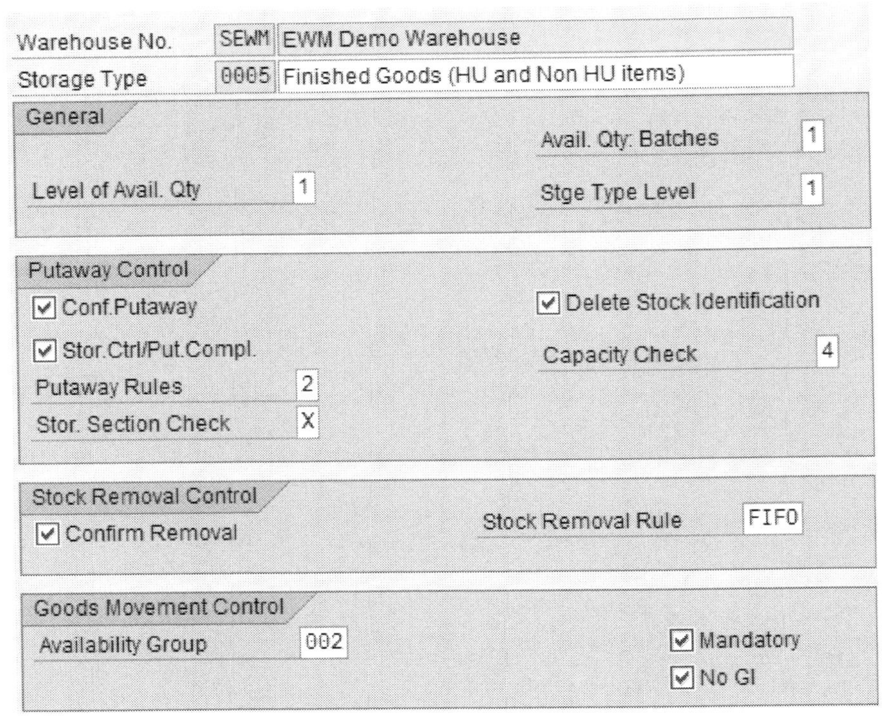

If the "Confirm Putaway" indicator is not active, the system will confirm the WT and WO in the background as soon as the WT is created.

The "Storage.Ctrl/Put.Compl" indicator controls the putaway status in the warehouse request. If this indicator is not set for final storage type, the putaway status will not be updated in the inbound delivery. For POSC, this has to be checked for the final storage types.

The following screenshot shows the settings done for work center (8001) storage type. In EWM, work center is a type of storage type, with storage type role “E—Work Center”. In the storage type, set the HU requirement as X.

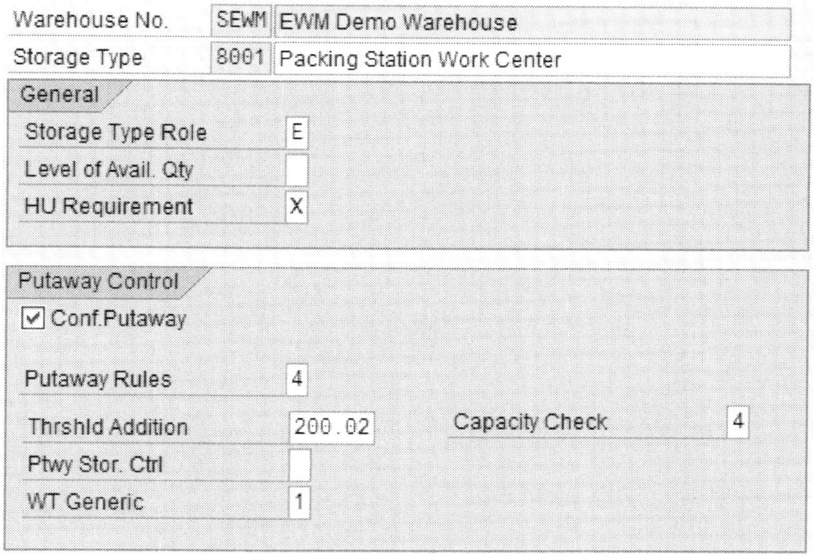

The following screenshot shows the settings done for GR staging area (9002). The storage type role defined for GR area is D—Staging area. Here also, the first external step has been assigned to this storage type.

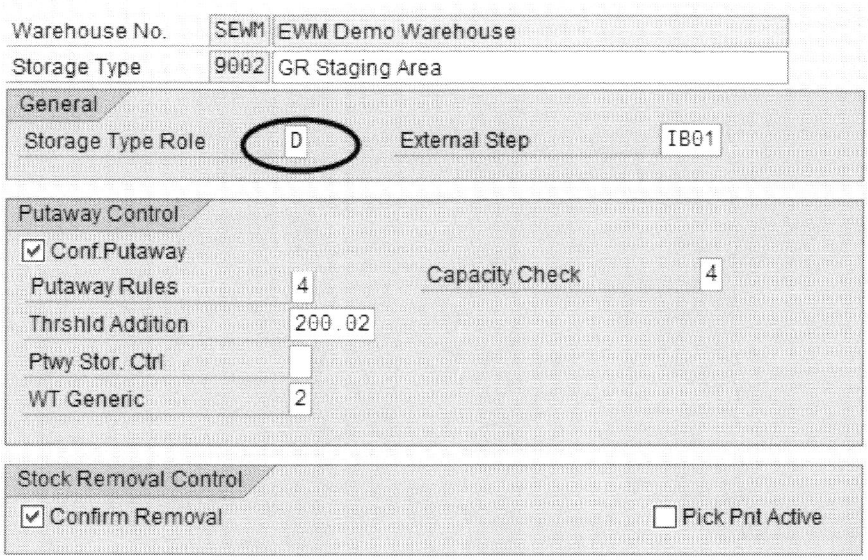

In EWM doors are also defined as a storage type. The next screenshot displays the settings done for GR doors (9030). An important parameter here is storage type role, which must be F for doors.

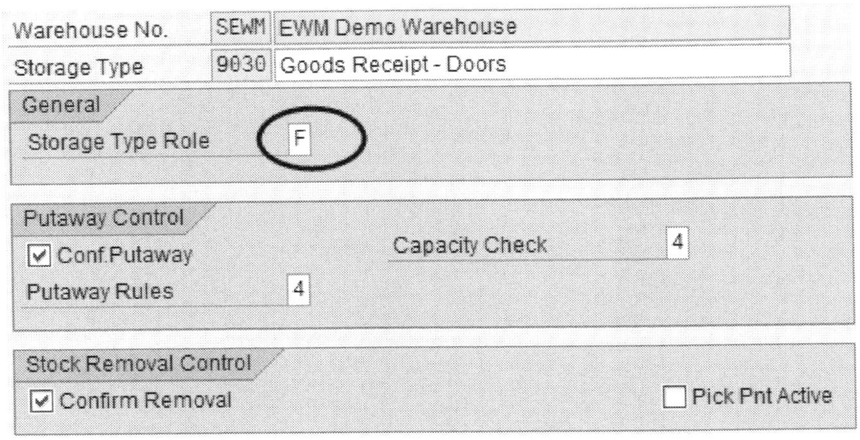

Storage Sections: Storage sections are covered in detail in chapter 5. The storage sections displayed here, created for each storage type. are only for reference and to facilitate understanding.

Menu Path: SPRO | IMG | Extended Warehouse Management | Master Data | Define Storage Section

Storage Sections

WhN	Typ	Sec	Description
SEWM	0005	0001	Heavy Parts
SEWM	0005	0002	Small Parts
SEWM	0005	0003	Damaged Stock
SEWM	8001	0001	Unpacked Goods
SEWM	8001	0002	Packed Goods
SEWM	9002	0001	General Staging Area 1
SEWM	9002	0002	General Staging Area 2
SEWM	9030	0001	Doors

15.1.7 Product Master data

For the above described POSC business scenario we have defined following two finished goods products (4000014282 and 4000014283) and one packaging product (5000005181).

	Whse Data Tab			Pkg Data Tab			
Prod. Number	**Proc. Type Det. Ind.**	**Put. Ctrl. Ind.**	**St. Sect. Ind**	**Packing Group**	**Std HU Type**	**Pack Mat Type**	**HU Type**
4000014282	01	HEVY	HEVY				
4000014283	01	SMAL	SMAL				
5000005181				PG01	BOX	Y007	BOX

In TCode /SCWM/MAT1, for finished products, assign the appropriate process type determination indicator, putaway control indicator (PACI), and storage section indicator (SSI) in "Warehouse Data

Tab." In this example, PACI and SSI "HEVY" is assigned to product 40000014282 and "SMAL" is assigned to 40000014283.

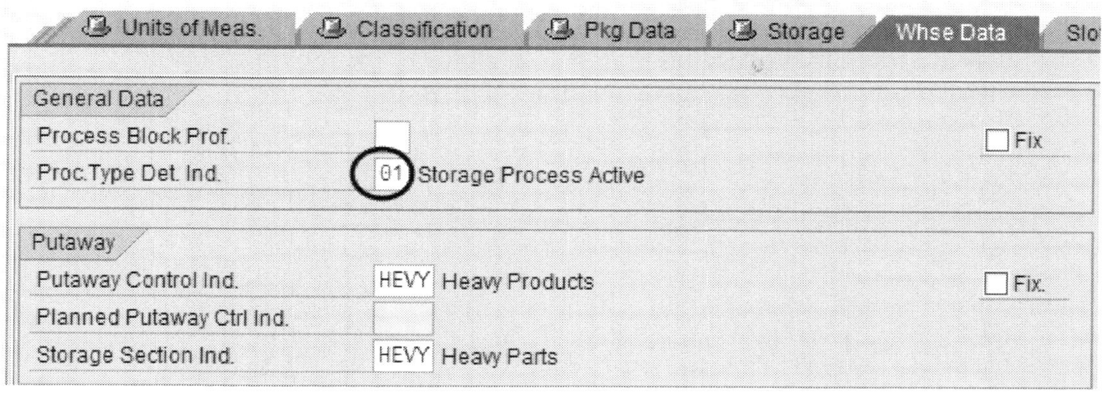

In order to create HUs, packaging products should also be created for the warehouse, but only the "Pkg Data" tab needs to be maintained. In this example product 5000005181 is defined as packaging product.

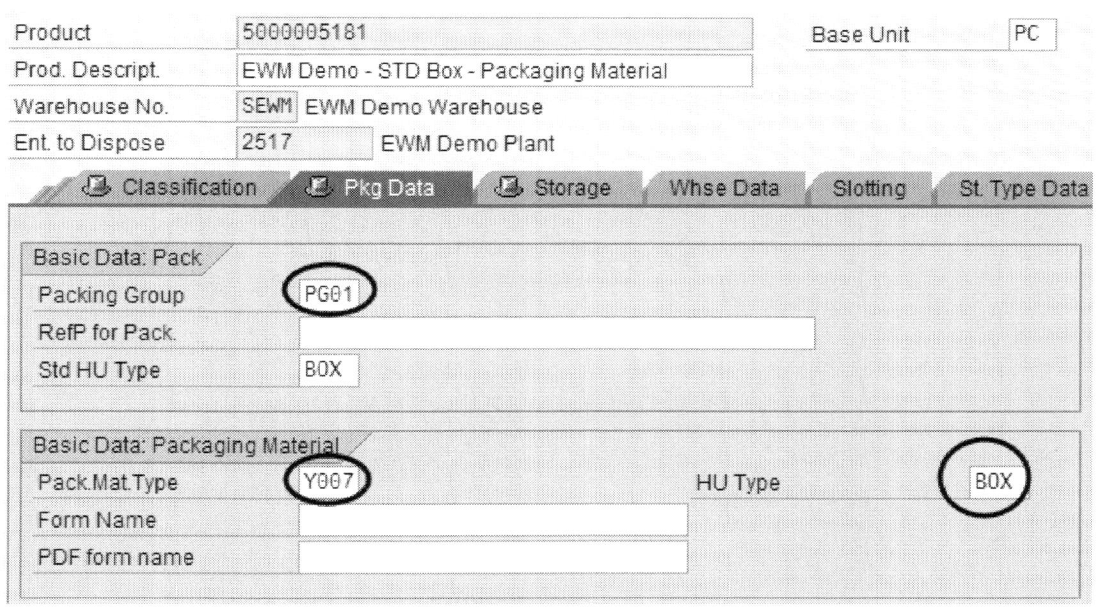

15.1.8 Storage Type, Section, and Bin Determination

Product master settings play an important role in the determination of storage type, storage section, and storage bins. These details have already been covered in earlier chapters. Here, only an overview of the required configuration settings will be covered.

15.1.8.1 Define Putaway Control Indicator (PACI)

Two indicators have been defined to differentiate the small products from the heavy products storage.

Menu Path: SPRO | IMG | Extended Warehouse Management | Goods Receipt Process | Strategies | Storage Type Search | Define Putaway Control Indicator

Putaway Control Indicator

War	PACI	Description	Stor
SEWM	HEVY	Heavy Products	
SEWM	SMAL	Small Products	

15.1.8.2 Define and Assign Storage Type Search Sequence for Putaway

The storage type search sequence indicator is used to assign appropriate storage types for the product putaway in a sequence. It is defined under **SPRO | IMG | Extended Warehouse Management | Goods Receipt Process | Strategies | Storage Type Search | Define Storage Type Search Sequence for Putaway**

Storage Type Search Sequence for Putaway - Definition

War	Stor	Description
SEWM	0005	Put Away in Storage Type 0005

Once the indicator is defined, the appropriate storage types and putaway sequence are assigned to it, as shown below. Multiple storage types can be assigned to the storage type search sequence.

Menu path: SPRO | IMG | Extended Warehouse Management | Goods Receipt Process | Strategies | Storage Type Search | Assign Storage Types to Storage Type Search Sequence

Storage Type Search Sequence for Putaway

WhN	Srch Seq.	Seq	Typ	STG	Evl	Description
SEWM	0005	1	0005			Put Away in Storage Type 0005

15.1.8.3 Specify Storage Type Search Sequence for Putaway

This menu is used to assign the storage type search sequence indicator to the combination of PACI and warehouse process type, along with other available indicators. Based on this storage type search sequence is determined for putaway.

Menu Path: **SPRO | IMG | Extended Warehouse Management | Goods Receipt Process | Strategies | Storage Type Search | Specify Storage Type Search Sequence for Putaway**

Search Sequence: Putaway											
WhN	PACI	Proc.	Qty Class.	Sto...	Type	Use	Ent.toDisp	Haz...	H...	Srch.Seq.	Putaway Rules
SEWM	HEVY	3065								0005	No Putaway Rule
SEWM	SMAL	3065								0005	No Putaway Rule

Here, both PACIs have been assigned to the same the search sequence. This way, both products will be stored in the same storage type, but in two different storage sections.

15.1.8.4 Optimize Access Strategy for Storage Type Search: Putaway

In EWM, various indicators influence the storage type search. To reduce the number of entries, an access strategy can be defined for the storage type search table. This can improve system performance. Each sequence number is an access combination that the system uses while determining the storage type search. The system will first use a more specific search, and then broaden to a more generic search.

Menu Path: **SPRO | IMG | Extended Warehouse Management | Goods Receipt Process | Strategies | Storage Type Search | Optimize Access Strategy for Storage Type Search: Putaway**

Optimization of Access for Stor.Type Determ. at Putaway											
WhN	Seq...	Put.Strat.	ProcTyp	Q	Stk...	Sto...	Use	Pa...	Ris...	Hzd...
SEWM	1	☑	☑	☐	☐	☐	☐	☐	☐	☐

15.1.8.5 Storage Section Search Sequence

Like with storage type search, the system can be defined to determine the appropriate storage sections for putaway. The storage section search starts after determination of destination storage type. The system uses the storage section indicator assigned in the product master to determine the allowed storage sections for product putaway. They are defined in menu path **SPRO | IMG | Extended Warehouse Management | Goods Receipt Process | Strategies | Storage Section Search | Create Storage Section Indicators**

Storage Section Indicators		
War...	Secln	Description
SEWM	HEVY	Heavy Parts
SEWM	SMAL	Small Parts

Once the storage section indicators are defined, they can be used in the storage section search sequence table to assign the appropriate storage sections and the sequence.

Menu Path: SPRO | IMG | Extended Warehouse Management | Goods Receipt Process | Strategies | Storage Section Search | Maintain Storage Section Search Sequence

Storage Section Search

WhN	Typ	H...	H...	SecIn	Seq...	Sec	EvlWh...
SEWM	0005			HEVY	1	0001	
SEWM	0005			SMAL	1	0002	

Here, notice the assignment of storage section indicators to the storage sections. In the product master, the storage section indicator "HEVY" has been assigned to product 4000014282 and "SMAL" to product 4000014283. In this configuration, "HEVY" has been assigned to storage section "0001—Heavy Parts," and "SMAL" to storage section "0002—Small Parts." This way, these two products will be stored in two different storage sections under storage type 0005.

15.1.8.6 Storage Section Check

In EWM, storage section search is not mandatory for putaway. This is defined in the storage type under option "Storage Section Check." During the storage section search if the storage section check is active, goods are putaway only in storage sections found as per the product master.

The storage section check can also be defined under **SPRO | IMG | Extended Warehouse Management | Goods Receipt Process | Strategies | Storage Section Search | Storage Section Check**

Storage Section Check and Haz. Subst. Mgmt per Storage Type

WhN	Typ	SC
SEWM	0005	X Storage section determination and check
SEWM	0006	
SEWM	0007	
SEWM	0009	

- X Storage section determination and check
- Y Storage section determination, no check
- No storage section determination or check

15.1.9 Staging Areas

Configuration of staging areas is covered in detail in chapter 5 under section 5.2.14. Please refer to this section for screenshots and for more details.

15.1.10 Work Center

Configuration of the work center is also covered in detail in chapter 5 under section 5.2.15. If a process step is performed at a work center, the system should also determine the work center where this step is to be performed. Therefore, it is important to assign the work center–related process step to the work center in the "Define Work Center" screen, as show below.

Menu Path: SPRO | IMG | Extended Warehouse Management | Master Data | Work Center | Define Work Center.

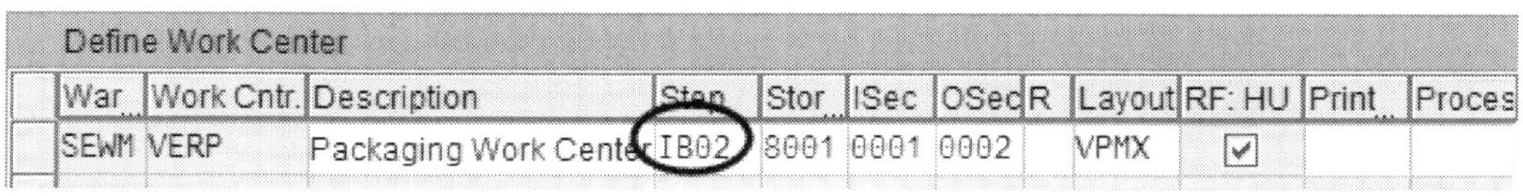

15.1.11 WOCR

Configuration of WOCR is covered in detail in chapter 12. This business scenario has used the standard SAP-delivered WOCR called "UL01—Unload." It is defined with the creation category "Load/Unload" and assigned to WPTs 3065 and 3060.

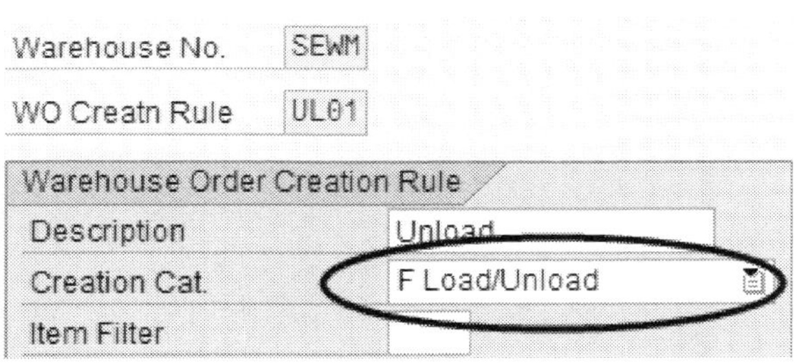

15.1.12 Determination of Consolidation Group

Consolidation group plays an important role in POSC. One of the ways the system determines that deconsolidation is required is based on different consolidation group from the putaway location. The system first determines the PACI, which helps to determine the storage type, storage section, and the bin location. The bin location information is used to determine the activity area. Activity areas contain the consolidation group.

At the time of putaway, if the HU contains multiple products, and they belong to different consolidation group, the system sends that HU to a work center for the deconsolidation process. Diagram 15.1.12A shows how the consolidation group is determined for the putaway activity.

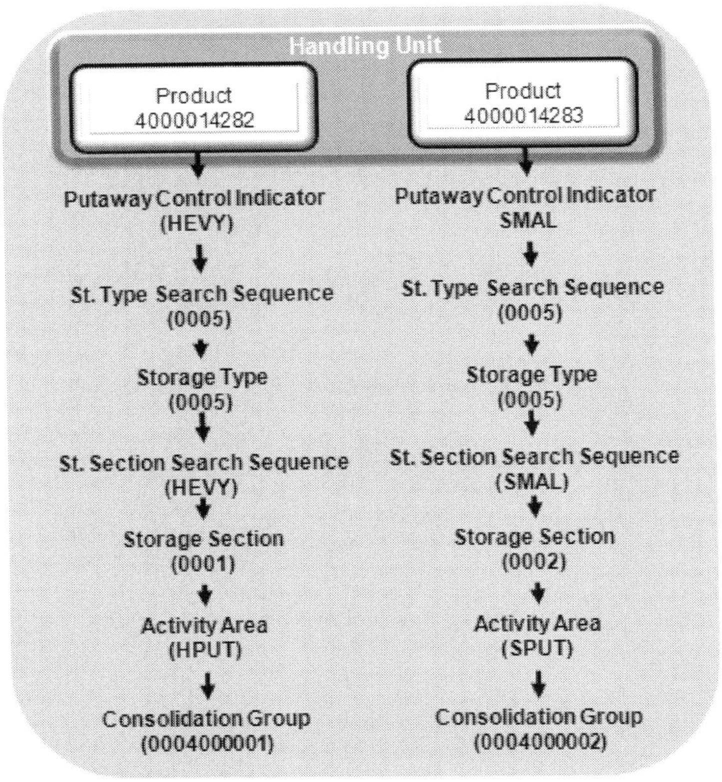

Diagram 15.1.12A – Determination of Consolidation Group

15.1.13 Exercise—POSC Scenario

In order to test the above explained POSC business scenario, the following data has been used:

a) Finished Materials—4000014282 and 4000014283

b) Packaging Material—5000005181

c) Vendor—1000030

d) Plant—2517, Storage Locations—NAFS and IAFS

15.1.13.1 Create Purchase Order in the ERP System

Create one purchase order (TCode ME21N) for two materials and select the appropriate confirmation key to create an inbound delivery.

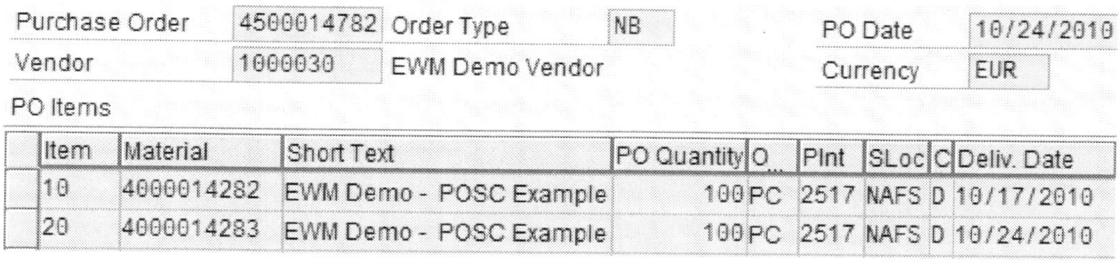

15.1.13.2 Create an Inbound Delivery in ERP System

In order to test POSC, create an inbound delivery (TCode VL31N) with reference to the purchase order and pack both materials into one HU. To pack products in the inbound delivery, use the "Pack" button located on the application toolbar. Upon saving, verify that inbound delivery is transferred to the EWM system.

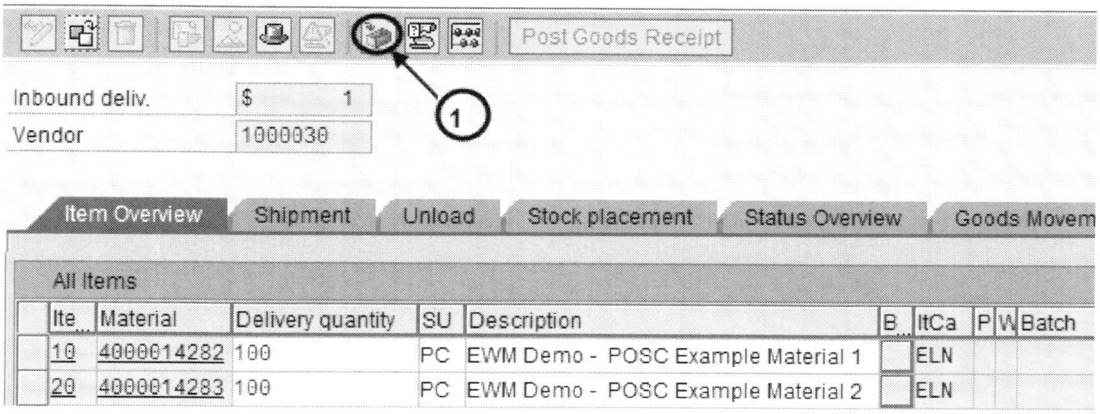

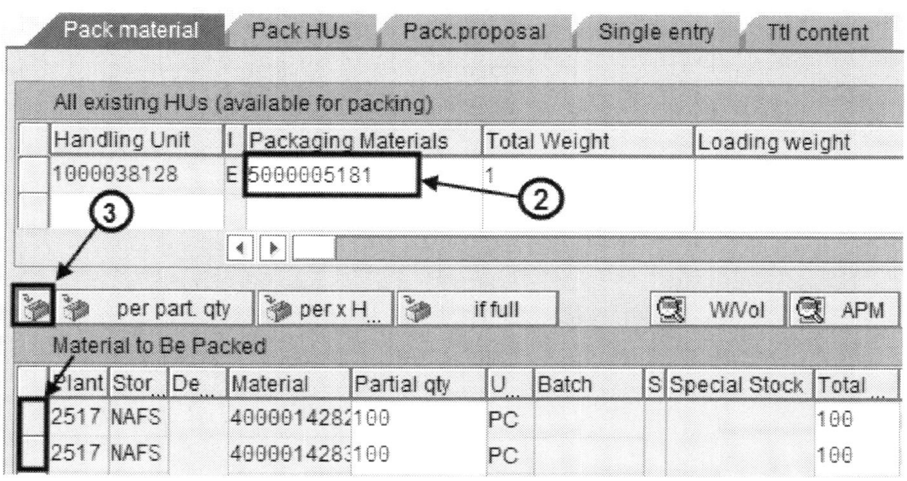

Select the materials to be packed and click on "Pack" button (step 3).

Once all the products are packed, click on "Save" button to create a delivery.

15.1.13.3 Locate ID in the EWM System

In TCode /SCWM/IDN, in the "Find" field, select the option "Inbound Delivery Notification," enter the ERP inbound delivery number in the text box, and click "Execute". Verify that IDN is active. If not, correct the IDN and click the "Activate" button.

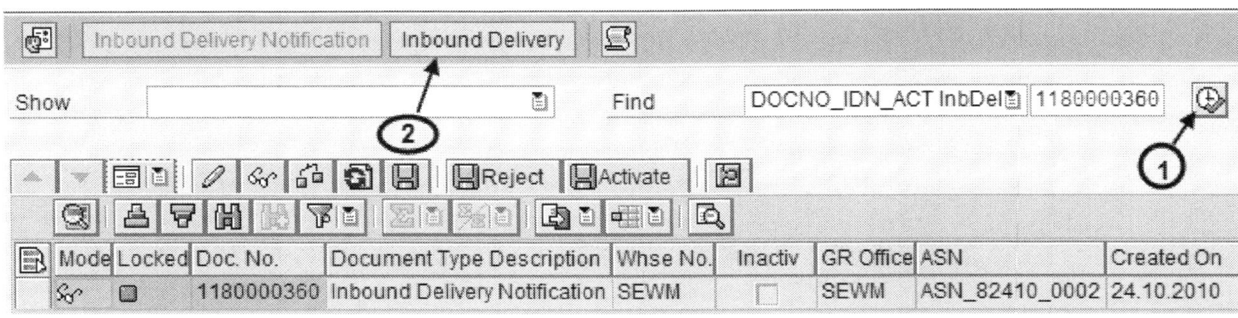

Click the "Inbound Delivery" button on the application toolbar. This will display the inbound delivery document created for the IDN.

In the ID screen, click the HU tab and verify that HU details are transferred to the EWM system. Verify the WPT, item category, stock type, and goods movement bin, if necessary.

Click the "Unload" button to unload the HU from the truck. This will create the multiple WTs for the delivery, which can be seen in the warehouse monitor.

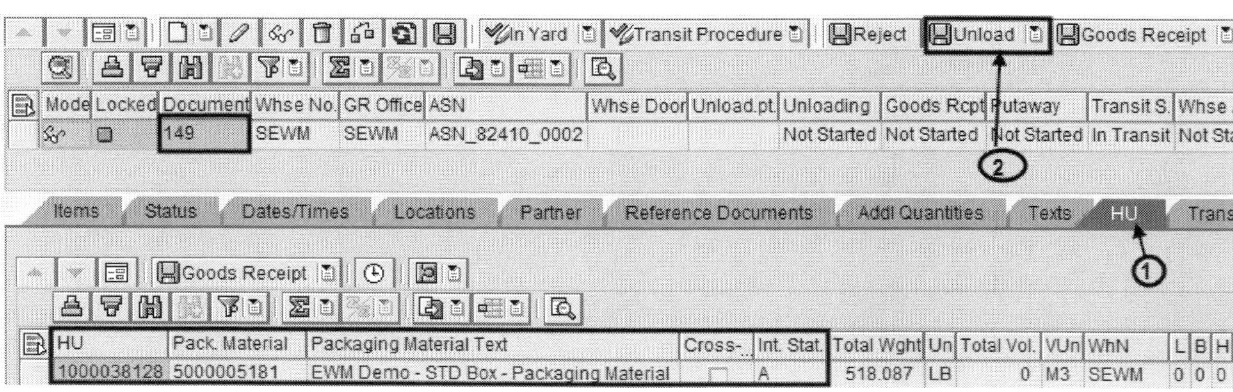

15.1.13.4 Display Warehouse Task

In the warehouse monitor (TCode /SCWM/MON), select the ID and click on the "Warehouse Task" button. This will display all WTs created for the inbound delivery. Notice the status "B—Waiting" for final putaway WTs. This means the system is waiting for the previous steps to confirm before the activating the final steps.

In this example, the system has created two HU tasks, the first for step IB01 to unload the HU from door 9030 to GR staging area (9002) and the second for step IB02 to move the HU from GR staging area to the work center (8001). The system also created two inactive tasks (one for each product with status B) to putaway the products in the warehouse. Notice the status "C—Completed" for the unloading HU task. This means the WO is created and confirmed for this task automatically.

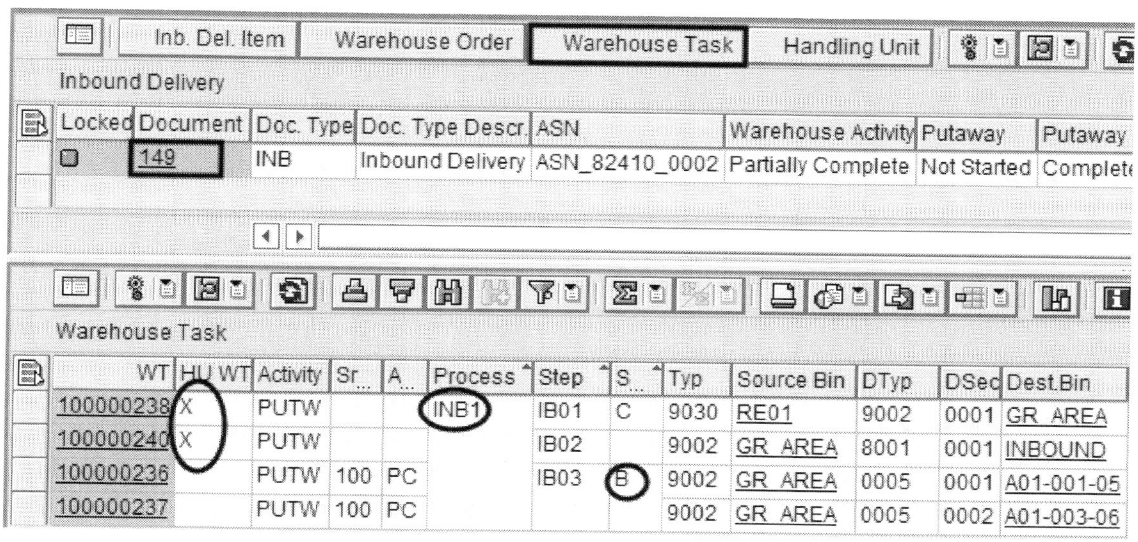

Notice the status "blank" for the HU task, which is created to move the HU from the GR area to the work center (8001). This means the WO has been created, and currently this task is active in the system.

15.1.13.5 Display WOs

In the warehouse monitor (TCode /SCWM/MON), select the ID number and click the "Warehouse Order" button to display all the WOs for the ID. As explained above, two WOs are created. One is confirmed, and the second one is open or active. The active WO has the status left blank.

Warehouse Order

Whse Order	WOCR	Creat.Cat.	Hdr WhsePT	Status	WO ActArea	Q	Wave	Created By	Created On
3000154	UL01	F	3060					RM0015	24.10.2010
3000153	UL01	F	3065	C				RM0015	24.10.2010

The following screenshot shows a stock overview before moving the HU to the work center. The HU and stock will show on the work center monitor only after confirming the WO.

Stock Overview

Typ	Stor. Bin	Product	Batch	ST	Incom. Qty	Outg. Qty	AvlQtyBUoM	Quantity	BUn
0005	A01-001-05	4000014282		F1	100	0	0	0	PC
0005	A01-003-06	4000014283		F1	100	0	0	0	PC
9002	GR AREA	4000014282		F1	0	100	0	100	PC
9002	GR AREA	4000014283		F1	0	100	0	100	PC

Click on the open WO number and click on confirm and save button. This will move the HU stock from the GR area to the work center storage type.

Check the status of the WTs, and the warehouse orders. The status of the final putaway WTs will remain "B" until the work center deconsolidates and confirms the new HUs. Notice that the system has now updated the source bin for final putaway as work center bin.

Warehouse Task

WT	HU WT	Activity	SrceTgtQty	AUn	Process	Step	Status	Typ	Sec	Source Bin	DTyp	DSec	Dest.Bin
100000238	X	PUTW			INB1	IB01	C	9030		RE01	9002	0001	GR AREA
100000240	X	PUTW				IB02		9002	0001	GR AREA	8001	0001	INBOUND
100000236		PUTW	100	PC		IB03	B	8001	0001	INBOUND	0005	0001	A01-001-05
100000237		PUTW	100	PC				8001	0001	INBOUND	0005	0002	A01-003-06

In the stock overview, the stock is now visible in the work center location in the inbound section.

Stock Overview

Typ	Stor. Bin	Product	Batch	ST	Incom. Qty	Outg. Qty	AvlQtyBUoM	Quantity	BUn
0005	A01-001-05	4000014282		F1	100	0	0	0	PC
0005	A01-003-06	4000014283		F1	100	0	0	0	PC
8001	INBOUND	4000014282		F1	0	100	0	100	PC
8001	INBOUND	4000014283		F1	0	100	0	100	PC

15.1.13.6 Deconsolidation Process

Go to TCode /SCWM/DCONS, enter the warehouse number and work center and click "Execute." The HU should be displayed with the product details in the work center monitor under "Section / Bin / HU/ Item" section.

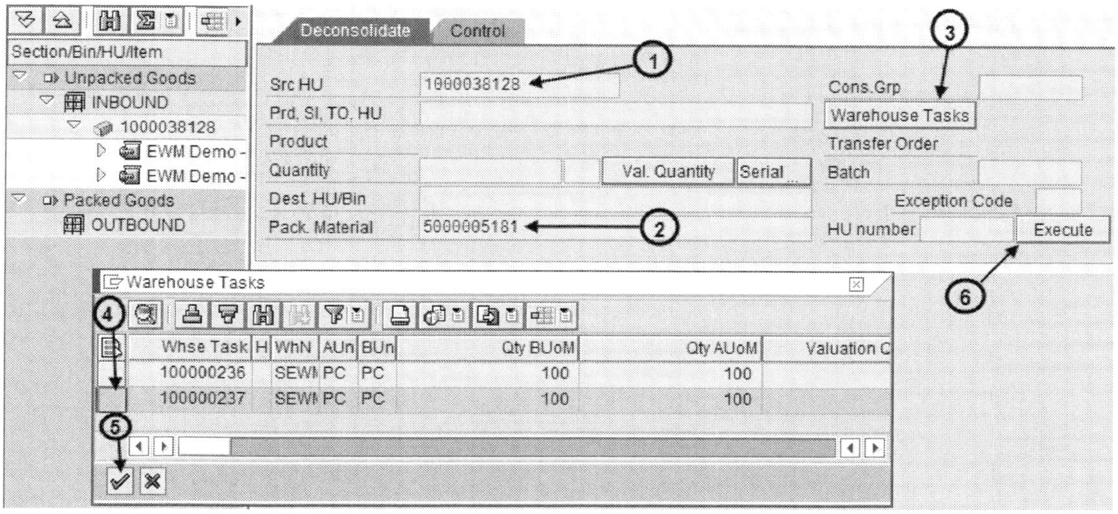

In the "Deconsolidate" tab, enter the HU number in the "Src HU" field, enter the packaging material, and click the WT button. This will display all the WTs assigned to the product. Once the actual deconsolidation task is completed and the product is packed into a new HU, select the appropriate WT and hit "Enter." During this process the quantity can be adjusted, if required. Finally, click the "Execute" button to create a new HU.

Based on the work center configuration, the new HU might remain in the same bin or move to the bin specified in the configuration. In this example, new HUs move to the outbound section. Repeat these steps for the remaining tasks or open packing activities. It is possible to leave partial stock in the parent HU or create new HUs for all stock. In this example, three new HUs were created from one parent HU, as shown below in the screen shot.

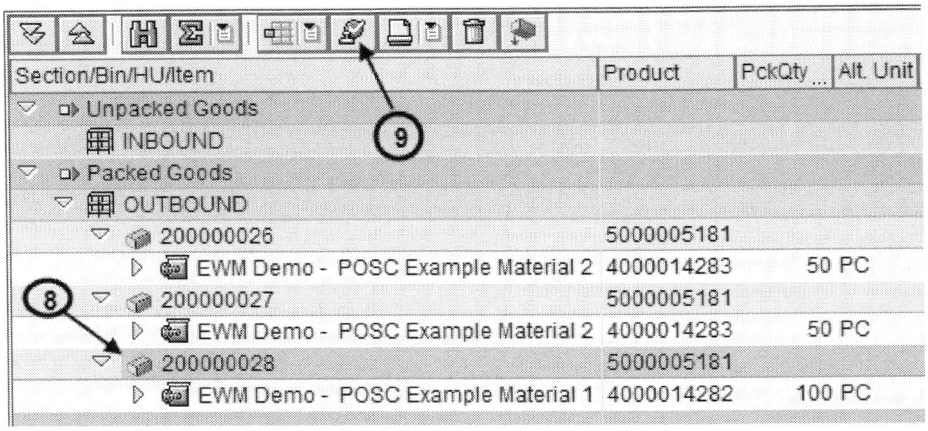

In order to complete the work center process, select the HUs created and click on the "complete process step for HU" button (step 9). This will activate the final putaway WTs and create the warehouse orders to move the products from the work center outbound section to the final destination bins.

For each newly created HU, the system will create a new WT. In this case, there are three open HU WTs with the status blank, with the updated source bin information.

Warehouse Task

WT	HU WT	Activity	Srce...	AUn	Proce...	Step	Status	Typ	Sec	Source Bin	DTyp	DSec	Dest.Bin
100000238	X	PUTW			INB1	IB01	C	9030		RE01	9002	0001	GR_AREA
100000240	X	PUTW				IB02		9002	0001	GR_AREA	8001	0001	INBOUND
100000236		PUTW	100	PC		IB03		8001	0002	OUTBOUND	0005	0001	A01-001-05
100000237		PUTW	50	PC				8001	0002	OUTBOUND	0005	0002	A01-003-06
100000241		PUTW	50	PC				8001	0002	OUTBOUND	0005	0002	A01-003-06
100000236		PUTW	100	PC			C	8001	0001	INBOUND	8001	0002	OUTBOUND
100000237		PUTW	50	PC				8001		INBOUND	8001	0002	OUTBOUND
100000237		PUTW	50	PC				8001	0001	INBOUND	8001	0002	OUTBOUND

15.1.13.7 Confirm Putaway WTs

WTs can be confirmed from the warehouse monitor (TCode /SCWM/MON) or, alternatively, using TCode /SCWM/TO_CONF. In the warehouse monitor, click on the WO and click the "Confirm Save" button. This will confirm the WTs and update the stock in the destination bins.

Warehouse Order

Whse Order	Status	WO ActArea	Created By	Created On	Created At	Q	Wave
3000158		SPUT	RM0015	24.10.2010	06:47:09		
3000159		SPUT	RM0015	24.10.2010	05:18:26		
3000160		HPUT	RM0015	24.10.2010	05:18:26		
3000153	C		RM0015	24.10.2010	05:18:26		
3000154			RM0015	24.10.2010	05:18:29		
3000155		SPUT	RM0015	24.10.2010	05:18:26		
3000156		SPUT	RM0015	24.10.2010	05:18:26		
3000157		HPUT	RM0015	24.10.2010	05:18:26		

15.1.13.8 Verify Warehouse Stock

If the HUs are allowed in storage type, they will show up in the stock under physical stock options. You can verify the stock in the warehouse monitor (TCode /SCWM/MON).

Physical Stock

Typ	Stor. Bin	HU	Product	Product Short Description	Quantity	BUn
0005	A01-001-05	200000028	4000014282	EWM Demo - POSC Example Material 1	100	PC
0005	A01-003-06	200000026	4000014283	EWM Demo - POSC Example Material 2	50	PC
0005	A01-003-06	200000027	4000014283	EWM Demo - POSC Example Material 2	50	PC

15.2 Layout-Oriented Storage Control (LOSC)

LOSC determines the internal routing based on the layout within the warehouse (intermediate locations). POSC is focused on the movement of the products, whereas LOSC is used to make sure that the products are moving accurately as per the physical layout of the warehouse.

LOSC is typically used in warehouses where the product cannot be moved to the destination bin directly due to the physical layout restrictions of the warehouse. For example, products stored in the mezzanine floor are received in the ground floor. In order to store the products in the mezzanine floor, they have to be transferred via elevator point. In such scenarios, LOSC is the better fit, as it creates tasks to move products from one location to another and provides product visibility in each of these areas. In the following sections, the LOSC configuration will be explained with this as an example.

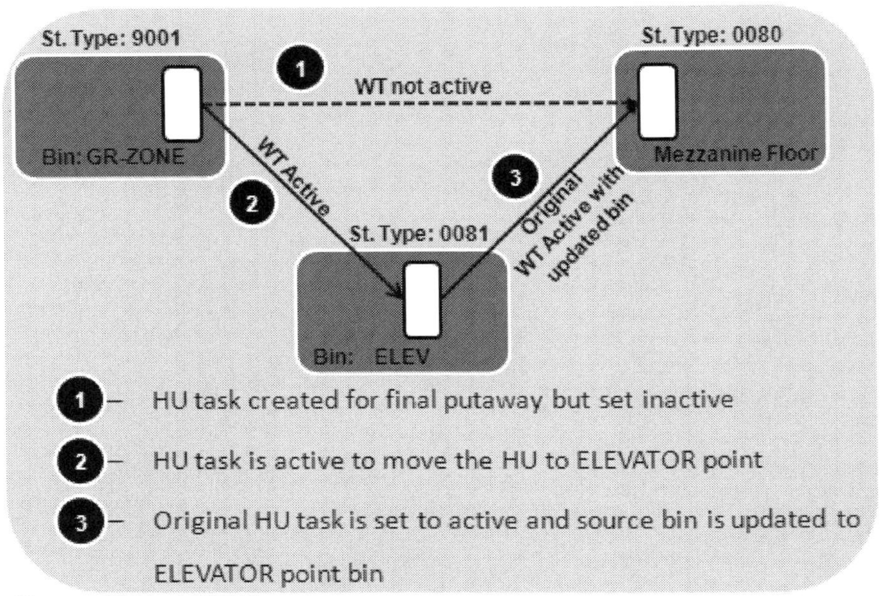

Diagram 15.2A – LOSC Example

Like POSC, LOSC works only with HUs. (The only exception is the process with ID points or picks points.)

LOSC Business Scenario

The business scenario is, products are packed in HUs in the ERP inbound delivery. In the warehouse, they have to be stored in the mezzanine/upper-level floor. The route followed in the warehouse to move the product to the upper level is via elevator point.

15.2.1 Configuration Requirement

By now, most of the basic configurations required to putaway the stock in the warehouse have been explained in detail both in chapter 14 and in this chapter under POSC section of this chapter. Hence, it will not be explained in detail here. Table 15.2.1A gives an overview of the configuration required to activate LOSC.

S. No	LOSC Specific Configuration	TCode	Transportable
1	Define Storage Types	SPRO	Yes
2	Define Layout-Oriented Storage Process Control	SPRO	Yes
3	Maintain Storage Type Search Sequence	SPRO	Yes
4	Define Control Indicators for Determining Warehouse Process Types	SPRO	Yes
5	Product Master Settings	/SCWM/MAT1	Yes
6	Determine Warehouse Process Type	SPRO	Yes

Table 15.2.1A - LOSC Configuration Overview

15.2.1.1 Define Storage Types

For LOSC, it is possible to use ID points and pick points for the intermediate point. Following screenshots will demonstrate how the final and elevator storage types can be configured.

Menu Path: **SPRO | IMG | Extended Warehouse Management | Master Data | Define Storage Type**

Storage type for Final Putaway: Here, the final storage type 0080, with HU requirement active, has been configured. This is a regular storage type with the role "Standard Storage Type."

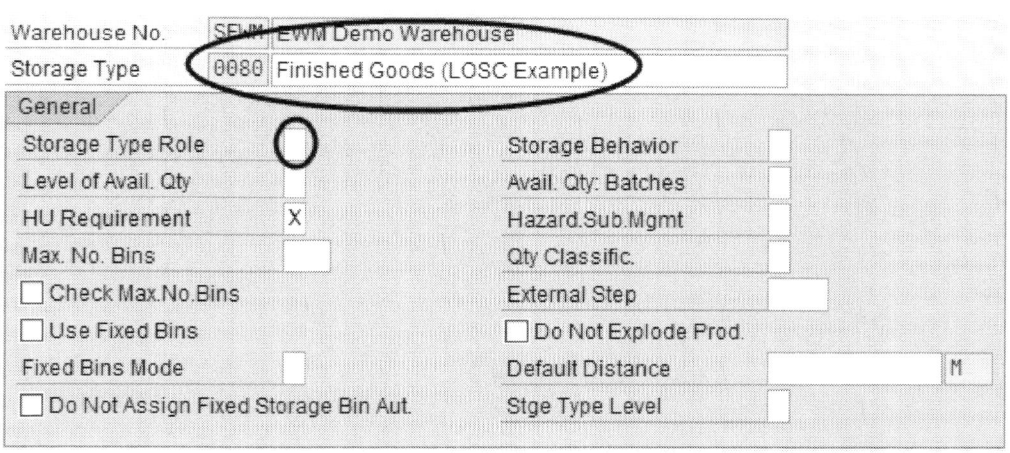

Under the putaway control section, the "Storage control/putaway complete" check must be active for LOSC for the final storage type.

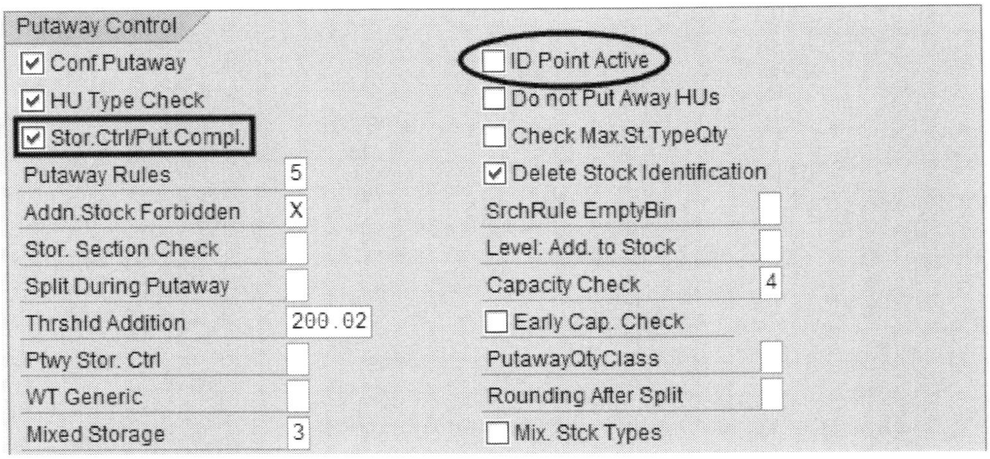

Storage type for Elevator staging area: We have defined this as a standard storage type. All general settings are same as for final storage type.

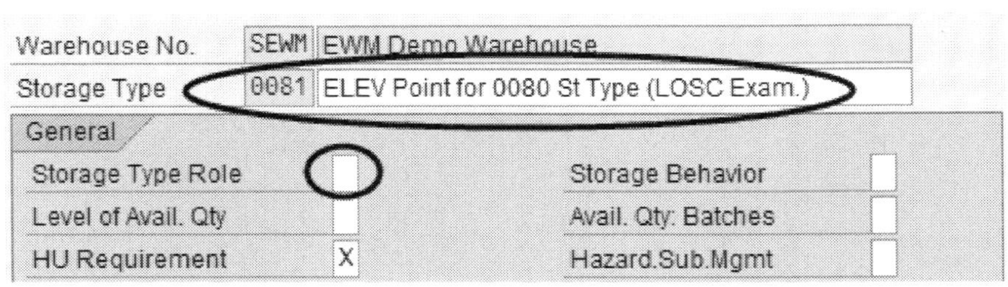

Under the putaway control section, the "storage control/ putaway complete" option is unchecked for elevator storage.

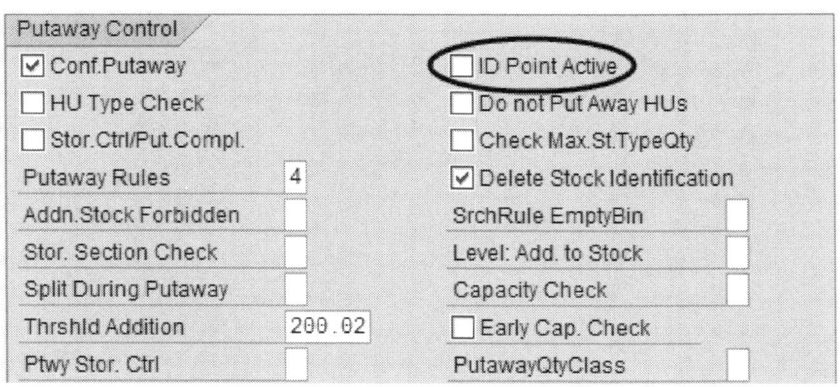

15.2.1.2 Define Storage Sections

More than one storage section can exist for each of these storage types. Here, one section has been defined for storage type 0081 and two sections have been defined for storage type 0080.

Menu Path: **SPRO | IMG | Extended Warehouse Management | Master Data | Define Storage Section**

Storage Sections

WhN	Typ	Sec	Description
SEWM	0080	0001	Fast-Moving Items
SEWM	0080	0002	Slow-Moving Items
SEWM	0081	0001	Elevator Area

15.2.1.3 Create Bins

More than one bin can be created for each of these storage types (TCode /SCWM/LS01). This example has one bin, created manually for elevator storage type called "ELEV."

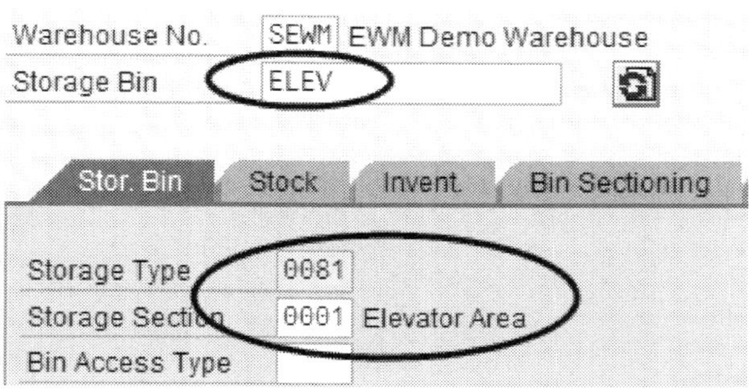

15.2.1.4 Define Layout-Oriented Storage Process Control

Based on the physical layout of the client's warehouse, consultants have to define the required LOSC settings for it. In the following screenshot intermediate storage type 0081 and bin ELEV is assigned to the destination storage 0080.

Menu Path: **SPRO | IMG | Extended Warehouse Management | Cross-Process Settings | Warehouse Task | Define Layout-Oriented Storage Process Control**

Layout-Oriented Storage Control

War	Sou	Sou	DTyp	De	Whole	HUT	S	Int. Storage Type	I	Int. Storage Bin	W	ID	Pick	Seg
SEWM			0080		Not F		1	0081		ELEV		☐	☐	

- **Source or Destination Storage Type:** This is used to control whether the LOSC is applicable while receiving and issuing the goods and whether the products need to be taken to the intermediate points or to the pick points.

- **Whole HU Indicator:** This is used to differentiate between moving a complete HU, an empty HU, or a partial HU.
- **HU Type Group:** This can be used to specify that a certain HU type should always be moved via some specific intermediate storage types.
- **Intermediate Storage Type:** Here, specify what the intermediate storage type will be.
- **Intermediate Storage Section/Bin:** This is optional. This can be used to specify where the products should be moved to. If this data is not maintained, the system will use the search sequence to determine the required data.
- **WPT:** The WPT defined here is used to create the WT to the intermediate storage location. This is required only for the pick point. The system doesn't use WPT for ID points.
- **Conveyor Technique Segment:** This is used only when working with the MFS.

15.2.1.5 Maintain Storage Type Search Sequence

In order to test this business scenario, the putaway control indicator has been set as 0080. We have used WPT 1010, which is a standard SAP-delivered process type.

Search Sequence: Putaway

WhN	PACI	Proc...	Qty Class.	Stoc...	Type	Use	Ent.toDisp	Srch Seq.	Putaway Rules
SEWM	0080	1010						0080	No Putaway Rule

In the storage type search sequence 0080, storage type 0080 has been assigned for final putaway.

Storage Type Search Sequence for Putaway

WhN	Srch Seq.	Se...	Typ	STG	EvlWh...	Description
SEWM	0080	1	0080			Put Away in Storage Type 0080

15.2.1.6 Allow HU Types for Storage Type

If the HU check is active in the storage type, you must allow the appropriate HU type for the storage type. During the transaction, the HU type will be derived from its packaging materials. For this scenario, the HU type "Box" will be used.

Menu Path: **SPRO | IMG | Extended Warehouse Management | Cross-Process Settings | Handling Units | Basics | Define HU Types for Each Storage Type**

HU Types per Storage Type

WhN	Typ	HU Ty...	HU Ty...	HU Ty...	HU Ty...	HU Ty...
SEWM	0080	E1	E2	BOX		

15.2.1.7 Define Control Indicators for Determining WPTs

It is not necessary that the new WPT control indicator be defined for LOSC; however, it is recommended to create one for POSC and one for LOSC. The indicator has been set as 05 for the LOSC storage process.

Menu Path: SPRO | IMG | Extended Warehouse Management | Cross-Process Settings | Warehouse Task | Determine Warehouse Process Type

Control Indicator for Warehouse Process Type Determination

War..	ProTypeDet	Description
SEWM	01	POSC Storage Process Active
SEWM	02	VAS Storage Process Active
SEWM	03	In-house Produced Materials
SEWM	04	Direct Putaway without Storage Process
SEWM	05	LOSC Storage Process Active

15.2.1.8 Product Master Settings

Maintain the appropriate values in the product master under the warehouse data tab (TCode /SCWM/MAT1). For this example, 05 has been used for the process type determination indicator, and 0080 for the putaway control indicator.

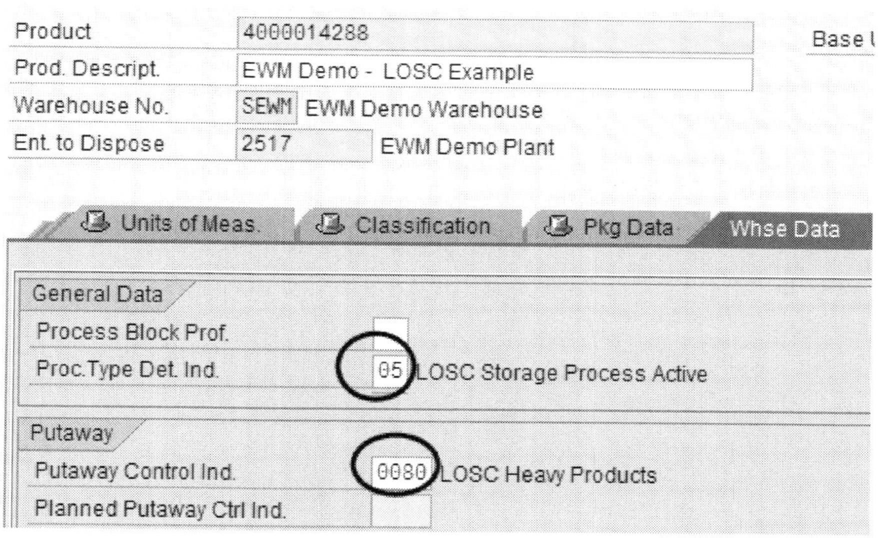

15.2.1.9 Determine WPT

Make an appropriate entry in the WPT determination table to determine the correct WPT as per the product master.

Menu Path: SPRO | IMG | Extended Warehouse Management | Cross-Process Settings | Warehouse Task | Determine Warehouse Process Type

Determination of Warehouse Process Type

War..	Doc.	Item...	Del.Prio.	ProTypeDet	Process Ind.	Wh...
SEWM	INB		0	01	No Special Pr	3065
SEWM	INB		0	04	No Special Pr	1010
SEWM	INB		0	05	No Special Pr	1010

15.2.1.10 Other Required Configurations

Along with the above configuration, it is recommended to verify the following configurations. They are covered in detail in the POSC section and in the previous chapter.

- Define or Generate Activity Areas for the Storage Types.
- Assign Consolidation Group to the Activity Area
- Define Search Sequence of Creation Rules for Activity Areas
- Define Work Center for Pick Point.
- Maintain Storage Section Search Sequence

15.2.2 Exercise—LOSC Configuration

In this section, the business scenario will be tested, starting from creating a purchase order in the ERP system. As a prerequisite, verify the material master, vendor master in the ERP system, and product master in the EWM system.

15.2.2.1 Create Purchase Order

To begin with, create a purchase order in the ERP system (TCode ME21N); verify the vendor, plant, and storage location for the entered product. The confirmation key for the PO line item should allow the creation of inbound deliveries.

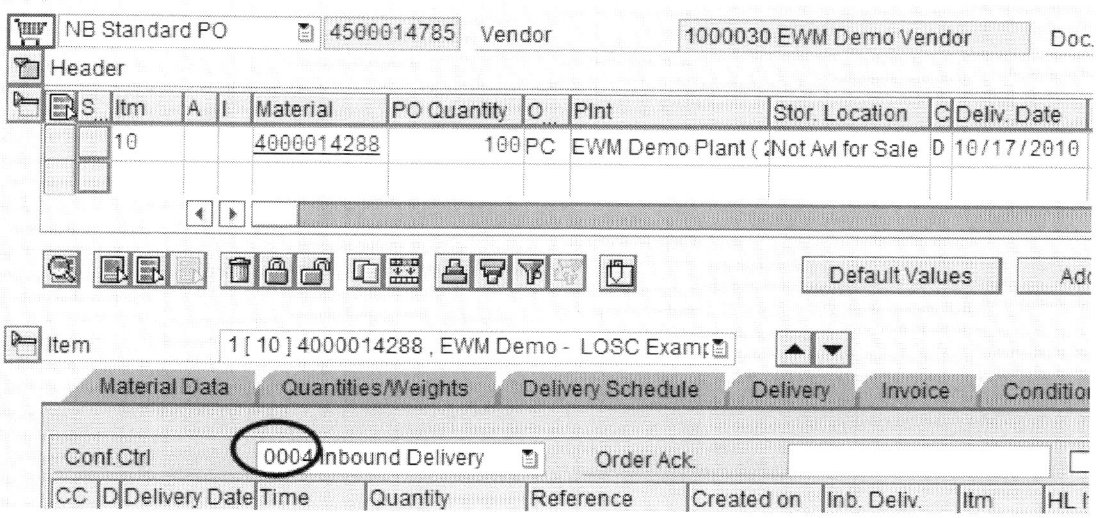

15.2.2.2 Create an Inbound Delivery

In TCode VL31N, enter the purchase order and ASN number in the external ID number field, and hit the "Enter" key.

In the delivery detail screen, enter the delivery quantity and click on the "Pack" button on the application toolbar to pack the product into HU. In the packing screen, pack the product into HU. Once the required data is entered, click "Save" to save the data in the inbound delivery. This will create an inbound delivery in the ERP system and will be transferred to the EWM system for further processing.

15.2.2.3 Verify IDN in the EWM System

Enter the ERP inbound delivery number and click the "Execute" button.

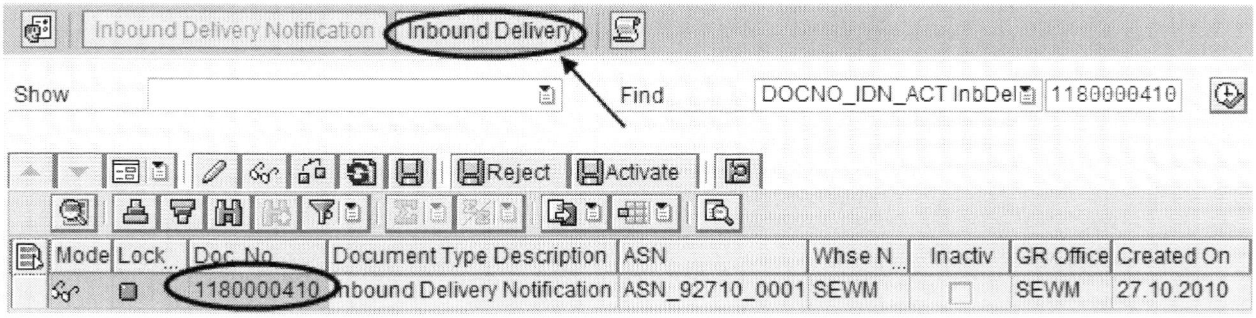

Select the delivery line item (TCode /SCWM/IDN) and click on the "Inbound Delivery" button on the application toolbar to locate the inbound delivery created in the EWM system.

15.2.2.3 Verify Inbound Delivery in the EWM System

As of now, LOSC will work only with HU-managed stock. In the inbound delivery (TCode /SCWM/PRDI), verify that the stock is HU managed by clicking the "HU" tab in the delivery detail section.

Once the data is verified, click the "Unload" button. This will update the status. In standard configuration, the WTs will not be created automatically.

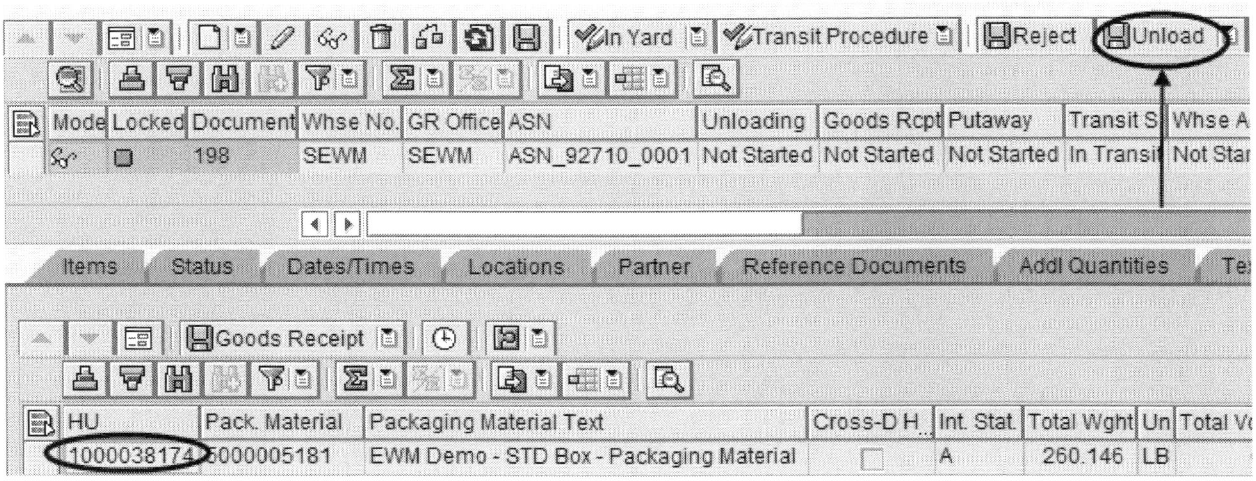

To create WT, click on "Inbound Delivery," "Follow-On Functions," and "Warehouse Task."

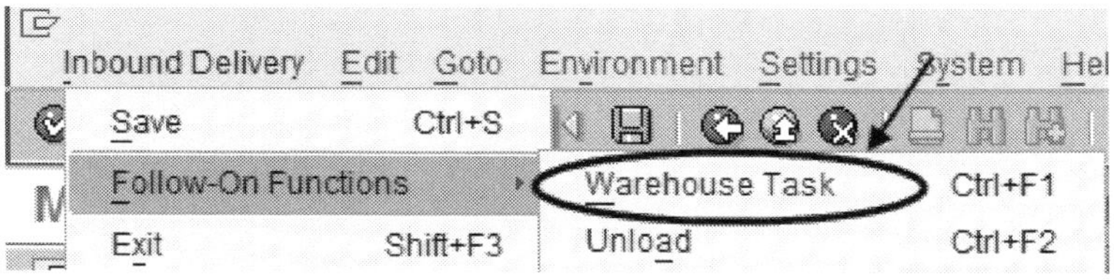

In the Warehouse Task "Create" screen, click the "Create + Save" button to create the WTs. For this business scenario, the system will create two WTs.

Click on "Message Log" to check the log created for the WT.

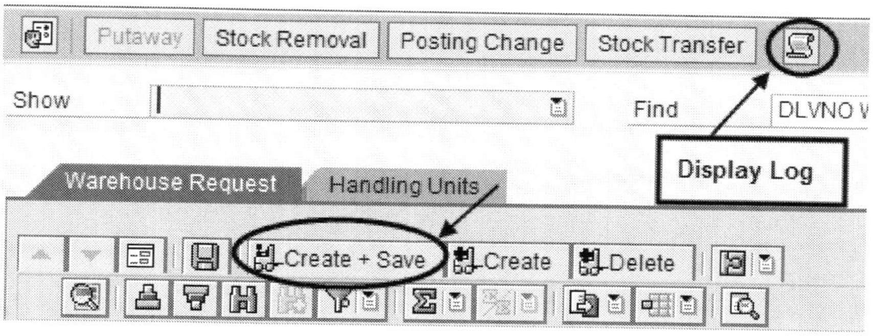

The system will show the determination of LOSC process and the details of the WTs created.

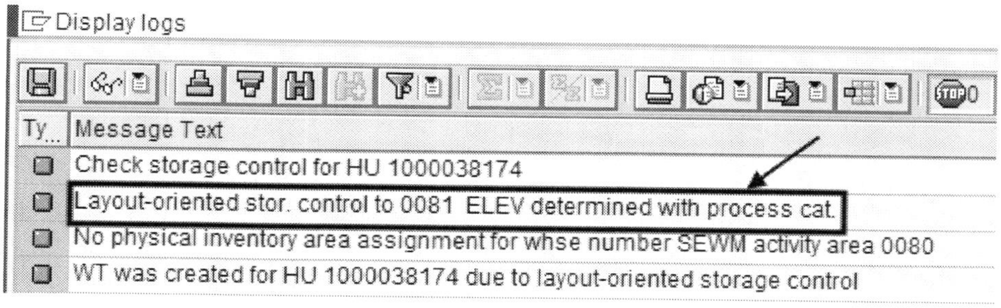

15.2.2.4 Process Warehouse Tasks

Go to TCode /SCWM/MON; enter the required details under "Inbound Delivery" to display the inbound delivery in the warehouse monitor. Select the inbound delivery line item and click on WT button. This will display the WTs created for the inbound delivery.

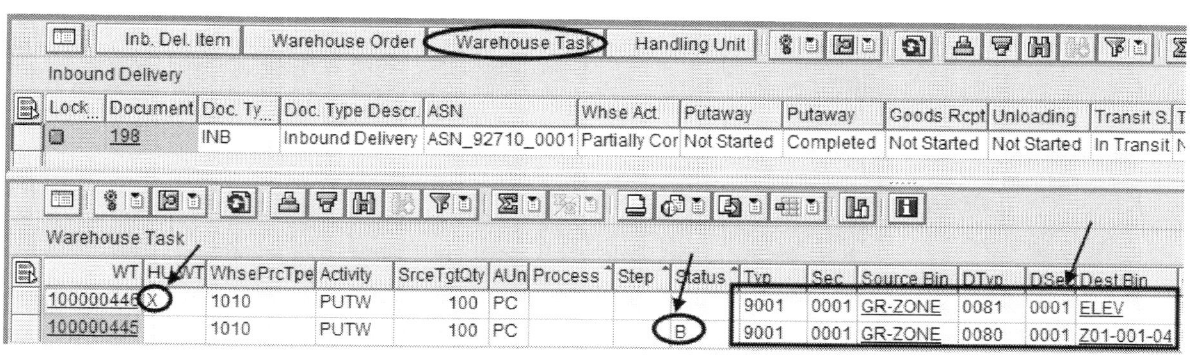

Note the source and destination location for each of the WTs and the status of the WT. The task to move products to the "ELEV" bin is active, and the final putaway task status is set to "B—Waiting." Click on the WO button to see the open warehouse orders.

Note that there is only one open WO for inbound delivery. Second WO will be created upon confirmation of the first WO.

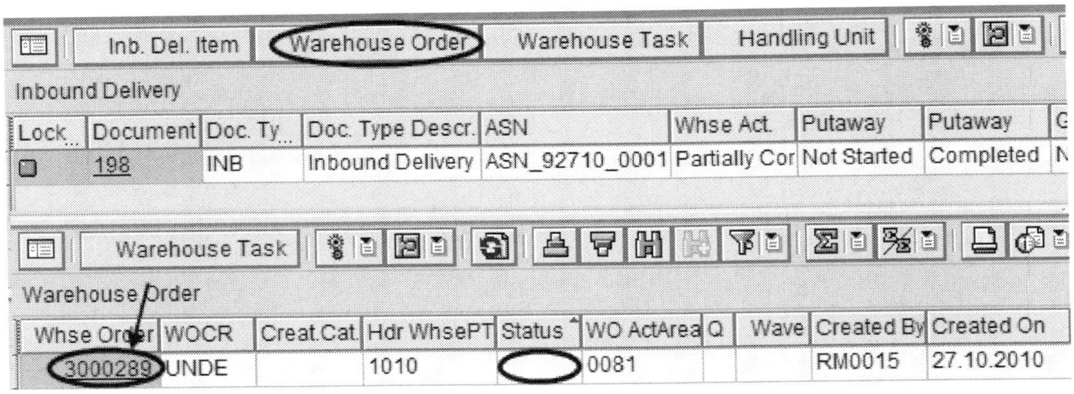

Click on the WO number and confirm the WO by clicking on the "Confirm + Save" button.

Upon confirmation of the WO, display the WT for the inbound delivery. Now the second WT is active, and the source information has been updated to "ELEV" storage type.

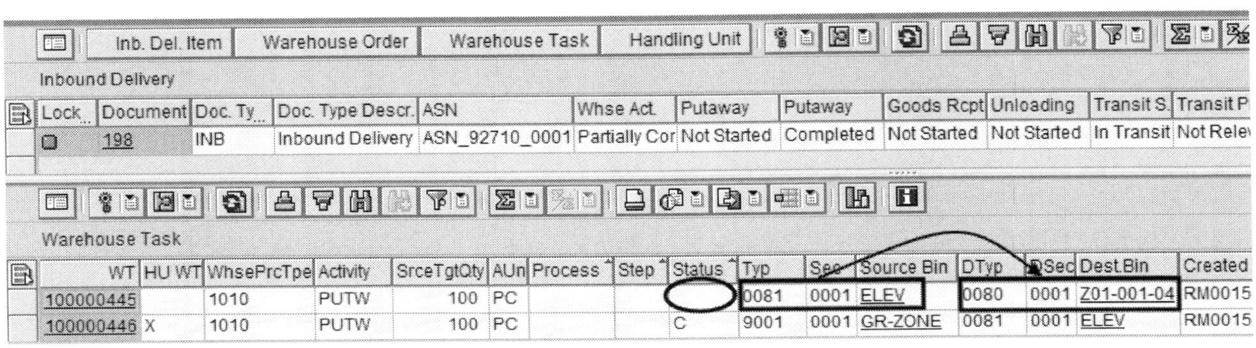

Click on the WO button to locate the open WO for the second WT. The system automatically creates a WO when the WT becomes active.

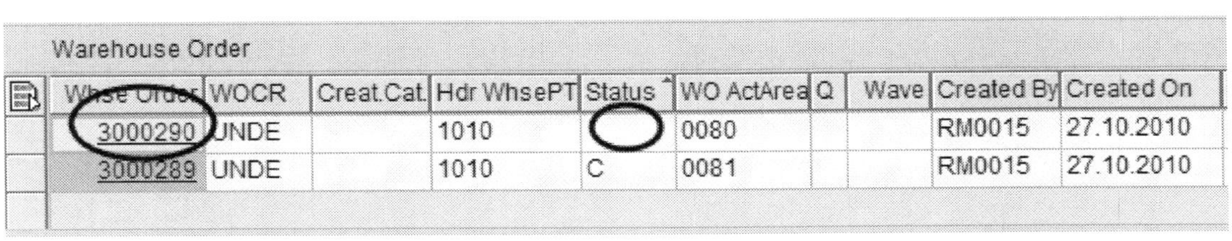

Click on the WO and click on the "Confirm + Save" button to confirm it. This will update the stock in the final storage type.

Verify the stock in the EWM and ERP systems. The stock should be now updated in the warehouse bin as well as in the ERP system.

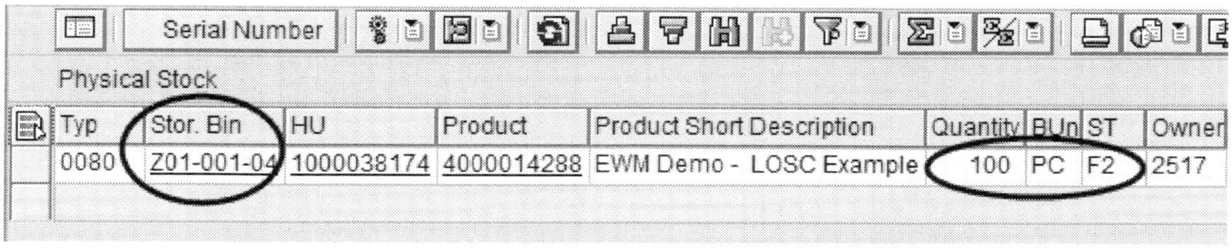

15.3 Using Both POSC and LOSC

In the very complex warehouse, it is possible to have scenarios where both POSC and LOSC combinations have to be configured to meet the warehouse requirements. In EWM, POSC and LOSC can be combined to determine the products' movements in the warehouse.

If POSC and LOSC are combined, the EWM system will execute the POSC settings first. The LOSC then checks whether the sequence of putaway process steps are possible in layout view, and, if required, the system will adjust the flow of the putaway or stock removal.

In the following business scenario, the POSC and LOSC methods have been combined.

Business Scenario for Combined POSC and LOSC

The products are packed in HU in the ERP inbound delivery. In the warehouse, products are stored on the second floor. The process followed in the warehouse is as follows: unload the HUs, move the HUs to the work center, and verify the packing in the work center. After verification, the HU has to be staged in the elevator area to move the products to the second floor. Finally, the products will be put away in the finished goods storage type.

Process flow for this business scenario is as follows:

- Unloading (IB01): Operator will unload the HUs from the truck and confirm in the EWM system. This will activate the WT to move the HU from the GR staging area to the work center area.
- Packing Verification (IB02): Operator will verify the HU and update the status in the system "Complete Process Step".
- Putaway (IB03): When the operator confirms packing verification, the system will locate the final putaway task. Because the LOSC is active, and product cannot be put away in the second floor without taking the HU to the elevator area, the system will create a new WT to move the HU from the work center region to the elevator area. The system will update the destination bin in the new WT and the source bin information in the final putaway task to the elevator area.
- LOSC Final Putaway: Once the elevator-related WT is confirmed, the final WT will be activated to move the product from the elevator area to the finished goods area.

15.3.1 Configuration Requirement

To demonstrate this business scenario, we have used the same configuration explained earlier in POSC and LOSC section with the following changes.

Create a new entry in "Maintain Storage Type Search Sequence" for PACI 0080 and warehouse process type 3065, as shown below.

Search Sequence: Putaway

WhN	PACI	Proc.	Qt	S	Type	U	Ent.t	H	Haz	Srch Seq.	Putaway Rules
SEWM	0080	3065								0080	No Putaway Rule

In the "Determination of Warehouse Process Type" menu, update WPT 3065 for Process Type Determination Indicator 05, as show below.

Determination of Warehouse Process Type

War	Doc	Ite	Del.Prio.	ProTypeDet	Process Ind.	Wh
SEWM	INB		0	01	No Special Pr	3065
SEWM	INB		0	04	No Special Pr	1010
SEWM	INB		0	05	No Special Pr	3065

15.3.2 Exercise—POSC and LOSC combination

To test this process, we will use the same material used for LOSC testing with the same settings. In the ERP system, create a purchase order and an inbound delivery. In the inbound delivery, pack the products into one HU.

In the EWM system, locate the inbound delivery and confirm the unloading activity by clicking on the "Unload" button. This will create the WTs for POSC process.

2 warehouse tasks were created

Verify the WTs in the warehouse monitor for the inbound delivery. Note the source and destination storage bins for final putaway. Note the process, step, and status of each WT.

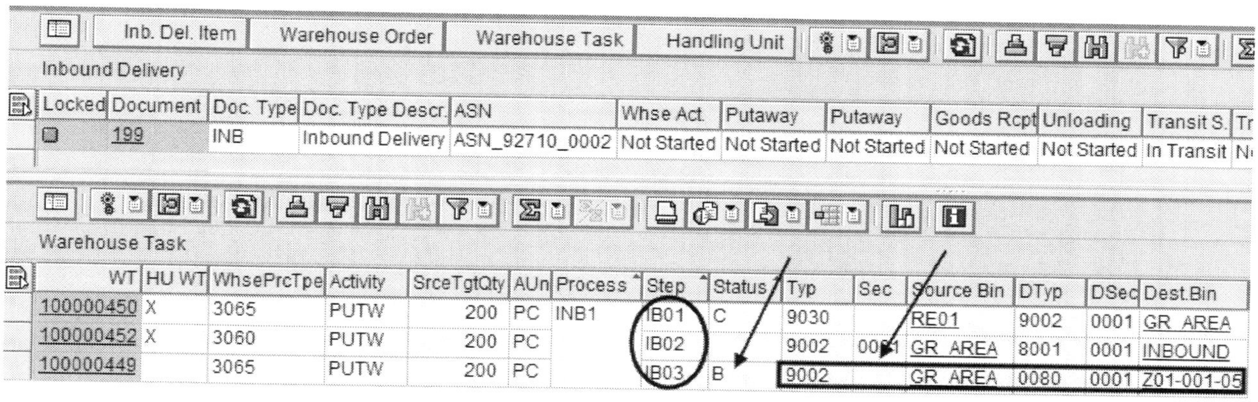

Inbound Delivery

Locked	Document	Doc. Type	Doc. Type Descr.	ASN	Whse Act.	Putaway	Putaway	Goods Rcpt	Unloading	Transit S.	Tr
	199	INB	Inbound Delivery	ASN_92710_0002	Not Started	Not Started	Not Started	Not Started	Not Started	In Transit	N

Warehouse Task

WT	HU WT	WhsePrcTpe	Activity	SrceTgtQty	AUn	Process	Step	Status	Typ	Sec	Source Bin	DTyp	DSec	Dest.Bin
100000450	X	3065	PUTW	200	PC	INB1	IB01	C	9030		RE01	9002	0001	GR_AREA
100000452	X	3060	PUTW	200	PC		IB02		9002	0001	GR_AREA	8001	0001	INBOUND
100000449		3065	PUTW	200	PC		IB03	B	9002		GR_AREA	0080	0001	Z01-001-05

Click the "Warehouse Order" button to display the WOs for the inbound delivery. Confirm the open WO.

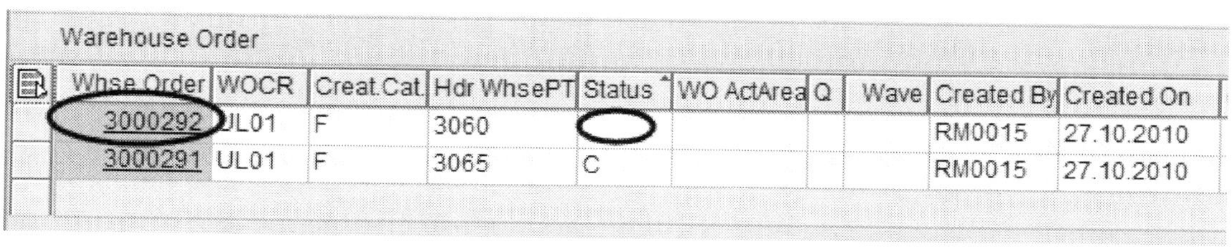

Warehouse Order

Whse Order	WOCR	Creat.Cat.	Hdr WhsePT	Status	WO ActArea	Q	Wave	Created By	Created On
3000292	UL01	F	3060					RM0015	27.10.2010
3000291	UL01	F	3065	C				RM0015	27.10.2010

Verify the WTs. Note the source bin details and status of the final putaway WT.

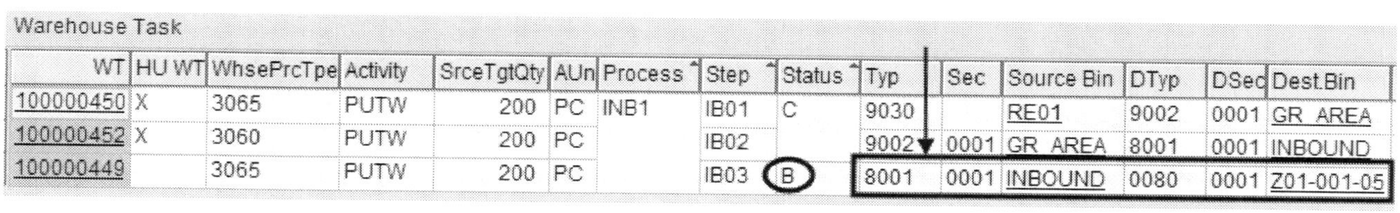

Warehouse Task

WT	HU WT	WhsePrcTpe	Activity	SrceTgtQty	AUn	Process	Step	Status	Typ	Sec	Source Bin	DTyp	DSec	Dest.Bin
100000450	X	3065	PUTW	200	PC	INB1	IB01	C	9030		RE01	9002	0001	GR_AREA
100000452	X	3060	PUTW	200	PC		IB02		9002	0001	GR_AREA	8001	0001	INBOUND
100000449		3065	PUTW	200	PC		IB03	B	8001	0001	INBOUND	0080	0001	Z01-001-05

Go to transaction /SCWM/DCONS and select the work center. The HU should be visible in the work center. Select the HU and click on complete process step for HU. This will create a new WT to move the products to the elevator area and will become active. The new WT is created because of the LOSC settings.

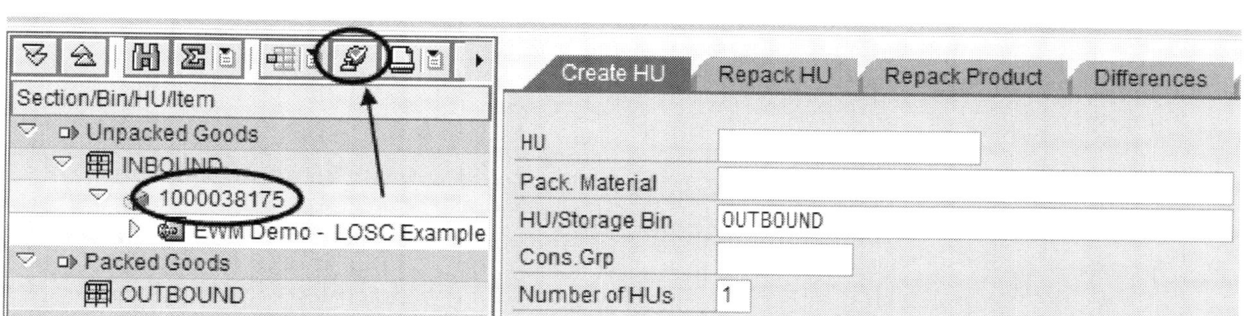

Verify the new WT, its source, and destination bin details. The system has updated the destination location of the new WT to elevator area. Note the WT status for final putaway—it is still set to waiting.

Warehouse Task

WT	HU WT	WhsePrcTpe	Activity	SrceTgtQty	AUn	Process	Step	Status	Typ	Sec	Source Bin	DTyp	DSec	Dest.Bin
100000450	X	3065	PUTW	200	PC	INB1	IB01	C	9030		RE01	9002	0001	GR AREA
100000452	X	3060	PUTW	200	PC		IB02		9002	0001	GR AREA	8001	0001	INBOUND
100000453	X	3065	PUTW	200	PC		IB03		8001	0001	INBOUND	0081	0001	ELEV
100000449		3065	PUTW	200	PC			B	8001	0001	INBOUND	0080	0001	Z01-001-05

Confirm the open WO to putaway the stock to the elevator storage area. This will change the status of the final WT to active, and the WO will be created to putaway the products in the destination bin. Confirm the warehouse order, which will update the warehouse bin stock and ERP system stock.

Warehouse Task

WT	HU WT	WhsePrcTpe	Activity	SrceTgtQty	AUn	Process	Step	Status	Typ	Sec	Source Bin	DTyp	DSec	Dest.Bin
100000450	X	3065	PUTW	200	PC	INB1	IB01	C	9030		RE01	9002	0001	GR AREA
100000452	X	3060	PUTW	200	PC		IB02		9002	0001	GR AREA	8001	0001	INBOUND
100000449		3065	PUTW	200	PC		IB03		0081	0001	ELEV	0080	0001	Z01-001-05
100000453	X	3065	PUTW	200	PC				8001	0001	INBOUND	0081	0001	ELEV

Verify the stock in the EWM and ERP systems. Stock should be now updated in the warehouse bin as well as in the ERP system.

Stock Overview

Typ	Stor. Bin	Product	Batch	ST	Incom. Qty	Outg. Qty	AvlQtyBUoM	Quantity	BUn
0080	Z01-001-04	4000014288		F2	0	0	100	100	PC
0080	Z01-001-05	4000014288		F2	0	0	200	200	PC

Summary

This section explained how to use POSC and LOSC methods for warehouse requirements. This completes the putaway process of EWM. The next chapter will explain how to process the outbound delivery in the EWM system.

Chapter 16: Outbound Delivery Processing

This chapter is broadly divided into three sections: basic goods issue, cancel picking, and pick denial. The basic goods issue section covers the configuration required for picking the products for the goods issue process. The cancel picking section covers how to put back the stock if there is a cancellation. The pick denial section covers how to manage exceptions at the time of picking.

16.1 Basic Goods Issue (GI) in EWM

The base document for the GI process is outbound delivery request (ODR). It gets created automatically in the EWM system when the ERP outbound delivery is transferred to the EWM system. If no errors are found in the ODR document, the system will automatically create the outbound delivery order (ODO) using PPF functions. In case of an error, the user can manually correct the error and activate the document, which will create the ODO in the system. ODO is essential for initiating the warehouse process. It is also called a warehouse request document for picking process. Chapter 10 already covered the process flow of EWM outbound process and the related documents in the outbound process.

This section will cover the required configuration for basic goods issue and how to process outbound-related documents in the EWM system.

16.1.1 Warehouse Process Type

Like with inbound delivery processing, when the outbound delivery order (ODO) is created, the system determines a WPT for each line item. Previous chapters have already covered the configuration and settings available for WPT in detail. Hence, those details will not be repeated here. Only the required settings for outbound delivery will be described.

The GI warehouse process type must have the warehouse process category as "2—Stock Removal," the activity selected as "Pick," and the destination location details. Destination details can also be optional, depending on the business scenario.

The following settings are optional and can be used, depending on the business requirements.

- SI Control: New stock identification
- Automatic Wave Determination: Yes, if working with picking waves
- Rough Bin Determination: Yes, if picking waves are defined by storage type

- Destination Storage Type/Bin: Used to specify the final destination location where the goods are staged or loaded from.

Menu Path: SPRO | IMG | Extended Warehouse Management | Cross-Process Settings | Warehouse Task | Define Warehouse Process Type

In standard SAP, WPT 2010 is configured for stock removal, which is used for direct picking from the source bin to destination staging area 9020.

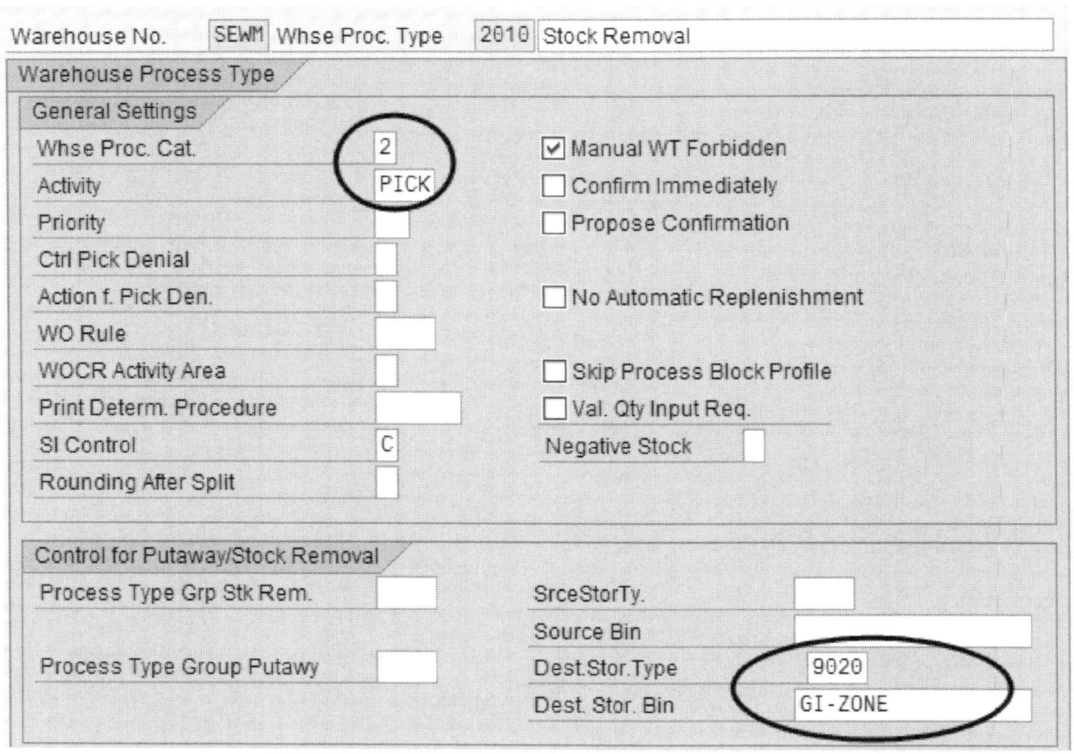

16.1.2 Warehouse Process Type Determination

WPT is determined for the combination of warehouse number, document type, item type, delivery priority, and process type control indicators. The warehouse number and document type are derived from the source document (ODR) and mandatory for determining the WPT. Other parameters like item type (derived from ODR), delivery priority (derived from ODR), and process type control indicators (derived from product master) are optional.

Menu Path: SPRO | IMG | Extended Warehouse Management | Cross-Process Settings | Warehouse Task | Determine Warehouse Process Type

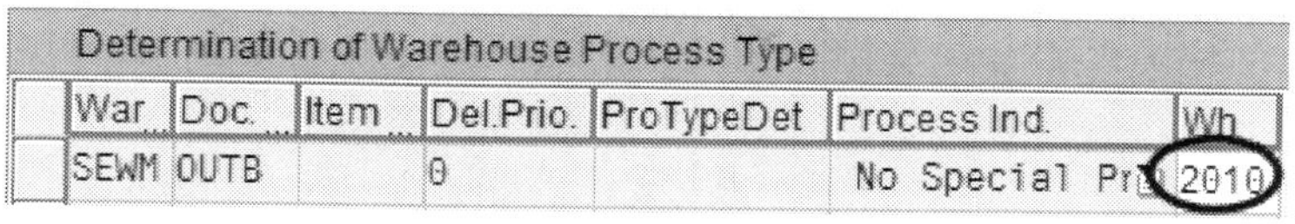

Determination of Warehouse Process Type

War	Doc.	Item	Del.Prio.	ProTypeDet	Process Ind.	Wh
SEWM	OUTB		0		No Special Pr	2010

16.1.3 Storage Type Determination

While creating pick WTs, the system determines the appropriate source bin from which the products have to be picked. In order to determine the appropriate source storage types, the storage types search sequence must be defined in the system. This sequence contains the list of storage types that system should search and the sequence in which they should be searched. Once the search sequence is determined, the system will search for available stock of products in each of the storage types in a given sequence until it satisfies the requirement quantity. The system can also be configured to allow partial picking or to terminate the picking processes in case of partial picking.

To define the storage type search sequence, follow menu path **SPRO | IMG | Extended Warehouse Management | Goods Issue Process | Strategies | Specify Storage Type Search Sequence**, click the "New Entries" button; enter the warehouse number, storage type search sequence, and the description as shown below.

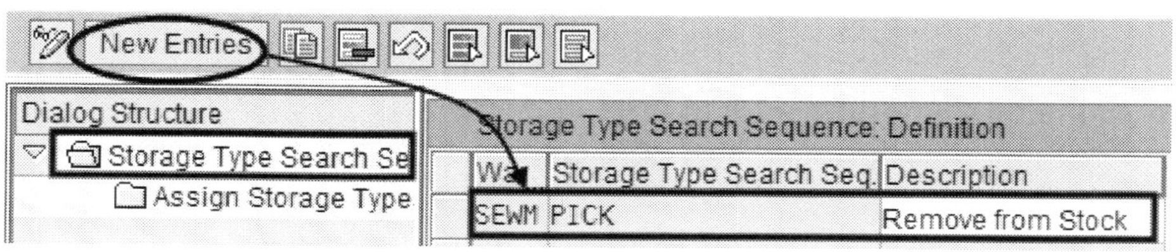

Storage Type Search Sequence: Definition

War	Storage Type Search Seq.	Description
SEWM	PICK	Remove from Stock

Select the storage type search sequence and click on the "Assign Storage Type" option under "Dialog Structure" to assign the storage types. The "New Entries" option can be used to add new storage types to the search sequence. If the stock in Transportation Units has to be considered for picking, check the TU checkbox active.

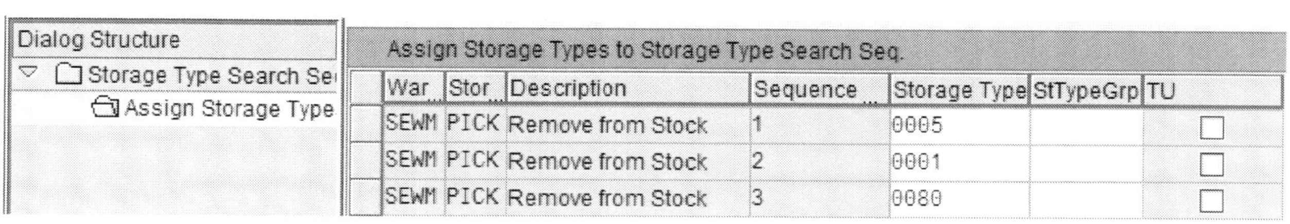

Assign Storage Types to Storage Type Search Seq.

War	Stor	Description	Sequence	Storage Type	StTypeGrp	TU
SEWM	PICK	Remove from Stock	1	0005		☐
SEWM	PICK	Remove from Stock	2	0001		☐
SEWM	PICK	Remove from Stock	3	0080		☐

16.1.4 Stock Removal Control Indicator (SRCI)

Like putaway control indicators, SRCI is normally used to control the product-specific storage type search and is defined in menu path **SPRO | IMG | Extended Warehouse Management | Goods Issue Process | Strategies | Define Stock Removal Control Indicator**

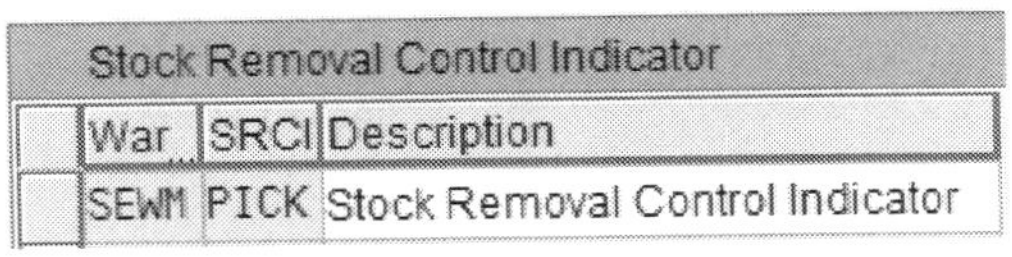

Stock Removal Control Indicator

War...	SRCI	Description
SEWM	PICK	Stock Removal Control Indicator

In the product master (/SCWM/MAT1), SRCI is assigned to the "Stk Rmvl Ctrl Indicator" field under the stock removal section of the "Warehouse Data" tab.

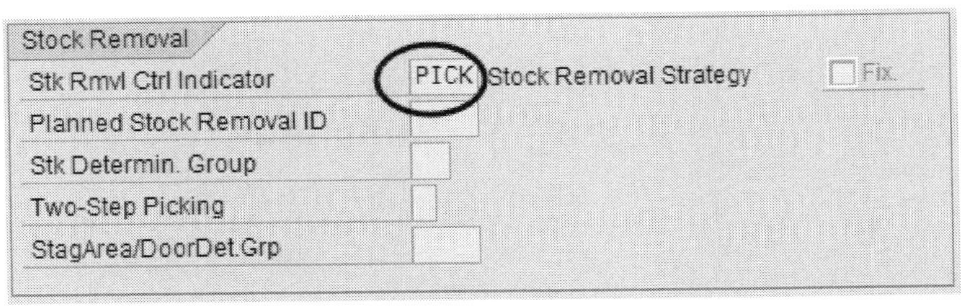

16.1.5 Determine Storage Type Search Sequence

Based on the parameters from ODO, the product master, and the hazardous material master data, the system determines the storage type search sequence and the stock removal rule. The following parameters are used to determine the storage type search sequence:

- Two-step picking: Derived from Warehouse/Product/Wave
- Stock removal control indicator: Derived from product master
- Warehouse process type: Derived from ODO
- Quantity classification: Derived from packaging specification
- Stock type/Group: Derived from ODO
- Sales order stock or project stock indicator: Derived from ODO
- Stock usage (consignment/subcontractor): Derived from ODO
- Hazard rating 1 and 2: Derived from ODO (i.e., hazardous ratings for the product)

Storage type search sequence determination is defined in menu path **SPRO | IMG | Extended Warehouse Management | Goods Issue Process | Strategies | Determine Storage Type Search Sequence for Stock Removal**

Determine Storage Type Search Sequence: Stock Removal

War...	2	SRCl	Wh...	Q	Stoc...	Tpe	Use	H...	HazRat2	Stor...	Re...
SEWM	☐		2010							SMAL	
SEWM	☐	PICK	2010							PICK	

16.1.6 Stock Removal Rule

The stock removal rule defines the sequence in which the quants should be sorted. For this, we maintain a sort field in the stock removal rule. The quant sorting can contain a maximum of thirty fields. For each field, this sorting can be ascending or descending.

Stock removal rules are stored in storage types, storage type groups, and storage type search sequence.

If the stock removal rule is stored in the storage type search sequence, then it applies for all storage types. If no rule is stored here, then the system considers the rule from the storage type group or storage type. To define the stock removal rule, follow the menu path **SPRO | IMG | Extended Warehouse Management | Goods Issue Process | Strategies | Specify Stock Removal Rule**

Dialog Structure
- Definition of Stock Remo
  - Stock Removal Rule

Warehouse No. SEWM
Stock Removal Rule FIFO

Stock Removal Rule

Sequ...	Sort Field	Descending
1	VFDAT	☐
2	WDATU	☐
3	LGPLA	☑
4	QUAN	☐

16.1.7 Optimization of Access Strategies for Storage Type Search Sequence

For a large range of products, stock types, and special stocks, the number of entries in the search sequence table will also be very large. To reduce the number of entries, an access strategy can be assigned to the storage type search sequence table. The system uses this access strategy to search storage type, as shown below:

- The system checks whether there is group assignment (for Wh. Process Type/Stock Type) and uses the group to read search sequence table.

- The system first attempts to read a completely qualified entry, meaning one that matches with all relevant indicators in the storage type search table.
- If the system cannot find an entry in the storage type search table, it attempts to reread this table, using the access strategy.

Menu Path: SPRO | IMG | Extended Warehouse Management | Goods Issue Process | Strategies | Optimization of Access Strategies for Stor. Type Determination in Stock Rmvl

Optimization of Access Strategy for Storage Type Determinatn

War...	Se...	2SP	RmvlD	Proc. Ty...	Q	S	Cat	Use	Ri...	Hzrd...
SEWM	1	☐	☑	☑	☐	☐	☐	☐	☐	☐
SEWM	2	☐	☐	☑	☐	☐	☐	☐	☐	☐

16.1.8 Exercise—Basic Goods Issue

This process can be tested, either starting with a sales order or by creating a delivery without reference in the ERP system. This example will start with a sales order.

16.1.8.1 Sales order: VA01

To begin testing the basic GI process, this exercise will create a sales order in the ERP system (transaction VA01). In the sales order, enter material, quantity, plant, storage location, sold-to party, and ship-to party, along with other required fields like sales order type, sales area information, and so on. The plant, storage location, materials, and shipping point entered here should belong to the EWM warehouse. Partners like ship-to party, sold-to party, freight forwarding agent, should have corresponding business partner data in the EWM system.

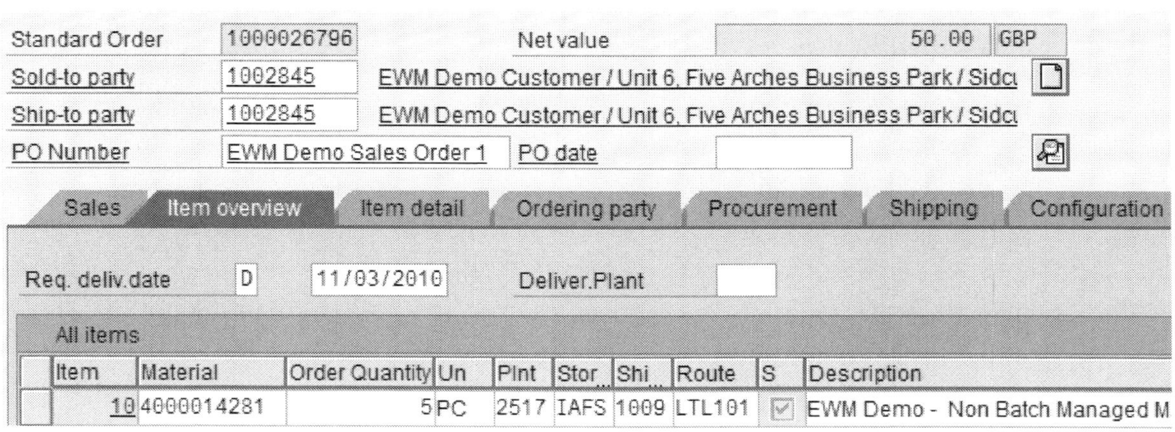

16.1.8.2 Create Outbound Delivery

An outbound delivery can be created directly from the sales order screen or from TCode VL01N. Like inbound delivery, outbound delivery created in the ERP system will be distributed to an EWM warehouse. Once the outbound delivery is saved, it cannot be edited in the ERP system.

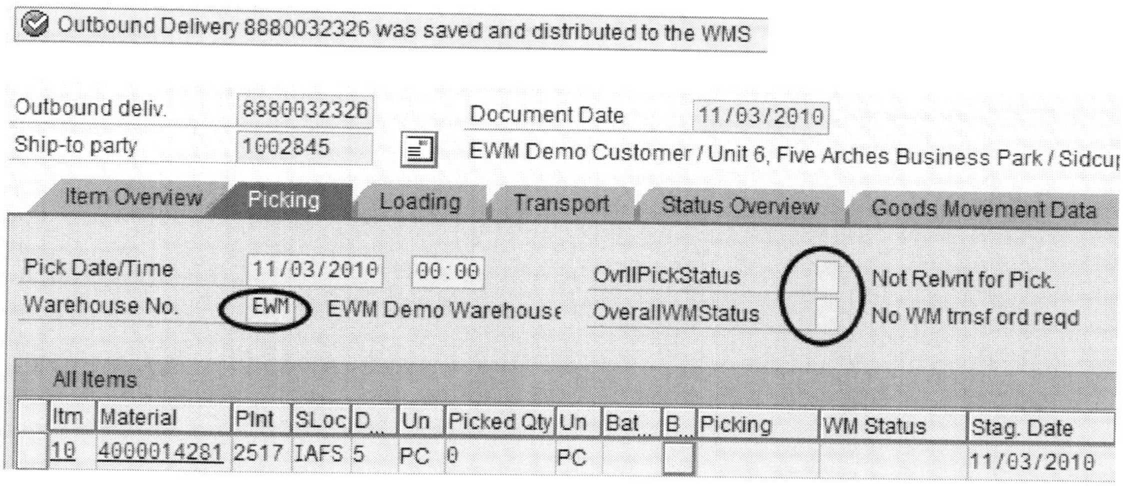

16.1.8.3 Outbound Delivery Request (ODR)

The outbound delivery transferred to the EWM system becomes an ODR document. It will have the same number as the ERP delivery number. The PPF actions can be set to create ODO automatically for an active ODR. If ODR is not activated due to some error, it can be activated manually by correcting the error. This will create ODO in the background. ODR can be viewed in TCode /SCWM/ODR.

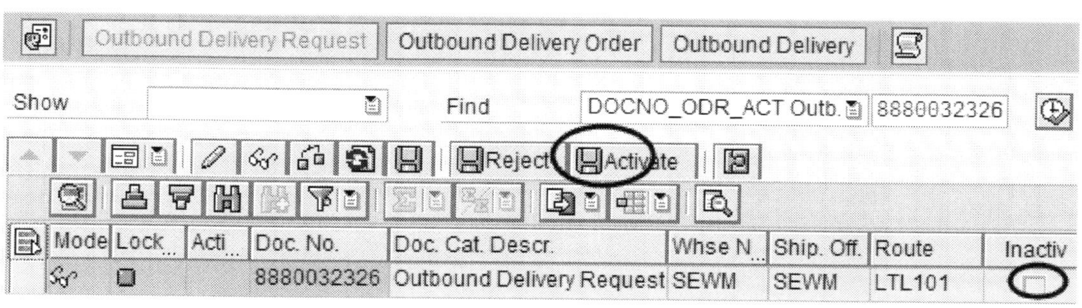

16.1.8.4 Outbound Delivery Order (ODO)

ODO can be located directly from the ODR screen (TCode /SCWM/PRDO) by selecting the ODR line item and clicking the "Outbound Delivery Order" button on the application toolbar. ODO is also called a warehouse request (WR) document. Various terms like picking, packing, loading, and GI describe the current status of the WT.

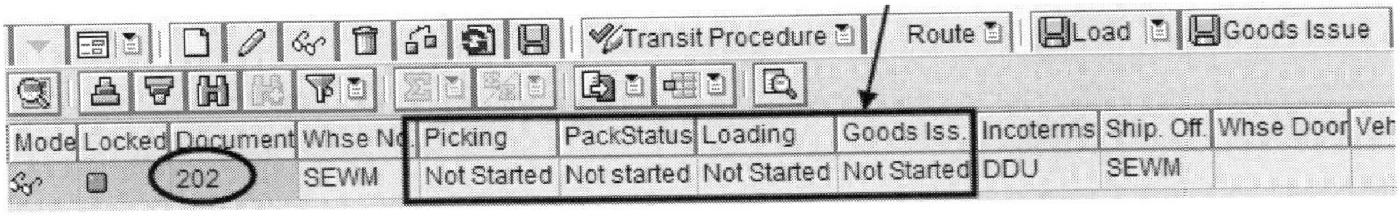

16.1.8.5 Warehouse Task

A picking WT can be created directly from the ODO screen or from menu path **SAP Easy Access | Extended Warehouse Management | Work Scheduling | Create Warehouse Task for Warehouse Request | Stock Removal for Outbound Delivery Order (TCode: /SCWM/TODLV)**

To create the WT, select the warehouse request and click on the "Create + Save" button. To verify the source and destination bin details, click the "Create" button, which will display the source and destination bin details for the WT. After the verification, click "Save" to create the WT.

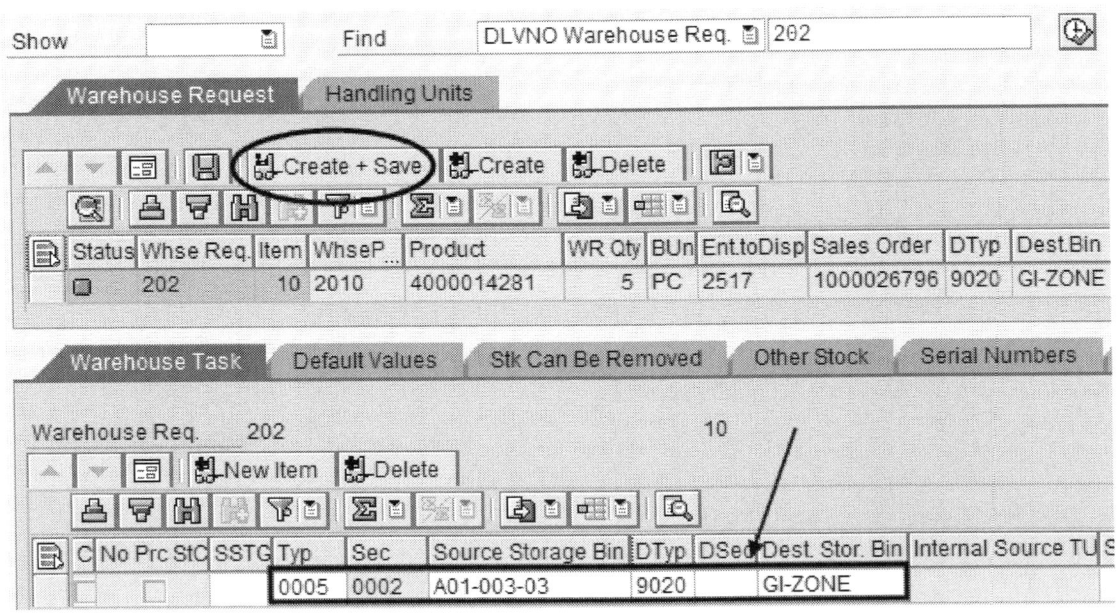

In the background, the WO will be created for the WT.

16.1.8.6 Warehouse Stock

In the warehouse monitor (TCode /SCWM/MON), verify the stock before confirming the warehouse order. A stock overview will be displayed as incoming stock in the GI area and outgoing from the source bins, as shown below.

Stock Overview

Typ	Stor. Bin	Product	Batch	ST	Incom. Qty	Outg. Qty	AvlQtyBUoM	Quantity	BUn
0005	A01-003-03	4000014281		F2	0	5	95	100	PC
9020	GI-ZONE	4000014281		F2	5	0	0	0	PC

16.1.8.7 Pack and Confirm WO

Packing of products during picking (Creation of Pick-HU) can be done manually (TCode /SCWM/TO_CONF), at the time of confirming the WO; or automatically in the background; or they can be packed in the work center, using POSC.

To create pick-HU manually, go to the WO confirmation transaction, enter the WO number, click the "Pick-HU" tab, click the "New" icon, enter the packaging material, and click the "Create" button with the HU icon. This will create the pick HU.

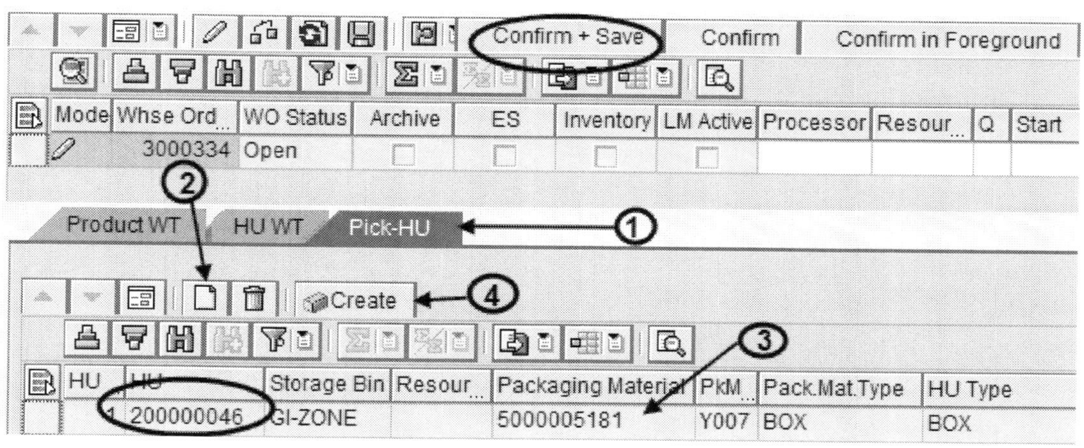

To confirm the WO, click the "Confirm + Save" button. The WO can also be confirmed in the foreground by clicking the "Confirm in Foreground" button.

When the WO is confirmed, the system will automatically pack the product into pick HU, as shown below in the screenshot.

16.1.8.8 Loading Activities

After the picking activities are completed and the products are staged in the goods issue area, usually the processes within the warehouse are complete; and the shipping activities like loading, yard management, and transportation begin. Yard management and transportation is part of "Advanced Concepts of EWM" book.

In EWM, loading of trucks can be performed in two ways.

- **Simple Loading: /SCWM/PRDO**

Once the picking WTs are confirmed and goods are staged in the GI area, they can be loaded onto the truck using simple loading. For simple loading, it is only necessary to update the loading status of ODO or HU. For this, select the ODO line item and click the "Load" button. This will update the loading status and show it as complete. In order to load Multiple ODOs, transaction "Process Vehicle (/SCWM/VEH)" or "Process TU (/SCWM/TU)" is available.

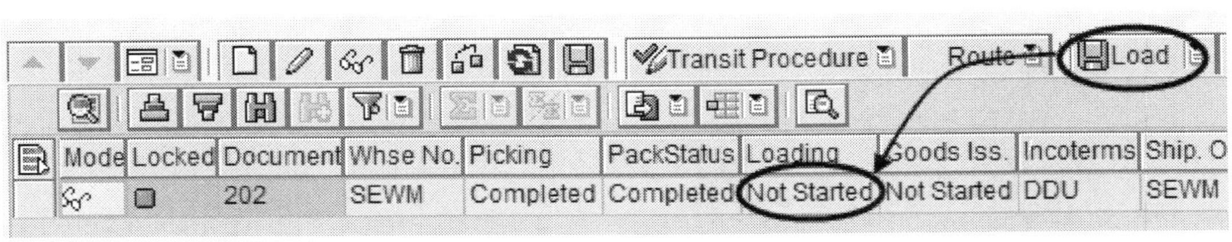

- **Complex Loading: /SCWM/LOAD**

For complex loading, a loading WT can be created manually in transaction /SCWM/LOAD. It can also be created automatically by storage control or through PPF actions when TU arrives at the door. In addition, loading rules can also be maintained, influencing loading time, while defining staging areas.

Once the loading WT is created and activated, WOs will be created automatically in the background. Confirming these WOs will be the same as confirming any other WO.

16.1.8.9 Post Goods Issue (PGI)

After the ODOs or HUs are loaded, GI can be posted for the delivery (TCode /SCWM/PRDO). However, for PGI, loading is not a mandatory step. GI can also be posted to multiple deliveries by posting "Goods Issue for Vehicle" (transaction /SCWM/VEH) or TU (transaction SCWM/TU).

Once the GI is posted, the GI status of the ODO gets updated to "Completed," and the system will create an outbound delivery document in the EWM system as proof of delivery. In the background, the system will also transfer the HU data to ERP delivery and will post the GI in the background.

When the truck leaves the warehouse yard, the transit status of the outbound delivery can be updated to "Out of Yard" by click the "Leave Yard" button.

16.1.8.10 Verify HU Data in the ERP Outbound Delivery

When the goods are issued in the EWM system, the system will automatically update the ERP outbound delivery with the HU data and post the GI. No further action is required in the ERP system.

The HU data can be verified on outbound delivery (TCode VL03N) by clicking on the "Pack" button in the outbound delivery.

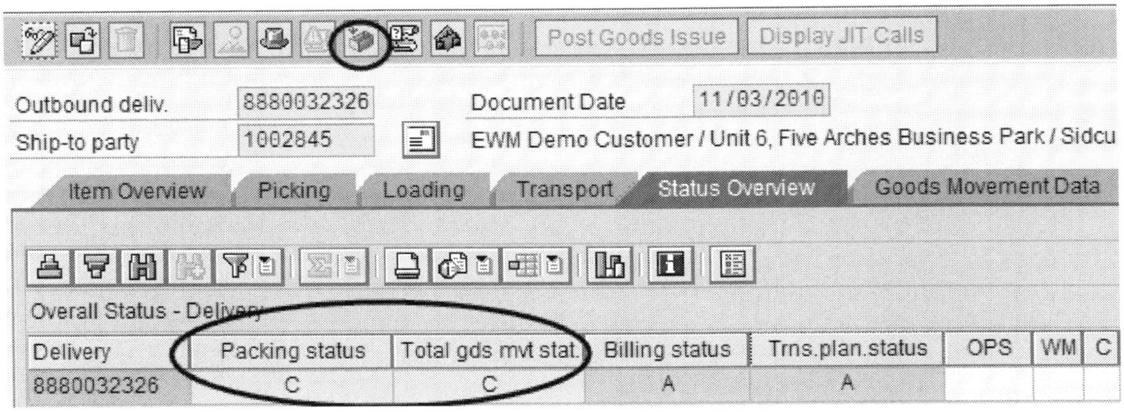

16.2 Cancel Picking

In certain circumstances, if it is necessary to reverse a confirmed task, users can perform "Cancel Picking." The following configuration should exist to perform cancel picking. In the Cancel Picking transaction, the user can release the picked stock and manually create an ad-hoc WT without reference; or release and create a WT in the foreground; or release and create a WT in the background for the put back quantity.

16.2.1 Define Warehouse Process Type for Putback

When picking is canceled, stock gets released from the delivery document and becomes available to putaway in the warehouse.

In the putback WPT, two important settings are warehouse process category (select value 7—posting change) and posting change bin (select value 2). Because in the EWM system, canceling the picking is part of the posting change process, the WPT should have posting change related values selected here.

Menu Path: SPRO | IMG | Extended Warehouse Management | Goods Issue Process | Cancel Picking | Define Warehouse Process Type for Putback

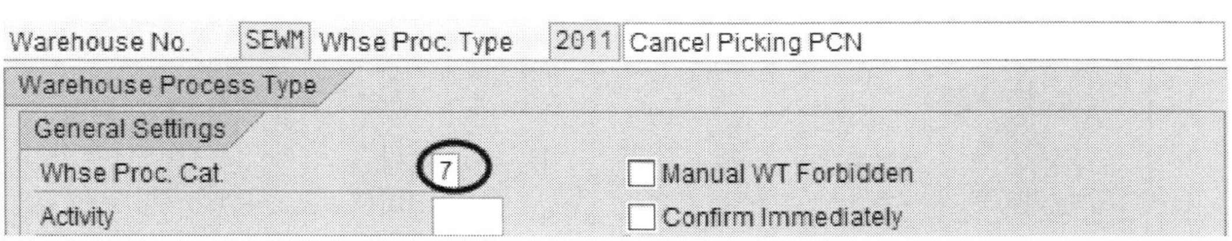

Settings for Posting Changes		
Post. Change in Bin	2	☐ Goods Mvmnt Before Warehouse Task
Exception Code		

16.2.2 Define Warehouse Number Control for Putback

This menu assigns the WPT defined for putback to the warehouse number. The system will use this process type as the default whenever the "Cancel Picking" transaction is executed.

Menu path: SPRO | IMG | Extended Warehouse Management | Goods Issue Process | Cancel Picking | Define Warehouse Number Control for Putback

Warehouse Number Control

War	Description	WPT Putbk
SEWM	EWM Demo Warehouse	2011

16.2.3 Specify Storage Type Search Sequence for Putaway

In order to automatically determine the destination storage bins for the putback WTs, a storage type search sequence must be specified for the putback warehouse process type.

Menu Path: SPRO | IMG | Extended Warehouse Management | Goods Receipt Process | Strategies | Storage Type Search | Specify Storage Type Search Sequence for Putaway

Search Sequence: Putaway

WhN	PAC	Proc.	Dt	Stoc	Type	Use	Ent.t	H	Srch Seq.	Putaway Rules
SEWM	SMAL	2011							0005	No Putaway Rule
SEWM	SMAL	3065							0005	No Putaway Rule

16.2.4 Cancel Picking

The menu path to access cancel picking is **SAP Easy Access | Extended Warehouse Management | Execution | Cancel Picking or TCode /SCWM/CANCPICK**

In the "Document Number" search field, enter the WR/ODO number containing the item that is to be canceled.

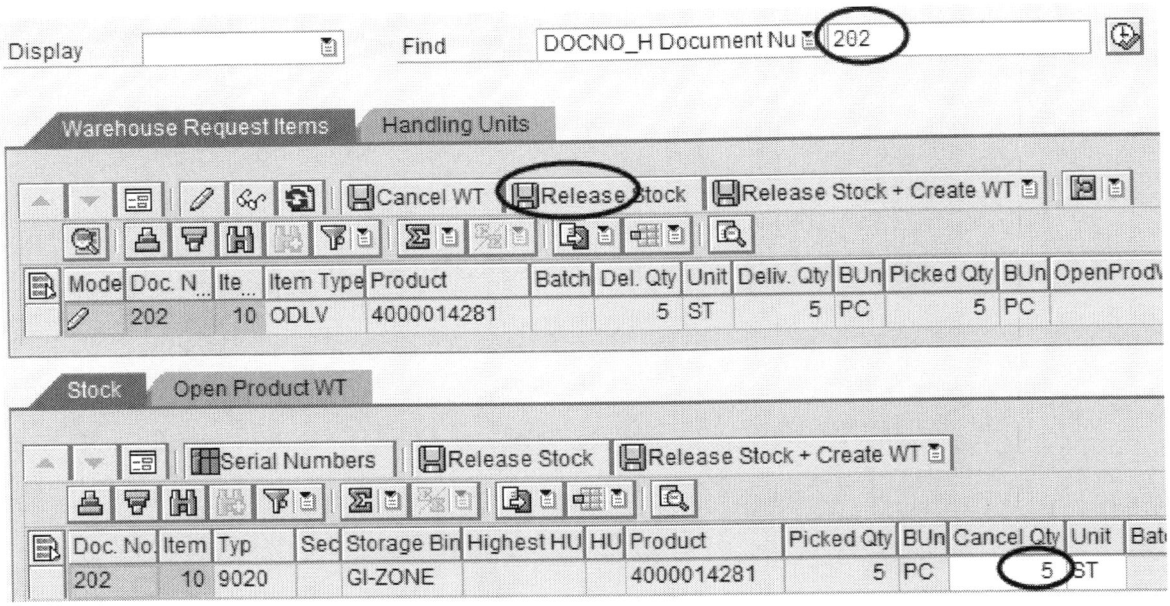

In the transaction, the following options are available:

- **Release stock:** To release the stock, select the WR item and click the "Release Stock" button. The system creates and confirms a WT for posting change, which releases the stock for putaway. This means that the stock remains in the GI bin and not reserved for picking. You need to create Ad-hoc Product Task manually (Bin-to-bin transfer) to send the stock back to storage types.

  If you click on "Release Stock + Create WT in Foreground," the system first creates and confirms a WT for posting change, which releases the stock. Also, the system opens user entry screen for creating Ad-hoc Product Task, where the destination bin details and WPT need to be entered.

  If you click on "Release Stock + Create WT in Background," the system first creates and confirms a WT for posting change, which releases the stock. Also, the system creates another putback task with the same WPT (in this example, it is 2011) and determines the destination bin automatically, with storage type search sequence and putaway strategy maintained for that WPT.

- **Cancel a partial quantity of the picked delivery quantity:** To do this, select the WR item, in the "Cancel Quantity" field in the Stock tab, specify enter the quantity that should be cancelled.

16.3 Pick Denial

In certain circumstances, it is possible that EWM cannot create a WT for the outbound delivery quantity, or that it can create a WT for only a partial quantity. This could be caused by various factors, such as the system cannot find stock, a storage bin is blocked for picking, and so on. Such exceptions can be managed in the EWM system using the pick denial function.

Pick denial can be used to trigger actions such as create a WT for partial stock, or do not create a WT for partial delivery quantity due to full delivery quantity requirement, or adjust the delivery quantity to WT quantity.

In the warehouse, a pick denial can happen in the following two situations:

- **Pick denial during WT creation:** At the time of WT creation, if the EWM system cannot find enough stock to meet the requested quantity, the system can be set up to trigger a pick denial. This typically happens if the warehouse stock is stored in the nonpicking relevant zones or if the product in the storage bin is blocked for some reason.
- **Pick denial at the time of WT confirmation:** In this case, the WT is confirmed with less quantity than requested, and no other stock can be found in the warehouse. This occurs when a discrepancy between the system quantity and actual quantity exists in the warehouse bin. In such scenarios, the system can be set up to automatically execute a pick denial.

In both cases, using a workflow, pick denial information can be forwarded to the ERP system so that the open quantity can be forwarded to another warehouse before the GI is triggered in the origin warehouse, thus providing better customer service.

16.3.1 Configuration of Pick Denial

The following configurations must exist in order to trigger pick denial.

16.3.1.1 Activate Pick Denial at Warehouse Number Level

The pick denial has to be activated at the warehouse number level.

Menu Path: SPRO | IMG | Extended Warehouse Management | Goods Issue Process | Pick Denial | Activate Pick Denial at Warehouse Number Level

Pick Denial at Warehouse Number Level

War..	Description	ActPickDen
SEWM	EWM Demo Warehouse	☑

16.3.1.2 Specify Pick Denial at WPT Level

The pick denial processing actions are configured at the WPT level, as shown below.

Menu Path: **SPRO | IMG | Extended Warehouse Management | Goods Issue Process | Pick Denial | Specify Pick Denial at Warehouse Process Type Level**

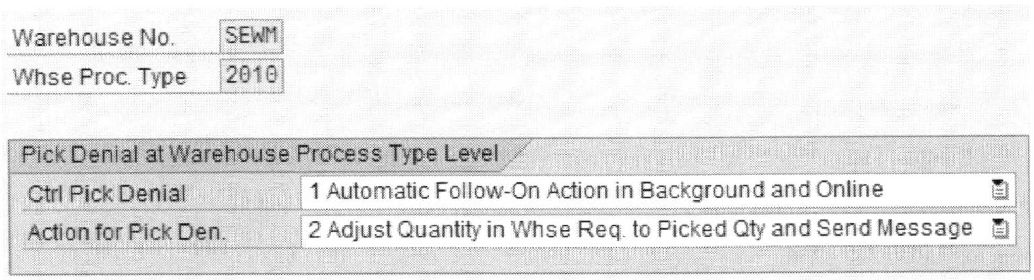

Settings available are:

- **Control Pick Denial:** This determines how pick denial is to run on dialog and background modes. Users can choose one of following options.

  i. **Warning for dialog, automatic follow-up action in background:** In the dialog, the system issues a warning. The predefined action to be performed after a pick denial can be changed. The follow-up action is performed automatically in the background.

  ii. **Automatic follow-up action in dialog and in background**: The system does not issue a warning message. Users do have the option to change the action performed after a pick denial.

- **Action for Pick Denial:** This determines what action is to be performed for pick denial, such as:

  i. Adjust warehouse request quantity to picked quantity

  ii. Adjust warehouse request quantity to picked quantity and send message

  The entry maintained in "Action for Pick Denial" will be defaulted in the WT creation transaction ("Pick Denial" tab).

16.3.1.3 Assign Internal Exception Codes to Exception Codes

The following menu can be used to assign internal exception codes to external exception codes. Internal and external exception codes are covered in more detail in the next chapter.

Menu Path: **SPRO | IMG | Extended Warehouse Management | Goods Issue Process | Pick Denial | Assign Internal Exception Codes to Exception Codes**

Assign Internal Exception Codes to Exception Codes

War...	Int.Exc...	Description	Exception	Description
SEWM	WR01	Adjust Delivery Quantity	PD01	Adjust Delivery Quantity
SEWM	WR02	Send Pick Denial	PD02	Send Pick Denial

16.3.1.4 Activate Workflow Process to Send Pick Den. to ERP Sys.

If the workflow process is to be triggered, it must be enabled for the required exception code. In this example, exception code PD02 is used communicate the pick denial to the ERP system and adjust the ERP delivery quantity.

Menu Path: SPRO | IMG | Extended Warehouse Management | Cross-Process Settings | Exception Handling | Define Exception Codes

Here, select the PD02 line for the warehouse, double-click on the "Define Exception Code" option in the dialog structure, and then double-click on the "Maintain Follow-On Action (Workflow)" option, as show below.

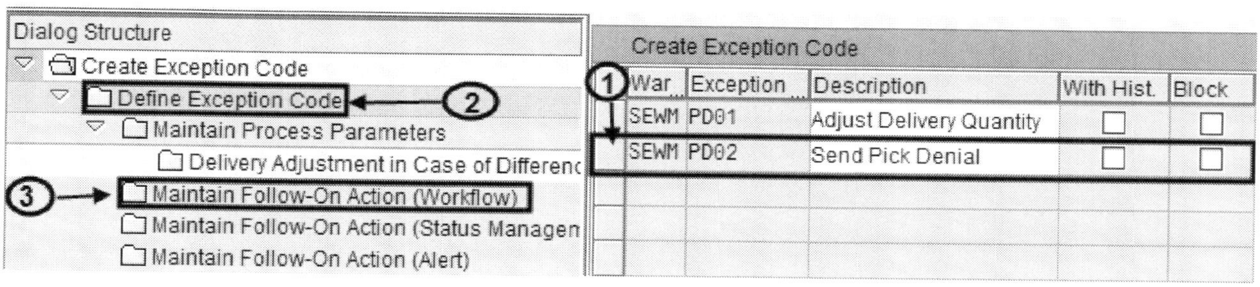

Here, verify that the "WF Start ID" and "Execution Control" fields are set to appropriate values. In the standard configuration, the value for "WF Start ID" is "WR03"; and for "Execution Control," it is "Execute WF Action."

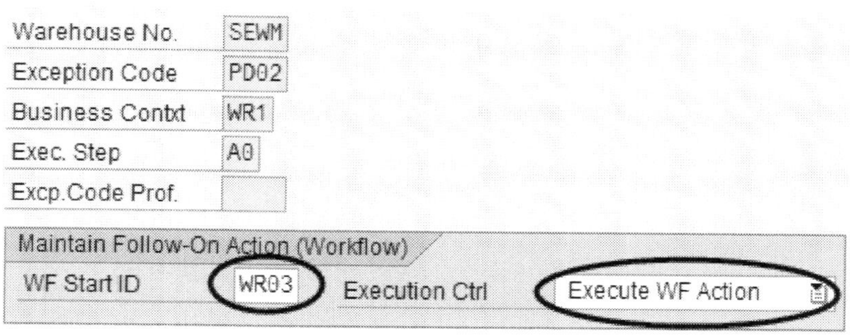

In the dialog structure, select "Maintain Workflow Connection," select the line WR03 for the warehouse, double-click on "Display Active Workflows," and verify that the "Type linkage active" check box is checked.

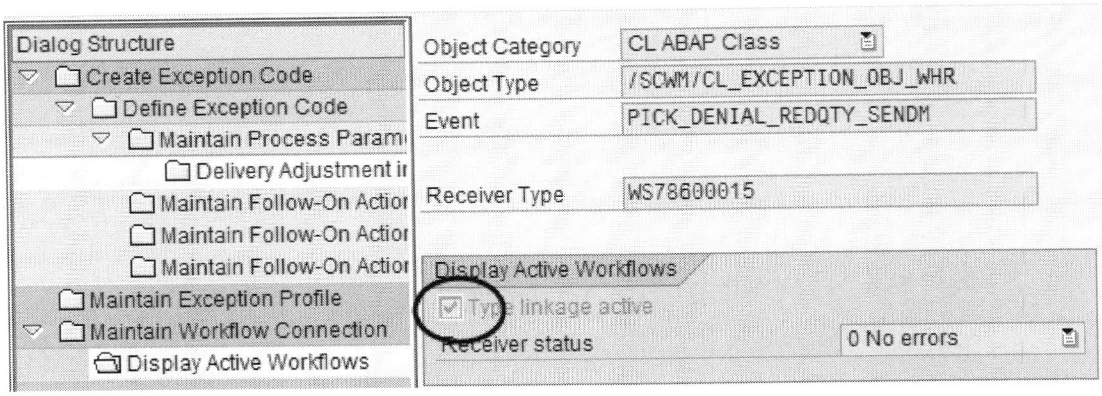

If the check box is not checked, type linkage can be activated in TCode SWE2.

16.3.1.5 Exercise—Pick Denial

In the following example, delivery is created for five PCs, but in the warehouse only three PCs are available. At the time of WT creation, the system will issue a warning message that WT is created for the partial quantity and will enable the "action for pick denial" field to enter the pick denial code.

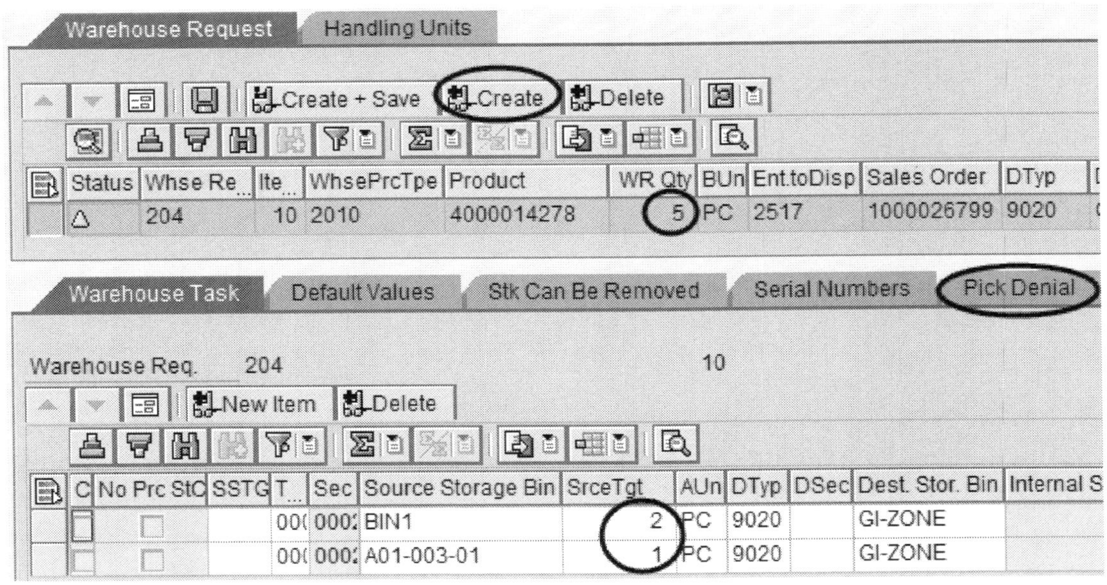

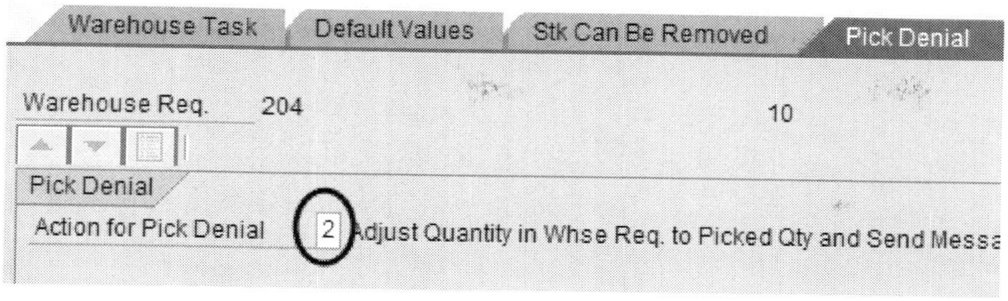

The code entered in the "Action for Pick Denial" field will create a WT and workflow item. When the workflow item is processed, the system will automatically adjust the WR quantity and ERP delivery quantity to the picked quantity. Workflow items can also be processed manually in TCode SWIA.

Notes:

If the requested quantity is available for picking, in the "Pick Denial" tab, the "Action for Pick Denial" field will be disabled.

16.3.1.6 Execute the Workflow Item Manually

To execute the workflow item manually, go to TCode SWIA or follow the menu path **SAP Easy access | SAP menu | Tools | Business Workflow | Development | Administration | Workflow Runtime | Execute Work Item without Agent Check**.

Here, choose the "Execute" button. This will display the results for all the workflow items.

In the resulting list, identify the work item text that belongs to the warehouse request. Select the line item with text "Dialog Step" (under "Work Item Type" column) for the WR document and click on "Execute or Execute without Check". This will trigger the configured workflow for the selected item.

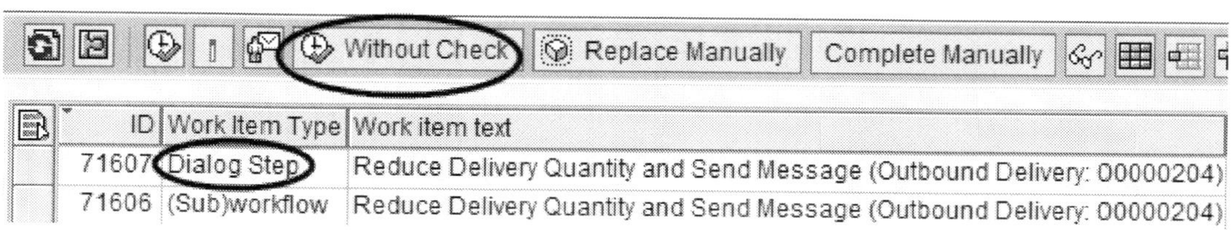

Notes:

In order to trigger the workflow, the required workflow customizing, and other settings like WF-batch user, event type linkage workflow tasks, workflows configurable customer processes has to be setup in the systems. This is done by the Basis team and workflow consultants and is not covered here.

Summary

This chapter has explained the required configuration for the basic outbound picking, loading, and GI posting. It has also explained how to reverse the picking and put the stock back in the warehouses. This chapter covered the required configuration for pick denial and different ways of triggering pick denial in the picking transaction.

Chapter 17: Exception Handling

Exception handling is a new feature in EWM and does not exist in ERP WM. This was introduced to bridge (or at least minimize) the gap between the physical data and system data and to take corrective actions for day-to-day warehouse exceptions.

In EWM, exception handling also enables the warehouse operator to continue the operation when an exception occurs by entering the exception code. Example: A warehouse operator has a pick task with a quantity of 10 from the ABC bin, but physically the bin is empty. The operator can enter the exception code and change the source bin; or trigger the replenishment for this bin and, after replenishment, pick the quantity; or send an alert to the warehouse supervisor to take further actions.

Because exception handling is fully integrated in the EWM system, it can be activated for all the warehouse process steps and can be entered in every goods movement transaction. This can also be connected to the following functions:

- **SAP Alert Framework**: Precondition is that the alert framework/notification engine has to be implemented through the SCM basis path.
- **SAP Status Management**: Precondition is that the SAP status management has to be implemented. (e.g., user status, status network possible, workflow connection).
- **SAP Workflow**: Precondition is that workflow has to be set up. (e.g., workflow customizing, WF-batch user, event type linkage workflow tasks, workflows configurable customer processes).

This chapter is broadly divided into two sections: business context and exception codes. Business context is the business process where an exceptional situation can occur. Exception codes are used to record and manage the exceptions that occur in almost every business process. Each section will cover the required configuration in detail.

17.1 Maintain Business Context for Exception Codes

Business Context is the business process where an exceptional situation can occur. Examples include confirmation of WT, PI count, and so on.

Table 17.1A shows an overview of the configuration that is covered under this section.

S. No	Configuration Items	TCode	Transportable
1	Maintain Exception Code Context	SPRO	Yes
2	Maintain Operation	SPRO	Yes
3	Maintain Internal Process Code	SPRO	Yes
4	Maintain Internal Exceptions	SPRO	Yes

17.1A - Configuration list for Business Context Definition

17.1.1 Maintain Exception Code Context

As of EWM 7.0, SAP has provided around twenty-five preconfigured exception code contexts, which cover most of the business requirements. These are client independent and not warehouse specific.

Menu Path: SPRO | IMG | Extended Warehouse Management | Cross-Process Settings | Exception Handling | Maintain Business Context for Exception Codes

The following is an example of the standard exception code contexts defined for confirmation of WT for the stock removal process.

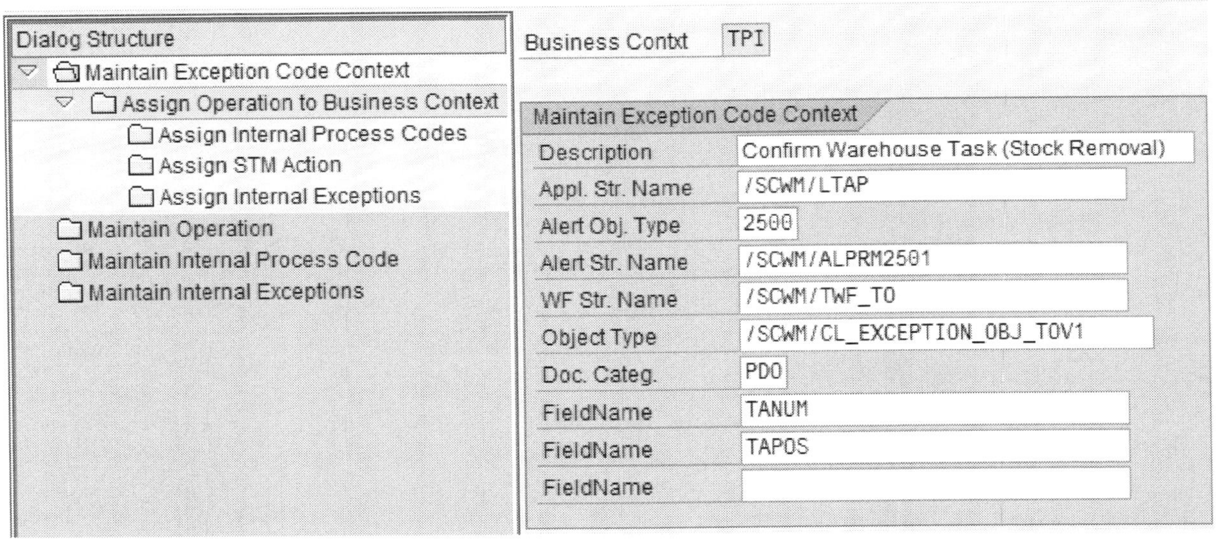

It consists of Application Structure for the import of different application data; Alert Object Type, which groups alert types according to the objects to which the alerts relate; Alert Structure Name for the dynamic transfer of application data in an alert; Workflow Structure Name (i.e., name of structure for persistent workflow data); Object Type, which is the identifier that specifies the type of an object (for example, by the name of a class, if the object is an instance of an ABAP object class) in a persistent object reference (POR) or local persistent object reference (LPOR); and the Doc Category, which is the classification of the different documents that the system can use for delivery processing.

17.1.2 Maintain Operation

Here, the operation represents the process execution step defined for a particular warehouse operation (business context). Examples include desktop product task, RF product task action on source data, and so on. As of EWM 7.0, SAP has provided around forty-six preconfigured execution steps (operation).

To display the list of operations, double-click on "Maintain Operation" in the dialog structure:

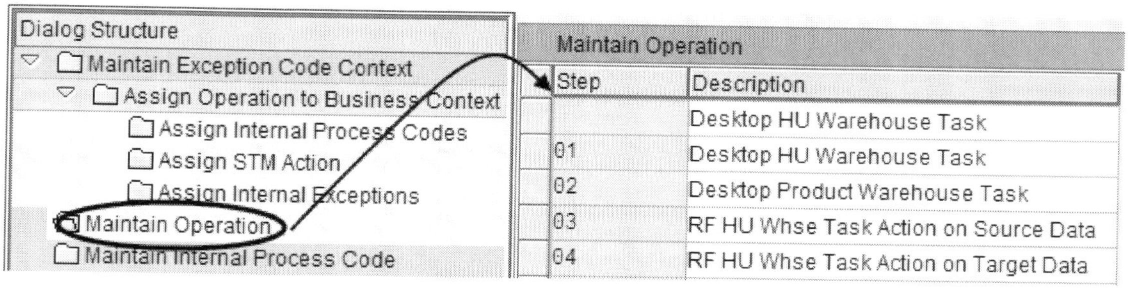

Once the operations are defined, they have to be assigned to the business context. To assign, double-click on "Assign Operation to Business Context" option in the dialog structure, click on "New Entries," and enter the appropriate operation as a step.

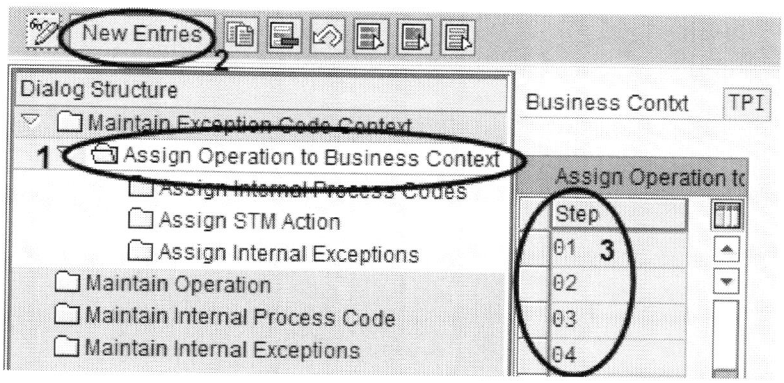

17.1.3 Maintain Internal Process Code

As of EWM 7.0, SAP has provided around forty-six internal process codes. It controls internal program reactions after an exception code is entered. After internal process codes are defined, they must be assigned to the appropriate exception codes. For example, CHBD—Change Destination Storage Bin is an internal process code. When an exception code that has CHBD as its internal process code is entered, the system permits changing the destination bin.

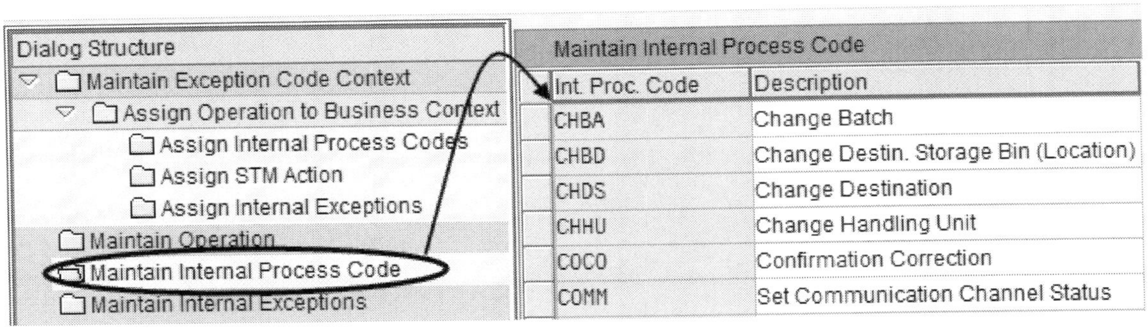

Next, the internal process code has to be assigned to the "Business Context". To assign, double-click on "Assign Operation to Business Context" in the dialog structure, select the appropriate step, and double-click on the "Assign Internal Process Codes" option in the dialog structure, as shown below.

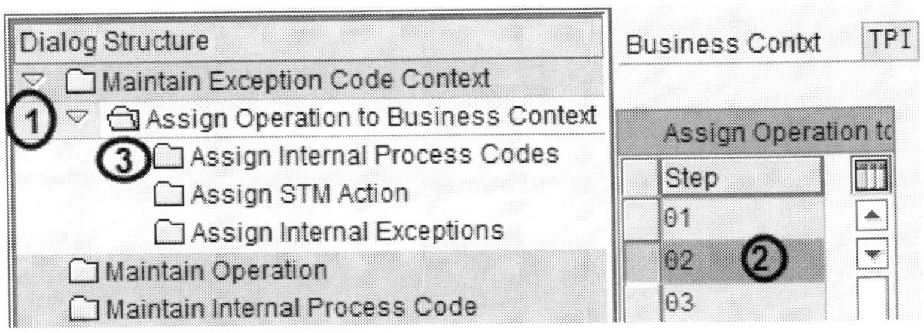

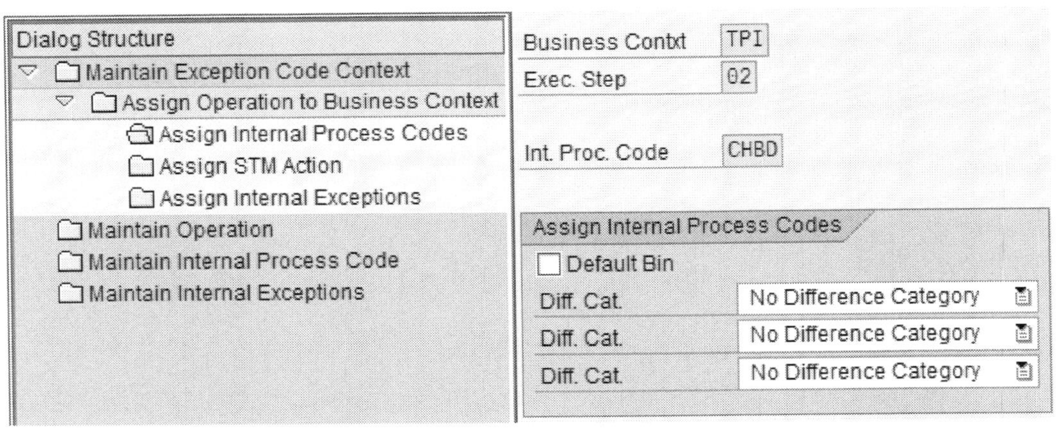

17.1.4 Maintain Internal Exceptions

Internal exception codes are automatically triggered when the system processes exception situations. SAP has predefined several internal exception codes in the EWM system.

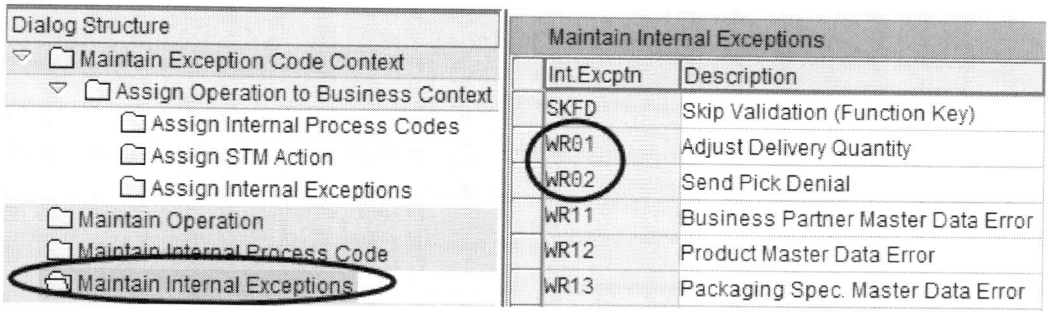

Internal exception codes are assigned to "Business Context & Operation." To assign, first select the step line in "Assign Operation to Business Context," then click on "Assign Internal Process Exceptions."

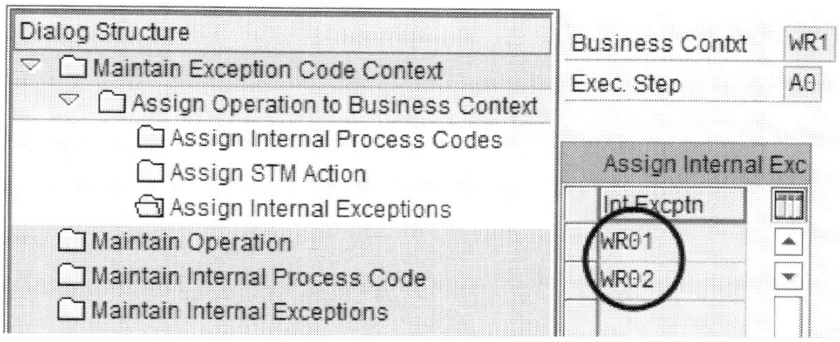

17.2 Exception Code

The exception code basically describes an exception situation in the warehouse. It provides advanced functionality to record and manage the exceptions that occur almost in every warehouse process. Table 17.2A shows an overview of configurations covered under the exception code definition.

S. No	Configuration Items	TCode	Transportable
1	Maintain Workflow Connection	SPRO	Yes
2	Display Active Workflows	SPRO	Yes
3	Create Exception Code	SPRO	Yes
4	Exception Code Profile	SPRO	Yes
5	Define Exception Code	SPRO	Yes
6	Maintain Process Parameters	SPRO	Yes
7	Delivery Adjustment in Case of Differences	SPRO	Yes
8	Maintain Follow-On Action (Workflow)	SPRO	Yes
9	Assign Internal Exception Codes to Exception Codes	SPRO	Yes
10	Assign Exception Code Profile to User	/SCWM/EXCUSERID	Yes

17.2A - Configuration Required to Define Exception Codes

For example, in the following screenshot, the picker wants to change the destination bin in the picking WT due to a last-minute change in the warehouse door assignment.

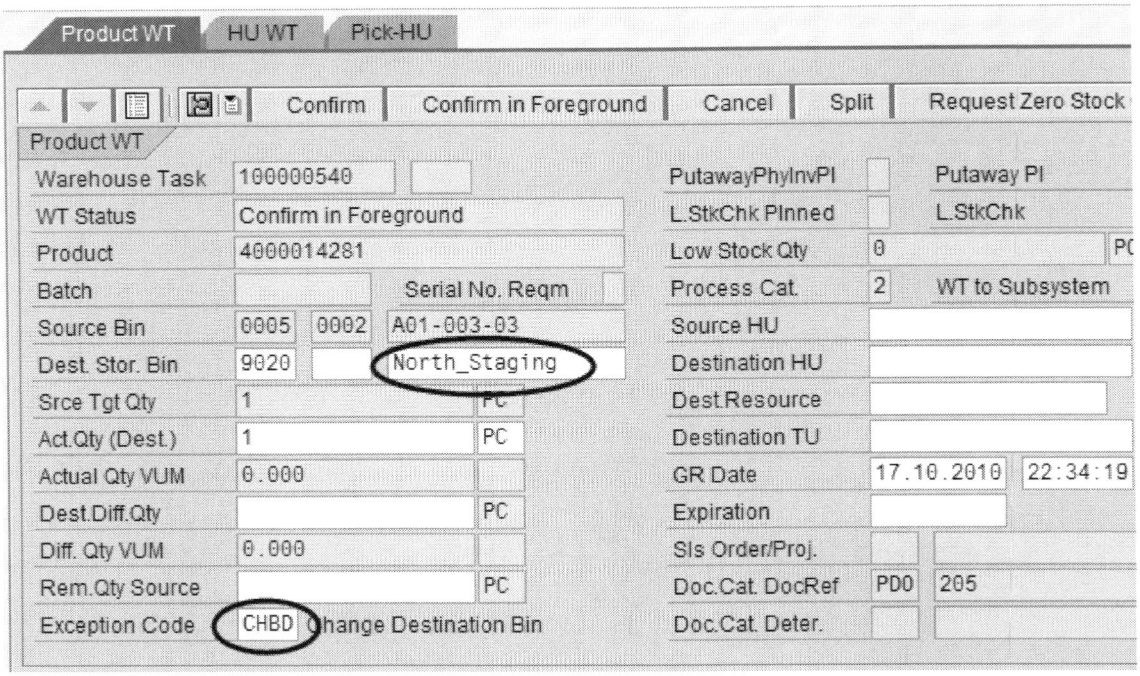

17.2.1 Maintain Workflow Connection

As explained earlier, in order to trigger the workflow, it is first necessary to define workflow connections. The connections defined here are warehouse specific. SAP has provided nine workflow connections. Users can copy them to their clients' warehouses, or they can define their own.

To copy the SAP-defined connection, click the "Maintain Workflow Connection" option in the dialog structure, click on "Select All Options," and then click the "Copy" option on the application toolbar. In the copy screen, change the warehouse number 0001 to the appropriate warehouse number. If there are any defined dependencies for the selected entry, the system will prompt the user before copying them. They can be copied automatically by selecting the "copy all" option.

Menu Path: SPRO | IMG | Extended Warehouse Management | Cross-Process Settings | Exception Handling | Define Exception Codes

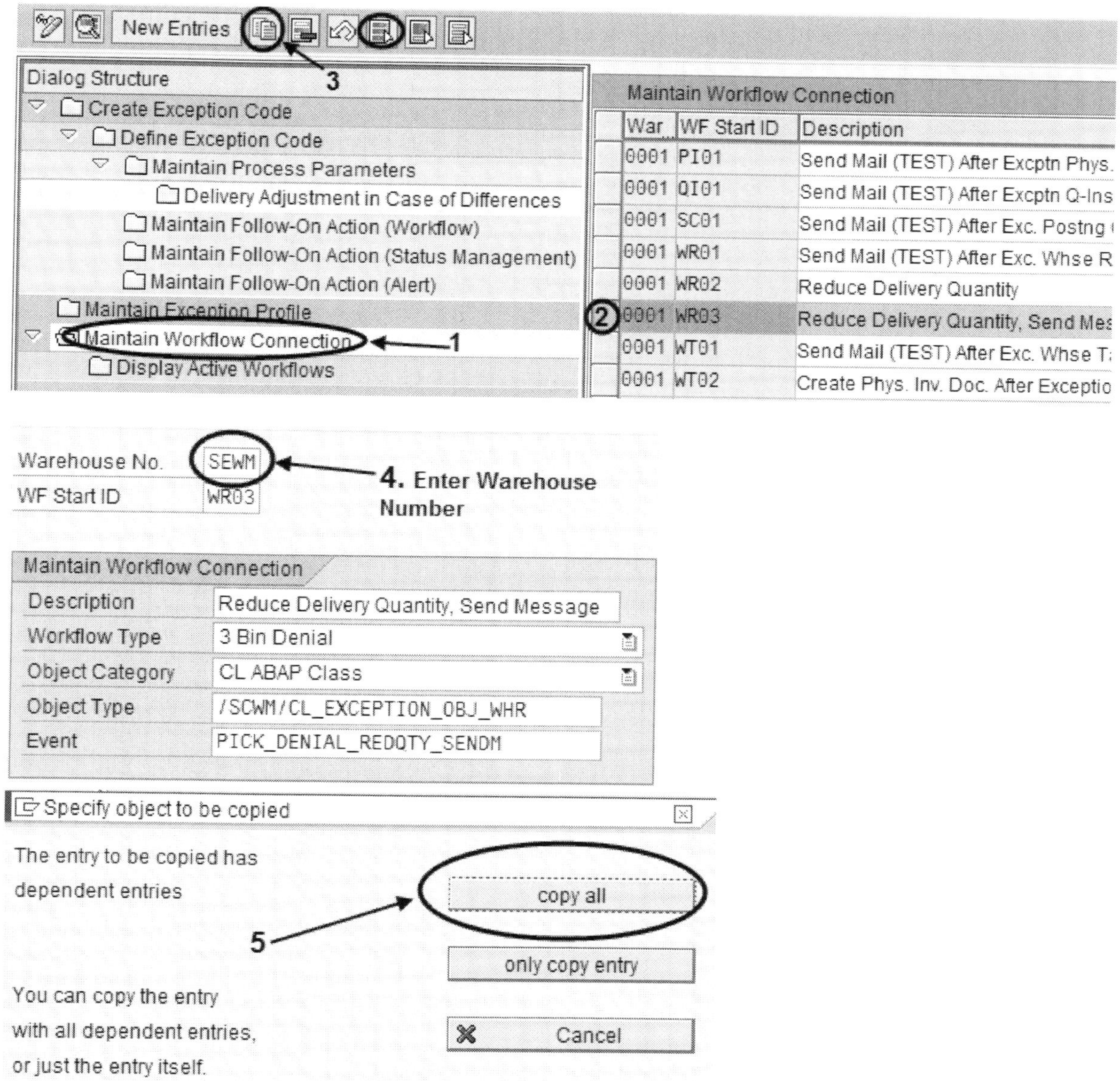

17.2.2 Display Active Workflows

In the dialog structure, select Maintain Workflow Connection; select the WF start ID, double-click on "Display Active Workflows," and verify that the "Type linkage active" check box is checked. This has to be checked to trigger the workflow. If the box is not checked, type linkage can be activated in TCode SWE2.

Menu Path: SPRO | IMG | Extended Warehouse Management | Cross-Process Settings | Exception Handling | Define Exception Codes or TCode SWE2

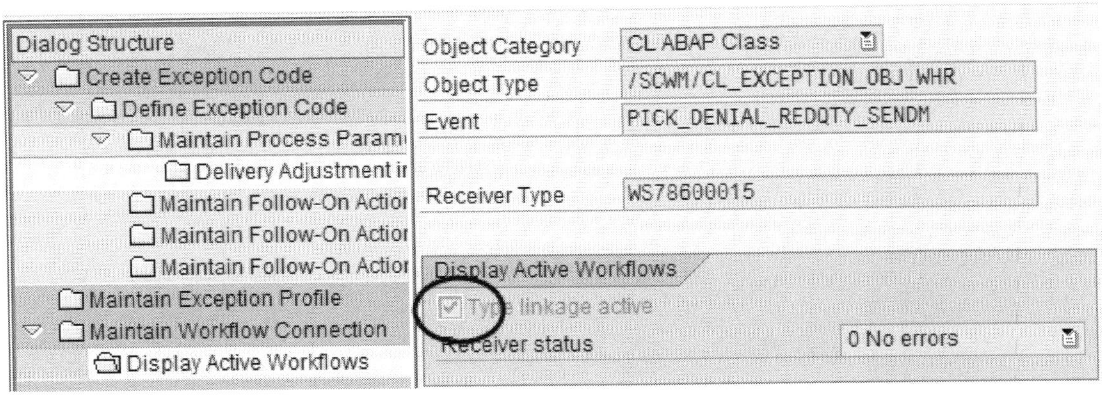

17.2.3 Create Exception Code

As of EWM 7.0, SAP has provided around seventy-five preconfigured exception codes and nine workflow connections, which can be copied to the user's warehouse. Users can also define their own exception codes and workflow connections. Exception codes defined in the system are warehouse dependent. To create an exception code, click on "New Entries" in the application toolbar. Check the "With Hist." check box. This saves the exceptions processed centrally and can be seen in the EWM monitor.

Menu Path: SPRO | IMG | Extended Warehouse Management | Cross-Process Settings | Exception Handling | Define Exception Codes

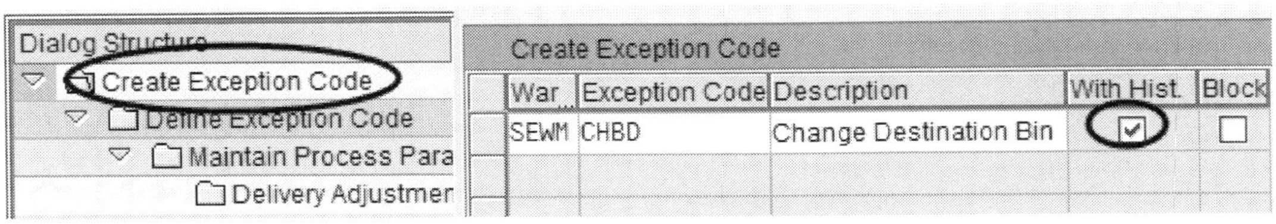

17.2.4 Exception Code Profile

Exception code profiles are used to restrict the availability of exception codes to a particular user.

In certain business scenarios, it may be necessary to prevent exception codes from being used by unqualified users. To do this, an exception code profile is assigned to each user. While executing the transaction with exception code, the system accesses the exception profile from the exception code and checks if this exception profile is assigned to the user.

Menu Path: **SPRO | IMG | Extended Warehouse Management | Cross-Process Settings | Exception Handling | Define Exception Codes**

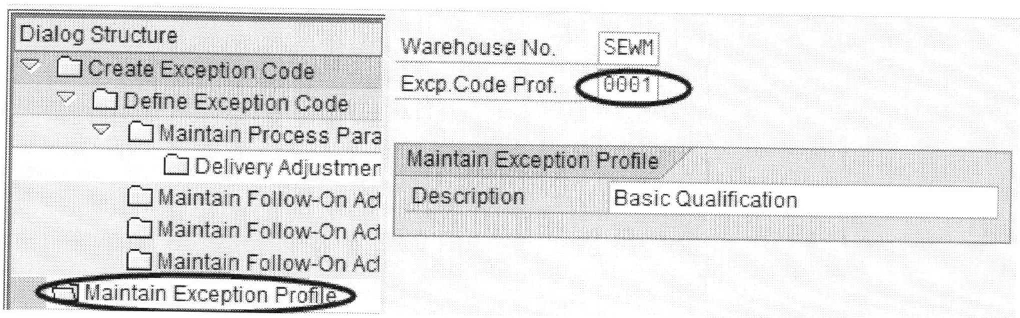

17.2.5 Define Exception Code

Here, the business context, execution step, and exception code profile are assigned to the exception code.

Menu Path: **SPRO | IMG | Extended Warehouse Management | Cross-Process Settings | Exception Handling | Define Exception Codes**

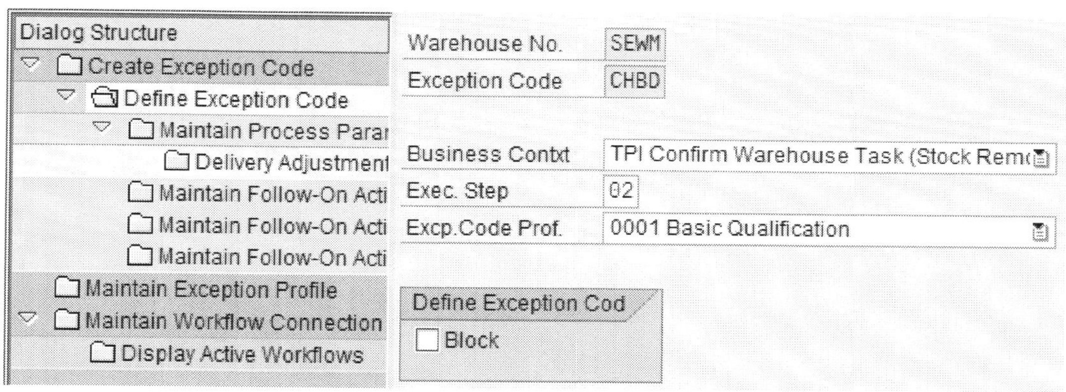

17.2.6 Maintain Process Parameters

Here, consultants can assign the internal process code, which was previously defined under "Maintain Business Context for Exception Codes." Weighting is used by the system to give priority to the exception code. Users can assign the value from 0, low priority, to 9, very critical.

Menu Path: **SPRO | IMG | Extended Warehouse Management | Cross-Process Settings | Exception Handling | Define Exception Codes**

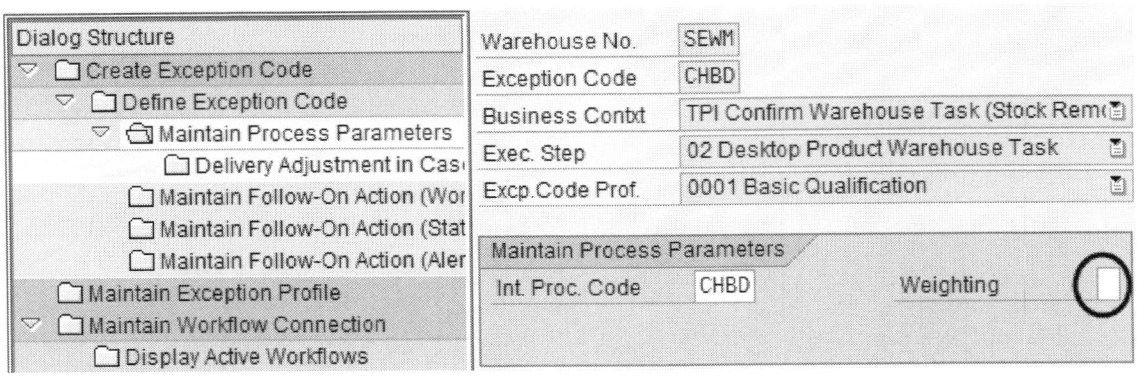

17.2.7 Delivery Adjustment In Case of Differences

If a delivery has to be adjusted with an exception code, the required settings must be made in the "Delivery Adjustment in Case of Differences" option.

Menu Path: SPRO | IMG | Extended Warehouse Management | Cross-Process Settings | Exception Handling | Define Exception Codes

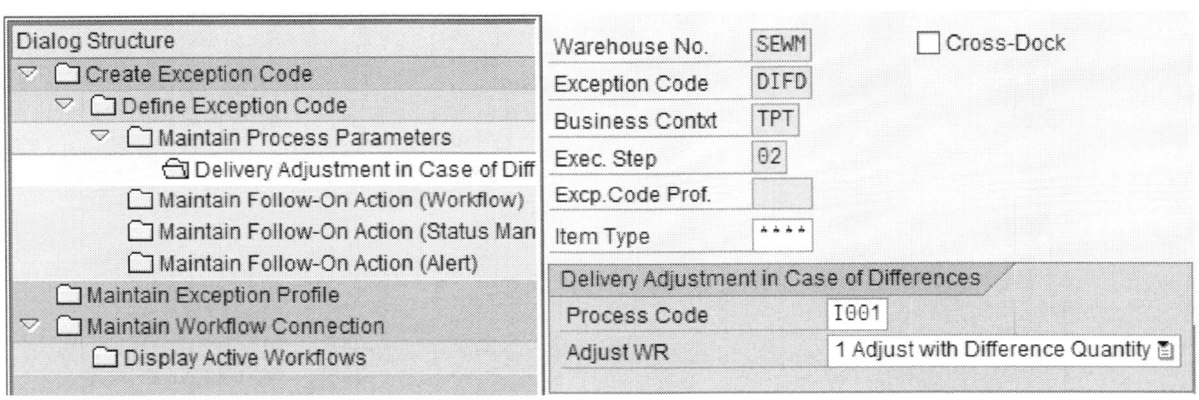

17.2.8 Maintain Follow-On Action (Workflow)

If the exception code requires workflow, assign the workflow start ID to the exception code.

Menu Path: SPRO | IMG | Extended Warehouse Management | Cross-Process Settings | Exception Handling | Define Exception Codes

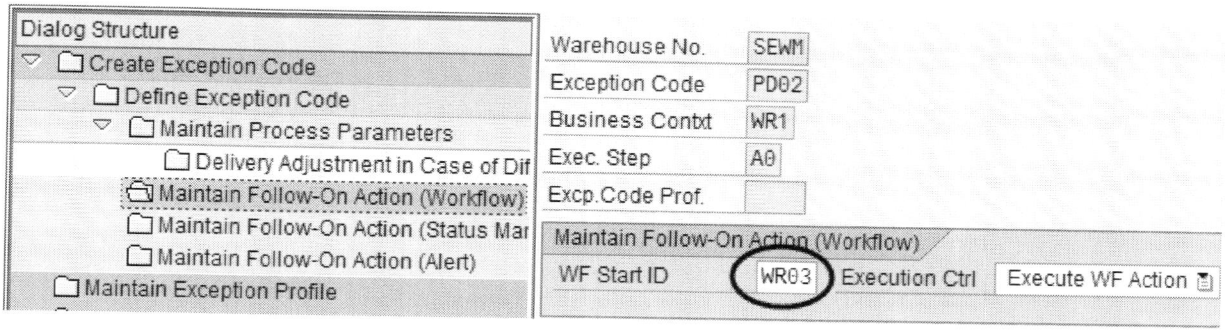

17.2.9 Assign Internal Exception Codes to Exception Codes

In "Assign Internal Exception Codes to Exception Codes" IMG activity, the relevant exception code is assigned to an internal exception code at the warehouse number level.

Assign Internal Exception Codes to Exception Codes

War	Int.Excptn	Description	Exception Code	Description
SEWM	WR01	Adjust Delivery Qu	PD01	Adjust Delivery Quantity
SEWM	WR02	Send Pick Denial	PD02	Send Pick Denial

17.2.10 Assign Exception Code Profile to User

To use an exception code profile, it must be assigned to the users.

Menu path: SAP Easy Access | Extended Warehouse Management | Settings | Assign User to Exception Code Profile or TCode /SCWM/EXCUSERID

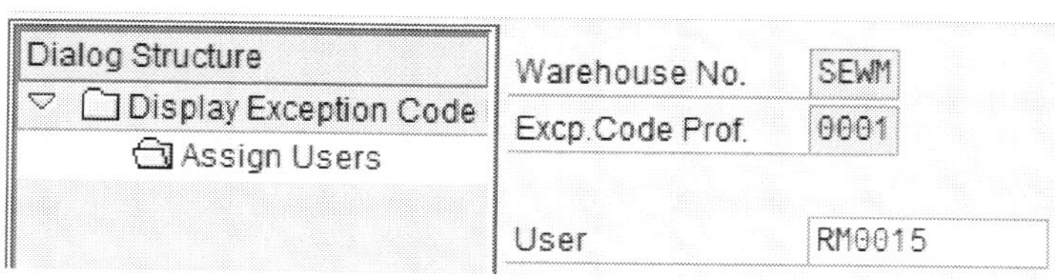

Summary

This chapter has explained how to configure exception codes. Chapter 16 demonstrated how to use exception codes during pick denial. Exception codes are mainly used at the time of outbound delivery processing or during PI.

Chapter 18: Post-Processing Framework (PPF)

The PPF is part of the SAP web application server. It is the successor to SAP's message control, which provides a wider functional scope, simpler connection to the applications, and greater flexibility. The greatest strength of the PPF is its flexibility. In general, it can be used to process different types of output types like printing, emailing, and faxing, or it can be used to trigger workflow, BADI, or follow-up actions.

In EWM, it is widely used in delivery processing, processing follow-up actions like automatic creation of WTs, posting of GRs and GI, and to print warehouse documents. This chapter explains the structure of PPF, process flow of PPF, and how to configure it, along with an example.

18.1 Process Flow of PPF

Diagram 18.1A explains the process flow of PPF.

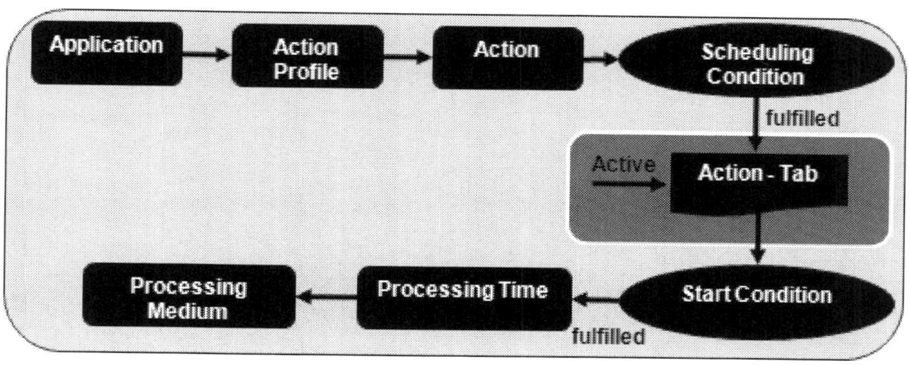

Diagram 18.1A – Process Flow of PPF

In the diagram:

- Application refers to the business transaction or process.
- Action profile contains the set of allowed actions with sequence of execution.
- Actions are generic business functions within a transaction. Actions define what to do (workflow/print), how to determine (condition techniques), when to process (on save/change), and how many times to process.
- Scheduling condition maintains the criteria for determining a particular action.

- The start condition is checked before the action is executed. The action is only executed when the start condition has been fulfilled. If no condition is defined, the system will consider that the condition is fulfilled.
- Processing time decides when a scheduled action is processed (immediately on saving application/through dialog).
- Processing mediums (types) are different ways the action is executed (call method, trigger workflow, smart form for print).

18.2 Configuration of PPF

Configuration for PPF actions can be done through respective application nodes in Customizing (example HU, WO) under menu path "Print" or in TCode SPPFCADM.

TCode SPPFCADM is mainly divided into three parts. They are applications, customizing, and cleanup inconsistencies. Under the application section, the PPF settings are defined for different transactions or processes. Action profiles and conditions are covered in detail later in this section.

In the following sections PPF settings are reviewed for a "New Delivery" application to give a better understanding of each of the PPF component.

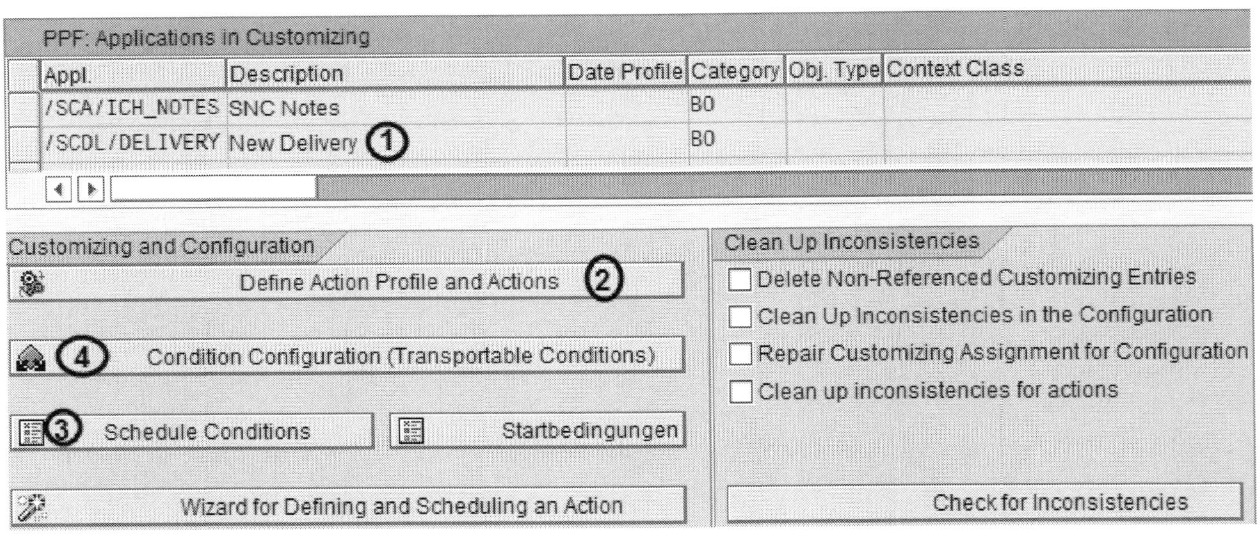

To begin, select the application line item "New Delivery—/SCDL/DELIVERY" in the application section. Click on "Define Action Profile and Actions" button in customizing section. This will display the defined PPF action profiles and actions for the new delivery.

18.2.1 Action Profiles and Actions

An action profile contains the set of allowed actions with their sequence of execution and the settings required for all the action definitions.

An action can be a function or a process that is scheduled for an application document under specific conditions and is started either immediately or later.

18.2.1.1 Action Profile

To see the action profile settings defined for the one of deliveries, select the "Action Profile" line and click on the "Details" button.

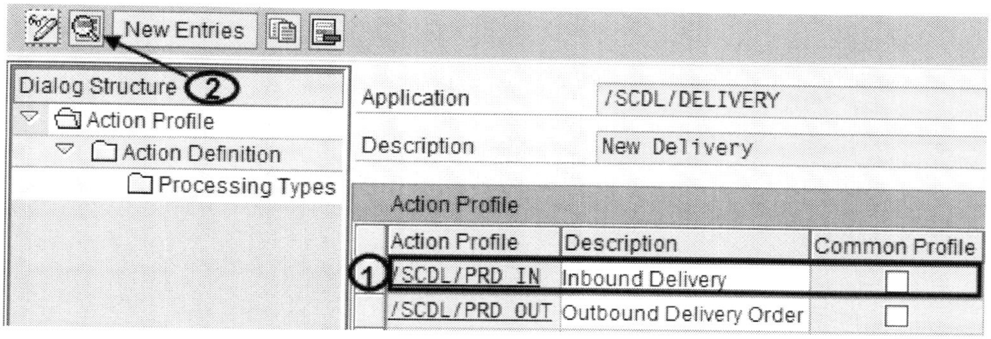

Here, category of the object type, the object type name, and the appropriate context class can be defined.

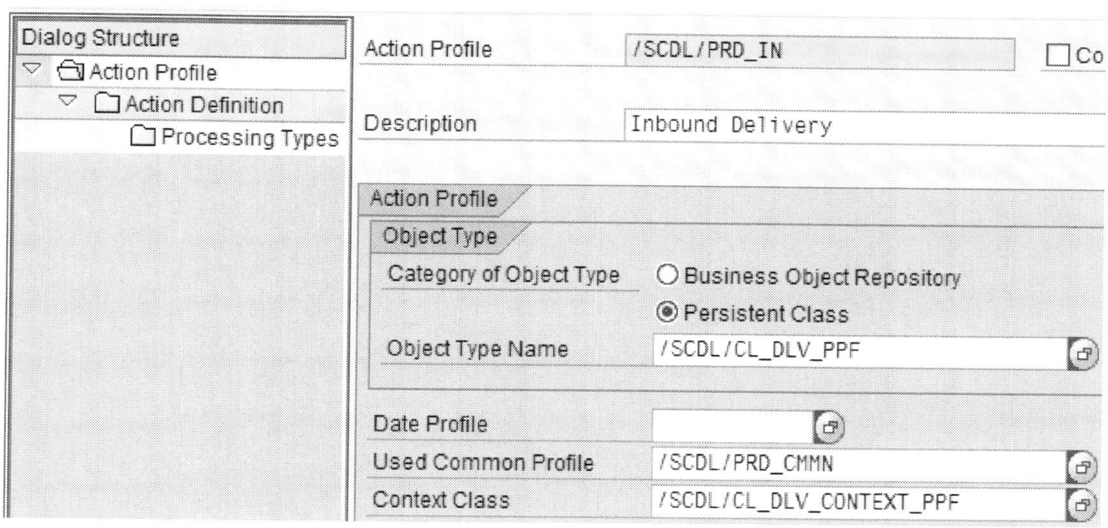

18.2.1.2 Action Definition

The action definition describes the content of an action independently of the processing type. It can be a function or a process that is scheduled for an application document under specific conditions and is started either immediately or later.

Actions can be determined both at the document header level and for single items. They can be performed in the background by the system, in foreground a user, or a group/organizational unit. The execution can either be started directly after the scheduling of the action or later. For example, actions might entail mail, fax, and so on.

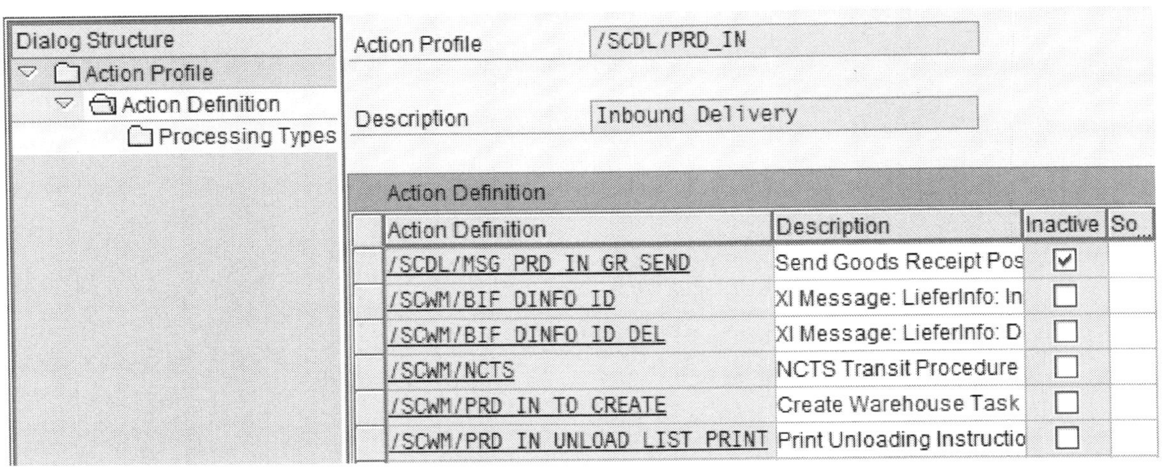

To see the details of the action definition, select the action line item and click the "Details" button. This has three tabs.

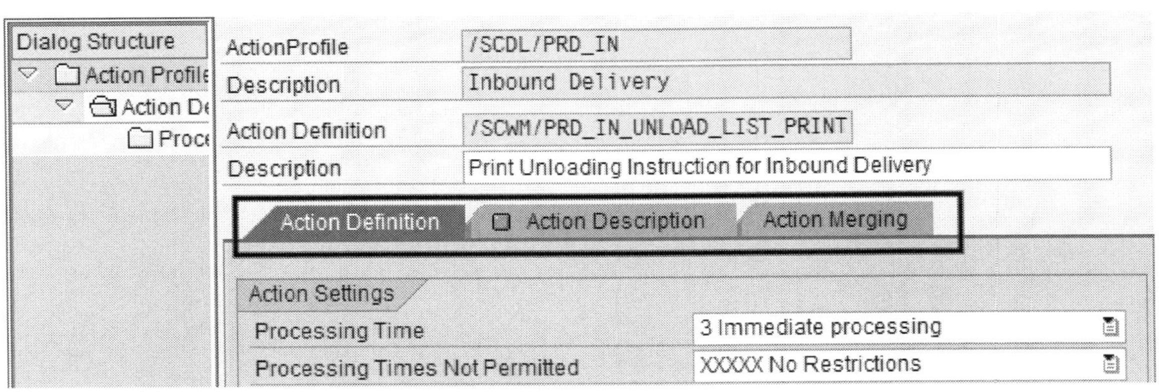

Under the "Action Definition" tab action settings, partner determination, and action determination need to be defined.

18.2.1.3 Action Settings

Under "Action Settings section" processing time, sort order, scheduling, and spool control can be defined.

The processing of an action can take place at different times. It can be started as soon as an action is scheduled—that is, after document posting—or it can be only scheduled initially. Processing can then be started later at a specific time, under specific conditions, or manually by a user.

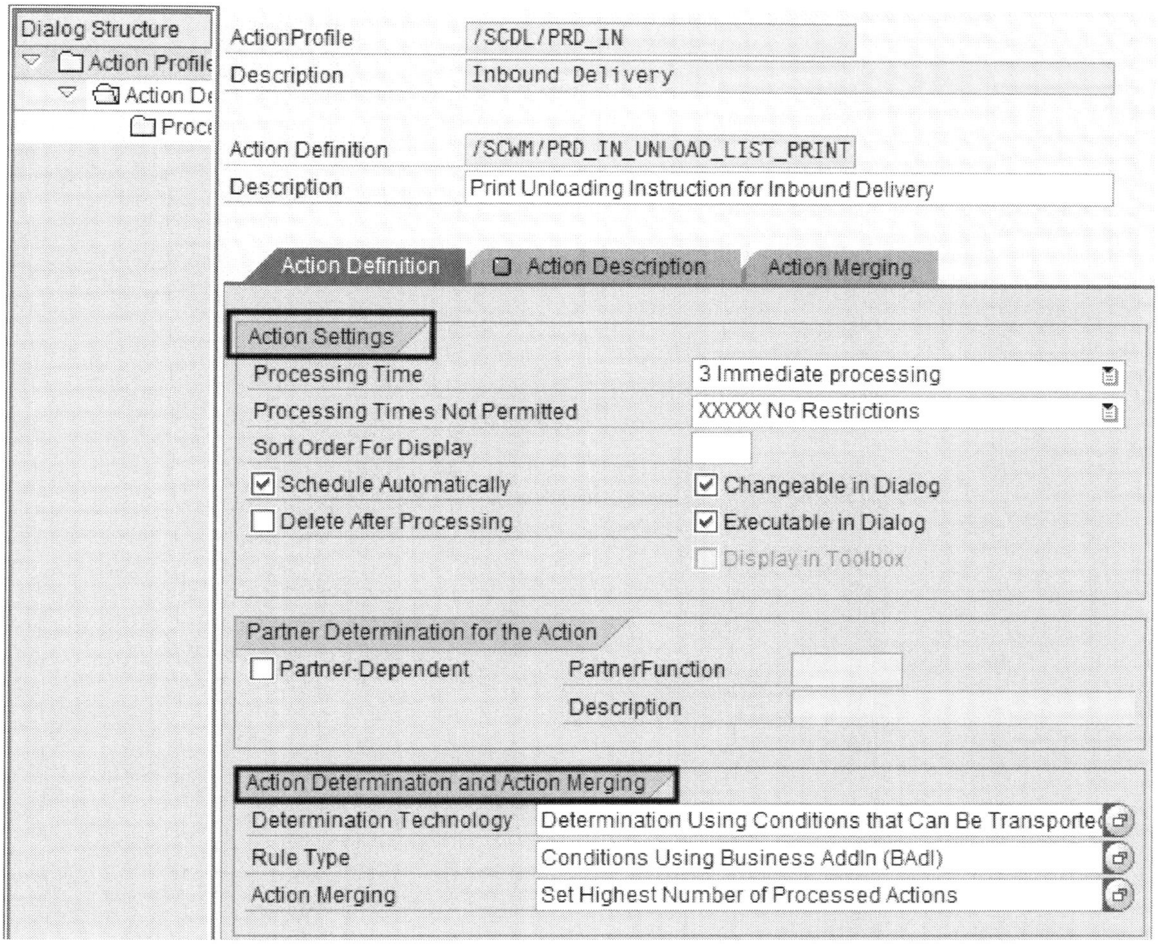

18.2.1.4 Action Determination

"Determination Technology" checks whether the conditions for scheduling the actions have occurred. It generates proposals for actions when specific conditions occur. This can take place automatically or manually. In case of automatic determination, it takes place when the application document is saved after relevant changes. It uses the attributes of a business object to check whether the conditions for scheduling actions apply. The actions found are inserted into the action list according to the merging rule. The technology used for determination is specified per action definition.

Determination using conditions can be implemented in the following ways. The standard determination uses workflow rules.

- Workflow condition editor.
- Business add-in EVAL_SCHEDCOND_PPF.
- Manual determination: Actions can be created, changed, or deleted manually when editing the application document. A new action is then inserted into the action list, according to the merging rule. Manually created actions are not changed or deleted by automatic action determination.

18.2.1.5 Action Merging

Action merging is always necessary if existing, unprocessed actions have to be merged with newly found actions. This is done if an existing document is changed, for example. Because the data has changed, actions that were found when creating the document can be omitted, and the new actions, which have not yet been executed, are added to the action list or the work list.

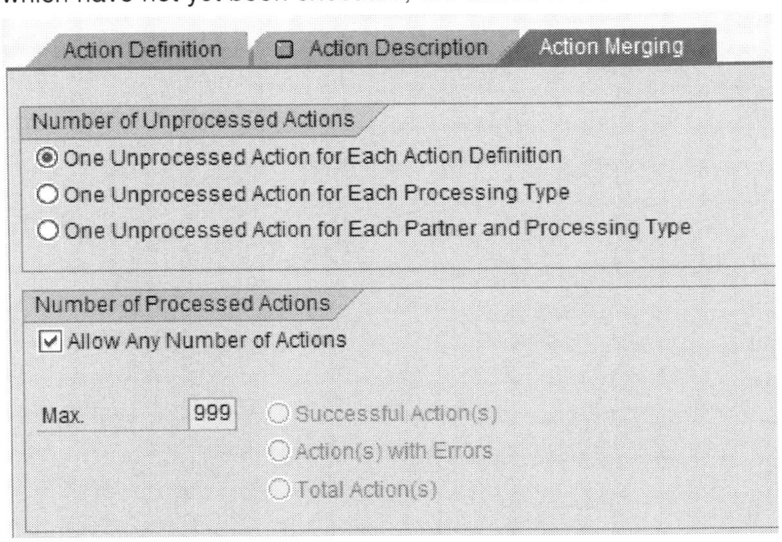

Under "Number of Unprocessed Actions" settings, the PPF provides several merge technologies but permits only one unprocessed action for each action definition, processing type, or partner and processing type. It covers the following situations:

- An action has been found and is not yet in the action list. It is inserted into the action list.
- An action has not been found but is in the action list. It is deleted from the action list and also from the database, if not changed manually.

- An action has been found but is already in the action list. If the existing action has not already been changed manually, the new action replaces the existing action.
- An action is executed a configurable maximum number of times. Any further actions found will not be executed.

18.2.1.6 Processing Type

Here, the processing type that is responsible for the execution of a particular action is defined. Examples include printing, faxing, sending, or starting a workflow.

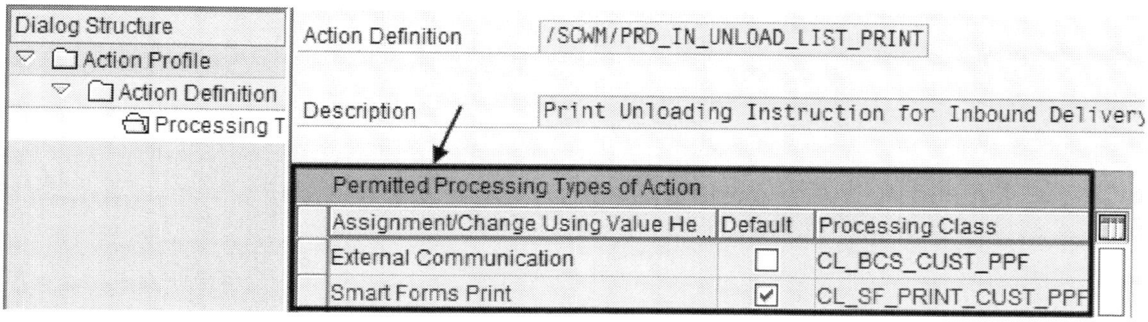

To add a new processing type, click the "New Entries" button, select the required item from the dropdown list in "Assignment/Change Using Value Help in List" and follow the steps. The dropdown list contains the following options:

- External Communication
- Method Call
- Smart Forms Fax
- Smart Forms Mail
- Smart Forms Print
- Trigger Alert
- Workflow
- XML Output of Confirmation
- XML Output of SA Release

For processing with method call, use the dropdown list to choose an appropriate method or BAdI. For workflow processing, enter a workflow template. For processing using Smart Forms, choose Smart Forms Print, Smart Forms Fax, or Smart Forms E-Mail and enter a form name, a processing class, and a processing method.

Depending on the selection, the system will display the required settings. For example, the following screenshot shows the print settings for process type "Smart Forms Print."

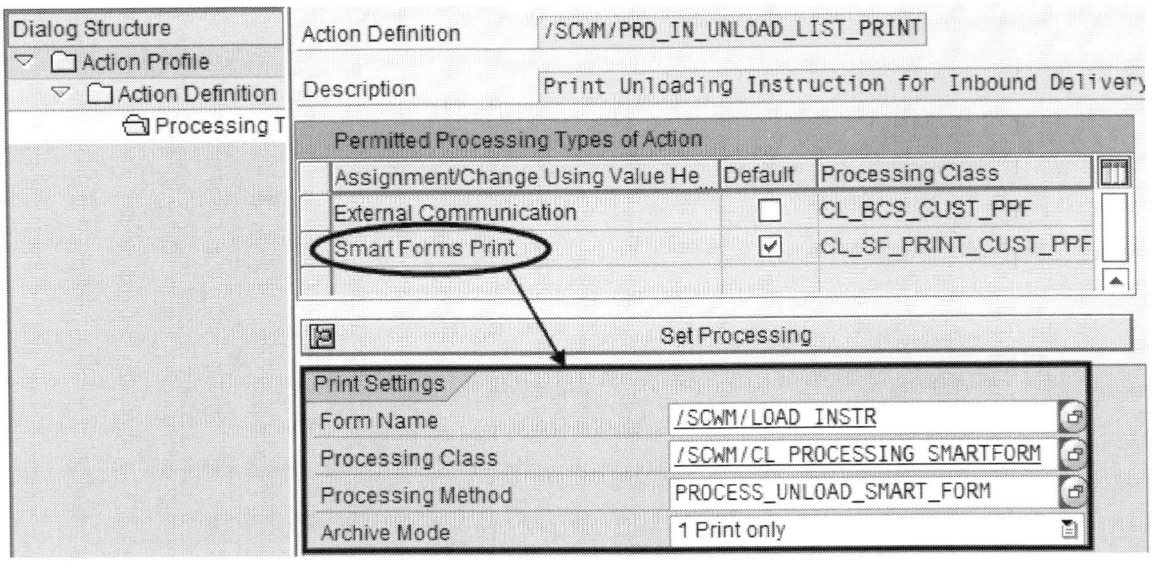

18.2.1.7 Assign Action Profile to Delivery Document Type

If the application is delivery, it is necessary to assign the action profile to the respective document type.

Menu Path: **SPRO | IMG | Extended Warehouse Management | Goods Receipt Process | Inbound Delivery | Manual Settings | Define Document Types for Inbound Delivery Process**

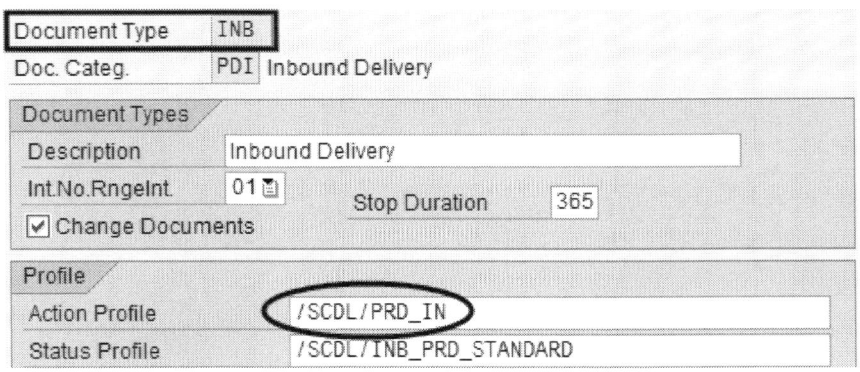

18.2.2 Maintain Condition Configuration

The next important configuration setting to trigger PPF is condition configuration. Either transportable or nontransportable condition configurations can be used.

The following example demonstrates how to maintain condition records to print unloading instructions for an inbound delivery.

In order to maintain condition records to print the unloading instruction, go to TCode SPPFCADM, select the application "New Delivery," and click on "Condition Configuration—Transportable Conditions."

Under the action profile, double-click on inbound delivery; in the action definition section, double-click on "Print Unloading Instructions for Inbound Delivery." Here, a printer can be assigned to print the unloading instructions in the "Processing Details" tab. In order to maintain the values, transaction should be in the change mode.

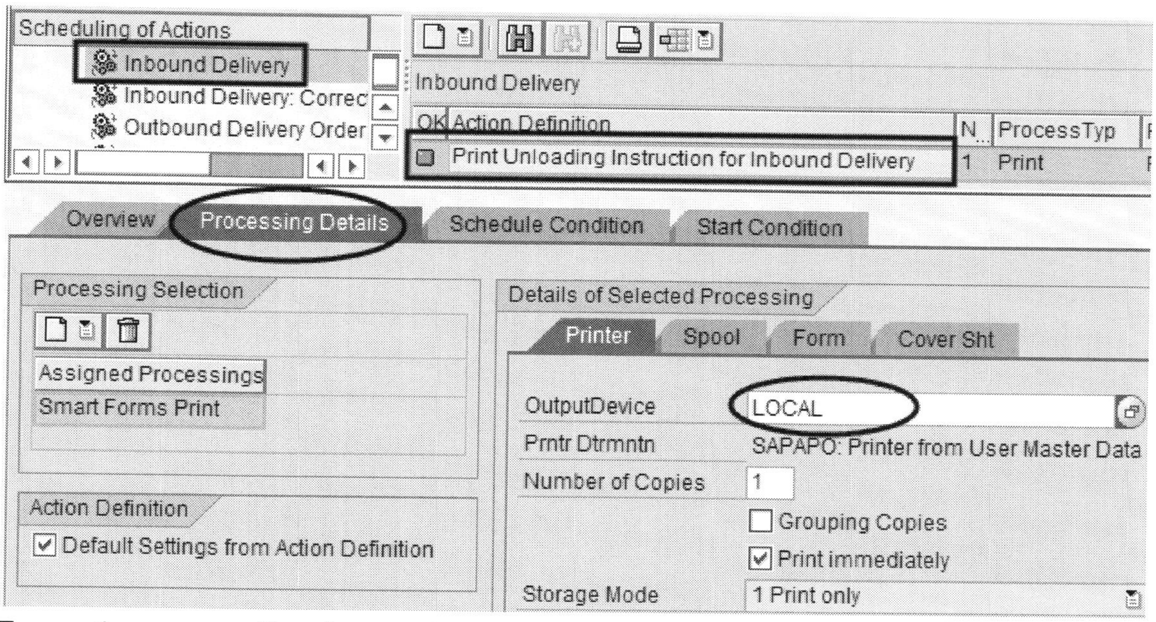

To use the user-specific printer settings, the printer details should be maintained in the user master data. Either /SCDL/PPF_ADD_DATA or /SCWM/EX_DLV_PRINT_PROFILE BADI can be used to determine the printers as well.

To verify the configuration, go to transaction /SCWM/PRDI, enter the inbound delivery, and click on the "Unload" button. If the above settings are maintained, this will trigger the automatic printing of unloading instructions.

The processed documents can be previewed from the PPF action tab. The unloading instructions can also be reprinted and previewed from the PPF actions tab.

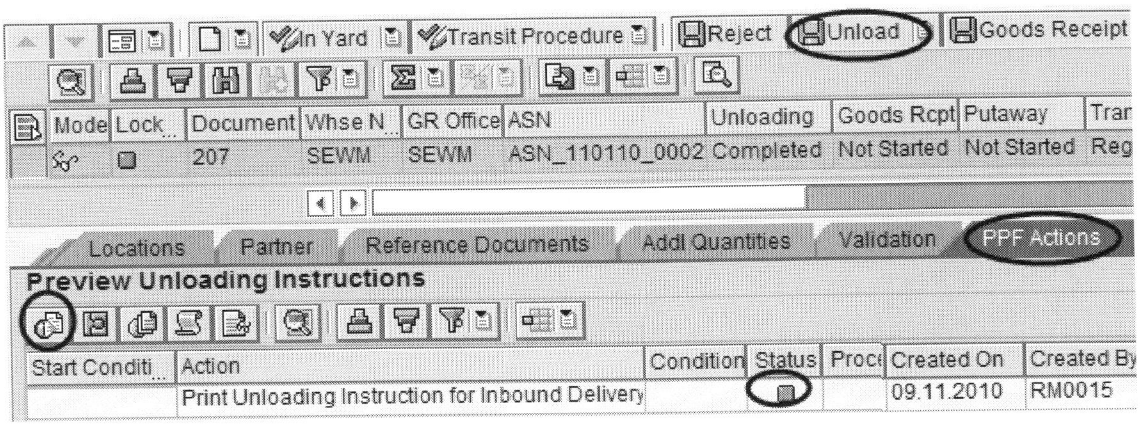

18.3 Processing of Outputs in EWM

TCode SPPFP makes it possible to manually process the outputs and to view all outputs that are scheduled, processed, or failed. Depending on user settings, previewing, printing, and reprinting the output can also be performed with this transaction.

Menu Path: SAP Easy Access | SAP Menu | Extended Warehouse Management | Delivery Processing | Actions | Process and Display PPF Actions or TCode SPPFP

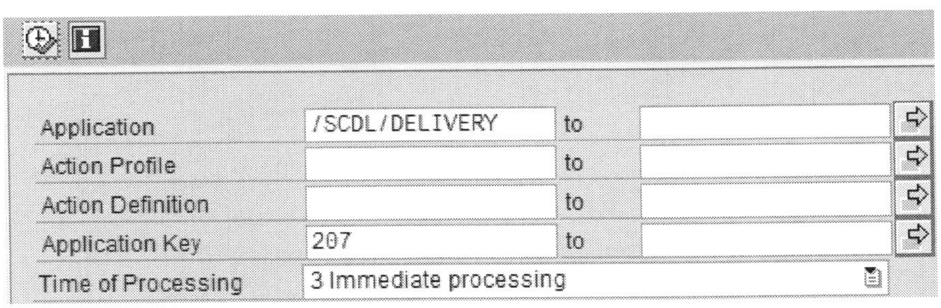

18.4 PPF Connections—Diagram

Diagram 18.4A provides an overview of how PPF components are connected to other applications and how actions are processed in the PPF framework. These components were already explained earlier in this chapter.

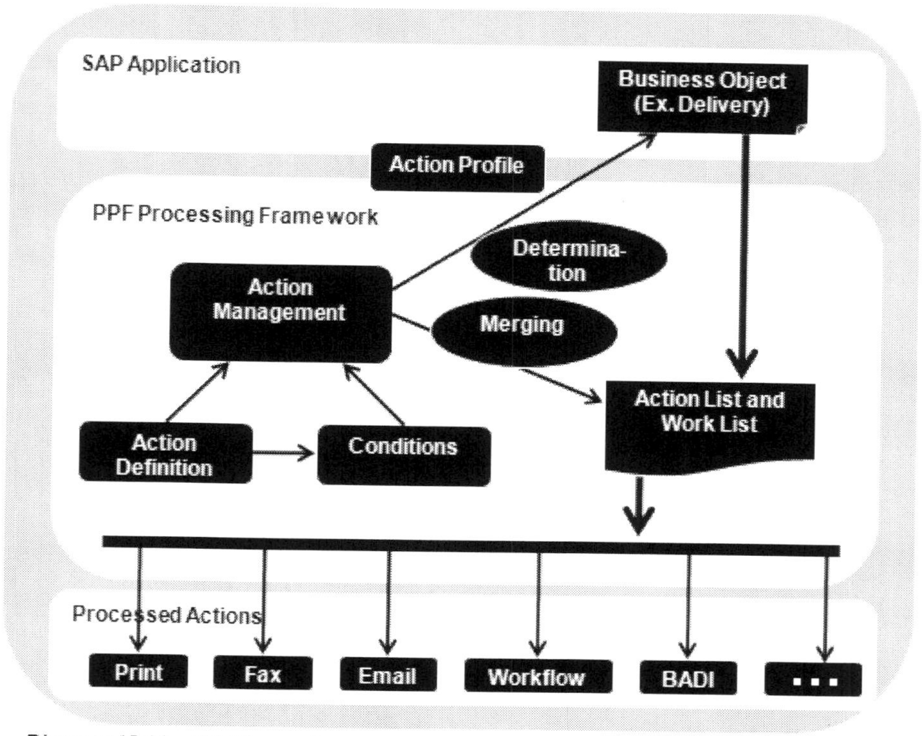

Diagram 18.4A – PPF Connections

Action List: Actions that have been scheduled by the determination for an application document are inserted in an action list. Users can display the action list and edit if required.

Work List: A work list contains actions that can be scheduled manually.

Notes:

i. In a few cases (like when printing a PI document, HU label, etc.), **the PPF configuration is more complex and requires additional configuration** like defining condition tables, access sequence, condition maintenance group, condition records, and so on. For easy understanding, this configuration is explained in detail in chapter 20, PI, under the "Print Physical Inventory Document" section.

ii. Depending on the PPF area, the following transaction may be useful and are available in the SAP easy access menu.

- /SCWM/PRHU5: Create Logical Conditions for Printing (HUs)
- /SCWM/PRWO5: Create Logical Conditions for Printing (Warehouse Orders)
- /SCWM/PRHU6: Create Condition Records for Printing (HUs)
- /SCWM/PRWO6: Create Condition Records for Printing (Warehouse Orders)
- /SCWM/PRPI_GCM: Create Condition Records for Printing (Physical Inventory)
- /SCWM/DLVPPFC: Maintain Condition Records for PPF Schedule Conditions
- /SCWM/PRT_CT_EXT: Enhance Print Condition Tables

Summary

This chapter explained what PPF is, why it is used, and how it can be configured in the EWM system. Because PPF is widely used in EWM, it is important for consultants to know how it works.

Chapter 19: Internal Warehouse Movements

Internal warehouse movements generally refer to PCNs, replenishments, and bin-to-bin transfers. Bin-to-bin transfers are also called as ad-hoc transfers. This chapter will discuss all three topics along with the configuration and example. By the end of each section, how to execute business transactions in each of these areas will also be explained.

19.1 Posting Change Notice (PCN)

PCN deals primarily with changes in information related to a warehouse stock, such as changing unrestricted stock to quality inspection stock, sales order stock to non-sales order stock, change in product or batch number, and so on. In most of these cases, the physical location of the stock doesn't change. It is only the status or the attributes of the stock that changes. In some cases, relabeling of the stock may be required in the warehouse. For all these stock status changes, EWM system creates a PCN document which needs to be processed to synchronize the stock between ERP and EWM system.

In the system, PCN can be triggered either from ERP or within EWM. Diagram 19.1A shows an overview of the process flow for PCN initiated in the ERP system.

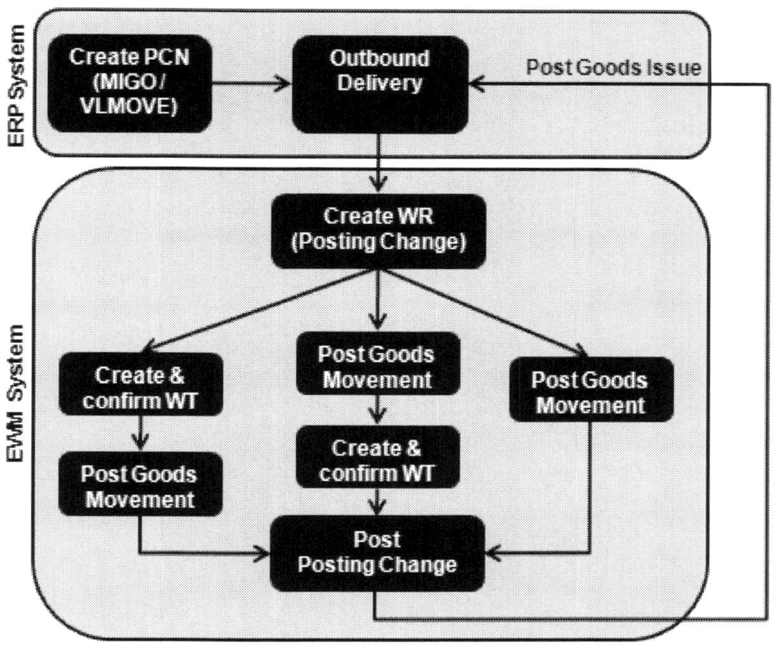

Diagram 19.1A – Posting Change Process (initiated in the ERP System)

In ERP, PCN can be initiated from various transactions. The most widely used transactions are "MIGO" for transfer posting, or "VLMOVE" for HUs. Both of these transactions will create an outbound delivery, which gets transferred to the EWM system and becomes a warehouse request document. In the warehouse, depending on the business requirements, the PCN-related warehouse request can be processed in three different ways.

- Create and confirm the WT, which will post the goods movement.
- First, post the goods movement and then create and confirm the WT for manual processing.
- Only post the goods movement. No WTs are created in this case.

The first two options are set up for manual processing, and the third option is completely automated. All these settings are triggered from the WPT. Only after the PCN document is processed in the EWM system, automatic goods issue will be posted for the outbound deliveries created in the ERP system.

On the other hand, a change can also be created directly in the EWM system. The goods movement for posting change created in EWM is communicated to the ERP system via the goods movement interface, as shown below.

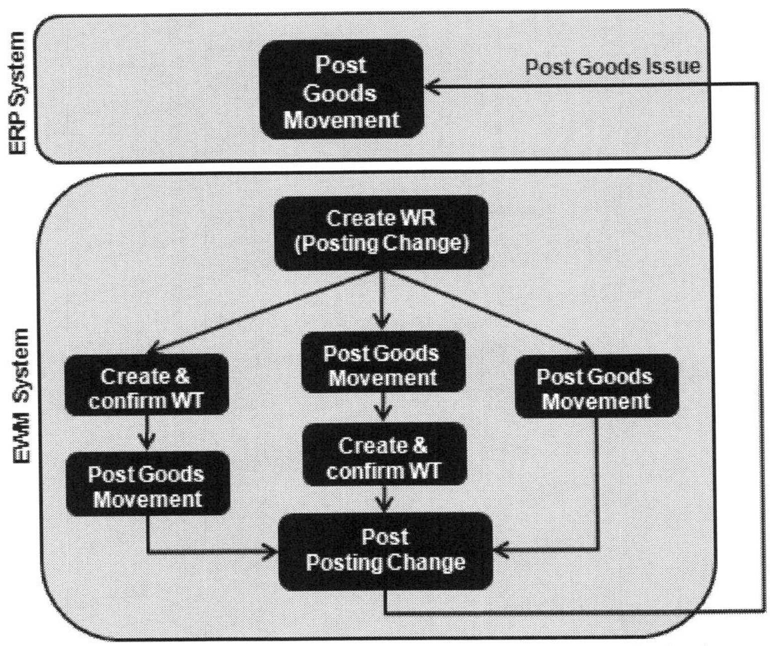

Diagram 19.1A – Posting Change Process (initiated in EWM System)

The following sections will discuss the configuration required for the PCN. Most of these configuration objects were already covered in detail in the earlier chapters. Hence, they will only be covered here with a brief note for such objects and will provide a screenshot and the configuration path for easy understanding.

19.1.1 Activities and Activity Areas

Activities and activity areas are required to process the PCN. Separate activity areas can be defined for PCN, or only an activity can be created and assigned to the existing activity area. Details on activities and activity areas were covered in chapter 5.

- **Define Activities**

Here, new activity can be defined or SAP delivered activity 'STCH" can be used. In either cases the processing category for the activity should be "7—Posting Change."

Menu Path: SPRO | IMG | Extended Warehouse Management | Master Data | Activity Areas | Activities | Define Activities

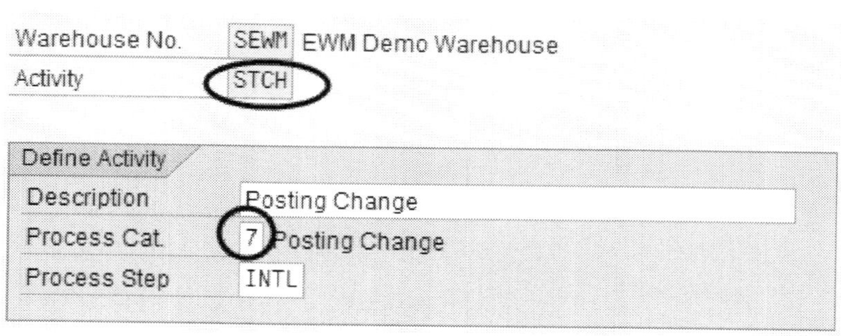

- **Define Activity Area**

In the following example, a separate activity area has been created for PCN for easy understanding.

Menu Path: SPRO | IMG | Extended Warehouse Management | Master Data | Activity Areas | Define Activity Area

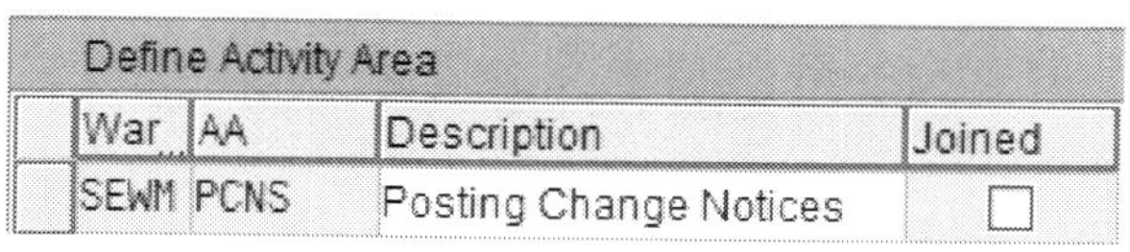

- **Assign Storage Bins to Activity Areas**

Under this section, the bins are assigned to activity areas. Because the PCN can be posted in the same bin, all the bins must be assigned to PCN activity areas.

	War	AA	Seq	Storage Type	Aisle Start	Aisle End	Level St	Level E	Bin	Bin
	SEWM	PCNS	1		A	Z	1	10	01	99

Activity Area

Menu Path: SPRO | IMG | Extended Warehouse Management | Master Data | Activity Areas | Assign Storage Bins to Activity Areas

▶ Define Sort Sequence for Activity Area

Because the PCN is generally only a notice of status change, and the products are not moved from the bin, it is not required to assign a sort sequence for the activity area. However, if a business requires bin movements, a sort sequence can be defined for the activity area to sort the bins.

Menu Path: SPRO | IMG | Extended Warehouse Management | Master Data | Activity Areas | Define Sort Sequence for Activity Area

Sort Sequence for Storage Bins

	War	AA	Activity	Seq	Stor	Sort Seq.	Sort Aisle	Sort Stack
	SEWM	PCNS	STCH	1				

▶ Sort Storage Bins (TCode /SCWM/SBST)

If the sort sequence is defined for the PCN activity area, the bins for the activity area must be sorted.

WhN	Storage Bin	Activity	Seq. No.	AA	Typ	Section	Sort Seq.
SEWM	A01-001-01	STCH	1	PCNS	0005	0001	1
SEWM	A01-001-02	STCH	1	PCNS	0005	0001	2
SEWM	A01-001-03	STCH	1	PCNS	0005	0001	3
SEWM	A01-001-04	STCH	1	PCNS	0005	0001	4
SEWM	A01-001-05	STCH	1	PCNS	0005	0001	5

19.1.2 Define Warehouse Process Type (WPT)

This section will cover the PCN-related settings required for the PCN-specific WPT. The standard SAP WPT for PCN is 4010.

Here, two important sections for PCN are "General Settings" and "Settings for Posting Changes."

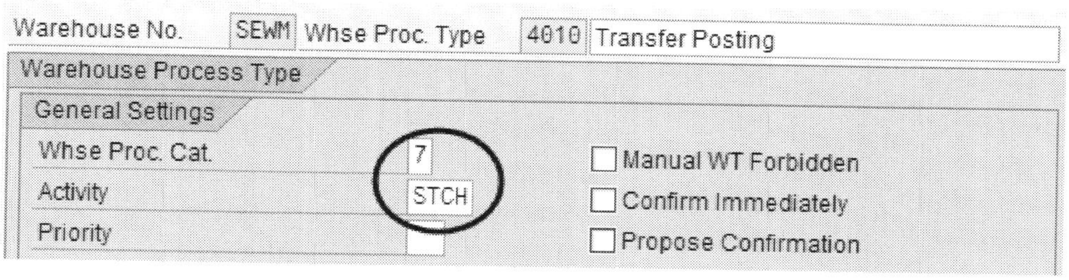

In the "General Settings" section, assign the warehouse process category as "7—Posting Change" and the activity defined for PCN.

In the "Settings for Posting Changes" section, the posting change bin setting, exception code, and the goods movement indicator, if the goods movement is posted before creating the WT can be defined.

"Posting Change in Bin" defines whether or not a WT should be created for PCN. If no inventory movement is required for the PCN, the value in this field must be blank. These settings can also be defined at the storage type level.

19.1.3 Define Document Types for Posting Change Process

SAP has provided document type TWPR for posting change. The standard delivered document categories are POR for posting change request and SPC for the posting change.

Menu Path: SPRO | IMG | Extended Warehouse Management | Internal Warehouse Processes | Delivery Processing | Posting Changes | Manual Settings | Define Document Types for Posting Change Process

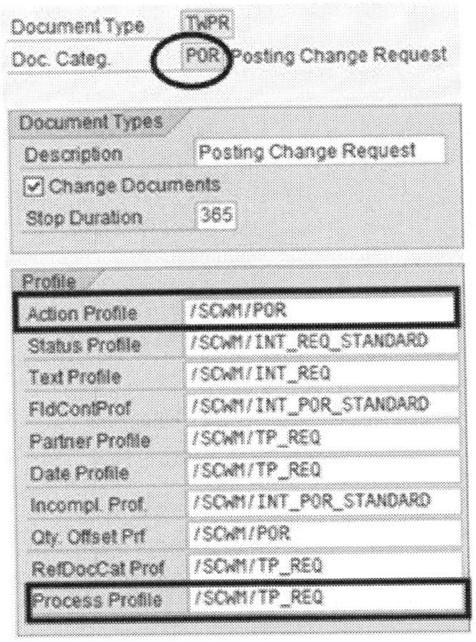

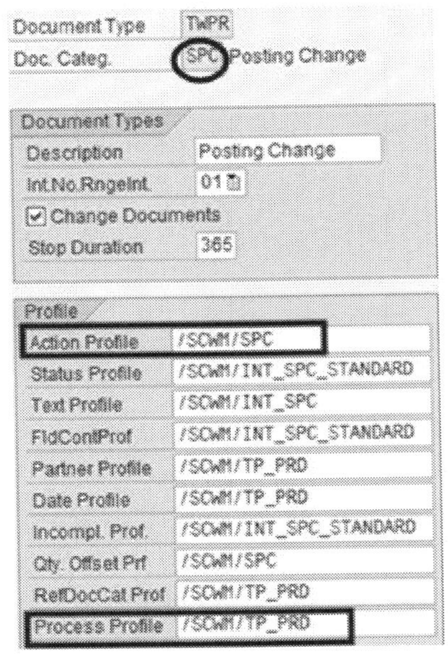

19.1.4 Process Profiles for Document Type

SAP has provided process profile /SCWM/TP_PRD for document category SPC and /SCWM/TP_REQ for document category POR. In the above menu, both of these categories are assigned to the document type TWPR. The processing profile describes how the processing of posting change request and posting change documents are controlled in the EWM system. The settings for process profiles can be viewed in menu path **SPRO | IMG | Extended Warehouse Management | Cross-Process Settings | Delivery Processing | Process Management and Control | Define Process Profile for Delivery Document Header**

Process Profile Delivery

Process Profile	Description	Process Profile	Creat	Predecess	Production	Scrap	Pickup	Inv Bef GI	Correction
/SCWM/TP_PRD	Std Posting Change	/SCWM/TP_PRD	A All	Predec	Disallc	Disal	Disa	D Disal	Disallc
/SCWM/TP_REQ	Stk Transfer Reqt Standard	/SCWM/TP_REQ	C Dis	A Predec	Disallc	Disal	Disa	D Disal	Disallc

19.1.5 Define Item Types for Posting Change Process

In addition to the document type configuration, item types for posting change documents must also be defined.

Menu Path: SPRO | IMG | Extended Warehouse Management | Internal Warehouse Processes | Delivery Processing | Posting Changes | Manual Settings | Define Item Types for Posting Change Process

The SAP-delivered item type for PCN is TWPR, the document category for posting change request is POR, and the document category for posting change is SPC.

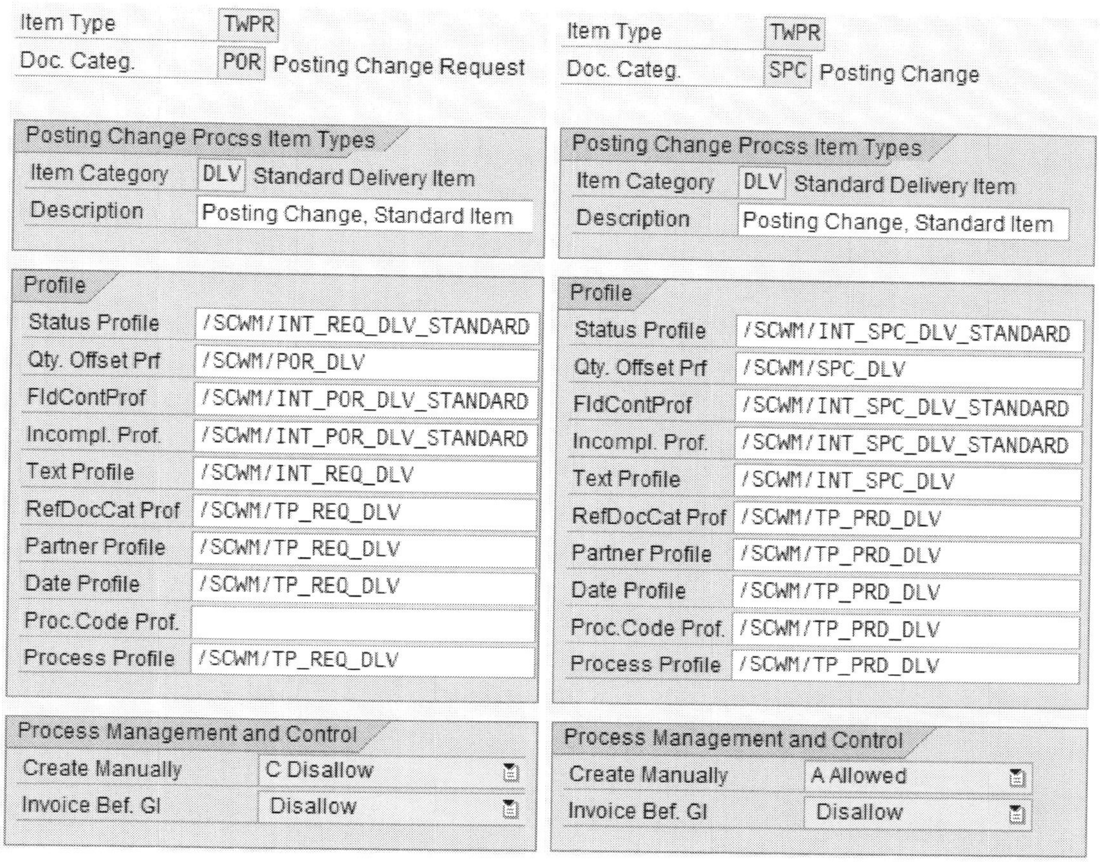

19.1.6 Map ERP Document and Item Type to EWM PCN Document Type

To get a posting change warehouse request document created in EWM for the ERP outbound delivery, the ERP document type and item type must be mapped to the EWM posting change document type.

Document types are assigned in menu path **SPRO | IMG | Extended Warehouse Management | Interfaces | ERP Integration | Delivery Processing | Map Document Types from ERP System to EWM**

Mapping Delivery Type - Document Type			
Business System	DocTypeERP	Cde Init. Com.	Doc. Type
	DTR		TWPR
	HTP		TWPR

In standard SAP configuration, two ERP document types (DTR and HTP) are assigned to EWM document type TWPR. No additional settings are required for these document types.

Item type mapping is done in menu path **SPRO | IMG | Extended Warehouse Management | Interfaces | ERP Integration | Delivery Processing | Map Item Types from ERP System to EWM**

Mapping of ERP Item Type						
Busine...	DocT...	ItmTpERP	Doc....	Diff.A...	CW Product	Item Type
	DTR	HSTP			☐	TWPR

19.1.7 Storage Type Search Sequence for Stock Removal

In order to determine the bin for PCN, it is necessary to assign a storage type search sequence to the WPT.

Menu Path: SPRO | Extended Warehouse Management | Goods Issue Process | Strategies | Determine Storage Type Search Sequence for Stock Removal

Determine Storage Type Search Sequence: Stock Removal											
War...	2	SRCI	Wh...	Q	Stoc...	Tpe	Use	H...	HazRat2	Stor...	Re...
SEWM	☐	PICK	4010							PICK	

19.1.8 Determine Warehouse Process Type

In case of custom WPTs, the WPT must be assigned to the document type.

Menu Path: SPRO | Extended Warehouse Management | Cross-Process Settings | Warehouse Task | Determine Warehouse Process Type

Determination of Warehouse Process Type						
War...	Doc....	Item...	Del.Prio.	ProTypeDet	Process Ind.	WhseP...
SEWM	TWPR		0		No Special Pr	4010

19.1.9 Maintain Delivery-Relevant Data in the ERP System

To initiate the posting change process in the ERP system, customer and vendor details for the movement type must be maintained in the ERP system. If the customer and vendor records do not exist for the plant, one dummy record can be created and transferred to the EWM system as a business partner. The ship-to party data defined here is used for outbound delivery, and the vendor number is used for inbound deliveries.

The configuration path to maintain vendor and ship-to party for the deliveries in the ERP system is **SPRO | IMG | Logistics Execution | Decentralized WMS Integration | Central Processing | Application | Define Interface to Inventory Management and Delivery-Relevant Data**

Here, double-click on "Delivery-Relevant Parameters for Reference Movement Type," locate the relevant movement types for posting change, and maintain the ship-to party and vendor number.

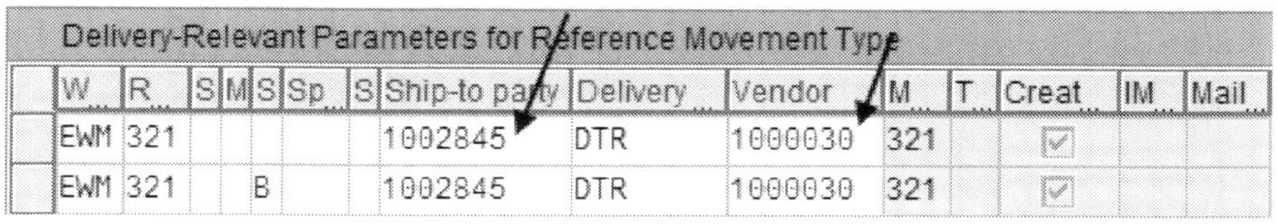
Delivery-Relevant Parameters for Reference Movement Type

W...	R...	S	M	S	Sp...	S	Ship-to party	Delivery...	Vendor	M...	T...	Creat...	IM...	Mail
EWM	321						1002845	DTR	1000030	321		☑		
EWM	321			B			1002845	DTR	1000030	321		☑		

19.1.10 Create Posting Change for Product in EWM

As discussed earlier, the posting change can be initiated either in the ERP system or in the EWM system. In the following example, it will be initiated in the EWM system.

To create a posting change document for a product, go to transaction **/SCWM/POST.** The menu path is **SAP Easy Access | SAP menu | Extended Warehouse Management | Work Scheduling | /SCWM/POST—Make Posting Change for Product**

In this transaction, users can create either a direct posting change or a posting change via a warehouse request. Changing the destination bin for PCN quantity is only possible with a warehouse request document.

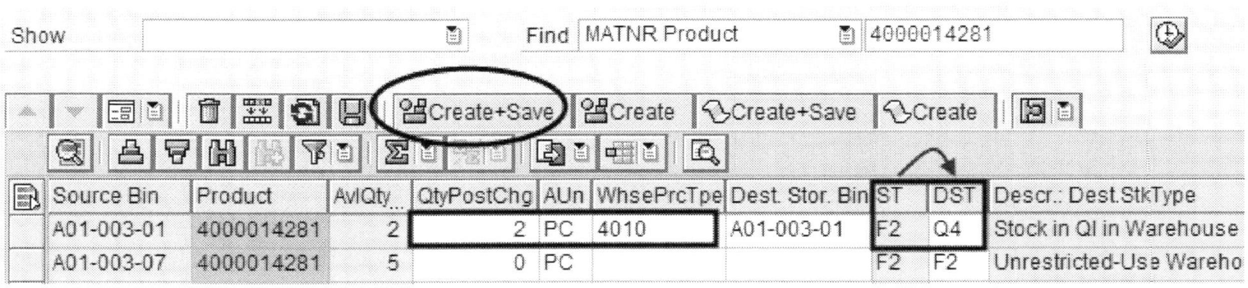

Source Bin	Product	AvlQty...	QtyPostChg	AUn	WhsePrcTpe	Dest. Stor. Bin	ST	DST	Descr.: Dest.StkType
A01-003-01	4000014281	2	2	PC	4010	A01-003-01	F2	Q4	Stock in QI in Warehouse
A01-003-07	4000014281	5	0	PC			F2	F2	Unrestricted-Use Wareho

Once the posting change is posted in the EWM system, information for PCN will be transferred to the ERP system via the goods movement interface. In the ERP system, the system will select the appropriate movement type to post the stock changes, based on the configuration, and will create a material document.

The following screenshot displays the material document posted in the ERP system for the stock change in the EWM system.

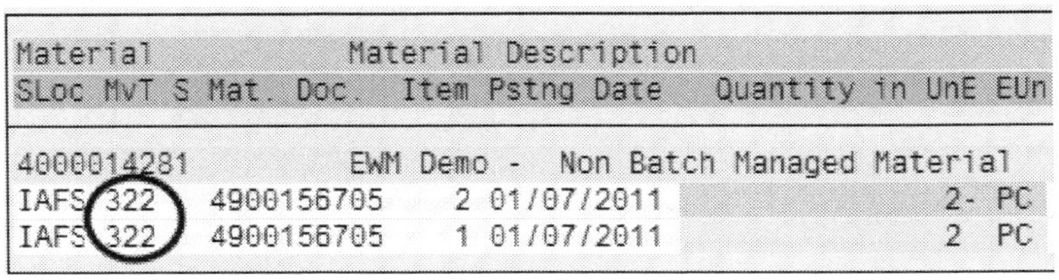

19.1.11 Create Posting Change for Product in the ERP System

Posting change can be initiated in the ERP from many transactions. The most widely used transactions are MIGO for transfer postings (without HU) and VLMOVE transaction for HU-related transfer posting. In case storage locations are EWM managed, the creation of posting change in the ERP system will trigger an outbound delivery and will be transferred to the EWM system. The standard delivery type for non-HU managed stock will be DTR; and for HU-managed outbound delivery, the delivery type will be HTP.

If the vendor and ship-to party data is not maintained in the configuration, users can manually enter these details in the MIGO transaction, as shown below.

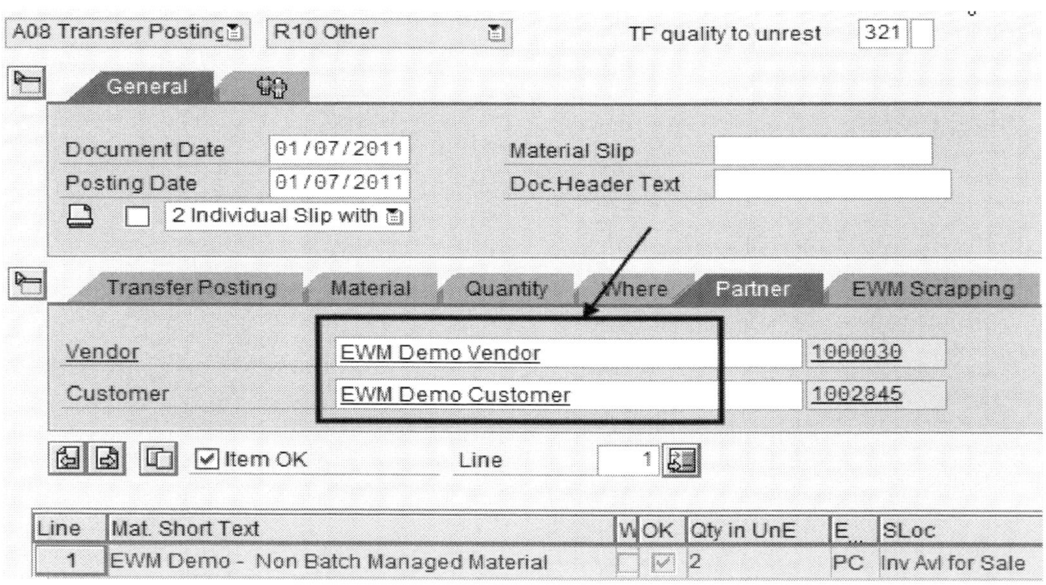

The delivery created in the ERP system will be transferred to the EWM system via qRFC. In the EWM system, it can be located in transaction **/SCWM/IM_DR** (menu path is **SAP Easy Access | SAP menu | Extended Warehouse Management | Delivery Processing | Posting Change | Maintain Posting Change Request**). Here, enter the ERP delivery number in the "Posting Change Requirement" field and click "Execute." This will display the posting change request document.

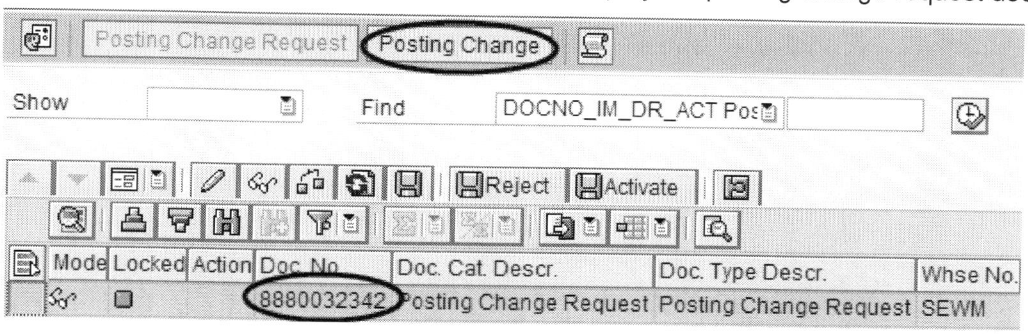

Select the document line and click the "Posting Change" button. This will create the posting change for the outbound delivery in the EWM system.

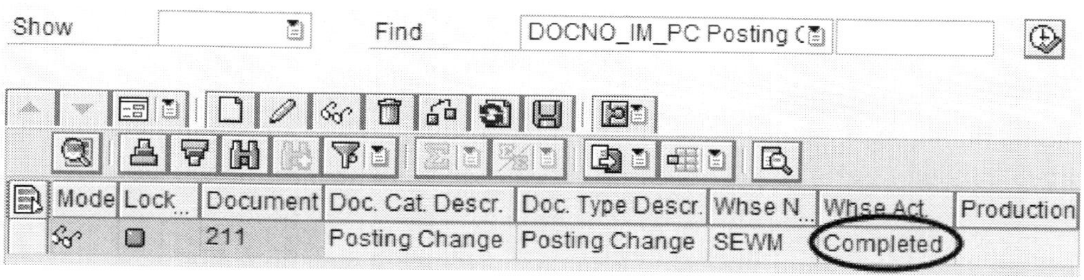

If the document is not processed automatically due to missing bin details, these details can be entered manually to process the document. To create WTs for PCN, the configuration must be set to create WTs, which can be created for the posting change document from menu path **Posting Change | Follow-On-Functions | Warehouse Task**

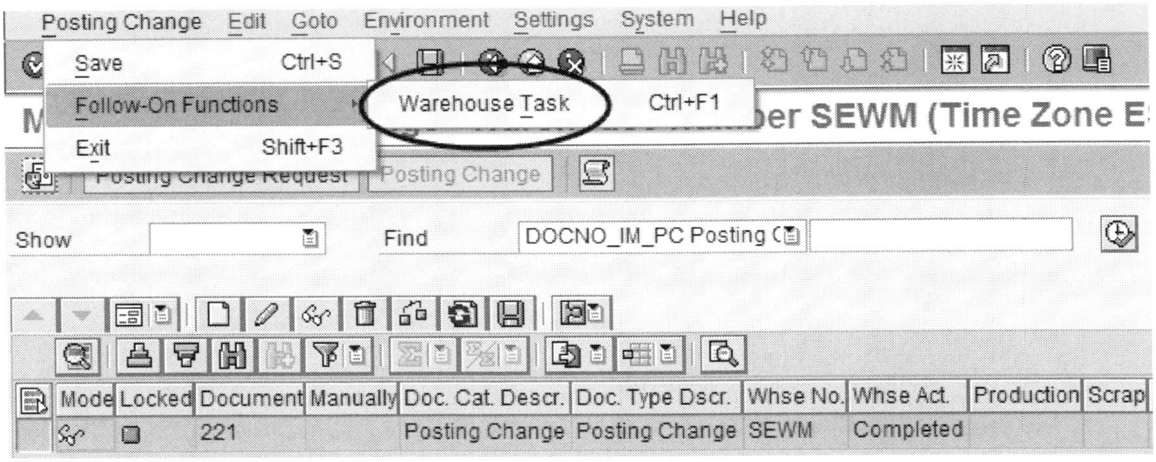

19.2 Ad-Hoc Stock Transfers

Ad-hoc stock transfers usually deal with the physical movement of products from one bin to another without a reference document. In the warehouse, this is also called bin-to-bin transfer. In EWM, TCode /SCWM/ADPROD can be used to transfer products and /SCWM/ADHU to transfer HUs.

Menu Path: SAP Easy access | SAP menu | Extended Warehouse Management | Work Scheduling | Create Warehouse Task without Reference | /SCWM/ADPROD—Move Product or /SCWM/ADHU—Move Handling Unit

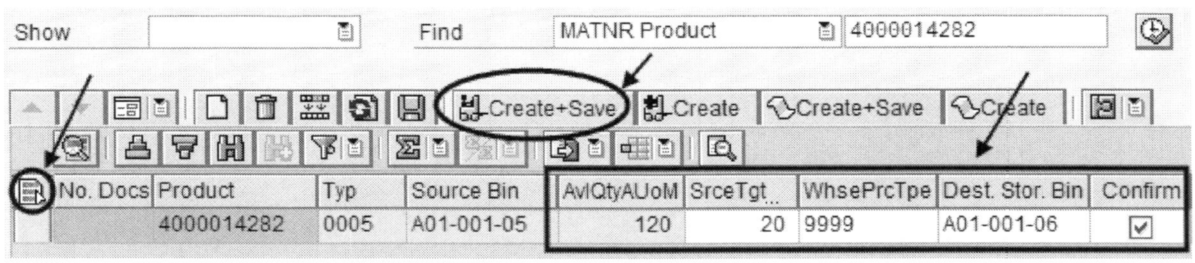

In this transaction, users can display the bin stock for the products. In order to move the stock from one bin to another, select the line items where the products should be transferred from, enter the transfer quantity, enter the WPT (SAP delivered process type is 9999), enter the destination bin, and check the "Confirm" checkbox to confirm the WT immediately. Finally, click "Create + Save" to create the WT. This will transfer the stock between bins.

19.3 Replenishment

Replenishment is a warehouse process that is used to ensure that there is enough stock available for picking. In this process, the picking bins are filled from one or more reserve storage areas.

In EWM, there are four basic methods of replenishment:

- Planned Replenishment
- Automatic Replenishment
- Order-Related Replenishment
- Direct Replenishment

For each storage type allowed replenishment types can be defined.

Planned and Automatic Replenishment

In both planned and automatic replenishment methods, the system uses the minimum, maximum, and replenishment quantities from the product master to trigger the replenishment process. The only difference between these two methods is that the automatic replenishment is triggered during the WT confirmation, whereas the planned replenishment is triggered manually or scheduled in the background as a batch job. Common features of planned and automatic replenishment methods include the following:

- Calculates replenishment quantity, according to maximum and minimum quantity of the product master
- Only started when the stock figure gets lower than the minimum quantity
- Rounds down to multiples of minimum replenishment quantity

Order-Related Replenishment

This method takes into account all open warehouse request (WR) quantities for products. The features of order-related replenishment include the following:

- Can be started online or in batch mode
- Calculates replenishment quantity according to open WR quantity
- Started when stock is lower than the required quantity.
- Rounds up to multiple of minimum replenishment quantity

- Exceeding maximum quantity is possible

Direct Replenishment

Direct replenishment is triggered from the exception code during a pick denial and is only possible for fixed-bin scenarios. The exception code is configured with an internal process code that will trigger the replenishment of the product. This is also called picker-directed replenishment.

The main features of the direct replenishment are as follows:

- Started during a pick denial when exception code points to the internal process code "Replenishment"
- Only possible for fixed-bin scenarios
- Calculates replenishment according to maximum and minimum quantity
- Assumes that the bin quantity is zero at the time of pick denial
- Rounds down to multiples of minimum replenishment quantity
- Picker performs the replenishment

The following sections describe the configuration required for the fixed-bin replenishment process. The example will refer to a simple business scenario where a primary storage type (0050) is replenished from several reserve storage types.

19.3.1 Define Storage Type

To test fixed-bin replenishment, define a storage type for fixed bins. SAP has provided storage type "0050—Fixed Bin Storage type" in warehouse 0001.

Menu Path: SPRO | IMG | Extended Warehouse Management | Master Data | Define Storage Type

In EWM, more than one fixed bin can be assigned per material. Under the general settings, enter the desired number of fixed bins per material and check the "Use Fixed Bins" check box.

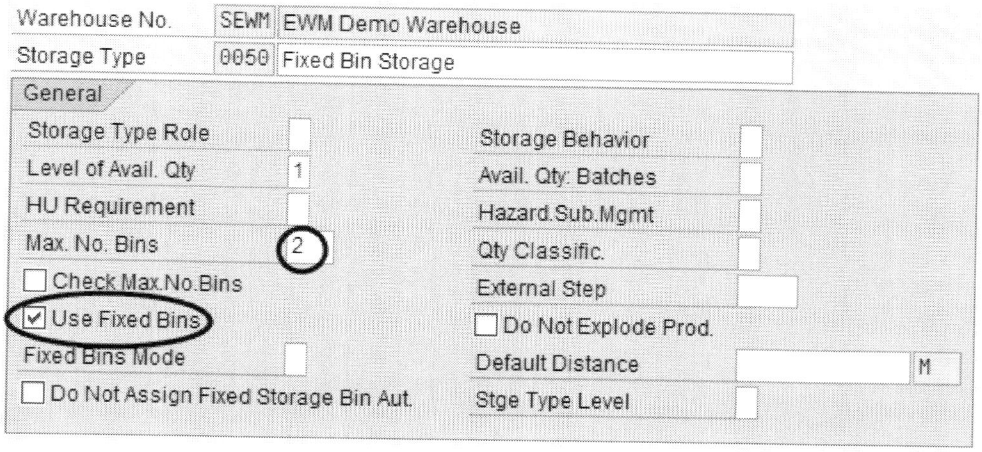

Under replenishment settings, select an appropriate replenishment level. Replenishment level "1—At Storage Type" means the product replenishment will be based on the total quantity available in the storage type. In this case, the system will consider minimum and maximum quantities defined in the product master to calculate the replenishment quantity. Users can also choose to replenish stock for individual fixed bins based on the minimum and maximum data defined at the storage bin. In this case, select the "Storage Bin Level for Fixed Bins" replenishment level.

19.3.2 Verify Activities and Activity Areas

Activities and activity areas are required to process the replenishment. Separate activity areas can be defined for replenishment, or an activity can be created and assigned to an existing activity area. More details of activities and activity areas were covered in chapter 5.

▶ Define Activities

The standard SAP-delivered activity for replenishment is REPL. The processing category for this activity type must be assigned to "3—Internal Warehouse Movements."

Menu Path: SPRO | IMG | Extended Warehouse Management | Master Data | Activity Areas | Activities | Define Activities

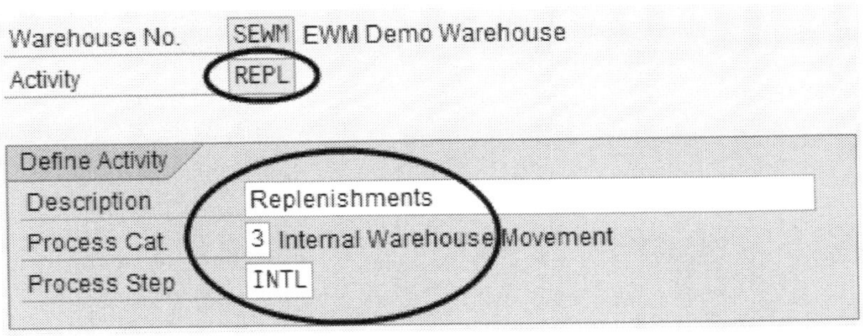

► Define Activity Area

Here, an activity area called "REPL" has been defined for easy understanding.

Menu Path: SPRO | IMG | Extended Warehouse Management | Master Data | Activity Areas | Define Activity Area

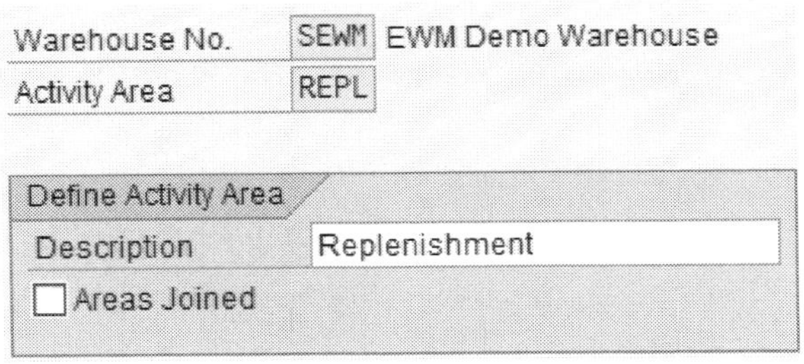

► Assign Storage Bins to Activity Areas

In this section, bins are assigned to the activity areas for the replenishment process.

Menu Path: SPRO | IMG | Extended Warehouse Management | Master Data | Activity Areas | Assign Storage Bins to Activity Areas

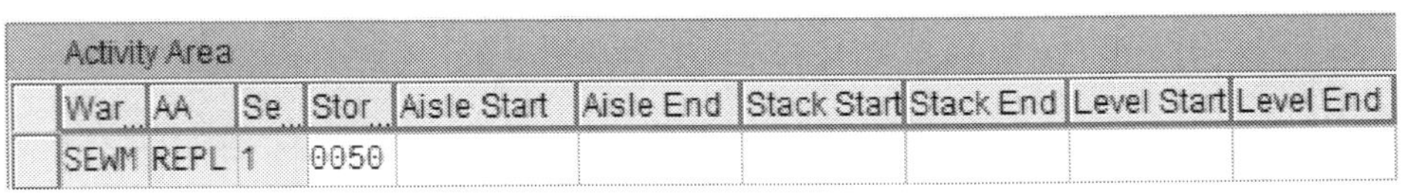

Activity Area

War	AA	Se	Stor	Aisle Start	Aisle End	Stack Start	Stack End	Level Start	Level End
SEWM	REPL	1	0050						

- **Define Sort Sequence for Activity Area**

Here, the sort sequence for the activity areas can be defined.

Menu Path: SPRO | IMG | Extended Warehouse Management | Master Data | Activity Areas | Define Sort Sequence for Activity Area

Sort Sequence for Storage Bins

War...	AA	Activity	Seque...	Stor...	Sort Seq.	Sort Aisle
SEWM	REPL	REPL	1	0050	1 Sort Sequence: Stack,	2 Descending

- **Sort Storage Bins (TCode /SCWM/SBST)**

If the sort sequence is defined for the activity area, the bins must be sorted before performing the replenishment.

WhN	Storage Bin	Activity	Seq. No.	AA	Typ	Section	Sort Seq.
SEWM	IX01-005-02	REPL	1	REPL	0050	0001	1
SEWM	IX01-005-04	REPL	1	REPL	0050	0001	2
SEWM	IX01-005-06	REPL	1	REPL	0050	0001	3

19.3.3 Define and Determine Warehouse Process Type

The predefined WPT for replenishment is "3010." Two important settings in this process type are the warehouse process category (i.e., "3—Internal Warehouse Movement") and the activity. Earlier chapters have already explained in WPT detail. The 3010 process type is available in SAP delivered template warehouse 0001 and can be copied the new warehouse.

Menu Path: SPRO | IMG | Extended Warehouse Management | Cross-Process Settings | Warehouse Task | Define Warehouse Process Type

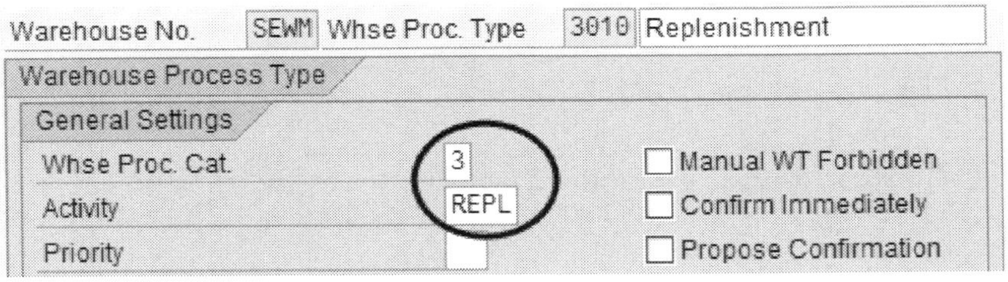

Under "Settings for Warehouse Request," verify the document and item types. The document and item types used for replenishment are "SRPL—Replenishment." They must be assigned to the warehouse process type. This document and item type is used when the warehouse request document created for the replenishment.

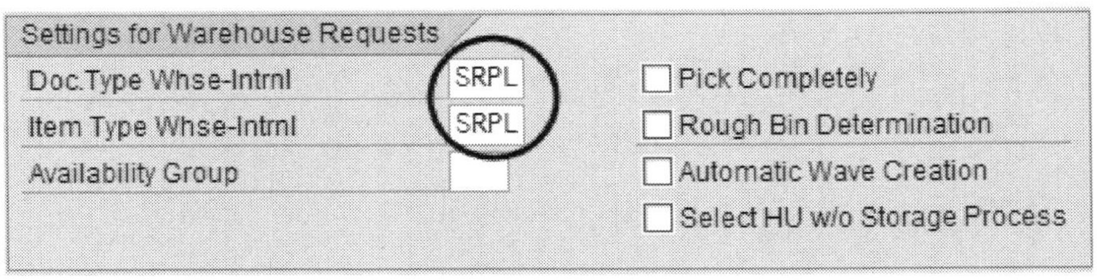

In order to determine the right WPT for replenishment, WPT must be assigned to the warehouse number and replenishment document type.

Menu Path: SPRO | IMG | Extended Warehouse Management | Cross-Process Settings | Warehouse Task | Determine Warehouse Process Type

Determination of Warehouse Process Type

War...	Doc. ...	Item ...	Del.Pr...	ProTyp...	Process Ind.	WhsePrcTpe
SEWM	SRPL				No Speci	3010

19.3.4 Activate Replenishment Strategies in Storage Types

The next important config step is activating the replenishment process for the storage types by assigning replenishment strategies. This menu defines the replenishment strategy, WPT, quantity type used, and WT creation settings for the storage type.

If the replenishment tasks are to be processed using wave functionality, the "WT Immed" check box should not be checked. The advantage of using wave functionality is that the replenishment-related wave can be released outside of peak picking hours. This might help the warehouse personnel manage their resources more effectively during peak hours.

Menu Path: **SPRO | IMG | Extended Warehouse Management | Internal Warehouse Processes | Replenishment Control | Activate Replenishment Strategies in Storage Types**

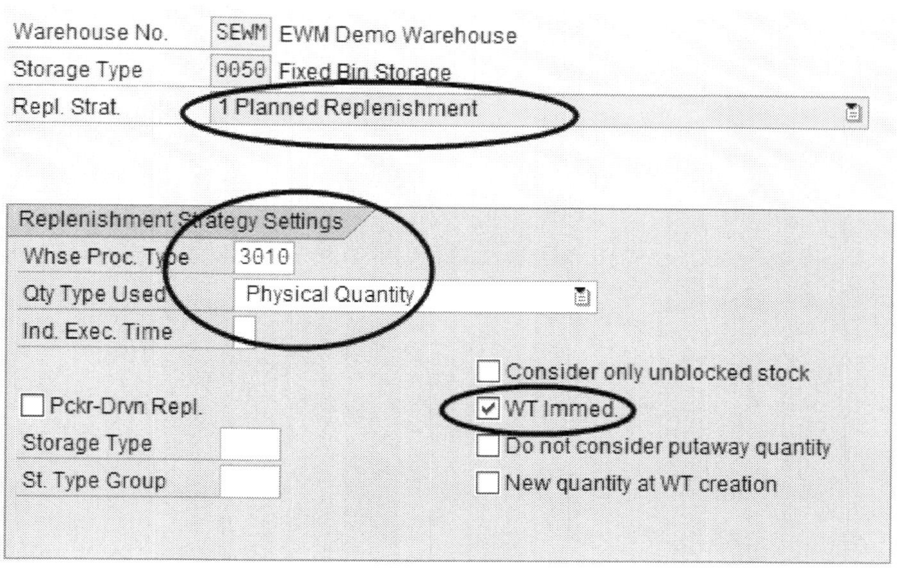

19.3.5 Specify Storage Type Search Sequence

This IMG activity defines a storage type search sequence for replenishment. While defining storage type search sequence, be sure that the storage type defined for replenishment (for example, 0050) is not included in the search sequence.

Menu Path: **SPRO | IMG | Extended Warehouse Management | Goods Issue Process | Strategies | Specify Storage Type Search Sequence**

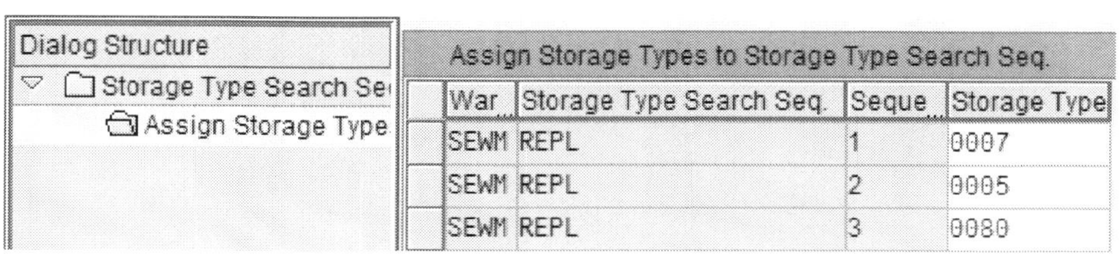

19.3.6 Determine Storage Type Search Sequence for Stock Removal

In order to determine the right storage type search sequence for replenishment, an appropriate entry must be made in the "Determine Storage Type Search Sequence for Stock Removal" table.

Menu Path: SPRO | IMG | Extended Warehouse Management | Goods Issue Process | Strategies | Determine Storage Type Search Sequence for Stock Removal

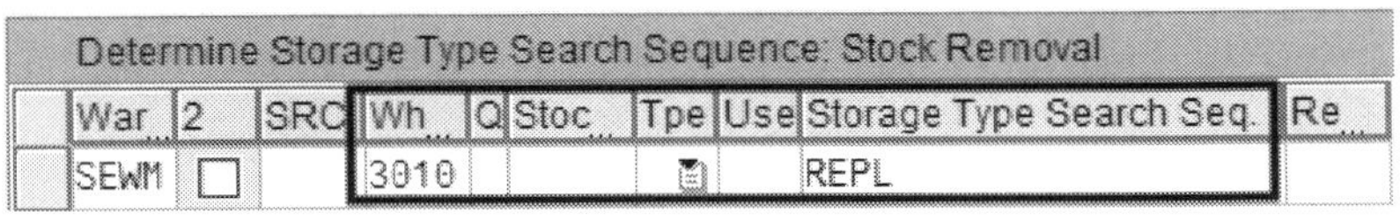

19.3.7 Maintain Fixed Storage Bin for a Product

For fixed-bin replenishment, the fixed bins must be maintained for products. In EWM, more than one fixed bin can be assigned under each storage type.

Menu Path: Easy Access | SAP menu | Extended Warehouse Management | Master Data | Storage Bin | Assign Fixed Storage Bins to Products or TCode **/SCWM/FBINASN**

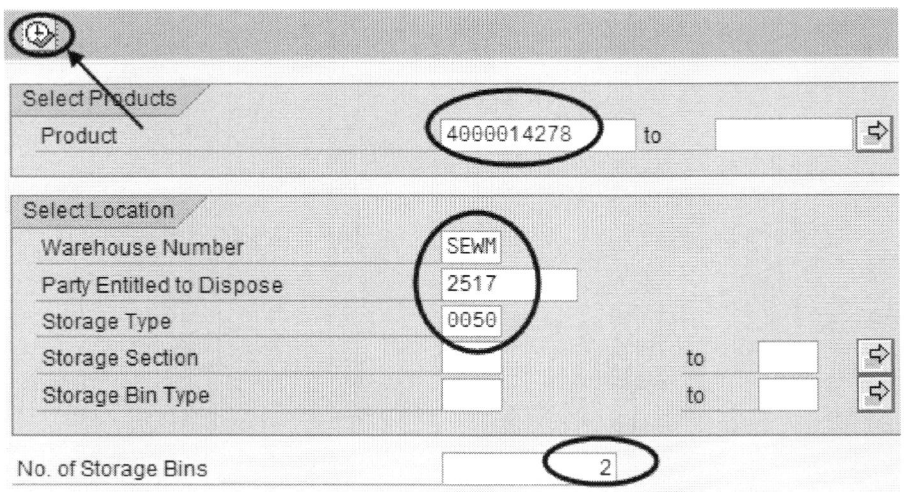

The transaction "Maintain Fixed Storage Bin" (TCode /SCWM/BINMAT) can be used to view or change the settings of the fixed bins.

To delete the fixed bin assignments, go to transaction "Delete Fixed Storage Bin Assignment" (TCode /SCWM/FBINDEL).

19.3.8 Create Storage Type View for Product Master

Depending on the replenishment type and/or the storage type settings (i.e., if the storage type settings are configured to consider the minimum and maximum quantities from the product master to calculate the replenishment quantity), it may be necessary to define the minimum, maximum, and replenishment quantity data in the product master.

Menu Path: SAP Easy Access | SAP menu | Extended Warehouse Management | Master Data | Product | Maintain Warehouse Product or **TCode /SCWM/MAT1**

Here, click on the "Storage Type Data" tab; enter the storage type, minimum replenishment quantity, minimum quantity, and maximum quantity, and click on "Adopt Data."

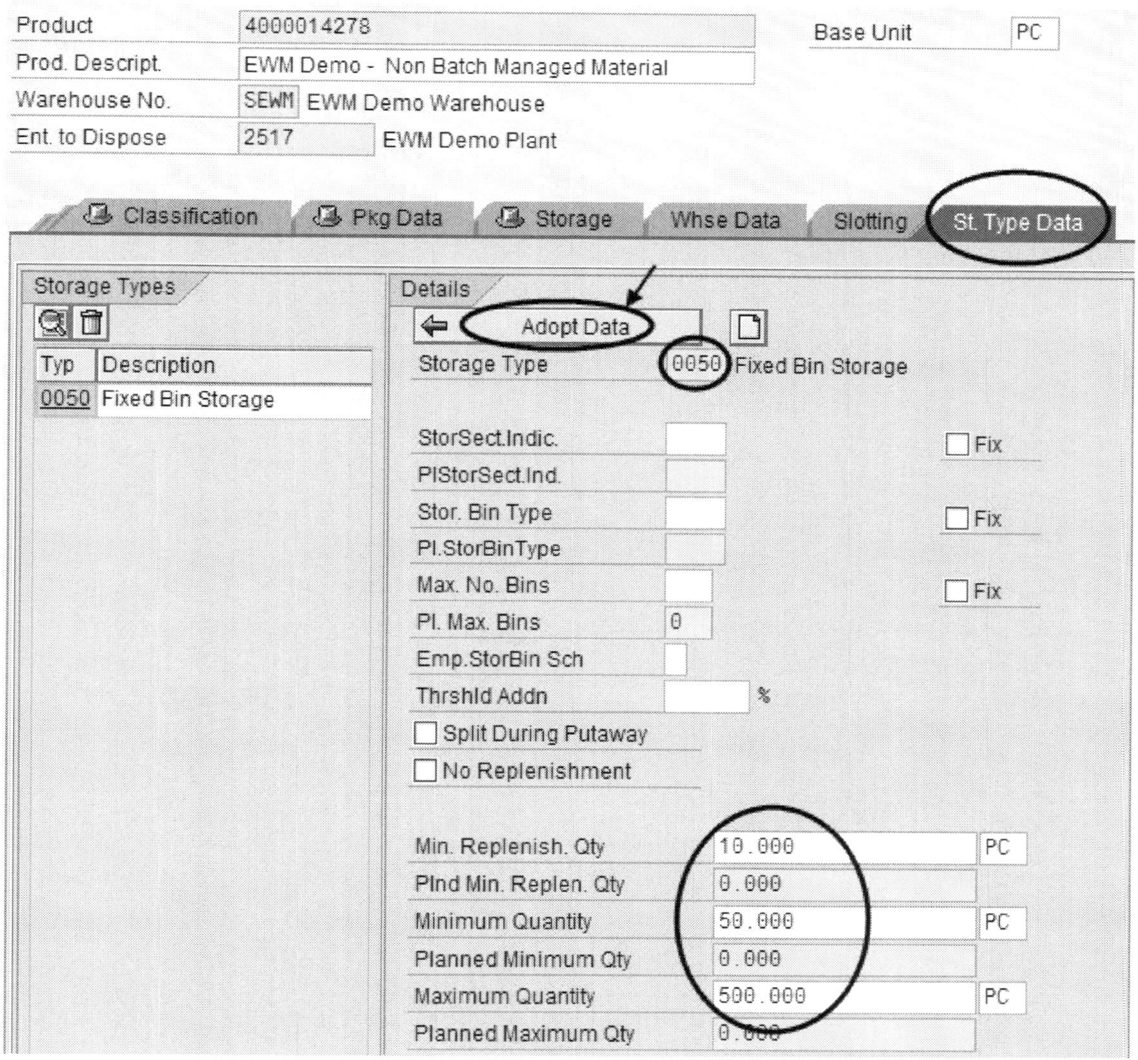

This covers all the settings required for the planned replenishment that needs to be maintained.

19.3.9 Execute Planned Replenishment

Planned replenishment can be executed from TCode /SCWM/REPL. The menu path is **SAP Easy Access | SAP menu | Extended Warehouse Management | Work Scheduling | Schedule Replenishment**

In this transaction, select the "Planned Replenishment" option; enter the warehouse number, party entitled to dispose, and product numbers, and click "Execute." This will display the planned replenishment items for the entered criteria.

Select the line items and click "Execute." This will create a warehouse request or WT, depending on the configuration settings.

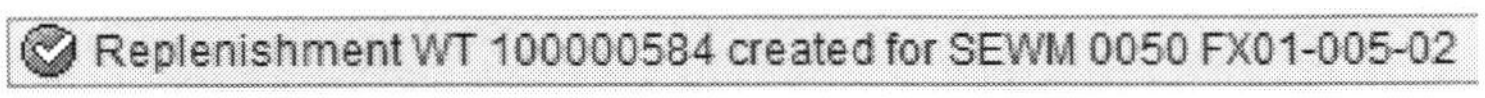

If the configuration is set only to create warehouse requests, use the transaction "Maintain Internal Stock Transfer" or TCode /SCWM/IM_ST to create a WT. Once the WT is created, verify the source bin, destination bin, and warehouse process type.

The TCode to confirm the WT is /SCWM/TO_CONF.

Summary

This chapter has explained posting change, ad-hoc stock transfers, and the different types of replenishment, along with the configuration and master data setup. The next chapter will cover PI in EWM.

Chapter 20: Physical Inventory (PI)

The PI process helps a company to keep control of the stock situation. Inventory needs to be kept track of for planning reasons, as well as because of legal requirements. In many companies, PI is mandated by the financial department or tax regulations, where the entire warehouse or all products must be inventoried at least once a year.

This chapter discusses in detail the process flow of the PI process, various PI procedures supported by EWM, and the configuration of PI methods. Here, consultants will also learn how to create PI documents, print count sheets, enter count results, and analyze and process of inventory differences in the EWM system. This chapter also covers how to use PPF functionality to print the PI document.

In EWM, physical inventory can be product specific or storage-bin specific. The difference between storage bin and product-specific counts is that in the storage-bin specific count, all of the products and HUs in that bin are counted; whereas in the product-specific count, particular products are counted that might exist in one or more bins or HUs. The product-specific count is used mostly for high-value products.

PI in EWM can be carried out for the following stock categories:

- Unrestricted stock in putaway
- Unrestricted stock in the warehouse
- Blocked stock in putaway
- Blocked stock in the warehouse
- Quality Inspection stock in putaway
- Quality Inspection stock in the warehouse

During the PI process, the relevant storage bins must be locked during the counting. However, this is not a requirement in the RF environment. As a prerequisite, at least one PI area must be created and assigned to the activity area.

In EWM, the warehouse is marked as completely inventoried once all the PI areas are counted. For product-specific inventory, a product is completely inventoried when all of the stocks of the product per physical inventory area and party entitled to dispose have been counted.

20.1 Physical Inventory Process Flow

PI documents contain the bins/products to be counted. They are usually created with inactivate status but can be activated at the time of document creation. In order to carry out the PI process, the PI document must be activated. The active PI documents can be printed using the PPF function and can be counted with or without RF framework.

After the initial count, a recount can be performed to determine any bins/products to be recounted. The recount selection can be based on value and/or quantity. After the inventory counting has been completed, the difference (if any) can be posted, completing the inventory process for that document. Diagram 20.1A provides an overview of the PI process flow in EWM system.

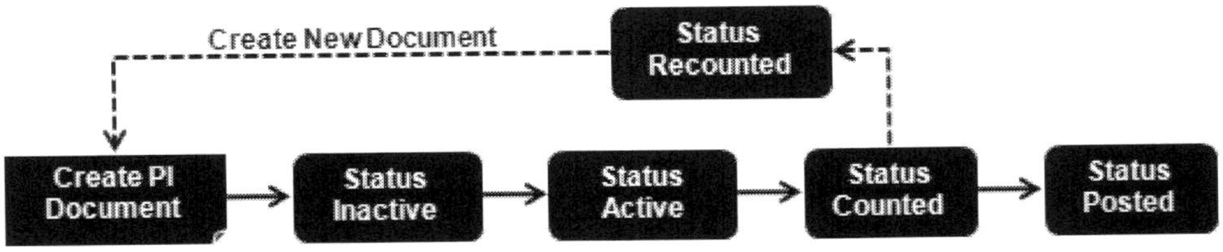

Diagram 20.1A – PI Process Flow

20.2 Physical Inventory Procedures

EWM supports the following three types of inventory procedures. All three can be implemented in the warehouse.

- Periodic Physical Inventory
- Continuous Physical Inventory
- Cycle Counting

20.2.1 Periodic Physical Inventory Procedure

Under this procedure, EWM supports both storage bin–specific annual PI and product-specific annual PI. Here, the stocks are counted on a certain day or within a fairly short period in this procedure. The stock movements can be blocked during this time.

20.2.2 Continuous Physical Inventory Procedure

This PI type is widely used in many warehouses and consists of the following inventory methods:

- Ad-Hoc Physical Inventory
- Low Stock Check

- Zero Stock Check
- Putaway Physical Inventory
- Storage Bin Check

20.2.2.1 Ad-hoc Physical Inventory

This is carried out at any time during the year to keep the physical bin stock in sync with the system stock. This method supports both product-specific as well as storage bin–specific inventory.

20.2.2.2 Low Stock Check

This is performed visually during WT confirmation, when the source bin contains only a small quantity after the stock removal. The low stock check is storage-bin specific. The quantity is defined in the form of a limit value that is based on the operative unit of measure for the product per storage type. The picker can check this stock level at a glance without having to do an explicit count. At the time of WT confirmation, picker can indicate that the low stock check has been executed in the RF or on the pick list. When the WT is confirmed, the system creates the PI document in the background on the basis of information in the WT.

20.2.2.3 Zero Stock Check (Storage-Bin Specific)

Zero stock check is a variant of the low stock check, with the limit value set as zero.

20.2.2.4 Putaway Physical Inventory (Storage-Bin Specific)

This is also similar to low stock check, but it occurs only at the time of putaway. It is carried out at the time of first putaway in the bin in the fiscal year. Here, the warehouse operator confirms during the first putaway that the stock in the storage bin matches the confirmed quantity in the WT after putaway. The system checks for the following conditions in this case:

- The storage bin is empty
- The stock is being putaway in the storage bin for the first time in the PI year
- Mixed storage is not permitted for the relevant storage type

If all conditions are met, the storage bin quantity becomes the same as WT quantity, and the system creates a PI document.

20.2.2.5 Storage Bin Check

Here, the actual stock of a product is not counted; instead, the operator checks whether or not a product is actually stored in the right storage bin. In many warehouses, this is not considered a PI method.

20.2.3 Cycle Counting Procedure

This is an inventory procedure in which only a small subset of stock is counted each day. It is an ongoing inventory procedure and is less disruptive than annual inventory, where the whole warehouse is counted within a short time frame.

EWM supports product-specific cycle counting. In cycle counting, the PI is carried out for products at regular intervals during a fiscal year. Here, the products are assigned to different classes (A, B, C, D, etc.), and the counting intervals for PI are assigned to these classes. This procedure allows fast-moving products to be counted more frequently than the slow-moving ones. The cycle counting indicator is maintained in the product master in the warehouse data view tab.

20.3 Physical Inventory Configuration

This section explains the required configuration and how to perform the basic PI transactions in the EWM system.

20.3.1 Define Physical Inventory Area

Physical inventory areas are defined first before doing any customizing settings for PI to specify whether:

- a putaway physical inventory is allowed (once per PI period)
- a low-stock/zero-stock physical inventory is allowed (once per PI period)
- a low-stock/zero-stock check is to be carried out when the WT is confirmed
- the document is to be posted automatically after the count (this depends on the user's allowed tolerance values)
- the book inventory is to be proposed at the time of the count and at the time of printout (does not apply to radio frequency environments)
- the product data is proposed for the storage-bin- specific physical inventory
- it is allowed to count a handling unit as complete
- the product data is included in printouts
- a serial number to be suggested when count results are entered

- Quantity threshold value for low-stock physical inventory or zero stock should be entered in the quantity field. If the value entered is zero, a zero check is triggered; otherwise, a low stock check is triggered. The unit of measure necessary to trigger the low-stock check is determined from the packing instructions

Menu Path: SPRO | IMG | Extended Warehouse Management | Internal Warehouse Processes | Physical Inventory | Physical-Inventory-Area-Specific Settings | Define Physical Inventory Area

Physical Inventory Area

Physic	Putaw	LSPI	LS Check	PstgAft	Dsp. Qty	Dsp.	HU	Print	Qty	Comp	Serial
0001	☑	☑	☑	☑	☑	☑	☑	☑		☐	☑

Once the PI Area is defined, in the dialog structure, double-click on "Permitted Document Types" and specify what types of PI procedures are allowed for the PI area. There can be more than one permitted document type for the PI area.

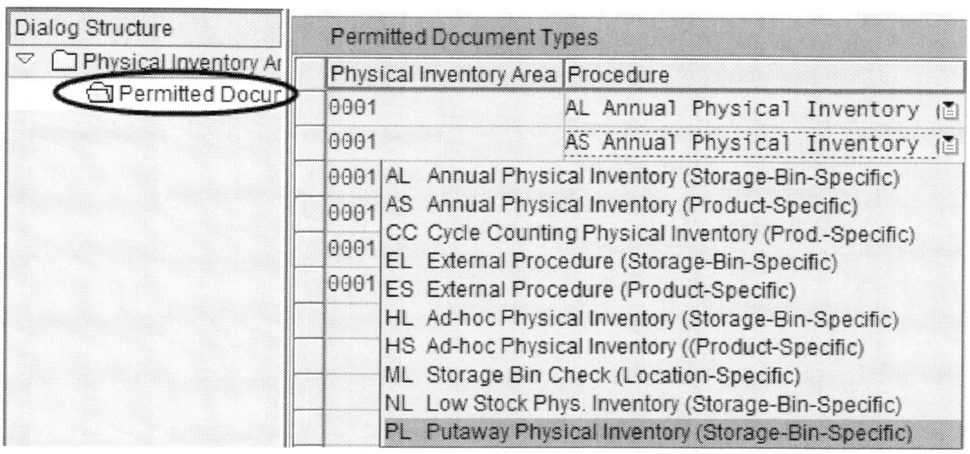

20.3.2 Configure Activities and Activity Areas

The following configuration has to be made in order to define a separate activity area for PI. For demonstration purposes, activity PHYS has been defined here. As the following topics have been covered several times in earlier chapters, they will not be covered in more detail here. All config items are located under menu path **SPRO | IMG | Extended Warehouse Management | Master Data | Activity Areas**

- **Define Activities**

Warehouse No.	SEWM	EWM Demo Warehouse
Activity	PHYS	

Define Activity

Description	Physical Inventory Movement
Process Cat.	4 Physical Inventory
Process Step	

- **Define Activity Area**

Define Activity Area

War	AA	Description	Joined
SEWM	PHYS	Physical Inventory	☐

- **Assign Storage Bins to Activity Areas**

Activity Area

War	AA	S..	Stor	Aisle Start	Aisle End	Stack Start	Stack End	Level Start	Level End	Bi..	Bin S
SEWM	PHYS	1		A	Z			1	10	01	99

- **Define Sort Sequence for Activity Area**

Sort Sequence for Storage Bins

War	AA	Activity	Se..	Stor..	Sort Seq.	Sort.Aisle	Sort.Stack	Dir.:Stack	Sort LEvel	PthDir.
SEWM	PHYS	PHYS	1							

- **Sort Storage Bins (TCode /SCWM/SBST)**

WhN	Storage Bin	Activity	Seq. No.	AA	Typ	Section	Sort Seq.
SEWM	A01-001-01	PHYS	1	PHYS	0005	0001	1
SEWM	A01-001-02	PHYS	1	PHYS	0005	0001	2
SEWM	A01-001-03	PHYS	1	PHYS	0005	0001	3
SEWM	A01-001-04	PHYS	1	PHYS	0005	0001	4

20.3.3 Periodicity of Storage Bin Check

This sets the interval in work days, according to which a new PI is to be executed along with the buffer time in work days. Menu path is **SPRO | IMG | Extended Warehouse Management | Internal Warehouse Processes | Physical Inventory | Physical-Inventory-Area-Specific Settings |Periodicity of Storage Bin Check**

Storage Bin Check

War...	AA	Int.	BT
SEWM	PHYS	30	5

20.3.4 Assign Physical Inventory Area to Activity Area

PI can be performed once PI area has been assigned to an activity area. Menu path is **SPRO | IMG | Extended Warehouse Management | Internal Warehouse Processes | Physical Inventory | Warehouse-Number-Specific Settings | Assign Physical Inventory Area to Activity Area**

Assign Physical Inventory Area to Activity Area

Ware...	AA	Physical Inventory Area
SEWM	PHYS	0001

20.3.5 Define Number Ranges for Physical Inventory Documents

In the system, each PI document is uniquely identified with the document number. The system assigns the number to the PI document from the number ranges defined for PI documents.

Menu Path: SPRO | IMG | Extended Warehouse Management | Internal Warehouse Processes | Physical Inventory | Warehouse-Number-Specific Settings | Define Number Ranges for Physical Inventory Documents

NR Object: WME Phys. Inv. Doc.

Intervals

No	Year	From number	To number	Current number	Ext
01	2010	00000000000700000000	00000000000799999999	0	☐

20.3.6 Specify PI-Specific Settings in the Warehouse

Menu Path: SPRO | IMG | Extended Warehouse Management | Internal Warehouse Processes | Physical Inventory | Warehouse-Number-Specific Settings | Specify Physical-Inventory-Specific Settings in the Warehouse

Physical Inventory-Specific Settings in Warehouse

War	Currncy	Cal	Fis	Procedure	Owner	Party to Disp.	Corr.Perm.	Allowed P	No Tol.	NRI PI
SEWM	USD	US	12	ZPIPRC	☑	☑	☑	1.00	☐	01

For each warehouse number, the following should be specified:

- **Currency unit to use**

  The currency unit is used in the calculation of the product value. The product values are used in the tolerance level checking during inventory counting and clearing. They can be transferred from ERP to EWM system manually in transaction /SCWM/VALUATION_SET. The menu path is **SAP Easy Access | SAP menu | Extended Warehouse Management | Physical Inventory | Periodic Processing | Determine and Set Process from ERP.**

  The values stored in the EWM system are used only for reference. If the values are changed in the ERP system, they have to be manually updated in the EWM system.

- **Factory calendar to use**

  The factory calendar is used to distinguish between working and nonworking days. This is required for cycle counting to calculate the intervals in working days to determine when the next count is scheduled.

- **Period (fiscal year) to use:** The fiscal year period is usually defined by the APO and FICO consultants.

  Menu Path SPRO | IMG | Advanced Planning and Optimization | Supply Chain Planning | Service Parts Planning (SPP) | Basic Settings | Maintain Fiscal Year Variants.

  The following is an example for fiscal year having four special periods.

Dialog Structure
- Fiscal year varia
  - Periods
  - Period texts
  - Shortened Fi

Fiscal year variants

FV	Description	Year-depend	Calendar yr	Number of post	No.of special periods
12	EWM Demo	☐	☑	12	4

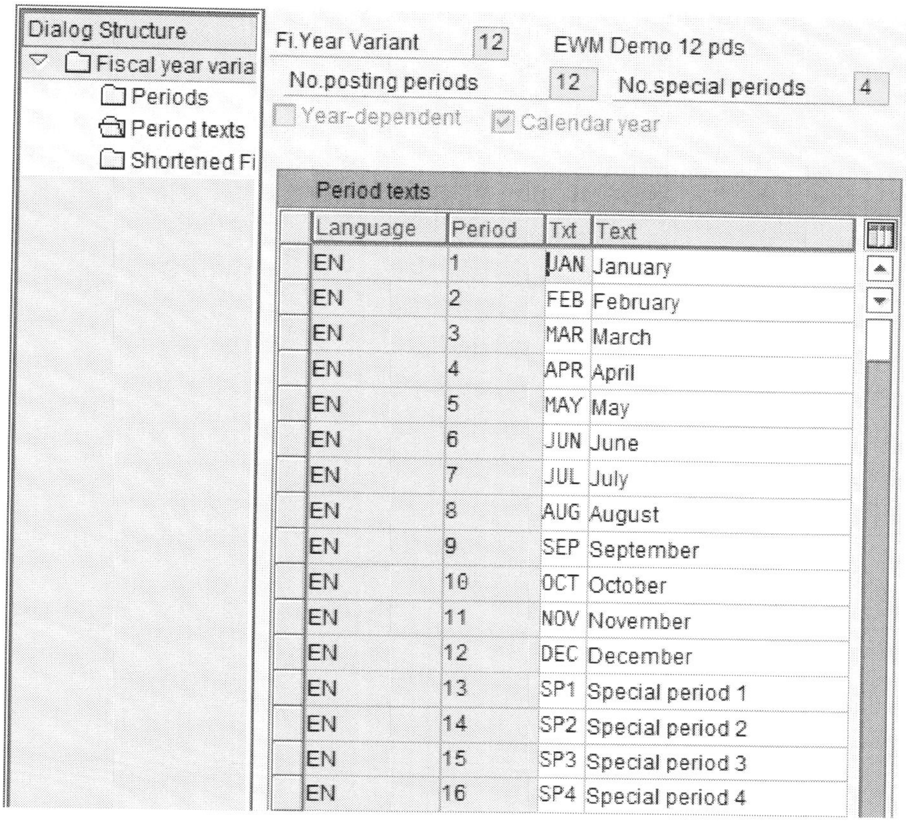

- **Determination procedure:** refers to the condition procedure for printing. Here, the "ZPIPRC" procedure has been defined, and the details are covered in section 20.3.17 under "Print Physical Inventory Document—PPF Action."
- **Number Range for PI documents:** used to generate unique number to the PI document.
- **Owner/Party Entitled to dispose:** if these parameters are selected, the owner and the party entitled to dispose are proposed in the PI count.
- **Correction Permitted:** This parameter should be selected if corrections to a PI document in the difference analyzer are to be allowed after the count has been posted.
- **Allowed Percentage and No Tolerance Check:** Here, a certain percentage of tolerance limits can be specified during the counting, which is used to prompt a warning message to the user to validate the entered count if necessary.

20.3.7 Configure Cycle Counting

For cycle counting, the following values must be maintained for each warehouse number.

- The cycle counting Indicator

- The interval in work days after which a new PI should be performed
- The buffer time in work days

Menu Path: SPRO | IMG | Extended Warehouse Management | Internal Warehouse Processes | Physical Inventory | Warehouse-Number-Specific Settings | Configure Cycle Counting

Cycle Counting Counting Cycle

War...	CC Ind.	InPI	BT
SEWM	A	30	5
SEWM	B	60	5
SEWM	C	90	5

20.3.8 Define Tolerance Group for Difference Analyzer

In this IMG activity, a value-based tolerance group can be defined for the difference analyzer. A later section will demonstrate how to assign this to users.

Menu Path: SPRO | IMG | Extended Warehouse Management | Internal Warehouse Processes | Physical Inventory | Warehouse-Number-Specific Settings | Define Tolerance Groups | Define Tolerance Group for Difference Analyzer

Definition of the Tolerance Group Difference Analyzer

War...	TolGr Diff. Ana	Value-Based Tolerance	Currncy	No Tol.	Wait Time
SEWM	HIGH	10,000.00	USD	☐	
SEWM	LOW	1,000.00	USD	☐	
SEWM	MEDIUM	5,000.00	USD	☐	

20.3.9 Assign User to Tolerance Group for Difference Analyzer

Here, tolerance groups are assigned to users for the difference analyzer.

Menu Path: SAP Easy Access | SAP Menu | Extended Warehouse Management | Settings | Physical Inventory | Assign User to Tolerance Group for Difference Analyzer

Warehouse No. SEWM

Assignment of User to Tolerance Grou

User	TolGr Diff. Ana...
RM0015	HIGH

20.3.10 Define Value Based Tolerance Group for Posting Differences

In this IMG activity, define value-based and quantity-based (percentage) tolerance values for each group for posting differences.

Menu Path: SPRO | IMG | Extended Warehouse Management | Internal Warehouse Processes | Physical Inventory | Warehouse-Number-Specific Settings | Define Tolerance Groups | Define Tolerance Group for Posting Differences

Definition of Tolerance Group "Post Differences"

War..	Tol. Group Po...	Allowed Perc	No Tol.	Value-Based Tol	Currncy	No Tol.	Alert Flag
SEWM	HIGH	50.00	☑	10,000.00	USD	☐	☐
SEWM	LOW	10.00	☑	1,000.00	USD	☐	☐
SEWM	MEDIUM	25.00	☑	5,000.00	USD	☐	☐

20.3.11 Define Tolerance Group for Recounting

In this IMG activity, for each warehouse number, define the PI tolerance groups for recounting, and assign value-based and quantity-based (percentage) tolerance values to these.

Menu Path: SPRO | IMG | Extended Warehouse Management | Internal Warehouse Processes | Physical Inventory | Warehouse-Number-Specific Settings | Define Tolerance Groups | Define Tolerance Group for Recounting

Definition of Toleranc Group "Recount"

War..	Tolerance Gro	Allowed Percen...	No Tol.	Value-Based Tol	Currncy	No Tol.
SEWM	HIGH	100.00	☐	10,000.00	USD	☐
SEWM	LOW	10.00	☐	1,000.00	USD	☐
SEWM	MEDIUM	50.00	☐	5,000.00	USD	☐

20.3.12 Assign User to Tolerance Group for Recount/Clearing

Here, the previously configured tolerance group for recount and clearing differences are assigned to the users.

The menu path is SAP Easy Access | SAP Menu | Extended Warehouse Management | Settings | Physical Inventory | Assign User to Tolerance Group for Recount/Clearing

Warehouse No.	SEWM

Assignment of User to Tolerance Group Posting and Recounting

User Name	AA	Tol. Group Po...	Tolerance Gro...
RM0015	PHYS	HIGH	LOW

20.3.13 Define Priorities

Priorities control the urgency of a PI document or an occurring difference in the system. PI documents having the greatest urgency are assigned the highest priority. The priorities must be defined for each warehouse. In EWM, a maximum of nine different priority values is possible.

Menu Path: SPRO | IMG | Extended Warehouse Management | Internal Warehouse Processes | Physical Inventory | Warehouse-Number-Specific Settings | Reason and Priority | Define Priorities

Definition Table of Priorities

War...	Priority	Prio Descrip.
SEWM	1	HIGH
SEWM	2	MEDIUM
SEWM	3	LOW

20.3.14 Define Reason for Physical Inventory

PI reason is used to control different tasks within the PI process. Priority is assigned to each reason.

Reason for Physical Inventory

War...	Reason	Description	Priority	PIL	Autom.	Active	No CW Qty
SEWM	CCIV	Cycle Counting	2	☐	☐	☐	☐
SEWm	LSPI	Low Stock Check	1	☐	☐	☑	☐
SEWM	PTPI	Putaway Physical Inventory	2	☐	☐	☑	☐
SEWM	STND	Standard Physical Inventory	2	☐	☐	☐	☐
SEWm	UNAS	Not Assigned	3	☐	☐	☐	☐
SEWm	UPLD	Unplanned Physical Inventory	1	☑	☐	☑	☐

- **PIL (product in location) indicator** is used to define whether the PI document can be ended with an exception during counting; that is, whether internal exception PRIL (standard PI with product in location) is permitted.

- **Automatic indicator** is used to define whether differences in PI are allowed to post in the difference analyzer immediately to the ERP system as a background job. If the indicator is not set, automatic posting is allowed.
- **Active indicator** is used to define whether PI documents should be activated at the time of creation.

Menu Path: SPRO | IMG | Extended Warehouse Management | Internal Warehouse Processes | Physical Inventory | Warehouse-Number-Specific Settings | Reason and Priority | Define Reason for Physical Inventory

20.3.15 Define Reason for Differences

Four types of differences can be assigned to each process, along with the reason and priority. They are as follows:

- Difference for a WT
- Change in difference for a PI document (COR)
- Difference for a receivable from a sales order (CO)
- Difference for a receivable from a stock transfer (STO)
- Difference for an inspection document (QI)

These values are used when displaying differences in the difference analyzer and during reporting.

Menu Path: SPRO | IMG | Extended Warehouse Management | Internal Warehouse Processes | Physical Inventory | Warehouse-Number-Specific Settings | Reason and Priority | Define Reason for Differences

Reason of Difference

War...	Process	Reason	Description	Priority
SEWM	CO Pending Claim from Sales Order	CUCL	Customer Claim	1
SEWM	COR Correction of a Difference	CORR	Correction	3
SEWM	QI Inspection Document	QIDF	Inspection Document	3
SEWM	STO Pending Claim from Stock Transf	STOC	Stock Transfer	1
SEWM	WT Warehouse Task	WTDF	Warehouse Task	3

20.3.16 Define Standard Reason for Each PI Procedure

When the PI document is created reason code must be assigned. If no reason code is specified, the PI document is created with the standard reason code from the PI procedure. Therefore standard reason code must be assigned to every PI procedure.

Menu Path: SPRO | IMG | Extended Warehouse Management | Internal Warehouse Processes | Physical Inventory | Warehouse-Number-Specific Settings | Reason and Priority | Define Standard Reason for Each Phys. Inv. Procedure

Definition of Default Reason per Phys. Inv. Procedure

War	Procedure	Reason
SEWM	AL Annual Physical Inventory	STND
SEWM	AS Annual Physical Inventory	STND
SEWM	CC Cycle Counting Physical Ir	CCIV
SEWM	HL Ad-hoc Physical Inventory	UPLD
SEWM	HS Ad-hoc Physical Inventory	UPLD
SEWM	NL Low Stock Phys. Inventory	LSPI
SEWM	PL Putaway Physical Inventory	PTPI

20.3.17 Print PI Document—PPF Action

Chapter 18 already covered how to print documents using PPF. This section will demonstrate how to use functionalities (like condition types, access sequence, condition records, etc.) to print the PI document along with the PPF action profile.

20.3.17.1 Create condition table

A condition table defines the combination of fields (the key) that identifies an individual condition record. A condition record is how the system stores the specific condition data entered in the system as condition records.

Menu Path: SPRO | IMG | Extended Warehouse Management | Internal Warehouse Processes | Physical Inventory | Print | Create Condition Table

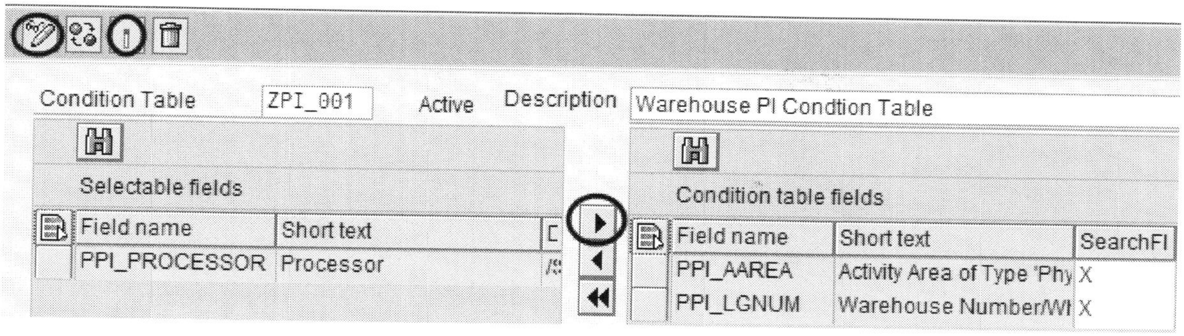

To create a condition table, click the "Change" button, enter the condition table name, description, and click the "Enter" button.

In the selectable fields section, select the desired fields to add them to the condition table and click on the right arrow key. This will add the selected fields to the condition table. Click the "Activate" button to activate the condition table.

20.3.17.2 Specify Access Sequence

The access sequence determines the sequence in which the condition records for a condition type are found and read. Here, the condition table is assigned to an access sequence.

Menu Path: SPRO | IMG | Extended Warehouse Management | Internal Warehouse Processes | Physical Inventory | Print | Specify Access Sequence

The default screen will be in display mode. Click the "Change" button; to make any changes. Click the "New Entries" button; enter the access sequence code in "Access Sequence," enter the description, and select "B Source: Local" for source.

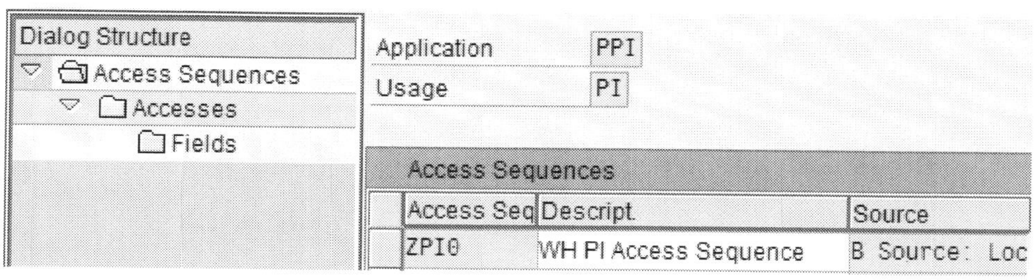

Hit the "Enter" key. Select the access sequence line and click on "Accesses" to assign the condition table.

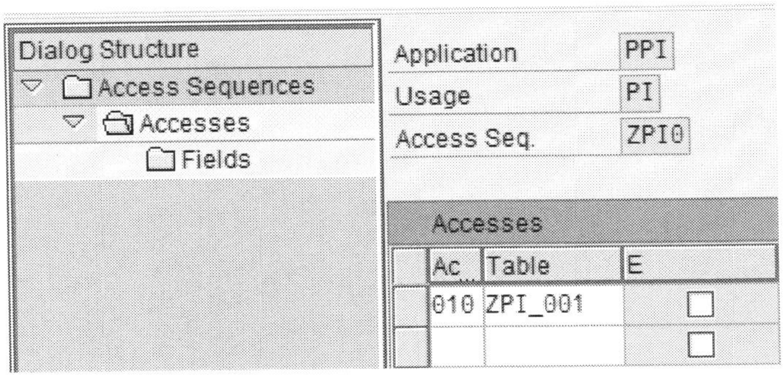

Hit the "Enter" key and click on "Fields" in the dialog structure. This will display all available fields in the condition table. Verify the fields and click on "Save" to save the changes.

20.3.17.3 Define Condition Types

In this IMG activity, define the condition types for printing PI documents with the PPF and assign an access sequence to every condition type. The access sequence contains a list of accesses to condition tables. The system searches through the condition tables for the appropriate key combination.

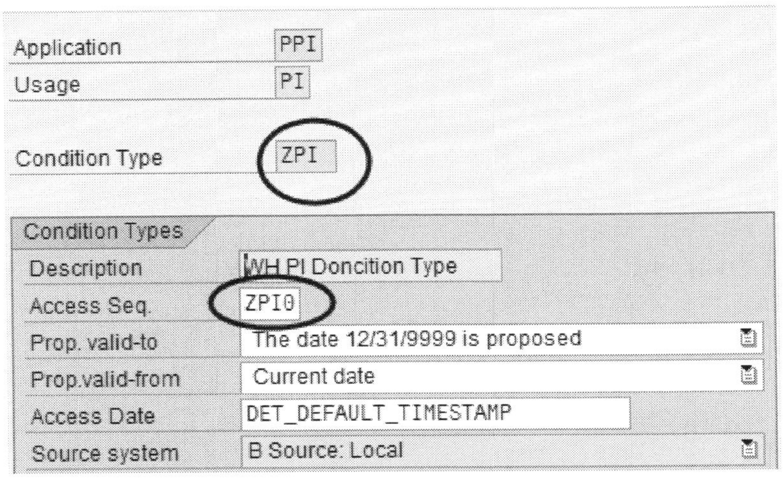

Menu Path: SPRO | IMG | Extended Warehouse Management | Internal Warehouse Processes | Physical Inventory | Print | Define Condition Types

20.3.17.4 Create and Change Determination Procedure

This IMG activity is used to create the PI determination procedure and assign the condition type to it.

Menu Path: SPRO | IMG | Extended Warehouse Management | Internal Warehouse Processes | Physical Inventory | Print | Create and Change Determination Procedure

To create determination procedure, click on "New Entries"; enter the procedure ID and the description.

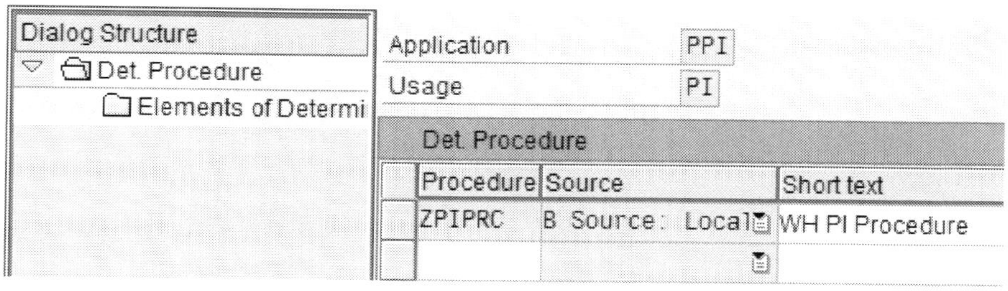

Hit "Enter," select the procedure, and double-click on "Elements of Determination Procedure" under the dialog structure. Here, the level sequence number is specified and assigned a condition type.

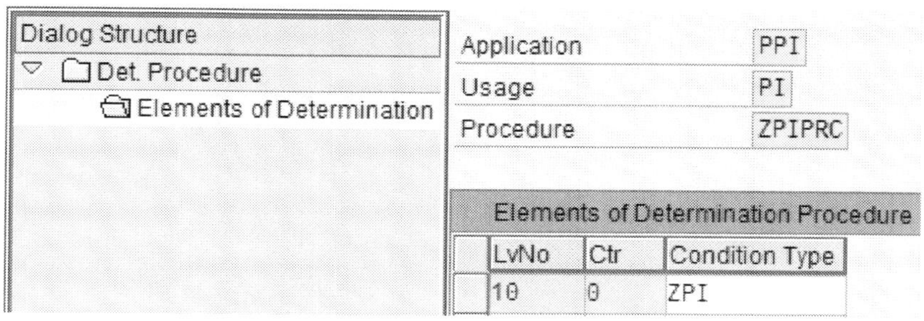

20.3.17.5 Assign Determination Procedure to the Warehouse

Once the PI determination procedure is defined, it has to be assigned to the warehouse number.

Menu Path: SPRO | IMG | Extended Warehouse Management | Master Data | Define Warehouse Number Control

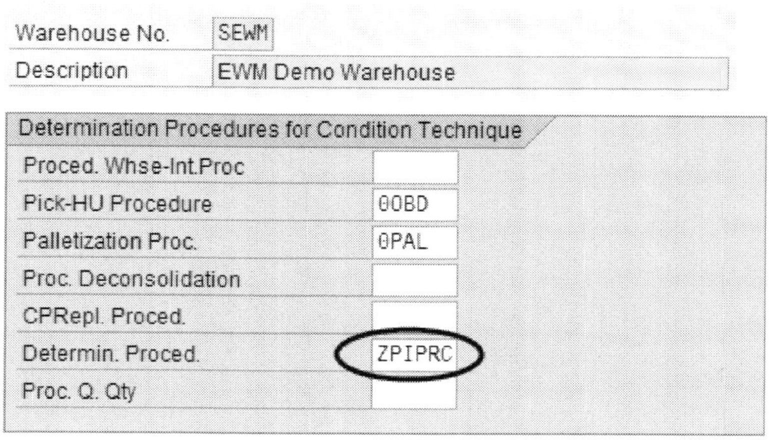

20.3.17.6 Create Condition Maintenance Group (CMG)

The condition maintenance group bundles condition tables and types for condition maintenance. In order to print PI document, it is necessary to define a CMG for the PI document and register it in maintenance context.

Menu Path: SPRO | IMG | Extended Warehouse Management | Internal Warehouse Processes | Physical Inventory | Print | Create Condition Maintenance Group

To define a CMG, click the "New Entries" button, enter maintenance group ID and description, and hit "Enter."

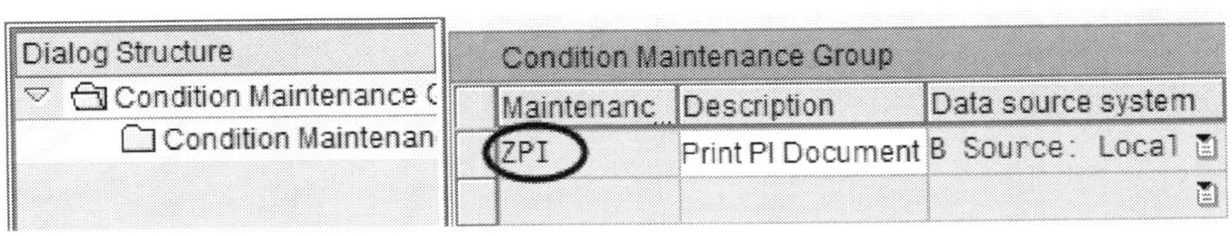

Select the entered line and click on the "Condition Maintenance Group—Detail" menu in the dialog structure. Here, enter the counter (usually defined in increment of tens), application, usage, condition table, condition type, and description. Application and usage are predefined in EWM. For PI, select PPI as an application and PI for usage.

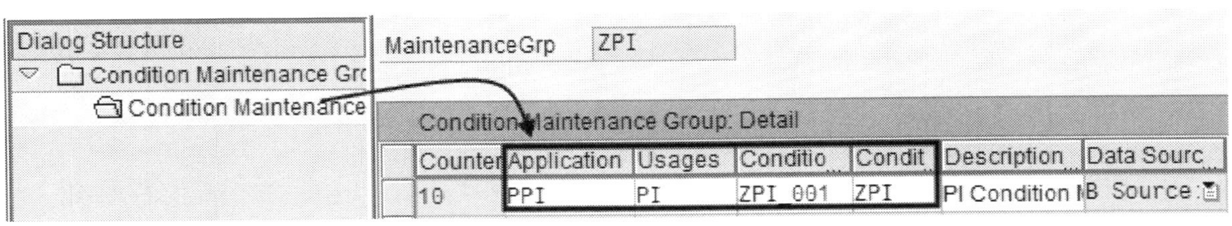

20.3.17.7 Register CMG

Finally, the CMG has to be registered in maintenance context. The predefined maintenance context to print various documents in EWM is CMG. The PI document CMG must be registered under this maintenance context.

Menu Path: SPRO | IMG | Extended Warehouse Management | Internal Warehouse Processes | Physical Inventory | Print | Register Condition Maintenance Group

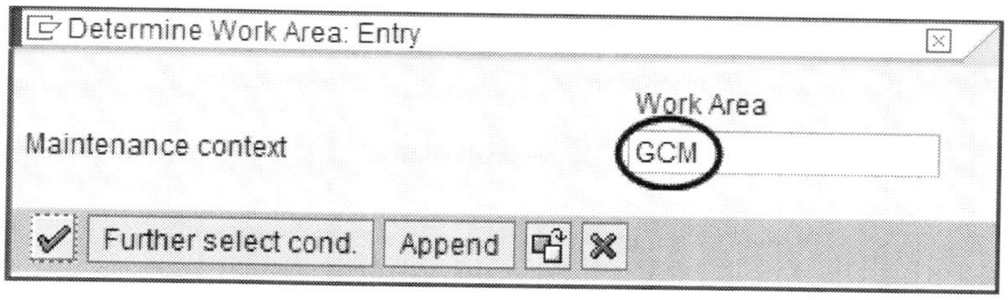

Here, in the work area, select value "GCM." To register the PI CMG, click on "New Entries", select the PI CMG in the “Group” field, hit “Enter” and click on “Save”.

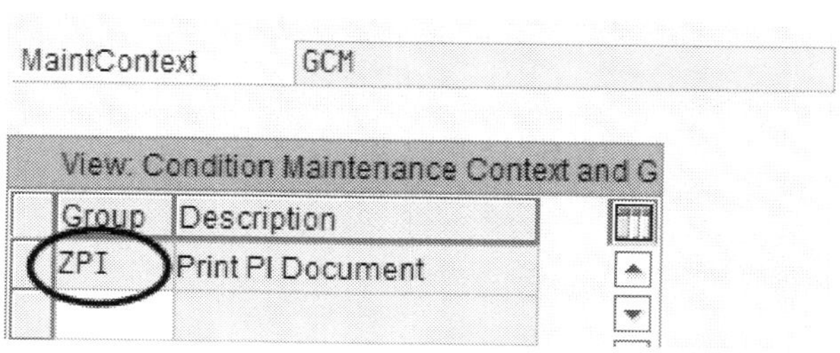

20.3.17.8 Specify Action Profiles for Printing Phy. Inv. Documents

In EWM, SAP has defined the "/SCWM/PI_COUNT" action profile for PI document. Custom action profiles, can be defined if necessary. The following screenshots show the settings for the predefined "/SCWM/PI_COUNT" action profile.

Menu Path: SPRO | IMG | Extended Warehouse Management | Internal Warehouse Processes | Physical Inventory | Print | Specify Action Profiles for Printing Physical Inv. Documents

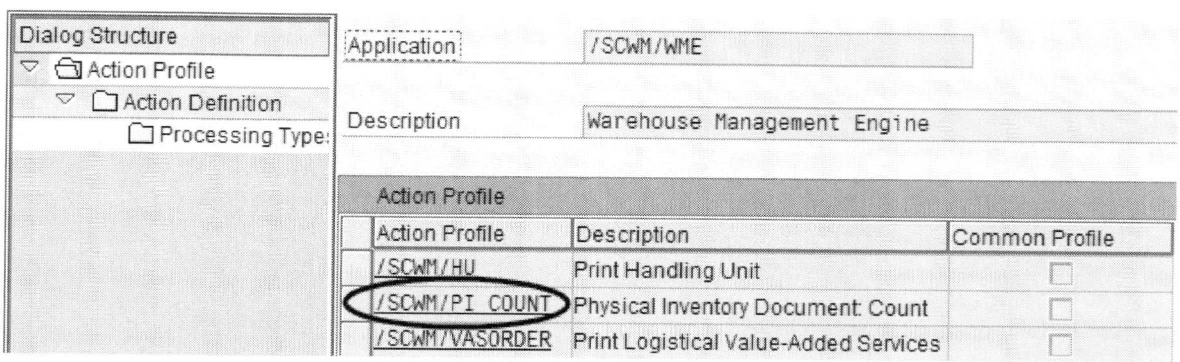

Select the line for action profile "/SCWM/PI_COUNT" and double-click on "Action Definition" to see the action settings.

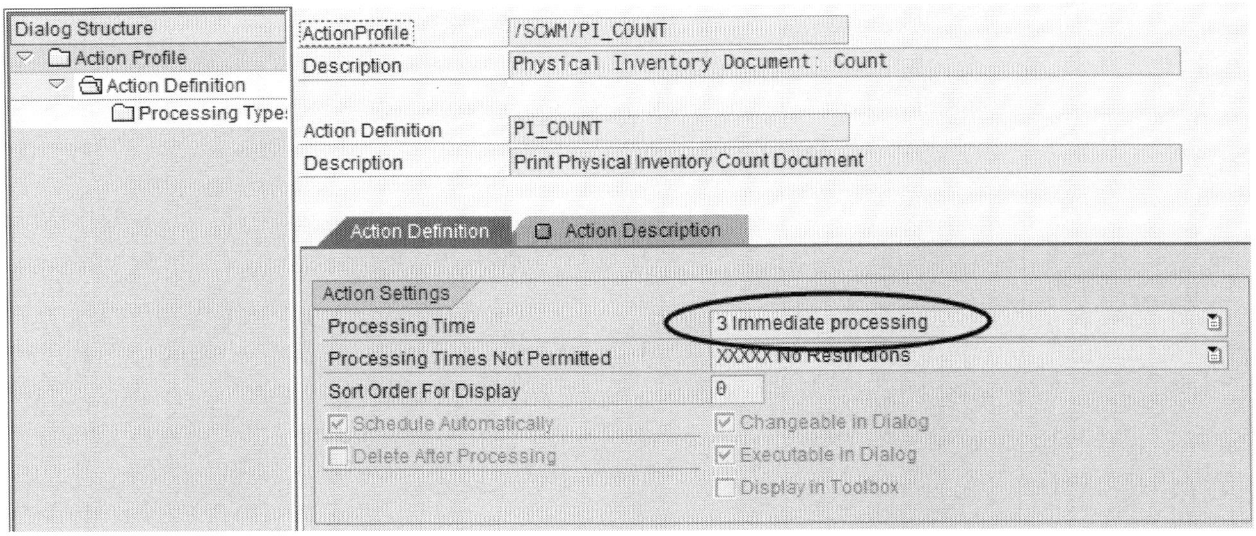

Double-click on "Processing Types" in the dialog structure and verify the processing details. There are no changes required for action profile /SCWM/PI_COUNT.

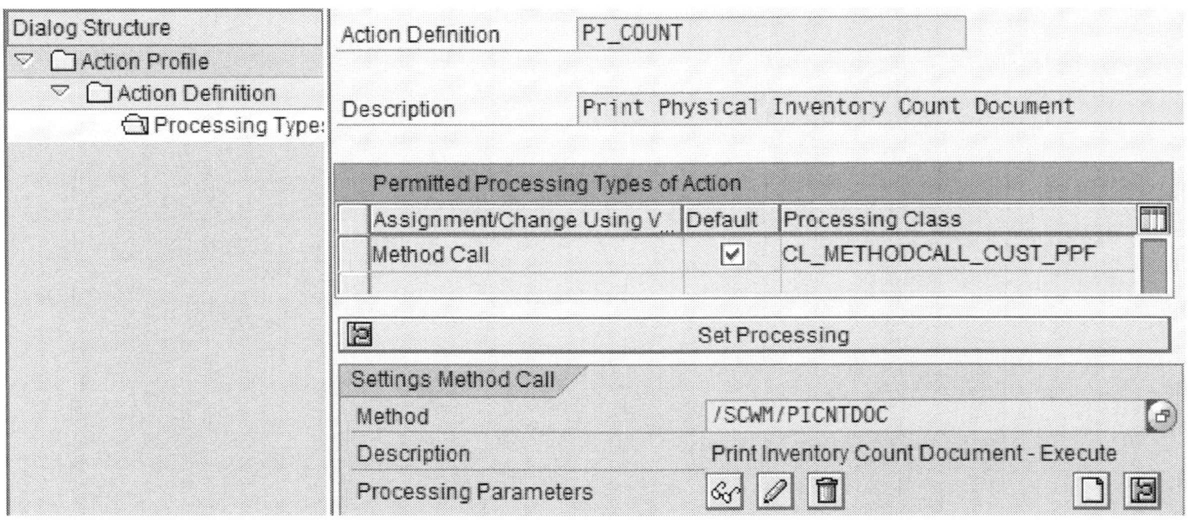

20.3.17.9 Specify Action Conditions for Printing PI Documents

This is covered in detail in chapter 18. In this menu start condition, scheduling condition, and processing requirements can be specified. There are no changes required to the predefined action profile.

Menu Path: **SPRO | IMG | Extended Warehouse Management | Internal Warehouse Processes | Physical Inventory | Print | Specify Action Conditions for Printing Physical Inv. Documents**

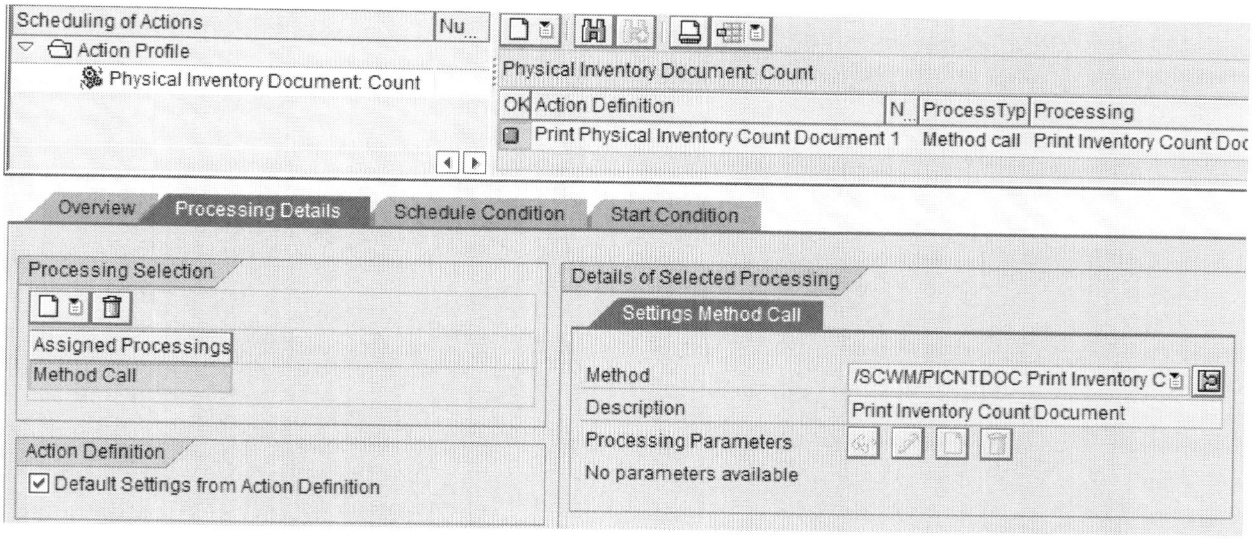

20.3.17.10 Maintain Warehouse-Specific Printing Parameters

In order to print PI documents, spool parameters have to be maintained for the warehouse number.

Menu Path: **SAP Easy Access | SAP menu | Extended Warehouse Management | Work Scheduling | Print | Settings | Maintain Warehouse-Specific Printing Parameters** or TCode **/SCWM/60000431**

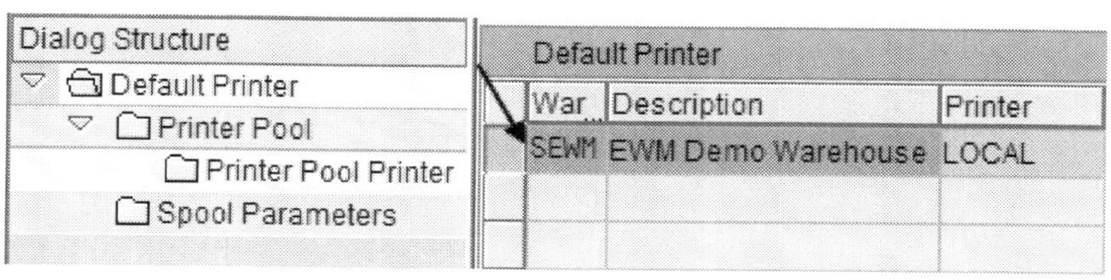

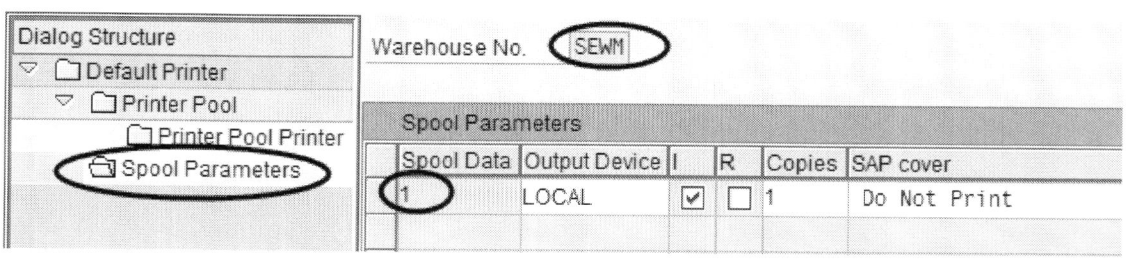

20.3.17.11 Create Condition Records for Printing (Physical Inventory)

In order to print the PI document, condition records have to be maintained for the warehouse number and PI area. The menu path to Maintain Condition Record is **SAP Easy Access | SAP menu | Extended Warehouse Management | Work Scheduling | Print | Settings | Create Condition Records for Printing (Physical Inventory)** or TCode **/SCWM/PRPI_GCM**

t maintain condition records, select "PPI" in the application field, select the maintenance group, and click "Execute."

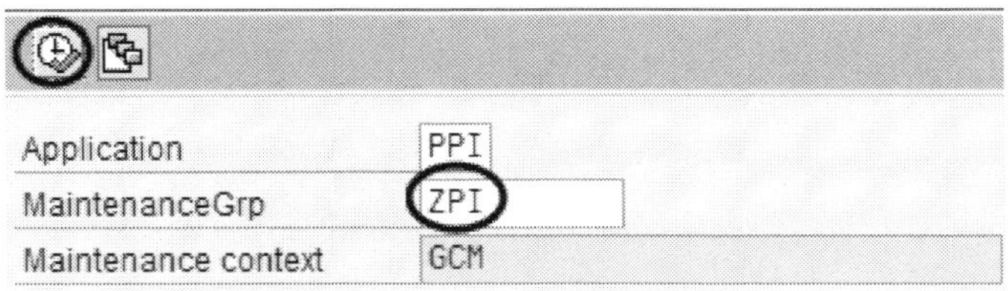

Select the condition type and maintain appropriate values for warehouse number, PI area, printer, spool parameters, and validity period fields. In the following example local printer is defined to print the PI documents.

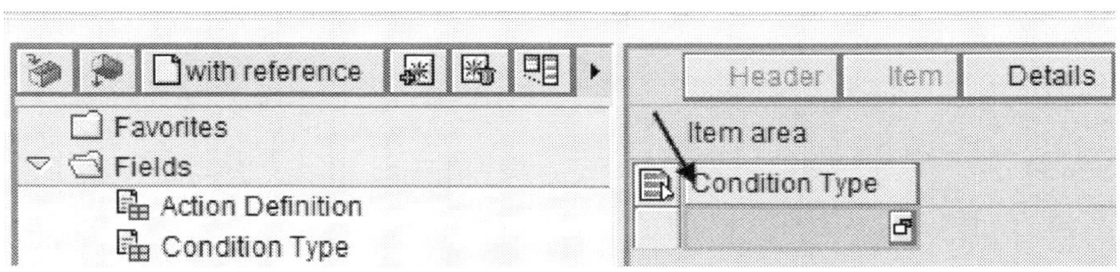

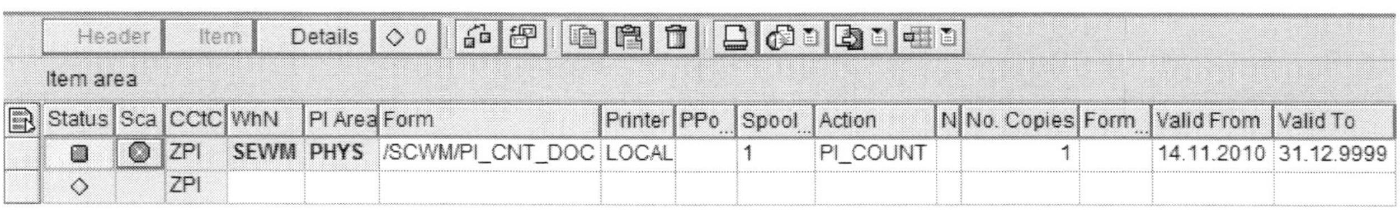

20.3.17.12 Print PI Document

In order to print PI count sheet use transaction /SCWM/PRPI_DOC. The menu path is **SAP Easy Access | SAP menu | Extended Warehouse Management | Physical Inventory | Periodic Processing | Print Physical Inventory Count Document—/SCWM/PRPI_DOC**

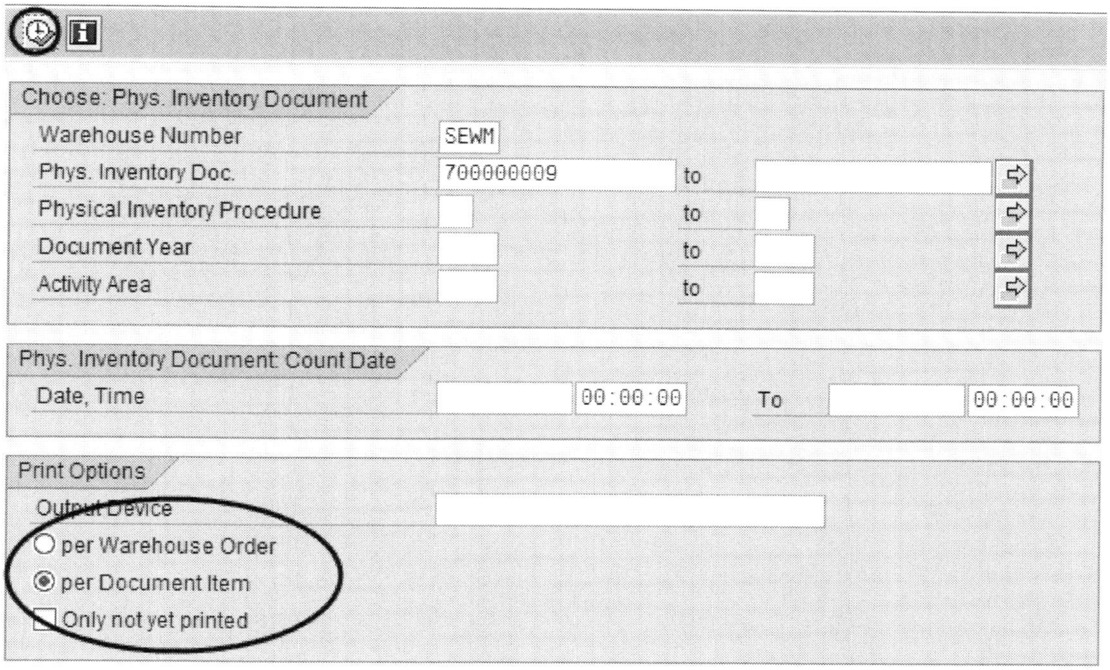

To print a particular PI document, select the radio button "per Document Item." This will provide the option to enter a PI document number.

20.3.18 Difference Analyzer

The difference analyzer is a tool available in EWM to analyze the stock count difference before posting to the ERP system. It also allows the users to post the differences to the ERP system, in which case stock will be adjusted in the ERP system and the financial documents will be created accordingly.

To prevent the difference from posting to ERP system, use the "Lock" feature in the difference analyzer; this keeps the difference from posting (both in foreground and background) accidentally until the locked item is released. Thus, additional investigation can be performed for locked items before posting the stock difference to the ERP system. This feature also has a provision to add the blocking reason and a note, which can be used for future reference or for further actions.

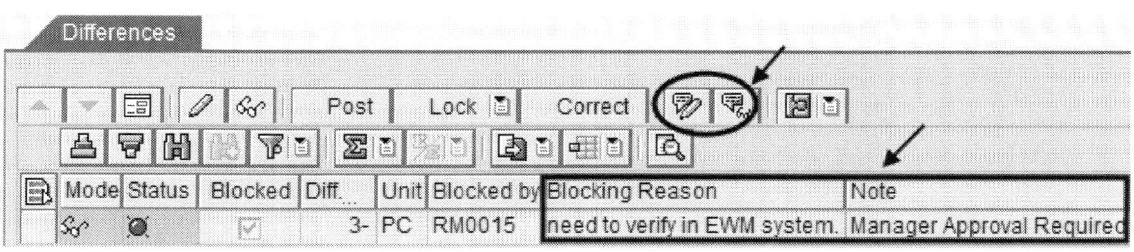

The difference analyzer displays stock differences that have occurred due to WT confirmation, PI document posting, or corrections made to the GR or GI posting in the ERP system. The stock differences are displayed at both a cumulative and an individual level. For the individual level, a link is provided to the document that caused the difference. At the cumulative level, differences are summarized or displayed in an aggregated way.

Menu Path: SAP Easy Access | SAP menu | Extended Warehouse Management | Physical Inventory | Difference Analyzer—/SCWM/DIFF_ANALYZER

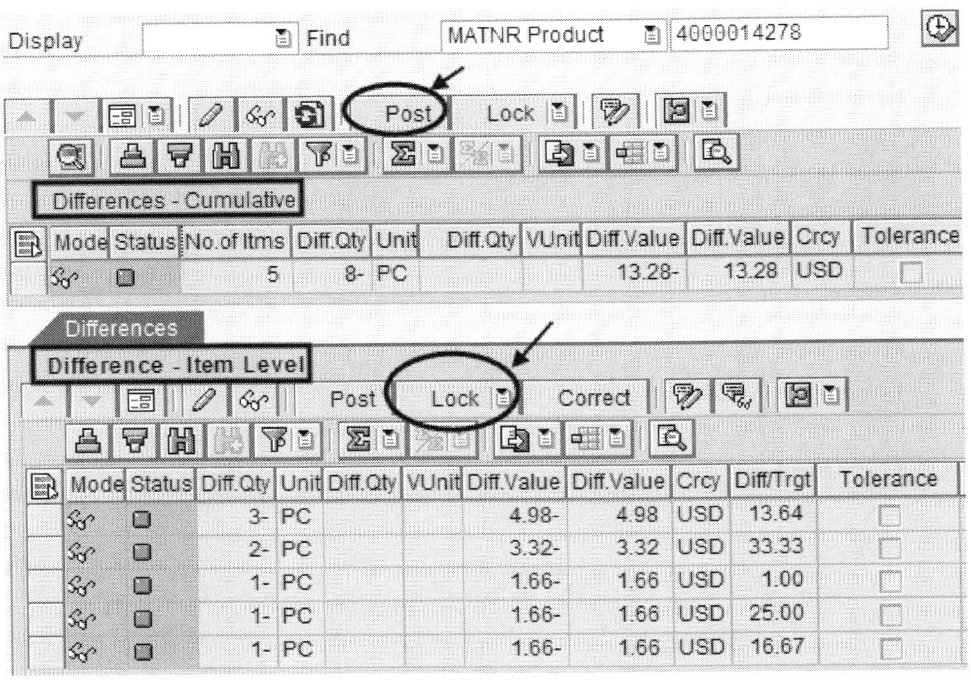

To post the differences to the ERP system, select the line items and click on the "Post" button. This will create the required material and financial documents in the ERP system. The transaction to list the material documents in the ERP system is MB51.

```
Material            Material Description
SLoc MvT S Mat. Doc.  Item Pstng Date    Quantity in UnE EUn

4000014278       EWM Demo -  Non Batch Managed Material
IAFS 712   4900156681   1 12/12/2010                  2  PC
IAFS 712   4900156681   4 12/12/2010                  1  PC
IAFS 712   4900156681   3 12/12/2010                  1  PC
IAFS 712   4900156682   1 12/12/2010                  3  PC
```

20.3.19 Other PI-Related Transactions

Along with PI transactions (like create, delete, count, and post), SAP has provided additional transactions that may be useful during PI. Some of them are explained below.

20.3.19.1 Determine and Set Prices from ERP

This transaction is used to download product prices from the ERP system to the EWM system. This information is used by the EWM system during tolerance checks (i.e., when PI documents and differences are posted to the ERP system. The menu path for this transaction is **SAP Easy Access | SAP menu | Extended Warehouse Management | Physical Inventory | Periodic Processing | Determine and Set Prices from ERP** or TCode **/SCWM/VALUATION_SET**

To download and save the prices in EWM, select all or required line items and click "Execute."

20.3.19.2 Stock Comparison ERP

This transaction is used to identify stock inconsistencies between the ERP and EWM systems. Inconsistencies can arise for various reasons like PI, confirm WT with difference, correction to GR or GI performed in the ERP system, and so on. This transaction compares the stock of both systems and displays the results. The menu path for this transaction is **SAP Easy Access | SAP menu | Extended Warehouse Management | Physical Inventory | Periodic Processing | Stock Comparison ERP** or TCode **/SCWM/ERP_STOCKCHECK**

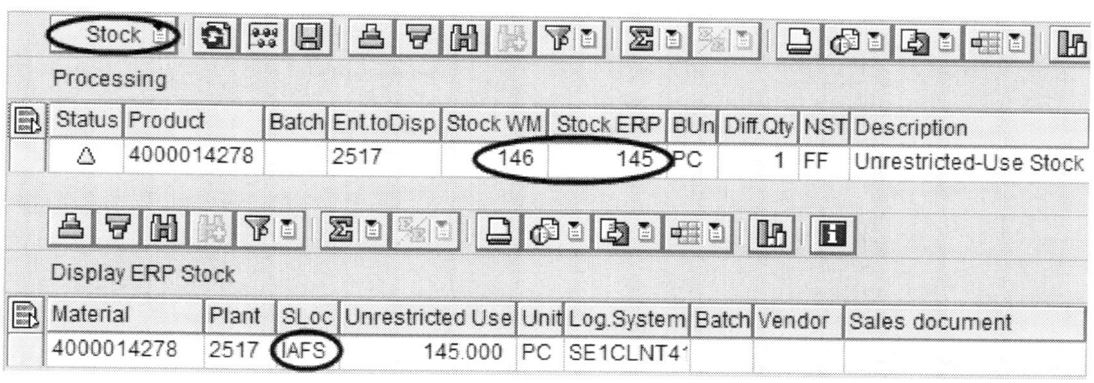

20.3.19.3 Upload/download Storage Bins and Count Data

As of SCM EWM 7.0, SAP does not provide a function for sample-based PI count. If this is required for the warehouse, it may be necessary to use a third-party system to determine which bin must be selected for sample-based counting. Transaction /SCWM/PI_DOWNLOAD can be used to download the storage bin and stock data from EWM system. Once bins are determined for counting, transaction /SCWM/PI_UPLOAD can be used to upload the storage bin data for which PI is to be performed in EWM. Also, using this transaction, counting can be carried out in the external system and the results uploaded to the EWM system.

The menu path for these transaction is **SAP Easy Access | SAP menu | Extended Warehouse Management | Physical Inventory | Periodic Processing**

20.3.19.4 Automatically Post Differences to ERP System

This transaction can be used to schedule a background job to post PI difference automatically to the ERP system. Like difference analyzer transaction, the system performs the tolerance check for the user who executes this transaction. The menu path for this transaction is **SAP Easy Access | SAP menu | Extended Warehouse Management | Physical Inventory | Periodic Processing | Post Differences to ERP System** or TCode **/SCWM/WM_ADJUST**

Notes:

i. It is recommended to use the difference analyzer transaction to analyze the stock difference before posting the difference to the ERP system. In transaction /SCWM/WM_ADJUST, users cannot analyze the difference in foreground.

20.3.19.5 BAPIs

In addition to these transactions, the following BAPIs can be used to develop custom logic creating, deleting, counting, and posting the PI documents.

- /SCWM/BAPI_PI_DOCUMENT_CREATE
- /SCWM/BAPI_PI_DOCUMENT_DELETE
- /SCWM/BAPI_PI_DOCUMENT_COUNT
- /SCWM/BAPI_PI_DOCUMENT_POST

20.4 Ad-Hoc PI Method

The above section covered the required configuration for PI. This section will show how to create and process ad-hoc PI in the non-RF environment.

20.4.1 Create an Ad-Hoc PI Document

The menu path to create an ad-hoc PI document is **SAP Easy Access | SAP menu | Extended Warehouse Management | Physical Inventory | Create Physical Inventory Document or TCode: /SCWM/PI_CREATE**

Click the "Default Values" button on the application toolbar, enter warehouse number, and select inventory procedure HL (Ad-hoc Physical Inventory (Storage-Bin-Specific)) or HS (Ad-hoc Physical Inventory (Product-Specific)).

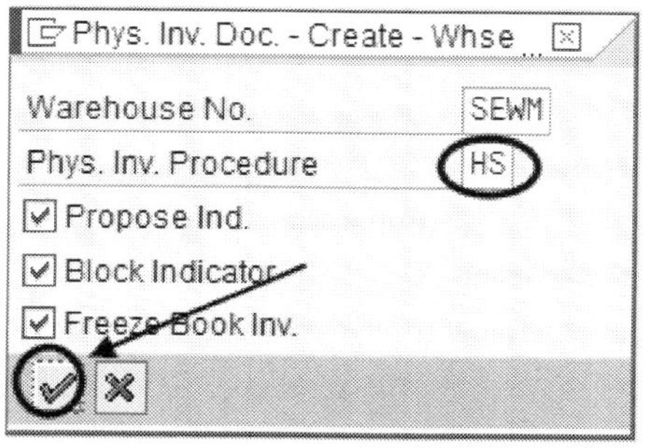

Based on the configuration and default values, the system will automatically default the settings of status, active, block indicator, and freeze bin to active or inactive for the proposed items. However, these values can be overwritten before creating PI document. In order to create a PI document, the status flag should be set.

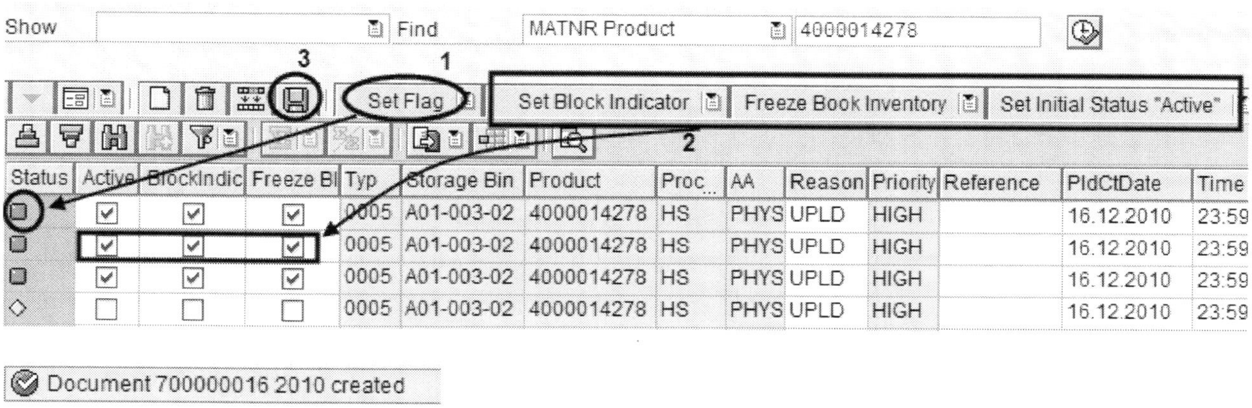

20.4.2 Enter Count Results

Once the PI document is created, users can enter or change the count in transaction /SCWM/PI_COUNT. The menu path for this transaction is **SAP Easy Access | SAP menu | Extended Warehouse Management | Physical Inventory | Enter Count Results**

To enter the count, the PI document must be activated. This can be done at the time of the PI document creation or in transaction /SCWM/PI_PROCESS—Process Physical Inventory Document.

To enter the count results, go to transaction /SCWM/PI_COUNT, enter the PI document number, select the line items, and click on "Count." In the popup window, enter the counter name and counting date. Double-click on the items, enter the counted quantity in the ". AUoU" field, and click "Save."

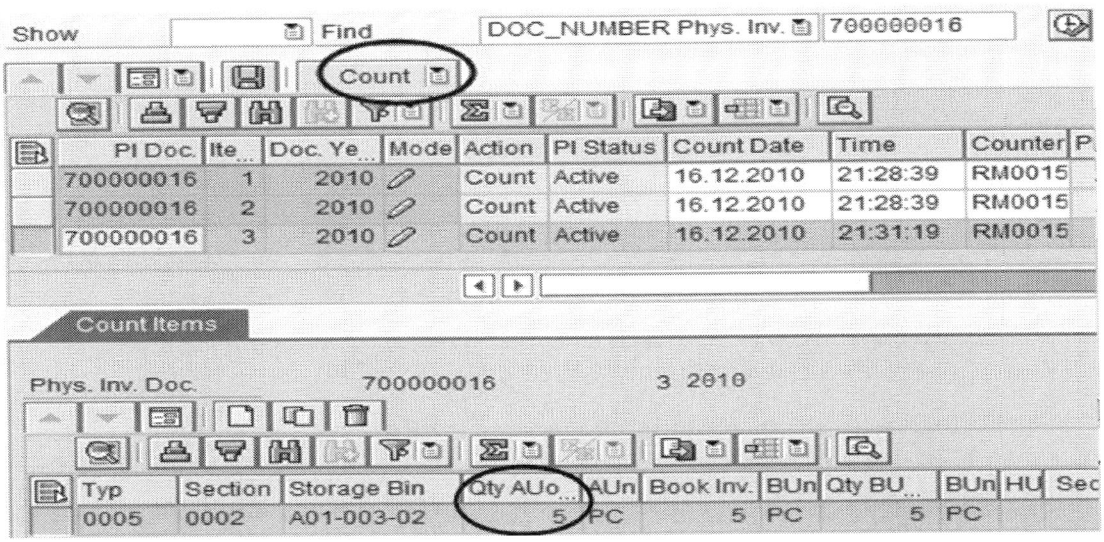

This will save the count results for the PI document.

20.4.3 Process PI Document

Transaction /SCWM/PI_PROCESS can be used to activate, change the count, initiate a recount, or to delete the PI document. If the counted stock matches with the system count, the system will automatically post the difference and unblock the bin (if the bin is blocked) for PI processing. If the difference is not posted automatically, users can select the line items and click "Post" to post the difference manually.

The menu path for this transaction is **SAP Easy Access | SAP menu | Extended Warehouse Management | Physical Inventory | Process Physical Inventory Document**

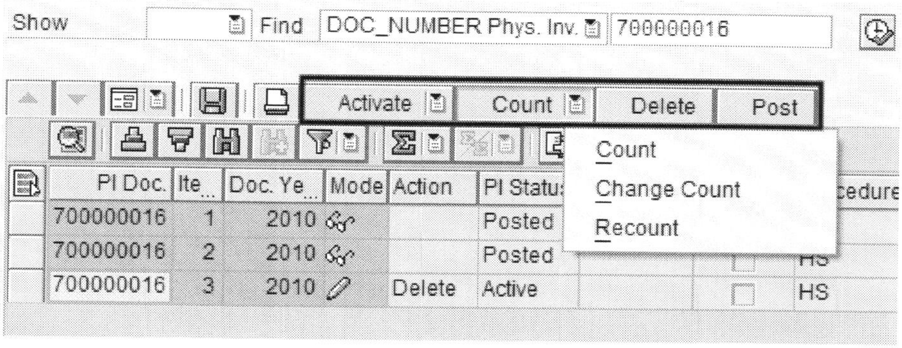

20.4.4 Difference Analyzer

Transaction /SCWM/DIFF_ANALYZER is used to analyze differences and post the differences to the ERP system. The details of the difference analyzer are covered in section 20.3.18. The menu path for this transaction is **SAP Easy Access | SAP menu | Extended Warehouse Management | Physical Inventory | Difference Analyzer**

In order to use this transaction, the user must be authorized for this transaction, and a tolerance limit must be assigned to the user ID in transaction /SCWM/PI_USER_DIFF—Assign User to Tolerance Group for Difference Analyzer.

20.5 Low Stock Check PI

Low stock check PI is performed visually during WT confirmation when the source bin contains only a small quantity after stock removal. The low stock check is storage-bin specific. The required configuration was discussed earlier in this chapter. In order to trigger low stock check, PI threshold value must be maintained for the PI area in **SPRO | IMG | Extended Warehouse Management | Internal Warehouse Processes | Physical Inventory | Physical-Inventory-Area-Specific Settings | Define Physical Inventory Area**

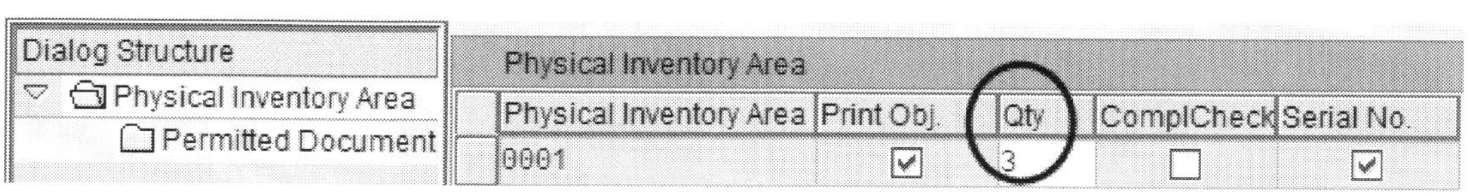

Low stock check is performed at the time of WT confirmation.

In order to demonstrate this functionality here, a bin-to-bin movement WT is created and low stock check is activated at the time of WT confirmation.

To create a WT for bin-to-bin transfer, follow the menu path **SAP Easy Access | SAP menu | Extended Warehouse Management | Work Scheduling | Create Warehouse Task without Reference | Move Product or Move HU.**

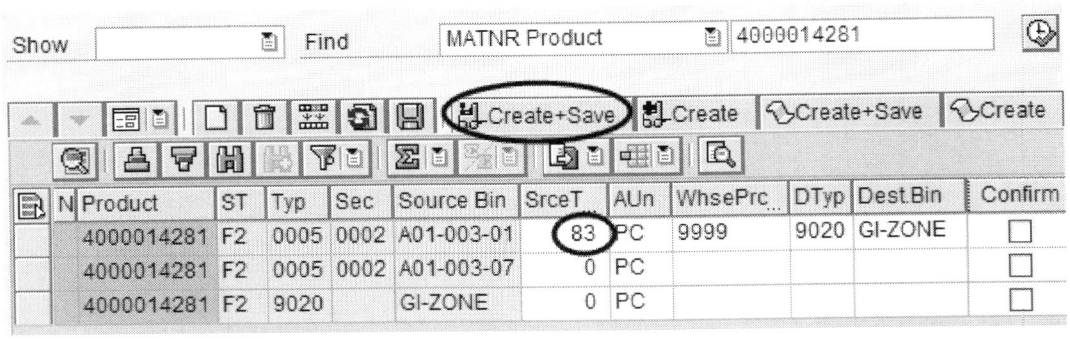

Once the WO is created, confirm the WO in menu path **SAP Easy Access | SAP menu | Extended Warehouse Management | Execution | /SCWM/TO_CONF—Confirm Warehouse Task**

Here, enter the WO number and click "Execute." In the details screen, switch to form view and confirm the WO in the foreground mode. Select "3—Low Stock Check Executed" in the "LStkCHK" field and enter the low stock quantity.

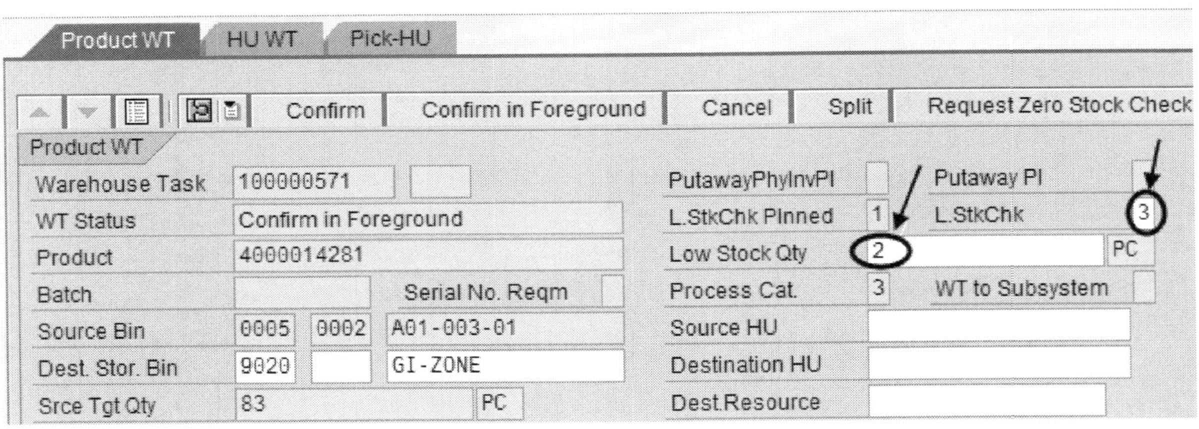

This will create a new inventory document with PI type NL. This document can be checked in transaction /SCWM/PI_PROCESS—Process Physical Inventory Document.

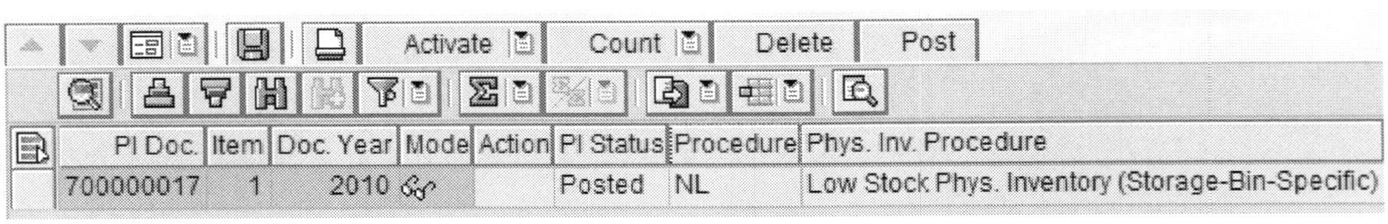

Any differences recorded can be posted to the ERP system in transaction /SCWM/DIFF_ANALYZER—Difference Analyzer.

20.6 Cycle Counting PI

The following configuration is required for cycle counting, along with the standard PI configuration. These were covered in detail earlier in this chapter; hence, they will not be covered again.

- Create Cycle Counting Indicators in IMG menu "Configure Cycle Counting."
- Activate the reason code for cycle counting in IMG menu "Define Reason for Physical Inventory." The standard defined code is CCIV.
- Assign default reason code for cycle counting inventory procedure (CC) in IMG menu "Define Standard Reason for Each Phys. Inv. Procedure."
- Update PI area to permit cycle counting in IMG menu "Define Physical Inventory Area" under "Permitted Document Types."

20.6.1 Update Product Master with Cycle Counting Indicators

In transaction /SCWM/MAT1, maintain cycle count indicators in the "Whse Data" tab for warehouse products.

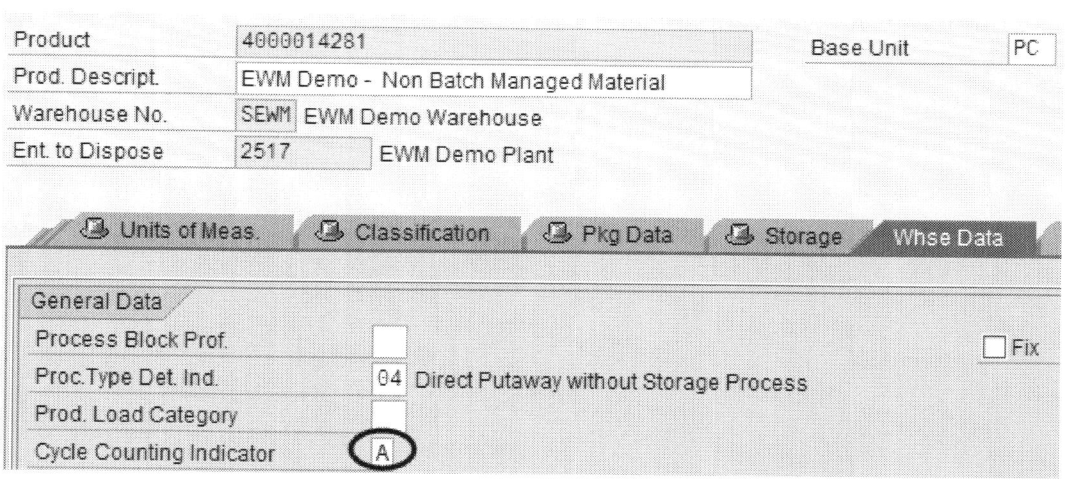

20.6.2 Create PI Document (Cycle Counting)

Transaction /SCWM/PI_CC_CREATE is used to create a cycle counting PI document. The menu path for this transaction is **SAP Easy Access | SAP menu | Extended Warehouse**

Management | Physical Inventory | Periodic Processing | Create Physical Inventory Document (Cycle Counting)

Here, enter the party entitled to dispose and other required filter values, and then click "Execute." Use the background mode to create the PI document directly in the background. If necessary, results can be viewed in simulation mode before creating the PI document by clicking on “Simulate” button.

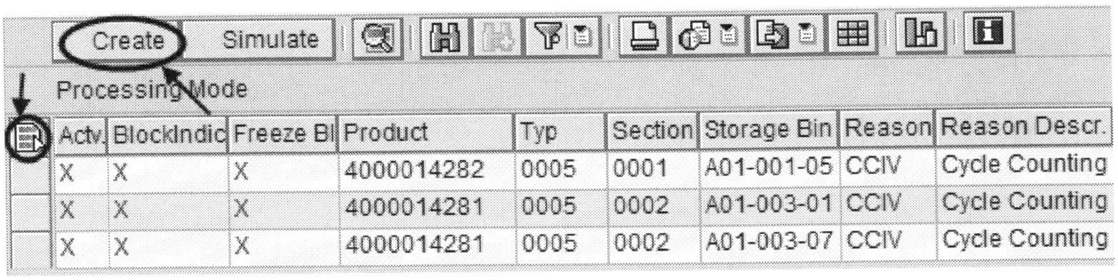

Actv.	BlockIndic	Freeze Bl	Product	Typ	Section	Storage Bin	Reason	Reason Descr.
X	X	X	4000014282	0005	0001	A01-001-05	CCIV	Cycle Counting
X	X	X	4000014281	0005	0002	A01-003-01	CCIV	Cycle Counting
X	X	X	4000014281	0005	0002	A01-003-07	CCIV	Cycle Counting

Once the document is created, users can enter the count and process it just like any other PI document.

Summary

This chapter described the various PI methods and the required configurations to setup the PI process in the EWM system. It also explained how to print the PI document using condition records and the PPF action profile, along with creating and posting PI documents. The chapter also demonstrated how to post the PI difference in the foreground and background under the difference analyzer.

Conclusion

We hope this book has helped you to strengthen your EWM concepts and basics. This book has extensively covered the basics of EWM, which is the foundation for any consultant who wants to grow stronger in EWM. Now that you have reached the end of this book, you might want to explore advanced concepts of EWM like labor management, RF configuration, kit to stock, kit to orders, cross-docking, value added services, yard management, and so on. You can find these topics in **http://help.sap.com | SAP Business Suite | SAP Extended Warehouse Management**. This will bolster your confidence and help you become a stronger consultant in the EWM market, where SAP has plans to continue investing in developing, supporting, and marketing this product.

About Advanced Concepts in SCM-EWM

We are currently in the process of developing content for *Advanced Concepts in SCM-EWM: A Step by Step Guide*, which will cover additional functionalities like labor management, slotting, rearrangements, warehouse cockpit, and RF functionalities. Similar to this book, the advanced topics book will also include configuration guide tables, detailed diagrams, full-screen snapshots, live examples and step-by-step procedures. Reading these two books will help you boost your confidence in the EWM area.

Tell Us What You Think!

We sincerely thank you for buying this book. As the reader of this book, you are our most important critic. We value your opinion and want to know what we're doing right, what we could do better, and what areas you'd like to see us publish in. Please email your comments to feedback@ewmguru.com. When you write, please be sure to include this book's title, subtitle, and the chapter number you are referencing, along with your name and email address. We will carefully review your comments and try to answer your questions promptly.

12025743R00278

Made in the USA
Lexington, KY
17 November 2011